A Dictionary of

INFORMATION TECHNOLOGY

The authors are highly indebted to their parents for providing the devotional encouragement, without which this book could not have been completed.

A Dictionary of

INFORMATION TECHNOLOGY

Arpit Sharma • Rajan Jain

CBS

CBS Publishers & Distributors Pvt. Ltd.

NEW DELHI • BANGALORE • PUNE • COCHIN • CHENNAI (INDIA)

ISBN : 81-239-0869-5

First Edition : 2003
Reprint : 2003, 2005, 2011

Published by Satish Kumar Jain and produced by V.K. Jain for
CBS Publishers & Distributors Pvt. Ltd.,
CBS Plaza, 4819/XI Prahlad Street, 24 Ansari Road, Daryaganj,
New Delhi - 110002, India. • Website: www.cbspd.com
e-mail: delhi@cbspd.com, cbspubs@vsnl.com, cbspubs@airtelmail.in
Ph.: 23289259, 23266861, 23266867 • Fax: 011-23243014

Branches:

- ***Bengaluru:*** Seema House, 2975, 17th Cross, K.R. Road, Bansankari 2nd Stage, Bangalore - 560070 Ph.: 26771678/79 Fax: 080-26771680 • e-mail: bangalore@cbspd.com
- ***Pune:*** Bhuruk Prestige, Sr. No. 52/12/2+1+3/2, Narhe, Haveli (Near Katraj-Dehu Road by Pass), Pune-411051 Ph.: +91-20-32404169 • Fax: 020-24464059 e-mail: pune@cbspd.com
- ***Kochi:*** 36/14, Kalluvilakam, Lissie Hospital Road, Cochin - 682018, Kerala • e-mail: cochin@cbspd.com Ph.: 0484-4059061-65 • Fax: 0484-4059065
- ***Chennai:*** 20, West Park Road, Shenoy Nagar, Chennai - 600030 e-mail: chennai@cbspd.com Ph.: 044-26260666-26202620 Fax: 044-45530020

Printed at :
J.S. Offset Printers, Delhi

Contributors

J.L. Sharma
M.Sc., Ph.D.
Reader, Deptt. of Chemistry,
Kirori Mal College,
University of Delhi, Delhi

Sadhna Vohra
Arch Communications,
Westboro MA 01581

Q. Zini
CNR-LAMEL, Bologna, Italy

Anna Mevoli
Centro Nazionale per la Ricerca,
Brindisi, Italy

Sandeep Srivastava
CEO, IYCWorld

Ajay Aggarwal
CEO, IYCWorld

Sanjay Singh
CEO, IYCWorld

Surender K. Jain
CBS Publishers & Distributors,
11 Darya Ganj, New Delhi

Vinod K. Jain
CBS Publishers & Distributors,
11 Darya Ganj, New Delhi

Satish K. Jain
CBS Publishers & Distributors,
11 Darya Ganj, New Delhi

Nand Kishore Garg
M.Sc., LL.B.
Chairman,
Maharaja Agrasen Institute of Technology,
Indraprastha University, Delhi

Major Gen. S.C. Goyal
B.Tech., MBA
Director,
Maharaja Agrasen Institute of Technology,
Indraprastha University, Delhi

B.N. Mishra
Emeritus Director,
Maharaja Agrasen Institute of Technology,
Indraprastha University, Delhi

Neeraj Garg
M.Tech., MBA
Director,
Maharaja Agrasen Institute of Technology,
Indraprastha University, Delhi

Rajat Srivastava
B.Tech., MBA
Maharaja Agrasen Institute of Technology,
Indraprastha University, Delhi

Baruna Bhatia
B.E., MSCE
Maharaja Agrasen Institute of Technology,
Indraprastha University, Delhi

Poonam Tandon
M.Sc., Ph.D.
Maharaja Agrasen Institute of Technology,
Indraprastha University, Delhi

Preface

This Dictionary of Information Technology presents a clear, convenient, and immediately accessible reference book. Every aspect of its conception and layout has been planned to help the user to find the scientific information he needs with minimum difficulty. It includes both British and US terms, as well as the terms used in other English-speaking countries.

The Dictionary contains a number of acronyms and their definitions. Commonly used symbols and abbreviations are also given. A set of short explanations of some of the OSI applications have also been included. The ISO standards are referenced as ISO nnnn, rather than the more familiar IS or DIS nnnn. The terms from the fields and disciplines, that impinge upon or overlap with Information Technology, have also been included. The authors have tried to strike a balance between the need to include the most important terms that technologists are liable to encounter and making a mistake of trying to compete with specialized books. Most of the terms come from a wide range of disciplines, such as Computer Hardware, Computer Languages and Programming, Data Processing, Database Management, Communications, Networking, Instructional Technology, Intelligence, Robotics, Internet & Intranet Engineering, Film and Television Production, Photography, Reprography, and Information Technology.

A term may have different meanings in different contexts. There may be as many meanings as there are areas of specialization. The authors have tried to establish core definitions that represent the variety of individual meanings. Also, many terms are used in different ways. The authors have tried to unite them without bias of giving the dominance over the other and have stated the connection among multiple usages. Restraint must prevail, particularly in a Dictionary such as this of modest proportions. The terms included have been selected in a somewhat pragmatic manner, partly on the basis of those most frequently encountered by the authors within the context of general usefulness of the subject. This Dictionary is expected to be a good source book not only for the students and teachers, but will also prove to be quite useful for persons working in the Information Technology.

The authors are grateful to the editors and programmers at IYCWorld.com who persuaded them to write the book and who helped shape the book in the present form. Mr. Rajiv Sikdar initiated the project, showed great editorial talent, and encouraged the authors in a number of ways. Mr. Virendra Aggarwal supported the project and provided wonderful support and kept the project moving. Mr. Rakesh Mani Tripathi contributed immensely in making strategic decisions.

The authors are also thankful to many people at CBS Publishers & Distributors, who participated with excellence and professionalism in the design and production of the book. Mr. Satish Jain, Managing Director, provided a big moral support and Mr. Vinod Jain, Production Director, took the challenge of providing technical and infrastructural support. Mr. Dharmvir did a superb job as production editor.

Finally, the authors are indebted to those who contributed their experience and knowledge.

AUTHORS

A

A. A DOS command that copies files that have archive bit, which is set with BACKUP and ATTRIB commands, set to a value of one. When /A is not used, BACKUP erases all files on the target disk and replaces them with those being copied.

A.nnn. A series of CCITT recommendations dealing with style, format, and terminology, presenting contributions to the CCITT study projects.

A/D. Analogue-to-Digital. 1. The process of conversion between an analogue and a digital signal.
2. A circuit used to convert information into digital form from an analogue input; used in digital voltmeters and similar devices.

AA. 1. Application Association; relationship between two AEs; same as a connection at supporting layers.
2. Abort Acknowledge Session PDU.

AA. One of the letter designations given to the most commonly used sizes of 1.5V batteries. Originally of North American nomenclature, this type of letter description has gained popularity over the International Electrotechnical Commission (IEC) letter/number system, as it is able to simplify the selection of batteries.

AAA. One of the letter designations given to the most commonly used sizes of 1.5V dry batteries.

AAESA-L. An open, unmodulated discussion list on the topic of educational service agencies.

AAR. Automatic Alternate Routing, in X.25 (or other) networks, the ability of the network to choose a non-congested or non-inoperative route when transmitting packets to a destination node; such routes will be selected based on criteria such as bandwidth, distance, and number of hops incurring propagation delay.

AARE. A-Associate REsoponse, the application protocol data unit which either accepts or rejects an ACSE association request.

AARQ. A-Associate ReQuest, the application protocol data unit which requests establishment of an ACSE association.

AB. Abort Session PDU, used to cause an abnormal release of session connection, or to reject an attempt to establish a session connection.

AberMUDs. The fantsy-game computer programs based on players killing each other rather than monsters or other artificial denizens of the game.

ABL. Atlas BASIC Language; the computer language designed for use on an Atlas computers.

ABM. Acronym for *A*synchronous *B*alanced *M*ode; used in the IBM token ring logical link control. Asynchronous balanced mode operates at the SNA data link control level and allows devices on a token ring to send data link commands at any time (and to initiate responses independently of each other).

ABME. ABM Extended.

abort branch. A special software routine, included in the controls for stationary baseline tracking robots, that constantly monitors the position of the tracking window. If at any time during automatic operation the robot's TCP coordinate in the tracking direction coincides with the coordinate of either limit of the tracking window, the robot control immediately initiates an abort branch that will direct the robot to exit from the part along a predefined safe path relative to the part.

ABP. 1. Actual Block Processor.
2. Advanced Business Processor.

ABRT. A-ABoRT, the application protocol data unit with which an ACSE association can be interrupted.

absolute address. An address in machine language that identifies a storage or a device without the use of any intermediate reference.

absolute delay. The time elapsing between the transmission of two synchronised signals from the same station or from different stations, as in radio, radar, or loran. By extension, the time interval between two such signals from any source, as from a generator.

absolute magnitude. The absolute magnitude of a complex quantity is the vector sum of the real and imaginary components of the quantity. *i.e.* it is the square root of sum of the squares of those components (*x*) I = root of $a^2 + b^2$, where (*x*) is the absolute magnitude, *a* is the real component, and *b* is the imaginary component.

abstract family of languages. AFL. A class of formal languages that is closed under all the following operations: Union, concatenation, Kleene-puls, intersection with regular set, A-free homomorphic image, and inverse homomorphic image. The motivation for the concept of an abstract family of languages is to investigate properties of classes of languages that follow merely from the assumption of certain closure properties. Each member of the Chomsky hierarchy is an abstract family of languages; all except type 2 are full.

AC PPDU. Alter Context Presentation PDU; the PDU used to add presentation context to or delete them from the defined context set on a given presentation association.

AC. 1. Access Control, the security for controlling what users have which rights in accessing resources such as entries in the Directory Service.
2. Application Context; the set of rules, which govern use of the ASEs to achieve a specific application functionality.
3. Association Control, managing the establishment and disconnection of associations between OSI entities.
4. ACept Session, PDU.

ACA PPDU. Alter Context Acknowledge Presentation PDU, PDU used to accept or reject modifications to the defined context set as proposed in an AC PPDU.

accelerator card. A self-contained device that enhances the processing speed through access to computer's central processing unit and memory by means of bus; used for special-purpose device access to the computer. Accelerator cards are often installed to speed up central processing unit, or the display of the video.

access charge. 1. Payments made by a long distance carrier to local telephone company for use of local facilities, and by telephone subscribers to obtain access to local networks.

2. The cost of accessing (gaining entry) to a network or computer system such as a public or industry bulletin board.

access code. A type of security check which requires a sequence of letters or symbols to be keyed in before entry (access) is allowed into the computer system.

Access Control List. *See* ACL.

access control. Any security device or entry system that is designed to restrict hackers or unauthorized users from entering certain sections of a computer room, computer network, or file. The control methods may include the use of passwords, magnetic entry keys, and electronic/photographic identification checks.

access denial. Access failure due either to the issuing of a system blocking signal by the telecommunication system, or to exceeding maximum access time and nominal system access time fraction during an access attempt.

access hole. The opening in a floppy disk which allows the read/write heads of a disk drive to make near-contact with the magnetic disk. In the traditional 5¼-inch disks, the access hole is always open and is susceptible to damage from dust and finger prints, while in the 3½-inch disks, the access hole is covered by an aluminium access gate, which is spring-loaded, and automatically opens when the disk is inserted into the drive.

access line. A circuit between subscriber and the switching centre. Any line giving access to a larger system or network. Also the private lines feeding a common control switching arrangement or enhanced private switched communications service switch from a PBX.

access method. The technique used for selecting records in a file, one at a time, for processing retrieval or storage. The access method is related to but distinct from the file organisation which determines how the records are stored. A number of different access methods are available mainly categorised as sequential access.

access points. A class of junction points in dedicated circuits outside plant. These are semi-permanent splice points at the junction of a branch feeder cable and distribution cables; used for testing, or for particular communications circuits.

access time. 1. In the telecommunication systems, the elapsed time between the start of an access attempt and successful access.

2. In a computer, the time interval between the instant when an instruction control unit initiates a call for data and the instant at which delivery of the data is completed.

3. The time interval between the instant at which data are requested to be stored and the instant at which storage is started.

ACD. Automatic Call Distribution, a specialised telephone system, or the service it provides, for handling many incoming calls; automatically distributes incoming calls to a number of different locations. It recognises and answers incoming calls according to instructions in a database, before sending the call to an operator or agent. It also offers management information on the type and volume of calls and efficiency of the agents.

ACDF. Abbreviation for the Access Control Decision Function.

ACEF. Abbreviation for the Access Control Enforcement Function.

ACF. Abbreviation for the Advanced Communications Function.

ACF/NCP. Advanced Communication Function/Network Control Program. In host based IBM SNA networks, it is the control software running on a communications controller that supports the operation of the SNA backbone network.

ACF/VTAM. Advanced Communication Function/Virtual Terminal Access Method. In the host-based IBM SNA networks, it is the control software running or a host computer that allows the host to communicate with networked terminals.

ACG. Automatic Code Generator.

ACI. Access Control Information, any information, including contextual, used in controlling access.

ACID. 1. Automated Classification and Interpretation of Data.

2. Atomicity, Consistency, Isolation, Durability; the properties used to characterise a transaction in transaction processing.

ACK. 1. Acknowledgement; a response sent to confirm receipt of a message.

2. A control flag specifying that Acknowledgement Number field in the TCP header is significant.

acknowledge character. 1. A transmission control character transmitted by a station as an affirmative response to a connecting station.

2. A transmission control character transmitted by a reviver as an affirmative response to a sender. An acknowledged character may also be used as accuracy control character.

Acknowledgement Number field. A field in the TCP header specifying the next sequence number the computer is expecting to receive.

acknowledgement. *See* ACK.

ACL. 1. Access Control List; A list of services available on a network; the usual means by which access to services is permitted or denied.

2. Application Control Language.

3. Audit Command Language.

ACL. Acronym for *A*dvanced *C*MOS *l*ogic. The further development of complementary metal-oxide semiconductors (CMOS) which offer low power-consumption, making them suitable for many computer and telecommunications devices.

ACM. Alterable Control Memory.

ACP. Allied Communications Publication; the publications of communication agreements among the English-speaking allies; e.g., ACP 127 defines the AUTODIN messaging service.

ACPI. *See* Advanced Configuration and Power Interface.

ACPM. Association Control Protocol Machine, the software that follows ACSE, modelled as a finite-state machine.

ACR. 1. Access Control Register.

2. Alternate CPU Recovery.

ACRE. *See* automatic call-recording equipment.

ACS. 1. Access Control Store; term used in Virtual Terminal.

2. Asynchronous Communications Server, shares modems on a LAN with multiple users for both incoming and outgoing calls.

3. Advanced Communication Service.

ACSE. Association Control Service Elements, part of the Application Layer, commonly used by many applications to establish the association between AEs.

ACT. 1. Advanced Communication Technology.

2. Active Control Technology.
3. Algebraic Compiler and Translator.

active open. A state in which TCP is attempting to initiate a connection.

ActiveX. A set of technologies that allows to create more interactive Web pages. It is a redesign of Microsoft's OLE technology that allows to open external programs and create active documents within another document. ActiveX technologies provide support for programs on both the client and server sides. It requires Microsoft's software to fully function because ActiveX controls are downloaded in to Internet Explorer or Netscape Navigator.

ActiveX controls. Applets that function as objects that can be embedded in HTML that provide interactive and user-controllable functions. These are small applications that run inside a Web browser. ActiveX controls can be viewed as the building blocks of an application. ActiveX controls can also function as servers. DCOM standard allows client and server controls to communicate with each other and distribute the workload across multiple networks.

AD. 1. Administrative Domain; in routing, a collection of names or addressed managed by the same organisation; i.e., a collection of hosts and routers, and the inter-connecting networks, managed by a single administrative authority.
2. ADdendum to a standard, separate document, which may correct problems with or add enhancements to a standard.
3. Activity Discard Session PDU; PDU that says an interrupted activity cannot be resumed.
4. Analog to Digital.

ADA. 1. Activity Discard Acknowledgement Session PDU, PDU that ways an Activity Discard PDU has been received.
2. Automatic Data Acquisition.
3. A high-level computer language, now widely used by the US Department of Defence. ADA is not an acronym, but the name of the girl friend of the 19th Century theoretical inventor of the computer Charles Babbage.

ADAPSO. Association of DAta Processing Service Organizations.

adaptive channel allocation. A process by which the capacity of a communication channel is multiplexed (shared) among several sources depending upon their relative requirements. The resource distribution varies with time to match changing requirements. The resource distribution varies with time to match changing requirements.

ADAS. Automatic Data Acquisition System.

ADB. Apple Desktop Bus; an interface standard for connecting input devices (such as keyboards and mice) to the Apple Macintosh family of personal computers. The each ADB port, 16 input devices can be connected, each offering a data transfer rate of 4.5 kilobits per second.

ADCCP. Advanced Data Communications Control Procedure, data link control procedure to be used with bit-oriented synchronous data communication links part of SDLC.

ADCON. A colloquial expression for ADdress CONstant; a value or expression used to calculate the real or virtual storage address of a memory.

added block. Any block or other delimited bit group delivered to the intended destination user in addition to intended user in addition to intended user information bits and delivered overhead bits.

add-in program. A software program designed to work in conjunction with an application program in order to extend the application's capabilities. For example, the spreadsheet program from Lotus called 1-2-3 can have an add-in program called *Allways.* It allows the 1-2-3 users to print reports using variety of fonts, lines, shadings, and other features.

ADDMD. ADministrative Directory Management Domain, similar to the ADMD of X.400, but DSAs for X.500.

address bus. The electronic channels along which the addresses of memory storage locations are transmitted internally from one system component to another, for example, from microprocessor to random-access memory (RAM). The size of computer's main memory is determined by the width of the address bus. An address bus of 20 wires wide can transmit 20 bits in parallel. However, because computers using binary numbers internally (zero and one) an address bus of 20 bits can identify and use a maximum of 2^{20} memory locations. This same equation applies to an address bus of 24 bits wide, giving a maximum RAM of 16 megabytes (2^{24}). DOS, a common operating system in personal computers, is limited to using only the first 640 kilobytes of RAM.

address format. 1. The arrangement of the address parts of an instruction.
2. The arrangement of the parts of single address such as those required for identifying a channel, module, or track on magnetic disk.

address mask. A set of numbers used to identify which parts of an IP address correspond to the network, subnet, and host portions of the address. Also known as subnet mask.

address messages. A message sent in the forward direction containing the signalling information required to route and connect the call. It includes address information class of service information, and additional information relating to user and network facilities. It also may contain the calling customer identity.

address modification. 1. Any arithmetic, logic, or syntactic operation performed on an address.
2. Altering the address part of a machine instruction by means of coded instruction.

Address Resolution Protocol. *See* ARP.

address signal complete. A signal sent in the backward direction indicating that signals required for routing the call to the called party have been received, and that no called party's line condition signals will be sent.

address space. The number of distinct locations that may be referred to with the machine address. For most (*i.e.,* binary) machines it is equal to 2^n, where n is the number of bits in the machine address. In many large machines the address space is larger than the number of physical or real addresses that are present in the system. Additionally, the number of bits available to specify an address is restricted and some form of address mapping or addressing scheme is used to obtain the machine address from the specified address.

address. 1. The destination of a message in a communication system.
2. A sequence of data characters designating the terminal equipment which is the origin or destination of data.
3. The location in storage of information in data processing system, *i.e.,* a character or group of characters that identifies a register, a particular part of storage, or some other data source or destination.

4. One or a group of characters specifying the recipient or originator of transmitted data. An address car also denote the position of data in computer memory or the data packet itself while in transit through a network. IEEE 802.3 and 802.5 recommend having a unique address for each device world-wide.

5. The unique identifier for a specific location on a network. There are many several types of addresses in common usage within Internet; for example, e-mail address is of the type:

webmaster@kmcollege.com; or
xyz@yahoo.com; or
abcd@hotmail.com; or
rjps@indiatimes.com; or
iycworld@iycworld.com

addressing. The method used to identify the location of a participant in a network. Ideally addressing specifies where the participant is located rather than who they are or how to get there. This is true for flat addressing, in which addresses are assigned independently of each other and carry no internal structure. More common, however is hierarchical addressing, in which addresses are grouped to reflect relationships among the addressed entities. Often the grouping reflects the physical topology of the network, so addressing and routing are interrelated. Sometimes the grouping reflects administrative or functional relationships (logical addressing) so addressing and naming are interrelated. In a system employing layered protocols, different forms of addressing may be used at different levels. The data link level may use addresses that identify specific stations on a multi-drop line. The network level uses addresses that identify the source and destination hosts associated with a packet. Higher protocol layers any use addresses that distinguish different connections or processes. Addresses may be fixed-length or extensible. In fixed-length addressing all addresses occupy a fixed number of digits. An example is Ethernet protocol, which uses 48-bit addresses. In extensible addressing the length of an address may vary from case to case. For example, in X.121 International data numbers are defined and these may be from 3-14 decimal digits in length.

ADF. Access control Decision Function, a function that applies access control policy rules to a requested action, the ACI, and the context in which the request was made, in order to provide access control decisions.

ADI. 1. Application DIrectory, prefix used to identify Directory functional profiles in the ISP taxonomy.

2. Access control Decision Information, that portion of access control information available to the access control decision function to make a specific access control decision.

ADIOS. 1. Automatic Digital Input/Output System.

2. Analog Digital Input/Output System.

ADIT. Analog Digital Integration Translator.

adjusted ring length. ARL. When a segment of Token Ring (in practice a dual ring) trunk cable fails, a function known as the Wrap connects the main path to the backup path. In the worst case, the longest path, would occur if the shortest trunk cable segment tailed, so ARL is calculated during network design to ensure the system will always work.

ADL. Automatic Data Link.

ADLC. Advanced Data Link Controller.

ADM. Adaptive Delta Modulation, a voice-to-digital sampling and encoding technique.

ADMA. Advanced Direct Memory Access.

ADMD. ADministrative Management Domain, a set of MTAs, owned and operated by an organization on behalf of others.

administrative domain. *See* AD.

ADMIS. Automated Data Management Information System.

ADPCM. Adaptive Differential Pulse Code Modulation, a ITU-TS standard technique for voice encoding and compression. It allows an analog to be carried within a 32Kbit/s digital channel.

ADPCM. Adaptive Differential Pulse Code Modulation, speech compression and digitizing method, at 32 K bps, that carries voice on a digital channel.

ADPP. Acronym for Automatic Data Processing Program.

ADPS. Acronym for Automatic Data Processing System.

ADSP. Apple Datastream Protocol, a transport mechanism for inter-process communications between Apple Macintosh and Dec Vax minicomputers.

ADT. 1. Application Dedicated Terminal. 2. Autonomous Data Transfer.

Advanced Configuration and Power Interface. ACPI. An open industry specification that defines a flexible and extensible hardware interface for the system board. Software designers use this specification to integrate power management features throughout computer system, including hardware, the operating system, and application software. This integration enbales Windows 2000 to determine which applications are active and handle all of the pwer management resources for computer subsystems and peripherals. ACPI design is essential to take full advantage of power management and plug and Play features in Windows 2000.

advanced IP address property sheet. The property-sheet on the Windows NT system where one can configure options such as multiple IP addresses and advanced security.

Advanced RISC. Advanced Reduced Instruction Set Computing; a specification for MIPS Computer System's RISC microprocessor-based computer platforms to provide products that scale from the laptop to the data centre, providing binary compatibility for application software. This specification was designed to complement X86-based industry standard personal computers, and give existing users a wide range of non-proprietary, standards-based computing alternatives. Acronym 'ARC'.

ADX. Automatic data Exchange.

AE. 1. Application Entity, an entity running part of an OSI application; it may consist of one or more ASEs.
2. Activity End Session PDU, that says there are no more data PDUs coming for this Session activity.

AEA. Activity End Acknowledge Session PDU.

AEF. 1. Address Extension Facility, field in X.25 call setup packet used when the Address Field cannot convey all necessary information.
2. Access control Enforcement Function, a function somewhere between the initiator and the target of a request that enforces the decisions reached by the access control decision function.

AEG. Active Element Group.

AEP. Application Environment Profile a POSIX term for a standardized profile that service the need of a specific application.

AET. Application Entity Title, identity of an application process in OSI name space; a descriptive name which unambiguously identifies an AE(1).

AF. Address Field, field in X.25/PLP call setup packet.
2. Audio Frequency.

AFC. Automatic Frequency Control.

AFF. Automatic Fast Feed.

AFG. Analog Function Generator.

AFI. Authority and Format Identifier, part of NSAP address. AFI specifies format of initial domain identifier, the authority that allocates IDI values, and syntax of domain-specific part.

AFIPS. American Federation of Information Processing Societies.

AFNOR. Association Francaise de NORmalisation, French national member of ISO.

AFO. Advanced File Organisation.

AFP. Apple Filing Protocol, a standard means of presenting the filing system of server to the user with a consistent Apple Macintosh interface.

AFR. 1. Automatic Field/Format Recognition.
2. Advanced Fault Regognition.
3. Attached FORTRAN Procesor.

AFSK. Audio Frequency Shift Keying; a modulation technique, which uses a kind of frequency modulation.

AFT. Application File Transfer, prefix used to identify FTAM functional profiles in ISP terminology; e.g., AFT11.

AFT11. The FTAM International Standardised Profile for basic file transfer.

AGC. Automatic Gain Control, a generic term used in describing circuitry which regulates signal amplitude in a telecommunications circuit.

agent. A software-driven process running on a communications or networking device that allows that device to participate in a network management system. For example, an SNMP agent running on a router provides the ability for the router to exchange information with an SNMP network management system using the SNMP protocol.

aggregate bandwidth. The total bandwidth of the channel carrying a multiplexed bit stream.

AGW. Advanced Graphics Workstation.

AH. Acceptor Handshake.

AHCS. Advanced Hybrid Computer System.

AIAG. Automotive Industry Action Group, a committee formed to coordinate EDI activities in the automotive industries.

AIB. Analong Input/output Board.

AIDC. Automatic Image Density Control.

AIL. Array Interconnection Logic.

AIM. 1. Advanced Information Manager.
2. Analog Input Multiplexer.

AIS. 1. Alarm Indication Signal, used in OSI Network Management.
2. Analog Input System.
3. Acron Interactive System.

AIT. Advanced Information technology.

AK. Acronym for Data AcKnowledge PDU in transport.

AKR. Address Key Register.

AKS. Associated Knowledge System.

AL. Application Layer, layer 7 of the OSI Reference Model; provides the means for application processes to use the OSI environment for communication between open systems.

Albert box. A window, which appears in graphical user interface systems to warn the user of an error or danger of possible error unless the problem is, attend to.

ALC. Adaptive Logic Circuit.

ALCOM. ALgebraic COMpiler.

ALCU. Arithmetic Logic and Control Unit.

ALD. Analog Line Driver.

Aldus PageMaker. The first page-layout program designed for personal computers. It helped the Apple Macintosh to lead in the desktop publishing race. The latest version of this package is PM-6.5.

alerts. Messages that Microsoft's LAN Manager network operating system sends under certain conditions. The three classes of alerts are admin alerts, error alerts and printer alerts.

ALF. Automatic Line Feed.

algebraic language. An algorithmic language, many of whose statements are structured to resemble the structure of algebraic expressions, for example, ALGOL, and FORTRAN.

ALGOL. ALGOrithmic Language. A colloquial expression for algorithmic language A programming language which uses algorithms to describe mathematical procedures. It is usually written in self-contained blocks which can be assembled in such a way that data storage is shared between many blocks.

algorithm. A process or set of rules necessary for a computer or intelligent device to perform a task, such as voice compression.

alignment. The adjustment of a device to certain tolerances to ensure it operates successfully. For example, the read/write head on a disk drive may require alignment to ensure it is correctly positioned to read a disk. Once a floppy disk is formatted on a disk drive, which is out of alignment, other disk drives may reject that floppy disk.

ALOHA NET. An early research network from which Ethernet originated.

ALOHA. Packet system, common carrier, collision detect; origin of Ethernet; so named because it ran on radios between islands; invented by N. Abramson, University of Hawaii.

ALP. 1. Abstract Local Primitive; in conformance testing, the description of control and observation to be done by the upper tester, but which cannot be directly mapped into abstract service primitives.

2. Arithmetic Logic Processor.

3. Assembly Language Processing.

4. Advanced Linear Programming System.

5. Automatic Language Processing System.

alpha test. The in-house testing of a new software package before it is commercially released. A second stage of testing is usually conducted outside the factory, and is known as a beta test.

alphameric display. A rectangle divided into a total of 14 segments which form all capital letters of the alphabet and all numbers from 0 to 9; commonly used to display information.

alphanumeric character subset. A character subset that contains both letters and digits and may contain control characters, special characters, and the space character.

alphanumeric data. Data represented by letters and digits, perhaps together with special characters and the space character.

alphanumeric. Pertaining to a character set that contains letters, digits, and usually other characters such as punctuation marks; synonymous with alphameric.

alphanumeric/alphameric. A generic term for alphabetic letters, numerical digits and special characters which are machine processable; used to designate a character-set which contains letters and punctuation marks.

ALQ. Almost Letter Quality, A term referring to the quality of printer.

ALS. 1. Application Layer Structure.

2. Arithmetic Logic Section.

alternate buffer. Two buffers are sometimes used to handle data I/O. These are alternated to achieve continuous throughput.

alternate routing. A safety technique, enabling communication to continue in case of node failure or congestion. The network design allows for alternate paths through the network to arrive at the same destination.

ALU. 1. Application Layer User, the end user of an OSI application, this may be either another computer program or a human user.
2. Arithmetic and Logic Unit.

AM. 1. Accounting management, the function that allows the use of a network-to be measured by the costs determined; this includes facilities for collecting accounting records and setting billing parameters.
2. Amplitude Modulation, a method of encoding signal carriers to carry the lower-frequency information (the signal) by varying carrier strength (amplitude).
3. Address Modifier.
4. Associative Memory.
5. Asynchronous Modem.

AM/FM receiver. A radio set that can receive either amplitude-modulated or frequency-modulated signals; usually, a band switch incorporates the demodulation-selection circuitry so that as frequency range is changed the appropriate detector is accessed.

AM/FM transmitter. A radio transmitter whose output signal may be frequency-or amplitude-modulated by a panel selector switch.

AM/FM tuner. A compact radio receiver unit which can handle either amplitude-or frequency-modulated signals and which delivers its low-amplitude-or output to a high-fidelity audio power amplifier.

AM/PSK. Amplitude Modulation with Phase Shift Keying, the method used to transmit higher baud rates over lower-rated telephone lines. This method constitutes a part of several modem function standards.

AMA. 1. Associative Memory Address.
2. Automatic Message Accounting.

AMC. 1. Automatic Message Counting.
2. Annual Maintenance Contract.
3. Autonomous Multiplexer Channel.

AMF. Account Metering Function, a term used in OSI Management.

AMH. Application Message Handling, prefix used to identify MHS functional profiles in the ISP taxonomy.

Amiga. A home computer developed by Commodore International. It is based on the Motorola 6800 microprocessor, and offers exceptional colour graphics and multi-channel stereo sound, making it well suited for playing computer games and composing music.

AML. Array Machine Language.

AMM. 1. Additional Memory Module.
2. Analog Monitor Module.

AMP. 1. Active Monitor Present; part of MAC frame in the Data Link Layer.
2. Associative Memory Processor.
3. AMPere, unit of electric current.

AMR. 1. Automatic Message Routing.
2. Automatic Message Registering.

AMS. 1. Advanced Memory Systems.
2. Asymmetric Multiprocessing System.

AMT. Advanced Manufacturing Technology.

AMVFT. Amplitude Modulated Voice Frequency Telegraph.

AN. 1. Abstract Number.
2. AlphaNumeric.
3. Accession Number.

ANA. Automatic Number Analysis.

analog computer. 1. A computer that operates on analog data by performing physical processes on these data.
2. A computer in which quantities of variable size are represented by another physical quantity such as voltage or position.

analog divider. A functional unit whose output analog variable is proportional to the quotient of two input analog variables.

analog input channel. The analog data path between the connector and the analog-to digital converter in the analog input subsystem. It may be noted that the path may include a filter, a analog signal multiplexer, and one or more amplifiers.

analog multiplier. A functional unit whose output analog variable is proportional to the product of two input analog variables. It may be noted that the term may also be applied to a device that can perform more than one multiplication, for example, a servo-multiplier.

analog output channel amplifier. An amplifier attached to one or more analog output channel, that adapts the output signal range of the digital-to-analog converter to the signal level necessary to control the technical process. It may be noted that if there is a common digital-to-analog converter in the subsystem, the amplifier performs the function of a sample-and-hold device.

analog. An analog signal is electrical and varies constantly in voltage, unlike a digital signal which varies between two constant values, usually denoted as 0 and 1. The value of analog signal varies all time during transmission, whereas a digital signal changes only between two set values without intermediate variations.

anchor. A place identified by words, sounds, or images, in a hypertext document, which holds the linked URL identifying a linked location. On selecting the anchor, browser client reads URL and the linked hypertext document is fetched and displayed.

ANI. Automatic Number Identification, a service that identifies the number from which telephone call originated.

anonymous file transfer protocol. AFTP. A protocol, which allows a user to retrieve data from archives in the Internet without establishing user ID and password on the computer, which contains the archive. Many systems now request the user's e-mail address as a password, in order to have better access tracking.

anonymous FTP server. An FTP server that allows anonymous login; however, today the World Wide Web often provides similar facilities.

ANSI. American National Standards Institute; defines US standards for the information processing industry. ANSI participates in defining network protocol standards and represents the US on other international standards-setting bodies like ISO.

antinoise carrier-operated circuit. A circuit that cuts off the audio output of a receiver while the station transmitter is in use. This may be accomplished in the automatic volume-control circuit of the receiver, or in the speaker or audio line.

anti-transmit-receive. ATR. A switch that automatically decouples a RADAR transmitter from its antenna during a receiving period; extra protection is thus provided from return echoes received by the antenna.

antivirus utilities. The utility programs designed for tracking viruses down, eradicating them, and also preventing their spread. These programs examine the boot sector and every file on a disk, identify viruses, if any, and attempt to remove them. Some of the common antivirus utilities are McAfee, Viruscan, Norton Antivirus, Virex, and Symantic Antivirus.

AOC. Automatic Output Control.

AOF. Advanced Operating Facility.

AOL. Application Oriented Language.

AOM. Application OSI Management, prefix used in specifying the subclass of profiles relating to OSI Management in the ISO taxonomy of SPs.

AOS. 1. Advanced Operating System. 2. Alternate Operate Service.

3. Alternate Option Selection in Transport.

AP. 1. Application Program.

2. Advanced Processor.

3 . Application Process, the software that does the information processing for some application in the Application Layer, OSI layer 7.

APAL. Array Processor Assembly Language.

APAM. Array Processor Access Method.

APC. 1. Adaptive Predictive Coding, a voice-to-digital encoding technique.

2. Advanced Personal Computer.

3. Associative Processor Control.

4. Automatic Phase Control.

APCI. Application Protocol Control Information.

APDU. Application Protocol Data Unit, PDU carrying data at the Application Layer.

API. 1. All Purpose Interface.

2. Application Program Interface, a standard interface specification, usually stating the functions providing in terms of arguments and results. In networking, an Application Program Interface also defines the method by which applications can take advantage of networking features. APIs in a network must be compatible to ensure programs are accessible to machines other than those they reside in. Some APIs, such as NetBIOS, are de facto standards.

APIA. Application Program Interface Association, a group writing APIs for X.400.

APIPA. Automatic Private IP Addressing, a technology available in Windows 98 that enables networked computers to self-configure TCP/IP without requiring a user to enter IP addresses, subnet masks, and so forth.

APL. 1. Algorithmic Programming Language.

2. Associative Programming Language.

APP. Associative Parallel Processor.

APPC. Advanced Program-to-Program Communications, set of IBM protocols also known as LU 6.2 and Type 2.1 architectures; best route across LANs algorithm used on the Internet It functions within SNA's APPN to support peer to-peer communications between work stations attached to SNA LANs and applications running on those workstations. It was added to SNA as part of the "new" SNA to support peer to-peer networking, unlike the traditional hierarchical SNA approach in which the mainframe acts as host or master and treats the other computer as a terminal or slave.

APPC/PC. A version of APPC developed by IBM to run on PC based Token Ring networks.

APPEND. A DOS command which appends file paths to the currently logged directory to enable the direct use of the files in the append file path without having to designate the file drive or directory.

append. To add a new record or data to the end of a file, database, character string, or list. From the Latin word *appendere* meaning 'to hang'.

APPEND/E. A DOS command which stores APPEND paths within the DOS environment. This is similar to path command, causing calls to files to search all appended file paths.

APPEND/PATH:OFF. A DOS command which prevents disc operating system from searching for a specified file outside the current drive and directory; when used, the drive and directory designation is ignored.

APPEND/PATH:ON. A DOS command which resets PATH to on.

APPEND/X:OFF. A DOS command used to turn off searches for and processing of executable files (such as those having the extension, such as .COM, .EXE, or .BAT).

APPLE. Associative Processor Programming Language Evaluation.

AppleShare. Apple system software that allows sharing of files and network services via a file server in the Apple Macintosh environment.

AppleTalk. The name given to Apple's original networking protocol; a seven-layer protocol stack developed by Apple for communications between its Apple Macintosh product range.

application layer. The layer of TCP/IP stack, which supports network applications and provides an interface to the local operating environment. It is the top layer in the OSI Reference Model comprising the interface between the OSI environment and a user's application. It does not contain applications, but provides a link from application software on one system to applications an another computer through the OSI environment. Several applications layers support different user tasks such as e mail and file transfer and transaction processing.

application program. A computer program which enables the processor (including both the hardware and the operating system software) to be applied to a task such as word processing, accounting, or database management.

application. A program, which performs a function directly for a user; e-mail, FTP, and Telenet are some of the examples of network applications. DOS, Windows, and UNIX, are some of the operating systems, on which applications run.

APPN. Advanced Peer to Peer Networking, an extension to SNA which routes information around the IBM network without help from the host, allowing systems to adjust dynamically to the topology of the network (dynamic routing). APPN keeps track of network topology, making it easier to connect and reconfigure. It also creates a directory of network nodes and other resources. APPN also allows for dynamic SNA networks, where nodes can join and leave the network as required, and session routes can be selected as needed.

APR. Alternate Path Re-entry.

APS. 1. Attached Processor for Speech.
2. Auxiliary Program Storage.

APSK. Amplitude and Phase Shift Keying.

APSP. Array Processor Subroutine Package.

APSS. Automated Program Support System.

APT. 1. Automatic Programming Tool.
2. Automatic Picture Transmission.

APU. 1. Analog Processing Unit.
2. Auxiliary Processing Unit.

AQL. Acceptance Quality Level.

AR. 1. Address register.
2. Arithmetic Register.
3. Associative Register.
4. Activity Resume Session PDU, PDU to continue to interrupted activity rather than start to resend it from the beginning.

ARA. Attribute Registration Authority, in the context of X.400 the organisation responsible for allocating unique attribute values of a single type within some portion of the global O/R address space.

Archie. A client/server utility that is used to locate files on anonymous FTP servers. Archie servers work by periodically searching every known anonymous FTP server on the Internet for the file names located on that computer. These file names are then sorted in to alphabetical order and placed in to a database that comprises the data a client can query from the Archie.

archived file. 1. A file that has been transferred to lower level in the memory hierarchy usually from magnetic disk to magnetic tape. The decision for this transfer to take place may be made as a conscious decision by the owner of the file or it may arise from the operations of the appropriate resource management.
2. A file stored on backing medium such as magnetic tape rather than being held permanently and under the control of a central processor; the file will be apart from the operating system's catalogue of current files but can be reconstituted as needed.

archiving. The storage of backup files and any associated journals, usually for a given period of time.

ARCnet. Attached Resource Computer Network; it has a topology and protocol of its own; it uses either twisted-pair wire or coaxial cable, and the star topology is formed with hubs attached to the network. The original ARCnet protocol was very slow, but it became popular because it was inexpensive, reliable, and easy to expand. fast ARCnet, like fast ethernet, increased the transmission rate to 100 Mbits per second and includes the ability to use fibre-optic cable.

ARCS. 1. Advanced Reconfigurable Computer System.
2. Automated Ring Code Search.

ARD. Application Remote Database, prefix used to identify RDA functional profiles in the ISP taxonomy.

ARF. 1. Alarm Reporting Function, a functional service of OSI Network Management that includes notification of faults or abnormal conditions generally leading to faults.
2. Automatic Report Feature.

ARL. *See* adjusted ring length.

ARM. Automated Route Management.

ARO. Automatic Recovery Option.

AROS. Alterable Read-only Operating System.

ARP PDU. Abnormal Release Presentation PDU; PDU that indicates receipt of an unexpected or unrecognized PPDU or session service primitive.

ARP. Address Resolution Protocol, an important TCP/IP protocol used to determine the physical address that corresponds to an IP address. It allows viewing the current contents of the ARP cache either of the local computer or of another computer. In addition, it allows the manual entering of desired physical/IP address pairs permanently. The entries in the ARP cache are by default dynamic, the entries are automatically added by ARP whenever a directed datagram is sent and a current entry does not exist in the cache. ARP operates only across a single physical network and is limited to networks supporting hardware broadcast.

ARPA. Advanced Research Projects Agency, now called DARPA. US government agency that pioneered packet-switching technology in conjunction with many universities and research facilities.

ARPANET. Advanced Research Projects Agency NETwork, developed by the eponymous research agency in the 1960s as the first packet switched network. It connects a large number of universities in the US and Europe, as well as commercial users. It helped in developing TCP/IP; the first large-scale packet-switching network, which grew from a university and research facility and eventually, split into the DDN and the Internet. Much of the original funding came from ARPA. The original ARPANet was shut down in 1990.

ARQ. Automatic Request for Correction.

ARR. 1. Address Record register.
2. Attributes for Representing Relationships, used in OSI Network Management.

array processor. 1. A specially designed computer used for mathematical calculations at very high speeds; once numbers are grouped together and made ready for mass calculations. The processing speeds are in the range of 5-100 MFLOP (million floating-point operations per second). Array processors became widely used in the 1980s, and today are used for applications such as CAT scanning. More common computer can only handle one-dimensional items of data. Super-computers are known as scalar processors.
2. Processors capable of executing instructions in which the operands can be arrays of data and not only single elements. It may be noted that in a special case where the array processor work on single elements, such elements are called 'scalars'.

ARS. 1. Audio Response System.
2. Automatic, or Alternate, Route Selection, telephony term.

ARSC. Automatic resolution Selection Control.

ARUP PDU. Abnormal Release User Presentation PDU, PDU indicating that the user of the Presentation service wants to end the association for some unexpected reason.

ARU. 1. Address recognition Unit.
2. Audio response Unit.

AS. 1. Advanced System.
2. Auxiliary Storage.
3. Activity Start Session PDU.
4. Application System.

ASC. Accredited Standards Committee, a division of ANSI. X3, T1, and X12 and ANSI ASCs.

ASCA. Automatic Subject Citation Alert.

ASCII file. A file consisting of characters that confirm to the American Standard Code for Information Interchange. This is the standard code used by most computer systems. It is comprised of a 7-bit code that represents 128 characters and control codes.

ASCII. American Standard Code for Information Interchange, ANSI X3.4-1977; a commonly used character set. These are normally padded out with an eighth bit that can represent parity to make up an eight-bit byte. This eighth bit can also be used to make ASCII support international character sets, extending the 128 possible seven-bit combinations to 256.

ASCP. Automatic System Checkout Program.

ASDC. Abstract Service Definition Convention, defined in CCITT X.407 (1988); defines the conventions used in describing distributed information tasks used in MHS.

ASE. Application Service Element, a set of communication capabilities, which support the interworking of Application Entities, using underlying, services where necessary.

ASES. Automated Software Evaluation System.

ASF. Automatic Sheet Feeder.

ASI. Addressing System International.

ASIC. Application Specific Integrated Circuit, a very large scale integrated (VLSI) circuit, custom-designed to perform one or more particular functions; the advantages include fewer discrete components, lower power consumption and increased reliability. These may be used in devices such as video machines, microwave ovens, and security alarms.

ASID. Address Space IDentifier.

ASK. Amplitude Shift Keying, a modulation technique that uses a form a amplitude modulation.

ASM. Address Space Manager.

ASN-1. Abstract Syntax Notation-1, a formal language used for describing and implementing ISO OSI protocols used in the automated implementation of protocol software. The protocol data units of most Application Layer standards like ACSE, FTAM, MMS, are defined using ASN-1.

ASP. 1. Associative Storing Processor. 2. Abstract Service Primitive, an implementation-independent description of an interaction between a service user and a service provider. 3. Attached Support Processor.

ASPER. Assembly Program for Peripheral Processes.

ASR. 1. Abstract test suite Selection Rules, the rules that govern the selection of test cases to run based on PICS in conformance testing. 2. Active Status register. 3. Address Shift register.

ASS. Analog Switching Subsustem.

assembly language. A computer-oriented programming language whose statements may be instruction or declarations. The instructions usually have a one-to-one correspondence with machine instructions.

ASSIGN. DOS command which reassigns the specified disk drive designations. It directs DOS to look at an assigned disk, rather than on the disk that is normally used by programs.

associative addressing. A method of addressing a location by what is in the memory rather than where it is. This is achieved by specifying something about the contents of the desired location rather than by a normal address. An associative memory (or content-addressable memory) is used to provide a search mechanism to match on partial memory contents for a word that satisfies the match. In some of the applications it may be permissible for more than one word to be found. The desired data will be in the close association or proximity, and most often as an additional field of the retrieved word.

associative storage. A storage device whose locations are identified by their contents, or by part of their contents, rather than by their names or positions.

ASU. Automatic Switching Unit.

ASV. Automatic Self Verification.

ASVS. Automatic Signature Verification System.

asynchronous communications. A method of transmitting data in which each transmitted character is sent separately. The character has integral start and finish start and stop bits so that the character can be sent at an arbitrary time, and separate from any other character. It is one of the most rudimentary type of communication, as the originating and receiving machines do not have to be synchronised. Cheap, reliable and common among computers, its disadvantage is the large number of extra bits needed for the data to be interpreted.

asynchronous communications interface adaptor. ACIA. A device that provides the data formatting and control to interface serial asynchronous data communications information to bus organized systems (*i.e.*, between a microprocessor and a modulator/demodulator).

asynchronous computer. A computer in which each event or the performance of each operation starts as a result of a signal generated by the completion of the previous events or operation, or on the availability of the parts of the computer required by the next event or operation.

asynchronous modem. A modem which is not capable of supplying the timing signals. All of the timing information must be supplied by the associated data terminal equipment.

asynchronous operation. 1. A sequence in which operations are executed out of time coincidence with any event. 2. An operation that occurs without a regular or predictable time relationship to a specified event.

asynchronous procedure. A procedure that can be executed concurrently with the calling part of the program. The word 'asynchronous' comes from the Greek and means 'not together in time'.

Asynchronous Transfer Mode. *See* ATM.

AT bus. Bus used in most of the IBM Personal Computer AT (Advanced Technology), or compatible machines, which employ 16-bit expansion bus, or possess AT-compatible slots. With the introduction of IBM's PC/AT personal computer, a broadening of the industry-standard bus structure occurred. The AT bus was just an extension of the original PC bus (62-pin bus connectors with 8 data lines used to pass a byte of data at a time. The AT bus contains exactly the same connection lines plus some additional ones that were required for the Intel 80286 microprocessor. In can accommodate most option boards that were designed for the PC bus. The major change with the AT bus involved the addition of another 8 lines for data transfer, bringing the total to 16. Most personal computers which use the AT bus have at least two connectors that are physically identical to those used on the older PC bus. The remaining connectors (option slots) are longer to accommodate option boards that require the full sixteen-bit-wide data bus.

AT. 1. Address translator.
2. Automatic Translation.
3. Modem control language for asynchronous dial-up modems designed by Hayes Microcomputer Products.

ATDM. Asynchronous Time Division Multiplexing; similar to TDM and STDM but with the circuit carrying asynchronous traffic, as distinct from STM; specified in numerous CCITT Recommendations.

ATE. Automatic Telephone Exchange.

ATF. Automatic Text Formatter.

ATLAS. A computer software for Automatic Tabulating, Listing And Sorting system; used for tabulating, listing and sorting.

ATM reciprocity. Ability to use cards from one credit card organisation or bank to obtain services from the Automatic Teller Machines of another body.

ATM. Asynchronous Transfer Mode, a cell-based data transfer technique in which channel demand determines packet allocation. ATM is a protocol designed by the telecommunications industry as a more efficient way to send voice, video, and computer data over a single network. It was originally conceived as a way to reconcile the needs for these different kinds of data on the telephone system, but the proponents of ATM arue that it can be implemented on computer LANs and WANs as well. In fact, this protocol is similar to Ethernet and token ring. ATM offers fast packet technology, real time, demand led switching for efficient use of network resources. It is also the generic term adopted by ANSI and the ITU-TS to classify cell relay technology within the realm of broadband WANs, specifically B-ISDN. In ATM, units of data are not time related to each other and, as part of the B-ISDN standard, is specified for digital transmission speeds from 34Mbit/s to 622Mbit/s. IBM currently offers ATM at non-standard 25Mbit/s format. ATM will be the high band width networking standard of the decade.

2. Abstract Test Method, one of the methods for conformance testing as defined in ISO 9646.

3. Automated Teller Machine, a cash machine, used in electronic banking.

ATME. Automatic Transmission Measuring Equipment; used in public networks to mean derives which measure signal quality.

ATOM. Automatic Transmission Of Mail.

ATP. Application Transaction Processing, prefix used to identify TP functional profiles in the ISP taxonomy.

ATR. Automatic Traffic recorder.

ATS. 1. Abstract Test Suite, in conformance testing, a test suite that is independent of any means of test, but uses specific abstract test method.

2. Administrative Terminal System; an obsolete text handling system.

at-sign (@). The separator for most of the e-mail addresses; it separates the user ID from domain name of the main computer.

attach. To make a device available for use by a system. On simple systems this may be achieved by engaging the appropriate plug and socket of the interface and putting the device into a state of readiness. In more complex systems it is often necessary to make the operating system aware of the type of device and the address of the connector to which it is attached. It is also necessary to ensure that the operating system has available the appropriate utility program for that device. In some designs the operating system can itself determine type and address of all peripherals that are electrically connected.

Attached Resource Computer Network. *See* ARCnet.

attached support processor. A term used to describe multiple computers, usually two, connected via channel-to-channel adaptors, employed to increase efficiency in processing many short duration tasks.

attenuation. The weakening of transmitted signals as they travel away from their point of origin. Amplifiers can recharge the signal up to a point.

atto-. Prefix denoting one million millionth; decimal prefix commonly used in association with a base unit in SI system of units, indicating a multiplication factor of 10^{-18} of unit.

ATTRIB. An external DOS command; used to change the attribute of a file.

ATU. 1. Address Translation Unit.

2. Autonomous Transfer Unit.

AU. 1. Access Unit, in the context of an X4.00 message-handling system, the functional object that links the MTS to another communication system, such as for accessing telex, telematics, or other service.

2. Adaptive Unit, supports a connection between an Integrated Services digital network and a public packet switch data network, in the context of ISDN.

3. Arithmetic Unit.

AUC. On-line AUthentication Certificate, information certified by a trusted authority, which after direct interaction with the authority may be used for authentication.

audio frequency. AF. Any frequency that can be detected by a normal human ear. This audible range extends from about 20-20000 Hz. In a communication system intelligible speech can be obtained if a frequency range from about 300-3400 Hz is reproduced; any frequency in this range is called voice frequency.

audio frequency-shift keying. AFSK. A system employed in telecommunications that uses audio frequency tones to modulate a carrier wave in order to convey a digital signal.

audio response unit. ARU. A device that can connect a computer system to a telephone and thereby provide a voice response to any enquiries received. The response is usually assembled by a computer from a prerecorded vocabulary of words.

audiotex. A service that allows a database host to pass data to a voice-mail computer, where it is interpreted and delivered as a natural, spoken-voice message.

audit trail. Data, in the form of a logic path linking a sequence of events, used for tracing the transactions that have affected contents of a record.

AUI. Attachment Unit Interface, the IEEE 802.3 specified cable and connector used to attach devices to a MAU; defined in Section 7 of the 802.3 standard. It may also refer to the interface between the physical layer and medium attachment unit.

AUNT. Automatic UNiversal Translator.

authentication. The verification of the identity of a user or process.

authorisation code. A unique multi-digit code identifying an authorised subscriber. The authorisation code is allowed only if the authorisation code is valid. The authorisation code is also generally used to identify the routing to be used to place the call and may also identify call restriction and class of service data.

authorisation. The permission for privilege based on identity; it is a part of authentication in a computer networking, where a person's access to services is based on his identity, and authentication procedure guarantees the use.

auto partition. A feature of 10 baseT; when 32 consecutive collisions are sensed by a port in a hub or concentrator from its attached work station or network segment, or when a packet that far exceeds the maximum allowable length is received, the port stops forwarding packets. The port continues to monitor traffic and will automatically begin normal packet forwarding when the first correct packet is received.

AUTO ABSTRACT. AUTOmatic ABSTRACT. Significant words from the title and sometimes the body of a document that describe its contents are selected and arranged in a meaningful pattern. The arrangement and selection by computer is carried out according to a specific programmed standard. Although not looking like an abstract prepared by humans, the autoabstract normally provides a good indication of what the document is about.

AUTODIN. AUTOmatic DIgital Network; US implementation of ACP-127, an allied Defence Messaging System.

automatic answering. Answering in which the called data terminal equipment automatically responds to the calling signal. The call may be established whether or not the called data terminal equipment is attended.

automatic bass compensation. Use of a resistor-capacitor network in conjunction with the gain control in an audio system to boost the volume of bass notes to compensate for the ear's inefficiency at low frequencies.

automatic call-recording equipment. ACRE. A device, which dispenses with the need for operator written 'tickets' detailing calls they handle. ACRE records the details automatically on magnetic tape for subsequent processing by computers.

automatic document request service. ADRS. A service provided by the British Library Automated Information Service (BLAISE), which permits subscribers at on on-line terminal to ask for the loan of, or copies of, documents from the British library lending division.

automatic frequency control. AFC. A device that automatically maintains the frequency of an alternating voltage within specified limits. Error-operated, the device normally consists of two parts, a frequency discriminator that compares actual with desired frequencies, and a reactor controlled by the discriminator in such a way as to correct any frequency error. A detector (such as a discriminator) operated from the turned circuit delivers a dc output voltage only when the circuit is operating above or below the signal frequency; otherwise, it has zero dc output. The dc output, when present, alters the value of a voltage-sensitive capacitor or a reactance tube connected across the tuned circuit to retune stage to desired frequency.

Automatic Private IP Addressing. *See* APIPA.

automatic programming. 1. The use of a high-level programming language. 2. Generation of programs automatically from a nonprocedural description of their desired effect. Thus in artificial intelligence we describe the required actions of a robot, and the system generates a program that will cause the required movements to take place. In commercial data processing we describe the various documents-orders, invoices delivery notes, etc.- and the relationship between the quantities involved, and the system generates a suite of programs to do the required processing. Automatic programming in this sense is at an early stage of development.

automatic repeat request. ARQ. An error control system for data transmission in which the receiving terminal can detect a transmission error and automatically transmit a request-repeat signal to the transmit terminal. The transmit terminal then retransmits the character code block or message until it is either correctly received or the error persists beyond a predetermined number of transmittals. Also known as automátic error correction.

automatic send-receive set. ASR. A combination of teletypewriter, transmitter and receiver, having the capability to transmit from either a keyboard or paper tape.

automatic storage allocation. A mechanism for allocating space to data objects only for the duration of the execution of their scope. It may be noted that automatic storage allocation is one form of dynamic storage allocation; another form is program controlled storage allocation.

autonomous built-in self test. ABIST. The ability of very-large-scale integration devices to automatically run a built-in self test software program.

AUTOPOLL. AUTOmatic POLLing; without interrupting the central processing unit, this hardware feature is able to process a list specifying the order in which a number of computer terminals are polled. It also handles negative responses.

AUTOPSY. Acronym for AUTomatic OPerating SYstem.

autoquote. AQ. Service provided for hotels by which billing information for calls originated from guest rooms is automatically transmitted to the receive-only teletypewriter at hotel.

AUTOSEVOCOM. AUTOmatic SEcure VOice COMmunications; a system utilising crypto-secure telephone instruments and high quality trunks.

AUTOVON. AUTOmatic VOice Network. The world-wide voice system; high quality trunks are used and different grades of priority pre-emption are provided.

AVA. Attribute Value Assertion, a statement that may be true, false, or undefined concerning the values of an entry in an X5.00 Directory.

AVC. Automatic Volume Control.

average access time. For a device such as hard drive, it is the amount of time it takes to position its read or read/write heads over any spot on the medium. It is important that the measurement be an average because access times can vary depending on the distance between the head's original location and their destination. Access time is a combination of two factors; the speed at which a disk spins, and the time it takes to move the heads form one track to another.

AVP. Attached Virtual Processor.

AVR. Automatic Voice Recognition.

AVT. 1. Application Virtual Terminal, prefix used to identify VT functional profiles in the ISP taxonomy.
2. Automatic Vision Testing.

AWS. Active Work Space.

B

B. 1. Bit. 2. Buffer. 3. Byte.

B.nnn. Acronym for the B-Series of CCITT Recommendations dealing with symbols and regular formats; for example, an international format for depicting dates [1991-09-26 (YYYY-MM-DD)], or the legal use of the term UTC (coordinated universal time-formerly Greenwich Mean Time).

BA. Binary Add.

BABBAGE. A machine oriented high-level language for GEC 4080 series of computers and their derivatives.

babble. Unwanted disturbing sounds in a carrier or other multiple channel system which result from the aggregate cross talk or mutual interference from other channels.

BAC. Basic Access Control, X.500 cases control defined in 1992 extensions, more comprehensive than Simplified Access Control.

BACE. Basic Automatic Checkout Equipment.

back end. The server part of a client/server application; it provides services across the network that have been requested by the client. For example, a back end may be a database server that responds to SQL requests from a workstation running a front-end application.

back space. One of the range of characters that form a specific code for any particular system (character set) that will cause the automatic back-spacing of an input or output device.

backbone. A high-capacity network that links together other networks of lower capacity. A local backbone network would typical y be an FDDI network acting as an in building backbone to link together multiple LANs. A wide area backbone network would typically use digital leased circuits and multiplexers or routers. The backbone network usually runs at a higher speed, and with a larger bandwidth, in comparison to the networks that branch off it.

background noise. The total system noise in the absence of information transmission independent of the presence or absence of a signal.

background processing. A general term for the processing of low-priority tasks such as printing. Processing only occurs when the computer does not have higher priorities such as those associated with real-time user interaction. Systems that are unable to perform multiple tasks (multi-tasking) carry out background processing during brief pauses in the system's primary (foreground) operations. The processing of high-priority tasks such as those associated with real-time user interaction on a multitasking computer is called foreground processing. This type of processing is performed without the opportunity for interaction with the user, within a system that provides for interaction by foreground processing. The jobs are submitted by users from terminals but are not processed immediately. They are placed into a background queue and run off, as resources become available.

background task. A secondary function perforated by a computer without interrupting its current or primary task.

background. 1. The area behind and outside the active window, including the desktop and any other application windows or icons.

2. Applications can run in the background. These applications are still running but they are not those in the active window and run without user intervention.

3. The counting rate of a counter tube caused by sources other than the caused by sources other than the one being measured. Due primarily to natural radioactivity in the soil, and cosmic rays.

back-haul. 1. The process of routing of a call, which appears to take an illogical path through network.

2. A link between a central office and a main microwave or multiplex station or between a ground satellite station or submarine cable terminal and switching centre controlling the circuits concerned.

backing store. Memory on which information is held for reference but not for direct execution; it is the lower part of the memory hierarchy in which the speed of access to the information stored is matched to the requirements of the system so as to achieve the greatest economy. The term may be used either in an absolute sense in which case it usually refers to a disk, or it may be used in a relative sense to refer to the device next down in the memory hierarchy. Also known as auxiliary memory; bulk memory; secondary memory.

backout. 1. The procedure for the removal of the updates done by a transaction that has either aborted, or that was in-flight at the time the system failed.

2. In programming, to return a file to an original state by deleting entries in the reverse chronological order to that in which they were inserted.

3. The act of retracting from a multilevel software program to return to base application screen or main menu.

4. In windows environment, the act of closing all the windows as one is retracting back to the base application screen, or main menu.

backpack. In recording, a lightweight, portable television-recording or camera signal-transmitting equipment.

backspace. To move backward one unit at a time.

backup copy. In computing, a copy of file or data set that is kept for reference in case the original file or data set is destroyed.

back-up domain controller. A server in a network domain that keeps and uses a copy of the domain's user accounts database to validate logon requests.

back-up server. Software or hardware which copies files so that there are always two current copies of each file. Also known as shadow server.

backup. Creating extra copies of files in case the original copies are damaged or destroyed. It has been suggested that the user should have at least three copies of important files, one on the hard disk, one on floppy, and another on any media stored off-site in fire-proof safe. That may be a little paranoid but consider what would happen if a particular file is lost.

2. The word backup is also used as a verb, to back up, *i.e.*, to make a copy in anticipation of future failure or corruption. Thus a dump forms a backup to be used in cases where a user's file has become unusable; the taking of the dump can be regarded as backing up the version on disk.

backus naur form. BNF. A formal computer language structure for the syntax phasing of other computer languages.

backward chaining. A commonly used method of deduction to draw inferences in an expert system, using the IF.....THEN rules.

backward chaining. One of several control methods for regulating the order in which inferences are drawn. In a rule-based system backward chaining is initiated by a goal rule. the system attempts to determine if the goal rule is correct. It backs up to the if clauses of the rule and tries to determine if they are correct. This, in turn leads the system to consider other rules that might confirm the if clauses. In this way the system backs into its rules. Eventually the back-chaining sequence ends when a question is asked or a previously stored result is found.

backward channel. A channel associated with the forward channel, used for supervisory or error control signals, but with a direction of transmission opposite to that of the forward channel in which user information is being transferred. It may be noted that in case of simultaneous transfer of information in both directions, this definition applies with respect to the data source under consideration. It may be noted that the backward channel is generally used for transmission of supervisory acknowledgement or error-control signals.

backward error correction. Error correction that occurs in a channel through the detection of errors by the receiver. The receiver responds to any errors in a block by requesting the transmitter to retransmit the affected block. Backward correction requires a return channel, in contrast to forward error correction.

backward LAN channel. In a broadband LAN, the channel assigned for uplink data transmission from the data stations to the head-end.

backward read. In memory systems, a technique used in a magnetic tape drive whereby data can be read when the tape is running backward.

backward recovery. A mode of system recovery in which transactions previously applied to a file are processed to reinstate file to an earlier condition.

bad sector. An area on a hard or floppy disk, which cannot store information accurately due to a manufacturing defect or damage caused by dust, scratches, fingerprints, and the like. Though the bad sectors on a floppy disk may mean the entire disk cannot be used; however, the operating system has the ability to ignore bad sectors on hard disks.

badge reader. A device designed to read in formation encoded into a small plastic card. It is often part of a data collection system in which each operator can be identified by the badge they present to the machine. It can also be used to control access to areas associated with electrically operated door locks and when built into keyboards and other parts of information systems it can control access to information. The badge is usually of plastic, or paper laminated between plastic, and may contain a photograph and other information in addition to what is encoded. The encoding takes many forms, some of which are proprietary and complex to achieve greater security. The most common form for data collection systems in an industrial environment was originally the punched badge: there were five standardized formats using the rectangular punched holes common to the 80-column punched card. The punched badge reader is being superseded by devices that sense information encoded by printed or characters by capacitive or magnetic elements embedded within the card or by magnetic recording on a strip of material on the surface.

bag. 1. An unordered collection of items where more than one instance of the same item is allowed.

2. Any data structure representing a bag. Representations are similar to those used for sets. In a set, however, it is only necessary to represent the presence of an element whereas in a bag it is also necessary to represent the number of times it occurs.

BAL. *See* basic assembler language.

balancing network. 1. A circuit used to simulate the impedance of a uniform two-wire cable or open-wire circuit over a selected range of frequencies.

2. A device used between a balanced device or line and an unbalanced device or line to transform from balanced to unbalanced or from unbalanced to balanced.

balancing. A test for equality between the values of two equivalent sets of items and a control total.

ballpoint. A Microsoft pointing device that incorporates both mouse and trackball technology, designed to be attached to laptop and notebook computers, enabling the user to work with a pointing device in areas where space is limited.

BALUN. 1. BALanced to UNbalanced transformer; the transformer employed to couple a balanced antenna to an unbalanced transmission line. These are often used so that the IBM 3270 terminals can run off twisted pair, or to allow the co-axial Ethernet to be operated over UTP.

2. A passive device that is used to match an antenna to a cable having different impedance.

BAM. *See* basic access method.

band communication satellite. Any of the bands of radio frequencies allocated for use by communication satellites.

Up-links to satellites, (in MHz):
5925-6425;
12500-12750;
14000-14500;
27500 - 31000.

Down-links from satellites, (in MHz):
3700-4200;
10700-10950;
12000-11450;
17700-21200.

band gap. Difference in energy between the valence and conduction bands of a semiconductor. Band gap of optoelectronic components determines their operating wavelengths.

band printer. An impact printer which employs a horizontally rotating band (belt), that contains characters (letters, numbers, and symbols). Hammers strike the ribbon and paper, hitting different characters on the band (which can be changed for different fonts). Print speed may exceed 600 lines per minute. An impact printer in which the character set available for printing is carried on a flexible band (on a belt).

band. 1. A range of frequencies between upper and lower limits; the section of the frequency spectrum lying between limits that are defined according to some requirement or to some functional aspect of a given signal or transmission channel. When used as a suffix the word is a contraction of bandwidth as in narrowband and wideband.

2. A set of tracks on a magnetic drum or on one side of a magnetic disc.

3. A loop of flexible material, in particular, the loop of steel tape that acts as font carrier in a band printer.

band-limited channel. A transmission channel with finite bandwidth. All physically realisable channels are band-limited.

bandwidth compression. A technique for reducing bandwidth which is generally required for the transmission by suppressing the redundant information.

bandwidth ratio. In a radio communication system the ratio, in decibels, equal to ten times the common logarithm of a quantity consisting of the occupied bandwidth of the entire baseband, divided by the assigned channel bandwidth.

bandwidth, nominal. Total bandwidth per channel. Four kHz for normal commercial speech channels of 300 to 3400 Hz; 3 kHz for the narrower channels used on some intercontinental submarine cable systems which use 16 voice channels per 48 kHz group instead of the usual 12 channels per group on FDM multiplexing.

bandwidth, x dB. A bandwidth such that beyond its lower and upper limits any discrete spectrum component or continuous spectral power density is attenuated by at least x dB relative to a given and predetermined zero dB relative to a given and predetermined zero dB reference level.

bandwidth. 1. The range of frequencies a transmission line or channel can carry: the greater the bandwidth, the greater the information- carrying capacity of a channel. For a digital channel this is defined in bit/s. For an analog channel it is dependent on the type and method of modulation used to encode the data.

2. Range of frequencies within which the performance of a device or system falls within given limits, with respect to a particular specified characteristic.

3. Difference between limiting frequencies of continuous frequency band.

4. The range of signal frequencies that can be transmitted by a communications channel with defined maximum loss or distortion. Bandwidth indicates the information-carrying capacity of a channel. For analog transmission this is usually expressed in kHz or MHz; for digital transmission the transmission rate, *e.g.*, bit/s, kbit/s, Mbit/s, is used. For an optic fibre system, bandwidth is usually given as its capacity to transmit information in a specific time for a specific length, *e.g.*, 10 Mbit/s/km.

bank switching. A technique for memory management commonly used in microcomputer systems that require more memory than the microprocessor can directly address. A typical 8-bit microprocessor can directly reference 16-bit address space (64K bytes). In systems requiring more than 64K bytes of memory, such as multi-user systems, bank switching can be used to overcome the addressing limitations of the microprocessor.

BAP. Basic Assembler Program.

bar code scanner. The optical character reader, a special optical pen is moved over printed bar code, the characters are read and translated into digital signals which are sent into a processor.

BAR. 1. Bar Address Register.
2. Buffer Address Register.

barcode. Code used for identifying an item, consisting of a sequence of thick and thin lines which can be read by an opto-electronic scanner.

barrel nut connector. *See* BNC connector.

10base-2. A wiring options for LANs.

10base-3. A wiring options for LANs.

10base-5. A wiring options for LANs.

10base-t. A wiring options for LANs.

base address. An address used as the origin in the calculation of addresses. While loading a program, base address is added to the address component of each instruction in order to obtain absolute addresses.

base band. *See* baseband.

base memory. The portion of memory set aside for general use in computer's random-access memory. Most personal computers running under DOS have a base memory of 640 kilobytes. The usable amount is much less because the operating system is also contained in the base memory.

base number. A quantity that specifies system of representation for numbers.

base station. A fixed radio transmitter/receiver which electronically relays signals to and from mobile voice and data terminals or handsets.

base unit. A unit that is defined in terms of a primary standard, *e.g.*, the unit of mass (kilogram) in SI units.

base. Region between emitter and collector of a transistor. Also the radix of a numbering system, such as 10 for decimals, 2 for binary, 3 for ternary.

baseband LAN. A local area network in which the data is encoded and transmitted without modulation of a carrier.

baseband modem. A special type of modem which transmits the modified digital signal, rather than modulating and demodulating a carrier signal. It is also called a 'short haul' or limited distance' modem.

baseband networking. Communication in which a digital signal is placed directly on the transmission medium without requiring a carrier, *i.e.*, without modulation. Only one signal may be present on the baseband cannel at a time. This type of signalling baseband signalling is also called *d.c.* signalling because in some baseband networks a continuous *d.c.* voltage is present when the data does not change. Baseband networks may use twisted pair or coaxial cables for data transmission. The Ethernet is a prototype local area network using baseband signalling on a coaxial cable.

baseband signalling. In communications, the transmission of a signal at its original frequencies.

baseband. A technique for transmitting a message at high line-speeds along a medium (such as a cable) only one signal at a time. Information is represented by changes in voltages. Baseband transmission cannot support video-conferencing and is only able to support limited graphics facilities through either twisted pair, coaxial, or fibre optics cables. A transmission medium through which digital signals are transmitted without complicated frequency shifting. Ethernet is an example of a baseband network. The digital input is applied directly to the transmission media without the intervention of a modulating device, which works well if there is wide bandwidth and distances no more than several hundred metres are involved. It is common in LANs and limited distance modems. All stations attached to the network have to participate in every transmission. Simpler and cheaper than Broadband, it permits only one "conversation" at a time as the whole of the bandwidth is used to transmit a single digital signal. Ethernet is a baseband network.

base-bound register. The hardware used for virtual-memory allocation. A base-bound register is associated with each segment of data or code and defines the position in physical memory of word zero for that segment the so-called base or datum and the number of words available to that segment, the so-called bound or limit (or alternatively the physical memory address of the next word after the end of the segment in which case it is a bounds register). Whenever a process attempts to access the memory segment the hardware of the system checks that the address of the word lies within the range:

$0 \leq$ word address $<$ bound;

and then adds the address to the value contained in the base register to give the physical address. The storage for the segment must be allocated in a contiguous area of memory. The base register used in the construction of relative addresses should not be confused with the base of a base-bound system; the result of modifying an address by a base register's contents is still an address within virtual memory space of the process, and is not necessary a physical address.

basic access method. BAM. Each input/output statement in this method of computer access initiates performance of a machine input/output operation.

basic additional teleprocessing support. BATS. A system used by some computer systems in the late 1960s to provide telecommunication-processing support.

basic assembler language. BAL. A non-complex computer program that translates an assembly language into object code, having no macros or conditional assembly instructions.

basic combined programming language. BCPL. A language developed to write a computer program that translates from a high level into object code for the combined programming language, this system's implementation language is available on a wide range of machines.

basic data access method. BDAM. Providing a non-queuing facility; a method employed by some computers of gaining access to data held in a backing store. Although not a primary store the backing store has in fact a larger capacity but a lower access time.

basic disk operating system. BDOS. An area in the memory map of a microcomputer using a control program for microcomputers disk operating system, having routines used by the system to access its system disk drives. It thus provides for file management.

basic identification number. BIN. The code having a three-colour-band system on the contact body of avionic rectangular connectors to identify each contact size.

basic indexed sequential access method. BISAM. A method employed by some computers to gain access to information held in a backing store, which is not a primary memory store. It is an fact a store that has a larger capacity but a slower access time.

basic input output system. BIOS. A group of routines comprising an area in the memory map of a microcomputer using a control program for microcomputers (CP/M) disk operating system (DOS), that is implemented when a user first gets the system up and running. The area is then called up by the operating system when it needs any input/output routines.

basic operating system. BOS. An operating system designed to run on IBM computers, this software, held resident on a disk, is associated with the execution of programs and the co-ordination of a computer system.

basic partitioned access method. BPAM. A method employed by computers to gain access to information held in a backing store, which is not a primary memory store, but a store that has a larger capacity but lower access time.

BASIC. Beginners All-purpose Symbolic Instruction Code, a computer language characterised by its ease of use and the ease with which it can be learned. It is the standard language used with microcomputers and is well suited to computer time-sharing. This computer language is designed to be easy to learn and suitable for youngsters. BASIC is not as commonly used today.

BASS. Basic Activity Subset of Session, a subset of the session service available that includes the activity management functional unit.

bass. Sound waves of frequencies at the lower end of the audio range, below 250 Hz.

BAT. File name extension for a batch file.

batch file/program. An ASCII text file which contains list of DOS commands and program names. When the batch file is run, the commands and programs are run in sequence just as if you had typed them at the MS-DOS prompt. Batch files are distinguished by their BAT suffix.

batch processing. A technique in which transactions are collected into groups so that they can be processed or updated as a single job. Where large database are involved, batch processing saves on computer time and avoids unnecessary computer interruption. In contrast, real-time transactions are made by the computer fast enough that records can be activated or updated immediately. The processing of data or the accomplishment of jobs, accumulated in advance, in such a manner that the user cannot further influence its processing while it is in progress. Batch working can be compared with real-time working in which transactions are delay between occurrence of the event and the eventual processing of relevant data. The term is also applied to background processing of jobs not requiring intervention by the user, which take place on many multi-access systems. Also known as dripfeed.

batch region. One of the several regions in main storage controlled by the operating system, where batch processing can be performed in a multiprogramming environment.

batch-header document. A document that accompanies and identifies a batch of input documents and that may be used to validate them. For example, a document that includes balances, control totals, hash totals or checksums.

BATS. *See* basic additional teleprocessing support.

baud rate. Speed at which information is transferred; generally referred to as bps now.

baud. Bits At Unit Density, derived originally from the name for the five bit code, BAUDOT; refers to (usually) bits per second; a unit of measuring the data-signalling rate or data flow. It is the instantaneous bit speed with which a device or channel transmits a character in serial transmission. Although strictly speaking it stands for signal speed, for practical purposes it is generally considered as interchangeable with bits per second. Reciprocal of the length in seconds of the shortest element of the code.

Baudot code. A special set of binary characters which use only 5 bits per character, forming 32 combinations (2^5). This was increased to 62 through the use of two special shift characters. It was mainly used to handle telex messages by common communications carriers. Its main disadvantage is the lack of an error checking bit.

bayonet nut coupling. BNC. A type of connector used for coaxial cable radio frequency interconnection. It employs a two-prong bayonet with a spring coupling unit. Bayonet nut coupling connectors are extensively employed within test equipment as they provide rapid connection/disconnection.

BB. Bubble Board.

BBD. *See* bucket-brigade device.

B-box. 1. Register that contains a quantity to be used under direction of the control section of computer hardware.

2. A device that permits automatic modification of an instruction address without permanently altering the instruction in the memory.

3. A register to an arbitrary integer, usually one which is added (or subtracted upon the execution of each machine instruction.

BBL. Basic Business Language.

BBS. *See* Bulletin Board System.

BC. 1. *See* Blind Copy.

2. Binary Code.

BCC. Block Check Character; a control character that is appended to blocks in character-oriented protocols; used for determining if the block was received error-free.

BCC. *See* block check characters.

BCD. *See* binary coded decimal.

BCDC. Binary Coded Decimal Counters.

BCH code. An error correcting code sometimes used with data transmission equipment.

BCL. Bar Coded Label.

BCPL. *See* basic combined programming language.

BCS. Basic Combined Subset of Session.

BCUG. Bilateral Closed User Group, a group of users that allows connections only among predetermined members based on previous agreements.

BDAM. *See* basic data access method.

BDCB. Buffered Data/Control Bus.

BDD. Binary to Decimal Decoder.

BDIC. Binary coded Decimal Interchange Code.

BDOS. 1. Batch Disk Operating System.

2. *See* basic disk operating system.

BDS. Building Distribution System, a building wiring system that uses a mix of wiring media to serve voice, data, and video applications.

beaconing. Token Ring process to recover network when any attached station has sensed that the ring is inoperable because of a hard error. Stations can withdraw from the ring if needed. A station detecting a ring failure upstream transmits (beacons) a special MAC frame used to isolate the location of error using beacon transmit and beacon repeat modes.

BECN. Backward Explicit Congestion Notification, a bit in a frame relay header to indicate that a node is experiencing congestion conditions.

BECS. Basic Error Control System.

BEEF. Business and Engineering Enriched Formula translator.

Bell 103. A standard for 300 bits per second full duplex communications using the AT&T Bell protoc over the public switched telephone network.

Bell 212. A standard for 1200 bits per second full duplex communications using the AT&T Bell protocol over public switched telephone network.

Bell integrated optical device. BIOD. An integrated optical circuit having both active and passive elements, which can be used as logic and control elements in various other devices (*e.g.* logic gates) depending on how they are interconnected during fabrication.

Bell System. Pre-1984 AT&T organisation including Bell operating companies. In 1984, wholly owned operating companies were separated from the other parts of AT&T. AT&T Communications, or ATTCOM provides long distance voice, data and video transmission services both within the US and other countries. AT&T Information Systems (ATTIS) is the principal marketing unit of AT&T Technologies. It provides information processing and distribution systems for business customers in addition to consumer product and services. Other sectors of AT&T include:

AT&T Network Systems,
AT&T Technology Systems, and
AT&T Bell Laboratories.

AT&T continues to hold a minority position in two of the original Bell Operating Companies (Southern New England Tel and Cincinnati Bell).

bell. One of the range of characters that form a specific code for any particular system (character set) that will initiate the sounding of a bell on a terminal device.

benchmark. Test of performance of a computer or peripheral device. While benchmarks can offer seemingly objective tests of performance, the best test is to use the computer or peripheral with the applications and files the user will actually be using.

BER. 1. Basic Encoding Rules of ASN; the standard rules for encoding data units described by ASN.

2. Bit Error Rate, the number of incorrectly transmitted or received bits divided by the total number sent in a given bit stream. It is usually expressed as a number referenced to a power of 10.

BERT. Bit Error-Rate Testing.

BES. Basic Executive System.

beta test. A second stage test of a new software package, outside factory, before its commercial release. The first stage test is conducted in-house and is called an alpha test.

beta. A conventional designation of pre-release software; a beta version of software is usually in secondary testing (alpha versions are earlier releases), and is sometimes publicly available, but sometimes only available to particular users (beta testers). Beta software is usually somewhat unstable, and may have more bugs than a regular release.

BEU. Basic Encoding Unit.

BEX. Broadband EXchange.

BF. 1. Bridge Function; a bridge repeats all traffic on either of two segments to the adjacent segment in network. 2. Beat Frequency.

BI. 1. Basic Index. 2. Batch Input.

bias distortion. Distortion affecting a two-condition (or binary) modulation in which all the significant intervals corresponding to one of the two significant conditions have uniformly longer or shorter duration than the corresponding theoretical duration.

bias error. An error due to bias, such as the error caused by a shrunken measuring tape; or in computation, an error caused by truncation.

bias. 1. A systematic deviation of a value from a reference value.
2. The amount by which the average of a set of values departs from a reference value.
3. Electrical, mechanical or magnetic force that is applied to relay, vacuum tube or other device to establish an electrical or mechanical reference level to operate the device.
4. Effect on telegraph signals produced by the electrical characteristics of the terminal equipment.

biased data. A distribution of records that is non-random with respect to the sequencing or sorting criteria.

biased. Pertaining to a process used in the generation of random numbers that is more likely to produce some numbers than others.

biax memory. A type of two-hole ferrite memory with the read and write wires running at right angles to each other.

bibliographic data processing program. BIDAP. A package of computer software, which has been designed to process information relating to the books, articles or reports. Normally the data covered is of authorship, title, and publication details.

BIDAP. *See* bibliographic data processing program.

bifurcation. Splitting in two, the term can be applied in computing in various ways. Bifurcation is the generic name for a collection of algorithms that initially convert a decision table into a tree structure, which can then be systematically encoded to produce a program. The bifurcation method involves choosing some condition *C* and eliminating it from the decision table to produce two sub-tables one corresponding to the when C is true and the other to when C is false. The method is then applied recursively to the two sub-tables. From this approach a decision tree can be built each node of the tree representing a condition and sub-trees representing sub-tables; leaf nodes identify rules.

Big Blue. A slang term used to refer to International Business Machines Corporation (IBM) whose corporate colour is blue.

BIL. Block Input Length.

BIM. 1. Bus Interface Module.
2. Branch Multiplexer.

BIN. *See* basic identification number.

binary coded decimal. BCD. Groups of binary digits representing decimal numbers, with each decimal number allocated four binary digits. This system is widely used in telecommunications computer projects. In this type of numerical representation in which digits are represented by binary numerals (1 or 0), and the individual figures of a decimal number are separately coded into binary form. The most common code used a presentation where 8-4-2-1 binary code groups are used. In this code twenty-three is represented as 0010 0011; in pure binary notation it would be 10111.

binary digit. Unit of information in two-level digital notation, may be 0 or 1.
2. A member selected from a binary set.

binary file. A file containing information that is in machine-readable form; it can be read only by an application. The term binary file, usually refers to a file that uses all 8 bits of each byte for information. Text files usually use only 7 bits, leaving the 8th bit as 0.

binary notation. 1. Any notation that uses two different characters, usually the binary digits 0 and 1; for example the grey code. The grey code is a binary notation, but not a pure binary numeration system. In the ordinary decimal system displacing a digit one position to the left means multiplying it by a factor of 10. In binary notation displacement to the left multiplies by a factor of 2. The binary number 1101 represents 1 unit, 0×2, 1×4, 1×8, *i.e.*, a decimal equivalent of 13.

2. The fixed-radix notation where the radix is two.

binary search. A dichotomizing search in which, at each step of the search the set of items is partitioned into two equal parts some appropriate action being taken in the case of an odd number of items. Synonymous with binary chop.

binary synchronous communications. BISYNC*:* In a data communications system, binary synchronous communications is the use of a set of control characters and sequences for the synchronised transmissions of binary coded data between stations. It is a low-level half-duplex communications protocol that allows any pattern of binary digits, including those normally used for control, to be transmitted in a block. Also called BSC.

binary system. *See* binary notation.

binary transfer. Method of transferring files to or from a remote computer in which all eight bits of each byte are transferred. In a text transfer, the eighth bit is ignored.

binary tree. 1. A finite set of nodes that is either empty or is such that firstly there is a single designated node called the root and secondly the remaining nodes are partitioned into disjoint sets, T_l and T_r, where each of these sets is itself a binary tree. T_l is called the left sub-tree and T_r the right sub-tree of the root. At level *h* of a binary tree there is a maximum of 2^h nodes. A binary tree of depth *d* thus has at most $(2^{d+1}-1)$ nodes and one with *n* nodes has a minimum depth of $\log_2 n$. The term binary tree is also used to describe any (ordered) tree of degree two.

2. Any data structure used to represent a binary tree. Each node would be represented by pointers to the left an right sub-trees as well as to data value associated with the node. The binary tree could then be represented as a pointer to its root node.

binary-to-decimal conversion. Conversion of a binary number to the equivalent decimal number, for example, the binary-to-decimal conversion of the binary number 111 is the decimal number 7.

binaural. The use of two separate sound channels on headphones so that the left-hand sound channel is heard only in the left ear, and the right-hand channel is confined to the right ear. The spatial dimension in binaural sound is not confined to the location of the sound source.

bindery. A database that contains definitions for entities such as users, groups and workgroups in Novel NetWare LAN network operating system. The bindery supports the design, organisation, and secure operation of NetWare environment.

binding. The process of linking a protocol to a network interface card or device driver.

bindings property sheet. The property sheet that allows enabling or disabling TCP/IP capability to communicate with higher level file sharing and network printing services.

binhex. A file format for encoding Macintosh binary files as text files, for easier transfer between computers. Binhex files usually have the suffix ".hqx" Almost all Macintosh communication programs will automatically detect and translate files in Binhex format.

BIO. Buffered Input/Output.

biochips. A kind of chip that can be used in place of silicon chip. It has been noticed that biochips employ organic molecules or genetically-engineered proteins for their main circuits, thereby allowing microscopic chips to be built which consume virtually no power. Two types of biochips are being researched; digital biochip, which will use organic molecules to turn the flow of electrons on and off to represent binary digits in the same way as silicon chips; and analog biochips in which protein enzymes would be used for graded responses to represent variable data (not based on the binary system).

BIOD. *See* Bell integrated optical device.

biometric security devices. A device which only allows access to a person after certain unique physical characteristics (physical signatures) of that person are entered into a computer system for verification. For example, a person's voice can be used to gain entry; a retinal scan verifier can be used to measure the eye's blood vessel pattern; a hand geometry verifier can be used to measure the length and width of fingers and their webbing; or a signature verifier can be used to store the dynamic characteristics of hand-written signature.

BIOS. Basic In/Out System. Part of an IBM or compatible computer than manages the flow of signals through bus.

biosensor. A biologically sensitive material immobilised in intimate contact with a suitable transducer system that converts the biochemical signal into a quantifiable and processible electrical signal.

bipolar transmission. Method of sending binary data in which negative and positive states alternate; used in digital transmission facilities.

bipolar transmission. Signalling method predominantly used for digital services. The signal carrying binary values alternative between positive and negative polarities.

BIPS. Billions of Instructions Per Second.

biquinary notation. A system similar to that used in the ancient abacus and also in some computers; each decimal digit is represented by two symbols, first is 0 or 1, the 1 representing decimal 5; the second is 0,1,2,3 or 4. Decimal 64 is therefore 1104. Some forms of biquinary use 7 digits for each decimal figure; 01 for less than 5,10 for 5-9 followed by 00001, 00010, 00100, 01000, 10000 for 0-4 and 5-9 so that each decimal figure is represented by 7 bits of which two only are always 1s, the others always 0s.

BIRS. Basic Information Retrieval System.

bis. Second version of a CCITT standard, e.g., V.26 bis.

BISAM. *See* basic indexed sequential access method.

BISDN. Broadband ISDN, high-bandwidth ISDN service that supports rates of 45 Mbps to 153 Mbps, using fixed-sized packets.

B-ISDN. *See* broadband ISDN.

BISYNC. BInary SYNchronous Communication, developed by IBM.

BISYNC. *See* binary synchronous communications.

bit error rate tester. A device for testing the reliability of a digital data communications link. BERT generates specific data patterns that are routed through a communications device for comparison at the receiving end. The errors are counted by the BERT.

bit error rate. BER. Number of erroneous bits divided by the total number of bits over a stipulated period of time. This is usually expressed as the number of erroneous bits per million introduced in the passage of single or parallel streams of binary digits (BITs) in a transmission path. Two examples of bit error rate are;

(a) transmission BER-number of erroneous bits received divided by total number of bits transmitted; and

(b) information BER-number of erroneous decoded (corrected) bits. BER is usually expressed as a number and a power of 10, *e.g.,* 2.5 erroneous bits out of 100,000 bits transmitted would be 2.5 in 10^5 or $2.5'10^{-5}$.

bit interleaving. A form of Time Division Multiplexing (TDM) for synchronous protocols, including HDLC, SDLC, BiSync and X.25 Bit interleaving retains the sequence and number of bits, so that correct synchronization is achieved between both ends.

bit mapping. A graphics display technique wherein each pixel (picture element) of the displayed image corresponds to one or more bits in the processor's memory. In a monochromatic display the number of bits corresponding to each pixel determines the number of grey-scale levels supported. If there one bit per pixel the image will be strictly black-and white with no shades of grey. In a colour display the number of bits per pixed determines how many colours can be displayed.

bit oriented protocol. BOP; refers to messages (*i.e.*, BOP messages) used in telecommunications, that are transmitted in frames, all messages adhering to one standard frame format.

bit rate. The speed, at which bits are transmitted over a communication link, usually expressed in bits per second.

bit sequence independence. Pertaining to a network that enables the transfer of digital data, as a sequence of bits, without placing any restriction upon the sequence of bits.

bit slice microprocessor. A microprocessor with a large scale integrated arithmetic logic unit; made from bit slices, and associated control unit.

bit synchronous operation. BSO. A mode of operation in which data circuit-terminating equipment, data terminal equipment, and transmitting circuits are all operated in bit synchronism with an accurate clocking system. Clock timing is delivered at twice the modulation rate, and one bit is released during one clock cycle.

bit. BInary digiT, pulse whose presence or absence indicates data. The smallest amount of information, consisting of two alternatives, either 0 or 1. It is one character of a digital word, and the position of the bit in word usually determines its significance. The number can be obtained by progressing right to leave across the columns and adding values when they appear. There are eight bits in one ASCII character.

bit-by-bit asynchronous operation. A mode of operation in which rapid manual semiautomatic or automatic shifts in the data modulation rate are accomplished by gating or slewing the clock modulation rate. The equipment may be operated at 50 bits/s one moment and at 1200 bits/s the next moment.

biternary transmission. A method of digital transmission in which two binary pulse trains are combined for transmission over a system in which the available bandwidth is only sufficient for transmission of one of the two pulse trains when in binary form. The biternary signal is generated from two synchronous binary signals operating at the same bit rate. The two binary signals operating at the same time to have a relative time difference of one-half the binary interval and are combined by linear addition to from the biternary signal. A decoding process returns the signals to the binary state.

bitmap. An image stored as a pattern of dots (or pixels).

BITNET. A network, which provides interactive electronic mail, interactive conversation, and file transfer facilities, using the store-and-forward protocol. Originally built on IBM hosts using IBM software for connections.

bits per inch. BPI. An expression of the density of data on a tape or disk memory-storage medium; number of binary digits over a specific length.

bits per second. BPS. A unit of measure of data flow. It is the instantaneous binary digit speed with which a device or channel transmits a character in serial transmission. For practical purposes the term is generally considered to be interchangeable with BAUD. One thousand bit/s is 1 Kbit/s.

bit-stuffing. A process in bit-oriented data communications protocols where a string of 'one' bits is broken by an inserted 'zero'. This 'zero' is added by the sender and removed by the receiver. This is done to prevent user data containing a series of 'one' bits from being interpreted as flag control character.

BL. Block Length.

BLA. Blocking Acknowledgement Signal.

black box. A device or system that has accessible inputs and outputs, but whose internal functions are unknown. All knowledge obtainable from a black box is derived solely from the output and input signals.

black clipping. In television and video, a control circuit in video cameras and recorders that is used to control the black level so that it does not affect or appear in the synchronisation portion of the video signal.

black signal. In communications, the signal produced by the facsimile scanning the darkest areas of a source document.

BLAST. Acronym for Boolean Logic And State Transfer.

BLDSC. British Library Document Supply Centre, formerly the British Library Lending Division.

BLERT. Block Error Rate Test.

BLISS. Basic Language for the Implementation of System Software.

BLOB. Basic Large OBject; all database management systems handle structured data such as part numbers and colour with ease, but they must go back to the file system for unstructured data such as text, graphics, and digitised data. A blob is a field in a record, like any other data element. It is subject to concurrency and transaction control. Unlike other fields, however, a blob has no size limit. Blob data is stored in the database, so it cannot be lost through a misguided file copy or backup. Most applications address data which is unstructured, or structured in ways that do not match the relational model. Blobs have been found to be quite useful in applications such as computer-aided design (CAD), computer-assisted software engineering, and office automation. For example, before blobs, CAD databases could only hold the names of files; component descriptions and graphics were kept in the files. Putting graphics data directly in the database as blobs reduces the number of files to open or close, and gives the benefits of transaction and concurrency control.

block check characters. BCC. Check bits used in line control procedures, which make up the later part of a block of transmitted information. They are generated by a checking process applied to the information part of the transmission.

block copy. To copy a file from one medium to another without changing its contents.

block factor. A measure of number of records contained with in a block.

block header. Bytes at the beginning of a block, used to describe the organisation of the file and the relationship between blocks.

block message. A message that is to be transmitted to two or more remote terminals.

block protector. A rectangular carbon block used on main distribution frames as lightning protection. The block is divided into two halves separated by a thin mica spacer or by a self-restoring insulating surface film. Lightning voltages jump the gap and discharge to ground. Also sealed glass tube with same external dimensions as carbon block containing electrodes, which operate as more efficient lightning arresters than traditional carbon blocks.

block transfer. The process of transferring one or more blocks of data in one operation. It may be noted that the block transfer can be done with or without erasing data from the original location.

block. 1. A group of bits or *n*-array digits transmitted as a unit. An encoding procedure is generally applied to the group of bits or *n*-array digits for error control purposes.

2. A string of records a string of words or a character-string to be treated as an entity.

3. A set of items such as words, characters, or digits, handled as unit.

4. A collection of contiguous records recorded as a unit; separated by inter-block gaps and each block may contain one or more records.

block-error rate. Number of blocks received with erroneous bits compared with the number of blocks received in an error-correcting data systems, the block error rate is a good indication of the through-put of a data system.

blocking factor. The number of records to be contained in a block.

blocking signal. A signal transmitted to the distant end of a communication circuit to indicate that it has been reserved for use or has been rendered unavailable for use.

blocking, external. When referring to a switching stage, the condition in which no suitable resource connected to that switching stage is available.

blocking, internal. In a conditional selection system the condition in which a connection cannot be made between a given inlet and any suitable free outlet owing to the impossibility of establishing a path.

blocking, poison. Traffic administrative assumption that a blocked call is held up to the total intended holding time and that if a trunk becomes idle, the call will seize it and use it for the remaining of the holding time.

blocking. 1. The combination of individual records in to blocks, usually to achieve greater input/output efficiency by reducing the number of peripheral operations.

2. In traffic flow, blocking occurs when the immediate establishment of a new call is impossible owing to the inaccessibility of facilities in the system being considered.

3. In connection with maintenance operations, the deliberate withdrawal from service of a circuit or other resource.

Bluetooth. The codename for technology specification for low-cost, short-range radio links between mobile computers, mobile phones, and other portable devices. It allows mobile phones, palmtops, and computers to communicate wirelessly with each other without manual intervention from user. A Bluetooth device has three components:

(a) a radio device that emit radio frequency waves;

(b) software which powers the hardware in which chip is embedded, and sends data to the radio device to be transmitted; and

(c) software or the protocol stack, which resides in the computer.

B-mail. An electronic mail utility provided by Banyan.

BMC. 1. Block Multiplexer Channel.

2. Bubble Memory Controller.

bmp. File name extension for a bit mapped image, a kind of graphics file.

BMTI. Block Mode Terminal Interface.

BMU. Basic Measurement Unit.

BNC connector. A cylindrical push-and-twist connector for connecting thin co-axial cable, such as 10Base2 "thin wire" Ethernet, and to link thin wire Ethernet to network interface cards, transceivers and other network elements. Said to be short for Bayonet Neill-Concelman after the developers of the connector. Also referred to as a Barrel Nut Connector.

BNF. Backus Naur Form, formal method for stating grammar or syntax rules. Also known as Backus Normal Form.

BNPF. Beginning-Negative-Positive-Finish, an older type of data-encoding output format for programmable read-only memory (PROM) programmers. *B* represents beginning, N is negative (1), *P* is positive (O) and *F* is finish. For example, 101010 is represented by BNPNPNPF.

BNT. Broadband Network Termination.

BOC. 1. Block Oriented Computer.

2. Bell Operating Company, the telephone company in US.

BOM. Beginning of Message, a byte or octet that signals the beginning of a Data Link Control message.

book message. A message to be transmitted to two or more remote terminals.

Boolean logic. Rules and concepts for comparing data conditions including LESS THAN, GREATER THAN, EQUAL TO, AND, OR, or NOT. Used often to specify the conditions of a search on a large set of data.

booster. A generator or transformer inserted in a circuit in order to increase or decrease the magnitude or to change the phase of the voltage acting on the circuit.

booting. Loading of operating system of a computer into the random-access memory from a storage device such as a floppy disk (in the case of a personal computer). This is generally an automatic loading procedure issued by the read-only memory chip. During the boot, several diagnostic tests are performed to check the working order of internal and external devices such as printers or disk drives.

bootstrap. 1. A sequence of instructions whose execution causes additional instructions to be loaded and executed until a complete computer program is loaded into storage.

2. To execute a bootstrap. It may be noted that the term 'bootstrapping' is also used for translating a compiler by using itself or a previous version as the translator.

BOP. Bit-Oriented Protocol, a data link protocol that is code transparent.

borrow digit. A digit that is generated when a difference in a digit place is arithmetically negative and that is transferred for processing elsewhere. It may be noted that in the positional representation system, a borrow digit is transferred to the digit place with next higher weight for processing there.

BOS. 1. Background Operating System.
2. Basic Operating System.
3. Batch Operating System.

BOT. Beginning Of Tape, the point to which a cartridge tape is rewound, as opposed to a beginning of information marker.

bot. A computer program that logs into a MUD and pretends to be a human being. Bots are generally frowned upon; asks the administrators of the MUD if they can run them.

bottleneck. A condition in which network data transfer is slowed significantly because of a problem with a network device.

bottom-up programming. The creation of software, by using a bottom-up approach, that is, by starting with the most basic or primitive subroutines and proceeding to higher level routines and programs while using the lower level ones, until the system is completed.

bottom-up. In automatic data processing systems engineering, pertaining to an approach to systems design, development or fabrication that starts with the lowest level components and gradually proceeds through high level components until the system is completed.

bounce. In transmission systems, to reflect a signal or the reflected signal itself. The reflection may occur from the end of a line, a point of sudden impedance difference, a dish, a target, or the surface of the celestial bodies.

bound mode. In an optical waveguide, a mode in which the field decays monotonically in the transverse direction external to the core and in which the power is not lost.

boundary routing. A 3Com proprietary name for a method of accessing remote networked locations, such as a bank branch office. Effectively a form of bridging, the idea is to reduce the need for technical expertise locally and the cost of equipment at the remote site and manage the communications from head office.

bounds checking. Testing of computer program results for access to storage outside of its authorised limits.

bounds register. A hardware register that holds an address specifying a storage boundary.

box. Flowchart symbol used to represent logical unit or operation within a system.

BP. 1. Batch Processing.
2. Bit Processor.

BPAM. *See* basic partitioned access method.

BPI. *See* bits per inch.

BPL. Binary Program Loader.

B-position. Peripheral equipment which due to fault condition sends desperate message as fast as it can usually operation in a loop.

BPS. 1. Bits Per Second, normally written in lowercase (bps) to avoid confusion with baud and bytes per second.
2. Basic Programming Support.

BPSK. Binary Phase Shift Keying, where a signal sends binary digits by shifting the phase of a signal; in effect similar to FM transmission in radio, but this technique is used in data communications by either modems or radio, etc.

BQL. Basic Query Language.

BRA. Basic Rate Access; provides ISDN users with access to two 64Kbit/s data channels, It is defined in ITU-TS Recommendation I.420

which covers a 2B + D-channel where the B channel is a 64Kbit/s channel, and the D-channel is the 16Kbit/s signalling channel.

branch. 1. A set of computer instructions that is executed between two successive decision instructions.
2. In the execution of computer program to select one from a number of alternative sets of instructions.
3. To select a branch as in 1.
4. A direct path joining two nodes of a network or graph.
5. Loosely, a conditional jump or departure from the implicit or declared order in which instruction are being executed.

BRI. Basic Rate Interface used with ISDN.

bridge. A network inter-connectivity device, connecting two separate networks at OSI Data Link Layer (Level Two Media Access Control Layer). Once bridging is accomplished, the bridge makes interconnected LANs look like a single LAN, passing data between the networks and filtering local traffic. There are two key classifications of bridge: those supporting Spanning Tree and, for Token Ring networks, those supporting source routing. Bridges connect networks using dissimilar protocols and do not interpret the data they carry. They control network traffic and security, filtering where necessary to boost network, performance and contain sensitive data to LAN areas.

Bridges are like routers in that they are used to interconnect local area networks (LANs) that are using the same media and a common protocol. his approach assumes that the networks to be interconnected define a consistent addressing scheme. They do not support protocol conversion or code conversion.

Bridges are implemented within both the physical layer (layer one) and the medium access control sublayer of the data link layer (layer two) of the OSI model. Bridges are capable of supporting speed conversion or flow control. A bridge monitors all traffic on the two sub-networks that it links, and allows two networks to communicate, even though they may have different topologies or communications protocols. Bridges are designed to comply with IEEE data link protocols and are able to support higher level protocols such as Xerox network system, TCP and DECnet. When data is transmitted on one of the network segments, the bridge checks the destination address of the data and consults the routing table. If the destination address is on the segment from which the data was received, the bridge ignores the data. If the destination address is on a different segment, the bridge forwards the data to the appropriate segment. If the destination address is not in the routing table, the bridge forwards the data to all segments except the segment from which it received the transmission. Filters traffic within a single network. They operate like a traffic cop to direct messages toward a destination and to exclude messages that are intended for other destinations. Like repeaters, they can join network segments. Unlike repeaters, they can extend the network by resending the signal.

broadband. 1. A term describing any network that multiplexes multiple, independent network carrier frequencies on to a single cable. It allows multiple simultaneous "conversations", since the independent networks operate on different frequencies and do not interfere with each other.

2. In LAN terminology, it refers to a system in which multiple channels access a medium, for example co-axial cable that has a large bandwidth using Radio Frequency (RF) modems. This may allow the co-axial cable to carry multiple separate LANs whose transmission is being modulated at different frequencies.

3. In cable television transmission, broadband describes the ability to carry 30 or more TV channels and is synonymous with wideband. Also known as wideband.

broadband ISDN. The proposed advanced version of ISDN, providing speeds of 155.52Mbit/s and higher. Standards and switching technology that will work this fast are under development. It promises universal coverage based on ATM/SDH technologies and optical fibre, supporting data, voice and video traffic. Also known as B-ISDN.

broadcast. The simultaneous transmission of data via a network from one terminal to a set of destinations or to all destinations.

brouter. A network inter-connectivity device, which bridges some packets and routes other packets; *i.e.*, it acts as both a bridge and a router; supports more than two LAN connections and uses Level Two addresses for routing. Bridge vendors mostly use the term. It can support multiple OSI Layer and also supports bridging capabilities for network traffic that cannot be routed; non-routable traffic. *See also* router.

brownout. A temporary decrease in the voltage level of power supplied to network devices. Also known as sag.

browse. In Windows, to look through files and directories. Some dialog boxes have a browse button, which opens another dialog box that lists files and directories so that you can easily select the file you want. World Wide Web service is accessed using client software called browsers, because it allows to drift from link to link without having to have a purposeful search.

BROWSER. BRowsing On-line With SElective Retrieval, a computer system data base able to offer ordinary English language searching of the documents that is holds.

BRS. Bibliographic Retrieval Services, an American service offering access to over 20 of most popular computer data files with information relating to books, articles or reports. Normally the information covered is of authorship, title, and publication details.

BS. Back Space, ASCII character 8 decimal or ^H (control H), means the print head should move back one space.

BSAM. Basic Sequential Access Method, a computer system with a large continuously updated file of information, abstracts or references concerning a particular subject (database).

BSC. Binary Synchronous Communications, the rules developed by IBM for the synchronous transmission of binary coded data as a serial stream of binary digits. Synchronisation is achieved by using control characters recognisable as bit patterns, which do not appear within the body of the message.

BSCA. Binary Synchronous Communications Adaptor.

BSELCH. Buffered SELector CHannel.

BSN. 1. Broadband Service Node.
2. *See* back-end storage network.

BSO. *See* bit synchronous operation.

BSS. Basic Synchronised Subset of Session.

BST. *See* byte serial transmission.

BSTMP. Batch Simple Message Transfer

Protocol, on BITNET, a specially formatted message envelope sent to a gateway virtual user address for further transfer to another BITNET host(s) as specified in the message address.

BTAM. Basic Telecommunications Access Method; the system used to control the transfer of data, in a computer system, between the main storage and local or remote terminals.

BTC. Block Transfer Controller.

BTD. Binary To Decimal.

BTE. Broadband Terminal Equipment.

BTF. Bulk Transfer Facility.

BTP. Batch Transfer Program; able to accommodate more than one terminal, a BTP controls data transfers from local or remote computer terminals, and allows for modification or deletion of records.

BTSS. Basic Time Sharing System.

bubble board. BB. An expansion board containing bubble memory, which functions as if it were a floppy or hard-disk drive.

bubble forming. A technique for writing to optical disks in which the laser raises the temperature of a point in the media to above 2000°C. The lower layer of the recording media vaporises and forces up the covering layer to a bubble.

bubble memory. The magnetic bubble memory storage; a bubble memory chip can have 10-100 times the capacity of the current generation of integrated circuit silicon chips. Intel has already produced a bubble memory chip capable of storing over four megabits. Although currently much more expensive to produce than integrated circuits, bubble memories are non-volatile, meaning they do not lose their data if the electrical current is turned off. Bubble memory consists of a chip of garnet coated with a thin layer of magnetic film on which a microscopic bubble is formed when magnetic field is applied. Using the basic principles of the binary system, the presence of a bubble represents 1 (on) whereas its absence represents 0 (off). A magnetic bubble memory stores data in the form of cylindrical magnetic domains in a thin film of magnetic material. An external rotating magnetic field propels these cylindrical domain bubbles through the film.

bubble sort. A form of sorting by exchanging that simply interchanges pairs of elements that are out or order in a sequence of passes through the file until no such pairs exist. The method is not competitive with straight insertion. Also known as exchange selection.

bubble. A solid-state storage device utilising magnetic domains in the garnet substrate. The domains, or the bubbles, are circulated within the substrate and are directed to the output by magnetic fields. Bubbles can be moved along at 100,000 bits per second, so fast access is possible to large stores of information and power failures do not mean that all the stored information is lost.

bucket. In memory systems, an area of storage that is referred to as a whole by some addressing system.

buffer. 1. An interface unit designed to link circuits together but not allow excessive or unwanted variations in one to affect the other.

2. Routine or storage used to compensate for a difference in rate of flow of data from one device to another.

3. An area of storage, that is reserved for temporary use in performing input/output operation. Data may be read from or written into the buffer storage area.

4. A temporary storage place for data designed to compensate for a difference in transmission speeds or to hold data when there is a difference in timing of events. It can be a software program, a storage facility, or a hardware device, ensuring the data always has somewhere to go, even if it has to be held up for while in the buffer until it can be transmitted to the destination.

buffered device. In memory systems, a device that has input/output elements queued to direct-access device before being written.

buffered input. The ability to enter new data or instructions into the machine before current operations is being completed.

bug. An error in a program or system; the word is usually used to mean a localized implementation error introduced at the requirements or system-design stage.

built-in. Pertaining to a language object that is declared by the definition of the programming language. Examples: The built-in function 'SIN' in PL/I, the predefined data type 'INTEGER' in FORTRAN.

bulk eraser. A device that can erase the signals recorded on the magnetic tape, without unwinding the tape.

bullet. In typography, a symbol (*) used to highlight a list of related items. Sometimes the full stop is used, but a bullet is usually much larger than a full stop, and raised above the baseline.

bulletin board system. BBS. The computers running with software, which allows callers to leave messages and accesses information much like an actual bulletin board. The bulletin board system are accessed via modem although some bulletin board systems can also be accessed through a network. Services that bulletin board systems can offer are electronic mail, conferences on topics of interest, and collections of documents (text files, pictures, and sounds). Bulletin board systems are often good sources for software, especially shareware and freeware utilities.

BUMP. Bottom Up Modular Programming.

bunching strip. In telephone switchboard operation, a strip of jacks connected in parallel, to facilitate the connection of multiple calls.

bundle jacket. The outer protective covering over a bundle of optical fibres.

bundled software. The software which is generally included with a computer system to boost the sales of the computer. A computer system which is specifically targeted to a profession (such as medial) is usually bundled with application-specific software suitable to that profession.

BUR. BackUp Register.

buried layer. A layer of high-conductivity semiconductor material diffused into substrate layer during the manufacture of bipolar integrated circuits and transistors. It is located below the collector and reduces the collector resistance.

burn-in. A part of a testing procedure which engages the computer system in a series of checks and operations to ensure that the semiconductor components are stable and error-free. Most computer manufacturers burn-in (test) all new products which come off a production line. When a product is relatively new, burn-in periods may exceed 100 hours. If testing confirms that the product is free from failure, the testing period decreases to 24 hours. Once a product is shipped from the factory or the warehouse to the remote subsidiary or the reseller, a second round of burn-in is conducted to ensure that the product is still stable.

burst error. An error pattern generally for a binary signal that consists of known positions where the digit is in error with the intervening positions possibly in error and possibly not. By implication, digits before the first error in the block and after the last error in the block are correct.

burst mode. 1. A system of obtaining full duplex bidirectional transmission of digital speech signals over a two-wire circuit. The two directions of transmission are separated in time by alternating the two directions. The penalty which has to has to be paid is the use of higher frequencies: if data enters the system at frequency D a typical burst frequency is 2.25 X D. Burst Mode working is sometimes called Ping-Pong Mode, or Time Compression Multiplexing. Burst Mode's principal rival way of transmitting digital speech signals in both directions on a 2-wire circuit is the hybrid system, this separates the two directions by hybrid balance circuits and the use of echo cancellers to ensure that there is sufficient near-end loss to enable proper detection of the far end signal.
2. The transfer of a packet of data from a peripheral unit to a central processing unit, with a start signal at the beginning and an end-of-burst signal at the end. The length of the burst can be varied to suit particular requirements.

bus arbitration. A procedure, which resolves the priorities among various units contending for the control of a common bus and that, passes control to the selected unit.

bus bar. A physical signal carrier that connects several parts of a computer.

bus network. A local area network in which there is only single path between any two data stations and in which data transmitted by any station are concurrently available to all other stations on the same transmission medium. It may be noted that the bus network may be a linear network, a star network, or a tree network. In the case of a tree or star network, there is a data station at each endpoint node. There is no data station at an intermediate node; however, one or more devices such as repeaters, connectors, amplifiers, and splitters are located there.

bus terminator. An electrical circuit connected at the end of a bus to hold it at predetermined signal level when it is not active, and also to ensure impedance matching and thus avoid unwanted reflections of signals.

bus topology. Kinds of network in which all devices are connected in a line to a single cable; a bus network has two distinct ends. All devices, which attached to a bus network, have equal access to it and they can see all the messages that are put on to the network. Each device determines which messages are intended for it alone, and selects those.

bus. 1. Part of a chip or circuit board designed to send and receive data. The bus on a computer's motherboard contains slots for expansion cards.
2. In transmission, part of a circuit, which is used in common from one of several to one of several circuit functions or modules. Sometimes it is called highway because much traffic flows along it.

business and engineering enriched formula translator. BEEF. A computer language employed in business and engineering applications. This is an enhanced version of formula translator (FORTRAN) computer language.

business game. An educational game on one or more of the financial or management disciplines. Also known as management game.

busy byte. A memory byte employed to prevent conflicts that can arise if processors, in multiprocessing systems, access the common blocks of memory.

busy hour. An uninterrupted period of one hour during which the average intensity of traffic of a telephone exchange or group of telephone circuits is at a maximum.

busy tone. Signal conveyed to a telephone calling party to indicate that the called telephone party or intermediate apparatus is reserved for use or it rendered unavailable for traffic.

butt coupling. The coupling of an optical fibre or optical element to another, by placing the end or face of one against the end or face of the other, so that an electromagnetic wave can be transmitted with a minimum power loss and a maximum transmission coefficient at interface.

buzz word. A word used for the sake of its sound alone.

buzz. An undesirable audible noise resulting from the interaction between sound and vision signals in a receiver.

BW. Band Width.

BWC. Buffer Word Counter.

BWT. Band Width Ratio.

Bx-cable. Insulated wires in flexible metal tubing used for bringing electric power to electronic equipment.

bylink. Special termination; particularly of automatic toll circuits, which gives rapid connection to registers thereby avoiding the use of delay signals or second dial tones.

bypass. BYP. Any arrangement of circuits which enables communications to be established directly between two organisations which would normally be expected to use the switched facilities of local telephone exchange.

BYSINC. Binary Communications Synchronous Protocol.

byte cipher feedback. The cipher feedback in which the segments transmitted and fed back to the shift register are one byte in length.

byte mode. A data transfer method between peripheral and central processor in which the unit is the byte. Compare burst mode in which a variable length package of data is sent in one burst.

byte multiplexer channel. A multiplexer channel that interleaves bytes of data from different sources.

byte serial transmission. BST. The transmission of data in which successive bytes follow one another in sequence. The individual bits of each byte may be transmitted serially or simultaneously.

byte. 1. A colloquial expression to describe an 8-binary digit word, in contrast to 'nibble', which is generally considered to be a 4-binary digit word. It is the amount of memory needed to specify one ASCII character; eight bits. Kilobytes (1000 bytes) and Megabytes (1,000,000 bytes) are generally used in describing the memory a computer utilises.

2. In data structures, a binary character operated upon as a unit and usually shorter than a computer word. It is the smallest addressable unit of storage.

3. In optical media, an eight-bit unit of compact disk data, representing one symbol before eight-to-fourteen modulation.

BZ. Branch Zip code.

C

.c. Extension for C programming language source code. these files should be retrieved in text/ASCII mode.

C. 1. A high-level and structured computer programming language developed for implementation of the UNIX operating system, and widely used for software development in the UNIX environment. It has been designed to optimize run time, size and efficiency.
2. The hexadecimal symbol for binary 1100, decimal 12; $C_{16} = 12_{10} = 14_8 = 1100_2$. 3. One of the letter designations given to the most commonly used sizes of 1.5-volt batteries.

C^{++}. An object-oriented high-level programming language based on the 'C' language. C^{++} has emerged as a standard for OOP on workstations and computers. It is a hybrid language; on one hand, it draws heavily from and is (with minor exceptions) a superset of C. On the other, it provides object oriented features that support high-level problem abstraction.

The C^{++} language is displacing research-oriented programming languages, such as Smalltalk, which run in interpreted environments. Several C^{++} translators have appeared in DOS implementations, mostly as front-end pre-processors for C compilers. However, code produced by a combination of a C^{++} pre-processor and a C compiler is not as efficient as code generated by a native code C^{++} compiler such as Bordland's Turbo C^{++} Professional. To make a significant difference in the way programmers write code; OOP systems must evolve from, rather than replace, traditional languages. Backward compatibility with both existing program code and programmer skills is important. C^{++} is a good example of this evolutionary approach.

Bordland's Turbo C^{++} is both a C^{++} and an ANSI C compiler. The compiler uses the source file extension ('.C' for C files; '.CPP' for C^{++}) to decide how to compile the file. Compiler options afford the programmer the flexibility to specify which language syntax the compiler should expect. This means that any number of lines of C code can be used in C^{++} programs without having to be reworked. Encapsulation, inheritance, and polymorphism are three cornerstone OOP concepts. Data hiding, constructors and destructors, stream input/output, overloading, type-safe linkage, and linkage specification are several other C^{++} features. It implements each of these ideas to provide the developer with a full-power object-oriented language.

C4. An abbreviation used to refer to the collection of activities performed by CAD (computer-aided design), CAM (computer-aided manufacturing), CAE (computer-aided engineering), and CIM (computer-integrated manufacturing). C4 applications are usually processor-intensive, often requiring math co-processors to help speed-up numeric calculations, and high-resolution graphics for faster image visualization. For quick response times, large amounts of random-access memory are required. C4 applications can work on different computer platforms, but the most popular include powerful personal computers, and engineering/technical workstations.

CA. 1. Call Number.
2. Card Alert.
3. Communication Adaptor.

CAAS. *See* computer-assisted acquisition system.

CABS. Computer Aided Batch Service.

CAC. Computer Aided Classification.

cache memory. 1. A type of memory that is used in high performance systems inserted between the processor and memory. The memory hierarchy on a system contains registers in the processor, which are the high-speed storage, and, at a slightly lower level of accessibility, the contents of the main memory. The cache is intended to reduce the discrepancy in accessibility between these two types of unit, and functions by holding small regions that map contents of main memory. Because of the combination of the cache memory's speed, size, and cache algorithm, over 85% of the data requests are performed with zero wait states. The basic steps to cache memory involve the microprocessor, which sends out a request for data. The cache memory controller intercepts it and checks and cache memory to see if the information is there so that it can be immediately accessed (this is known as a cache hit). If the information is not there, it is called a cache miss, and the cache memory controller reads the data from the slower system memory. The information is then copied into cache memory as it is sent to the processor so that all subsequent requests for that information can be read from cache memory, at zero wait states.
2. A special purpose buffer storage, smaller and faster than main storage, used to hold a copy of instructions and data obtained from main storage and likely to be needed next by the processor.

cache miss. An unsatisfied request by the microprocessor for code or data in the cache. Upon a cache miss, the cache requests from the main system memory not only the code or data requests by the microprocessor, but several additional bytes of code or data as well. This is called a line. Line is a string of bytes that is moved from main system memory to the cache when the cache memory is updated. It is the basic unit or minimum amount of code or data transferred between the main system memory and cache. A larger line size increases the number of bytes of code and data copied from main system memory into the cache memory on an update. Increasing line size can increase cache performance by taking advantage of software's locality of code principle. Since program code and data is mostly sequential, it is very likely that the next item requested by the microprocessor will be within the line of the previous memory request. Generally, increasing line size increases hit rate. However, increasing line size is a trade-off with other system factors. If the line size exceeds the system data bus width, then multiple memory accesses will be required. This will take time and monopolize the memory bus. The processor will have to add wait states if it requires the memory bus when the bus is not available. 'Replacement policy' refers to how the cache memory is updated upon a cache miss. This is important when the cache already contains data. Replacing data that will be needed later will cause a lower hit rate and decreased microprocessor performance.

caching-only server. A server that responds to queries from clients on the local network for name resolution requests and stores that information in its cache in case a request for that information is made again. Caching-only servers are not registered with InterNIC as DNS servers, so other DNS servers do not know about it.

CACS. Computer Aided Communication System.

CAD. 1. Computer-Aided Dispatch, a system in which hand written incident cards and conveyor belts in radio dispatching operations are replaced by alphanumeric keyboards and cathode ray tube terminals.
2. Computer-Aided Design.

CAD/CAM. Computer-Aided Design/ Computer-Aided Manufacture, a method of production employing designs provided by a computer aided design system held in a memory device, to produce finished products by computer or numerical controlled machinery.

CAD/CAT. Computer-Aided Design/ Computer-Aided Test, a method of production employing designs provided by a computer aided design system held in a memory device, to provide final testing of a finished product under control of a computer. Tests are most often undertaken by automatic test equipment.

CADD. Computer-Aided Design and Drafting; specialized hardware and software tools which produce drawings conforming to engineering conventions.

CADIS. Computer Aided Design of Information System.

CADS. Computer Analysis and Design System.

CAE. Common Application Environment, a term encompassing what is needed to achieve portability and interoperability of application software.

CAF. Computer Aided Fraud.

CAI. Common Air Interface, in radio communications, the electromagnetic wave distortion; CT2 international mobile communications standard which allows any compliant equipment to be used on any network of the same type. CAI compliant telepoint handsets from different vendors may therefore be used on a telepoint network.

CAI. *See* computer-aided instruction.

CAIP. Computer Assisted Indexing Program.

CAIRS. *See* computer-assisted information retrieval system.

CAK. Command Access Key.

CAL. 1. Computer- Aided Learning.
2. Computer Animation Language.
3. Common Assembler Language.

call collision. A term used in telephony, referring to contention that occurs when data terminal equipment and data circuit equipment simultaneously transfers a call request packet and an incoming call packet specifying the same logical channel. The DCE will proceed with the call request and cancel the incoming call.

call control character. In data operations, a character of an alphabet, or a part of it, which is used for call control. It may be used in conjuction with defined signal conditions on other interchange circuits.

call control procedure. The entire set of interactive signals necessary to establish, mauntain, and release a data call.

call directing code. A routing and identifying code in a message switching system, which ensures that a message is routed to the required terminal station and automatically, starts up the printer at the station.

call forwarding. A service feature available in some switching system where calls can be rerouted automatically from one line to another or to an attendant.

call forwarding busy line. A service feature in which an incoming call is automatically routed from one line to another or to an attendant.

call indicator. CI. A flagging device in a computer system that shows when branching or transfer of control to a specified closed subroutine has taken place.

call processing. The system and process that sets up the intended connection in a switching system. A system scans the trunk and station ports for any requests for service. It then checks the stored instructions and look-up tables and sets the connection up accordingly.

call transfer. Service whereby a call to a subscriber's number is automatically transferred to one or more predetermined alternative numbers when the called number is busy or does not respond.

call. 1. Action of bringing a computer program, a routine, or a subroutine into effect, usually by specifying the entry conditions and jumping to an entry point.
2. In computer programming to execute a call.
3. An attempt to reach user, whether or not successful.
4. To transfer control to a specified closed subroutine.
5. A transmission for identifying the transmitting stations for which the transmission is intended.

call-back. In data transmission a facility which enables the originator of a call attempt to a busy terminal to request the network to establish the call when the busy terminal becomes free.

call-in time. CIT. A period of time during which the control of digital computer is transferred from a main routine to s sub-routine. The period has been inserted into a sequence to fulfil a subsidiary purpose.

CALTRANS. A programming language related to FORTRAN.

CAM. *See* computer-aided manufacture.

CAMA. Centralized Automatic Message Accounting.

CAMC. *See* computer-automated measurement and control.

CANCL. Short form of the word 'CANCeL'. This status word is used to indicate that a remote system has deleted information previously transmitted.

CAP. 1. Card Assembly Program.
2. Computer Aided Production.
3. Cellular Array Processor.

capability. The access right of a device to access a memory store for the transfer of program/ data. It limits the access of various memory blocks to specific devices to minimize the possibility of program/data corruption being input to the system.

CAPS. Computer Aided Problem Solving.

CAR. 1. Channel Address Register.
2. Computer-Aided Retrieval.

card cage. A framework in which circuit boards can be mounted. It comprises channels in to which the boards can be slid and sockets and wiring by means of which they are interconnected.

card feed. The mechanism, which places data cards one at a time into correct position for reading or punching.

card punch. A machine used to punch a pattern of holes in a punch card.

card reader. A machine that senses the data encoded on card and translates it into binary code that can be transmitted for further processing. The various types of card readers include:

(a) magnetic card reader,

(b) slot reader, and

(c) chip card reader.

card. 1. An electronic printed circuit board designed to slot into a computer's expansion bus.

2. Any small, wafer-like set of circuits which can be plugged in (or inserted into) a device. For example, printers have font cards, and earlier compuers had sound cards; laptop computers offer memory expansion though small, credit-card sized memory cards.

CARD. Compact Automatic Retrieval Device.

carriage return. CR. 1. The action of moving a carriage back to the beginning of a line on a printer or teletypewriter.

2. A key on many computer systems or teletypewriters, the operation of which returns the carriage or transmits a carriage return character, from which the computer transmits a line feed characters which in turn generates a new line.

Carrier Sense Multiple Access with Collision Detect. *See* CSMA/CD.

carrier sense multiple access/CD. Method of controlling access to a shared transmission path, particularly in local area networks. A generally similar procedure is proposed to be used in ISDNs. Terminals listen to a signaling bus and wait for it to be free before they signal. In the event of simultaneous seizure a garbled echo will cause the terminal to stop transmission.

carrier signal. The underlying frequency or frequencies that are to carry information. They are modulated through one or more modulation techniques to impose information on the signal.

carry. CY. 1. The action of transferring a carry digit.

2. One or more digits, produced in connection with an arithmetic operation on one digit place of two or more numerals in positional notation that are forwarded to another digit place for processing there.

3. The number represented by the digit or digits in (2).

4. The command directing that a carry be forwarded.

5. To transfer a carry digit.

cartridge drive. Either a tape transport for handling cartridge tape, or a disk drive for handling disk cartridges.

cartridge font. *See* font cartridge.

cartridge tape. The tape carried in a magnetic tape cartridge; the term is generally used in reference to the 3M-type cartridge.

cascade. In Windows, a way of arranging open windows on the desktop so that they overlap each other, with the title bar of each window remaining visible.

cascading menu. A menu that opens from a command on another menu. In Windows, a command that opens a cascading menu has a right arrow next to it. Also known as hierarchical menu or submenu.

CASD. Computer Aided System Design.

CASE. 1. Computer-Aided Software Engineering; a set of graphic-text tools designed to implement software engineering from formal specifications, through rigorous testing, to highly-automated code generation. Typical CASE applications include module management, project management, and compilers.
2. Common Application Service Element, obsolete term for what has developed into ACSE.

Cassegrain antenna. A high-gain parabolic antenna in which the main feed is not at focus of the dish but near its surface, pointing towards a small sub-reflector located near the focus.

CAT. Computer-Aided Telephony, any of a variety of new services relying on DTMF technology, for example, computer information systems, which are actuated by "touch-tone" keypad.

Category 3. Cablling standard for UTP voice grade cabling specified by the EIA/TIA 568 standard for use at speeds up to 10Mbit/s including 10BaseT Ethernet.

Category 4. Cablling standard specified by EIA/TIA 568 for use at speeds up to 20Mbit/s including 16Mbit/s Token Ring.

Category 5. Cablling standard specified by EIA/TIA 568 for use to speeds up to 100Mbit/s including FDDI (TP PMD), 100baseT and 100baseVG-AnyLan, and potentially ATM at 155Mbit/s.

CATV. CAble TeleVision, the cable system covering defined areas, such as the franchises to install and operate a cable system granted by the Cable Authority and Department of Trade and Industry, offering TV channel output and, increasingly, local loop digital telephony services.

CAW. *See* channel address word.

CBEMA. Computers and Business Equipment Manufacturers Association, secretariat to ANSI-Accredited Standards Committee X3, Information Processing Standards.

CBI. Computer Based Instruction.

CBL. *See* computer-based learning.

CBSM. *See* computer-based message system.

CBT. Computer Based Training.

CBX. Computerized Branch eXchange, a term used in telephony indicating an automated switching site.

CC. 1. Courtesy Copy, also known as Carbon Copy in electronic mail.
2. Connection Confirm, PDU accepting a connection, usually qualified with the layer, *i.e.*, CC TPDU is the Transport Layer CC. 3. Country Code, in the X.400 specification, a two-character alphabetic code used for the country name standard attribute; examples are US, HK, and SE(2).

CCA. Conceptual Communications Area, term used in Virtual Terminal.

CCAP. Communication Control Application Program.

CCB. 1. Channel Control Block.
2. Communication Control Block.

CCC. 1. Clear Channel Capability, a communications channel used for control signaling.
2. Central Communications Controller.

CCD camera. A solid-state camera using charge-coupled device for transforming a light image into a digitized image. It is similar to CID camera, except that its method of operation forces readout of pixel brightness in a regular line-by-line scan pattern. It has a readout station, and charges are shifted along until they reach it.

CCD. 1. Computer Controlled Display.
2. Cash Concentration and Disbursement, term used in EDI.

CCIR. Consultative Committee for International Radio, a committee under the ITU that creates Recommendations on radio communications.

CCITT. Consultative Committee on International Telegraph and Telephone, with 160 member nations, headquartered in Switzerland. CCITT has been replaced by the ITU.

CCP. *See* console command processor.

CCR. 1. Commitment Concurrency, and Recovery, a common ASE used to ensure that a number of tasks can be performed atomically.

2. Customer Controlled Recognifiguration, carrier bandwidth allocation by user on ISDN.

CCS. Common Channel Signaling, signaling between central office switches in telephone networks using out-of-band signaling.

CCS7. Common Channel Signaling 7, Bellcore's version of CCITT Signaling System 7.

CCT. CNMA Conformance Testing, a project for developing European OSI test suites.

CCTA. Government Centre for Information Systems, U.K. government body that produces the U.K. GOSIP. Formerly known as Central Computer and Telecommunications Agency.

CD. 1. Collision Detection, detecting when signals have been transmitted at the same time from different entities on the net.

2. Capability Data Session PDU, PDU that carries session user data while not within an activity.

3. Current Data, object class used in performance monitoring in Network Management; specifies information like the time interval and types of data to be collected.

4. Committee Draft, ISO term for a standard that has not yet stabilized enough to become a Draft International Standard; formerly called a working Draft.

CDA. 1. Capability Data Acknowledgement Session PDU.

2. Command and Data Acquisition.

CDC. 1. Code Directing Character. One or more routing indicators used in telecommunications at the start of a message to determine its destination.

2. Call Directing Code; an identifying call, usually two letters in length that is transmitted to an outlying receiver to turn on its printer automatically.

CD-E. A compact disk optical storage system, which allows the user to write, erase and rewrite data to or from the disk, as is possible with a floppy disk.

Cdex. A utility which can record Digital Audio (DA) tracks from CD into the files. The recorded audio tracks can be stored as WAV or MP3 (MPEG-1 Audio Layer-3) files. It utilizes the Adaptec's ASPI library Manager to communicate with the CD-ROM device. The latest version of Cdex can be downloadedat: http://www.cdex.n3.net.

CD-I. Compact disk interaction; a standard for interactive compact disk systems used, for example, in interactive training systems, which involve music, video, animation and speech. CD-I can quickly respond to commands from the user.

CDF. *See* channel definition format.

CDL. 1. Common Display Logic.

2. Computer Design Language.

CDMA. Code-Division Multiple Access, a type of multiplexing to allow access to one medium by several stations.

CDP. Central Data Processor.

CD-R. A compact disk storage system synonymous with WORM (*w*rite *o*nce *r*ead *m*any times) systems.

CDR. Call Detail Recording, telephony term for accounting information about individual calls.

CD-ROM. Compact Disk Read Only Memory; an optical secondary storage device that uses compact disk technology to store upto 750 megabytes of data on a single a compact disk (4.7 inches in diameter). CD-ROMs are used to store software, pictures, audio and video files, encyclopedias and dictionaries because upto 3,75,000 pages of information may be condensed onto one disk. Some compact disks can be only be read, while others can be written on. WORM (write once read many times) is a particular types of technology which allows a disk sector to be written over only once. If a file is updated, then the new information is written on new tracks. The old information cannot be erased, but becomes inaccessible. Although CD-ROM is a read-only technology, its large storage capacity and low price make it an effective way to distribute large capacity database reference material. Data on a magnetic hard disk is stored in concentric circles, Called tracks, with each track divided into a given number of sectors. The sectors near the center are physically shorter than those on the outside. A CD-ROM, on the other hand, stores data in a single spiral-shaped track. This one track is divided into many segments, each of equal length. To properly read data, the rotational speed of the optical disk must increase when the read head gets closer to the center, the decrease as the head moves back out. The typical data access time is ~0.5-1.5 s.

CDS. Conceptual Data Store, term used in Virtual Terminal.

CDT. Control Data Terminal.

CE. Communications Entity, the aspects of an implementation pertaining to communications functionality.

CEC. Commission of European Communities, permanent civil service of the European Commission that makes policy decisions. An important stimulus and source funding for OSI programs, e.g., the Conformance Testing Service projects and EWOS.

CEI. Connection End-point Identifier, identifies the terminator of a connection at a service access point.

cell animation. An animation technique which uses a fixed background, over which clear sheets of celluloid are changed to produce the illusion of movement. This is commonly used in cartoon films. The same effect can be derived from a computer such as the Macintosh, using an animation program (such as MacroMind Director) to produce cell animation. In the same way that cell animation saves the cartoonist from having to re-draw the background with every frame, MacroMind Director saves a lot of disk storage space.

cell relay. Generic term for a protocol based on small fixed packet sizes capable of supporting voice, video and data at very high speeds. Information is handled in fixed length cells of 53 octets.

cell. 1. An address, location in memory, or a register, usually capable of holding a binary number. It is sometimes a location capable of holding one bit.

2. The data blocks used by ATM; the cells are exactly 53 octets long.

3. An area in a cellular radio system that is served by a transmitter.

4. A position on a spreadsheet, in which the data or the formula may be entered.

Cello. A program that allows full access to the information resources of the Internet. It can run World Wide Web, Gopher, FTP, CSO/ph/qi, and also runs other protocols through external clients and gateways. It can be used to view hypermedia documents, including text, sounds, and movies.

cellular mobile radio telecommunications system/service. CMRS. Automobile radio system using low-power transmitters providing coverage in a limited area but linked (usually by cable) with other similar transmitters operating at different frequencies. The whole system enables radio frequencies to be reused economically, and enables good telephone service to be provided in moving automobiles by switching control from one transmitter cell to another as the mobile moves across an area.

CEN/CENELEC. Comite Europeen de Normalisation/CEN Electro-technique.

central display unit. CDU. A device providing a visual representation at a single location of data obtained from a number of geographical locations.

central file. May be thought of as a single electronic reservoir or data-deposit, containing a central information file, index and all major application files.

central input output multiplexor. CIO. A centrally located device that takes low-speed inputs or outputs from terminals and combines them into one high-speed data stream, for transmission between an external source and a computer.

central processing element. CPE. An element that can provide a complete 2, 4 or 8 binary digit slice across the data processing section of a computer. It enables functions to be executed in one, rather than several, micro-cycles.

central processing unit. CPU. The portion of a computer that controls the operation of the whole system, where instructions are executed and computations performed. It contains the main storage, arithmetic unit and special register groups. Sometimes also known as control processor Unit. In telephone switching systems, memory usually is elsewhere.

With the wider use of microprocessors and distributed control, central processing unit now tend to be used for administrative tasks and the more complex diagnostic tasks only, typically those requiring access to large data stores. Sometimes central processing units are used on a cluster or multiprocessor basis. One advantage claimed for this approach is that the traffic handling capacity of the exchange can be increased in stages as the network grows.

central. A position in a network or system, which is connected with, or is in communication with, all other points in the network or system.

centralized operation. Operation of a communication network in which transmission may occur between the control station and tributary stations, but not between tributary stations.

CENTREX. CENTRalized EXchange, a telephony service that provides private network-like features to business customers via public network central office switches.

centronics interface (cable). *See* parallel interface.

centronics interface. A parallel interface with 36-pins that will transmit 8-data bits simultaneously, originally made by Centronics Company, a printer manufacturer. It has become widely used as a parallel interface standard.

CEP. Connection End Point, terminator at one end of a connection within the service access point of given OSI layer.

CEPI. Connection End-point Identifier.

CET. Computer-Enhanced Telephony, enhancement of otherwise audio-deteriorated telephonic signals.

CF. 1. Conversion Facility, translation services between different protocols provided by access unit or gateway. 2. Central File.

CFA. Computer Family Architecture.

CFB. Cipher FeedBack.

CFC. Channel Flow Control.

CFD. Compact Floppy Disk.

CFDD. Compact Floppy Disk Drive.

CFF. Critical Flicker Frequency, the highest frequency at which a flicker can be detected on CRT display.

CFG. File name extension for a configuration file.

CFSK. Coherent Frequency Shift Keying.

CGI. Computer Generated Image.

CGM. Computer Graphics Metafile, an interchange format for exchanging graphics data between computer graphics systems and graphical output devices, specified in the US Nist-App and in CALS.

challenge handshake authentication protocol. CHAP. A protocol that negotiates secure form of encrypted authentication by using Message Digect 5 (MD5). It uses challenge-response with one-way MD5 hashing on the response. By supporting CHAP and MD5, network dial-up connections is able to securely connect to almost all PPP servers.

CHAMP. Communication Handler for Automatic Multiple Program.

channel access. In local area networks, the method of gaining access to the communications channel that links all the devices. Common channel access methods are polling, token ring, and connection.

channel address register. CAR. A storage location that provides information to access a path to a particular register, location or unit of memory where information is stored.

channel address word. CAW. A word that provides and access path to a particular register, location or unit of memory where information is stored.

channel bank. A part of the carrier-multiplex terminal that performs the first step of modulation.

channel control block. CCB. A set of locations in memory containing information that is accessed by various programs and provides control of the input or output of data via a channel.

channel definition format. CDF. The XML application behind push technology; instead of browsing from Web site to Web site, and form Web paage to Web page with in that site, the user takes out a subscription to a particular content provider. Instead of pulling Web pages, the user allows some one else to push pages for him.

channel gate. A device for connecting a channel to a highway, or a highway to a channel, at specified times.

channel group. 12-voice channels, frequency division multiplexed into a signal frequency band, 48 kHz wide.

channel modulation. First stage of modulation in a frequency division multiplex carrier system; the translation of a voiceband to its appropriate frequency band in the basic twelve-channel group.

channel noise level. dB_m1. The ratio of the channel noise at any point in a transmission system to some arbitrary amount of circuit noise chosen as a reference. This ratio is usually expressed in decibels above reference noise, abbreviated signifying the reading of a circuit noise meter, or in adjusted decibels, abbreviated dB_a, signifying circuit noise meter reading adjusted to represent an interfering effect under specified conditions.
2. The noise power density spectrum in the frequency range of interest.
3. The average noise power in the frequency range of interest.

4. The indication on a specified instrument. The characteristics of the instrument are determined by the type of noise to be measured and the application of the results thereof.

channel service unit. CSU. 1. In US, the data transmission equipment to repeat the signal from carrier and ink to CPE. Vendors add value to channel service units by adding performance monitoring and management.

2. In Europe, channel service units are sold for their value features like diagnostics and performance monitoring.

channel, television. Numbered frequency bands used for broadcasting of television signals. Low numbered channels utilize VHF frequencies between 54-88 MHz; higher numbers utilize higher UHF frequencies in the 200 MHz and 500-900 MHz ranges.

channel. CHNL. 1. The smallest subdivision of a circuit, which provides a single type of communication, service. *e.g.*, a voice channel, a telegraph channel, a data channel. Note however that a channel is a unidirectional path, so a telephone circuit includes both directions of transmission and the entire associated relay sets etc whereas channel is the one-direction transmission path only. Several channels may share a common carrier, as in frequency division and time division systems; in these cases each channel is allocated a particular frequency band or a particular time slot which is reserved for it.

2. A complete facility for the transmission, emission or reception of signals, *e.g.*, a television channel or a radio channel.

3. The portion of a storage medium that is accessible to a given reading or writing station, *e.g.* track, band.

4. A particular path or specific frequency band in communications used for the reception or transmission of signals.

5. The means of performing two-way-alternative communication in one pre-assigned direction.

6. A connection between two nodes in network.

7. In communication theory, the part of a communication system that connects a data source to data acceptance equipment.

8. In a computer or data-processing system a route along which information travels.

9. In a field-effect transistor, the region connecting a current source to the point where charge carriers leave.

10. In information theory that part of a communications system that connects the message source with the message sink.

11. An individual path in a transmission medium, that is separated from other paths, *e.g.*, a multi-pair cable.

CHAP. *See* challenge handshake authentication protocol.

character interleaving. A form of TDM used for asynchronous protocols. This can be used either with extra channels, or by carrying RS232-C control signals.

character interval. The total number of unit intervals, including synchronizing information error checking, and control bits, required to transmit any given character in any given communications system. Extra signals not associated with individual characters are not included.

character recognition. The process of machine's recognizing typescript. The two main methods used for machine recognition of characters are; optical character recognition (OCR) and magnetic ink character recognition. optical character recognition is cheap to produce (ordinary typewriters can be used) but prone to error, especially if documents are soiled or creased. MICR needs special print fonts but is more trustworthy. MICR characters are printed using ink impregnated with magnetizable particles. The documents go through a magnetizing stage before they are presented to an automatic reader. There are no international standards for print font for use with either procedures as yet.

character set. 1. A finite set of different characters which are agreed upon and considered to be complete for some purpose, e.g., each of the character sets in ISO Recommendation R646, 6- and 7-bit Coded Character Sets for Information Processing Interchange.

2. The set of character that is handled by a specified machine. The set usually includes the English alphanumeric characters, special characters and operation characters the entire are graphic characters, and various control characters. Graphics characters thus denote a printed mark or a space while control characters produce some particular effect.

3. An ordered set of unique representations called characters, such as the 26 letters of the English alphabet.

character subset. A selection of characters from a character set, comprising all characters that have a specified common feature; for example in each of the character sets of the International Standards Organization (ISO) Recommendation R646 (6-and & bit coded character sets of information processing interchange), the digits 0 and 9 may constitute a character subset.

character. CHR. 1. A member of an agreed-on set of elements that is used for the organization control or representation of data. Characters may be letters, digits, punctuation marks, or other symbols, often represented in the form of a spatial arrangement of adjacent or connected strokes or in the form of other physical conditions in data media.

2. A letter, digit or other symbol that is used as part of the organization, control, production of text, or representation of data. A character is often in the form of spatial arrangement of adjacent or connected strokes.

characters per second. CPS. 1. The number of individual letters, numerals or other symbols which are printed in one second; usually this abbreviation occurs when describing the speed of characters-at-a-time printers.

2. A measure of the rate of transmission normally between a computer and terminal devices. As various numbers of binary digits are required to represent a character, there is no simple correlation between bits per second and CPS.

chassis. A mechanical system, designed to provide a supporting and/or enclosing medium for electronic equipment. The system may be equipped with supporting structures to carry standard-sized circuit boards in addition to a motherboard or backplane into which the boards are inserted and connected via sockets. Alternatively, the individual components may be hardwired onto tag strips attached to the chassis. For safety reasons, the metal parts of a chassis should be permanently connected to a local zero-voltage reference or ground. In some equipment, however it is more convenient to connect the chassis to one side of the a.c. or d.c. line (mains) supply; the equipment is then said to have a hot chassis. The chassis may also be left unconnected or floating.

CHATS. Call Handler for Advanced Telephone Services.

CHCU. Channel Control Unit.

check bit. A bit (zero or one) this is added to a byte so that when transmitted, all byte will have the same parity. For example, EBCDIC letter 'A' is represented by 11000001. Note this has three ones, therefore an odd number. If using odd parity, the check bit would have to be a '0' so that the quantity of ones remain an odd number (110000010). Should the byte be received at the other end showing an even number of ones (110100010), then the computer knows that the information was corrupted during transmission. Errors could still occur it the incorrectly transmitted byte contained two reversing errors which coincidentally and erroneously resulted in an odd number of ones. However, the probability of this occurring is very low. The same principles apply when the sending and receiving devices are configured to accept even parity, where the number of ones must always be even.

check box. A small square box that appears in a dialog box and that can be selected or cleared; found in graphical user interfaces (GUIs). When the check box is selected, an X appears in the box (alternately, it can be darkened, or identified as selected in another way). A check box represents an option that you can turn on and off.

check digit. 1. In a character or word, one or more redundant digits, which depend on one another such that is one digit changes, a malfunction, can be detected.

2. When carried along with a machine word, one or more digits used in relation to other digits in the word as self-checking or error-detecting code.

check. 1. A means of verifying the accuracy of data transmitted, manipulated or stored by any unit or device in a computer system.

2. A process of testing the corrections of machine operations, the existence of certain prescribed conditions within a computer or the correctness of the results produced by a program.

checksum. A 16-bit calculated field used to ensure detection of corrupted datagrams. It is used for verifying the accuracy of transmitted data. A checksum is a computed value calculated from the contents of a packet. This value is sent along with the packet when it is transmitted. The receiving system computes a new checksum based upon the received data and compares this value with the one sent with the packet.

chemical markup language. CML. An XML application that, together with the Jumbo Java applet, allows chemical formulae and molecular models to be described and viewed with a Web browser.

CHILL. A high-level computer language used particularly for real-time applications such as the control of electronic telephone exchanges.

chip carrier. A high-density package for very large scale integration integrated circuits. It may be a lead-less chip carrier, a lead-less ceramic chip carrier, a pin grid array or a lead-less land grid array. There are many different sizes available.

chip creep. A situation in which integrated circuits gradually lose contact with their sockets because of changes in temperature.

chip. 1. A small section of a single crystal comprising capacitors, resistors, microprocessors or other devices manufactured on small pieces of semiconductor usually silicon,

ceramic or other materials. Chips are often called integrated circuits.
2. Chip Hermetically In Plastics; the microprocessors or other devices, cut from larger wafers, usually silicon, and hermetically sealed within the plastics or resinous material.

CHKPT. ChecKPoinT, a point of time during a machine run where processing is halted momentarily to allow the variables of the run to be recorded on magnetic tape.

CHNL. CHaNneL, used in several contexts. *See* channel.

CHOL. Common High Order Language.

chooser. On Macintosh, the facility that controls the selecting of printers, file servers, and other network devices.

CHP. CHannel Processor.

CHR. *See* character.

chrominance. The comparison of colours of equal luminance.

CHRP. Common Hardware Reference Platform.

CI. 1. Call Indicator.
2. Chain Index.
3. Communication Interface.

CIB. 1. Channel Interface Bus.
2. Command Input Buffer.

CICP. Communication Interrupt Control Program.

CICS. Customer Information Control System, a system that provides an interface between operating systems, access methods and applications programs to allow remote or local display terminal interaction with the database of the central processor.

CIDA. Acronym for Channel Indirect Data Processing.

CIDR. Classless Internet Domain Routing, a routing protocol for working with multiple class C addresses.

CIE. Customer-Initiated Entry, term used in EDI.

CIF. 1. Central Index File.
(a) A centrally located table containing a set of key characters, treated as a whole, that identify the actual disk records in another permanent disk file.
(b) A central file of terms in an automatic retrieval system that is searched by a computer.
2. Central Integration Facility. A centrally located device whose output function is proportional to the integral of the input function with respect to a specified variable.

CIF. Central Information File.

CIL. Call Identification File.

CILE. Call Information Logging Equipment.

CineWeb. An audio/video player for standard movie and audio files (AVI, MOV, MPG, WAV, MID, and MP2)on Windows systems. One can create standard movies using Weblisher and MegaPEG.

CIO. *See* central input output multiplexer.

CIOCS. Communication Input/Output Control System.

CIOCS. *See* communication input/output control system.

cipher. The pseudo-random signal resulting from the combination of an intelligence signal and akey signal.

cir. Committed Information Rate, used in a frame relay to allow the network to monitor traffic form a given device and decide what traffic may be discarded in case of congestion.

circuit switching. The transmission technique in which a physical circuit is established between sender and receiver before transmission takes place. When the transmission is complete, the circuit is freed.

CISC. Complex Instruction Set Computing, a central processing unit architecture in which a large number of instructions are hard coded into the chip. Older central processing units were CISC chips.

CIS-COBOL. Compact Interactive Standard COBAL; a version of the programming language COBOL that runs on many of the popular personal computers above the hobby level. CIS-COBOL has been implemented for the 6809, 8080, 8086, and similar microprocessor chips making it widely available. A particularly important point is that CIS-COBOL programs are portable between different micros, thus making it a very useful language for the development of program packages on the commercial market.

CIX. Commercial Internet eXchange, an association of Internet providers.

CI. Connect Indication, primitive to indicate that a connection has been requested by the service user at the peer service access point.

CL. 1. ConnectionLess-oriented, used as a prefix with connectionless protocols and services.
2. CLassification code.
3. Command Language.
4. Current Loop.

CLA. Communication Line adaptor.

CLASS. Custom Local Area Signal Services, a telephony term.

Classless Internet Domain Routing. *See* CIDR.

CLB. Central Logic Bus.

CLC. 1. Central Logic Control.
2. Communication Line Control.

CLI. Calling Line Identification, a service available on digital phone networks that tells the person being called which number is calling them. The central office equipment identifies the phone number of the caller, enabling information about the caller to be sent along with the call itself; synonymous with Automatic Number Identification (ANI). See also Command Line Interface.

CLID. Calling Line IDentification, a term used with ISDN, equivalent to Caller ID.

client. A computer using services or resources provided by a remote machine, called a server. Often, communications software will have a separate version for the client, or guest, and the server, or host.

client/server architecture. A network architecture in which clients request data, programs, and

client/server computing. The division of an application into two parts; a front end client and a back end server. It allows multiple front ends running on a PC or Unix workstation (client) to access the same SQL based server database at the same time over the LAN. The aim is to off-load as much processing as possible to the intelligent desktop leaving only the shared information and the software for managing it at the central server. An application that is running in such a fashion with client and server linked by a LAN is termed a bifurcated application.

client/server network. A server-centric network in which some network resources are stored on a file server, while processing power is distributed among workstations and the file server.

client-side scripting. Creating scripts that are executed in the user's Web browser. It is typically small program embedded within an HTML document. Whenever a Web browser that supports client-side scripting encounters one of these scripts, it executes the program by interpreting the commands.

CLIP. 1. Calling Line Identification Presentation, ISDN supplementary service for presenting the ID of the calling party.
2. Cellular Logic Image Processor.

ClipArt. Images that are available for use on computers. Companies have begun to sell collections of ClipArt that may be useful in business, desktop publication, etc.

clipboard. A temporary storage location used to transfer data between documents and between applications. Typically, you transfer data to the Clipboard by using an application's Copy or Cut command, and inserting data from the clipboard by using the application's paste command. In Windows, Clipboard Viewer is used to view the contents of the clipboard. On the Macintosh, Show Clipboard is choosen from the edit or window menu of most applications.

CLIR. Calling Line Identification Restriction, ISDN supplementary service for restricting presentation of the ID of the calling party.

CLLM. Consolidated Link-Layer Management, in frame relay, a way for the network to send control messages to user devices.

CLM. Communications Line Multiplxer.

CLNP. ConnectionLess-mode Network Protocol, sometimes referred to as OSI IP; the Internet IP was the initial input to ISO in the development of this standard.

CLNS. ConnectionLess-mode Network Service, the OSI datagram service in which each packet must carry the destination address.

clone. Software or hardware which is almost identical to an original. The term 'IBM clone' usually refers to a personal computer which performs and functions in the same away as an IBM personal computer. PS/2 was designed using a new bus architecture called Micro Channel Architecture (MCA) which meant existing industry software and peripherals could not function on PS/2 Compaq and eight other manufacturers (dubbed as 'Gang of Nine') joined forces to maintain the industry-standard architecture (ISA), and further developed it to take advantage of the 32-bit bus structure of the Intel 80386 and 80486 microprocessors. Extended ISA became known as EISA. Today, the term 'IBM-compatible' is confusing, and it has become common to refer to personal computers, and personal computer system, as industry-standard computers.

Close Box. On Macintosh, small square in upper-left hand corner of a window that allows to Close that window.

CLP. Communication Line Processor.

CLS. Communication Line Switch.

CLT. 1. Communication Line Terminal.
2. Computer Language Translator.

CL-TK. CLaim ToKen, MAC frame.

CLTP. ConnectionLess Transport Protocol, the OSI protocol that uses end-to-end transport addressing, via the Transport Selector, and error control by way of a checksum, but does not guarantee delivery or flow control.

CLTS. ConnectionLess Transport Service; uses end-to-end transport addressing and error control, but does not guarantee delivery or flow control.

CLU. Computer Logic Unit.

cluster controller. An IBM device that allows multiple 3270 terminals to be linked directly to a host computer, or into a SNA network using a communications controller.

cluster. A group of sectors on a disk. DOS allocates disk space to files in clusters.

CM. 1. Central Memory.
2. Configuration Management, set of functions in Network Management to control and exchange data with NEs.

CMA. Communications Managers Association, a generic type of user groups for users of telecom products.

CMIP. Common Management Information Protocol, format for the transfer of management information between open systems; defined in ISO 9596.

CMIP/CMIS. Common Management Information Protocol/Common Management Information Services, OSI connection oriented network management protocol and set of services; well accepted in WAN and telecommunications world, they have not yet been widely adopted for LAN management.

CMIS. Common Management Information Service, the service interface to CMIP; describes the services to carry management information for many management function areas.

CMIS/CMIP. Common Management Information Service/Common Management Information Protocol.

CMISE. Common Management Information Service Element, common ASE to support system management exchanges.

CMND. *See* command.

CMOS RAM. Complementary (symmetry) Metal-Oxide Semiconductor Random-Access Memory, a kind of random-access memory, which uses special low-powered chips with battery backup, allowing information to be saved after the power is turned off. The batteries can last up to three years. Along with memory size and type of peripheral devices, CMOS RAM also keeping track of the time and date. One of the main reasons for using CMOS is to conserve power, but this does not just relate to reducing electricity consumption, nor does it necessarily relate to minimizing battery operation. The main reason for conserving power is to be able to put more functionality into a smaller space. Reduced power consumption allows the use of smaller and lighter power supplies. With less heat generated, denser packaging of circuit components is possible, and expensive fans and blowers can usually be eliminated. A cooler running chip is more reliable, since most random and wear-out failures relate to high temperature. In addition, lower power dissipation allows more functions to be integrated onto the chip.

CMOS. Complementary Metal Oxide Semiconductor, a small section of RAM used to hold certain hardware configuration parameters in IBM and compatible computers.

CML. *See* chemical markup language.

CMOT. CMIP over TCP/IP.

CN. 1. CoNect Session PDU, PDU that requests establishment of a Session connection.

2. Country Name, used as one of the attributes in X.400 names; may be either alphabetic or numeric.

CNC. CoNCentrator, a communications device that allows a number of Network Elements to share a smaller \number of physical ports for connection to a communication network.

CNMA. Communications Network for Manufacturing Applications, a project sponsored by ESPRIT to develop advanced networks for automation in manufacturing areas.

CO. 1. Central Office, in telephony, the main switching office in district.

2. Customer Owned, in telephony, equipment not owned by the network service provider.

3. Connection-Oriented, used as a prefix for connection-oriented protocols and services.

co-axial cable. A cable comprising a central wire surrounded by a second tubular screening of fine wire; associated with IBM for linking terminals and other devices needing high-speed links. Coaxial cable is often used in Ethernet networks; both thick (10Base5) and thin (10Base2) Ethernet cables are coaxial. It is difficult to add or remove devices from a coaxial LAN as the cable is unwieldy and thick so is being superseded by UTP.

COBIS. Computer Based Instruction System.

COBOL. Common Business-Orientated Language. A computer language designed for commercial data processing such as accounting and financial work. It is a specific language by which business-data processing procedure may be precisely described in standard form. This language that was developed by; CODASYL. COBOL program is divided into four divisions of which the most important are the data division and the procedure division. In the data division, the programmer defines the files to be used by specifying their record structure. The procedure division is made up of statements grouped into sentences, paragraphs and sections. These statements define manipulation of data from the current record(s) of one or more files. Input-output is defined in terms of complete records so typical program reads a record from its input file, processes it, and writes record to its output file, repeating this sequence until the whole file is processed. A powerful feature allows data definition to specify editing that will take place as side-effect of output, *e.g.,* suppressing non-significant zeros.

COC. Central Office Connection, the connection of a circuit (phone or data) at the phone company office to the local loop (subscriber).

COCC. Character Oriented Communication Controller.

code conversion. 1. Conversion of character signals or groups of character signals in one code into corresponding signals or groups of signals in another code.

2. A process for converting a code of some predetermined bit structure (*e.g.*, 5,7, or 14 bits per character interval) to a second code with approximately the same number of bits per character interval. No alphabetical significance is assumed in this process.

code extension character. A control character used to indicate that one or more of the succeeding coded elements are to be interpreted according to a different code. It may be noted that the code extension characters are described in ISO 646 and ISO 2022.

code, access. Digits that must be dialed in order to gain access to a particular circuit or facility. A PABX extension user, for example, often has to dial 0-9 to access the public network.

CODLS. COnnection-mode Data Link Service.

COED. Computer Operated Electronic Display.

COFF. Common Object File Format.

collision detection. Devices at each end of link are designed to detect collisions instantly and attempt to resend. This is the principle on which CSMA/CD is based and the access control method for Ethernet. An alternative is to resend if there is no acknowledgement of receipt from remote device.

collision. The result of two devices on a shared transmission medium, like Ethernet, transmitting simultaneously. Data is corrupted and both devices must retry their transmissions. A delay mechanism used by both senders drastically reduces the chances of another collision.

.com. File name extension for a command file, the program file that is activated when the filename is brought to the command line by the user or another program.

COM port. A connection on an IBM or compatible computer, usually named

COM1, where you plug in the cable for a serial device. Common serial devices are printers and modems. Serial ports are smaller than parallel ports and usually contain 9-pins.Also called a serial port.

combinational logic element. A device having at least one output channel and one or more input channels, all characterized by discrete states, such that at any instant, the state of each output channel is completely determined by states of input channels.

COMBS. Customer-Oriented Message Buffer System, a term used in EDI.

COML. COMmercial Language.

command key. A key found on the keyboards of some computers which often modifies the action performed when pressing another key in combination with it. On a Macintosh, the command key is marked with the Mac Apple symbol and a symbol resembling a cloverleaf.

command line interface. CLI. Accessing a computer based on typing commands rather than selecting icons and menu items.

command line. Commands typed to run an application. The user can type commands at an MS-DOS prompt or in the Run dialog box in the Program Manager of Windows. Interfaces in which the user types commands rather than choose them from a menu, are often called command line interfaces. MS-DOS has a command line interface while Macintosh does not.

command prompt. Usually refers to the MS-DOS prompt; the character or characters that appear at the beginning of the command line (usually "C."), indicating that the computer is ready to receive input.

command. 1. A word or phrase usually found in a menu, that is choosen to carry out an action. A command is choosen from menu, or type a command at the MS-DOS prompt.
2. A mathematical or logic operator; an instruction.
3. An electronic pulse, signal, or set of signals to start, stop, or continue an operation, or the execution of a program.
4. A mathematical or logic operator; an instruction.
5. The portion of an instruction word which specifies the operation to be performed.

commercial language. Generally procedural, this type of computer language is designed for data processing, accounting and financial work (such as COBOL).

communicating word processor. CWP. A computer having copying and communications facilities. It can send information to and receive pages of text in seconds from another word processor by means of a network, which allows rapid inter-office or site-to-site text communications.

communication input/output control system. CIOCS. A group of routines which automatically control the performance of input/output operations an direct other functions, in a computer system that handles on-line, real-time applications (*i.e.*, a communications system).

communications adaptor. A hardware feature on most processors and terminals that permits telecommunications lines to be attached. It converts data from parallel to serial for output, and from serial to parallel for input.

communications controller. A switching unit central to the implementation of host-based IBM SNA networks. The network is built around a backbone of inter-linked communications controllers to which host computers and control units are attached.

communications data processor. CDP. A device that has the capability of performing the reduction, summarizing, or input and output, of transmitted data originating from another point. A specialized I/O processor is used to control a number of communication lines and/or communication devices. These lines/devices operate slowly in comparison to computing speeds so that one communication processor is usually multiplexed across a large number of lines/devices. Communication processors are used for the handling of data (in blocks, packets, messages datagrams, etc.) for purposes of protocol, error checking and correction, acknowledgment, and buffering. They are now (mostly) programmed computers; earlier generations tended to be less general wired-program systems. Communication processors are sometimes called concentrators, transmission control units or front-end processors.

communications manager. An individual often underpaid and invariably over-worked, dedicated to providing cost effective, ultimately flexible networking to users.

communications satellite. An orbiting vehicle which relays signals between communications stations. It may be:
(a) active communications satellite- a satellite which receives, regenerates, and retransmits signals between stations; and
(b) passive communications satellite- a satellite which reflects communications signals between stations.

communications server. A specialized network server that provides access to external networks, communications facilities and hosts that cannot be directly connected to the LAN. Typically, it will enable workstation users running appropriate workstation software, such as terminal emulation software, to access asynchronous communications links and typically modems attached to the communications server.

communications storage unit. A single- or dual-drive diskette system used for storing messages received on line or other locally-prepared information ready for transmission.

communications system. A collection of individual communications networks, transmission systems, relay stations, tributary stations, and terminal equipment capable of interconnection and inter-operation to form an integral whole. These individual components must serve a common purpose, be technically compatible, employ common procedures, respond to some form of control, and in general operate in unison.

communications toolbox. Extension of Apple Macintosh operating system; provides protocol conversion and the drivers needed for communications tasks.

communications. 1. The process of transferring information in various forms from one point, person or device to another.
2. The information thus received.
3. Information transfer according to agreed conventions.

community antenna relay service. CARS. The 12.75-12.95 GHz microwaves frequency band, which the FCC has assigned to the CATV industry for use in transporting television, signals.

COMPAC. Computer Program for Automatic Control.

compact disk. An audio disk system in which the disk if only one seventh of the total area of a conventional record or disk, although a single side can play for an hour. Information is carried or encoded as spiral groove of pits ad flats in digital form. The compact disk carries a total of over five billion digital sound signal binary digits not including additional bits that are used for speed control and error correction tasks.

compact floppy disk drive. CFDD. The disks that have been designed in such a manner so as to match and drive each size of compact floppy disk and are direct, plug-compatible replacements for conventional mino floppy disk drives. The rotation speed, data transfer rate, recording capacity per track and other specifications are exactly similar to those of the mini floppy disks, so the existing floppy disk controllers can be employed.

compact floppy disk. CFD. A smaller form of floppy disk, being 3, 3.25 and 3.5 inches rather than the conventional mini disk sizes of 5 and 5.25 inches. CFDs have a rigid hard plastic shell (measuring 80 X 100 X 5 mm) with a shutter on the case that automatically opens and closes when the case in inserted or pulled out of a compact floppy disk drive system.

compile. 1. To translate a computer program expressed in problem-oriented language into a computer-oriented language.

2. To prepare a machine language program from a computer program written in another programming language by making use of generating more than one computer instruction for each symbolic statement, or both, as well as performing the function of an assembler.

compiler. A program which translates source code written in a particular programing language into computer-readable machine code that can be executed on its own. Compare with Interpreter.

COMPUSEC. COMPUter SECurity, security to protect information in and access to a computer system.

computer graphics. A mode of computer processing and output in which a significant part of the output information is in pictorial form. The information may range from a simple histogram or other plot of information to a complex map or engineering design annotated with alphanumeric and displayed in colour. The output may be via a visual display terminal or as a permanent record via a printer/plotter or *x-y* recorder. Suitable input devices include data tablets and light pens. The computer can be made to manipulate the information, *e.g.* straighten lines, move or delete designated areas, expand or contract details, etc.

computer interface unit. CIU. A unit that provides a common boundary between automatic data processing systems. In communications and data systems, it may involve code. Format, speed or other changes as required.

computer logic. The basic organization, design, and wiring used to realize a particular computer logic is therefore concerned with the design of building blocks or components, both logical and physical and with the logic design involved in realizing a particular set of machine-code instructions; this may include the provision of facilities such as microprogramming whereby the set of basic instructions can be altered.

computer micrographics. Methods and techniques for recording on microforms data produced by a computer or for transforming data recorded on microforms into a form suitable for computer use.

computer output microfilm. A microfilm printer that will substitute directly for a line printer or tape output by taking output directly from a computer. It may also be referred to as computer output microfilmer, computer output microform, computer onto microfilm, computer output on microfilm, computer output microfiche or computer onto microfiche.

computer. An automatic device capable of accepting information, applying prescribed processes to the information, and supplying the results of these processes. The instructions are stored in a memory. The most widely used and most versatile of these devices is the digital computer.

computer-aided design. CAD. The application of computer technology to the design of a product, or the design itself. A computer-aided design uses as inputs both the appropriate technical knowledge of individuals who enter design criteria, edit results and otherwise test and modify the design and also accumulated information from libraries of standards for components, element sizes, regulations, etc., *e.g.* standard ICs for a digital design system, standard pipe lengths and fittings for hydraulic or piping system. Processing of data from the inputs takes place in at least two phases:

(a) certain interactive programs are invoked by the technical designer during the design process these results being generally displayed on a visual display unit;

(b) programs are applied that may take considerable periods of running time to analyze tolerances clearances, electrical characteristics, etc., the results of these runs being displayed back to the technical designer.

The output from a computer-aided design system consists of printouts of specifications and other information, and machine-readable files that are passed to computer aided manufacturing (CAM) systems and computer-aided testing systems. Examples of output to a CAM system are computer-produced artwork for printed circuit boards or computer-produced tapes for automatic component insertion and board drilling.

computer-aided engineering. CAE. Specialized hardware and software tools which help develop products faster by assisting designers and engineers with the design, development, calculation, analysis, testing, and experimentation of new products.

computer-aided instruction. CAI. The original term for on-line use of a computer to administer instruction directly to one or more people. In many areas CAI has come to mean computer-based drill and practice; in other areas any computer-based tutorial, particularly one aimed at teaching the use of particular computer or program is referred to as CAI.

computer-aided learning. CAL. The use of computer in a system that is employed to aid students in a course of programmed learning.

computer-aided manufacture. CAM. A manufacturing production process resulting in finished products, controlled by a computer or numerical controlled machinery.

computer-aided retrieval. CAR. The use of computers in document-retrieval systems to replace the simple manual look-up reference systems.

computer-aided tomography. CAT. Image processing of body tissues through the computer analysis of X-ray data.

computer-assisted acquisition system. CAAS. A computer system used to assist libraries in their acquisition of material.

computer-assisted information retrieval system. CAIRS. A computer system that provides information to users in response to their requests. The computer has files containing information that can be searched for particular items, in response to the definition of particular user needs.

computer-automated measurement and control. CAMC. A standard that defines the physical sizes of modules and racks, as well as defining power supplies, module address lines, data lines control code for the deletion of information used in American standard code for information interchange.

computer-based learning. CBL. A structured course of teaching and learning the relies on the use of a computer.

computer-based message system. CBSM. A term used to describe the communication via electronic mail of keyboarded material which also includes the idea of electronic mailboxes.

computer-orientated language. A programming language requiring little translation. This type of program usually runs efficiently on a related computer, but requires extensive translation for use on another variety of computer.

computer-sensitive language. A programming language written so that is it totally or partially dependent on the type of machine used.

COMSAT. 1. COMmunications SATellite. An artificial unmanned satellite in earth orbit that provides communication links between locations on Earth which can be widely separated. It accepts and relays suitably modulated signals between earth stations. 2. COMmunications SATellite Corporation. A privately owned American corporation established by statute as the exclusive international satellite carrier and representing the US in the International Telecommunications Satellite Consortium.

COMSEC. COMmunication SECurity, security against threats to the communication of Information Technology; this involves protection of data in transit, authentication of originators and recipients, non-repudiation of origin, receipt, and content integrity.

concentration. A technique used to get the most out of a composite multiplexer link. Usually a statistical multiplexer, or concentrator, is used to focus channel inputs onto the composite ink by removing the portions of the transmission carrying no data.

concentrator. A central chassis into which various modules, such as bridging, supervisory, 10BaseT and other peripheral cards are plugged. It permits to position machines closer together on the network cable than you could otherwise. If a twisted-pair cable is used, a concentrator is needed.

CONFIG.SYS. A text file that DOS reads when booting which instructs the computer about the configuration of the machine. Config.sys contains configuration commands, which enable or disable system features, set limits on resources, and extend the operating system functionality by loading device drivers.

congestion. A condition occurring when the load exceeds the capacity of a data communication path. It is experienced when a busy signal is received while dialing the modem, or when an error message is received that no ports are available for the service.

connectionless service. Transport of single datagram or packet of information from one network node to destination node or multiple nodes without establishing network connection.

connection-oriented. Transport of packets of information from one network node to a destination node following an established network connection.

CONP. Connection-Oriented Network Protocol.

CONS. Connection-Oriented Network Service, requires that a connection be established before data can be transferred between two entities on the network.

consistency. In transaction processing (TP), a computer transaction is said to provide integrity of operation and data when the transaction passes the ACID (atomicity, consistency, isolation, durability) test. A transaction has 'consistency' when it successfully transforms the system and the database from one valid state to another. Consistency in a transaction processing system stems mainly from correct application programming (for example, always debiting and crediting the same amount). Because the transaction processing system provides atomicity for the transaction, the application programmer can concentrate on the consistency of the application programs from a business standpoint.

console command processor. CCP. An area in the memory map of a microcomputer using a control program for microcomputers disk operating system that allows the user to converse with the operating system by using the command syntax. Thus the user can accomplish various tasks which include listing a directory on a disk or executing a program file on a disk simply by using the terminal that is tagged on the system.

console. Workstation from which the operation of a computer system can be monitored and controlled. In current systems, the console is usually a desk-height surface supporting a keyboard and one or more VDUs and reference documents. There may also be a number of other switches and indicators mounted on a panel. In early systems, the control unit at the console was often a teleprinter. As systems became large and more sophisticated the consoles first became more complex and then much simpler as the development of operating systems advanced.

constant voltage transformer. CVT. A transformer than can provide a substantially constant value of voltage independently of the current supplied to it.

contact input. A binary input to a device generated by opening or closing a switch. It may be noted that the switch could be either mechanical or electronic.

contention. The process whereby multiple users make requests for transmission bandwidth across a transmission link but the pool of bandwidth is less than the aggregate amount of bandwidth the users could request between them. Contention is used to resolve which users gain access to the bandwidth. When this s applied to multiplexers, it is concerned with the multiplier's ability to allow a number of channels to contend for transmission bandwidth that is less than the sum of all the channel rates.

continuous-path control. Methods that are divided into three basic categories based on how much information about the path is used in the motor control calculations. These are:

(a) The conventional or servo-control approach which uses no information about where the patch goes in the future (this is the control design used in most industrial robots and process control systems).

(b) The preview control, synonymous with feed-forward control, which uses some knowledge about how the path changes immediately ahead of the robot's current location, in addition to the past and present tracking error used by servo controller; and

(c) the path planning approach synonymous with the trajectory calculation approach, where the controller has available a complete description of the path the manipulator follows from one point to another, achieving a highly accurate coordinated movement at high speed.

control character. Any one of 32 special hardware-control characters and symbols available in ASCII (sometimes invisible) which are used to control a communications process, or a peripheral device such as a printer. Control characters may be used to instruct the printer to advance paper, or move one line. They can also be used to signify the start and finish of a data transmission. A character whose occurrence in a particular context specifies a control function. It may be noted that:

(a) control character may be recorded for use in subsequent action.

(b) A control character is not a graphic character but may have a graphic representation in some circumstances.

(c) Control characters are described in ISO 646 and ISO 6429.

control panel. In Windows, OS/ Presentation Manager, and within the Macintosh system, a utility menu (desk accessory) which allows the user to set the parameters when using the computer and its peripheral devices. For example, the control panel allows the user to adjust the volume, colors on the screen, cursor speed, and mouse-movement speed.

control point. A program that manages APPN network node and its resources, enabling communications to other control points in the network.

control read only memory. CROM. The memory designed and micro-programmed to decode control logic, this special type of read-only memory (ROM) is an important component in several types of two-chip microprocessors; one chip contains central processing unit and other a CROM.

control section. A main sequence of instructions or data in a computer program, that can be transferred, deleted or replaced with a control section from other program segments.

controlled path system. CPS. A method that takes advantage of the computational capability of the computer to provide the operator with coordinated control of the robot axes when teaching the unit. It also allows control of total position, velocity and acceleration control of the robot end effector along a desired path between programmed points when in the replay or automatic mode of operation. When teaching the robot, controlled path system coordinates the axes in a manner that permits the operator to position and orient the end effector at desired points without having to individually command each robot axis. When teaching, the operator does not have to generate the desired path but only programs end points.

conventional memory. In an IBM PC or compatible computer, up to the first 640K of memory in your computer. MS-DOS by default uses only this memory to run programs.

converter. A repeater that also converts from one media type to another, such as from fiber to copper. Often called a media adapter.

CoolFusion. A plug-in that plays streaming video for Windows (AVI) files. Using CoolFusion, the user may preview AVI video in real-time as it downloads on Windows 95 systems.

cookies. The objects that enable Web page authors to save some state information about the user who just visited their site. In general, when a user requests Web page from a server, that page is sent to the the user's Web browser. After the page is sent, no record of the event is saved, except for the small mention in the access log file. Because the access log file is not set up for keeping track of and supplying this information to the Web server, there is no practical record kept of what page the user requested or any of the actions the user took. A cookie is a simple record that is stored on user's machine in a cookie.txt file.

Copland. A new version of Macintosh system software under development scheduled to be released by 1997.

COPP. Connection-Oriented mode Presentation Protocol.

coprocessor registers. Registers in coprocessors, which are used to improve the performance of numeric applications. For example, connecting an Intel 80287 or 80387 numeric coprocessor to an 80386 microprocessor effectively adds these registers to the 80386. While numeric coprocessor recognizes integers, packed decimals, and floating point formats of various lengths, internally it holds all values in an eight-deep, 80-bit-wide floating point 'register stack'. Numeric instructions may implicitly refer to other registers. The 'status register' maintains the top of stack pointers with flags that identify exceptions (for example, overflow) and condition codes that reflect the result of the last instruction.

coprocessor. An additional processor chip, which increases the computer's speed by handling specialized chores such as math or graphics. A personal computer may use a math coprocessor to more efficiently handle specialist mathematics-intensive applications, or a video coprocessor optimized for faster video imaging. For computations using binary-coded decimals, and floating point calculations, a microprocessor can perform at speeds of up to 100 times faster when a numeric coprocessor is used (handling approximately 80 bits at a time). Floating point operands are large, and the useful set of operations on them is quite complex; many thousands of transistors are required to implement a standard set of floating point operations such as those defined by IEEE standard 754. The variety of functions that could be implemented in a coprocessor is unlimited and more than one coprocessor could be used in a system if the primary processor has been suitably designed. For instance, one coprocessor could provide high-speed math processing and another could provide database management primitives. An example of coprocessor is Intel 8087, which is a math chip designed to work with both 8-bit-bus 8088 and 16-bit-bus 8086 processors.

COPS. Connection-Oriented mode Presentation Service.

copy protection. A set of hidden instructions and commands embedded into a software program by the manufacturer. Copy protection is designed to prevent unauthorised duplication of the software contained on a diskette.

copy. To reproduce data in a new location, replacing the information that was previously stored there without altering the source of the original data. This is often done to guard against loss or corruption of the records.

copyright. The right to prevent copying of a book, information, software or manufacturing process. It protects the form in which the idea is expressed. Most of the computer software are considered to be protected under the law of copyright.

COR. Confirmation Of Receipt, used in the network service.

CORAL. Computer Online Realtime Application Language, a programming language based on Algol 60. Although described as a real-time language, it has no built-in facilities for parallel processing, synchronization, interrupt handling etc.

CORBA. Common Object Request Broker Architecture,

core memory. The memory of a computer that a directly addressable by the central processing unit.

core, magnetic. Devices used as stores for binary information; magnetic material cores arranged in a matrix formation, threaded with write wires and a read wire. Ferrite stores of this nature were at one time common in computers and in the control circuitry of telephone central offices.

COS. 1. Cassette Operating System.
2. Compatible Operating System.
3. Corporation for Open Systems, an international not-for-profit consortium of venders and user organizations based in the US. Their goal is to promote OSI and ISDN standards, mainly through providing conformance testing and education.

COSCL. Common Operating System Control Language.

COSINE. Cooperation for open Systems Interconnection. Networking in Europe, a Wan cosponsored by the CEC and started in 1990.

COSS. Committee on Open Systems Support Services, a subcommittee with ISO SC21.

COTP. Connection-Oriented Transport Protocol.

COTS. 1. Connection-Oriented Mode Transport Serivce; transport service is defined in CCITT X.214 and ISO 8072; the protocol is given in CCITT X.224 and ISO 8073.
2. Commercial Off the Shelf, a product that follows the standards and therefore does not need to be tailored to fit each application and user.

CP PPDU. Connect Presentation PDU, PDU requesting establishment of a Presentation association.

CP. Customer Premises.

CPA PPDU. Connect Presentation Accept PDU.

CPCS. Check Processing Control System.

CPDS. Computer Program Design Specification.

CPE. Customer Premises Equipment, equipment residing at customer site; used to connect to a public network.

CPE. *See* central processing element.

CPF. Control Program facility.

CPFM. Continuous Phase Frequency Modulation, one of several modulation techniques used to signal on a carrier frequency.

CPI. Computer to PBX Interface.

CPIW. Customer Provided Inside. Wiring, when the phone compnay is not responsible for problems with the telephone wiring inside the building.

CPS FORUM. COS/POSI/SPAG, a forum to promote international harmonization of conformance testing and certification across North America, Europe, and Japan.

CPS. Characters Per Second, a measurement of throughput.

CPS. 1. *See* characters per second.
2. *See* controlled path system.

CPU. Central Processing Unit, refers either to the principle microchip that the computer is built around (such as the Pentium or Power PC chip) or the box that houses the main components of the computer.

CR. 1. Connect Request, refers to the transport PDU requesting a connection, often followed by an indication of the layer referred, to, for example, CR TPDU.
2. Carriage Return character, usually shorthand for both carriage return and line feed.

cracker. An individual, who attempts to access computer systems without authorization, such persons are often malicious, as opposed to hackers.

CRAM. Card random Access Memory.

crash. A sudden, unexpected cessation of activity by the computer, accompanied by a sudden, unexpected increase in activity by the system administrator; caused by someone running huge, unimportant program just as your small, critical program is about to finish.

Cray-1. A powerful mainframe computer capable of executing over 80 million operations per second. Cray-1 is known as supercomputer. It was developed by former Control Data Corporation's employee.

CRC. Cyclic Redundancy Check, a method of detecting errors in the serial transmission of data. A check-sum calculation used to verify the contents of a data frame; a 4-byte (32bit) checksum value for the frame. The sending computer calculates a CRC value for the frame and encodes it in frame. The receiving computer then recalculates CRC and checks the CRC field to see if the values match. If the values do not match, some data is lost or changed during transmission.

CREN. Corporation for Research and Educational Networking, academic computers network formed by the administrative merger of BIT-NET and CSNET.

Crescendo Plus. A MIDI player that uses QuickTime's built-in MIDI synthesizer to play the music. It downloads the MIDI sound file and plays it as a continuous sound loop.

CRF. Communication-Related Function, a function providing the means for cooperating processes in different open system to communicate.

CROM. *See* control read only memory.

cross-connect. An ATM switch usually comprising three functional areas. System control The central control unit, which also provides the management interface of the system; the ATM "fabric block" providing the system switching capacity; termination groups to provide the external interfaces and the functions of the ATM layer of the network node. Each of these functional system areas is configured according to the specified needs of the respective network node. Each functional area usually has its own monitoring and control units for safeguarding the high availability of the complete system.

cross coupling. The coupling of a signal from one channel, circuit, or conductor to another, where it becomes a undesirable signal.

cross modulation. Interference when a carrier signal becomes modulated by an interfering and unwanted signal as well as being modulated by its wanted signal.

cross-ring. Ringing of the bell of a second, undesired caller after one caller has already been rung.

crossover network. A type of filter, which divides an incoming signal into two, or sometimes more outputs, with higher frequencies to one output, and lower ones to another.

cross point. A single element in an array of elements that comprises a switch; a set of physical or logical contacts that operate together to extend the signal in the switching network.

cross-talk. Unwanted interference from another adjacent communications channel. The signal from the adjacent channel is inserted into the original communications channel.

cross-talk level. Effective power of cross-talk signal, expressed in decibels.

crowbar. A short-circuit or low resistance path placed across the input device.

crown, cabinet. The space at the top of an equipment cabinet, normally reserved for terminal blocks.

CRT controller. Necessary electronic circuitry to control CRT display. Several controller ICs such as Intel 8275, Intel 8276, Intel 82706, Intel 82716, Intel 82786, and Motorola 6845 are available.

CRT terminal. An assembly of CRT (cathode ray tube) display unit, keyboard, CRT-refresh RAM, CRT controller, and USART or UART for communication with the computer. CRT terminals contains one or more built-in microprocessors to control and co-ordinate the keyboard, CRT display unit and data transmission from the terminal to the computer, and vice-versa. The data are entered into the computer through keyboard. Each entered character is displayed on the CRT screen, so that the user can see what he has entered. When the data are keyed in, they are held in a small memory called buffer, within the terminal itself.

cryptanalysis. The steps and operations performed in converting encrypted messages in to plain text without initial knowledge of the key employed in the process.

cryptochannel. A complete system of crypto-communications between two or more points; analogous to a radio circuit.

cryptographic. Pertaining to equipments or systems that encode data to conceal real meanings.

cryptology. The scientific study of hidden, disguised, or encrypted communications; embraces communications security and communications intelligence.

CS. 1. Coordinated Single-layer (abstract) test method, one of the abstract test methods used in conformance testing; uses a test management protocol for controlling coordination between the upper and lower testers.

2. Channel Status.

CSDN. Circuit-Switched Data Network.

CSE. Coordinated Single-layer Embedded (abstract) test method, a variation on the CS test method in conformance testing.

CSL. 1. Code Selection Language.

2. Computer Simulated Language.

3. Computer System Laboratory, part of NIST; develops FIPS; sole source of computer and communications standards for US federal agencies.

CSMA. Carrier Sense Multiple Access; all devices on the network connect directly to the cable and are free to transmit at any time. CSMA is used usually with collision detection.

CSMA/CA. Carrier Sense Multiple Access with Collision Avoidance, a method of network access not covered by OSI standards and used in AppleTalk networks; prevents stations from sending traffic at the same or nearly the same time.

CSMA/CD. Carrier Sense Multiple Access with Collision Detection, the access method used in Ethernet. All nodes are attached to a single cable and contend equally for access to the transmission medium. If two nodes attempt to send data at the same time, they "sense" each other's signal and immediately stop sending. They will both try to send again after waiting a random number of microseconds.

CSMA/CP. CSMA with Collision Prevention (e.g., LDDI).

CSMC. Communications Service Management Council, one of the functional committees involved in the management of so-called smart buildings or shared tenant service (STS).

CSN. Circuit-Switched Network, essentially the telephone system (including public data circuit service); circuit switching means to make a connection between two points.

CSNET. Computer Science NET, a research computer network mainly in the United States but with some international nodes; recently merged administration with BITNET to form CREN.

CSPDN. Circuit-Switched Public Data Network, a CCITT term describing a public network that employs circuit-switching technology.

CSR. Channel Select Register.

CSS. 1. Conceptual Signaling and Status store, term used in Virtual Terminal.

2. Controlled Slip Second, an attribute used in performance management to indicate a count of one-second intervals containing one or more controlled slips.

3. Character Start Stop.

CSSFE. Controlled Slip Second Far End, an attribute containing a count of one-second intervals containing one or more controlled slips received at the far end.

CSTA. Computer-Supported Telecommunications Applications, standards being developed by ECMA technical committee 32, task group 11 for cooperation between computers and switches.

CSU. Channel Service Unit, a data communications device used on digital circuits.

CT. Collection Time, period used in the summarization function of system management as the time period during which data is gathered and computations for the summarization calculations are performed.

CT1. First generation analog domestic cordless telephone (non-cellular).

CT2. Two-way digital cordless telephony technology, particularly relevant to cordless PBXs. In its public guise, it becomes a one way telepoint service now no longer available in the UK but prevalent in the Far East.

CT3. Ericsson's proprietary cordless telecommunications system.

CTC. Channel-To-Channel.

CTD. Commulative Transmit Delay, the delay of the Network Layer Entity, all lower-layer entities, and the effects of the access line transmission rate.

CTI. Computer Telephone Integration, a generic name for the technology automatically relating computers and PABXs via applications such as ACD, power dialing, IVR and other customer facing or agent facing services. So known by older, proprietary names CIT (Computer Integrated Telephony) and CSTA (Computer Supported Telephony Applications).

Ctrl. Control key; a key which is pressed in conjunction with other keys to activate a program command to minimize keystrokes when using an application. For example, in WordStar, a whole line can be deleted by placing the cursor anywhere on the line and pressing the control key together with the 'Y' key. In other programs, the control key acts in a similar way to the Alt (alternate) key to maximize the use of the keyboard. In WordPerfect, pressing the first function key (F1) allows the user to restore information recently deleted.

Shift F1 activates the setup screen; Alt F1 activates the thesaurus; while control, F1 enables the user to exit to the DOS shell.

CTS. 1. Clear To Send, one of the signals or contacts assigned under the RS-2332 specification, which when asserted signals that the DCE is ready to transmit data.
2. Conformance Testing Service(s), a series of programs funded by the CEC starting in 1986 to develop conformance-testing services for OSI.
3. Conversational Terminal System.

CTS-LAN. CTS Local Area Network, one of the original CTS programs.

CTS-WAN. CTS Wide Area Network, one of the original CTS programs; developed abstract tests and testing services for FTAM and X.400.

CTV. 1. Community Telivision.
2. Coloured TeleVision.

CU. 1. Control Unit.
2. Croostalk Unit.

CUDN. Common User Data Network.

CUE. Computer Updating Equipment.

CUG. Closed User Group, in X.25, an arrangement whereby a group of hosts do not accept incoming call requests from unknown addresses.

cursor. An icon on the screen that moves when the computer's mouse is moved, allowing the user to "point" to a command or position on the screen. It may point to a link where one can click to jump to a new information. In a hyperlinked document, it may represent a place where one can provide input from the keyboard. Also known as pointer.

CU-SeeMe. A videoconferencing protocol produced by Cornell University, enables real-time video and audio connection over TCP/IP; supported on Macintosh and PC platforms.

custom calling service. The provision of enhanced services to small business users and resendintal telephone lines.

custom chip. An integrated circuit chip designed for a specific task.

customer-recorded information service. A service provided to the customers tht has ability to distribute information transmitted from recording equipment to calling subscribers.

CUT. Control Unit Tester.

cut-over. To transfer a facility from one circuit or system to another.

cut-off. The act to fail to provide satisfactory transmission at a particular cut-off frequency.

cut-off waveguide. Lowest radio frequency that can effectively be carried by a waveguide.

cut-off relay. Relay used to disconnect a subscriber's loop from a line circuit.

cut-off wavelength. The shortest wavelength at which only the fundamental mode of an optical wavelength is capable of propagation.

CV. Code Violation, used in performance management in Network Management.

CVCP. Code Violation, CP-bit Parity, count of when a CP-bit parity violation is detected; used in performance management.

CVCRC. Code Violation, cyclic Redundancy Check, count of when CRC violations are detected; used in performance management.

CVFE. Code Violation, Far End, count of one-second intervals containing one or more code violations received at the far-end terminal; used in performance management.

CVM. COBOL Virtual Machine.

CVP. Code Violation, P-bit, count of P-bit parity violations; used in performance management.

CVR. Computer Voice Response.

CVT. 1. *See* constant voltage transformer.
2. Communication Vector table.

CW. 1. Call Waiting.
2. Command Word.

CWI. Call Waiting Indicator.

CWP. Communicating Word Processor.

CX. Central Exchange.

cyberspace. The place where data is stored, processed, and moved through vast data communications networks. This is a technological, cultural, as well as economic fashion that is growing all over the world.

cyborg. In the MUD terminology, it is defined as "part man, part machine"; it means that your clint is doing some of the work for you.

cycle. In computers, the basic time unit ofd a central processing unit.

cycle stealing. A technique in which a peripheral uses one or more processor cycles to access main storage, locking out the processor from main storage for that duration.

cyclic access. An access mode to stored information whereby access can only be achieved at certain times in a cycle of events. A magnetic disk is an example of a device with cyclic access.

cyclic distortion. A kind of distortion thatis neither characteristic, biased, nor fortuitous, and that generally has a periodic character.

Cyclical Redundancy Check. *See* CRC.

cycling. Not steady on a specified level, but searching between the limits in an automatically controlled system.

cylinder machine. In printing, a machine bed from which impressions are made by a cylinder.

cylinder. On a magnetic hard disk, the vertical column of tracks, which occupy the same relative position on the disk pack, but on different disks (one above the other). On a double-sided disk, a cylinder includes track 'X' on one side and track 'X' on the other side. The surface of a disk is divided logically into concentric circles radiating from the centre, where each concentric circle is called a track. The group of same tracks on all disks is collectively called a cylinder. In an assembly of magnetic disks, the set of all tracks that can be accessed by all the magnetic heads of a comb in a given position.

CYMB. Cyan, Yellow, Magenta, and Black, the colour-model used for specifying the color of printed matter. This corresponds to the four colors of inks used in most color printers. *See also* RGB and HLS, common models used to specify colours on monitors.

cyrillic alphabet. The Russian alphabet derived from Greek and incorporating characters expressing Slavic sounds.

cystadyne reception. A kind of radio reception in which a crystal dectector is polarised by battery, which gives the negative resistance.

D

d. A decimal prefix commonly used in association with a base unit in the SI system of units indicating a multiplication factor of 10^{-1} of that unit. Although it is not one of the multiples that increase in steps of 10^3 preferred by SI, it is used and limited to occasions where the recommended prefixes are inconvenient.

D. Decision table language, used in programming.

D.nnn. D Series of CCITT Recommendations dealing with intercontinental telecommunications circuits, specially the tariffs and accounting charges.

da. DecA. A decimal prefix used in association with a base unit in the SI system of units indicating a multiplication factor of 10^1 of that unit. Although this particular prefix is not one of the multiples that increase in steps of 10^3 preferred by SI, it is used and limited to occasions where recommended prefixes are inconvenient.

DA. Destination Address, network address of hosts being called for a network connection. *See also* data acquisition; direct access; and differential analyser.

DAA. *See* data-access arrangement.

DAC. 1. Digital-to-Analogue Conversion, the process of converting a digital signal to an analogue form. 2. Digital-to-Analogue Converter, a unit that provides analogue output channels from digital input signals. 3. Data Acquisition and Control System, a variety of real-time applications, process control, and high-speed data acquisition can be handled by DAC. Individually designed, each system is tailored to meet specific requirements.

DAC. Dual Attachment Concentrator, types of circuit interface equipment used in FDDI.

DACD. Directory Access Control Domain, a sub-tree portion of Directory governed by the same access control information.

DACS. Digital Access and Cross-connection System, telephony term.

DAD. Draft ADdendum, DADn, an ISO term denoting addenda to International Standards documents which have not yet passed final balloting to become stable.

daemons. The programs that execute in the background and performs services when required. The daemons are usually started when the computer is turned on. When a request arrives, the daemon reads the request and acts on it. The daemons return the bounced mail, make sure that the programs that are supposed to run at certain times wake up and run, and so on. The mailer daemons are getting more and more sophisticated these days.

DAF. 1. Distributed Application Framework, a model for describing and developing distributed applications currently being developed by CCITT, to be coordinated with ISO'w Open Distributed Processing work.
2. Acronym for the Directory Authentication Framework.

daily activity report. DAR. A report generated by computer concerning the daily uses and operation of programs, routines and subroutines.

daisy chain. A method of connecting devices on a bus. On a daisy-chained bus, devices not requesting a signal respond to it by passing it on. The daisy chain scheme permits assignment of device priorities based on the electrical position of the device on the bus.

daisy wheel. A sectored wheel (resembling a daisy) with characters (letters, numbers, and symbols) protruding from the tips of each sector; used to strike a ribbon, which in turn hits the paper to make high quality impressions at speeds of up to 55 characters per second. Daisy wheels are interchangeable, and available in different font styles. Daisy wheels were used with the electronic typewriters.

DAL. 1. Data Address Line.
2. Direct Address Line.

DALK. DAta Link Controller.

DAM. *See* direct-access memory.

damage assessment routine. DAR. A component of a computer operating system (OS) that endeavours to make a recovery from a software failure.

DAN. Departmental Area Network, a generic term referring to a network serving an entire department.

DAP. 1. Directory Access Protocol, the protocol used between a DUA and a DSA to provide access to the directory service.
2. Document Application Profile, profile of exchange format for SGML.

DAR. *See* daily activity report.

DAS. *See* data-acquisition system.

DASD. Direct Access Storage Devices, generally disk drives, particularly high-speed ones.

DASM. *See* direct-access storage media.

DassiII. A message based signalling system following the ISO based model developed by BT to provide multi-line IDA interconnection to the BT network.

DAT. 1. File name extension for a configuration file.
2. Duplicate Address Test, used in the MAC layer.

data acquisition. DA. The process undertaken by data acquisition system, where data is collected at one system location from various other locations. It is then converted into digital information for operating, supervisory or accounting records.

data authentication. A process used to verify the integrity of transmitted data, especially a message.

data bank. A comprehensive data file usually stored on a direct access device, and offering access to a large number of users. Often connected to and updated by a real time system.

data bus. An electrical path that connects the central processing unit, memory, andd the other hardware devices on the motherboard. Actually it is a group of parallel wires; the number of wires in the bus affects the speed at which data can travel between the hardware components. Because each wire can transfer one bit at a time, an 8-wire bus can transfer 2 bytes, and a 32-bit bus can transfer 4 bytes at a time.

data circuit terminating equipment. The communications equipment installed in a user's premises responsible for establishing, maintaining and terminating a connection. A modem is an example.

data circuit. A means of two-way data transmission between two points comprising associated transmit and receive channels;

(a) between data switching exchanges, the data circuit-terminating equipment, depending on the type of interface used at the data switching exchange;

(b) between data terminal installation and a data switching exchange and/or concentrator, the data circuit includes the data circuit-terminating equipment at the data terminal installation end and may also include equipment similar to a data circuit-terminating equipment similar to a data circuit-terminating equipment at the data exchange or concentrator location;

(c) either physical or virtual data circuits may be established.

DATACOM. DATA COMmunications.

data communication. The movement of encoded information by means of electric transmission systems via one or more data links according to a protocol.

data communications control unit. DCCU. Messages that are received by a central terminal unit are scanned by the data communications control unit, and transferred to the central processor unit.

data communications equipment. DCE. Any piece of equipment that interfaces with a data communications network; usually used in reference to a modulator demodulator (MODEM).

data compression utility. A program specifically designed to abbreviate sequences of bits in order to make files as small as possible. PKZip and WinZip are some of the most popular data compression utilities.

data compression. A technique used to reduce the size of data being transmitted without losing any of the original information. Compressed data must be decoded at the receiving end of the communications path in order to extract the original information.

data concentrator. A functional unit that permits a common transmission medium to serve more data sources than there are channels currently available within transmission medium.

data connection. The interconnection of a number of data circuits on a tandem basis by means of switching equipment to enable data transmission to take place between data terminal equipment:

(a) Where one or more of the data circuits which are interconnected is a virtual data circuit, the overall connection is known as a virtual data connection.

(b) The overall connection includes the data circuit terminating equipment at the respective data terminal installation locations.

data control block. DCB. A storage, a holding control, or status information employed by file management routines when storing and retrieving data.

data control. The section of the centre responsible for verifying that data input to or output from a computer has been correctly assembled and processed.

data corruption. Unwanted changes (impairment) of data (or a program) as they are being transmitted, such as the loss of data codes from a message when it is being read from a disk. This may be caused by the accidental loss of power during disk access, or due to noise or faulty equipment.

data definition. A term commonly used in the job control language, where it is employed to connect external input/output devices to an internal named file or data set associated with a particular step used in a computer program.

data defragmentation. When a file is copied to disk, the operating system tries to put it all in one place, in one or more contiguous sectors. If later, data is added to the file, however, the sectors nest to the original may no longer be available. In this case, the operating system puts the data somewhere else on the disk. Thus the file is said to be defragmented, because its parts are physically separated. In such cases it its longer time to read the file from the disk. A utility program that defragments files on a disk can speed up the disk drive.

data dictionary. DD. A central master file often used in conjunction with a database management system, containing data descriptions (metadata) that can be used in multiple databases and shared by multiple software applications and products. Storing data definitions in a data dictionary keeps programmers and database administrators from having to make dozens of changes throughout the entire database. For example, if a database contains several sub-databases, where each sub-database assumes a ZIP code (post code) field of five numeric characters, then the database administrator can change each of those fields to accommodate longer length ZIP codes simply by changing the master stored in the central data dictionary.

data diddling. Computer crime which involves the unauthorised alteration or manipulation of data. A data diddler is one who, to his/her advantage, falsifies information such as bank transaction records and university grades.

data encryption key. DEK. The key used for the encryption of message text and for the computation of message integrity checks.

data encryption standard. DES. A security system used for the protection of sensitive data; this security algorithm specifies implementation in hardware for maximum security. Data is passed through a complex circuit by means of a user-supplied key, outputting a cipher text that is a non-linear function of the original data, which is then virtually impossible to regenerate without knowing the key.

data event block. DEB. Memory control locations that have information accessed by programs, to provide control of asynchronous processing. The information is modified to indicate the progress of a particular event.

data exchange unit. DEU. The component used in communications; it accepts data from a number of input channels, and sorts it according to priority and destination, at the same time performing checking and error routines.

data file. *See* document.

data flow. The transfer of data between constants, variables, and files accomplished by execution of statements, procedures modules, or programs.

data format. A description of the way in which data are held in a given field, record or file. Specifying, for example, if it is alphabetic or numeric.

data frame. A package of data transmitted over an Ethernet network.

data input bus. DIB. Some microcomputers have a DIB, a mechanism in which data and address information is transferred between the switch register and the processor, also between processor and the memory, the memory and the input/output interface and the processor and the input/output interface.

data input-voice answerback. A communications system where a user inputs, via a data terminal, to a computer and receives a voice answerback output of a synthesised or recorded voice.

data interchange format. A standard file format developed by Software Arts to enable database and spreadsheet programs which are able to support data interchange files to exchange files successfully.

data leakage. The term used to identify computer crime which involves the output (leakage) of confidential information. This can be done by employees who copy files on to floppy disks and sell these to interested parties. Usually, the data is encrypted (coded) so that it is not recognised as being confidential information, should be criminal be searched.

data level. Pertaining to the rank of a particular data element in a hierarchy of elements as a record.

data link control. A discipline or protocol comprising a set of rules used by computers or terminals when communicating, in order to ensure the orderly transfer of information.

data link escape character. The use of a control character combined with one or more succeeding characters to form an escape sequence and the development of extra data communications control operations.

data link escape. The withdrawal of a communication circuit that is used for the transmission of data in a coded form, in conjunction with data processing equipment.

data link layer. The second layer of the OSI (Open Systems Interconnection) reference model. The data link layer deals with the composition of the frames of data sent out on the network, the error-free transmission of those frames between two network nodes, and the protocols for getting those transmissions onto the network medium. In its definitions for local area networks, the IEEE 802 Committee divided the data link layer into two sub-layers: logical link control (LLC), and medium access control (MAC). The current relevant standards are IEEE 802.2 (LLC), IEEE 802.3 (CSMA/CD), IEEE 802.4 (token bus), and IEEE 802.5 (token ring).

data Link Switching. *See* DLS.

data link. A direct serial data communications path between two devices without intermediate switching nodes; i.e., an assembly of terminal installations and the interconnecting circuits (which operate to specific standards) which permit information to be exchanged between the terminal installations. The standards relate to the transmission codes, transmission modes and controls to be used. The assembly of the parts of two data terminal equipment that are controlled by a link protocol, and the interconnecting, data circuit, that enable data to be transferred from a data source to a data ink.

data manipulation operation. In most software applications, an operation such as data retrieval, data insertion, data deletion, data modification.

data module. A removable and hermetically sealed disk pack that incorporates a read/write assembly and magnetic disks.

data PBX. A switching system for data traffic that allows terminals and workstations connected by individual cables to Data PBX selectively to link to one or more host computers over asynchronous circuits with contention.

data processing centre. A collection of automatic data-processing equipment systems along with operators, in one centralised area under a single management group.

data processing machine. In general, a machine that can store and process numeric and alphabetic information.

data processing node. In a computer network, a node at which data processing equipment is located.

data processing standards. The written guide lines and procedures laid down for data processing as well as for the other aspects of computing. A number of committees were formed , that were concerned with these standards, and have now been brought into line with corresponding International Standards Organisation (ISO) standards.

data processing system. A number of components and sub-assemblies connected together to receive, transmit, or store data. Many systems can also process information to a set protocol of mathematical formulae and produce results in the desired manner.

data processing. A general term describing the organisation of data in a desired manner by automatic or semi-automatic means. Also sometimes a generic term for computing in general; information is received, stored, acted upon mathematically, and transmitted as in a computer system; the form, location, meaning, appearance or any other aspect of the data may be changed.

data recovery utility. The software needed to recover the erase data from a disk. It recovers data files that have been mistakenly deleted or some how rendered unusable.

data retrieval. The selection and extraction of data from a file, following search or file for specified record keys.

Data Service Unit. *See* DSU.

data set control block. A storage location, containing information necessary for the control of one data set, that is needed to describe and manipulate the data set in a direct-access device.

data sink. The equipment that accepts data after transmission and perhaps checks the data and originates error- and system-control signals.

data statement. The part of source language program, used to specify the format of a data item to be used in that program.

data storage. The use of any medium to store data; in general, it implies to the on-line storage of the data.

data terminal equipment. 1.A unit, at a data station that can receive transmitted data signals and/or transmit data. It can also control information transfer according to the protocol of the data link network.

2. Any piece of equipment at the beginning or end of a communications path. It can be a terminal or computer or the end user of a telephone circuit.

data transfer rate. The number of bits, characters or blocks per unit time passing between corresponding points in a data transmission system. data transfer speeds are usually expressed in bits per second.

data transmission. 1. Transmission of data from one part of a system to another.

2. The sending of data means of signals send over a telecommunication network, from a data source to a data sink. The data are transferred via a telegraph, telephone or radio circuit using specially designed equip-

ment; the characteristics of the circuit in use will largely govern the rate at which data are transmitted.

data validation. The process of checking and correcting data to reduce the number of errors entering a data processing system. Usually carried out by an edit program prior to the main processing programs.

data. A general term used to denote any or all facts, letters symbols, and numbers that refer to or describe an object, idea, situation, condition or other factor. In general use data are the elements of information that can be processed by a computer. The term data is the plural form of datum.

data-access arrangement. DAA. A small wall-mounted enclosure which contains an isolating transformer, that has been designed to prevent signals harmful to a direct-dial telephone network from being sent down the network lines. A DAA is required in the USA to protect the network from some customer-owned modulator demodulators (MODEMs). Also known as a direct-access arrangement.

data-acquisition system. DAS. A system that acquires data at one computer or system location from various other locations and then converts is into digital (D,4) information.

data-base access method. DBAM. A generic computing term used to describe various processes such as direct access and random access.

data-base index. DBI. An index used by the System Development Corporation (SDC), provides information to all the files of computer information held by the organisation. It is employed to help in the selection of a suitable database for a user requirements.

database management system. DBMS. The primary control software used in manipulating computer information files.

database manipulation. The changing of information in a database, such as adding, changing, and deleting data.

database server. A database installed as a back-end or server component of a client-server system, which can be accessed over a LAN by one or more client, or front-end applications through the use of query language, typically SQL. The server part of the program is responsible for updating the records, ensuring that multiple access is available to authorised users, protecting the data and communicating with other servers holding relevant data. The client end of the program requests records and then modifies them, while the server tracks records down for the client and adds new ones.

database. A data file so structured that all logical relationships may be expressed between records and that is independent of any particular application. Thus the program accessing the database do not themselves place constraints on the organisation of the data it contains. It may be the collection of information of technical or commercial importance to an organisation. Database information held in a computer-accessed memory is usually subdivided into pages, with each page accessible to all users unless it belongs to a closed user group. The word however, covers catalogues on a library shelf as well as facts stored in computer memories. Database management systems allow users to define entries, such as fields and indexes that are used to describe and work with data. These are collectively referred to as metadata which are 'data about actual data'. Database definition is normally the responsibility of a trained database administrator. For example, if a database contains several sub-databases, where each sub-database assumes a ZIP code field of five numeric characters, then the database administrator can change each of those fields to a accommodate longer length ZIP codes simply by changing the master stored in the central data dictionary.

data-circuit terminating equipment. DCE. An active unit in a data station or terminal that connects data transmission line to the terminal equipment. The interface unit controls all connections and provides signal or code conversions if required.

DATACOM. DATA COMmunications.
1. A general term used for devices or systems that transmit data from one point to another.
2. A data communications service covering and linking more than 60 cities in the US.

data encryption standard. DES. One of the effective ways of data security involving encoding and decoding the data; often used in messaging systems such as electronic mail. It can encode the message in more than 72 quadrillion ways. Because a special software key is used to decode the message, the possibility of unauthorised interception of the message is lreduced. In many messaging systems, DES encryption takes place even without knowledge of the user.

datagram. A term referring to the self-contained entity of data carrying sufficient information to be routed from source to destination computer without reliance on earlier exchanges between the source and destination computers and transporting network. The datagram is a connectionless, single packet message or item of data that can traverse a network at OSI Level 3, the network layer. It typically does not involve end-to-end session establishment or delivery-confirmation acknowledgement. As well as the information within the datagram, there is a destination network address and usually a source network address.

data-handling equipment. A system of devices that can be either automatic or semi-automatic, used for the collection, transmission, reception and storage of information.

dataphone digital service. DDS. A communications service provided by the Bell System which eliminates the need for modulator-demodulators (MODEMs) by transmitting data in a digital form rather than an analogue.

data-retrieval language. DRL. A computer language used in an information retrieval system, whereby information can be searched for particular items, in response to the definition of particular user needs.

data-sensitive fault. A fault that is revealed as a result of the processing of a particular pattern of data.

data-set label. The identification given to a storage location containing information necessary for the controls of one data set.

data-set ready. A line on a modulator demodulator (MODEM) which informs the transmitting terminal that the signal received is perfect order.

data-switching exchange. A particular section of a computer network, which allows the transmission of discrete packages of information. It performs switching and routing functions and normally consists of a mini- or a microcomputer.

data-transmission system. A series of devices, circuits or modulator/ demodulators (MODEMs), that can translate or transfer information from one position to another.

data warehouse. The massive collection of information related to an organisation, often stored in gigabytes or terabytes of data. It can include all data that is relevant to the running of an organisation. A key step in setting up a data warehouse is data scrubbing. Data warehouse can be valuable resource for serving the needs of workers/coustomers/users.

DAU. 1. Data Access Unit.
2. Data Adaptor Unit.

DAV. 1. DAta Valid; recognition given in a computer data entry system indicating that data entered has passed extensive arrays of data validation and error checking features.
2. Data Above Voice. A system of digital data transmission that carries information on a frequency above that used for voice transmission.

DB. 1. DataBase.
2. Decibel.
3. Decimal to Binary.

DB25. The most common of the "D-type" connectors, commonly used with EIA RS-232 equipment.

DBA. DataBase Administrator.

DBAF. DataBase Access Facility.

dBASE. A database management program designed for personal computers; the second version, dBASE II, was designed by C. Wayne Ratliffe, an engineer at the Jet Propulsion Laboratory. dBASE II included advanced database management systems (DBMS) features, including relation database management. In 1984, dBASE III was introduced for IBM and industry-standard personal computers, and two years later, dBASE Plus provided an easy-to-use menu-driven system. In 1988, Ashton-Tate released dBASE IV which included a Structured Query Language (SQL), an improved menu-driven interface, and new report-generation capabilities. Many buts were found in the first version, damaging the company's credibility. Version IV.1 solved these problems, and established dBASE as a leading database program.

DBCB. DataBase Control Block.

DBCL. DataBase Command Language.

DBCS. DataBase Control System.

DBDL. DataBase Definition Language.

DBI. *See* data-base index.

DBIN. Data Bus IN.

D-bit. Delivery confirmation bit, used in X.25.

DBM. DataBAse Management.

DBMS. DataBase Management System, a package to provide controlled access to structured data. Some of the popular DBMS for personal computers include:
dBase for DOS
dBase for Windows
Access and Visual Fox Pro
Lotus Approach
R:BASE for Windows from Microrim.

DBOS. *See* disk-based operating system.

DBP. DatBase Processor.

DCA. Document Content Architecture, IBM approach to storing documents as two types of document group: draft documents and final form documents. For presentation, the draft document is transformed into a final document through an office system.

DCB. *See* data control block.

DCC. 1. Data Country Code, a three-digit number for country allocated by ISO 3166, used as the first three digits in an X.121 address.
2. Data Communications Channels.
3. Direct Computer Control.

DCCS. Distributed Capacity Computing System.

DCCU. *See* data communications control unit.

DCD. 1. Data Carrier Detect, a specific position in the definition of the RS-232 physical specification which is

true, when a modem (or other equipment) detects a signal carrier of the designated frequency for its protocol.
2. Dynamic Computer Display.

DCE. 1. Data Circuit-termining Equipment, e.g., a modem; the complement of DTE.
2. Distributed Computing Environment; an OSF term for one of the portable environments they are creating. It comprises a suite of software utilities and operating system extensions that will, in theory, create applications on networks of heterogeneous hardware- personal computers, Unix workstations, minicomputers and mainframes. The DCE is the product of the OSF. The DCE is designed to simplify the building of heterogeneous client/server applications and provides seven general services: Remote Procedure Call, Security, Naming (directory), Distributed File System, Threads, Time and PC Integration. DDE (Dynamic Data Exchange), Microsoft messaging specification. When DDE-compliant applications are combined, dynamic documents can be created which update each other as data changes.

DCF. Data Communications Function block, the means by which management information is communicated between function blocks.

DCL. Digital Command Language.

DCN. 1. Data Communication Network, a communication network within a managed network that supports data communication functions.
2. Distributed Computer Network.

DCP. Data Collection Processor, a communications device that provides concentration, protocol conversin, and operations functions in a telecommunication management network.

DCOS. Data Collection Operating System.

DCPP. Data Communications PreProcessor.

DCS. 1. Defined Context Set, a set of presentation context sets agreed to by the presentation service users and presentation service provider.
2. Distributed Computer System.
3. Digital Cross-connection System, used in a telecommunication management network used to cross-connect the subportions of communications channels, possibly changing the rate.
4. Data Collection ystem.
5. Data Communications Service.

DCTL. Direct-Coupled Transistor Logic. A particular type of logic circuit that employs only direct-coupled transistors as active elements. DIAGRAM.

DD. 1. Double Density, refers to the recording technique which enables a floppy or hard disk to store twice the amount of data as a single density medium allows.
2. Data Dictionary.
3. Data Demand.
4. Digital Data.

DDA. 1. Domain Defined Attribute, in X.400, O/R Name attributes defined and used by a specific mail service or group of users, as opposed to the standard attributes.
2. Digital Differential Analyser.
3. Direct Data Attachment.

DDB. Distributed Data Base.

DDC. *See* direct digital control.

DDCE. *See* digital data conversion equipment.

DDCMP. Digital Data Communication Message Protocol, DecNet-specific Link Level protocol that operates at Layer Two of the digital network architecture.

DDCS. Data Definition Control System.

DDD. Direct Distance Dialling, telephony term meaning that a user can dial a number outside the local area without needing operator assistance.

DDF. 1. Data Description File.
2. Database Definition File.

DDFII. Data Description File for Information Interchange.

DDL. Data Definition Language.

DDM. 1. Distributed Data Management Architecture, IBM SNA LU 6.2 transaction providing users with facilities to locate and access data in the network. It involves two structures: DDM Source, and DDM Target. The source works with a transaction application to retrieve distributed data and transmits commands to the Target program on another system where the data that has been requested is stored. The target interprets DDM commands, retrieves the data and sends it back to the source that originated the request.
2. Digital Display Markup.

DDMBS. Distributed Database Management System, a DBMS distributed across multiple computer systems.

DDN. 1. Defence Data Network, large US network that currently follows the TCP/IP protocols that grew out of ARPANET. Due to become dual-suite with the OSI protocols in 1992.
2. Digital Data Networks.

DDP. 1. Decentralised data processing. This is the opposite of centralised data processing and involves the gathering, storing and processing of data at various remote locations of a large computer environment. This became popular in 1970s when minicomputers were decentralised and could process data independently, yet still had access to the host.
2. Digital Data Processor.
3. Distributed Data Processing.

DDR. Data Descriptive Record, the header preceding a DDFII.

DDS. Dataphone Digital Service, set of standards covering ISDN DS-0, 1, 2, and 3.

DDS. *See* dataphone digital service.

dead zone unit. An analogue computer unit designed to give a constant output signal over a predetermined range of input signals.

deadlock. In transaction processing, a situation in which two or more transactions are simultanesously waiting, each one unable to proceed without access to resources already held by the other. If occurs when two users each have a lock on a separate object. Each wants to acquire a lock on the other user's object.

DEB. *See* data event block.

deblocking. The action of making the first and each subsequent logical record of a block of information available for processing.

debugger. A program or part of a program, which helps in locating and correcting errors (bugs) in program code. It executes each command in a program one step at a time, so the programmers can walk through the source code on screen and track down hard-to-find logic errors. It is said that the original bug was in fact a moth, which found its way into an early computer and caused it to malfunction.

debugging. Detecting, locating, and correcting logic errors found in computer programs. Diagnostic routines are performed to locate error which can often be removed (debugged). The term was coined when programmes found an insect (but) lodged in the circuits of ENIAC (first large-scale electronic digital computer) causing the computer to malfunction.

decimal notation. Normal to-the-base-10 figures. Although computers operate on a binary basis (to the base 2, *i.e.*, either 0 or 1) it is common when normal decimal numbers are to be operated upon (*i.e.*, in most telephone exchanges) for computers to use binary numbers in groups of four, each group of four representing one decimal digit. This system is called binary coded decimal notation.

decision content. A logarithmic measure of the number of decisions needed to select a given event among a finite number of mutually exclusive events.

decision element. DE. In a computer, the circuit which undertakes a logical function on binary digits of input information and provides a result in its output.

DecNet. Proprietary peer-to-peer network technology originally developed for use in wide area networking by Digital Equipment Corporation and evolved to include significant Ethernet-based LAN capabilities. It is the implementation of the Digital Network Architecture (DNA).

decoding. For PCM, a process in which one of a set of reconstructed samples is generated from the character signal representing a sample.

decollating. The automatic or manual removal of carbon paper from continuous stationery or other multi-part documentation.

decompression. Any procedure for relieving the pressure or compression.

DED. Double Error Detection.

DEDS. Dual Exchangable Disc Storage.

default button. In some dialog boxes, the command button that is selected automatically if you press Enter or Return. In graphical user interfaces, (GUIs) default buttons have a bold border around them.

default directory. In DOS or other computer applications, the directory which is automatically available when the application is first switched on. Default directory may be changed, and when this is done the new directory becomes the current directory.

default drive. The drive which first becomes available when an application is switched on. The default drive may be changed, and when this is done, the new drive from which all files are retrieved (or written to) becomes the 'current' drive.

default route. An entry in a routing table, used to direct packets addressed to networks not explicitly listed in the routing table.

deference. A process by which a data station delays its transmission when the transmission medium is busy to avoid collision with ongoing transmission.

degauss. On monitors, a process that demagnetises the metal components in the CRT, thus eliminating image distortion that can result from magnetic charges acquired by the components. Some new monitors degauss automatically whenever you turn on your monitor.

Dejanews. One of the searcable Usenet news archive; particularly good resource for e-mail address of a single individual on Internet. it can also be used to have access to Britannica encyclopedia.

DEK. *See* data encryption key.

DEL. 1. DELete. The action of removing or eliminating information, normally the removal of a record from a master file or the removal of a computer program from a memory after use.

2. DELete character; a control character that is synonymous with backarrow used to indicate that a previous character is to be ignored.

3. DELay. (a) The time interval between the initiation of a signal and its reception; the time a pulse takes to traverse an electronic circuit or device. (b) In a computer the time taken to prepare or process data. (c) In data communications, the slowing

down of information in a channel for a specified period of time.

delay. *See* DEL.

delete. *See* DEL.

delimiter. A symbol such as a comma (,) which is used to mark the end of one section of information, and the beginning of another. This is especially used when transferring or converting files from one application (or environment) to another. The delimiter (in this example the comma) acts as guide. One or more characters used to indicate the beginning or the end of a character string.

DEM. DEModulator; a device used in communications, and consists of a circuit or piece of apparatus that extracts an original signal (or intelligence) from a modulated carrier wave with the minimum of distortion.

demand paging. The transfer of a page from auxiliary storage to real storage at the moment of need.

demand priority. Access method providing support for time-sensitive applications such as video and multimedia as part of the proposed 100BaseVG standard offering l00Mbit/s over the voice-grade UTP cable. By managing and allocating access to the network centrally, at a hub rather than from individual workstations, sufficient bandwidth for the particular application is guaranteed on demand. Users, say its proponents, can be assured of reliable, continuous transmission of information.

Demand Protocol Architecture. *See* DPA.

demand. Pertaining to an input/output technique whereby blocks of data are read (demand reading) or written (demand writing) as they are required; no buffers are allocated and input/output does not proceed in parallel with processing.

DEP. Data entry Panel.

dependent compilation. The compilation of a source module using all the necessary interface and context information from related source modules. It may be noted that the interface and context information is used by the compiler to check validity and to resolve references.

DER. Distinguished Encoding Rules, another type of encoding rules for use with ASN.1.

DERS. Data Entry Reporting System.

DES. 1. Data Encryption Standard, the US government standard encryption alogrithm.

2. Distributed End System, spreading an application over many computer systems; usually the systems communicate over a net work like a LAN using connectionless mode.

DES. *See* data encryption standard.

descending order. When sorting information in descending (decreasing) order, items are arranged from the largest to the smallest (4,3,2,1) or from the last to the first (d,c,b,a). Depending on the software program, other characters including punctuation marks and symbols may interfere with 'dictionary' sort, causing words like 'A/UX' to be placed before 'abacus'. When sorting data in ASCII, all capitalized words are placed before lower case letters.

descending sort. The arranging of data in a way that places the highest value first and the least last. For example, a descending sort of the numbers 1 to 10 will result in: 10, 9, 8, 7, ... 1; the letters A to Z will result in: Z, Y, X, W, ... A.

description. In specification description language: the implementation of the requirements of a system. Descriptions consist of general parameters of the system as implemented and the function description (FD) of its actual behaviour.

desktop. The term for the screen background in most graphical user interfaces (GUIs) on which windows, icons, and dialog boxes appear.

destination code. Complete 10-digit number comprising (3-digit NPA code + 3-digit CO code + 4-digit station number), which pinpoints the location of a telephone in North America. Also called a telephone address.

destination file. A file selected to receive the output data of a particular run.

destination-code indicator. Data, common channel signalling: information sent in the forward direction indicating whether or not the destination code is included in the destination address.

destructive read-out. The phenomenon of data being lost when it is read from a storage device, all recording of its being destroyed.

DET. Data Terminal Equipment; the complement (oposite) of DCE.

DETAB. DEcision TABle; used for the analysis of various problems, a DETAB contains a list of the possible courses of action, alternatives or selections that can be made.

detail flowchart. A flowchart specifying the solution to a problem in great detail and from which a program can be readily coded.

DEU. 1. Data Entry Unit.
2. Data Encryption Unit.
3. Data Exchange Unit.

deviation. 1. In an FM signal, the amount of carrier frequency shift away from its unmodulated frequency during modulation. Deviation is usually expressed in kilohertz and is directly proportional to the amplitude of the modulating signal.
2. The amount by which a quantity drifts from its proper value, *e.g.*, an allowable frequency deviation of +10 Hz in a MHz carrier.

device controller. An expansion board used to control devices which were not connected to the original computer configuration. If second disk drive is later added to a personal computer, a device controller may be required to manage it. The program which enables DOS to work with the device is known as device driver.

device driver. In the context of computer networking a device driver is a software module forming part of a computer operating system, or software that interacts with the operating system. It aims to control communications equipment, such as a LAN network adapter card and facilitate the transfer of information to and from the network. Other examples of device driver programs include software to support the activities of printers, disks and mice. A device driver is installed when the system is initialised, either by the operating system (base device driver) or through an installable device drivers include a mouse driver, graphical/video monitor driver, communications port driver, printer driver, and network adapter card driver.

device status word. A computer word that contains binary digits, the condition of which indicates the particular status of various devices.

device. A component of the system's hardware configuration, such as a modem, printer, mouse, sound card, or disk drive.

DFB. Distributed FeedBack., a type of injection laser, whose wavelength of radiative longitudinal-mode oscillations is determined by the corrugation period of the structure and not by its material composition.

DFR. Document Filing and Retrieval, a standard being developed by ISO/IEC JTC1/SC18/WG4 to enable multiple users to communicate with a remote documnt filing and retrival server.

DFT. *See* diagnostic function test.

DHCP client. A computer that contains TCP/IP software and is not manually configured with TCP/IP parameters.

DHCP server. A computer that is capable of configuring DHCP client computers with an IP address, a subnet mask, and optionally other TCP/IP configuration parameters.

DHCP. Dynamic Host Configuration Protocol, the protocol used for automatically assigning TCP/IP configuration parameters to computers. The computer receiving configuration information is considered as the DHCP client, whereas the computer supplying configuration information is considered as DHCP server. It is possible configure the DHCP client with additional configuration settings such as IP addresses for default gateway, DNS servers, and WINS servers. DHCP is especially important where many workers carry notebook computers. Using manually configured IP addresses on the notebook allows the computer to network using TCP/IP on only one network.

DHP. Document Handler Processor.

DI. Data Input.

DIA. Document Interchange Architecture, an IBM term defining the sets of functions needed for document handling in an IBM environment, including storage and distribution.

diagnostic function test. DFT. A particular computer program employed to test the reliability of a system.

DIAL. Display Interface Assembly Language.

dialogue box. A message box in the form of small window, which appears in a graphical user interface environment, asking the user to select certain options or answer questions before a requested function can proceed. Dialog boxes usually request a response such as Ok to continue, or Cancel to stop an operation. For example, when printing a document, a dialogue box may ask the user to nominate the paper size, document orientation (landscape or portrait), and output quality.

DIB. 1. Directory Information Base, the information held in the Directory.
2. *See* data input bus.

dibit. A pair of binary digits which can be represented by a single modulation condition in a data transmission system, such as four-phase modulation. The four possible states for a dibit are 00,01,10, and 11.

dichotomizing search. A search in which an ordered set of data elements is partitioned into two mutually exclusive parts, one of which is rejected; the process is repeated on the accepted part until the search is completed. In digital computer practice, locating an item in a table of items which are arranged by key values in serial order. The required key is compared with a key halfway through the table; according to this relational test, half of the table is accepted and again divided for comparison, and so on until the keys match and the item is found.

DID. 1. Digital Information Display.
2. *See* direct inward dialing.

DIDAD. DIgital DAta Display.

DIDO. Data Input/Data Output.

DIF. Device Input Format.

differential backup. Unlike an incremental backup in which the volume's structure is scanned for all files created or modified since the date of the last backup (copying only those that have changed), a differential backup records only the differences between a baseline version of a file and an updated version. This mode of backup is useful in applications, which make relatively small numbers of random changes to a large file.

DIGICOM. A colloquial expression for DIGItal COMmunications system. It is a collection of units and devices which transmit information from one point to another in a digital form.

digit place. In a positional representation system, each site that may be occupied by a character and that may be identified by an ordinal number or by an equivalent identifier.

digit. Any one of the symbols of integral value used in a system of numbering, each individual digit is used to designate a quantity smaller than the number base itself.

In the decimal system, the ten digits are 0,1,2,3,4,5,6,7,8,9.

In the binary system the digits are 0 and 1.

In digital transmission, a digit may be represented by a singal element, characterized by the dynamic nature, discrete condition and discrete timing of the element.

2. In equipment used for digital transmission, a digit may be represented by a stored condition being characterized by a specified physical condition; it may be represented as a binary magnetic condition of a ferrite core.

digital. Pertaining to the representation of data or physical quantities by means of digits or discrete quantities.

digital data. The data represented in digital form, e.g., a sequence of light pulses in an optical fibre.

digital circuit. A circuit which transmits information signals in digital form between two exchanges. It includes termination equipment but not switching stages.

digital communications. The transfer of information via a sequence of signals may, for example, take the form of two different voltage levels on a wire or the presence or absence of light in fiber-optic light guide. It can be made arbitrarily insensitive to external disturbances by means of error control methods.

digital data communication message protocol. Governing parallel, serial-synchronous, or serial-asynchronous data transmission and reception, this uniform discipline is used for the transmission of data between stations in a multi-point or point-to-point data-communication system.

digital data conversion equipment. DDCE. The equipment employed in the conversion of digital data into a form other than digital.

digital data transmitter. A package of computer software designed to assist in the isolation and correction of errors in a routine or program.

digital differential analyser. DDA. 1. An incremental computer that employs a digital integrator for computing the data.

2. A differential analyser that employs digital representations for all analogue quantities used.

3. Having specific circuits designed to carry out mathematical integration, a digital differential analyser is part of a digital computer.

digital display. 1. A display of digital orientated numerals.

2. Generally on a cathode-ray tube, a visual display of numeric, alphabetic or graphic material.

3. Information that is provided in digital form.

digital filling. The addition of a fixed number of digits to a digital signal to change the digit rate from its existing nominal value to a higher predetermined nominal value. Added digits are not used to transmit information.

digital microcircuit. A miniaturised electronic circuit fabricated with inseparable interconnections and elements; designed to accept at its input terminals particular logic states. These are converted according to set logic equations or function tables, and passed to the output terminals.

digital multimeter. DMM. A digital multimeter essentially converts an analogue, or continuous, signals into a series of digital representations of sections of that signal. It ensures that the resultant display is an accurate assessment of the signal amplitude. DMM with its wider range of functions has largely superseded the digital voltmeter.

digital multiplex switching system. Providing a digital circuit switched service for voice and data transmission; the digital multiplex switching system family of devices makes use of pulse code modulation and time division multiplexing.

digital output. An output signal, representing the magnitude of an input signal, that is produced in the form of a series of discrete quantities coded to represent digits.

digital panel meter. A device that provides in digital form, a display of any particular quantity of event that has been measured or recorded. Two preferred types are light-emitting diode displays for their self-illumination and, and liquid crystal displays.

Digital Private Networks Signalling System. *See* DPNSS.

digital representation. The use of discrete signals to represent data in the form of characters and numbers.

digital signal. A signal with only two values, normally 0 and 1, during transmission, unlike an analog signal whose values constantly vary.

digital sum variation. An expression of the difference between the maximum and minimum values of the digital sum of a coded signal.

digital. Pertaining to the use of discrete signals to represent data in the form of characters and numbers. Data processing makes use of the fact that all the digital representation can be achieved using binary numbers. The sets of bits can be grouped together to represent numbers with some other base or characters.

digitizer. A device that scans pictorial material such as photographs, diagrams, or maps, and converts them into digital data which can be stored by a computer and represented on a computer screen.

DIMM. Dual Inline Memory Module. A type of pre-assembled RAM unit, used in some new computers, including the Macintosh PCI models. DIMMs support a wider data path than SIMMs, allowing faster memory access.

dimmed. A term usually used in GUIs to indicate that a particular command is not available or is disabled. Also sometimes referred to as grayed out.

dino. Some one who has been around for a long time. Such people tend to reminisceabout dead or non-existent MUDs that were especially fun.

DIP. Display Information Processor.

DIP switch. Dual Inline Package. Small on-off switches mounted in computer hardware for purposes of user configuration. When adding expansion cards to computers, DIP switches must often be set to make the card compatible with computer's configuration.

DIPE. Distributed Interactive Processing Environment.

DIR. Data Input Register.

direct access. DA. 1. The facility to obtain data from a storage device, or to enter data into a storage device in such a way that the process depends only on the location of that data and not on a reference to data previously accessed.

2. A memory device that allows a memory location to be accessed independently of its position and information in various stores be accessed in the same amount of time.

direct attachment. IBM term for linking a device or LAN directly to a host computer through an appropriate Control Unit, like cluster controller.

direct conversion method. The process of moving from the old systems to the new systems, in which all users stop using the old systems at the same time, then begin using the new. This option is fast, but can be very disruptive.

direct coupling. Direct connection of one circuit point to another for signal transmission, *i.e.,* without intermediate capactiors or transformers. Because coupling devices aren't used, direct coupling provides transmission of dc as well as ac.

direct dialling-in. DDI. The facility that allows a telephone caller direct access to any particular public automatic business exchange (PABX) extension without involving the exchange operator. Also known as direct inward dialling.

direct digital control. DDC. An automated action in a computer control system whereby the signal to a final control element is obtained by digital device. Such elements are used to perform process control tasks for production systems.

direct distance dialling. DDD. Information conveyed that automatically establishes, controls, supervises and releases a long-distance telephone call. It enables the telephone user to call outside his local area without operator assistance. In the India and many other countries, this is called subscriber trunk dialling (STD).

direct inward dialling. DID. *See* direct dialling-in.

direct memory access controller. DMAC. A circuit or device, now available on a single chip, providing control over applications that require data to be transferred into a computer memory rather than going through the central processor unit. DMAC can improve performance in larger systems with a number of peripherals, by completely controlling block transfers between input/output circuits and the system memory.

direct memory access. DMA. A technique employed to provide the high-speed transmission of data between a computer peripheral and the computer memory without having to go through the central processor unit. Data is exchanged at maximum memory speed and several access methods to the memory are possible.

direct numerical control. DNC. The system created by a number of numerical control machines being connected to a common memory. The memory provides data, from stored machine programs, on demand to the numerical control machines.

direct outward dialling. DOD. The condition that allows PABX extensions to dial an external number without requiring the assistance of the particular exchange's operator.

directory. A record containing details of the location of the file in backing storage, that is accessed by the operating system. In databases, it refers to a file that stores relationship between records in other files. The directory conatins an overview of the data held, and since it occupies less storage than the data files searches and operations performed on directory are more efficient than those performed on data files themselves.

directory routing. A routing method that employs a directory at each node.

DirectParallel cable access. A feature of Windows 2000 that supports computer-to-computer connections using standard and enhanced (ECP) parallel ports, employing Parallel Technologies's Basic or fast parallel cables.

direct program control. An input/output operation that allows the direct control of a device by software programs.

direct-access memory. DAM. A particular type of memory device that permits the access of a memory location independently of its position. The items stored can therefore be accessed in the same amount of time whatever their position.

direct-access storage devices. DASD. A device that allows access time for any stored information on the particular medium to the independent of its location. Generally primary computer memory is direct, disks have pseudo-direct access and tapes have sequential access.

direct-access storage media. DASM. Capable of storing information and computer programs, these media allow rapid access to individual elements. The access is independent of the location of the element required and of the location of the last element of data accessed.

direction keys. Keys used at times to navigate around the screen- especially in text areas. Direction keys have arrows pointing up, down, right, and left. Also known as arrow keys.

directory. Part of a structure for organising your files on a disk. A directory can contain files and other directories (called subdirectories). Directories are often referred to as folders on computers with GUIs. The Directory is a physically distributed yet logically centralised database. A directory user agent (DUA) is available to provide access to the Directory f or a user. Directory system agents (DSAs) are the processes which hold the information contained in the Directory and can provide a centralised view of the data by chaining directory requests from the initial DSA to that DSA containing the desired information. The DUA interacts with a DUA by way of the Directory Access Protocol (DAP). Two DSAs communicate with each other by way of the Directory System Protocol (DSP). The most common initial use of the X.500 Directory will be for message handling systems. The Directory can be used for both storing MHS user names, addresses, and for storing information needed by the message transfer system for locating destination message transfer agents. Additional information such as passwords for both users and MTAs can also be stored in the Directory. Other OSI applications such as File Transfer, Access, and Management and Network Management are looking at using the Directory as well.

DIS. Draft International Standard, an ISO term meaning that the standard has passed the first round of ISO balloting for stabilisation.

DISA. 1. Data Interchange Standards Association, secretariat for ANSI ASC X12, providing administrative management for publication and maintenance of standards related to EDI.

2. Direct Inward Switch Access, controls acceptance of third-party billing, calls, etc., on a telephone switch.
3. Defence Information Systems Agency, formerly known as DCA.

disk cache. A portion of main memory, which temporarily stores information that, is frequently requested from the disk drives. It improves the speed of disk-intensive applications such as database management programs.

Disk cache should not be confused with memory cache. It is a software utility that manages hard-disk intensive operations by copying data from the hard disk into the much faster system memory and functions as an interface between the system and the hard disk. It is based on the principle that, most of the time, data is requested sequentially rather than randomly. Conceptually, the process of utilising the system random-access memory, as a buffer is similar to the way in which cache memory works.

Disk cache allows the data read from a sector on the hard disk to be accessed at the access speed of system memory which can be up to 500 times greater than that of the hard disk.

disk crash. Any hardware or software malfunction that may lead to the inaccessibility of disk data.

disk drive. The mechanism that holds and spins a disk, reading and writing data to it.

disk interface. An interface that specifies electrical connections between a controller and the disk drive.

disk pack. An assembly of magnetic disks that can be removed as a whole from a disk unit, together with a container from which it must be separated when operating.

disk server. A device equipped with disks and a program permitting users to create and store files on those disks. Each user has access to their own section of disk on the disk servers. The aim is to give users access to disk space that they would not normally have on their computers. The disk server is linked to the computers via LAN. The next level of sophistication would be a file server.

disk. *See* diskette.

disk. The US spelling for disc.

disk-based operating system. DBOS. Software loaded in a computer which allows it to control the operation of all activities related to the use of magnetic disks in the system.

diskcomp. Disk comparison, DOS and OS/2 command that checks all the information contained on two different disks so as to compare and report on whether the contents are identical.

diskcopy. Unlike copy command, which duplicates only specified files, diskcopy is a DOS and OS/2 command which makes a complete and identical copy from one disk to another, including all hidden DOS or OS/2 files. The disks must have identical formats.

diskette. A medium for storing information. Information stored on a disk remains there even when computer is turned off, unlike information stored in memory (RAM). A floppy disk can be inserted and removed from a floppy disk drive, whereas a hard disk is permanently mounted inside its drive. Diskette are often called floppy disks or simply floppies. The most common uses of diskettes are for:

moving the files between computers that are not connected through communications hardware;

loading new progrms on to a system; and

backing up data or programs, the primary copy of which is stored on a hard disk drive.

diskless workstation. A workstation attached to a LAN that has neither floppy nor hard disks, but relies on disk storage provided by a file server attached to the same LAN. When the diskless workstation is first initialised, it uses a remote boot program stored in a remote boot prom/eprom on its network adapter card to initialise a session with the file server. The workstation then loads its operating system, such as MS-Dos, from the server and executes the normal server login procedure.

DISOSS. DIStributed Office Support Systems, IBM software typically forming part of IBM Office System Node.

DISP. 1. Directory Information Shadow Protocol, the protocol that supports shadowing of information between DSAs, defined in the 1992 extensions to X.500.

2. Draft International Standardized Profile.

dispersion. 1. The chromatic or wave length dependence of a parameter. Also, the process by which an electromagnetic signal is distorted because the various frequency components of that signal have different propagation characteristics. Signal distortion in an optical waveguide is caused by several dispersive mechanisms; waveguide dispersion material dispersion, and profile dispersion. In addition, the signal suffers degradation from multi-mode distortion, which is referred to as multi-mode dispersion.

2. The scattering of microwave radio radiation by raindrops, or similar obstructions.

3. The separation into the components of an electromagnetic wave with different frequencies.

4. The allocation of circuits between two points over more than one geographic or physical route.

display adaptor. Hardware that converts (adapts) information in video memory to video output.

display command. A command that can be used to control a display device.

display console. A control device that includes a display device and one or more input units, such as keyboard, joystick, control ball, or light pen. The device is usually equipped for use by a human operator.

display field. A specified part of the storage space of a display buffer or a specified area on a display surface that contains or displays a set of characters that can be manipulated or operated upon as a unit.

display file. A sequence of instructions similar to a computer program to be executed by the processor in a display device.

display frame. A specified portion of the area of dispaly surface available for viewing.

distributed computing environment. *See* DCE.

distributed computing. Trend of having centralised computers to bring processing power to the desk top; often confused with the distributed processing.

Distributed Data Management Architecture. *See* DDM.

distributed database. A collection of different data repositories that looks like a single database to the user.

distributed database. A database stored on more than one networked computer. The database is split up across these machines, and not replicated.

distributed function. 1. The use of programmable terminals, controllers, and other devices to perform operations that were previously done by the processing unit such as managing data links, controlling devices and formatting data

2. Functions such as network management, processing and error recovery operations that are dispersed among the nodes of a network, as opposed to functions that are concentrated at a central location.

distributed name service. A technique for storing network node names so that the information is stored throughout network, and can be requested from, and supplied by, any node.

distributed processing. An approach that allows one application program to execute on multiple computers linked together by a network. The networked computers share the work between them.

Distributed Queue Dual Bus. *See* DQDB.

distributed-intelligence microcomputer system. DIMS. A method of multiprocessing which assigns to different processors fixed tasks allocated by software algorithms; tasks include input/output controller activities, data concentration, information processing, and remote communications.

DIT. Directory Information Tree, the logical structure of the DIB.

dithered colour. A colour produced by a pattern of differently coloured dots that simulate the desired colour. A solid colour on one device (such as a 256-colour monitor) may be a dithered colour on another device. Also knows as nonsolid colour.

DIU. Digital Input Unit.

DIV. Data In Voice system.

DIX. Digital Intel Xerox, origin of the Ethernet Blue Book.

DL. 1. Data Link Layer, layer-2 of the OSI Reference Model.

2. Distribution List, a predefined list of recipients in MHS, sometimes carried in the Directory service.

DLA. Data Link Adaptor.

DLC. Data Link Control, the upper part of the Data Link Layer, concerned with error detection.

DLCI. Data Link Connection Identifier, used ot identify and route each frame in frame relay and LAPD, made up of service access point identifier and terminal end point identifier.

DLCN. Distributed Loop Computer Network.

DLE. Data Link Escape, ASCII character 16 decimal or ^P (control P); not a printed character but a "control" character.

DLI. Digital Line Interface.

DLL. 1. File name extension for library files used by a program.

2. Data Link Layer, layer 2 of the OSI Reference Model.

DLM. Data Linking Module.

DLS. Data Link Service, the service provided by layer 2 of the OSI Reference Model; provides independence from the physical layer and transparent transfer of the DLS user data. It is an enhancement to source routing which transports source route packets over a resilient IP/OSPF network and provides local termination of LLC2 sessions to avoid LLC timeouts in large or busy networks. It is the ideal mechanism for mixed LAN-to-LAN and interactive SNA traffic since it can recover from network problems quickly using OSPF. It is rapidly becoming accepted as a major standard.

DLSAP. Data Link Service Access Point.

DLSDU. Data Link Service Data Unit.

DM. 1. Delta Modulation, voice-to-digital sampling and encoding technique.

2. Disconnected Mode, HDLC.

DMA. Direct Memory Access, a technique for high-speed data transfer between device such as LAN network adapter card and the computer memory. DMA bypasses the Central Processing Unit of the computer, PC or workstation, allowing the device to transfer a block of information directly across the bus into system memory.

DMAC. *See* direct memory access controller.

DMD. Directory Management Environment, OSF term for one of the portable environments.

DMI. Definition of Management Information, part of the SMI of OSI management, ISO 10165-2.

DMI. Desktop Management Interface, a set of APIs outlined by the DMTF, comprising three components: service layer, component interface and management interface.

DML. Data Manipulation Language, part of SQL, SQL-DML, part of ISO IS 9075.

DMO. Domain Management Organisation, an organisation that manages a DMD and has responsibility for maintaining the associated portion of the DIB.

DMOS. *See* double-diffused metal-oxide semiconductor.

DMP. Direct Memory Processor.

DN. 1. Distinguished Name, one of the names of an object that uniquely identifies this object in the directory. 2. Domain Name.

DNA. Digital Network Architecture, the network architecture of Digital Equipment Corporation with eight layers. DNA is similar in structure to OSI at lower levels, except that the top three layers of the DNA correspond to the top two layers in the OSI model.

DNA. *See* Digital Network Architecture.

DNC. *See* direct numerical control.

DNS configuration property sheet. The property sheet that allows to enter a host name for the computer and to enter the domain name to which it belongs in the host and domain fields respectively.

DNS. Domain Name System, a hierarchical distributed database that allows centralised control of domain names and local control of resources. DNS allows for local control of names within the assigned domain name. DNS servers throughout the world work together to form a database where detailed information is located on DNS servers that are local to the company or organisation, which owns the domain name. It allows the user to retrieve files and documents from computers that might be located anywhere in the world. After an organisation registers a domain name, the domain can be further subdivided, as desired by the organisation. DNS servers throughout the connected Internet implement a hierarchical namespace that allows sites freedom in assigning machine names and addresses. DNS also supports separate mappings between mail destinations and IP addresses.

DNZ. Xerox Networking Systems, Xerox's proprietary networking software.

do pitch. The maximum resolution of a monitor, which is determined by the size of smallest dot it can display. To ensure that light does not spill from one dot to the next, a metal sheet is used as a shadow mask. The finer the perforation in mask, higher the resolution. Very high-resolution monitors use a dot pitch of 0.28 mm or less.

DOAM. Distributed Office Applications Model, an umbrella for several layer 7 applications, including DPA, DFR, MOTIS, and RDT.

DOC. File name extension for a word processor or information file.

document comparison utility. A program used to compare two documents on disk. It is especially useful when a copy of a document is given to another person to edit on disk.

When the document is returned, the author is able to identify the changes made by comparing the two documents using the utility. The result is displayed on the screen, highlighting new words or sentences. Text which was deleted is also displayed with a line through it on the screen for easy identification and comparison.

document format. In word processing, a set of codes which describe the parameters of the working area, including fonts, line spacing, margins, headers, and footers.

Document Interchange Architecture. *See* DIA.

document-oriented computing. The workgroup computing that is organised around the goal of producing some kind of corporate document.

document processing. A complete system for creating, editing, printing, binding, and packaging a document. This may include automated indexing, table of contents, and referncing. Document processing thus goes one step further than word processing which is limited to the automated process of creating, editing, and outputting words for letters, reports, and the like.

document reader. A character reader whose input data is the text from specific areas on a given type of form.

document window. In most graphical user interfaces (GUIs), a window within an application window. There can be more than one document window open at a time.

document. A data file; whatever you create with an application, including information you type, edit, view, or save. A document may be a business report, a picture, or a letter and is stored as a file on a disk.

document-retrieval system. DRS. An information-retrieval system in which the contents of a document are indexed by means of key-word-in-context terms.

Domain Name System. *See* DNS.

domain name. An alphanumeric name associated with an IP address through TCP/IP's DNS name service system. The first part of the name identifies or is related to a company or organisation. The second portion of the domain name is a suffix such as com, edu, gov, mil, net, or org, that provides a mean of classification.

domain. A group of nodes on a network that form an administrative entity. It could also be a number of servers grouped together and named to simplify network administration and security. Every computer on the LAN belongs to at least one domain. Being logged in on one domain, however, does not limit resources in other domains to which the user has access permissions.

DOP. Directory Operational binding management Protocol, the protocol to support the management of operational bindings between two DSAs in the 1992 extensions to X.500.

DOPS. Digital Optical Projection System.

DOS. Disk Operating System, comprising a suite of programs managing disk-based computer system. It controls the computer's transfer of data to, and from a hard or floppy disk; frequently combined with the main operating system. DOS schedules and supervises work, allocating computer resources and the operation of peripherals. Many versions of DOS exist; Microsoft's MS-DOS is the most common. DOS 3.1 was the first version of MS and PC DOS able to support LAN functions separate, of course, from the network's own operating system, notably including record and file locking which is now standard on multi-user systems.

DOS/VS. Disk Operating System/Virtual Storage.

DOS-LAN Manager. DOS version of Microsoft's network operating system LAN Manager. It gives named pipes (an applications interface) support to DOS machines, enabling them to use the client/server environment.

dot address. The common notation for the IP addresses of the form A.B.C.D.; where each letter represents, in decimal, one byte of a four-byte IP address.

dot prompt. A dot (.) used as the symbol or character visible on the screen which represents a 'ready state, asking the user for a command. In DOS, the common prompt is calld a 'C' prompt. This is the letter 'C' followed by a colon, a back-slash sign and greater-than sign (C:\>).

dot-matrix printer. A printer which, instead of having a type wheel, has five or more carefully spaced and segmented wires, elements of which are pushed against the printing paper under the control of solenoids so that a dot-pattern is printed for each character. Variants of this technique use tiny inkjets, sometimes with a matrix of up to 20×15 spots per letter enabling suitably programmed printers to print characters.

dot-matrix. A two-dimensional pattern of dots used for constructing a display image. In printing, it refers to the pattern of dots used as a basis for character formation in a dot-matrix printer.

double-click. Clicking a mouse button twice in quick succession.

DOV. Data Over Voice, where data is transmitted over a voice circuit, either exclusively or simultaneously, without the subscriber hearing the data portion (requires special equipment).

down. In computer terminology, pertaining to a device or system that is inoperative.

down time. The period during which a system is non-functional due to hardware or software malfunction.

downline. The direction from a central or controlling node to a remote node in a hierarchical network, or (sometimes) the direction away from the current node without respect to hierarchical ordering. The word is often used as a verb: to download or to downline load, *i.e.* to send programs or data from a central or controlling node to a remote node in a network. The remote node may not have facilities to store the programs or data permanently, in which case the downline load would be necessary, each time the remote node is restarted. When the remote node does have permanent storage facilities, downline loading may be used to supply newer versions of programs or data to the remote node.

downlink. Transmission from a satellite to an earth station.

downloadable font. *See* soft font.

DP. Draft Proposal in ISO, obsolete term, replaced by CD for Committee Draft.

DPA. 1. Demand Protocol Architecture, a technique for loading protocol stacks dynamically, as they are required. It is associated with adapter cards in workstations and servers. Only the protocol stacks that are needed for a particular communications sessions are loaded. Examples of stacks that could be loaded include TCP/IP, XNS, SPX/IPX and NetBIOS.

2. Document Printing Application.

DPCM. Differential Pulse Code Modulation, a voice-to-digital sampling and encoding technique.

DPI. Dots Per Inch; used for expressing density with which a printer can print or a monitor can display. Describes the size of the pixels or dots of ink.

DPNSS. Digital Private Networks Signalling System, signalling standard for digital private networks within the UK formulated jointly by BT and PABX manufacturers.

DPSK. Differential Phase Shift Keying, a modulation technique that uses a form of phase modulation.

DQDB. Distributed Queued Dual Bus, a dual-strand, fibre-optic-based technology, which operates over tens of kilometres. A queuing system maintains transmission order. Some similarity with ATM encourages evolution between the technologies.

DR. 1. Delivery Report, used to confirm that a message was delivered to the recipient User Agent in X.400.
2. Disconnect Request Transport PDU.
3. Data recorder.

DRA. Data Resource Administrator.

drag. An action performed using a mouse; used to move icons on the screen and in selecting commands from menus. Position the cursor/ pointer on an item, press and hold the mouse button, move the cursor to a new location (by sliding the mouse), and then release the mouse button.

DRAM. *See* dynamic random-access memory.

DRD. Data Recording Device.

drift compensation. For a common channel signaling system; the process of adjusting for the difference in relationship of the backward acknowledgement information contained in the acknowledgement signal unit to the forward signal units it acknowledges which occurs as a result of drift in the bit rates of data channels.

drip-feed. A technique whereby transactions are collected into groups so that they may be processed or updated as a group to save computer time. Sometimes this technique is known as batch processing.

drive circuit. In the optical fibre transmission systems, the electrical circuit that drives the light emitting source, modulating it in accordance with intelligent-bearing signal.

drive letter. The letter assigned to a drive on an IBM or other compatible computer, for example, A, and B usually refer to floppy drives, while C to a hard drive.

drive mirroring. A fault-tolerance feature that sets up primary and secondary partitions on two disks using the same disk controller. The operating system treats these partitions as a single logical drive. Data lost from one partition can be recovered from the other. In drive mirroring and duplexing, drive verification is the process of ensuring that data on a primary partition and a secondary partition are identical. The drive that duplicates data on the primary memory is called that secondary partition. This is invisible to operating system which sees the primary and secondary partitions as single logical drive.

driver. 1. A file used by a particular program to execute commands to operate peripherals such as a printer or monitor.
2. A device that supplies a useful amount of signal energy to another device to insure its proper operation; e.g., a current drive for a magnetic-core memory, an oscillator driving a loudspeaker (a siren), etc.
3. A power amplifier stage that supplies signal power to the higher-powered amplifier stage.
4. In a digital computer, a stage that increases the output current or power of another stage.

DRL. *See* data-retrieval language.

DRMS. Data Resource Management System.

drop cable. A cable that links a network adapter to the external transceiver attached to a co-axial LAN such as Ethernet. Also known as an Attachment Unit Interface cable or transceiver cable.

drop cap. In printing, the letter at the beginning of a line of text, that is set to a larger size and extending into the lines of type below.

drop-in. 1. The reading of a spurious signal whose amplitude is greater than a predetermined percentage of the nominal signal.

2. An error in the storage into or the retrieval from a magnetic storage device, revealed by reading of a binary character not previously recorded. This is result of a fault condition, often imperfect erasure of data previously on the medium and will generally be a problem only in inter-record gaps (elsewhere it will be dealt with by the same means provided for drop-out): magnetic tape and disk systems normally have means of identifying and coping with this problem.

drop-out. 1. In magnetic recording technology (disk and tape), the loss of one or a sequence of bits due to a fault condition, most frequently a flaw in the recording medium. Magnetic tape and disk systems employ some form of redundancy to detect and frequently correct the resulting data errors.

2. A momentary loss in signal, causing errors and loss of synchronization especially with telephone line data transmission; defined as an unexpected drop of at least 12 dB for more than 4 milliseconds. Bell standard allows no more than two such dropouts per 15-minute period.

3. A failure to read a binary character from magnetic storage, generally caused by defects in the magnetic storage, generally caused by defects in the magnetic media, or failure in the read mechanism.

DROS. Disk Resident Operaing System.

DRP. Directory Replication Protocol, used to provide shadowing capabilities between two DSAs, in the Directory; part of the 1992 extensions to X.500.

DRPF. Decimal Reference Publication Format, a string of upto 40 decimal digits used to represent NSAP address.

DRS. *See* document-retrieval system.

drum printer. The printer with a rapidly rotating drum (cylinder), which contains a complete raised characters set in each band around the cylinder. Each character position along the text line contains a band of raised character set. There is a magnetically driven hammer in each character position of the line. The printer receives all characters to be printed in one line of the text from the processor. The hammer hits the paper and ribbon against the desired character on the drum when it comes in the printing position. Its speed varies from 200 to 2000 lines per minute.

DS. 1. Directory Service, the service provided by the Directory to users, defined in the X.500 series of Recommendations.

2. Distributed Single-layer [(abstract) test method], one of the abstract test methods used in conformance testing.

3. Document Storage, provides additional storage for a telematic terminal; similar to a message store for Telematic servies.

4. Draft Standard.

DS-0. Sub-T1 message header protocol, for 64-kpbs transmission rate.

DS-1. T1 message header protocol, for 1.544-Mbps messaging.

DS-2. T2 message header protocol, for 6.312-Mbps messaging.

DS-3. T3 message header protocol, for 44.736-Mbps messaging.

DSA. 1. Directory System (Survice) Agent, an OSI application process which is responsible for a part of the Directory Information Base.
2. Digital Service Area, telephony term.

DSAP. Destination Service Access Point, used in LLC.

DSB. Double SideBand, an advanced from of SSB.

DSBSC. Double SideBand Suppressed Carrier, a more advanced from of SSB.

DSBT. Double Sideband Transmission.

DSD. Data Structure Definition, defines the Virtual Terminal Conceptual Communications Area.

DSE. 1. DSA Specific Entry, information a DSA holds associated with the name of a Directory entry, other than the name itself.
2. Distribted Single-layer Embedded, a variation on one of the abstract test methods used in conformance testing.
3. Data Switching Equipment, usually refers to equipment on X.25 network.
4. Digital Switching Exchange, a node in a telecommunications network.

DSP. 1. Directory System Protocol, used between DSAs in the Directory.
2. Domain-Specific Part, part of the NSAP address that is used within a given addressing authority's domain.
3. Digital Signal Processor, special-purpose microprocessor used in communications devices.
4. Defence Standardised Profile, proposal to write US Department of Defense profiles in the ISP formation.

DSS. Digital Signal Standard, a method for paired public and private keys to be used to authenticate an originator and the data of a mesage.

DSSDU. Expedited Session Service Data Unit.

DSU. Data Service Unit, data transmission equipment used to interface to a digital circuit at user site. It converts the user's datastream, such as X.21 to E1, or T1 for transmission through the CSU, which is often contained, functionally within the DSU device. Data service unit can convert data to or from a native port on a router to an E1, E2 or E3 leased line, primary rate ISDN or SMDS, DSU functionality can be built into devices such as some routers or multiplexers. In Europe the DSU can convert El bandwidth into RS.449, X.21, V.35 or other serial interface via a router. Data service unit with an HSSI interface will deliver E2 or E3 bandwidth from the WAN to an HSSI router on a LAN.

DT. 1. DaTa, PDU in Transport that carries data.
2. Document Type.

DTAM. Document Transfer, Access, and Manipulation, provides for ODA/ODIF document transfer; the CCITT T.4.00, T.431, T.432, T.433, and T.441 recommendations, similar to but not the same as ISO 10166.

DTD. 1. Document Type Definition, the header on an SGML formatted document which declares SGML tags used in the document and the actions to be executed on encountering each tag in each possible target output device.
2. Data Transfer Done.

DTE. Data Terminal Equipment, a piece of equipment where a communications path ends; user's equipment is collectively termed DTE and can include PCs and display terminals.

DTI. Department of Trade and Industry, U.K.; produces a number of publications on open systems under its Technology Transfer Programme, including a comprehensive review of OSI products available in Durope.

DTMF. Dual Tone Multi-Frequency, a term for push button dialling; technology used to generate several distinct tone patterns in a touch-tone phone or equipment which emulates a phone. The pushed button makes a tone, actually the combination of two tones of high and low frequency. They are necessary to access advanced network features such as call barring and call forwarding.

DTP. 1. Data Transfer Protocol. 2. Distributed Transaction Processing. 3. DeskTop Publishing.

DTR. Data Terminal Ready, one of the pins or contacts assigned under the RS-232 specification; when true, indicates the hardware is ready to receive and/or send.

D-type. A connector employed in both the data processing and telecommunication industries. Available in sizes from 9 to 37 ways, it is usually used for interconnecting between equipment or for connecting different assemblies within one unit. The name derives from the elongated D shape of the pin housing.

DU. Data Unit, information exchanged as a single unit between entities.

DUA. Directory User Agent; OSI application process which represents a user in accessing the Directory, X.500.

dual drive. A floppy disk drive for two disks using only one spindle motor and one positioner.

dual diversity. The simultaneous combining of, or selection from, two independently fading signals and their detection through the use of space, frequency, angle, time or polarization characteristics.

dual homing. The connection of a terminal so that it is served by either of two switching centres. This service uses a single directory number.

dual operation. Of a Boolean operation, another Boolean operation whose result, when performed on operands that are the negation of the operands of the first Boolean operation, is the negation of the result of the first Boolean operation. Disjunction is the dual operation of conjunction.

dual port memory. A memory that is capable of receiving two concurrent access requests. Depending upon the internal memory organisation, responses may or may not be simultaneous. Close-coupled multiprocessor systems use these memories.

dual processor. A multiprocessor system with two central processors. Use of this term sometimes implies a two-processor system in which one processor is redundant so that the total system but is not intended to be executed.

dual scan display. A variant of a passive matrix display in which the top and bottom half of the screen are refreshed simultaneously, allowing the screen to be refreshed twice as fast, yielding better display quality.

Dual Tone Multi-Frequency. *See* DTMF.

duct. An underground tube or tunnel in which the cables are installed.

dumb device. A computer, or device, usually a terminal, that can only transmit or receive data to or from a servicing computer.

dumb terminal. A computer which allows communications with other computers, but does not enhance the data exchanged, or provide additional functions, such as upload or download.

dummy section. The part of a computer program that translates a source program written in assembly language into object code. It contains data declarations but does not reserve space for that data.

dump. 1. A hard-copy printout (or output to secondary storage) listing contents of primary storage available in the central processing unit. Data can be dumped in hexadecimal format or English-like code. A dump is usually requested by a programmer when a error is detected in a program or operating system.

2. In a system handling large numbers of users' files stored on magnetic disk, one of the periodic records of the state of the disks that are made on magnetic tape in order to protect against accidental overwriting or mechanical failure of the disks.

3. A printed version of the contents of system memory taken when a system crash has occurred. In principle it is possible to determine the immediate cause of a system crash by studding the dump and determining the reason for any inconsistencies in its contents. In practice, this may be difficult even with the assistance of dump analysis software.

dumpster diving. A method of obtaining confidiential information by examining the contents of the legitimate user's dusbins, etc.

duodecimal. 1. Characterized by a selection, choice, or condition that has 12 possible values or states.

2. Pertaining to a fixed-radix numeration system having a radix of 12.

DUP. Disk Utility Program.

duplex signalling. A signalling system which occupies the same cable pair as the voice path, but does not require any special type of filtering.

duplexing. A fault-tolerance feature that sets up primary and secondary partitions with identical data using separate disk controllers. Drive duplexing provides protection against errors caused by a faulty controller or faulty disk. In drive duplexing and mirroring, drive verification is the process of ensuring that data on a primary partition and a secondary partition are identical. The drive that duplicates data on the primary memory is called the secondary partition. This is invisible to the operating system which sees the primary and secondary partitions as a single logical drive. Also known as drive duplexing.

durability. In transaction processing, a computer transaction is said to provide integrity of operation and data when the transaction passes the ACID (atomicity, consistency, isolation, durability) test. A transaction has 'durability' if all the changes that it makes to the database becomes permanent when the transaction is committed. ACID properties and the ability to recover data (after a failure) make transaction processing a distinct style of computing for which unique software products have been developed, such as VAX ACMS and DECintact systems, and CICS system.

DUS. Diagnostic Utility System.

DUT. Device Under Test.

DUV. Data Under Voice, a method for carrying data and voice on the same connection.

dye-sub printer. The printer utilising dye-sublimation technique, in which a ribbon containing panels of colour is moved across a focused heat source that is capable of subtle temperature variations. The heated dyes evaporate from the ribbon and diffuse on specially coated paper where they form area of different colours. The variation in colour are related to intensity of the heat applied. The dye-sublimation printer produces 300 dpi. unlike thermal wax transfer printer, its dots are not of the same size. At lower temperatures, smaller dots are produced.

dynamic adaptive routing. The automatic rerouting of traffic based a sensing and analysis of current actual network condition.

dynamic allocation. An allocation that is made dynamically, *i.e.* while the system is running rather than statically at the time of first initiating the system.

dynamic characteristics. The relationship between the current from one electrode and the voltage on another, under dynamic conditions.

dynamic debugging technique. A computer technique that makes use of a debug program, especially designed for continuous debugging of user-written programs.

dynamic equilibrium. 1. The state of balance between two or more constantly varying quantities.
2. Tendency of two current-carrying circuits to maintain at a maximum the magnetic flux linking them.

dynamic flip-flop. A flip-flop (bistable multivibrator) which is kept on by recirculating an ac signal. The device may be switched on or off, however, by a signal pulse.

Dynamic Host Configuration Protocol. *See* DHCP.

dynamic link. Particularly useful in database management, a link which ensures that by using an update command, all data changed in one program are automatically changed in another program, thereby keeping the data consistent.

dynamic margin. Step-by-step attenuation is applied to a data test signal; the amount of attenuation added when the receive end gives total errors or wipeout is noted, this becomes the benchmark for future trouble isolation.

dynamic memory. A form of volatile semiconductor memory in which stored information is degraded with time; most common example is dynamic RAM (random-access memory) where the logic state to be entered in each cell is stored as a voltage on the small capacitance associated with the gate of the MOS output transistor for the cell. The voltage decays away with time because of leakage currents in the cell, and so it must be refreshed (*i.e.* recharged) periodically by external circuitry.

dynamic node address. A patent of AppleTalk under which each node assigns itself a unique address code each time it is initialized. Conventionally, nodes are assigned fixed addresses that do not change.

dynamic password. An access control method based on the use of random numbers; effective against reply attacks. One of the users is given a device, but having a protected data encryption standard key. This key is also stored in protected form in the computer system. After log on, the user is challenged by a random number. this number is entered in to the device to produce a response number, which in turn is keyed in to the computer by the user.

dynamic programming. The mathematical theory and planning of multi-stage decision processes.

dynamic RAM. A kind of dynamic memory which stores data on the capacitances between gate and source of MOSFET.

dynamic random-access memory. DRAM. A form of memory, which requires its contents to be, updated at least every one thousandth of a second because the capacitors, which are used to represent memory states lose their electrical charge very quickly. It is called dynamic because information is stored only temporarily, the dynamic random-access read/write memory (RAM) must be continually rewritten or refreshed. Storage is made in the form of the parasitic leakage's that are experienced in integrated circuits. DRAM chips (also known as dynamic RAM) are very small, cheap, and relatively simple to manufacture, but they are becoming unpopular among manufacturers since the introduction of static RAM (SRAM) chips, or even SDRAM, which can retain their contents (without the need to refresh) until the power is switched off. Microprocessors operating at clock speeds above 25 MHz, need DRAM with access times faster than 80 ns (80×10^{-10}s). DRAM devices use one transistor and one capacitor to store each bit as a charge. The reduced logic required to store each bit makes DRAM significantly denser than SRAM, allowing more bits per chip. Silicon die and the package of DRAM is also smaller than SRAM, allowing more DRAM chips to be mounted on a single board. DRAM technology, however, has two disadvantages with respect to SRAM technology. The first is performance. CMOS (complementary metal-oxide semiconductor) SRAM chips are much faster than CMOS DRAM chips.

dynamic range. 1. In a transmission system, the difference in decibels between the noise level of the system and its overload level.

2. The difference in decibels between the overload level and the minimum acceptable signal level in a system or transducer.

dynamic routing. The process for selecting most appropriate path or route for a packet or datagram to travel around a network. In this method, the routing information is supplied dynamically through routing protocols. At the end of each leg of the journey of the packet across the network, the router decides on the most appropriate path for the packet or datagram to follow if there are multiple routes available. This is done using network status information gathered from around the Internet and passed from router to router using routing information protocols.

dynamic scanning. In optical fibre transmission systems, a technique in which a fibre bundle is vibrated about a fixed point with reference to the impressed image in order to render the fibre pattern less visible at the output end.

dynamic signature verifier. A biometric security device, which is used to store the dynamic characteristics of a hand-written signature so that a positive identification can be established before entry to a computer system or a room, is permitted.

dynamic storage. 1. A device storing data in a manner that permits the data to move or vary with time so that the specified data or not always available for recovery. Magnetic drum storage and disk storage are dynamic non-volatile storage.

2. The available storage left within the partition after the task set is loaded.

DYSTAC. Dynamic Storage Analog Computer.

DYSTAL. Dynamic Storage Allocation Language.

E

E. 1. The hexadecimal (HEX) symbol for binary 1110, decimal 14;

$E_{16} = 14_{10} = 16_8 = 1110_2$.

2. Exa. A decimal prefix used in association with a base unit in the SI system of units indicating a multiplication factor of 10^{18} of that unit.

3. Symbol for erlang, a unit of telecommunications traffic intensity.

E1. European standard for high-speed data transmission at 2.048Mbit/s; 32-64Kbit/s channels is provided.

E13B. In character recognition, magnetic ink character recognition font consisting of 10 numerals and four symbols. It is widely used in cheque sorting and banking.

E²PROM. Electrically-Erasable Programmable Read-Only Memory; using only silicon and its derivatives plus metals, this device employs the floating-gate tunnel oxide cell structure in which electrons tunnel to and from a floating gate. It is a field programmable read-only memory (FROM) in which the cells may be erased electrically and may be re-programmed electrically. Also known as EFPROM.

EA. *See* effective address.

EAE. *See* extended arithmetic element.

EAP. *See* extensible authentication protocol.

EAPROM. *See* electrically-alterable programmable read-only memory.

EARN. European Academic Research Network, a pan-European agency that oversees the interconnectivity of its member's networks. Member networks use a BITNET technology to connect universities and research labs in Europe.

earth station. Transmitting or receiving point for satellite transmission.

EasyCAD2. A software package published by Evolution Computing of Arizona, US. It is a two-dimensional CAD (computer-aided design) program written in assembly language to allow the use to produce drawings from basic layouts to full engineering specifications for many commercial fields, including architectural, mechanical, electrical, and electronics. It uses floating-point math for precise, near-infinite zoom, and includes online help, pull-down menus, a text editor for writing user-script, and macros. It also has utilities for file sharing among CAD and desktop publishing programs such as Aldus PageMaker and Ventura Publisher, and writes PostScript and HPGL files. To operate effectively, Easy CAD2 requires 640 kilobytes of random-access memory, a graphics adaptor, monitor, and a mouse or digitising tablet.

EAX. Electronic Automatic eXchange, a telephone exchange employing modern techniques such as digital switching, in which communication between subscribers is effected without the intervention of exchange operators.

EBAM. Electronic Beamed Access Memory.

EBCDIC. Expanded (or Extended) Binary Coded Decimal Interchange Code; an 8-binary digit code, similar to American Standard Code for Information Interchange, that uses the eighth level as an information bit. The code is used to represent 256 letters, numbers and special characters. It allows the representation of control codes and graphics in a logical format. It was created to represent data in particular types of data processing and communications terminal devices. Most Internet hosts use ASCII encoding; however, EBCDIC code is encountered if the data is transferred via tape or other physical media to or from a large IBM installation. Most systems translate EBCDI to ASCII during FTP or other electronic transmission.

EBM. Extended Branch Mode.

EBR. Electron Beam Recording, a process that employs an electron beam to store and read information on a particular target. These targets are normally silicon dioxide and electrostatic charges actually store the data.

EC. 1. Error Count.
2. Error Correcting.

ECAD. Electronic Computer Aided Design.

ECAP. Electric Circuit Analysis Program.

ECC. Error Correction Codes, generation term for methods such as parity bits and CRC to detect and correct bit errors in digital communications.

echo cancellation. A technique used in high-speed modems to isolate and remove unwanted signal energy created by echoes of the transmitted signal. (An echo is the return of a transmitted signal). It would be noticeable by its absence on transatlantic or other time-differentiated phone conversations.

echo check. A way of establishing the accuracy achieved during the transfer of data over a data link, computer network, etc. When data is received, it is stored and transmitted back to its point of origin in the transmission loop where it can be compared with the original data.

echo return loss. The difference, in dB, between the level of a composite-frequency signal sent into a circuit and the level of the echo of that signal as it reaches the point of application. The signal normally contains all frequencies between 500 Hz and 2500 Hz at equal amplitudes.

echo suppresser. In data communications, the conventional telephone networks have echo suppressers to inhibit annoying echoes during telephone conversations. These devices detect the presence of a voice signal in one direction and inhibit signal flow in the opposite direction. These devices prevent full-duplex data communications and must therefore be suppressed for data transfer.

echo tolerance. Subjectively obtained figures for the loudness of an echo which can be tolerated and how this varies with the delay before the echo is heard. If the echo is heard only one or two milliseconds after the words have been spoken a loss in the echo path of only 3dB is sufficient, but if the delay is longer the echo signal has to be attenuated much more before it is considered tolerable, *e.g.*. 30dB for a 100 ms delay.

echo. A wave, which has been reflected or otherwise, returned with sufficient magnitude and delay to be perceived. An effect, which can be experienced on long distance, calls. It is usually associated with relatively long round-trip delay in the four-wire portion of the circuit so that the disturbing sound is perceived as being separate in time from the wanted sound. The phenomenon of echo primarily affects the talker and not the listener. In television echoes appear as ghosts displaced to one side or another of the primary picture. The characters typed on the keyboard of a data terminal will not appear on the display of the terminal unless they are echoed. The echoing may be done locally by the terminal itself, by a modem, or by intervening communication processor.

echoplex. In data communications, the method employing an echo of the received data for error checking. A computer, receiving data from communication link operating in a full-duplex mode, returns the received data to the transmitter thus allowing it to verify that data was correctly received.

ECN. Explicit Congestion Notification, bits in frame relay header that indicate a not is experiencing congestion.

ECS. *See* error-correcting system.

ECSA. Exchange Carriers Standards Association, secretariat to T1.

ED. 1. EWOS Document, usually proposed European profiles.

2. Expedited Data Transport PDU, a small Transport PDU that is transferred and processed with higher priority than normal data PDUs and will be delivered before any subsequently sent Transport PDU.

3. Exception Data Session PDU, used to put the Session Protocol Machine into an error state.

EDAT. Expedited Data Acknowledgement Transport.

EDC. 1. External Disk Channel.

2. External Drum channel.

3. Error detection and Correction.

edge card. In computing, a circuit board with contact strips along one edge. It is designed to mate with an edge connector.

edge connector. A multi-way socket, whose contacts are arranged according to a standard pattern. It is capable of accepting a standard-sized circuit board having contact areas that are formed along its edge and can mate with corresponding contacts in the socket. Connections to various points on the circuit board may then be made indirectly via the socket.

edge emitting LED. A light-emitting diode with a spectral output that emanates from an edge, having a higher output efficiency and greater coupling efficiency to an optical fibre, or integrated optical circuit, than a surface emitting LED.

EDI. Electronic Data Interchange, electronically transferring data in a predetermined form. Many different forms have been defined for use by different industry groups.

EDIFACT. Electronic Data Interchange For Administration, Commerce, and transport, one of the common EDI formats and one that can be carried over X.400 with X.435.

EDIME. EDI Message Environment, an object-oriented environment for EDI over X.400.

EDIMG. Electronic Data Interchange MessaGing.

EDIMS. Electronic Data Interchange Messaging System; an X.400 message store that supports the EDI MS attributes.

EDIN. EDI Notification, in EDI over X.400, service message containing information about receipt or non-receipt of an EDI message.

edit. 1. To prepare data for a later operation; editing may include the rearrangement or the addition of data, the deletion of unwanted data, format control, code conversion, and the application of standard processes such as zero suppression.

2. To enter, modify, or delete data.

EDIUA. EDI User Agent, that component of an EDI messaging service that represents the EDI user in submitting and accepting delivery of EDI messages over X.400.

EDI User. An X.500 directory object class defined in Annex H of X.435.

EDN. Expedited Data Negotiation facility; implies support of the interrupt procedures in the Network Layer.

EDP. *See* electronic data processing.

EDPE. Electronic data Processing Equipment.

EDPM. *See* electronic data-processing machine.

EDPS. *See* electronic data-processing system.

EDS. 1. Electronic Data System.

2. *See* error-detecting system.

3. *See* exchangeable disk store.

EDS. *See* exchangeable disk store.

EEI. External Environment Interface, the interface between an application platform and the external environment in an Open Systems Environment. An example EEI is a user interface.

EEL. *See* exclusive exchange line.

EEMS. Enhanced Expanded Memory Specification; most computers running under DOS having a random-access memory limitation of 640 kilobytes. To expand on this memory limitation, EEMS was introduced by Ashton-Tate (Borland), AST, and Quadram to enhance an earlier version of expanded memory called Lotus-Intel-Microsoft Expanded Memory Specification (LIM EMS). Since the release of LIM EMS Version 4.0, enhancement issues have been solved, making it the dominant standard.

EEPROM. *See* electrically-erasable programmable read-only memory.

EET. *See* equipment engaged tone.

EETDN. End-to-End Transit Delay Negotiation facility.

EF. Electronic Filing.

EFD. Event Forwarding Discriminator, an OSI management object that allows a system to select whether to send event reports and, if so, where to send them.

effective address. EA. The location or unit in a computer, where information is stored that is actually used for the execution of an instruction; i.e., the address actually used during instruction execution and derived as a result of instruction modification. This may differ from that of the instruction in storage.

effective algorithm. An algorithm that is effectively computable. The study of whether or not effective algorithms exist to compute particular quantities forms the basis of the theory of algorithms.

effective data transfer rate. The average number of bits, characters, or blocks per unit time transferred from a data source and accepted as valid by a data sink; expressed in bits, characters, or blocks/second, minute, or hour.

effective instruction. The instruction executed as a result of the modification of the basic instruction.

EFI. Error Free Interval.

EFS. 1. Extended Facility Set, used with Virtual Terminal.

2. External File System.

EFT. Electronic Funds Transfer, a way to transfer money between different banking institutions using electronic means.

EG CAE. Expert Group for Common Application Environment, the technical groups within EWOS developing a CAE profile.

EG CT. Expert Group for Conformance Testing methodology, the technical group within EWOS working on conformance testing issues in co-operation with ETSI TC ATM.

EG DIR. Expert Group on DIRectory, the technical group within EWOS working on OSI directory profiles, a joint activity with ETSI STC TE6.

EG FT. Expert Group on File Transfer and access, technical group within EWOS working on FTAM profiles.

EG LIB. Expert Group for LIBrary applications, the technical group within EWOS developing OSI profiles for library applications.

EG LL. Expert Group for Lower Layers, the technical group within EWOS working on lower-layer profiles, in co-operation with ETSI STC TE7.

EG MHS. Expert Group of MHS, the technical group within EWOS working on X.400 profile development.

EG MMS. Expert Group developing Manufacturing Message Specification profiles within EWOS.

EG NM. Expert Group for Network Management, the technical group within EWOS developing agreements on Network Management.

EG ODA. Expert Group developing Office Document Architecture profiles within EWOS.

EG TP. Expert Group on Transaction Processing, the technical group within EWOS developing profiles on OSI Transaction Processing.

EG VT. Expert Group within EWOS working on Virtual Terminal profile development.

EG. Expert Group, a working group within EWOS focused on a particular area of interest.

EGP. Exterior Gateway Protocol, a routing protocol used between gateways on the Internet.

EHF. Extremely High Frequency, in radio communications, the band higher than super high frequency.

EIA/TIA 568. The EIA/TIA's most famous standard specifying a maximum horizontal cable run of 90 metres, allowing 10 metres for hub and device attachment resulting a total cable length of 1000 metres. Its related Service Bulletins TSB 36 and 40 define three categories of cabling system for data communications: Categories 3, 4 & 5.

EIA/TIA. The US Electronics Industries Association and Telecommunications Industries Association which have merged. EIA is a trade organisation for the electronics industry that concentrates on hardware interface standards. Best known for the RS232C and RS422 standards that specifies the electrical characteristics of interconnections between terminals and computers or between two computers.

EIDE. Enhanced Integrated Drive Electronics, a newer version of the IDE standard for hard drives.

EIES. Electronic Information Exchange System; a set up in the US, which connects a number of groups together; it provides electronic mail (E-COM), teleconferencing and personal electronic communications, whilst monitoring their use and impact.

eight level. Any binary code using 8-bits, in addition to start and stop pulses, for each character.

EIS. Electronic Information Security.

EISA. Extended Industry Standard Architecture, a 32-bit adaptation of the 8/16-bit buses originally developed by IBM and now standard in almost all computers that use Intel 8086 and 80X86 chips. EISA bus is a joint development from Compaq and other computer manufacturers.

EIT. Encoded Information Type, in X.400, an indication of the body part types being carried.

EIUF. European ISDN Users Forum.

EKS. Electronic Key System.

ELAN. ESPRIT Local Area Network.

ELD. Edge Lit Display.

ELE. Equivalent Logic Element.

electrically-alterable read-only memory. EAROM. A specialised random-access read/write memory that can be programmed by writing into the array and then generally used as a read only memory. The devices have a fast read cycle of around 1.5 microseconds and a much slower write cycle of about one millisecond. Other qualities are as EAPROMs.

electrically-erasable programmable read-only memory. EEPROM. Using only silicon and its derivatives plus metals, this device employs the floating-gate tunnel oxide cell structure in which electrons tunnel to and from a floating gate. It is a field programmable read-only memory in which the cells may be erased electrically in one second and may be reprogrammed electrically. It can also be erased and reprogrammed up to a million times. This memory device in general makes practical such applications as altering remotely, by telephone, microprocessor system programs. Also known as E^2PROM.

electromagnetic wave. The resultant effect obtained from the interaction of an electric field and magnetic field. The interaction causes energy to be transmitted in a particular direction. It is a kind of disturbance which propagates outward from any electric charge which oscillates, or is accelerated; far from the charge it consists of vibrating electric and magnetic fields which move at speed of light and arc at right angles to each other and to the direction of propagation.

electronic data interchange. The interchange of information using electronic messaging system; a form of paperless data transaction that is rapidly expanding.

electronic data processing. EDP. The conversion of data by electronic equipment into a form, that is able to be processed by computers. Electronic data processing is a term used more often in the US whilst data processing is more often used in the UK and Europe.

electronic data-processing machine. EDPM. An individual unit or device that is part of electronic data processing system, or can provide standalone electronic data processing.

electronic data-processing system. EDPS. A collection of electronic data processing machines that are capable of performing electronic data processing functions.

electronic exchange. An automatic telephone exchange that makes use of solid-state switching and computing equipment.

electronic filing. A computer-based system for the storage, cataloguing, and retrieval of documents; the files in an electronic filling system are generally stored on magnetic disk or tape; some systems use microfilm techniques for bulk storage of data.

electronic funds transfer system. EFTS. A term referring to various electronic communications systems that is able to transfer financial information from one point to another. The term can encompass automated clearinghouses and point-of-sale systems.

electronic mail and message system. EMMS. Services in com munications system or network such as electronic mail, teleconferencing, word processor communication and videotex.

electronic mail. A method of transferring information (often text messages) from one computer to another over a network. The wide use of communications and local area networks has made sending and receiving electronic messages possible. The messages can be sent locally within the computer network, or via telephone networks to remote sites. Recipients can read the message at their convenience, then perform one of many options such as printing the message, forwarding it, answering it, or deleting it. This is a fast and efficient way to communicate, as text and graphics files can be attached to the message, and is available either as a value-added services from providers such as GEIS and IBM, or on LAN systems. E-mail programs generally combine various features such as:

a text editor for writing and editing messages;

an address book for storing names and e-mail addresses;

ability to transfer outbound messages to a post office server;

ability to transfer inbound messages from a mail server; and

a message manager that organises and stores the sent and received messages.

Also known as electronic text transfer; e-mail.

electronic materials information services. EMIS. A store of information held on computer files concerning material properties and material supply; produced by Information Services.

electronic memory. A memory in which read and write operations are entirely electronic, includes ferrite cores, magnetic bubbles, and MOS devices.

electronic message system. First used as a description of communication made using terminals in a communications network or system. It is now generally employed to describe specialised services such as electronic mail, teleconferencing, word processor communication and videotext.

electronic surveillance. The receipt, analysis, and evaluation of signals obtained from scanning a designated volume of space with electronic equipment such as receivers, radar, and infrared scanners. Electronic surveillance devices may be ground-based or airborne, side looking or forward-looking, or area searching. They are employed to monitor, intercept, classify, and analyse all electromagnetic transmission and radiation from or in a given area.

electronic switching system. ESS. Originally a term for Bell System computerised telephone exchange. In general, a switching system with components that utilise semiconductor devices, such as transistor combinational circuits (logic elements), semiconductor diode matrices, and integrated circuits to perform the selection and switching of circuits.

electronic warfare. The use of electronic devices for determining the existence and disposition of enemy's electronic aids to warfare; destroying or degrading the effectiveness of an enemy's electronic aids to warfare; preventing the destruction of effectiveness of friendly electronic aids.

electronic waveform synthesiser. EWS. A signal generator, which delivers an alternating or pulsating signal whose waveform may be tailored by means of adjustable circuit components.

ELF. Extremely Low Frequency.

EMA. Electronic Mail Association, founded in 1983, a North American association which monitors US government regulations affecting electronic mail and provides liaisons with similar international associations.

e-mail. *See* electronic mail.

EMC. Extended Multiplxer Channel.

EMIS. *See* electronic materials information services.

EMMS. Electronic Mail and Message System.

EMP. ElectroMagnetic Pulse, a type of high-capacity electrical disturbance emitted by lighting, certain generators, or nuclear detonation which, like RFI, can interface with or damage equipment or signals.

EMPM. Electronic Manuscript Preparation and Markup, Z39.59-1989, similar to ISO 8879 (SGML).

EMS. 1. Element Management System, the level of a network management system concerned with collecting network management information from, and setting parameters on the network elements. Network elements consist of data communications and telecommunications equipment.
2. Expended Memory Specification.
3. Electronic Mail System.

emulation mode. A special mode in which a device such as a printer can emulate the actions of a different device. Communications programs commonly emulate terminals.

emulation. 1. A process by which a computer imitates the actions of another computer, so that the imitating system accepts the same data and executes the same computer programs as the imitated system. The imitating computer system accepts the same data, executes the same programs, and achieves the same results as the imitated computer system.
2. Use of programming techniques and special machine features to permit a computing system to execute programs written for another system.

en block signalling. A method of signalling in which address digits are transmitted in one or more blocks, each block containing sufficient address information to enable switching centres to carry out progressive onward routing.

enable pulse. A pulse that must be present to allow other signals to be effective in certain electronic logic circuits. The term is now used to describe an electronic logic function it was originally used in an analogous manner in connection with core stores, where the coincidence of two pulses is required to change the state of a core; one of the pulses is the write pulse and can be common to a number of cores. An enable pulse is simultaneously applied to a particular core and thus enables the write pulse to change the state of that core.

encapsulation. The process of sending data encoded in one protocol format across a network operating a different protocol, where it is not possible or desirable to convert between the two protocols. For example, where Ethernet LANs attach to an FDDI backbone, it is not possible to convert between the different packet formats, so the Ethernet packet is encapsulated in its entirety inside an FDDI packet as it crosses the bridge on to the FDDI network. When the encapsulated Ethernet packet reaches the bridge connecting the destination Ethernet LAN to the FDDI network, the Ethernet packet is stripped out of the FDDI packet and put, unchanged, on to the destination Ethernet LAN. Also known as protocol tunnelling.

encipher. To convert plain text into an unintelligible form by means of a cipher system.

encode. 1. To apply a code, usually one consisting of binary digits that represent individual characters or group of characters in a message.

2. To convert data by the use of a code or a coded character set in such a manner that reconversion to the original form is possible, even if exact reconversion is not possible.

encoder. A functional unit that has a number of input lines such that not more than one at a time may carry a signal and a number of output lines such that any number may carry signals, and such that the combination of output signals serves as a code to indicate which input line carries the signal.

encryption. The conversion of plain text into a disguised or unintelligible form by means of a cryptosystem.

end distortion. In start-stop systems, the shifting of the ends of all mark pulses from their proper positions in relation to the beginnings of the start signal.

end node verification. A feature of TCP/IP in which two computers are actually communicating; these are called end nodes because they are at each end of the chain passing message, and are responsible for acknowledging and verifying transmission.

end of medium. A specific control character used to indicate the physical end of a data medium. It normally allows sufficient time for the user to adjust or change the system of operation.

end of text. A specific control character employed to indicate the end of transmission of a piece of text.

end of transmission block. A control character employed to indicate the termination of finish of transmission of a group of words or records treated as an individual unit.

END. A computer statement used to denote the end of a computer program.

end-around-carry. EAC. A type of carry that is required when a radix-minus-one complement representation of integers is used and two integers so represented are summed. If a carry is generated at the most significant end of the two numbers, then this carry must be added to the digit at the least significant end of the result to give the radix-minus-one complement representation of the sum.

end-around-shift. EAS. Another name for circular shift. The movement of data out of one end of a storage unit or register and re-entry of the data into the other end.

end-order traversal. Another name for post-order traversal.

end-to-end encryption. The use of one encryption to protect a transaction all the way from a user to the process being invoked in the destination computer system, and vice versa.

energiser. A hardware or software mechanism that is used as an aid in testing the behaviour of a subsystem. It is intended that the energiser should drive the subsystem in a way that simulates its actual application, and should at the same time analyse responses from subsystem in order to detect any erroneous behaviour.

Enliven. A server-based technology for streaming 2-D animation sequences for Windows 95 and Windows NT servers. It competes against RealAudio and Shockwave to provide fast downloading and real-time playing of animations with sounds.

ENQ. A colloquial term derived from ENQuiry, a special control character used in data communications. It has been designed to elicit a response from a remote station or terminal. The response usually required is some form of identification and/or operating status.

ENSDU. Expedited Network Service Data Unit.

entry point. An IBM network management term; an entry point provides management functions for itself and the devices attached to it. It has to be an SNA-addressable unit, allowing it to participate in network management by monitoring its own environment and exchanging information and messages with a Focal point.

environment variable. Environment information, such as a drive, path, or filename, associated with a symbolic name that can be used by MS-DOS. You use the MS-DOS SET command to define environment variables.

EO. End Office, the telephone office that terminates the user access line.

EOA. End Of Address; a specific control character used to indicate the finish of characters that are not text, *i.e.,* they are address information, employed on a transmission line.

EOB. End Of Block, control character used to indicate the finish of a group of words or records treated as an individual unit, employed on a transmission line.

EOC. Embedded Operations Channel, a channel for carrying operations messages as a part of a communications.

EOF. End Of File. 1. A mark used at the end of a quantity of data to indicate its completion.
2. A computer statement that indicates the end of a file of information.

EOJ. End Of Job. 1. A status condition that exists in a system when a particular. job has been completed.
2. A computer statement that indicates the end of a task or job.

EOL. 1. End Of Line; a specific character that indicates the termination or finish of a group of records.
2. End of Life.

EOM. End Of Message, a byte or octet that signals the end of a Data Link Control message.

EOR. 1. End of Reel; a character or word employed to indicate the termination or finish, in multi-reel magnetic tape file, of all but the last reel.
2. End Of Record; a computer statement used to indicate the finish of a record or a set of records.
3. End Of Run; a computer statement used to indicate the finish of a computer run.

EOS. Element Of Service, a functional description of a feature in message handling system.

EOT. 1. End Of Transmission, a bit which indicates the last PDU when Transport segmentation is used to carry an SDU too big for a single TPDU. It denotes the end of a data transmission to or from remote terminal and resets stations in the transmission line to control mode.
2. End Of Tape, a special mark that can be either a specific code on the magnetic tape (MAGTAPE) or a physical indicator used to show the physical end of a reel of tape. The physical indicators can be in the form of an easy-to-see reflective strip or a transparent section.
3. End Of Text, a byte or octet that. signals the end of user test in a Data Link Control message.

EOTC. European Organisation for Testing and Certification, related to ECITC.

EOV. End Of Volume. 1. A marker that indicates finish of a physical volume.
2. A computer software routine that comes into operation and takes control when the situation in EOV (1) is indicated.

EPF. Electronic Power Feed.

EPL. Encoder Programming Language.

EPOS. Electronic Point Of Sale, the interfaces used to debit bank cards or credit cards in stores.

EPR. Error Pattern register.

EPROM. 1. Erasable Programmable Read-Only Memory, a computer chip which can be erased and written to but which will not lose its information when a computer is turned off. EPROMs that use metal-oxide semiconductor (MOS) technology can be erased by ultra-violet light through a small window in the top of thier packaging. The first ROMs contained cell arrays in which the sequence of ones and zeros was established by a metalization interconnection mask step during fabrication. Thus, users had a supply ROM vendor with an interconnect program, so that the vendor could complete the mask and build the ROMs. Set-up charges were quite high. To avoid this high set-up charge, manufacturers developed a user-programmable ROM (PROM). The first PROMs used fusible links that could be melted or 'burned' with a special programmer system. Once burned, a PROM was just like a ROM.
2. Electrically Programmable Read-Only Memory.

EPU. Executive Processing Unit.

EQ. EQual to, a comparison of two values that state whether a second value is equal to the first.

equipment engaged tone. EET. A tone heard by a caller if any part of a telephone network is overloaded and the call cannot be completed. An engaged tone or busy tone is used for this purpose in many systems replacing an EET, although the busy tone actually indicates that a called party is busy.

ER. 1. *See* error recovery.
2. ERror transport PDU.

E-R-A. Entity-Relationship-Attribute, a data model (ANSI) which allows only binary relationships; mandatory part of IRDS, FIPS 156.

erase. 1. To obliterate information from any storage medium, *e.g.,* to clear or to overwrite.
2. To remove all previous data from magnetic storage by changing it to a specified condition that may be an unmagnetized state or predetermined magnetized state.

ERD. Qvent Report Discriminator, a management object to allow selection of potential event reports about other management objects.

ERF. Event Report Function, a function of OSI Network Management.

ergonomics. The study of physical relationship between people and their tools, such as computers. It has been helpful in designing the furniture of computer user, and also suggests the preventive measures to avoid damage to the eyes. Desks that allow proper keyboard height and special ergonomic keyboards have been developed to prevent carpal tunnel syndrome, a kind of repetitive stress injury.

ERIPAX. Wide area X.25 network, from Ericsson Business Communications AB, Stockholm.

ERJE. Extended Remote Job Entry.

erlang. A unit expressing intensity of traffic in telecommunications. One continuously engaged line has a traffic flow of 1 erlang; if the average number of calls made at any one time is 12, then traffic intensity is 12 erlang.

ERMF. Event Report Management Function, in OSI Network Management, the ability to control what events are reported and when the notifications are sent.

ERP. Error Recovery Procedure.

error burst. In data communications, a series of consecutive errors. It is not unusual for errors to occur in-groups or clusters.

error control. A means of ensuring that information received across a transmission link is correct. The techniques involved typically use error detection to detect if the transmitted data has been corrupted. The error control technique involves asking data to be retransmitted until a correct version is received.

error correcting. EC. The process of detecting invalid characters that will not conform to a set of rules. The construction of the rules is held in an error-correcting code.

error correction code. A code used by most memory controllers, including those in VAX systems, to detect memory errors. Error correction code (ECC) detects errors in a manner similar to parity checking, but ECC goes one step further by correcting many of the errors it detects. The most common ECC logic is called single-error correction, double-error detecting (SEC-DED). This means that the ECC will correct single-bit errors and detect double-bit errors. ECC dramatically decreases the number of system failures caused by memory errors because most memory errors involve only a single bit. ECC generates a number of check bits for each unit of data and appends these check bits to the data before it is written to memory. If SECDED implementation of ECC is used, a 32-bit long word will have 7 check bits appended to it. An error-detecting code designed to allow for automatic correction of certain types of errors.

error correction. A technique to restore data integrity in received data that has been corrupted during transmission. Error correction techniques involve sending extra data along with the original data being sent. It allows the correct form of the data to be reconstructed from the extra information if the original has been corrupted. This extra information is calculated using particular error correction algorithms such as Hamming Code. It allows errors to be detected and the original data reconstructed. This is sometimes termed forward error correction.

error detection. A set of techniques that can be used to detect errors in received data; such techniques include parity checks involving parity bits, checksums or a Cyclic Redundancy Check.

error message. In computing, a statement indicating that the computer has detected an error in the translation or execution phase of a program.

error rate. The frequency of occurrence of errors, defined as the ratio of bits incorrectly received to the total number of bits received.

error recovery. ER. A system of procedure that has been designed to overcome the deviation of a computed or a measured quantity from the theoretically correct or true value.

error routine. In programming, a routine that is entered when an error condition arises during execution. The error routine may simply produce error message, or it may attempt to recover from the error condition so that processing can continue.

error syndrome. In codes, a word indicating that a code word is correct or incorrect.

error trapping. Pertaining to a program that takes over control when an error occurs in the system.

error. A discrepancy between a computed or measured value and some objective standard.

error-correcting system. ECS. A system employing an error-correcting code and is so arranged that some or all the signals detected as being in error are automatically corrected at the receiving terminal before delivery to the data sink. In a packet switched data service, the error correcting system might result in the retransmission of one or more complete packets should an error be detected.

error-detecting code. A code in which each code representation conforms to specific rules of construction so that their violation indicates the presence of errors.

error-detecting system. EDS. A system employing an error-detecting code and so arranged that any signal detected as being in error is either deleted from the data delivered to the data sink, in some cases with an indication that such deletion has taken place, or delivered to the data sink together with an indication that the signal is in error.

ERT. Expected Run Time.

ES. 1. End System, a system originating or receiving the data, usually a system with a full seven-layer stack. 2. Errored Second, used in performance management in Network Management.

ES. *See* expert system.

ESA. Errored Second, type A, used in performance management in Network Management.

ESAFE. Errored Second, type A, Far End, used in performance management in Network Management.

ESB. Errored Second, type B, used in performance management in Network Management.

ESBFE. Errored Second, type B, Far End, used in performance management in Network Management.

ESC. Escape, control character.

escape character. A special symbol, part of a character set, employed to show that following characters belong to a different character set from those that have gone before.

ESCP. Errored Second, CP-bit Parity, used in performance management in Network Management.

ESCRP. Errored Second, Cyclic Redundancy Check, used in performance management in Network Management.

ESDI. Enhanced Small-Device Interface. One type of hard drive specification for IBM PC and compatible computer.

ESE20. Electronic Storage Element Model 20; a non-volatile storage device developed to offer a speed of 1 megabit DRAM technology, combined with availability advantages of magnetic disk storage. ESE20 is capable of servicing up to 300 input/output requests with average access times of 1.6 ms. It stores 120 megabytes and is available in a 60-inch-high storage array cabinet designed to hold two disks, with a total of 240 megabytes. In the event of a power loss, all data in the ESE20's memory arrays is safely transferred onto an internal Winchester disk in minutes, using an internal power supply.

ESF. Extended Superframe Format, framing structure defined under DS-1 interface specification to support a maintenance channel.

ESFE. Errored Second Far End, used in performance management in Network Management.

ESH. End System Hello, an ES-IS PDU that contains a list of NSAP and SNPA addresses for the sending ES, along with a holding time for the information.

ESI. Externally Specified Index.

ES-IS. End System to Intermediate System, protocol to provide a means of dynamically and automatically updating routing information maintained by the machines in an OSI network.

ESP. Errored Second, P-bit, used in performance management in Network Management.

ESPL. Electronic Switching Programming Language.

Espresso. One of the ten SPEC (System Performance Evaluation Co-operative) benchmarks drawn from real-world applications including scientific and engineering areas, focussing on system performance, memory, input/output, graphics, networking, multi-user, and commercial applications. Espresso is one of a collection of tools for the generation and optimisation of programmable logic arrays (PLAs). Specifically, it is an application that performs heuristic Boolean function minimisation. Espresso does not involve any floating point operations; it is categorised as an integer-intensive, it also provides insight as to how logic simulation and routing algorithms can be expected to perform on a given platform. Espresso performs set operations such as union, intersect, and difference. Sets are implemented as arrays of unsigned integers, and set membership is indicated by a particular bit being on or off. The set operations are implemented as logical (and) or (or) sequences. The sets typically contain fewer than 200 members. Espresso takes as input a Boolean function and produces a logically equivalent function, possibly with fewer terms. Both the input and output functions are represented as truth tables. The time taken to run a set of 7 input models is the measure of performance. Each model is run in sequence and the 7 elapsed times is the measure of interest. The application consists of approximately 9000 source code lines white compile into 69 kilobytes of instructions and 13 kilobytes of static data on an Apollo DN 3000 (12 MHz 68020/68881 system). Additional data space is dynamically allocation at run time. Amount of dynamically allocated memory depends upon the specific problem that espresso is solving, but is less than one megabyte. Consequently, espresso executes without paging even on system with small physical memory subsystems.

ESS. 1. Electronic Switching System, a switching technology, commonly used with PBXs.

2. Echo Suppression ystem.

ESTELLE. Extended State Transition Language, a formal technique for description of distributed or concurrent-processing systems, especially OSI processes, i.e., protocol and service specifications.

ET. 1. Exchange Termination, an ISDN user node termination connection.

2. *See* End Of Text.

ETC. Extended Text Compositor.

ETG. EWOS Technical Guide, explanatory or tutorial documents produced by EWOS.

Ethernet switching. A technique utilises the advantages of a parallel networking architecture to current contention- based Ethernet LANs. Each LAN can be segmented each with its own 10Mbit/s path. When users on different segments exchange data, an Ethernet switch dynamically connects the two separate Ethernet channels without interfering with other network segments. The switch can create multiple independent connections between separate segments, allowing multiple parallel data exchanges. This multiplies network bandwidth without modification to Ethernet end station hardware or software. Once disparaged by other vendors, it now forms part of the portfolio of the major hub and router manufacturers.

Ethernet. A popular networking technology featuring 10Mbps transmission speeds, running over thin coaxial (10Base-2), thick coaxial (10Base-5), or twisted pair (10Base-T) cables. Ethernet supports TCP/IP, AppleTalk (EtherTalk), Novell Netware, and other communication protocols. It is a baseband CSMA/CD network running on coaxial cable with a transmission rate of 10 megabits per second. It works well under light to moderate usage but suffers under heavy use from high collision rates. An Ethernet connection is significantly more reliable medium than a standard communication line. The protocols that run on an Ethernet network provide for fault detection and retransmission in the same way that wide area networks do. Segmentation, redundancy of Ethernet adapters, and redundancy of Ethernet connectors can protect against faults. Bridges can automatically select an alternate path to link two Ethernet segments in extended local area network. Manufacturers of hardware for the Ethernet protocol include Novell and 3Com.

Ethernet/802.3. A modified version of the original Ethernet specification which was approved by IEEE standard 802.3. Ethernet/802.3 (also called 'Ethernet/IEEE.) employs baseband signalling and Manchester phase encoding at a 10-megabits/s data rate using a broadcast bus topology. The medium is defined as a 0.4-inch, heavily shielded, 50-ohm cable which extends in segments of up to 500 m.

EtherTalk. An implementation of the AppleTalk communications protocol that runs over Ethernet.

e-time. Execution time; the time it takes the arithmetic/logic unit to execute (perform) the instructions after the central processor executes a computer program. This is part of the machine cycle.

ETIS. Electronics Telephone Inquiry System, an operator-based service that allows users to ask for telephone or fax numbers; the service is by country and is provided by PTTs or network providers.

ETS. 1. European Telecommunications Standards.

2. Executable Test Suite, in conformance testing, a test suite implemented on a particular MOT.

3. Electronic Tandem Switching.

ETSDU. Expedited Transport Service Data Unit.

ETSI STC TE3. Technical group within ETSI working on MHS.

ETSI STC TE6. Technical group within ETSI working on OSI Director.

ETSI STC TE7. Technical group within ETSI working on lower layers.

ETSI TC ATM. ETSI Technical Committee for Advanced Test Methods.

ETSI. European Telecommunications Standards Institute, created in 1989 by the European PTTs; now also contains manufacturers, user groups, and research bodies.

EUNET. European Unix NETwork.

EUROSINET. The EURopean Open Systems Interconnect NETwork, regional member of OSIONE, an association and network to demonstrate the interoperability of OSI products.

EUTELSAT. Satellite consortium of 26 European PTTs.

EUUG. European UNIX Users Group, the European association or support group for UNIX, involved with promoting open systems.

EV. European Videoconferencing Experiment, a research project with public video rooms controlled by various PTTs throughout Europe.

evaluative database. In online information retrieval, a full-text database that also offers evaluations of document contents.

even parity. An error-checking technique used in asynchronous communications in which the number of '1' bits must add up to an even number. A parity bit is used to signal to the computer that the bits in a byte have been transmitted correctly. To do this, an extra bit (check bit) is added to the byte. For example, the EBCDIC letter 'A' is represented by 11000001. This has three ones, and is therefore an odd number. The parity (check) bit would have to be a 1 so that it becomes an even number (110000011). Should the byte be received at the other and showing an odd number of ones (for example 110100011), then the computer knows that the information was corrupted during transmission. Errors could still occur if the incorrectly-transmitted byte contains two reversing errors which coincidentally and erroneously resulted in an even number of ones, but the probability of this occurring is very low.

event control block. ECB. A group of words or records treated as an individual unit that indicates the status of predictable events and take appropriate action where necessary.

EVM. Extended Virtual Machine.

EVR. Electronic Video Recording.

EVS. European Videoconferencing Service, the successor to EVE, with over 1000 public videoconference rooms throughout Europe.

EWS. *See* electronic waveform synthesiser.

EX. 1. EXchange.
2. EXpedited Data Session PDU.

exalted-carrier reception. A method of receiving either amplitude or phase modulated signals in which the carrier is separated from the sidebands, filtered and amplified, and then combined with the sidebands again at a higher level prior to demodulation.

EXCEL. A spreadsheet program developed by Microsoft Corporation offering presentation graphics with a selection of typefaces, colours, and area shading. It is available with Microsoft Office 97, and is used for making data sheets and data analysis. Some of the recent features incorporated in Excel include Natural Language Formula, Page Break Preview, Functional Suggestions, Lookup Wizard, and improved Workbooks.

exception. An error or fault condition that makes further execution of a program meaningless. If the programming language permits, occurrence of an exception will cause a break in the normal flow of control to an exception handler.

excess-3-code. An 8421 code for which the weighted sum of the four bits in each code words is greater than the decimal digit represented by that code word.

exchangeable disk store. EDS. A generic term used to describe storage disks that are capable of being removed from a computer and replaced by others.

exclusion. 1. The dyadic Boolean operation whose result has the Boolean value if and only if the first operand has Boolean value 1 and the second has Boolean value 0. 2. A logic operator having the property that if P is a statement and Q is a statement, then P exclusion Q is true if P is true and Q is false, false if P is false, and false if both statements are true. P exclusion Q is often represented by a combination of AND and NOT symbols such as P Q. Synonymous with NOT-IF-THEN operation.

exclusive exchange line. EEL. A single telephone line that provides services to an individual subscriber and has only one exchange number. Also known as a direct exchange.

exclusive-NOR gate. An electronic logic gate whose output is logic 0 (false) only when one of its inputs is logic 1 (true) and all the others are logic 0, otherwise the output is logic 1. It implements the logic operation of equivalence and has the same truth table. Like exclusive OR gate it can be used as simple digital comparator. Also known as equivalence gate.

exclusive-OR gate. An electronic logic gate whose output is logic 1 (true) only when one of its logic is logic 1and all others are logic 0 (false), otherwise the output is logic 0. It therefore implements the logical exclusive-OR operation and has the same truth table. Like the exclusive-NOR gate it can be used as a simple digital comparator. Also known as nonequivalence gate.

EXCP. Execute Channel Program.

EXDC. External data Controller.

.exe. File name extension for executable file, a program file that is activated when the file name is brought to the command line by the user for another program. These files should be retrieved in binary mode.

EXEC. 1. EXECutive statement. A job control character that labels the load module to be executed along with specific job steps.

2. EXECute; to carry out the operations specified by a particular instruction or routine.

execute phase. The time during a program run in which the target program is actually being executed.

execute. *See* EXEC.

execution states. The various states in which a computer system may be operating; these states have differing degrees of ability or privilege attached to them. There may be two or more states. In simplest case, there is a supervisor state and a user state. With more than two execution states at different levels, different degrees of privilege may be granted. These states can represent some of the used resources in an access matrix.

execution time. 1. The time taken by the arithmetic/logic unit to execute an instruction. This is part of the machine cycle. Also known as e-time.

2. Time needed for the execution of a particular computer program.

3. Any instant at which the execution of a particular computer program takes place.

exhaustivity. The extent to which a document is analysed to establish the subject content that has to be specified for search and indexing purposes. The greater the proportion of concepts covered the greater the exhaustivity.

exit point. The point at which the control leaves a subroutine.

exit. In programming, an instruction which upon execution, relinquishes all further control by that program.

expanded binary coded decimal interchange code. *See* EBCDIC.

expanded memory. Memory beyond the 640K limit of usable RAM in DOS, which conforms to the Lotus-Intel-Microsoft (LIM) specifications for expanded memory. This memory is available only to DOS applications that can support it. It is an older standard, which is being replaced by extended memory.

expander. In communications, a device that expands the range of amplitudes of speech signals.

expansion card. In computing, a card added to the system in order to mount additional chips or circuits so as to expand the system capability. In a microcomputer, an expansion card normally connects directly to the system bus.

expansion slot. One of the various slots in most personal computers which are connected to the mother-board and offer the ability to connect expansion cards (circuit boards) to improve the computer's capabilities. These may include a memory expansion card which provides additional random-access memory, a colour card which allows the connection of a colour monitor, or a graphics card which improves the resolution of the monitor. Each board must be placed in the expansion slot. The number of expansion devices, which may be connected is only limited to the number of expansion slots available. To overcome slot limitations, multi-function boards were designed to maximise on the capability of each slog by providing more than one function per board.

expert system. ES. 1. The computer system capable of performing at, or near, the level of human expert.
2. Any computer system developed by means of a loose collection of techniques associated with artificial intelligence research. Therefore, any computer system developed by means of an expert system building tool (even were the system to be so narrowly constrained that it could never be said to rival a human expert).
3. A computer program that performs a specialised, professional task even beyond the level of human expert. Because their functioning relies heavily on large bodies of knowledge, expert systems are sometimes known as knowledge based systems. Since they are often used to assist the human expert, they are also called intelligent assistants.

EXPIO. EXPander Input/Output.

expired password. In computer security, a password that must be changed by the user before login is completed.

exploratory data analysis. A term used to denote techniques for looking at numerical data with a view to discerning pattern. This type of analysis is open-ended and makes few prior assumptions about the nature of any pattern that may be found. Graphical techniques are frequently used.

explosion. In online information retrieval system, a technique employed in online searching whereby a search may be expanded form a particular term to include all those below it in the hierarchy.

exponent. In a floating-point representation, the numeral that denotes the power to which the implicit floating-point base is raised before being multiplied by the fixed-point part to determine the real number represented; for example, a floating-point representation of the number 0.0001234 is 0.1234-3, where 0.1234 is the fixed-point part and -3 is the exponent.

exponentiation cipher. In data security, a cipher in which the encryption/decryption processes involve raising plaintext/ciphertext messages to specified powers in modulo arithmetic.

EXR. EXecute and Repeat.

extended addressing. Any of several methods that permit access to memory with address space larger than the address space normally accessible in an instruction.

extended area service. Extension of toll-free area to include nearby exchanges in return for accepting a higher tarrif.

extended arithmetic element. EAE. A central processor element in a microprocessor that is implemented by hardware to multiply, divide and normalise functions.

extended binary coded decimal interchange code. *See* EBCDIC.

extended BNF. A notation for defining the syntax of a programming language based on BNF (Backus normal form). The main disadvantages of BNF are that the repetition has to be expressed by a recursive definition, and options and alternatives require auxiliary definitions.

Extended Industry Standard Architecture. *See* EISA.

extended memory. Any amount of memory above the base configuration of 1 Mb with which Intel 80286 and 80386 microprocessors are usually equipped. Extended memory is especially useful with OS/2, an operating system capable of taking full advantage of the benefits of extended memory. When using DOS, a memory manager must be used to break through the 640 kilobytes barrier.

extended-memory manager. On an IBM or compatible computer, a program that prevents different applications from using the same part of extended memory at the same time.

extended result output function. The function that allows the facility for displaying or printing the result of a calculation in successive operations where the number of digits in the result exceeds the output capacity of the calculator.

extensible authentication protocol. EAP. An extension to the Point-to-Point protocol; developed in response to an increasing demand for remote access user authentication that uses other security devices. It provides a standard mechanism for support of additional authentication methods within PPP. By using EAP, support for a number of authentication schemes may be added., including token cards, one-time passwords, public key authentication using smart cards, certificates, and others.

extensible language. A programming language having the property of extensibility, *i.e.*, having the capability to accept definitions of new constructs.

extension header. An optional header, following the main header in an IPv6 datagram. It may contain additional information that may not be needed in all cases.

extension. 1. The period and up to three characters at the end of a filename. An extension usually identifies the kind of information a file contains. For example, text file often have the extension .TXT. Derived from the MS-DOS operating system but the convention is often used in other operating systems to help quickly determine the file type.

2. A special file used on Macintosh computers to add extra functionality to the system; stored in the extension folder of the system folder.

exterior gateway protocol. EGP. The protocol used by a gateway in one autonomous system to advertise the IP addresses of networks in that system to a gateway in another autonomous system.

exterior router. The non-core router between autonomous networks; it maintains routing information about its own and neighbouring autonomous networks, but does not have a map of the complete inter-network. Exterior routers use the exterior Gateway Protocol, but the newer routing protocols that serve exterior routers are commonly referred to as EGPs.

external blocking. The condition in which no suitable resource connected to that switching stage, is accessible.

external data file. In data structures, a file containing data that is stored separately from the program that processes it.

external device address. *See* external device.

external device. Any device that is subsidiary or peripheral to a computer system, usually a terminal or other remote device. In some I/O instructions the designation of an external device is made by specifying a number that distinguishes that device from all others. This number is often called the external device address although, strictly speaking, it is not an address in true sense.

external fragmentation. A kind of fragmentation that arises when memory is allocated in units of arbitrary size. When a large amount of memory is released, part of it may be used to meet the subsequent request, leaving an unused part that is too small to meet any further requests.

external hard disk. A hard disk equipped with its own power supply, casing, and cables used primarily as a portable unit. Since the introduction of 'removable' hard disk cartridges capable of storing up to 44 megabytes of data, external hard disks have been losing their popularity. An internal hard disk is on housed inside a computer, operating on the computer's own power supply.

external interrupt. In computing, an interrupt not caused by an event in the instruction sequence that is interrupted; one caused by the device external to the processor.

external label. In memory systems, an identification label attached to the outside of a file medium holder.

external memory. A backing store, which is under the control of central processor but is not necessarily, connected permanently to it. It holds data in a form directly acceptable to it, to minimise access time delays.

external modem. A modem equipped with its own power supply, casing, and cables, which plugs into a computer's serial port. Many modern personal computers, especially notebook and laptop models, are being manufactured with internal modems.

external storage device. Any type of storage device that is connected to and controlled by a computer but is not integrated within it. Generally, the external storage devices are peripheral units such as tape transports or disk drives. The external storage device can be shared by more than one computer.

externally specified index. ESI. Enabling a computer system to become a central message-switching centre, for a variety of remote devices, this facility automatically routes messages to and from a main store. It achieves this without the programme sequence of the central processor unit being disturbed.

extraneous component. A usually undesired inherent effect which results from the physical nature of a component or device and, which it is the concern of engineering to minimize.

extremely-high frequency. EHF. Frequencies occurring between 30 GHz and 300 GHz, forming part of a larger continuous range of frequencies. These are considered by international agreement to be radio frequencies in band number 11 and have wavelengths between 1mm-1cm.

extremely low frequency. radio signals with frequencies below 300 Hz; used for radio telecommunications.

EXTRN. EXTeRNal reference, an indication of where to find single variable from a range, or where to find an item which is not defined in a particular computer program, segment or subroutine.

eye-legible copy. In micrographics, a microform record that contains title, or other lettering, legible to naked eye.

F

f. Symbol for focal length of a lens.

F.nnn. The F Series of CCITT Recommendations, developed by Study Group I. They describe the services provided by Administrations; these include telegraph and mobile services, telematic services, and message handling and directory services.

FA. Field Address.

fabrication. The assembly of parts into a structure.

FAC. File Access Control.

FACE. Field-Alterable Control Element.

face. In printing, the design of a particular type font.

FACOM M-190. The world's first fourth-generation large-scale computer system based on large-scale integration (LSI) semiconductor technology introduced by Fujitsu in 1974. This system featured ECL (emitter-coupled logic)-LSI with 100-gates-per-chip integration and 700-picosecond-per-gate propagation delay time. In 1977, Fujitsu introduced a medium-scale computer system TTL (transistor-transistor logic)-LSI device with an integration of 600 gates per chip. Today, All FACOM M-series models are designed to be used as the host computers in an advanced network architecture-Fujitsu Network Architecture (FNA)-that anticipates future online data processing requirements.

facsimile communications. FAXCOM. A telecom service that allows for the transmission of written, drawn or typed graphics over a direct distance-dialling network.

facsimile. FAX. A system used for electronic transmission of printed images. During operation the image is scanned by equipment at the transmitting station, transmitted and then reconstructed by the receiving station and finally duplication as hard copy on paper. Earlier facsimile systems were exclusively analog, but the recent ones employ digital techniques for data encoding and transmission.

FACT. *See* fast access current text.

factorable code. An error-correcting code that can be considered as the result of several coding stages, the output of each being encoded by the next. Constituent codes are the factors of the original compound code.

FADS. Fortran Automatic Debugging System.

FADU. File Access Data Unit, data unit carrying FTAM information about accessing a file system directory tree or sub-tree.

fail-safe. The automatic termination and protection of programs and/or processing systems when the hardware or software failure is detected in the system.

fail-soft. Denoting or relating to a computer system that can continue to provide a reduced level of service in spite of the occurrence of a single fault. The system is then said to be in a state of graceful degradation.

failure recovery. A software-aided procedure that allows the restart of a failed system in a way that either eliminates or minimises the amount of incorrect system results.

failure. A condition in which some portion of a computer system is unable to perform its prescribed function. The term fault is used as a synonym for failure but sometimes refers to the actual (physical) cause of the inability.

fake code. An English-like language used instead of flowcharting when designing a computer program. This is sometimes known as pseudo-code.

FAKS. File Access KeyS.

FAL. File Access Listener.

fallback. 1. The backup procedures to be used in the event of services or machine failure.

2. The ability of a modem to use a lower speed communications standard if connection is not possible with the standard being used.

fall-time. The time required for a logic circuit to change its output from a high level to low level.

false drop. In information retrieval, the selection of a wrong data item, usually caused by an error in the specification of the selection criteria. Also called false retrieval.

FAM. 1. Fast Access Memory.

2. File Acces Manager.

FAMOS. Floating-gate Avalanche-injection Metal-Oxide Semiconductor, a particular type of erasable programmable read only memory that erases by use of ultra-violet light and has an avalanche-transport mode. It has silicon-gate metal-oxide semiconductor field-effect transistors that have no connection to the floating gate, and memory operation depends upon charge transport effected by avalanche injection from a source or a drain.

FAN. Facility Area Network, a network which services only one specific industrial/commercial facility.

fan-in. 1. The maximum number of inputs that can be connected to a processing unit.

2. The maximum number of acceptable input lines to a logic gate or logic device.

fan-out. The maximum number of devices that can be safely driven by the output from a logic gate or logic device (which have only a limited ability to drive other devices from their output terminals). If the fan-out is exceeded the voltage levels corresponding to a logic 1 and a logic 0 become more similar and errors are more likely.

FAP. Failure Analysis Program.

FAPL. Format And Protocols Language.

FAQ. Frequently Asked Questions, a document containing answers to a set of frequently asked questions. Such information is stored in an anonymous FTP archive.

FAQS. FAst Queuing System.

FAR. File Address Register.

FARNET. Federation of American Research NETworks.

fast access current text. FACT. An electronic library system, capable of producing documentation facsimile (FAX) copies from microfiche via a telephone network.

fast core. A type of core store that has a lower access time than the device used for working store in the same processor.

fast Ethernet. 100Mbit/s technology for workstation LANs from eponymous Fast Ethernet Alliance, which includes 3Com and synoptics. It has been adopted by the IEEE as the basis for the 100BaseT Ethernet standard.

fast Fourier transform. FFT. Any realistic periodic signal can be represented as the sum of sine waves having various amplitudes and phases. This sum, although an infinite series, converges quickly. To include transients or non-periodic functions, the method for Fourier-series analysis is extended. In such a case the infinite-series becomes a continuous function expressed as an integral, known as the 'Fourier transform'. To make available a method whereby calculations can be performed by computer, the Fourier transform (an infinite series) is provided with a finite range, known as the fast Fourier transform.

fast interactive retrieval system technology. FIRST. An information retrieval technique that provides a system having the ability to allow the searching of computer files that contain particular items of data. The search is implemented under real time operator control.

fast packet switching. A WAN technology capable of transmitting data digitised voice and digitised image information. It makes use of short, fixed length packets (or cells) that are all the same size. The underlying switching technology is based on the statistical multiplexing of data and voice in fixed length cells. Any of these packets could carry digital voice, data or digital image information. All the packets travel at Level Two of the OSI Model, and routing is performed based on the Level Two addressing. Fast packet is an effective way of making best use of available bandwidth. It offers the benefits of conventional multiplexing techniques and circuit switching techniques. It is one of the transmission technologies being developed for use with B-ISDN. The switch used to route packets in a fast packet network is termed a fast packet switch. Also, fast packet technology can carry data transmissions that enter the network using a frame relay access method. For particularly high speed networking, an implementation of fast packet switching known as ATM is being commercially developed.

FastCAD. A software package published by Evolution Computing of Arizona, United States. It is a powerful CAD (computer-aided design) program with advanced drawing and editing features such as associative dimensioning. The program offers 16 line styles, 256 layers and 64 fill styles. Users can plot different drawings on a single sheet of paper with the plot assembly feature. FastCAD uses floting point numbers to represent entities (such as circles, lines, squares, and polygons) thus enabling the largest entity in a drawing to be over one million times larger than the smallest. It also includes online help, pull-down menus and a text editor for writing user-scripts and macros.

fast-recovery diode. A diode in which very little carrier storage occurs and that may therefore be used to give an ultra-high speed of operation. Fast-recovery diodes may be formed as an *p-n* junction diodes fabricated from a direct-gap semiconductor, such as gallium arsenide, in which minority-carrier lifetimes are very much smaller than in silicon.

fat zero. A significant charge packet used in charge-coupled devices that corresponds to zero input sample.

FAT. 1. *See* file allocation table.

2. An application which is compiled with code to run on two platforms, for example both the 680×0 based and PowerPC based Macs.

fault detection. Determination, normally by detection of a failure in a check, that a fault has occurred in a logic circuit, arithmetic circuit, or an information transfer.

fault threshold. A prescribed limit to the number of fault in a specified category which, if exceeded, requires appropriate action. It may be noted that the actions may include notifying the operators, running diagnostic programs, or reconfiguration to exclude a fault unit.

fault tolerance. A method of making a computer system or network resilient to faults or breakdowns to avoid lost data and downtime. System failure can occur in any element of the computer system, including hardware, software, people, and environment. For servers this involves such techniques as disk mirroring, disk duplexing or mirrored servers. For LANs and WANs it may involve the use of multiple redundant transmission links.

fault. An event in which a system operates contrary to its specifications, although this may not always be visible to users of the system.

fax server. A specialised IVR system, which sends facsimile messages to a fax machine designated by DTMF tones. What amounts to a database of fax text resides in the server that is accessed via a user's DTMF phonepad. Requests result in the fax pages being delivered to the chosen fax and the subscriber charged a fee.

FAX. A facsimile transmission.

FAX/Data modem. A modem which can handle FAX protocols and also transmit data. Some older modems can only either sends faxes or receive them; most can do both.

FAXCOM. *See* facsimile communications.

FAXEN. Two or more transmissions of or by a FAX, plural of FAX.

FB. 1. Fixed Block.

2. File Block.

FBA. Fixed Block Architecture.

FC. 1. Frame Control, a control field employed in a number of IEEE and ISO local area network protocols.

2. File Code.

3. File Conversion.

FCB. File Control Block.

FCC. 1. Frame Check Character.

2. Federal Communications Commission, government agency that regulates interstate and international telecommunication policy originating within the US.

FCG. Format Computer Graphics, prefix used to identify Computer Graphics Metafile interchange format functional profiles in the ISP taxonomy.

FCL. 1. Feedback Control Loop.

2. Format Control Language.

FCS. Frame Check Sequence, used to check the integrity of a frame in frame relay and HDLC.

FD. 1. File definition.

2. Floppy Disc.

3. File Directory.

FDB. File Data Block.

FDCS. Functionally Distributed Computing System.

FDDI. Fibre Distributed Data Interface (sometimes Digital Interface); a high-speed (100Mbps) LAN standard; specification for fibre network, *i.e.*, backbone, using three fibres (transmit, receive, and one spare) and counter-rotating token ring protocol.

Each ring carries data at a rate of 100 Mbit/s using a 125MHz transmission frequency. It has been standardised by the American National Standards Institute (ANSI). An FDDI network has two modes of attachment: a device may be single attach station, attached to one ring, or a dual attach station, attached to both rings. Typical applications of FDDI are in the area of high-speed LAN backbones.

FDEP. Formatted Data Entry Program.

FDI. Format DIrectory, prefix used to identify Directory Data Definitions interchange format functional profiles in the ISP taxonomy.

FDM. Frequency Division Multiplexing, the method of allowing several signals to operate simultaneously on a given communications channel by transmitting each with a different carrier frequency.

FDMA. Frequency Division Multiple Access.

FDOS. *See* floppy-disk operating system.

FDP. Fast Digital Processor.

FDRAM. Fount Description random Access Memory.

FDT. Formal Description Technique, formal languages developed to describe technical processes.

FDX. Full DupleX, simultaneous bi-directional telecommunications, the mode in which people tend to (fail to) communicate.

FE. 1. Format Effector.

2. Front End.

FECN. Forward Explicit Congestion Notification, bit in a frame relay header that indicates that a node is experiencing congestion.

feed. 1. To feed data or media into a system of peripheral.

2. A device for moving media, usually tape or cards, to position at which the data can be read.

feedback control loop. A method of control, employed in control systems, in which a portion of the output derived from a system is fed back to the input circuit in order to control the output signal in a desired manner.

feedback queue. A form of scheduling mechanism often used in multi-access systems. The individual processes are allocated quantum of time on the processor. A process once started is allowed to run until it has exhausted its quantum, until it initiates a transfer on the peripheral device, or until an interrupt generated by some other process occurs.

feedback register. A shift register consisting of several cells, in which the first cell has its input supplied by a combination logic function of the parallel outputs of several cells and of a possible external output.

feedback. 1. The return of part of out put of a, process, or system to the computer as input for another phase, especially for self-correcting or control purposes.

2. Transmission of current/voltage from output of a circuit or device back to the input, where it interacts with the input signal to modify operation of the device. Feedback is positive when it is in phase with the input, negative when it is out of phase.

3. To input the result at one point in a series of operations to another point; it allows a system to monitor its actions and make corrections.

feeder. A transmission line used between a transmitter and an antenna. A device for delivering materials to a processing unit.

feed-forward register. A shift register consisting of a number of cells, several parallel outputs of which are combined in a combination logic function.

FEP. Front-End Processor, a machine designed to handle communications functions for a host computer.

FERPM. FTAM Error Recovery Protocol Machine, implementation of the finite-state machine to handle error recovery in FTAM.

FEXT. Far-End CROSS(X)Talk. 1. Observation and measurement at a remote terminal in a communications system of unwanted energy transfers between one circuit and another which allow unwanted energy to travel in the same direction as the wanted signal.
2. In optical fibres, the similar condition can be experienced as in (1). Measurement is at the receiving end of a given fibre when optical power is inserted into an adjacent fibre at its transmitting end.

FF. 1. Form Feed, ASCII character 12 decimal or ^L (control L); moves the print head to the top of the next page. 2. Flip Flop.

FFM. Fast File Manager.

FFT. *See* fast Fourier transform.

FGC. Fifth Generation Computer.

FHD. Fixed-Head Disk.

FHDS. Fixed-Head Disk Storage.

FHSF. Fixed Head Storage Facility.

FI. File Interchange, application Layer file transfer.

Fibonacci search. A dichotomising search in which the number of data elements in the set is equal to a Fibonacci number or is assumed to be equal to the next higher Fibonacci number and then at each step in the search the set of elements is partitioned in accordance with the Fibonacci series. It has an advantage over the binary search in slightly reducing average movement of a sequentially accessed data medium such as a magnetic tape.

Fibre Distributed Data Interface. *See* FDDI.

fibre distribution frame. A type of optical fibre connector panel, whereby distribution and jumper cables, usually of a single fibre each, which can splice or connect optical transmitters to optical receivers, are able to be joined.

fibre optics. The activity and technology of the passive guidance of ultraviolet, visible or infra-red light through predetermined paths along transparent flexible fibres. These fibres provide a path for a single beam, of light or in multiples, such as the transportation of a complete image. The fibres are provided either singly or in a cable bundle.

fibre-optic cable. A thin strand of glass that transmits pulsating beams of light instead of electric frequencies. When one end of the strand is exposed to light, the strand carries the light to the other end, bending around corners with only a minute loss of energy along the way. It can easily carry data at more than a billion bits per second, and is immune to electromagnetic interference.

fibre-optic communications. A communication system that provides for the carrying of a signal from one point to another by the use of optical fibres or fibre optics.

fibre-optic transmission system. A system of transmission that uses small-diameter transparent fibres through which ultra-violet, visible or infrared light is passed.

FIDONET. An international network of amateur BBS (Bulletin Board System) operators who operate world-wide.

field data code. A standardized data transmission code consisting of seven data bits plus one parity bit.

field programmable logic array. FPLA. An arrangement of logic circuits in which the internal connections of the gates can be programmed by the use of a higher than normal working current, can therefore be programmed by the user. Fusible links are used for programming the logic configuration and the high current is passed through the links to achieve the required logic design.

field programmable read-only memory. A read-only memory that is programmed by fusing or burning out particular critical interconnections at specific storage locations. The programming can be completed by the customer using special equipment.

field. 1. A commutative ring containing more than one element and in which every nonzero element has an inverse with respect to the multiplication operation. Apart from their obvious relationship to arithmetic involving numbers of various kinds, fields play a very important role in discussion about the analysis of algorithms. Results in this area mention the number of operations of a particular kind, and those operations are usually related to addition and multiplication of elements of some field.

2. An item of data consisting of a number of characters, bytes, words, or codes that are treated together, *e.g.*, to form a number, a name, or an address. A number of fields make a record and the fields may be fixed in length or variable.

field-alterable control element. FACE. A chip employed in some microcomputer systems to permit the user to write micro-programs. It allows for field micro-programming in low-volume applications and each system has a writeable control store, a logic unit and a display-and-debug unit.

FIFO. *See* first-in first-out.

fifth-generation languages. The computer languages that include artificial intelligence and expert systems. These systems are intended to think and anticipate the needs of their users, instead of just to execute a set of commands.

figures shift. A function initiated by a figure shift character and performed by a teletype that causes the machine to make a physical movement to the upper case in order that numbers symbols and upper case characters can be printed.

file allocation table. A table used by DOS to locate the blocks in which it writes data to a disk. When DOS stores data on a disk, it usually breaks the data into smaller sections of data (clusters) and writes them to various places on the disk. The location of each section is recorded in a file allocation table, which keeps control of all the clusters recorded on different sectors. File storage is actually allocated on the disk (by the file system) in fixed sized areas called blocks. Normally a block is the same size as a disk sector. Files are created by finding and reserving enough unused blocks to contain the data in the file. Two file allocation methods are currently in widespread use. The first method allocates blocks (for a file) from a sequential pool of unused blocks. Thus, a file is always contained in a set of sequential blocks on the disk. As files are created, updated, and deleted, these free-block pool become fragmented (separated from one another). When this fragmentation occurs, it often becomes impossible for the file system to create a file although there is a sufficient number of free blocks on the disk. At this point, special programs must be run to 'squeeze' or compact the files, in order to re-create a single contiguous free-block pool.

file defragmentation. The rewriting of all the parts of a file on contiguous sectors (one after the other). When files on a hard disk are being updated, the information tends to be written all over the disk. This fragmentation causes delays in file retrieval. Defragmentation is the reversal of this process. Special defragmentation programs like Disk-Express and DOS Rx perform automatic defragmentation, providing up to 75% improvement in the speed of disk access and retrieval.

file fragmentation. The storage of a file in non-contiguous sections, called 'clusters'. Even though DOS stores the locations of these clusters in the file allocation table (FAT), fragmentation leads to extra movement of the read/write head and degradation in disk performance. A greater disk reading and writing efficiency (up to 50%) can be realised by using a defragmentation utility, which rewrites the files on a disk so that they are placed in contiguous clusters.

file locking. 1. In local area networking a file may be set so that only one user can access it at a time.
2. In word processing and similar applications, a file may be locked through the use of a password so the access is only available to those who know the password.

file management system. A collection of computer programs or an on-line executive program that provides management of files. They allow for the creation, deletion or retrieval of files by name from a bulk storage device.

file processing. The periodic updating of the master files to bring about the effects of current data.

file protection. A method of protecting files against unauthorised access by other users.

file separator. 1. An indicator or flag employed to show the boundary between one collection of related records treated as a whole unit (file) and another.
2. A control character employed to indicate or flag the boundaries of a group of contiguous locations (or columns on a card) which contain a particular item of data or a group of related pieces of information.

file server. A computer attached to a LAN that runs a network operating system. This lets the file server regulate communications among the workstations connected to it across the LAN, and to manage shared resources available on the file server, such as hard disk storage and printers. A file server may be dedicated: the computer is used only as a file server; or non- dedicated: the underlying computer that the LAN network operating systems runs on is used for another task simultaneously, for example as a workstation.

file sharing. Provisions in the networking software, which allows more than one user to access the same file.

file transfer protocol. FTP. Permitting transfer between different computers, file transfer protocol is a formalisation of the methods by which the two parties communicate.

file transfer. The transfer of a file from one computer to another in a network; the data may be moved either by opening a network connection directly to the destination, or by passing the data together with control information to a message-switching file transfer relay.

file updating. Incorporating changes to the data in a file without altering its structure or significance. This is one of the most fundamental operations in data processing.

file. A program, document, utility-anything that is not hardware on a computer. A file might contain a memo, a drawing done in a graphics application or a program itself.

fill character. Another name for ignore character.

FILO. First In Last Out.

filter. A database management (DBMS) feature for displaying and browsing a selected list or subset of records from a table. The visible records satisfy a condition that a user sets. It is called filter because it tells the DBMS to display those records that satisfy the condition, while hiding or filtering out, those that do not.

FIMS. *See* functionally-identifiable maintenance systems.

FIN. A control flag used in the process of closing a TCP connection.

final selector. A telecommunications switching unit that has one inlet and provides direct access to a number of subscribers' lines via its outlets. Operation can be by external or internal controls.

final signal unit. A group of information and check binary digits, normally subject to a single error detecting process, that are used in the common-channel signalling or multi-unit messages. The International Telegraph and Telephone Consultative Committee (CCITT) have designated a signal unit system No.6 which consists of 28 bits, the last being used for error-detection purposes.

finder. An essential component of the Macintosh system software. The Finder provides the interface to the Macintosh. It is the program that is running when you start the Macintosh, which allows you to view, lists of and manipulates files.

FINGER. A program that displays information about a particular user (or all users) logged on to the local system or on a remote system. It typically shows full name, last login time, idle time, and terminal location.

FIO. Field Input/Output.

FIPS. Federal Information Processing Standard, a standard created for the US government.

FIR. File Indirect Register.

firewall. A hardware device that protects a network from unauthorised Internet accesses. It runs on the computer where the private network connects to public networks (such as Internet). Such programs are used to protect internal computers from access or attack by external computers. The firewall limits access to authorised users and systems by filtering packets as they come in based on the source or destination address, as well as an application's TCP/IP port.

firmware. In memory systems, a program or data that has been permanently stored in the computer memory (*i.e.*, ROM, PROM, EROM, or EPROM). This method of implementing software contrasts with programs held on magnetic media, that must first be loaded into the RAM memory of the computer before they can be used.

first fit. A method of selecting a contiguous area of memory that is to be allocated for a segment. The free-space list is scanned in order of starting address, and the allocation made from the first free area whose size exceeds that of the request.

first normal form. In databases, a property of a relation, in a relational database. A relation is in first normal form if it does not have any repeating groups, that is, the data can be expressed in the form of a flat file.

first read rate. FRR. The mode of operation of a bar code scanner, which translates codes on the first pass. The scanner is known as a 'first read rate' scanner.

first silicon. Electronic chips developed from the first masks; mainly used for testing and debugging.

FIRST. *See* fast interactive retrieval system technology.

first-generation. Refers to the vacuum-tube computer technology employed commercially between 1951-1958. The first-generation era started with the introduction of UNIVAC I, which was originally built for the US Bureau of Census for tabulating the 1950 census. Its inventors, John Presper Eckert and John Mauchly, started their own company which was later taken oven by Remington-Rand (later known as Sperry Corporation, and today called Unisys Corporation). They produced general-purpose electronic computers for businesses that needed to automate their payroll processing and other labour-intensive transaction processing applications.

first-in first-out. FIFO. In memories, tables, stacks or lists, a method of storing and retrieving data or items. Information is deposited at one end, and removed from the other, enabling the oldest entry to be retrieved first.

FIT. File Inquiry Technique.

FIX. Federal Internet Exchange, A connection point between the US governmental-based Internets and the Internet.

fixed data. 1. The data, text, or format instructions entered initially and available for subsequent reuse in documents.

2. The data that is written on the display screen of a visual display unit but cannot be altered by the user.

fixed disk. *See* hard disk.

fixed head disk. In memory systems, a read/write head that cannot be moved relative to the centre of the disk. A large number of these heads are usually incorporated into an assembly so that there is a head per track, and such drives may be referred to by this expression. The advantage of a fixed head is that the average access time is reduced to the time for half a revolution since there is no track seek time required. Some drives have both fixed and moveable heads.

fixed radix system. A radix numeration system, in which the entire digit places, except perhaps the one with the highest weight, has the same radix. 1. The weights of successive digit places are successive integral powers of a single radix, each multiplied by the same factor. Negative integral powers of the radix are used in the representation of fractions.

2. A fixed radix numeration system is a particular case of a mixed radix numeration system.

fixed routing. A method of routing messages in data communications, in which the behaviour of the network is predetermined, taking no account of changes in traffic or network components.

fixed-length code. The code in which a fixed number of source symbols are encoded into fixed number of output signals. It is usually a block code.

fixed-length record. A record that always has the same length as all other records, with which it is logically or physically associated.

fixed-point notation. A representation of real numbers in which the positions of the radix point is fixed. The position of the point determines the absolute precision of the representation. If the point is fixed at the right-hand end of the number then all the fixed-point numbers are integers.

fixed-width font. A font in which all characters has uniform widths, such as Courier. Contrast with proportional font. Also known as mono-spaced font.

FL. Fault Allocation.

FL/1. Function Language one.

flag. 1. A variable whose value indicates the attainment of some designated state or condition by an item of equipment or a program. The flag is subsequently used as a basis for conditional branching and similar decision processes.
2. In desktop publications, the designed title of the publication as it appears in the beginning at page one.
3. In computing, a signal set up to indicate that a specific condition has occurred, when the buffer is full.

flagging. In video recording, the television picture distortion caused by incorrect video tape playback head-timing coordination.

flash card. In micrographics, a document introduced during the recording of a microfilm to facilitate its indexing.

flexible algebraic scientific translator. Device enabling a user to writer a computer program in an algebraic format by translating complex statements into Beginner's All-purpose Symbolic Instruction Code (BASIC).

flexible manufacturing system. Controlled by numerical control machines linked into computer numerical control system, an flexible manufacturing system makes use of robot-controlled transport of production work between machine stations.

FLIP. Floating Point Interpretive Program.

flip-chip. A thick semiconductor chip with extended bonded pads, enabling it to be flipped over and mounted upside down on a suitable substrate, such as a thin-film circuit.

flip-flop. A combination of two inter-connected active devices (*i.e.*, bi-stable) or two inter-connected logic gates. As long as power is available an flip-flop circuit can be used to store one binary digit of information permanently.

flipover. An optical effect in television in which the picture appears to turn from left to right, or vice versa, to reveal a picture on the reverse side.

flippy floppy. A floppy disk that can be flipped over so that a single-sided drive can read either side.

floating point base. In a floating point representation system, the implicit fixed positive integer base, greater than unity, that is raised to the power explicitly denoted by the exponent or represented by the characteristic and then multiplied by the mantissa to determine the real number represented. Example: In the example of entry 'floating point representation' the implicit floating point base is 10.

floating point package. FPP. A set of computer software routines that are necessary to perform floating point arithmetic.

floating point unit. FPU. A coprocessor that provides hardware routines for mathematical function, to be used with a CPU that does not have those functions built in. The 680x0 and 80x86 line of CPU chips had FPU chips available. Current CPUs (such as the PowerPC and Pentium chips) incorporate floating-point functions and do not need a separate FPU.

floating point. A notation to represent decimal numbers that is employed to help simplify arithmetic calculations by moving the decimal or binary point from left to right. For example, 234,000,000 can be shown as 2.34,8 as it is equal to 2.34×10^8.

floating probe. A test electrode (wire or plate) inserted in a discharge tube at a desired point to sample the potential gradient, but which acquires a misleading negative charge with respect to the gas cloud, because electrons (travelling faster than the positive ions) tend to accumulate on the probe.

floating-carrier modulation. A type of amplitude modulation in which amplitude of the carrier wave does not remain constant but is automatically varied in a manner dependent upon the amplitude of the modulating wave, which is averaged over a short time period. The modulation factor therefore remains almost constant. Also known as controlled-carrier modulation.

flooding. A routing method in data communications in which each node replicates incoming packets and sends copies to its neighbours, thus ensuring that the actual destination is reached in least time.

floppy disk. A mass-storage device employing a soft flexible (floppy) diskette coated with magnetic material onto which information is recorded. The disk(ette) is driven so that is rotates inside a cardboard jacket and cut-outs are provided for a moving head and index hole information. Currently, floppy disks are generally 3.5" wide. The protective covering on 3.5" disks is hard plastics. The media inside is the same floppy material as that inside the older 5.25" disks. Floppy disks also come in different densities and care must be taken to use a disk of appropriate density. Floppy disks are noted for their relatively slow speed, small capacity, and low price.

floppy-disk controller. Controls the transfer of data to and from a floppy disk. Floppy-disk controllers can interface both single-density and double-density disk drives and are able to interface up to four double-density drives. High-performance disk controllers can feature automatic seek, read and write operations, select lines for multiple heads, programmable loading and unloading of heads, control lines for phase-locked loops generally required for disk-drive circuitry and operate on a 5 volts power supply unit.

floppy-disk operating system. FDOS. 1. An operating system that has been developed to permit source programs written and edited at the system keyboard, to be stored on floppy disks. The assembled programs are stored on the disk in binary form. A typical FDOS package can consist of dual drive floppy disk, interface, software, documentation and cable. 2. A combination of areas in the memory map of microcomputer using a control program for microcomputers disk operating system. The areas are the basic input/output system and the basic disk-operating system.

FLOTOX. A colloquial expression for FLOating gate Tunnel OXide. A principle employed in electrically-erasable programmable read-only memories in which electrons tunnel to and from a floating gate.

flow control. The procedures for controlling the rate of transfer of data between two points in data network, such as between a protocol converter and a printer. This avoids data loss when a recipient device's buffer is full. Buffers play an essential role in overall flow control in a network.

flowchart symbol. A symbol used to represent operations, data, flow direction, or equipment in a flowchart.

flowchart. A set of diagrams outlining the logical flow of a computer program using a standard set of block-shapes to represent different operations. ANSI symbols have been universally accepted as the standard set of flowchart symbols. For example, a diamond represents a 'decision' and a rectangle represents a 'process'. Readily available templates are used as drawing aids. A graphical representation in which symbols are used to represent such things as operations, data, flow and equipment, for the definition, analysis, or solution of a problem.

flowline. A line representing a connecting path between the symbols in a flowchart to indicate a transfer of data or control.

fluid logic. A means of implementing logic functions, not by normal use of electronic circuitry but by the flow of incompressible fluids through tubing containing intersections and constrictions. The logic gates so formed are useful in situations in which high electromagnetic interference prevents the use of electronic components. Also known as pneumatic logic.

FM. 1. The functions that allow detection, isolation, and correction of abnormal operations of the network.
2. Frequency Modulation, varying the frequency of an alternating current (sine wave) carrier signal to convey information.

FML. File Manipulation Language.

FMLF. File Management Loading Facility.

FMPS. Functional Mathematical Programming System.

FMVFT. Frequency-Modulated Voice Frequency Telegraph.

FN. 1. FiNish Session PDU, used to request an orderly release of a session connection.
2. Forwarded Notification, a type of EDI notification that says an EDI message was forwarded to another recipient.
3. Functional Network.

FNC. Federal Networking Council, US, the body responsible for coordinating networking needs among federal government agencies, especially those networks using TCP/IP and the Internet.

FNP. Front End Network Processor.

FO. Fibre Optics, a medium that can carry high data speeds.

focal point. An IBM Network management term; it consolidates the functions needed to manage centrally all parts of a network. It provides an end-to-end network view and receives information from entry points and service points. NetView is IBM's key implementation of the focal point.

FOCAL. Formula CALculator.

FOD. Format Office Document, prefix used to identify Office Document interchange format functional profiles in the ISP taxonomy.

FOIL. File Oriented Interpretive Language.

folder. A graphical representation of a directory or subdirectory. On the Macintosh and some other graphical user interfaces (GUIs). Folders contain files and other folders.

FOM. Fibre Optic Modem.

font cartridge. A font contained in a cartridge that physically plugs into your printer. Font cartridges are used by laser printers such as those in the HP LaserJet family, but some dot-matrix printers also use font cartridges. Unlike down-loadable fonts, a ROM cartridge does not use random-access memory, which is volatile (lost when the power is switched off).

font family. A group designation that describes the general look of a font. For example, the Roman font family contains proportionately spaced fonts with serifs.

font size. *See* point size.

font. A set of letters, numbers, punctuation marks, and symbols that are a given size and design. Some fonts can be scaled to any size while others are a fixed size. Outline fonts, TrueType fonts and PostScript fonts are examples of scaleable fonts.

footer. Text that appears at the bottom of document pages when they are printed. Compare with header.

forbidden combination. A combination of bits that is not valid according to the criteria set by the programmer or system designer.

forced release. A facility in a telecommunications system that enables a traffic carrying device or circuit to be released arbitrarily, quite independently of any release action taken by the caller or the called party.

foreground. The area of the Screen that the active window occupies. Contrast with background.

FOREM. File Organisation Evaluation Model.

forgiving system. A software package designed in such a manner so that the mistakes made by the users can be easily corrected.

form feed. 1. A control character that provides regulation of the demands of a printer to feed forms.

2. A mechanical form-positioning system on printing device that automatically locates and positions continuous stationery.

form. A document in which certain items have been pre-coded and against which variable information is entered into the computer system.

formal language. In programming, a language defining the set of symbols, alphabets, and set of strings of those symbols. The significance of formal language in programming is that a given program may be considered as a string of the formal language.

formal logic. The study of the structure and forms of valid argument without regard to the meaning of the terms in the argument.

formal semantics language. A language used for computer-orientated languages that is employed as machine-independent language. It intergenerates compilers for specific machine and contains formal semantics.

format effector. A specific control character used for the control of the layout or position (format) of printed or displayed information.

format. 1. Preparing a disk for use by your hardware and operating system. Also called Initialising. 'Format a:' is a user-command that instruct the computer to initialise the disk in drive 'A' by placing magnetic patterns called tracks (each track is divided into nine sectors which can each store 512 bytes). Double-sided, double-density disks are formatted to contain 40 tracks with 360 sectors on each side. Formatting a disk may take up to five minutes. Some diskettes can be purchased already formatted.

2. Formatting also refers to the way text is set up on a page (underlining, bold, indenting, etc. In word processing, graphics, spreadsheets, and database programs, the way in which data is arranged within the application, including margins, indents, fonts, and tabs.

3. Formatting, The initialisation of a data medium such that a particular computer system can store data in and subsequently retrieve data from the medium.

4. In data structures, the defined structure of the pattern of information that is recorded in a computer system. It involves the predetermined mandatory order, organisation or position of symbols in a computer

instruction, data or word, data transmission message etc.

formatted dump. In computing, a dump in which certain data areas are isolated and identified.

formatting. An operation that initialises blank disks; initiating data is written so that tracks are divided into sectors; no file can be written to the disk until formatting has been performed.

forms-capable browser. WWW browser that allows the users to fill in the blanks, in questionnaires and other user response items. Most GUI browsers are form-capable.

FORTRAN assembly program. A procedurally orientated formula translator computer software system.

FORTRAN. FORmula TRANslator, computer-programming language originally conceived by International Business Machines and developed for scientific analysis and mathematical problems; widely used language in scientific environments; also used for commercial/business applications.

forwarding. Passing e-mail from one mailbox to another, particularly when the user is not reading mail regularly on the first system.

FOSDIC. Acronym for Film Optical Sensing Device for Input to Computers. A device to enable a computer memory to receive information from a microfilm storage medium.

fourth-generation languages. The special purpose programming languages that are easier to use than the third-generation languages. With these languages, programmer can create applications rapidly.

fourth-generation. Refers to the general present-day technology used in computers. This generation was originally introduced in the 1970s and offers, at lower-cost, increased performance through solid-state circuits, miniaturised microprocessors, and advanced integrated circuits. The computer revolution can be traced back to 1969 when Intel Corporation, then a small Californian company, commissioned Marcian E. Hoff to develop a general-purpose logic chip. It was called the Intel 4004 and dubbed the first microprocessor. It was built to enhance the capabilities of ordinary calculators. By 1971, when the fourth generation became evident, Altair 8800 was produced to become the world's first commercially available microprocessor. The small group formed Micro Instrumentation and Telemetry Systems (MITS) and later hired Bill Gates, a Harvard student, to install the BASIC programming language on the 8800. Later in the 1970s, Apple Computer was born, and Stephen Wozniak and Steven Jobs offered their first computer in kit form. Later models (Apple II) were pre-assembled. VisiCalc was launched in 1978, and adopted by Apple as a business spreadsheet package which gave rise to functional business computing.

In 1981, IBM introduced their microcomputer called the IBM Personal Computer. The fourth-generation became characterised by micro-miniaturization with silicon chips smaller than a shirt button containing over a million circuits. Use of metal oxide semiconductor (MOS) internal memory, and improvements in software, saw over 100 firms manufacture computer system units. Companies like Compaq and Apple have specialized in microcomputers, while Digital Equipment Corporation and Data General have focused on minicomputers. Third-generation programming languages like BASIC and FORTRAN gave way to fourth-generation programming languages, enabling executives to access the information they needed through decision support system (DSS), without having to rely too heavily on management information systems personnel. Today, computing is still growing at a very fast rate. The development of very-large scale integration (VLSI) seems inadequate when compared to ultra-large-scale integration (ULSI) offering billions of circuits. The development of technology, which is called 'fifth-generation', is now available.

FOX. Field Operational X.500, a project funded by U.S. DARPA to provide X.500 DIrectory services in the NREN/ Internet.

FP. Functional Profile, a statement defining a group of standards, options, and parameters to accomplish one or more specified functions.

FPAD. Facsimile PAD, PAD for transmission of FAX protocol messaging.

FPF. Facility Parameter Field.

FPLA. *See* field programmable logic array.

FPP. *See* floating point package.

FPU. *See* floating point unit.

FQDN. The name generating by concatenating a host name with a domain name by the addition of a dot character.

FR. Frame Relay, a high-speed simple protocol for delivering variable length message segments from source to destination. Uses bandwidth on demand, and is suitable for image data.

fractional services. Bandwidth available from carriers in increments of 64Kbit/s.

fragment. A piece of packet; when a computer is forwarding an IP packet to a network that has a maximum packet size smaller than the packet being forwarded, it is forced to breakup the packet in to multiple fragments.

fragmentation. The creation of many small areas of memory, which arises, as memory is allocated to and then, released by processes. The portions of unallocated memory tend to become so small that they fail to satisfy any request and so remain unused.

frame of reference. A set of reference axis for defining the position of a point or body in space. A frame of reference in the four-dimensional continum consists of an observer, a coordinate system, and a clock to correlate positions with times.

frame relay. A data communications interface originating from ISDN designed to provide high speed frame or packet transmission with minimum delay and efficient use of bandwidth. It is a variation on the X.25 interface and form of fast packet switching. It derives its name from using the Data Link or 'frame' OSI layer Two to route or 'relay' a packet directly to its destination instead of terminating the packet at each switching node. This eliminates processing overheads and increases throughput speed. Based on the ITU-TS Lap-D standard, it uses variable-length packets and applicable only to sub-broadband, T3/E3 or lower, data transmission. Like Ethernet, or token ring, frame relay assumes that connections are reliable. It does not have error detection and error control within the network, which helps to speed up the protocol. When errors occur frame relay relies on higher level protocols for error control. Frame relay is often viewed as a replacement for X.25, primarily for LAN-to-LAN busy traffic. Voice over frame relay is available, but the subject of debate. It will also become an access method for ATM-based WANs.

frame. The data package created at the network access layer according to the specifications of the physical network. It refers to a group of bits sent over a link; contains the header and trailer information required by the physical medium. A frame may contain control and addressing information, as well as error detection, for example CRC information, and the forward error correction information. The size and composition of frame varies according to the protocol; often used synonymously with packet.

frame-capable browser. WWW browser that allows the independent display of multiple resources on the same Web page.

framing. In a local area network, a data packet which 'encloses' raw data and tells the network equipment of the data's origin, its intended recipient and other important control information. Each networking system has different protocols for framing messages. Ethernet, for example, uses a frame composed of multiple 'fields' which contain such information as the preamble (used for hardware synchronisation), addressing information, message data, and a cyclic redundancy check (used to make sure the frame was correctly received).

Freenet. A community-based bulletin board system with e-mail, information services, notice board, interpretative communications, conferencing, and many other similar functions.

freeware. Software that is provided without charge.

F-region. The second lowest of principal regions of the ionosphere, with an altitudes at night of approximately 300 km. In daytime, the region is divided into the lower F1 region and higher F2 region. Also called F-layer.

fremodyne detector. An FM detector which is essentially a conventional AM circuit detuned to one side of resonance (slope-tuned) to demodulate a frequency-modulated signal.

frequency-division multiple access. FDMA. A technique enabling communicating devices at various different location to share a multi-point or broadcast channel. It allocates a different frequency to each user.

frequency-division multiplexing. FDM. A method of multiplexing in which more than one signal is transmitted on a channel by dividing the available transmission frequency into narrower bands. A number of separate single channels are thus derived from splitting up a wider bandwidth into several narrower bandwidths.

frequency-shift keying. A form of frequency modulation where the frequency is made to vary without interrupting the carrier at the instant limiting intervals of modulation (*i.e.*, the significant conditions of the modulating digital signal), between a set of predetermined discrete values called the 'mark' and the 'space' frequencies. Generally, frequency-shift keying is used in telecommunications for lower speed devices such as teleprinters.

frequency-shift pulsing. A technique of signalling, used in telecommunications, which makes use of a frequency shift between 1070 Hz and 1270 Hz. This particular type of signalling is used with narrow-band systems, such as teletypewriter switching networks.

FRICC. Federal Research Internet Coordinating Committee, U.S., replaced by FNC.

FRMR. Frame Reject, HDLC/LAPD frame.

front-end. The client part of a client/server application that requests services across a network from a server, or back end. It typically provides an interactive interface to the user, for example, a data entry front end, allowing data to be entered into a server by SQL.

front-end processing. The transformation of information prior to processing information.

front-end processor. FEP. A programmed-logic or stored-program device that interfaces data communication equipment, data processing systems, or other pieces of major equipment with an input-output bus or storage device and a data processing computer. The interface between a mainframe computer and the outside world. It is normally used to remove some of the necessary processing load from the computer.

front-to-back ratio. In communication systems, a ratio of parameters that is used in connection with antennas, rectifiers, or other devices, in which signal strength, resistance, or another parameter in one direction of the transmission or electric current flow is compared with that in the opposite direction.

FRR. *See* first read rate.

FS. Functional Standard, a profile that may specify requirements for more than one protocol layer.

FSCB. File System Control Block.

FSCR. Field Select Command Register.

FSG. Format SGML, prefix used to identify SGML interchange format functional profiles in the ISP taxonomy.

FSK. Frequency Shift Keying, a technique for modulating data that use two frequencies. Frequency shifts between two frequencies are generated when binary digital level changes. So one particular frequency is used to represent binary one, and second frequency is used to indicate a binary zero. FSK is used in low speed modems when, in full-duplex transmission, two different frequencies are used in each direction, resulting in four different frequencies being used.

FSL. Formal Semantic Language.

FSM. Finite-State Machine, a method of describing a process by defining the states and what input will cause a transition to a new state, often used in describing the Protocol Machine for OSI standards.

FSOS. Free-Standing Operating System.

FSP. Frequency Shift Pulsing.

FSR. File Storage Region.

FST. File Status Table.

FTAM. File Transfer Access and Management, ISO 8671 standard which plays a key role in integrated message handling as the vehicle for interchanges of EDI information between applications. FTAM controls the transfer of whole files or parts of files between end systems. FTAM defines a virtual filestore in order to avoid dealing with the internal file structure of the end system. Local formats are converted into the virtual filestore format for transfer purposes. One end system initiates the file transfer or access, while the other end acts as a responder and provides access to the file and management of the virtual filestore. Different document types may be supported as well as different types of file transfer and file access. FTAM profiles have been written for simple, positional, and full file transfer and simple and full file access; there is also a profile for management. ISO 8571 is a four-part standard containing a general introduction, definition of the virtual filestore, the file service definition, and definition of the file protocol. FTAM was one of the first OSI applications to make full use of Association Control Service Elements (ACSE) and the Presentation Layer.

FTF. 1. Face to Face; refers to a meeting where all participants are in the same location at the same time, as opposed to communications by electronic means, such as teleconferencing or computer-based conferencing.
2. Fault Transfer facility.

ftp. A command used to start the FTP client program. It may be entered as such, or is followed by IP address or domain name.

FTP. File Transfer Protocol, the TCP/IP standard, high-level protocol for transferring files from one computer to another; usually implemented as applications level programs, FTP uses Telnet and TCP protocols. It can also create and remove directories and display contents of directories. The user runs an FTP program on one computer while other computer runs an FTP server program such as FTP daemon, on UNIX box, or an FTP service on other platforms. Most FTP client programs are command-line based, but the graphical versions are also in use. Most FTP client implementations allow entering either UNIX-based commands or DOS-based commands. Actual command available depends on the client software being used. Anonymous FTP servers allow users to login without password, specifying "guest" as the user, and then copy whatever is available.

FU. Functional Unit, in protocols like Session and the above layers, the capabilities that are negotiated during connection establishment.

full duplex. 1. A channel capable of transmitting in both directions at the same time.
2. The property of a communication system or any equipment, to communicate simultaneously in two directions; *i.e.*, each of its ends can simultaneously transmit and receive.

fully associative cache. A cache architecture in which each item of information from main system memory is stored as a unique cache entry. For a given cache size, a fully associative cache is the highest performance cache architecture. There is no relationship between the location of the information in the data cache RAM (random-access memory) and its original location in main system memory.

fully-automated cataloguing technique. A library system that combines computer control of documents, along with storage on microfilm and a computer output microfilm facility.

fully-automatic information retrieval system. A retrieval system that provides automatic searching of computer files containing information, in response to the definition of a particular user's needs.

fully-connected network. A network in which each node is directly connected to every other node. Thus, each node is connected to $n-1$ branches where n is the number of nodes in the network. The number of branches is given by $n(n-1)/2$.

function code. 1. A code indicating the types of process to be applied.
2. The codes that control the typesetting as distinct from those that produce characters.

function control. The control of an operation to be performed by a system, such data recording or data processing device.

function generator. 1. A signal generator whose output is any of several selectable waveforms (*e.g.*, sine, square, triangular, step-pulse) and frequencies (or repetition rates).
2. An analog computer circuit that produces a variable based on a mathematical function and one or more input variables.

function key. In peripherals such as keyboard, a key (such as SHIFT, ENTER or SEND) that result in actions such as line feed. In communications, function keys may cause the transmission of signal not associated with a printable or displayable character. On a standard personal computer keyboard, the function keys are usually marked F1 through F12.

function signal. A set of signal elements that is used to transmit or represent a function-control character that actuates a control function, such as carriage return, line-feed, letters shift, or figures shift.

function. A kind of subroutine, that enables the programmers to define higher-level operations.

functional description. The actual behaviour of the imlementation of functional requirements of the system in terms of internal structure and logic processes within the system.

functional languages. A class of programming languages and a subclass of declarative languages that is based on lambda calculus.

functional profile. A defined stack of ISO OSI Layer elements, such as GOSIP, maps or top. Functional profiles were developed in order to ensure that, when defined, ISO OSI stacks could inter-operate. Due to the different protocol elements at each OSI layer, it was possible to define stacks that were syntactically correct, but would not be able to exchange information due to differences at particular layers. A functional profile that has been defined as a standard is a standardised

functional signalling link. A communication link together with its transmission-control functions and other associated controls.

functional unit. Any hardware, software, or firmware that has a specific purpose or is capable of performing a specific function, such as data processing system, computer program, or fiberscope.

functionally-identifiable maintenance systems. FIMS. A system of block diagrams organised in such a manner that it can direct non-technical personnel to a replaceable unit. The unit can range from a computer to a printed circuit board, or to a simple repairable circuit.

fuzzy set. A set in which membership can be expressed as a continuum of values between 0 and 1. A value of 1 corresponds to definite membership, a value of 0 corresponds to definite non-membership.

fuzzy theory. A branch of logic designed specifically for representing knowledge and human reasoning in such a way that it is amenable to processing by computer. Thus, fuzzy theory is applicable to expert systems, knowledge engineering, and artificial intelligence.

G

4GL. 4th Generation Language; characterised by an integrated, visual design environment and the use of parameters and connections between pre-built objects to build applications without the use of grammatical constructs. By definition, a 4GL is human readable language only through examining the objects and their parameters, and does not simply produce text editable code. Oracle Forms and Oracle Reports are 4GL languages.

G. Giga, one thousand million; 10^9.

G.nnn. The G Series of CCITT Recommendations dealing with characteristics of communications media, for example, coaxial cable, wave-guides, satellite services, FDM, PCM, etc.

G3, G4. Two commonly used standards for facsimile communications.

GAB. Graphic Adapter Board.

gain. 1. The measure of the ability of an electronic circuit, device, or set-up to increase the magnitude of a given electrical input parameter. It is generally measured in decibels.

2. The ratio of output power of an amplifier system to the input power.

gain compression. Small reduction in repeater gain under load conditions; it is significant in systems with a large number of repeaters in tandem.

gain hits. The short duration surges in power, that cause errors in data transmission. Generally, a gain hit is a surge of more than 3 dB.

GAL. Generic Array Logic.

galioping pattern memory. A microprocessor test technique for generating successive patterns.

gallium arsenide devices. Semiconductor integrated-circuit devices that are implemented using gallium arsenide as the intrinsic semiconductor material in preference to, say, silicon. Gallium arsenide has certain advantages over other semiconductor materials, in particular in the fabrication of optical and optically complex devices such as light-emitting diodes and opto-isolators.

gallium arsenide. GaAs. A direct-gap 3-5 semiconductor material that can be used for high-speed applications. It has a relatively large band gap and high carrier mobility. It is difficult to work with since diffusion of impurities into the material is a tough task. Epitaxy or ion implantation must therefore be employed to produce areas of different conductivity type. Its main uses have been for microwave devices, but lately it has been employed for metal semiconductor field-effect transistors (MESFETs) used in high-speed logic circuits.

game theory. A method of analysing situations in which competitive participants are each seeking to make decisions to maximise their own gains at the expense of other participants.

gamma match. A linear transformer for matching a coaxial feeder to a half-wave antenna. The outer conductor of the cable is connected to the centre of the radiator, and an extension of the centre conductor runs for a short distance parallel to the radiator, making a right-angle bend before connecting to the radiator. In this way, a short section of impedance-matching transmission line is formed by the extension of the centre conductor and the portion of the radiator that is parallel to it. This arrangement takes its name from its resemblance to a capital gamma (Greek letter) lying on its side.

gamut. In graphics, the range of colours that can be displayed on a given monitor.

GAN. Global Area Network, a network which covers a planet; although meant to indicate many nodes, technically one node in each hemisphere constitutes a GAN.

gap loss. In memory systems, the loss of signal from a magnetic disk reading head when it is not directly in line with the information that has been recorded.

gap. 1. On a magnetic tape, any gap between groups of signals recorded on magnetic tape, but usually the inter-block gap.

2. In memory systems, the space between the read or write head and the recording media.

3. An air gap in a magnetic circuit that increases the inductance and saturation point.

4. The space between the electrodes in an electron tube.

GAP. *See* general assembly program.

garbage. 1. Information in a memory that is no longer valid or wanted. It is usually the result of memory compaction operations. The removal of this superfluous information from the memory is known as garbage collection and is usually associated with memory compaction.

2. In television and video, the interference of audio and/or video signals on adjacent frequency bands.

3. Radio frequency spill-over interference onto adjacent frequency bands.

GAT. Generalised Algebraic Translator.

GATE. Generalised Algebraic Translator Extended.

gate array chip. A computer chip made for general use, yet it can be customised to specifications by adding a final interconnecting layer at the end of its manufacturing process.

gate. 1. A device or circuit with one output channel and one or more input channels, such that the output channel state is completely determined by the input channel states expect during switching transients.

2. A combinational logic element having at least one input channel.

3. The input(control) electrode of a field-effect transistor or thyristor device.

4. A signal that triggers the passage of other signals through a circuit.

gateway exchange. A telephone exchange that allows the connection of international exchanges with a national network.

gateway property sheet. The property sheet that allows to add IP addresses for a gateway by entering the IP addresses and choosing the add button. One can enter multiple IP addresses for multiple gateways; the first IP address is considered the default gateway.

gateway software. In online information retrieval, the software that acts as an interface between end users and online databases. It offers automatic dialling and logon, offline search formulation, downloading and may allow text or data processing.

gateway. A network connectivity device (router) that connects a local area network (LAN) to larger area network. This term is sometimes also used for a router, which performs same kind of protocol conversion. A gateway supports a full stack of the relevant protocol, such as SNA, DecNet, ISO, TCP/IP, and can covert to a non-seven-layer protocol, such as async or BSC. It is typically used to provide access to wide area networks over asynchronous or X.25 links from a LAN environment. Examples include pads and protocol converters. Gateway transfers information between physically separate networks that are based on differing protocols (e.g.,, between Internet and AppleTalk networks). It performs high-level information translation, while routers provide low-level.

Gateway-to-Gateway Protocol. *See* GGP.

GB. 1. Gigabit; 10^9 bits.
2. Gigabytes; 10^9 bytes.

Gbps. Gigabits per second; an information transfer or signalling rate of 10^9 binary digits per second.

GBT. Generalised Burst Trapping.

GCH. Giga CHaracters.

GCI. Graphic Command Interpreter, provides plotting function on computers.

GDB. Global DataBase.

GDDL. Graphical Data Definition Language.

GDF. Group Distribution Frame.

GDM. Global Data Manager.

GDMO. Guidelines for the Definition of Managed Objects, part of the SMI of OSI Management that specifies how managed objects shall be defined and what notational tools shall be used.

GDMS. Generalised Data Management System.

GDS. 1. Graphics Data Syntax, OSI, refers to facsimile transmission standards such as CCITT G4.
2. Graphic Data System.
3. Graphic Design System.

GDSF. Generalised Data Structure definition Facility.

GDT. *See* graphic display terminal.

GE. Gateway Exchange.

GEL. General Emulation Language.

general assembly program. GAP. Allows programs to be written in symbolic code rather than in the absolute machine language of a computer.

general organisational environment. An organised collection of techniques and procedures for operating a computer, which resides on a disk, employed with ICL computers.

generalised information-retrieval language. GIRL. A computer language employed in the searching of stores of data held on computer files. It has been developed by the US defence Nuclear Agency.

general-purpose computer. A generic term for computers that can be used for a number of purposes, rather than dedicated to a specific function or functions.

general-purpose interface adaptor. Able to interface between an IEEE-488 standard instrument bus and a microprocessor unit, the general-purpose interface adaptor enables many instruments to be interconnected and thus remotely automatically controlled or programmed.

general-purpose interface bus. 1. In computing, a bus widely used to

facilitate the connection between a computer and the wide range of peripheral devices.
2. A bus that connects instruments, including the connectors, the signal lines and the voltage level on lines, the functions used by the instruments interfaces to exchange data control messages and protocols. The mechanical specification defines the cable and connectors, the electrical specification defines the voltages, and current values required being compatible with transistor logic.

general-purpose scientific document writer. The software capable or producing complex hard copies for scientific use, this computer output; the device can deal with mathematics and graphics.

general-purpose simulation program. A high-level computer programming language. Each natural language instruction corresponds to a number of machine code instructions. It permits the use of notations with which the user is already familiar.

general-purpose. Pertaining to a system that can be applied to a variety of tasks without essential modification.

general register. An internal addressible register in a central processing unit, that can be used for temporary storage.

generator. 1. In programming, a program that creates other programs that carry out specific tasks.
2. A machine that converts mechanical energy into electrical energy. Also known as electric generator; dynamo.

generic unit. A possible parameterised model of a language construct from which, at translation time, a language construct proper is derived. It may be noted that there is some analogy between generic units and macro-definitions: the language construct derived from the generic unit corresponds to the statement sequence replacing a macro call and is referred to as a 'generic instantiation'.

genlock. In televisions, a device for synchronising video signals generated from different sources.

GFI. 1. General Format Identifier, a field in the X.25 frame that specifies the format of the packet, the first four bits in a packet header; GFl contains the obit, Dbit and modulus value.
2. Guided Fault Isolation.

GFLOPS. Giga Floating-point Operations Per Second.

GFP. Generalised File Processor.

GGP. Gateway-to Gateway Protocol, the earliest internetworking routing protocol on the Internet. The protocol, which core gateways use to exchange routing information, GGP implements a distributed shortest path routing computation.

GIF. 1. Graphic Interchange Format; a popular file format for graphic images, created by CompuServe. GIF format features image compression.
2. File name extension for bit mapped image, a kind of graphics file.

gigabit. One billion bits. Also known as billibit.

gigabus. A term used to describe the bus-based parallel processing capabilities of Elxsi's System 6400 which operates at 320 gigabytes per second.

gigabytes. Number of bytes, given by:
$1024 \times 1024 \times 1024$ bytes, or
1,099,511,627,776.
It may be expressed as 10^{24} megabytes. The storage capacity of a large Al system reaches the G-byte level. Also known as G-byte.

gigahertz. A frequency of one thousand million hertz.

GIGO. Garbage In, Garbage Out; signifying that a program working on incorrect data produces incorrect results; produced as a result of undesirable input information of data, GIGO is unwanted and meaningless information carried along in the storage of a computer.

gimbal. The frame in which a disk slider is mounted; permits limited roll, pitch, and vertical translation - but not yaw, longitudinal translation, or lateral translation. The gimbal is usually fabricated from stainless steel for high strength and compliance, and rigidly attached to the access arm.

GINO. Graphical INput/Output, a package of FORTRAN subroutines for computer graphics. The GINO subroutines define a language for the production of elaborate graphics, including three-dimensional objects viewed in various projections.

GIP. General Information Programme.

GIPS. Ground Information Processing System.

GIRL. *See* generalised information-retrieval language.

GIRLS. Generalised Information-Retrieval and Listing System.

GJP. *See* graphic job processor.

GKS. Graphical Kernel System, defines the basic building blocks for generating graphical objects, e.g., lines and circles.

GKS-3D. Graphical Kernel System in Three Dimensions.

global backup. A backup procedure for a hard disk where the entire contents of the hard disk are copied onto another secondary storage medium such as floppy disk or tape cartridge.

Global System for Mobile communications. *See* GSM.

G-LOTOS. Graphical Language for Temporal Ordering Specification.

GMAP. General MacoAssembly Program.

GML. Generalised marup language.

GMSS. Graphical Modelling and Simulation System.

GMT. Greenwich Mean Time, standard for time; all other time zones are offset from here.

GN. 1. Given Name one of the attributes within the personal name used in X.400 naming.

2. Group Number.

GNM. Generic Network Model, a model of network management that is applicable across different telecommunications technologies.

GO. Generated Output.

Gods. A software term for the people who own MUD database, the administrators. The Gods can do whatever thy want to whomever they want whenever they want. Also known as janitor.

GOL. General Operating language.

Golay codes. A family of perfect linear error-correcting block codes, of which the most important is the binary (23,12) Golay code. There is also a ternary (11,6) Golay code. Golay codes can be arranged to be cyclic.

Gopher. A menu-based client/server utility program used to navigate and display content from throughout the Internet. It allows people who are familiar with content to develop catalogues on Gopher servers that other people can use to access information. Using gopher, the client burrows through the Internet to various sites where one can access documents and services. In addition to text documents, some gopher clients can give you access to pictures, sounds, and interactive sessions. This service, in many respects, has been replaced by the World Wide Web (WWW) service, though it provides the user with very quick responses, because it is totally character-based and is not burdened with downloading graphics as is the case with World Wide Web.

gopherspace. The collection of documents available from Gopher servers, to what is available based on the menu selections has been made in the client.

Goppa codes. A family of linear error-correcting block codes. The most important classes of Goppa codes are the Reed-Solomon codes and the binary Golay (23,12) code. Goppa codes are not in general cyclic.

GOPS. Giga Operations Per Second.

Gorizont. In communications, a series of Russian C-band geostationary satellites.

GOS. Grade Of Service, generic, refers to choices in certain characteristics of service such as priority, throughout, etc.

GOSIP. Government Open Systems Interconnect Profile, country specific ISO OSI functional profiles that have been defined as part of national procurement policies. The US has US GOSIP, which is defined as a Federal Information Processing Standard. The UK has UK GOSIP, which is defined by the Central Computer and Telecommunications Agency. The various GOSIPS as published by the US, UK, Japanese governments, and are all slightly different.

GOST. CIS (formerly the USSR) State Committee for Standards.

GOTO statement. A programming tool that exists to allow structured programmers to complain about unstructured programmers. A branch instruction in high-level language; causes the normal flow of control to be broken by designing explicit successor statement, usually identified by a label. Modern programming practice avoids the use of GOTO statement since its use makes programs more difficult to follow, the flow of control being less visibly explicit.

Government Open Systems Interconnect Profile. *See* GOSIP.

GPA. General Purpose Array.

GPD. General Protocol Driver.

GPDC. General Purpose Digital Computer.

GPF. General Protection Fault; in Windows, the memory protection hardware detected an illegal memory instruction from a program, causing the program to crash.

GPIB. General-Purpose Interface Bus.

GQ. Generation Qualifier, one of the attributes within the personal name in X.400 naming.

GR/PR. Graphical Representation/Phrase Representation.

grabber hand. In HyperCard and graphics programs, grabber hand is a cursor image that looks like small hand. It can grab text or graphics to move them to a place directed by the user.

grade of service. A measure of service provided by Internet Providers during a period of an hour in which the average traffic intensity is at maximum. It is usually expressed as the ratio of telephone calls liable to failure at the first attempt due to equipment limitations.

grammar. One of the principal ways of specifying an infinite formal language by finite means; the grammar consists of a set of rules that may be used to derive one string from another by substring replacement. The strings of the specified language are obtained by repeated application of these rules, starting from some initial string.

grammar-checking program. In word processing, software package, that aids operators to check the common grammatical errors in a document.

Gramme ring. A type of armature for a motor or generator, consisting of an iron ring onto which is wound a coil of wire, each turn being connected to a commutator bar.

graphic character. One of the 127 different shapes that can be generated in a character rectangle as part of a image. There are alphanumerics characters to provide text and graphics characters to provide an elementary, mosaic type of pictorial representation. There are three sets-alphanumerics, contiguous graphics, and separated graphics, each of the 96 display characters, some of which are common.

graphic display terminal. GDT. A visual display unit that permits the user or operator to display graphics information.

graphic job processor. GJP. A feature of a computer program for job control, which allows job control statements and other associated information to be entered via a remote visual display unit.

graphic structure input. GSI. Permitting the direct searching of a store of information held on a computer file, graphic structure input methods are used concerning scientific material and data.

graphical kernel system. GKS. A standard defined in ISO GKS 7.2 for computer systems. Comprising a set of basic functions for graphical input/output on vector and raster devices, GKS makes for portability of application programs between installations, savings in programming effort and simplified viewing of a variety of display devices. It can support several work stations in parallel.

graphical user interface. GUI. A way of interacting with a computer based on graphics instead of text. GUIs use icons, pictures, and menus, and use a mouse as well as a keyboard to accept input. It is the collection of graphical icons, menus, clipboards, desk accessories, and alert boxes, each accessible through the use of a mouse. The graphical user interface was first featured in the Apple Lisa in 1983, and made computing much simpler (especially for novices). The Macintosh, using the Motorola 68030 microprocessor, led the way with the graphical user interface until Microsoft launched Windows and Presentation Manager for Intel 80386 microprocessor. In contrast, a character user interface (CUI) only displays characters on the screen; pronounced as 'gooey'.

graphics files. The graphics programs save files in different formats. There are two basic groups in to which these formats can be divided: bitmap and vector formats. Graphics files are composed of either a grid of dots, called bitmap, or a set of vectors, which are mathematical equations describing the positions of lines.

Most common bitmap formats are: BMP, PICT, TIFF, JPEG, and GIF.

Most widely used vector format is Encapsulated Postscript (EPS).

graphics language. A programming language used for processing and display of graphic data.

graphics packages. Software packages designed for graphics applications. They require the user to interact in real time or to produce a command file, or program, which is processed by the package to produce the graphic display. There are five major categories of graphics software; these include:

Paint Software
Photo-manipulation Software
Draw Software
Computeriaided drafting software
3-D modelling software.

No single graphics software is capable of performing all the possible functions.

graphics. 1. The ability to present data in the form of graphs, drawings, pictures, diagrams, etc.

2. In filming, printed or hand-painted titles, charts, graphs, etc.

GRASP. Generalised Read and Simulate Program.

GRD. GOSIP Register Database, an online database facility developed by NIST to provide up-to-date information in the registers associated with US GOSIP.

GRED. Generalised Random Access Device.

Grey code. A binary (n, n) block code having the following properties:

(a) there are 2^n codewords, each of length n bits;

(b) successive codewords differ by the complementation of a single bit, *i.e.*, Hamming distance between them is unity.

A Grey code can be conveniently represented by its transition sequence, *i.e.*, the ordered list of bit positions that change when moving from one codeword to the next. Grey codes are used in encoding the positions of shafts, wheels, etc., in order to avoid the problems that would arise when several digits were supposed to change at the same time. They are also used to represent intensity or brightness levels. Also spelled as Gray code.

grey level array. An array of numbers, each of which in Grey code represents the level of brightness in the corresponding area of a visual scene. The Grey-level array might represent the output of a television camera or similar device.

grey marketing. Marketing and/or distribution of software and hardware, without prior permission of the copyright owner. The concept of grey marketing involves unauthorised dealing for commercial gain. Software piracy, on the other hand, is colloquial expression used world-wide to describe the criminal act of making or distributing for financial gain an unauthorised copy (or copies) of a copyrighted software product.

grey scale. A scale that assigns values to the range of grey tones that exists between black and white. In computer graphics systems using monochrome monitors, the shades of grey which are used to enhance the contrast of design elements. Grey scales are formed by varying the intensity of each picture element (pixel) on the screen. Some monitors use colours other than white, such as green or amber. The term grey scale also refers to the scanners. To read images, a scanner shines a bright light onto the paper. Arrays of small components called 'charge-coupled devices' then measure the amount of light reflected from all areas of the page. The amount of image detail, or resolution, that can be scanned is dependent on the density of the charge-coupled devices. Also spelled as grey scale.

GRID. 1. General Format IDentifier in X.25 PDUs.

2. Graphical Interactive Display.

GRIP. General Retrieval of Information Program.

group. 1. In data structures, a set of related records that have same value for a particular field in all the records.

2. In the context of network security, a group is a set of users who share common permissions for one or more resources. Individually assigned user permissions take precedence over those assigned through groups.

3. An assembly of 12 telephone channels forming a 48-kHz frequency band of carrier trnasmission system.

Group 4. The international standard for

high-speed, high-resolution facsimile transmission as defined by CCITT as a switched digital 64 kilobits-per-second ISDN technology.

group channel. Twelve voice grade in the FDM carrier system.

group delay. A modulated radio frequency signal consisting of a group of waves, within an overall wave envelope which may travel at slightly different velocities. The group delay is the time of propagation of the modulated wave envelope transmited between two points.

group delay distortion. In the propagation of a signal, the distortion that is caused by the transmission medium due to the difference in propagation velocity among the different frequencies that comprise the signal. Thus, the resulting dispersion will distort the received signal as it appears to be different from the dispatched signal. This result in spreading of the signal during transmission in the medium, as different parts of signal arrive in a time sequence relatively different from the sequence they were originally dispatched.

group distribution frame. GDF. In a frequency division multiplexing system, a frame that provides for interconnection apparatus used in the twelve transmission channels assembled in frequency band 60-108 kHz.

group index. For a given mode propagating in the fibre, the velocity of light in a vacuum divided by the group velocity of the mode.

group link. The whole of the means of transmission using a frequency band of specified width (48 kHz) connecting terminal euipment. The ends of the links are the points on group distribution frame to which the terminal equipment is connected. It may include one or more group sections.

group mark. A special character used in a write instruction to designate the beginning or end of a group of words, characters or records in storage. It enables the group to identified to be processed and addressed as a unit. In the case of repeated fields, the group mark often indicates the number of repetitions of such fields.

group reference pilot. The frequency waves transmitted to help maintain and adjust a system. It is applied where transmission channels are assembled into groups, accompanying the group until they are separated into their individual channels.

group separator. A special character used to designate the beginning or end of a group of words, characters or records in a store. It enables the group to be identified and be processed and addressed as a unit.

group velocity. The velocity of propagation of the enevelope produced when an electromagnetic wave is modulated by, *i.e.*, mixed with, another wave of different frequency. The group velocity may be regarded as the velocity of information propagation, and energy propagation.

groupware. The applications that involve group interaction across a network; Lotus Notes and Microsoft Exchange are the two popular groupware packages.

GSI. *See* graphic structure input.

GSL. Generalised Simulation Language.

gsm mapping. Short for generalised sequential machine mapping. A function that is the response function of a generalised sequential machines, and therefore generalises the notion of sequential function. Without constraining the machine to have a finite state-set, generalised sequentially is equivalent to the following property of initial subwords preservation: for all *u,v* in *I, f(uv)* has the form *f(u) w* for some *w* in *O,* where *I* and *O* are sets of all input and output stings.

GSM. 1. Global System for Mobile communications, 2-way, pan-European digital cellular system. Its specification is in line with ISDN and ITU-TS System-7 signalling and approved by almost all countries. GSM operates at 900MHz and is a fore-runner to the mass-market Personal Communications Networks, based on the same set of standards. GSM services include current digital subscriber services and the unique Short Message Service - a superior form of paging offering up to 160 alphanumeric characters with guaranteed delivery.

2. Graphic System Module.

3. Group Special Mobile, European public mobile radio-network for terminal devices.

GSR. Global Shared resources.

GSS. Graphic Support Software.

GSS/RSS. Generation Support Statements/Reception Support Statement, within ODA, statements about what functions an implementation claims to support.

GT. Give Token Session PDU, PDU used to change assignment of currently owned tokens or to introduce a sequence of concatenated SPDUs.

GTA. Give Token Acknowledgement Session PDU.

GTC. Give Token Confirm Session PDU.

GTD. Graphic Tablet display.

GTN. Government of Canada Telecommunications Network.

GTO. Graphics Text Organiser.

GTP. Graphics Transform Package.

GTX. Graphics within TeXts.

guard band. 1. The narrow unoccupied band of frequencies at the upper and lower limits of an assigned channel; its purpose is to prevent adjacent-channel interference by maintaining separation between channels.

2. Unused bandwidth separating channels to prevent crosstalk.

3. In backing storage, blank portion of the magnetic tape that separates two sets of information, thus preventing signal interference.

guarding. The function of preventing the false operation of a device.

guard time. Empty time interval used to separate time division multiple access bursts.

guard tone. A tone generated by a high-speed modem dial-up modem to ensure that there is sufficient bandwidth available on the PSTN circuit for transmission.

guard. In radar and sonar communication systems, to maintain a continuous receiver watch and transmitter ready for immediate use.

guarded frequency. A transmission frequency that is not to be jammed or interfered with because of the value of the information being derived from it.

GUI. Graphical User Interface, an interface, which describes the screen display that first welcomes a user and with which the user interacts during the computer session. A GUI makes use of Windows, Icons, Menus and Pointers, so-called WIMP systems, such as Microsoft Windows, GEM and X-Windows. Apple's GUI is particularly notable and be-spoke GUIs are becoming popular.

Guillemin line. A network that produces almost square pulses with very sharp rise and fall times.

GULP. General Utility Library Program.

gulp. A group of bytes, procesed as a single unit or word.

GUS. Guide to the Use of Standards, a guide written by SPAG.

H

.h. Extension for C programming language header files. These files should be retrieved in text/ASCII mode.

H channel. The ISDN packet switched channel on Basic Rate Interface, designed to carry user information streams at different speeds, depending on type:

H_0=384Kbit/s;
H_{11}=1536Kbit/s; and
H_{12}= 1920Kbit/s.

H.nnn. The H. Series of CCITT Recommendations deals largely with unusual uses of telephone-type circuits, such as videoconferencing, simultaneous voice and telegraph, VFT, and facsimile.

H261. ITU-TS standard for video compression, known as Codes for Audiovisual services at N′ 384Kbit/s. It sets a common algorithm for converting analog video signals to digital, operating at or above 384Kbit/s.

HA. *See* half-add.

HAB. Home Address Block.

hacker. A person who makes a conscious effort to gain illicit access to a computer system owned by another person or corporate entity. Hackers break access codes by clandestine means, such as studying the material written on waste paper from thrash bins, gaining access to computer rooms, talking to operating personnel, conducting trial-and-error routines, and using their knowledge of computer operating systems. These days hackers enjoy in accomplishing difficult tasks and learn more about networking and computer systems.

half-add. HA. A computer instruction that carries out binary digit-by-binary digit half additions. The operation is by a half-adder device where two inputs are received and two outputs are produced representing the sum and the carry.

half-adder. A digital logic circuit with two input terminals and two output terminals. The output terminals are called the sum and carry outputs. The sum output of a half-adder circuit is the exclusive-OR function of the two inputs. That is, the sum output is zero when the inputs are the same and 1 when they are different. The carry output is the AND function of the two inputs. It is 1 only when both inputs are 1. The half-adder circuit differs from the adder in that the half-adder will not consider carry bits from previous stages.

half-baud coding. HBC. A modified full-baud coding process that consists of representing a 0 by a zero-level voltage in the bipolar sequence of the pulses and a 1 by alternate positive or negative pulses in the bipolar sequence. These pulses return to the zero level at the midpoint of the baud.

half-bridge. 1. Apple Computer terminology for a device linking LANs over a low-speed link such as a telephone line or X.25 link. It is called half-bridge, as one is required at each end of the link.

2. A bridge rectifier having diodes in two arms and resistors in the other two. The efficiency of the half bridge circuit is less than that of the conventional bridge rectifier. This is because the resistors tend to dissipate some power as heat as the current flows through them. The half-bridge operates over the entire alternating-current input cycle, and is therefore a form of full-wave rectifier.

half-circuit. Term used when different administrations share the cost of a major submarine cable system.

half-duplex operation. An operation that makes use of a half-duplex circuit. The operating method may employ a circuit that is designed for duplex operation but can only be operated alternately in each direction because of the limitations of the terminal equipment.

half-duplex transmission. The transmission in either direction but only in one direction at a time.

half-duplex. HDX. 1. A circuit or system that can transmit in either direction, but not both directions at once. The circuit is designed for duplex operation, but is limited by the nature of the terminal equipment to use in alternate directions only.

2. A method of transmitting information over a communications channel, in which signals may be sent in both directions, but only one way at a time. This is sometimes referred to as local echo. Half-duplex operations can use a 2-wire or a 4-wire circuit, and either a dial-up or a dedicated line. When a half-duplex 2-wire circuit is used, the transmitted and received data alternately travel through the same inter-office and toll trunks. As the direction of the data transmission changes, the transmitter and receiver circuits in each station must turn on and off. When a half-duplex 4-wire circuit is used, the data transfer is still in one direction at a time, but the transmitted data travels over a totally separate trunk circuit from the received data.

half-echo suppresser. The equipment in which speech signals in one path control suppression of reflected waves (echoes) in the other path, but the action is not reciprocal.

half-height drive. A space-saving disk drive that occupies only half the height of the original disk drive first used in the IBM Personal Computer.

half-reflection. The reflection that occurs at the interface between one transmission medium and another when half of the optical power of the incident wave is reflected and half is transmitted.

half-wave transmission line. A section of the electromagnetic feed line, which measures an electrical half wavelength. At frequencies above 20 MHz, where half-wave sections of transmission line have reasonable length, these sections are often used in place of coils and capacitors as resonant circuits.

halo antenna. A special form of horizontal half-wave antenna; consists of a dipole whose elements have been bent into circle so that the circumference of the circle is 1/2 electrical wavelength. The ends of the dipole are insulated from each other at the opposite side of the circle from the feed point. The halo antenna is used in the very-high-frequency part of the radio spectrum.

halo. The dark area surrounding an unusually bright object, caused by over loading of the camera.

ham. A popular name for amateur radio operators.

HAM. Hierarchical Access Method.

Hamming code. An error detecting and correcting digital data transmission code; it uses special binary words in which the number of corresponding bit positions which differ in adjoining binary words is always the same.

Hamming distance. The number of symbol positions in which two equal-length symbol sequences are different.

HAMT. *See* human-aided machine translation.

hand-held device markup language. HDML. An XML application intended for displaying information (including Web pages) on pocket electronic devices such as mobile phones, equipped with display screens.

handshake. A method of error control in which data transmitted over a forward channel are returned over a backward channel and checked with the stored data originally transmitted, usually on an immediate and continuous basis. Handshaking is becoming increasingly universal in electronic communications because it drastically improves the signal-to-noise ratio. The handshake can be part of the protocol itself or an introductory process: the computers wishing to talk to each other set out the conditions they can operate under. Sometimes, handshake is just a warning that a communication is imminent.

hanging indent. A text format in which the first line of each paragraph is flush left, while all other lines are indented to the next tab stop.

hang over. The time between the end of a voice signal in one direction and the reopening of the voice channel in the other direction.

hang up. 1. A state in which a program has come to an unexpected halt, *e.g.*, because it is trying to read data from a device that is not connected to the processor.

2. In the context of time-sharing systems, the signal received by the program when a remote terminal breaks its connection (hangs up the telephone).

HAR. Home Address Register.

hard copy. 1. Printed (on paper) output, such as computer-generated reports. These are tangible and permanent records, such as printed invoices, statements, and reports.

2. A document that can be read without magnification or other technical aids and that is usually portable. Note Hard copies are commonly used to reproduce the image displayed.

hard copy. A permanent copy of the display image that can be read directly by humans or machines and can be easily transported.

hard disk. In memory systems, a permanently installed high-capacity, direct-access storage device with a rigid magnetic disk. Hard disks are noted for their speed and high capacity. High packing densities and data rates demand that the disk rotate at high speed with the read/write heads of the order of 1 mm above the disk surface. These days hard disks capable of storing 28GB of data are available.

hard hyphen. In word processing, a command used to force proper nouns like 'Hewlett-Packard' to appear on the same line (unbroken) even when the word reaches the end of a line.

hard line. A form of coaxial cable with 100% shielding continuity. The perfect shield is obtained because the outer conductor of the hard line is made from metal tubing. It is not as flexible as coaxial cable with a braided-wire outer conductor.

hard space. In word processing, a command used to ensure that particular combinations or words are not broken even when the first word is at the end of a line. This is particularly useful when using numbers and symbols. For example, a hard space command ensures that a long number like '400,787,870', or a measure like 20 Mb is not broken.

hard wired. Referring to functions built into the computer's firmware or read-only memory for processing certain information (such as arithmetic) at higher speeds. Hard-wired functions improve the computer's performance for that particular function, but go against the theory of most computer scientists who prefer computers to contain logic circuits that are general in nature, relying instead on software programs for instructions. In data communications, 'hard wired' refers to a communications link (such as a remote telephone line or local cable) that permanently connects two nodes, stations, or devices.

hardware address. In networking, each computer has an address specific to the technology. These hardware addresses are mapped to the assigned IP address and sometimes domain address as well.

hardware handshaking. Hardware (usually a modem cable) which handles handshaking (data flow control) automatically. Most new modem cables have hardware handshaking.

hardware. A term used to describe the actual circuitry that makes up the device. The wiring, circuit boards, integrated circuits, diodes, transistors, and resistors comprise the hardware. So do the operator interface devices, such as display terminals, printers, and keyboards. Contrast with software.

hardware profile. A set of instructions that tells the Windows 2000 which devices to start, or what settings to use for each device, when computer is switched on. Hardware profiles are especially useful in portable computers. Hardware profiles can be managed by double clicking System in control panel., clicking the Hardware tab, and clicking Hardware Profiles.

Hargelbarger code. A convolutional code designed to enable burst errors to be corrected if there are relatively long error-free intervals between the error bursts. Parity check bits, spread out in time, are inserted so that an error burst is not likely to affect more than one of the groups whose parity is checked.

harmonic analyser. A device capable of analysing a periodic function from its graph in terms of Fourier series corresponding to the function.

harmonic analysis. Breaking a complex wave in to the sum of a fundamental and various harmonic frequency signals.

harmonic attenuator. A circuit, device, or method of operation-such as filter, tuned amplifier, special biasing, or special bypassing-for reducing the amplitude of harmonics.

harmonic distortion. The presence of frequencies at the output of a device, caused by non-linearity within the device, which are harmonically related to a single frequency applied to the input of the device.

harmonic emission. Spurious emission at frequencies, which are whole multiples of those, contained in frequency band occupied by an emission.

harmonic function. A mathematical function, which can be used to describe the curves used to represent waves, whose amplitudes at particular constant intervals of time, distance, or other abscissa parameters have a specific constant value, such as sine wave.

harmonic generator. A device capable of generating signals which are harmonics of an input fundamental frequency.

harmonic suppression. An expression for the degree to which harmonic energy is attenuated, with respect to fundamental frequency, in the output of a radio transmitter. The term is also used to denote the process of minimising harmonic energy in the output of a signal generator.

harmonic. Having a frequency that is integral multiple of the fundamental frequency.

harmonic, even. Fundamental frequency multiplied by an even number.

harmonic, odd. Fundamental frequency multiplied by an odd number.

harmonics, triple. Odd harmonics, which are multiples of three.

harp antenna. A kind of broadband, unbalanced ground-plane antenna; the radiating power of the antenna is vertically polarised, and consists of a number of different vertical conductors of various lengths. The conductors extend upward from a common feed line, giving antenna the appearance of a harp. Harp antennas are most practical at the very-high frequencies, where the element lengths are easily manageable, allowing construction from metal rods or tubing.

hartley. A unit of logarithmic measure of information content; equal to decision content of a set of 10 mutually exclusive events that are expressed as a logarithm to the base 10.

hash. The meaningless signals added to the information signals, in order to comply with requirements for standard block length for items in the store or program.

hash total. A summation of one or more corresponding fields of transmission that would not usually be totalled.

HASQ. Hardware-Assisted Software Queue.

Hay bridge. A circuit designed for the purpose of measuring the value of an unknown inductance. It also gives an indication of the *Q*-factor of the inductor under test.

HB. Hexadecimal to Binary.

HBC. *See* half-baud coding.

HBEN. High Byte ENable.

H-bend. A gradual change in the direction of the axis of a waveguide, throughout which the axis remains in a plane parallel to the direction of the magnetic field transverse polarization. Also known as H-plane bend.

HC. 1. Hard Copy.
2. Host Computer.
3. Hybrid Computer.

HCC. Hardware Capability Code.

HCF. Host Command Facility.

HCG. Hardware Character Generator.

HCI. Host Computer Interface.

HCP. Host Communications Processor.

HCR. Hardware Check Routine.

HDD. Head Down Display.

HDDR. High Density Digital Recording.

HDDS. High Density Data System.

HDLC. High Level Data Link Control, an ISO standard set of protocols for carrying data over a link with error and flow control; defining Data Link Layer, layer 2 of OSI; similar to IBM's SDLC, versions of HDLC are under development for multi-point lines.

ITU-TS later adapted HDLC for its Link Access Protocol used for X.25 networks. It is a bit-oriented data link control procedure under which all data transfer takes place in frames. Each frame ends with a frame check sequence for error detection. There is a control field at the beginning of each frame that allows error detection, and data link set-up and data link termination. HDLC is a misnomer, as it is not a high level protocol.

HDML. *See* hand-held device markup language.

HDMR. High Density Multi-track Recording.

HDOS. Hard Disc Operating System.

HDVS. High Definition Video System.

HD-WDM. High-Density-Wave Division Multiplexing.

HDX. Half Duplex, non-simultaneous bi-directional telecommunications, the preferred mode in which people speak with each other.

head crash. An accidental contact of a magnetic head with the surface of rotating data medium, thereby leading to malfunction of the magnetic disk drive in which the access arm touches the rapidly spinning disk, causing permanent damage thereby causing data to be lost. This some times occurs due to excess heat, moisture, or sudden drop in pressure.

head loading zone. A peripheral area on each magnetic disk surface where heads are positioned to proper flying height for reading and writing data.

head/disk assembly. An assembly which includes magnetic disks, magnetic heads, and an access mechanism all enclosed in a container.

head-end. A central point or hub in broadband networks that receives signals on one set frequency band and retransmits them or another. Every transmission has to go through the head-end in a broadband network. The head-end is the piece of hardware that enables a network to send and receive on the same piece of cable. In CATV technology, the head-end is the control centre for a cable system where signals are processed and sent for distribution down the cable system.

header. The bunch of protocol information enclosed with the data at each layer of protocol stack. The control information added to the beginning of a transmitted message. This may consist of packet or block address, destination, message number and routing instructions. It appears at the top of every page of a document when it is printed. A header is also a part of e-mail message.

head-up display. An arrangement of equipment that projects images into a pilot's line of sight. It uses a cathode-ray tube to provide comprehensive information on height, speed, heading and altitude.

heading. The control information that characterises an inter-personal message in a message handling system.

heat sink. A device that helps to remove excess heat from the electronic devices by means of conduction, convection, and radiation. The use of heat sink increases the power-dissipating capability of a transistor, tube, integrated circuit, or other active device. it is made of a metal, usually aluminium or iron, and is an excellent conductor of heat. When a heat sink is used, it is necessary that the component be thermally bonded to the device.

hectometric wave. An electromagnetic wave that is in the medium frequency subdivision of the frequency spectrum, ranging from 300 to 3,000 kHz.

helical antenna. An antenna in the form a helix; when the helix circumference is much smaller than one wavelength, the antenna radiates at right angles to the axis of the helix. When the helix circumference is equal to one wavelength, maximum radiation is along the helix axis. Helical antennas are ideally suited to satellite communications because the circular polarization of the transmitted and received signals reduces the amount of fading as the satellite orientation changes. The sense of the circular polarization can be made either clockwise or counter-clockwise, depending on the sense of the helix.

helical filter. A quarter-wave device often used at very-high and ultra-high frequencies as a bandpass filter. A shielded enclosure contains a coil, one end of that is left either free or connected to variable capacitor. The filter sections are tuned to slightly different frequencies, resulting in a very little attenuation throughout the passband, but steep skirts and high attenuation outside the passband. Helical filters provide a high *Q*-factor, which is important in the reduction of out-of-band interference.

hello screen. The first screen-display obtained when an application package is run.

HELP. 1. A method of operation of a computer, terminal or processor; the user is guided by the HELP mode, which indicates instructions on a visual display unit. The mode enables user with no programming experience, to perform functions or obtain information by using single keystrokes. 2. Highly Extendable Language Processor.

hemispheric beam. A satellite beam pattern with a footprint that is capable of covering up to 20% of the earth's surface; used for providing television coverage in rural areas.

HERS. Hardware Error Recovery System.

hertz antenna. Any horizontal, half-wavelength antenna, the feed point can be at the centre, at either end, or at some intermediate point. It operates independently of the ground, is therefore a balanced antenna.

hertz. The SI unit of frequency. The angular frequency in radians is equal to approximately 6.3 times the frequency in hertz.

Hertzian wave. An electromagnetic wave that has a frequency which is lower than 3,000 GHz and that is propagated in free space without a waveguide.

heterochronous. A relationship between two signals such that their corresponding significant instants do not necessarily occur at the same moment. Thus, two signals that have different nominal signalling rates do not stem from the same clock or from homochronous clocks, are usually heterochronous.

heterodyne detector. A detector that operates by beating the signal from a local oscillator against the received signal. This form of detector is more often called a product detector, and is required for the reception of continuous wave, frequency-shift-keyed, and single-sideband signals.

heterodyne frequency. The sum of, or the difference between two frequencies produced by combining the two in a modulator or similar device.

heterodyne reception. The reception of radio signals by a beat method which results in incoming signals being combined with locally generated signals of almost same frequency as the incoming signals, thus producing a beat note at audible frequency.

heterodyne. A term denoting the production of beats in a radio receiver by the combination of received wave with a locally generated wave of slightly different frequency.

heterogeneous computer network. Computer network in which computers have dissimilar architectures but nevertheless are able to communicate.

Heterogeneous LAN Management Specification. *See* HLMS.

heterogeneous networking. The networking of computers from different vendors, or the running of different operating systems.

hex dump. A programmer's trouble shooting aid that prints out (for the purpose of analysis) the hexadecimal values of the data.

hexadecimal system. A system of number notation to the base 16; most commonly used set of digits representing hexadecimal notation system are 0 to 9 and then A,B,C,D, E and F. There are some other systems not so widely used that employ letters other than A-F for the last six digits.

hex-Intel format. In data structures, standard format for storage of binary information on magnetic tape or disk.

HF. High Frequency, in radio, the bandwidth below VHC.

HICLASS. HIerarchical CLASSification, one in which terms are provided with a designation and arranged in a hierarchical order. Items are split into initial sets, and then into successively finer sets. The Dewey decimal classification system uses this method.

hidden codes. In word processing and similar programs, formatting codes which are transparent to the user. This ensures that the working screen is not cluttered with codes and commands. Some programs like Wordstar and WordPerfect allow the user to reveal and edit the hidden codes for greater control over the document.

hidden file. A file that is not intended to be viewed in a directory listing. In MS-DOS, the system files IO.SYS and MSDOS.SYS are hidden; in Windows, the swap file. Some operating systems allow the user to hide files so that they can only be accessed if the name is known.

hidden line. A line segment that represents an edge obscured from view in a two dimensional projection of a three-dimensional object.

hierarchical database. A database that allows records to be related to one another on one to *n* mapping; records are thus interrelated by a tree structure.

hierarchical indexed sequential access method. HISAM. A technique of organising store of information entered on a computer file, that can be held on a disk.

hierarchical menu. A secondary menu that appears while dragging and holding the cursor over an item in a menu. It gives you choices of options that apply to the item you are selecting in the menu. Also known as submenu or cascading menu.

hierarchical network. A computer network (resembling a star network) which is controlled by a large host computer (usually a mainframe) with several smaller computers (perhaps minicomputers) connected to the host computer, but also acting as sub-hosts to a group of workstations of microcomputers. A network with one host at its hub, which is the major processing centre, and one or more satellite processing units. IBM's SNA was originally designed as an hierarchical network.

hierarchy. A data structure consisting of sets and subsets; each subset has a lower rank than the data of its sets.

High level Data Link Control. *See* HDLC.

high memory area. HMA. The first 64K of extended memory in an IBM PC or compatible computer. This area is used by Windows and by some applications. MS-DOS can also be "loaded high"- loaded into the HMA to make more room in conventional memory.

High Speed Synchronous. *See* HSSI.

high threshold logic. HTL. A type of microcomputer logic employed in industrial environments, where the electrical noise level can be quite high. Digital systems operated in such environments must have a high threshold in order to ignore these noise spikes, and thus not provide false operation. The high threshold logic gate is a development of diode transistor logic.

high. The most significant half (that containing the most significant digits MSD) of a microcomputer memory location or pointer. Normally, 0-7 portion of 16 binary digit (BIT) word.

high-C circuit. A tuned circuit having high capacitance and low inductance at a given frequency. Such a circuit is characterised by high selectivity and low voltage.

high-frequency trimmer. 1. A low-value variable capacitor operated in parallel with a usually front-panel tuning capacitor to set the high-frequency end of the tuning range. 2. A small variable capacitor used in conjunction with a larger tuning capacitor the function of which is to permit precision tuning of the larger device.

high-frequency. HF. In radio systems, the HF bands lie between 1.6 and 30 MHz, and are popular because relatively long distances can be covered at low cost, under relatively light traffic conditions.

high-L circuit. A tuned circuit having high inductance and low capacitance at given frequency. Such a circuit is characterised by low selectivity and high voltage.

high-level data link control. A formalised method of communications, in which information is considered as a stream of binary digits, allowing data transparency via bit stuffing.

high-level language. HLL. A computer programming language resembling natural language using symbols and command statements that an operator can read, but is not English. Each statement represents a powerful series of computer instructions; some of the examples of high-level languages include:

Beginners All-Purpose Symbolic Instruction Code (BASIC),
Common Business-Orientated Language (COBOL), and
FORmula TRANslator (FORTRAN).

High-level languages may be classified into two broad groups: procedural and nonprocedural. In case of procedural languages, the programmer is still concerned with the manner in which the task is to be operated, but he need not to specify the detailed computer steps.

highlighted. Indicates that an object or text is selected and will be affected by your next action. Highlighted text appears in reverse video on monochrome monitors and in a chosen colour on colour monitors. The highlighted objects may change colour or be surrounded by some sort of selection cursor.

high-noise-immunity logic. A specific design of logic circuits for use in application where transients are likely to be present producing a noisy environment. They can protect complementary metal-oxide semiconductor circuits from transients and static electricity, and compatible with a number of analogue circuits.

high-order mode. In the electromagnetic wave propagation in a waveguide, a mode of propagation in which high solutions to the wave equations are represented in the wave, whether be transverse electric, transverse magnetic, or transverse electromagnetic waves.

high-pass filter. HPF. A filtering device that permits only those components in Fourier transform domain whose frequencies lie above some critical value to pass through with little attenuation, all other components being highly attenuated. A highpass filter is a combination of capacitance, inductance, and/or resistance, that is intended to produce large amounts of attenuation below a certain frequency and little or no attenuation above that frequency. Highpass filters are used in a variety of situations in electronic apparatus. One of the common uses for the highpass filter is at input of a television receiver; cut-off frequency of such a filter is about 40 MHz.

High-Performance File System. *See* HPFS.

high-*Q*. For a component or circuit, a high value for ratio *X/R* (reactance to resistance). This is a relative term, since a particular numerical value of *Q* considered high in one situation might be regarded as low under other circumstances. High-Q filters are desirable in situations where the response must be confined to a single signal, or to a very narrow range of frequencies. In general, high-Q circuits require low-loss inductors and capacitors, and the resistance should be as low as possible.

high-speed duplication. The production of one or more copies from a master document at a speed much faster than the original recording.

high-speed memory. A computer peripheral device that is capable of retrieving information at compara-ively faster rate than other memory units connected to a computer system.

high-speed metal-oxide semiconductor. HMOS. A metal-oxide semiconductor technology employing high-scaling techniques to increase density and performance beyong that of *n*-channel semiconductor and *p*-channel metal-oxide semiconductor technologies.

high-speed multiplex link. A high-speed link in data communications, over which many signals are combined and subsequently separated at the far end of the circuit.

high-speed printer. A printer that is able to operate on line and has a speed of operation compatible with data processing and computer speeds.

high-speed reader. A device that converts information from one storage medium into another. In general a card reader operating at speed more compatible with the speed of computation and data processing so that is may operate on-line.

high-speed skip. The rapid vertical advance of a form on a printer to the areas where the information is to be printed.

high-voltage power supply. A form of power-supply unit that can provide a high-voltage supply output from a lower-voltage input. A typical high-voltage power supply is found within a domestic television receiver and is used to provide the cathode-ray tube element voltages.

highway. 1. A bus that is capable of carrying a digital serial-coded bit stream with time slots allotted to each call on a sequential basis.

2. In a computer system, the means for interconnection between the computer

system and process interface system. It may be noted that a bus may be used as highway. A common path or a set of parallel paths, over, which signals from many channels, can pass. The separation of calls and messages is generally achieved by time-division multiplexing.

HILI. HIgher-Level Interface.

HIM. Hardware Interface Module.

HIP. Host Information Processor.

HISAM. *See* hierarchical indexed sequential access method.

hiss. Audio noise, in which the amplitude is peaked near the midrange or treble regions. It is always heard in active audio-frequency circuits. In audio equipment the hiss is generated as a result of random electron or hole movement in components.

hit rate. The faction of references to one level of memory hierarchy that must otherwise be fulfilled in the less accessible levels within the hierarchy. Thus, for a cache memory the hit rate is the fraction of references that do not result in access to main memory.

hit. 1. A momentary line disturbance in data communications, which is capable of corrupting the characters being transmitted. 2. A momentary interference in an audio signal.

HK. ISO 3166 alphabetic country code for Hong Kong; these country codes are used in X.400.

HL. 1. High Level.
2. Host Language.

HLAIS. High Level Analog Input System.

HLCO chart. High/low/close/open chart; a chart used in presentation graphics to simultaneously plot the highest value, the lowest value, and open/close (begin/end) or average value of events such as the weather or the movement of stock prices for a given period.

HLI. Host Language Interface.

HLL. *See* high-level language.

HLML. High Level Microprogramming Language.

HLMS. Heterogeneous LAN Management Specification, the network management specification developed by IBM and 3Com; provides underlying structure for developing network management products, which can function with a variety of network operating systems and adapter cards.

HLP. File name extension for a help file.

HLPI. High Level Programming Interface.

HLQL. High Level Query Language.

HLS. Hue, Luminance, and Saturation. A Model for specifying colours used for monitors. Television uses this model; also, common in computer applications is RGB. CYMB is used for printers. HLS is also called HSI (hue, saturation, intensity) or HSV (hue, saturation, value).

HMA. *See* High Memory Area.

HMI. 1. Human-Machine Interface, term used in network management when talking about a user interface.
2. Hardware Monitor Interface.

HML. Human-Machine Language, command language for user interfaces.

HMM. Hardware Multiply Module.

HMO. Hardware Microcode Optimiser.

HMOS. *See* high-speed metal-oxide semiconductor.

H-network. A network of 5-impedance; two connected in series between upper input terminals, and one shunted between the junctions of the series connected impedance. The H-configuration can be used in the construction of bandpass, band rejection, high-pass, and low-pass filters. Also called H-pad, balanced tee-network, and balanced tee-pad.

HOB. Hierarchical Operational Binding, relationship between two DSAs when one contains the naming context immediately superior to a naming context of the other and holds a subordinate reference to the subordinate DSA.

HOL. 1. High Order Language.
2. *See* human oriented language.

hold mode. That operating mode of an analog computer during which integration is stopped and all variables are held at the value they had when this mode was entered.

holographic memory. A storage device that records binary information in the form of holograms, which are produced (as interference patterns) on photographic or photochromic media by means of laser beams, and are read by means of low power laser beams. The advantage of a hologram is the way in which the image is dispersed over the recording surface so that dust or scratches do not totally obscure data though they may reduce the contrast.

home banking. In applications, the use of a domestic communications terminal, usually view data, to perform transactions on user's bank account.

home bus. A small-area network in domestic environments for the transmission of video, audio signals and control information around a building. The transmission medium may be coaxial or optical fibre, or a combination of these.

home key. A programmable cursor control key found on all standard keyboards. Its functions depend on the particular application used. In word processing, the home key (in conjunction with arrow keys) is used to move cursor to the beginning of a line, or to the top or bottom of a page.

home page. In WWW terms, the base hypermedia document for an individual or organisation. From this page there may be other pages of information or resources listed.

homogeneous multiplex. A multiplex structure in data communications, in which the information bearing channels are transmitted at the same data-signalling rate.

hook transistor. A type of four layered *p-n-p-n* device in which the outer *p* and *n* layers serve as emitter and collector, the inner *n*-layer being the base. This places a *p*-layer between the base and collector, resulting in a transistor that provides high alpha as a result of carrier multiplication by the additional junction in the collector layer.

hop limit. The number of remaining router hops a datagram might take before it is discarded; hop limit is specified in the IPv6 main header and then decremented at each router stop.

hop. 1. A transmission path in communications, from one point on the earth to another via the ionosphere without any intermediate reflections from the earth's surface.
2. In routing, a server or router that is counted in a hop count.

HOP. Hybrid Operating System.

hop count. The number of routers a message must pass through to reach its destination. It is used to determine most efficient network route.

horizontal blanking. The blanking out of the retrace path area on the screen during horizontal retrace of a raster scan on a cathode ray tube.

horizontal sync pulse. HSP. The pulse in television, that follows the front porch in the composite colour video signal. It is used to synchronise the sweep circuits of the receiver with those of the camera.

horizontal synchronisation. In televisions, the picture signals must be synchronised at the transmitter and receiver. The electron beam in the television picture tube scans from left to right and top to bottom. At any given instant of time, in a properly operating television system, the electron beam in the receiver, picture tube is in exactly the same relative position as the scanning beam in the camera tube. This requires the synchronisation of horizontal as well as the vertical position of the beams. When the horizontal synchronisation in a television system is lost, the picture becomes totally unrecognisable.

horizontal tabulation. A specific control character that causes the position of print of a printer to be pushed forward to the next allocated position in the same line of print.

horn antenna. The microwave antenna formed by flaring out the end of a waveguide. It is used for the transmission and reception of signals at ultra-high and microwave frequencies. There are several different configurations of the horn antenna, they all look similar. It provides a unidirectional radiation pattern, with the favoured direction coincident with the operating of the horn. The horn antenna is characterised by a lowest usable frequency; feed system generally consists of a waveguide, which joins the horn at its narrowest point. They are often used in feed systems of large dish antennas. The horn is pointed toward the centre of the dish, in the opposite direction from the favoured direction of the dish. When the horn is positioned at the focal point of the dish, extremely high gain and narrow-beam radiation are realised.

host computer. HC. 1. In a network, a computer that primarily provides services such as computation, data base access, or special programs or programming languages.

2. Primary or controlling computer in a multiple computer installation.

3. A computer used to prepare programs for use on another computer or on another data processing system; for example, a computer used to compile, link, edit, or test programs to be used on another system.

host ID. A portion of the IP address, which refers to a node on the network. Each node within a network should have an IP address that contains a unique host ID.

host name. A single name used to identify a computer; usually it has a meaning such as location, usage, or ownership. Host names are said to occupy flat name-space, which means there is no hierarchy or vertical structure associated with the name.

host processor. A minicomputer or mainframe attached to a network providing services to network users. It controls all, or a part of the user application network.

hot fixing. Ability to detect and mark bad sectors of a disk, then assign alternate disk sectors during routine LAN operation. This automatically updates the original defect map.

hot key. A keystroke or combination of keystrokes intended for activating a RAM-resident program on IBM PC and compatible computers. In computing, a feature of a distributed processing emulation package which enables a user to switch automatically from a session, with the local microcomputer's operating system to a session with the host by pressing a single key.

hot list. A stored collection of URL's that can be accessed by the browser client for easy use. Sometimes, it is called bookmark.

hot mode. A technique in communication security, in which each terminal is required to generate continuously messages or dummy messages.

hot spot. 1. The places in a Web document that are entry points linking a page to another pages via URLs. Hot spots look different than other words or pictures on a Web page. They may have a different colour and appearance..

2. In communications, a region in which reception is much better than in the immediate surroundings. The effect can be caused by the addition of several components of a signal because of geographic location of the area. It can also be caused by unusual good earth conductivity. Sometimes the cause is unknown. A receiving hot spot is not necessarily a good transmitting location.

hot swap. The ability of a device to have parts removed after, for example, a slot-in card or fan failure, without affecting its operation. Many of today's hubs offer hot swapping without bringing down the network to charge a component.

howl. An unpleasant high-pitched audio-frequency tone heard in receivers that is caused by unwanted electric or acoustic feedback.

HPAD. Host-Packet Assembler/Disassembler, used to connect hosts to a network.

h-parameters. Parameters of the four-terminal network equivalent of a transistor. They are called hybrid parameters (thus, *h*) because of their appearance in mesh and nodal equations. The basic *h*-parameters are h_{11}, input resistance with output short-circuited; h_{12}, reverse voltage ratio with input open-circuited; h_{21}, forward current gain with output short-circuited; and h_{22}, output conductance with input open-circuited.

HPF. High Pass Filter.

HPFS. High-Performance File System, an OS/2 file system that has faster input/output than the file allocation table file system; it does not restrict file naming to eight characters with a three character extension; and is compatible with the FAT file system.

HP-IB. Acronym for Hewlett-Packard Interface Bus, an implementation of IEEE-488 standard for digital interfacing of programmable instrumentation made by Hewlett-Packard.

H-plane bend. *See* H-bend.

.hqx. Extension for compressed Macintosh files. These files should be retrieved in binary mode and decompressed by a Macintosh decompression program.

HRDP. Hypothetical Reference Digital Path.

HRM. Hardware Read-in-Mode.

HRPF. Hexadecimal Reference Publication Formal, the symbol / (slash) followed by a string of up to 40 hexadecimal digits used to represent an NSAP address.

HRS. Host Resident Software.

HSDB. High Speed Data Buffer.

HSI. *See* HLS.

HSP. 1. High Speed Printer.

2. *See* horizontal sync pulse.

HSR. High Speed Reader.

HSSC. High Speed Selector Channel.

HSSI. High Speed Synchronous Serial Interface, the interface for transferring data to or from a WAN leased line, or to and from a LAN via an HSSI-capable DSU and HSSI router.

HTB. Hexadecimal To Binary.

HTL. *See* high threshold logic.

HTML. Hyper Text Markup Language; the language used to "mark up" hypertext and hypermedia documents and then stored with those documents on World Wide Web server and transmitted upon request to a web browser client to be displayed. This language is used to define the locations and characteristics of each element of the page. HTML has been developed with the vision that all manner of devices should be able to use information on the web. Computers with graphics displays of varying resolution and colour depths, cellular telephones, hand-held devices, speech input and output devices, computers with low/high bandwidth, and so on. Each version of HTML attempts to reach greater concensus among industsy. It is an application of Standard Generalised Markup Language (SGML), an ISO standard for defining the structure and managing the contents of any digital document.

HTTP. HyperText Transport Protocol; the underlying protocol, which supports the linking and transfer of hypermedia documents that makeup the webs; used for transferring HTML and related files, usually from WWW sites.

hub. A network connectivity device that brings media segments together in a central location; the centre of a star topology network or cabling system. A multi-node network topology that has a central multiplexer with many nodes feeding into and through the multiplexer or hub. The other nodes do not usually directly interconnect. LAN hubs are increasingly popular with the growth of structured cabling and the need for LAN management.

hue. Position of a colour along the colour spectrum; for example, purple is between red and blue. Luminance and saturation also affect the appearance of a colour.

hum modulation. Unwanted modulation of a signal by hum arising in an audio frequency system. It results in noise or the distortion of output.

hum. Undesirable low-frequency currents interfering with a desired signal and usually caused by the poorly screened alternating main supply. Hum is the presence of 60- or 120 Hz modulation in an electronic circuit. It can occur in the carrier of a radio transmitter, in a radio-frequency receiving system, or in an audio system. When filtering is inadequate in the output of a power supply, hum is often introduced into the circuits operating from the supply. With half-wave power supplies, the hum has a frequency of 60 Hz; with full-wave supplies, the frequency is 120 Hz. Both of these frequencies are within the range of human hearing, and produce objectionable modulation.

human oriented language. HOL. The computer language that has more affinity with a human language than a machine language.

human-aided machine translation. HAMT. In machine applications, a computerised system capable of automatically translating text from one spoken language to another. It requires human intervention only to resolve ambiguities of syntax and semantics as well as problems arising from non-literal usage.

hunting. The fluctuation of a controlled signal about its desired value that results from over correction by a control device. In reality, the stable desired value is never achieved.

HVTS. High Volume Time Sharing.

HWI. HardWare Interpreter.

hybrid device. A component or circuit that uses two or more different technological forms of design

hybrid integrated circuit. HIC. An integrated circuit embodying both integrated and microminiature discrete components, *i.e.,* one coming both monolithic and thin-film construction.

hybrid junction. A waveguide or transmission line arrangement having four ports that, when terminated in their characteristic impedance, have the property that energy entering any one port is equally transferred to two of the remaining three ports. The hybrid junction is used as a mixing or dividing device.

hybrid system. A system capable of accommodating both digital and analog signals.

hybrid. 1. A component, device, circuit, apparatus, or system, that uses two or more different technological forms of design, each of which is normally used in different application and not usually combined in a given requirement. An integrated circuit that uses both microminiature discrete components and integrated components is often called a hybrid integrated circuit, even though all the components are solid-state. Computers that use both analog and digital techniques are often called hybrid computers. A switch that makes use of relays and transistors might be called a hybrid switching circuit.

2. Equipment used to convert four-wire transmission to the two-wire transmission and vice versa.

Hyper Text Markup Language. *See* HTML.

hypercard. Application toolkit, which provide an easy method of creating hypertext presentations. It does not require the user to have any programming experience to create or customise information in the form of graphics, text, music, video, and animation.

hypermedia. A superset of hypertext, which includes images and sounds. It is employed for computer-aided instruction (CAI), inter-connecting series of text, graphics integrated video, interactive laser disks, animation, and sound. Hypermedia is especially useful for expert systems when diagnosing, monitoring, interpreting, controlling, designing, planning, and testing. Using a fast-access disk drive, any part of a document can be linked to another, without having to close the working document, or manually search each document.

HYPERNET. HYPER NETwork, a genetic term used to describe a number of computers interconnected to form a network capable of transmitting information at megabaud rates.

HyperTalk. The software command language used to write programs for the Macintosh HyperCard application, enabling it to integrate video, interactive laser disks, animation, and sound, while fully implementing object-oriented programming standards.

HyperText Transport Protocol. *See* HTTP.

hypertext. A form of non-sequential text retrieval, which interconnects a series of documents so, that retrieval and immediate cross-referencing is possible. It is an inter-connected web of textual information; the text that points to other text and allows to jump around in the text without necessarily reading it in a specific manner; the anchored links within the document can point to other places within that document or within other documents. Using a fast-access disk drive, any word or section of a document can be linked to another, without having into close the working document, or manually search each document. For example, a stock control system written in hypertext could enable the user to select a product number and gain immediate access to the sales history or mechanical reliability associated with that product.

Hytelnet. A DOS-based tool for working with Telnet; presents menus of library catalogs and other resources that allow public access through Telnet.

I

I. 1. Input.
2. Instructions.

I.100. Series of CCITT recommendations providing general introduction about the concepts of integrated digital network services.

I.200. Series of CCITT recommendations providing general introduction about the concepts of integrated digital network services.

I.nnn. The CCITT I. Series of Recommendations; deal entirely with ISDN.

I/O address. Locations within input/output address space of an IBM or compatible computer, used by a device, such as a printer or modem. The address is used for communication between software and device.

I/O control system. *See* input/output control system.

I/O controller. *See* input/output controller.

I/O interface. *See* input/output interface.

I/O port. *See* input/output port.

I/O processor. *See* input/output processor.

I/O register. *See* input/output register.

I/O. *See* input/output.

I/O-bound. *See* input/output-bound.

I/OC. Input/Output Controller.

I^{2}L. Integrated Injection Logic; a semiconductor-device technology for a logic family, fabricated using bipolar techniques. It is also called merged transistor logic (MTL). In I^{2}L circuits the electrode areas of individual bipolar electrode areas of individual bipolar transistors are merged into a single area, this is then common to each transistor. This permits a higher packing density of individual devices in a single chip and a reduction in the complexity of chip fabrication. Integrated injection logic is said to be capable of offering the low cost and low power consumption of CMOS, but it is yet a largely unproven technology. Also written as IIL.

I^{3}L. Insoplanar Integrated Injection Logic.

IA. 1. Indirect Address.
2. Interchange Address.
3. *See* immediate addressing.

IA-1. 1. International alphabet 1.
2. Image Array Processor.

IA-2. International alphabet 2; standard telegraphy code.

IA-5. 1. International Alphabet 5.
2. The most common body part type in X.400; 7-bit communication code; the international equivalent to ASCII.

IAB. 1. Internet Activities Board, the technical body that sets policy and standards for TCP/IP and the connected Internet suite of protocols. Its task forces are the IETF and IRTF.

2. Internet Advisory Board.
3. Interrupt Address to Bus.

IAD. Initial Address designator.

IAL. International algebraic language. A computer language which was the predecessor of algebraic-orientated language (ALGOL).

IAM. *See* initial address message.

IANA. Internet Assigned Numbers Authority.

IAP. Internal Array Processor.

IAR. Instruction Address register.

IAS. 1. Immediate Access Store.
2. Interactive Application System.

IB. 1. Identifier Block.
2. Instruction Bus.
3. Interface Bus.

I-band. The band of frequencies in the range from 8 to 10 GHz, comprising 10 numbered channels each of which is 200 MHz wide. These frequencies overlap with parts of the old X-band and H-band.

IBC. Integrated Block Controller.

I-beam cursor. Appearance of cursor/pointer in graphical user interfaces (GUIs) when it is positioned over an area in which text can be entered.

IBG. InterBlock Gap; the magnetic tape units spin reels at very high speeds so that, just like a car, the tape units need to slow before coming to a halt. To cater for this, blanks are left between records or blocks. Once a high-speed search is completed, the magnetic reel gradually slows. The gaps ensure that the desired data block is not accidentally passed, requiring a rewind. The gap is called InterBlock Gaps (IBG) or InterRecord Gaps (IRG).

IBM Cabling System. *See* IBMCS.

IBM Personal System/2. A line of personal computers developed by IBM in 1986 employing new operating system called OS/2, used with Intel 8086, 80286, 80386, 80486, and 80586 microprocessors, operating on IBM's Micro Channel Architecture.

IBM token-ring. A baseband star-wired ring network developed by IBM. It is uses the token-passing access method and runs at 4 megabits per second.

IBM XT. The computers introduced in 1983 by IBM; XT (Extended Technology), based on the Intel 8088 microprocessor, and a 16-bit data bus. The original XT models offered a clock speed of 4.77 megahertz, a speed now considered too slow for modern business and personal applications. The later computers based on the Intel 8088 microprocessor are called turbo XTs, offering a 10-megahertz clock speed.

IBM. International Business Machines, one of the largest manufacturers of computers in the world. IBM set the standard for DOS machines. Currently, many companies make clones of IBM's personal computers which are often called compatibles.

IBMCS. IBM Cabling System, the cabling system introduced by IBM in 1984 based around Shielded Twisted Pair (STP) cabling.

IBOL. Interactive Business Oriented Language.

IBT. *See* isochronous-burst transmission.

IBX. Integrated Business Exchange.

ICA. 1. International Communications Association, professional organisation for telecommunications managers.
2. *See* integrated communications adaptor.

ICAI. Intelligent Computer Assisted Instruction.

ICAM. Integrated Computer Aided manufacturing.

ICB. Internal Common Bus.

ICC. IEEE International Conference on Communications.

ICCS. Inter Computer Communications System.

ICD. International Code Designator, a 4-digit identifier for an organisational authority responsible for allocating values in the domain-specific part of an NSAP address.

ICF. Integrated Control Facility.

ICG. Interactive Computer Graphics.

ICI. Interface Control Information, information transferred across a service boundary from an entity in one layer to the entity providing service at the layer below to coordinate their activity.

ICM. Instruction Control Memory.

ICMP. Internet Control Message Protocol, a part of the IP protocol, used to handle errors and to control messages at the IP level; the key protocol that resides within the Internet layer. Routers usually use this protocol. ICMP also includes an echo request/reply used to test whether a destination is reachable and responding. It allows status messages to be generated by an internetworking gateway, indicating a variety of error or unusual conditions.

ICN. Integrated Computer Network.

icons. 1. The graphical screen elements displayed on the screen of a graphical user interface to identifier, and execute one or more commands when selected with a mouse or other pointing device.

2. In database management, a particular description code used to identify a file as being unique in some way. For example, in a library system, data on a book featuring motor vehicles may contain the identifier 'turbo'. When a search is conducted, 'turbo' can be used as a descriptor to search all titles containing information pertaining to turbo technology.

3. One or more characters used to identify or name a data element and possibly to indicate certain properties of the data element.

4. A lexical unit that names a language object; such as the names of variables, arrays, records, labels, procedures, etc. It may be noted that an identifier usually consists of a letter optionally followed by letters or digits.

ICOS. Interactive COBOL Operating System.

ICOT. ISDN COnformance Testing working group.

ICP. Initial Connection Protocol.

ICR. 1. Intelligent Character Recognition, the software similar to OCR, but it learns to recognise different fonts and character styles, so is more efficient. Useful to make paper documents accessible via GroupWare.

2. Indirect Control Register.

3. Input Control Register.

4. Interrupt Control Register.

ICS. *See* integrated communication system.

ICSU. Intelligent Channel Service Unit, a data communications device used on digital networks.

ICT. Image Creation Terminal.

ICU. 1. Instruction Control Unit.

2. Interface Control Unit.

ICW. 1. Interrupted Continuous Wave.

2. Interface Control Word.

ID. 1. IDentifier, a protocol element used for identification, used in many different protocols with a classifier.

2. Identification.

3. Instruction Data.

I-D. Internet-Draft, the working documents of the IETF, its areas, and its working groups. As the name implies, Internet-Drafts are draft documents, that are valid for a period of six months and may be updated, or made obsolete by other documents at any time.

IDA. 1. Integrated Digital Access, the means of providing digital access for subscribers to the BT ISDN service.

Two versions: single line IDA and multi-line IDA are available.
2. Integrated Disc Adaptor.
3. Integrated data Access.

IDAPI. Integrated Database Application Programming Interface, a standard from Borland and others providing a standard interface to a wide range of databases. It is supposed to be a superset of ODBC.

IDB. Input Data Buffer.

IDC. 1. Insulation Displacement Connector.
2. Integrated Disc Control.
3. Internal Data Channel.

IDCC. Integrated Data Communications Controller.

IDD. Integrated Data Dictionary.

IDDD. International Direct Distance Dialling, an automatic system of calling telephones beyond the local area, enabling subscribers to make international calls.

IDE. 1. Integrated Drive Electronics, a kind of hard drive specification for IBM PC and compatible computers, also used in some Macintoshes.
2. Interactive Data Entry.

IDEA. Interactive Data Entry Access.

identification. A computer, data processor or telecommunications label that can consist of a code number or code name which serves to uniquely identify a record, block, file or other unit of information or data.

identifier. A character or group of characters in communication and data processing systems, which is used to identify or name an item of data and to indicate certain properties of that data. The kind of element that may be named depends on the programming language; it may be variable, data structure, procedure, statement, higher level unit, or the program itself.

ideogram. In a natural language, a graphic character that represents an object or a concept and associated sound elements. Example: A Chinese ideogram or a Japanese Kanji.

IDF. 1. Intermediate Distribution Frame, a connecting apparatus for communications circuits.
2. Integrated Data File.
3. Image Description File.

IDI. 1. Initial Domain Identifier, part of the NSAP Address; identifies the network addressing domain from which domain-specific part values are allocated.
2. Intelligent Dual Interface.

IDL. Information Description Language.

idle character. A control character transmitted on atelecommunication line when there is no information to be transmitted. The idle character is not displayed or printed by the terminal.

idle signal unit. A group of information and check binary digits used in common-channel signalling during a period when no signal messages are free of transmission.

idle state. In data communication, a checking character or bit sent when no other messages are being sent. It provides verification that the link is still functioning and may also provide synchronisation data.

idle time. That part of operable time during which a functional unit is not operated.

idle. A period during which a computer or system stays switched on and available but is not in operation.

idling current. The current flowing in a device during a standby period, as opposed to operating current. Also known as standby current.

idling frequency. In a parametric amplifier, the difference between the signal frequency and pump frequency.

IDMS. *See* integrated data management system.

IDN. *See* integrated digital network.

IDOS. Interactive Disc Operating System.

IDP. 1. Integrated Data Processing.
2. Industrial Data Processing.
3. Input Data Processor.

IDP. Initial Domain Part, part of the OSI network address containing the AFI and IDI; identifies the addressing authority for the overall NSAP Address.

IDS. *See* intelligent disk server.

IDU. Interface Data Unit, a unit of data passed across the service boundary from one layer entity to the entity providing the service at layer below, or vice versa.

IEEE 1003.0. One of the IEEE POSIX working groups that has a charter to produce a guide that will accomplish the following: identify elements needed for a comprehensive application portability environment; explore standards that exist to address these elements; and determine whether these standards can be successfully integrated.

IEEE 1284. Bi-directional Printer Cable. This is the specification for a standard parallel printer cable.

IEEE 802. IEEE project to develop physical and software LAN standards, begun in 1980 to ensure compatibility between manufacturers.

IEEE 802.2. The Data Link standard for use with IEEE 802.3, 802.4 and 802.5 standards. It specifies how the basic data connection should be set up over the cable.

IEEE 802.3. The IEEE standardisation of Ethernet; a physical layer definition that includes specification for physical cabling plus method of transmitting data and controlling access to the cable. It uses CSMA/CD access method on a bus topology LAN.

IEEE 802.4. The IEEE standardisation of Token Bus; a physical layer standard that uses the Token Ring passing access method on a bus topology LAN; used by LANs implementing the Manufacturing Automation Protocol; older ArcNET operates in a similar way but does not follow 802.4, but ArcNET supporters have been trying to get the technology ratified by IEEE without success.

IEEE 802.5. The IEEE standardisation of IBM Token Ring; LAN physical layer standard that uses the Token Ring passing access method on a ring topology LAN.

IEEE 802.6. Standard defining an SMDS-based, short-packet ATM transmission.

IEEE. Institute of Electrical and Electronic Engineers, a US publishing and standards organisation responsible for many LAN standards such as the 802 series.

IEF. Instruction Execution Function.

IESG. Internet Engineering Steering Group, executive body within IETF.

IETF. Internet Engineering Task Force, a guiding body, composed of over 40 working groups, that helps develop new policies and protocols to be used on the Internet, specifically short-term needs; a part of the IAB.

IF and only IF statement. The formula of the form $A=B$ where A and B are also appropriate well formed formulas.

IF. 1. A statement used in many computer languages. A reserve word, signifying the beginning of a conditional statement.
2. *See* intermediate frequency.

IFA. Integrated File Adaptor.

IFAM. Inverted File Access Method.

IFEP. Integrated Front End Processor.

IFF. Identification Friend or Foe, a system used to indicate whether and aircraft is equipped with a transponder that replies with codes signal to an interrogation initiated by the IFF system.

IFIP. International Federation for Information Processing; much of the work of this group is sent as input for standards work in ISO and CCITT.

IFLA. International Federation of Library Associations and Institutes.

IFM. Interactive File Manager.

IFP. Integrated File Processor.

IFS. 1. Internal File System, a file system on the local computer, possibly internal to the software packages. 2. Interactive File Sharing.

IF-THEN-ELSE. A program statement often used in high-level computer languages. If the IF statement is correct, a THEN statement has the meaning that a following expression is to be executed. When the expression is untrue, the ELSE expression is executed.

IFU. Interworking Functional Unit, a term used in several OSI specifications, describing a discrete part of a protocol between two interworking entities.

IGES. Initial Graphics Exchange Specification, specification that defines a standard exchange format for graphical documents; part of NIST-APP.

IGFET. *See* insulated-gate field-effect transistor.

IGMP. Internet Group Multicast Protocol that host functions for multicasting applications such as audio, video, and shared-document real-time teleconferencing over Internet and other IP environments.

ignore character. A character used in transmission to fill an otherwise empty position and whose value is thus ignored. Also known as fill character.

IGOSS. Industry-Government Open Systems Specification, a proposed profile to combine MAP/TOP, GOSIP, and other industry OSI profiles.

IGP. Interior Gateway Protocol, term applied to any protocol used to propagate network accessibility and routing information within an autonomous system. There is no single standard IGP, but RIP is one of the most common.

IGRP. Internet Gateway Routing Protocol, a proprietary gateway protocol used by Cisco routers.

IIL. See I^2L.

IIOC. Intelligent Input Output Channel.

IIU. Instruction Input Unit.

IJS. Interactive Job Submission.

IL. Instruction List.

ILAN. Industrial Local Area Network.

ILC. Instruction Length Code.

ILD. *See* injection laser diode.

ILL. InterLibrary Loan, an international standard protocol, developed by libraries, to provide standards and procedures to allow loans of library books and other items between libraries all over the world.

illegal character. Any character not in the character set of a given machine or of a given programming language.

illegal instruction. An instruction that has an invalid operation code. It is sometimes deliberately inserted in an instruction stream when debugging in order to have a program halt at a particular point.

ILLS. InterLibrary Loan System.

ILP. 1. Intermediate Language Processor.
2. Intermediate Language Program.

IM. 1. Instruction Memory.
2. *See* isochronous modulation.

IMA. Invalid memory Address.

image antenna. A hypothetical, mirror-image antenna, that is supposed to be located as far below the ground as the actual antenna is above the ground, and in an inverted position, as if it were a reflection of the actual antenna.

image following. A data compression technique for images in which the coordinates of non-white pixels are stored.

image impedance. The property of a network in which the load impedance is seen looking in to the output terminals with the generator connected to the opposite end, and the generator impedance is seen looking into the input terminals with a load connected to the opposite end.

image inverter. An image rotator in the fibre-optic systems, which rotates the image by 180 degrees.

image lag. An image that remains on the screen for a short duration after the camera has been moved.

image printer. A printer that composes an image of a complete page before printing.

image rollover. A method of having a picture change when the user moves mouse pointer over the image. This action provides the user action feedback, adding another level of interaction and dynamics to the Web page. A common use of rollover technique is in navigational bars, which are composed of images. When the user moves the mouse pointer over one of the menu options, the image might change in some manner, designating that user is about to select that option.

image rotator. A coherent bundle of fibres in fibre-optic systems, the output end of which can be rotated with respect to the input end. Thus, twisting the bundle along its length and rotating the output image permits image rotation.

image scanner. An input device that converts images in to electronic form; the sensor determine the intensity of the reflected light from the page, and the light intensities are converted to digital data that can be viewed and manipulated by the computer. Also known as graphics scanner.

image setter. A professional typesetting machine capable of recognising the PostScript (or any other page description language) commands for type and graphics output (on film or paper) exceeding 1200 dots per inch (compared with 300 dots per inch for most laser printers). Due to the high investment cost of image setters, service bureau have been set up where customers can take their diskettes for high-resolution processing, in the same way film processing labs operate.

image transfer constant. A number depicting the transfer of power by an impedance network. It has the same value regardless of the direction of transmission through the network.

image. In data processing, a copy in memory of data that exists elsewhere.

IMAP. Interactive Mail Access Protocol, which allows the Internet users to browse and read their e-mail on the remote mail servers without, unlike POP2/POP3, having to transfer, and be responsible for storage of read/ stored messages.

IMI. Intermediate Machine Instruction.

IMIL. International Management Information Library, a registry of managed objects for OSI Network Management, still in the developmental stages.

IML. Information Manipulation Language.

immediate access store. IAS. A memory device in which the access time for any location is independent of the previous access and is usually of the same order as the cycle time of the processor.

immediate addressing. IA. In data processing, a method used to refer data that is located in address field of an instruction. Strictly, this is not a method of generating an address at all; it does not provide a reference to the desired data in a way that is both compact and requires less memory reference time.

immediate data. In software, data that are contained in an instruction word rather than in a storage location specified by an address in the word.

immediate instruction. An instruction that contains the value of an operand rather than its address. It may be noted that the operand is then called an immediate operand.

IMP. 1. Integrated Message Processor. 2. *See* interface message processor.

impact printer. Any device such as typewriter, that make use of mechanical impact to print characters onto paper.

IMPACT. Information Market Policy ACTions, a CEF-funded program aimed at establishing European-wide markets for information services.

implementation. The phase-4 of software development life cycle, in which the new hardware and software are installed in the user environment. The activity of proceeding from a given design of a system to working version of that system, or the specific way in which some part of the system is made to fulfil its function. With software, the use of the term implies that all major design decisions have been made so that the implementation activity could be relatively straight forward.

implicant. A product term that covers at least one of the standard sum of product terms in Boolean function but will introduce no new standard sum of product terms. An implicant that includes a standard product of a function that is not otherwise included is called prime implicant.

implicit declaration. A declaration caused by the occurrence of an identifier and in which the attributes are determined by default.

import. To move an item or file into an application or environment which is different from that native to it. The file is converted to the new format while attempting to change as little as possible about the appearance of the file when printed. For instance, MS Word for the Macintosh is able to import files from a few MS-DOS word processors.

IMPS. InterPersonal Messaging System, X.400, composed of MTS, IPM-UAs, AUs.

impulse noise. Noise of large amplitude consisting of random occurrences of energy spikes, having random amplitude and bandwidths, whose presence in a data channel can be a prime cause of errors.

IMS. *See* information management system.

IMSP. Acronym for Integrated Mass Storage Processor.

IMU. Information management Unit.

IM-UAPDU. Interpersonal Message User Agent Protocol Data Unit.

3½-inch disk. A magnetic flexible disk fully-enclosed in a rigid plastic casing and used as a secondary storage medium for personal computers. This 3½-inch disk was developed by Sony Corporation and introduced by Apple Computer Corporation in their Apple Macintosh range. IBM, Compaq, and other leading computer manufacturers followed suit. The 3½-inch disk has almost entirely replaced the 5¼-inch disk, as it offers several advantages. For example, 5¼-inch disk has an exposed section, which can be easily damaged by dust, fingerprints and other particles. Whereas each 3½-inch disk employs an automatic aluminium gate which only opens after the disk has been inserted into the disk drive. Another advantage of the smaller disk is the ease of write-protecting.

in phase. Pertaining to signals that have zero phase shift relative to each other, such as two sinusoidal waves of the same frequency whose maximum and minimum values coincide.

IN. Intelligent Network, a sophisticated network capable of recognising the profile (authorisation, services) of its users or subscribers. Carriers offering advanced services will increasingly offer IN services, particularly as the boundary between fixed and mobile networks becomes blurred.

in-band signalling. A communications technique in which the part of a signal bearing the data control information is contained within the bandwidth of the signal it is controlling.

incidence matrix. A representation of a graph *G* employing a matrix in which there is a row of each matrix *v* of *G*; entries on this row are just the vertices that are joined by an edge to *v*.

in-circuit emulator. A device that actually replaces a microprocessor by connecting directly to the circuit board. The device has a hardware/software capability for the real time input/output debugging of chips. The emulated microprocessor can be stopped, its memory locations can be examined and modifications as well as other alterations can be carried out.

in-circuit emulator. A tool for use in designing systems incorporating micro-controllers. Using an in-circuit emulator, the system designer can interactively control and examine the state of the system at any chosen time. This is essential for speeding up the debugging process and enhancing the system designer's productivity. The tool is easy to use and provides not only the capabilities of the target processor, but also a set of debugging capabilities to facilitate.

in-circuit test. The examination of discrete components and integrated circuits as part of a complete circuit. This can be done statistically in a non-energised state and dynamically in an energised state. The term is used generally in association with tests via automatic test equipment.

incoming message. A message transmitted from a server or host to the terminal computer.

incremental compiler. A compiler that compiles partial programs, and compiles additional statements for a previously compiled program, rather than compiling the whole program.

incremental integrator. A digital integrator modified so that the output signal is maximum negative, zero, or maximum positive when the value of the input is negative, zero, or positive, respectively.

indent. The distance between the beginning or end of a line of text and the margin.

independent compilation. The compilation of a source module not using the interface and context information from related source modules. It may be noted that when independently compiled units are eventually combined, it may be necessary to check interface and context information for validity.

independent side-band transmission. ISB. The transmission of the frequency bands above and below a carrier frequency, each independent of the modulating signal of the other side band. The system is limited by the difficulty of separating the two signals at the receiver.

indeterminant system. A logic system whose logic states are unpredictable.

index register. A register that can be specified by instructions that use indexed addressing. An index register is usually controlled by one or more instructions with the ability to increment or decrement the register by a fixed amount, to test the register for equality with a specified value and to jump to a specified location when the equality is achieved. It may be noted that an index register may also be used as a counter to control the execution of a loop, to control the use of an array, for table look-up, as a switch, or as a pointer.

index. 1. A symbol or a numeral used to identify a particular quantity in an array of similar quantities; for example, the terms of an array represented by X_1, X_2,..X_{100} have the indexes 1,2,...100. respectively.
2. In programming, a subscript of integer value that identifies the position of an item of data with respect to some other item of data.
3. A list of the contents of a file or of a document, together with keys or references for locating the contents.
4. A table used to locate the records of an indexed sequential data set.
5. To move machine part to a predetermined position, or by a pre-determined amount, on a quantized scale.
6. The value held in an index register.
7. An integer value selecting a particular element of an array.

indexed addressing. A method of generating an effective address that modifies the specified address given in the instruction by the contents of a specified index register. The modification is usually that of addition of contents of the index register to the specified address. The automatic modification of the index register contents results in an orderly progression of effective addresses being generated on successive executions of the instruction containing the reference to the index register.

indexed file. A file whose organisation uses an index. The index may be separated from the file, or located within the file. An index may be based upon the data item on which the file is ordered, if the file is sequential.

indexed processing. The use of directory (index) of key numbers of all files on a magnetic/optical disk. Before searching the entire disk for the record key, the index can be consulted for the address (location) of the file.

indexed sequential access method. ISAM. A method that provides keyed access for rapid and direct retrieval of information from a fast and continuously updated file of information in a computer system.

indexed sequential. A method in which computer files are organised on a direct access storage device. A directory is compiled with the address of each record along with its identification, thus permitting the fast access of a relevant record.

indicator. A bit or bit configuration that may be inspected to determine a status or condition.

Indigo 2. A higher end Indigo designed for 3D graphics.

Indigo. RISC-based workstation made by Silicon Graphics that supports high-speed 2-D graphics and digital audio. The Indigo uses display PostScript.

indirect referencing. A mechanism for referencing via a data object the value of which points to the referenced language object. This term also applies to the use of the mechanism. The referencing may be done along a chain of data objects in which each data object, except the last, points to the next, the last data object pointing to the referenced language object.

industrial process control. A data acquisition and control system that can provide great flexibility, as it can accept various types of process data, and a number of output signals and format of data that a computer may exercise.

Industry Standard Architecture. *See* ISA.

Indy. A lower-end workstation from Silicon Graphics.

infection. The obvious or undetected presence of a virus or Trojan in a computer system. Infections can remain dormant for some time, then become activated to display error messages, or erase entire databases. Trojan is the name given to any computer program which contains purposefully-hidden special codes written to intentionally cause damage. Unlike viruses, Trojans cannot duplicate themselves within a system.

inference. The formal method of reasoning that underlies logical deduction. Rules of inference provide means whereby a theorem-prover program may use earlier results, theorems, or axioms to derive new results.

inference engine. Software used with an expert system to examine data with respect to the knowledge base and to select an appropriate response.

infinite loop. A repetitive process often created by accident that causes the computer to continue to perform a given segment of a program indefinitely. It can only by intervention from outside the computer program in which the loop is included.

infix notation. A method of forming mathematical expressions governed by rules of operator precedence and using paired delimiters such as parentheses, in which the operators are dispersed among the operands; each operator indicating the operation to be performed on the operands or the intermediate results adjacent to it. If it is desired to distinguish the case in which there are more than two operands for an operator, the phrase 'distributed infix notation' may be used.

INFO. Information Network and File Organisation.

infographic. An image developed using various graphics tools and designed to impart maximum amount of information to the viewer.

INFOL. INFormation Orientated Language, high-level computer language structured around the provision of information; permits notation to be used by operators.

INFOR. INFormation Oriented Language.

informatics. Science dealing with the collection, transmission, storage, processing, and display of information.

information carrier. Any medium, such as compact disk or magnetic tape, etc., by which information is carried from its point of origin to its point of utility.

information channel. The hardware establishing the link between terminals in a data transmission system.

information flow analysis. The tracing of the flow of specific information types through an information system to determine whether the controls applied to the information are appropriate.

information hiding. A principle employed in computer programming for design of program modules; only the information essential to the user of the module is made available, while the details about how the module is implemented, are hidden.

information management system. IMS. A group of procedures organised as a system that is able to carry out a number of processes upon information, including maintenance and organisation cataloguing, locating, storage and retrieval.

information networks. The interconnection of a physically dispersed group of databases linked via telecommunications so that the total information resource may be shared by a larger number of users.

information orientated language. *See* INFOL.

information processing language. IPL. A computer programming language that provides for the processing of data representing information and the defining of the meaning of the processed information.

information processor. In computing, a device that stores information and instructions, receives input data or signals, processes the input and stores information according to its stored program and delivers the output information signals. The term computer is a misnomer because a vast majority of the computers are not concerned with mathematical operations, but with the processing of textual information or communication and control signals.

information provider. IP. In the context of view data systems, this is an organisation or an individual that provides data for the systems store of information held on computer files.

information rate. The number of symbols emitted by a source per second multiplied by the average information content per symbol.

information retrieval automatic language. *See* INFRAL.

information retrieval language. IRL. A computer programming language that is used for the cataloguing of large amounts of data all related to one specific area of interest. It allows for the retrieval of all or part of this data quickly and precisely.

information retrieval system. IRS. A system which provides particular items of data requested by users. Modern systems employ files of information that can be searched for specific items, in response to the definitions of particular user needs.

information retrieval. The methods, techniques and processes employed in searching particular computer files for specific items of information, in response to specific user needs.

information separator. IS. A special character used to designate the logical boundaries between items of information in data records.

information storage and retrieval. ISAR.
1. The process of storing and retrieving data.
2. A computerised system that provides information to the users in response to the requests. The processes employed in the system use the searching of computer files for particular items of information, in response to specific user needs.

information superhighway. The vast communication link, that allow access to government, industry, research, commercial and educational data banks for all users; it is similar to Internet, but provides a single high-speed link in place of a network of systems.

information system. The organised collection, processing, transmission, and dissemination of information in accordance with defined procedures. It may be manual or automatic.

information technology. IT. The techniques associated with handling information; it involves the use of telecommunications systems and computers in handling and processing the data, including the application, acquisition, storage and dissemination of pictorial, audio and numerical data.

information theory. The theory concerned with information rate, channel capacity, noise and other related factors affecting the information transmission. Initially the theory was developed for electrical communications, but now it is also applied to business systems and other areas concerned with information units and the flow of information in networks.

information. The meanings assigned to data by the agreed conventions used in its representation. If the contents of the message are known prior to its receipt then no new information is conveyed.

information-bearer channel. A channel capable of carrying both control and message information; it usually operates at a greater signalling rate than that required solely for user's data.

INFRAL. INFormation Retrieval Automatic Language, a computer language that permits the user to produce lists of groups of documentation information from indexed data.

INGA. Interactive Graphics Analysis.

inherently ambiguous language. A context-free language that has no non-ambiguous grammar.

inhibit. To prevent a process from taking place, that is, an inhibit input prevents a logic element from carrying out its defined function.

INI. File name extension for a configuration file. *See* initialisation files.

initial address message. IAM. The first signal message transmitted in a telecommunications call set-up process, in common-channel signalling. It contains all the information necessary to identify the called person or the route to be taken.

initial program load. IPL. Each time a computer is switched on, it must go through a formal loading (initialising) procedure known as booting or 'initial program load'. This occurs when the computer's operating system is installed. A section of this software also allows the computer to communicate with the user.

initial program loading. An initiation process that allows a computer program or operating system into a computer with data records. Once the self-loading routine is established in memory, the program can proceed under its own control, loading and executing other programs.

initial signal unit. The first of a group of information and check binary digits of a multi-unit signal message used in common-channel signalling.

initialisation files. 1. In Windows, files with the extension .INI. They contain information that defines your Windows environment.

2. Files which load when the computer starts up which change the way the computer normally behaves; called INITs on the Macintosh. One INIT allows you to access MS-DOS disks on the Mac. Another makes Oscar the Grouch sing whenever you throw trash away.

initialisation. 1. The operations required for setting a device to a starting state, before the use of a data medium, or before implementation of a process.

2. The process of assigning initial values to variables before the start of a computation. Many programming languages provide a facility for specifying initial values when a variable is first declared.

initialise program loading. A routine of initialisation used in various intelligent controllers and computers.

ink jet printer. A printer that produces images by spraying ink on to the page; it prints at moderate speeds and is cost effective.

in-line program. A program that is written sequentially, *i.e.*, without loops.

in-line recovery. In computing, a recovery in which the affected process is resumed from a safer point preceding the occurrence of the error.

in-line. In computing, a method of processing data without their previously having been edited or stored.

INP. Integrated Network Processor.

input area. The area of main memory that is currently allocated to hold incoming data. The processing system usually retrieves the data from input area and transfer it to a working area or register prior to its processing. The result of processing may be written to an output area. Subroutines are usually organised so as to replenish the input area from a source such as an input peripheral or communication line and clear the output area by transfer to baking store.

input-bound. Pertaining to a system in which the speed of performance is restricted by the rate at which data input may be entered.

input device. Any device that transfers data, programs, or signals to a processor system. Such devices provide the man-to-machine interface, the keyboard being most common device. The current devices include data tablets, data collection terminals, speech recognition units, magnetic card readers, and document readers.

input field. In peripherals, an unprotected field on the display surface of a visual display in which data can be entered, modified, or erased.

input port. In data communications, an interface used for transferring information into a computer.

input primitive. An item of data obtained from an input device such as a keyboard, choice device, locator, pick device, or valuator.

input protection. For analog input channels, the protection against overvoltages that may be applied between any two input connectors or between any input connector and ground.

input subsystem. That part of a process interface system that transfers data from the technical process to the process computer system.

input. 1. Energy or information delivered or transferred to a circuit or device.

2. The terminals of a device or circuit to which energy or information is applied.

3. To deliver or transfer energy or information to a circuit or device (as to input data from a computer peripheral to memory).

4. A signal transmitted from a peripheral device to central processing unit.

input/output control system. IOCS. 1. Computer software specifically designed to control input/output operations and communications between peripheral equipment and a central processor unit. The main areas of communications that are concerned include device allocation, error recovery and file identification. An input/output control system comprises a set of computer routines that can also direct other functions such as error correcting checkpoint label processing and restart.

2. A number of routines which a system analyst or programmes can use in a source program for handling input and output for tapes, cards and printers. Also known as I/O control system.

input/output controller. IOC. A device that controls interactions between a processing unit and input/output equipment. There are two portions to the controller: one controls actions of tape, card and printer equipment and the other is designed for the random processing of records stored on direct access devices. Also known as I/O controller.

input/output interface. In peripherals, an interface that can transmit or interrupt signal from a peripheral device to the central processing unit. Also known as I/O interface.

input/output port. A specially designed chip in a computer that is housed in the central processing unit data bus, enabling an external device to be connected to the computer for input/output operations. Also known as I/O port.

input/output processor. IOP. A device that is capable of handling normal data input/output control and sequencing. Also known as I/O processor.

input/output register. IOR. A memory location that accepts information from outside a computer at a particular speed and presents the information to a computer calculating unit at a normally higher speed. Also known as I/O register.

input/output. I/O. The devices, media or operations that are employed to pass information in or out, or both, of a computer or system.

input/output-bound. Pertaining to computer applications in which there is relatively, little processing compared to the amount of reading or writing to external devices. Also written as I/O-bound.

input-bound. Pertaining to a system in which the speed of performance is restricted by the rate at which input may be entered into it.

input-limited process. A process whose speed of execution is limited by the rate at which input data is obtained.

inquiry station. IS. A terminal from which information can be retrieved from a database. In most of the cases the terminal has a keyboard and display, but there may also be ancillary devices such as badge reader. An enquiry station may also update information as the result of an action arising from an enquiry, such as a railway booking terminal.

inquiry. A request for information from storage that may be initiated at a local or remote computer by using keyboard or similar device.

inscribe. To encode a document by printing information that is readable by both a person and a machine.

insert module. A module which, when inserted into equipment of a system, enables it to perform additional functions.

insert. The additions of characters, words, sentences, paragraphs, etc., into a copy during word processing.

insertion gain. The gain resulting from the insertion of a transducer in a transmission system, expressed as the ratio of the power delivered to that part of the system following the transducer to the power delivered to that same part before insertion. If more than one component is involved in the input or output, the particular component used must be specified; usually expressed in decibels. If the resulting number is negative, an insertion loss is indicated.

insertion loss. Loss of energy or gain by placing certain devices or subcircuits-filters, impedance matches, or equalisers, etc., in a circuit. It is usually expressed in decibels.

insertion point. The vertical bar in a text area which indicates where the typed text will be entered.

insertion test signal. Test signals introduced to unused lines during the time interval between two fields in which the television picture is suppressed (field blanking) to monitor, test and measure the working of the system and to networks.

installable file system. A file system that can be installed in place of the usual file allocation table file system, such as the high-performance file system.

installation program. A utility program used to install software programs onto the hard disk. The installation program is usually packaged with the application software and used to simplify and automate the loading process of an application, which may use more than ten diskettes to contain the program.

installation. A general term for a particular computing system in the context of the job it performs and the staff who manages it.

instantiate. In object-orient programming, to create an object with all the attributes and methods associated with a specific class.

instruction control unit. ICU. A specially designed device that contains a read-only memory storing the micro-instructions and address control logic for branching. This part of a computer enables instructions to be retrieved in the correct order, interpreted and applied.

instruction counter. A multi-bit device which temporarily sores information that monitors the location in a memory (address) of the current instruction is used to input information in the memory-address register.

instruction cycle. Sequence of obtaining an information stored in computer memory and then executing it.

instruction format. The allocation of the bits of a machine code instruction to the operation code, operands, etc. An instruction word is normally made up of a combination of an operation code and some way of specifying an operand, most commonly by its location or address. Some operation codes deal with more than one operand; the locations of these operands may be specified using any of the many addressing schemes.

instruction register. A device that temporarily stores the current instructions which are being decoded and executed by the central processor unit section of a computer.

instruction sequencing. The order in which the instructions in a program are carried out; normally the sequence proceeds in a linear manner through the program, and the address of the instructions is obtained from the program counter in the control unit. The sequence is interrupted when a branch instruction is executed; at such instances, the address of the branch instruction is inserted into the program counter and the process continues.

instruction set. The totality of instructions that a computer is capable of performing; the list of all the operation codes and the permitting addressing scheme pertinent to each.

instruction. Description of an operation, that is to be performed by a computer; consists of a statement of an operation to be performed, and some methods of specifying operands and the disposition of result of the operation.

insulation displacement connector. IDC. A type of connector and connector system that provides a self-stripping contact. The contacts are normally in the shape of a 'U' formed by two parallel cantilevered beams or legs with sharpened tips. The majority of flat cables for use with IDC systems are manufactured on 0.005 mm centres. A complete flat cable with as many as the 64 conductors can be terminated in one process.

INT. INTerrupt.

INTAP. Interoperability Technology Association for Information Technology, Japan. A national agency, funded by MITI to deal with OSI products and research.

INTAPNET. The Japanese regional member of OSIONE, and association and network to demonstrate the interoperability of OSI products.

integral controller. A communication unit built into a mini-frame computer.

integrated accounting package. An accounting software program that links all the accounting software program that links all the accounting functions together, including the general ledger, accounts receivable, and accounts payable, plus other mainstream functions like payroll and inventory. The advantage is that any transaction entered in one section of the program will result in an automatic update of other related areas.

integrated capacitor. A fixed capacitor in which one plate is a layer of material diffused into the substrate; the dielectric, a thin oxide film grown on top of the first layer; and the other plate, a metal layer deposited on top of the oxide film.

integrated circuit. IC. A circuit whose components and connecting wires are made by processing distinct areas of a chip of semiconductor material, such as silicon. Integrated circuits are classified according to construction, a few being monolithic, thin-film and hybrid. A single-package complete circuit is able to perform at least one, sometimes many, complete functions. This interconnected array of components is fabricated from a single crystal of semiconductor material by etching, doping and diffusion. Generally, ICs are known by their circuits' complexity as follows:

small-scale integration (SSI),
medium-scale integration (MSI),
large-scale integration (LSI),
very-large-scale integration (VLSI),
extra-large-scale integration (ELSI).

In MOS integrated circuit the active devices are MOSFETs, which operate at low currents and high frequencies. A very large number of MOSFETs can be packed together on one silicon chip, *i.e.,* MOS circuit have a high packing density. They also consume very little power. The development of MOS technology has allowed extremely complex functions to be performed on a single chip. In bipolar integrated circuits, the components are bipolar transistors and other devices that are fabricated using the *p-n* junction properties of semiconductors. Compared with MOS circuits, bipolar circuits have higher operating speeds but have the disadvantages of high power consumption and low packing density.

integrated communication system. ICS. A system incorporating two or more autonomous communication systems combined into one single system, so that none of the original autonomy remains.

integrated communications adaptor. ICA. Integrated adaptor that permits connection between multiple communication lines and a processing unit.

integrated computing. The concurrent use of data by two or more software packages.

integrated data processing. IDP. 1. A computer system processing concept in which the processing of data is organised, correlated and systematic, embracing all the data processing requirements in a particular area of interest.

2. A system where all procedures are linked by a computer employed for the processing of data.

3. Treating data processing requirements as a whole, this system tries to reduce or eliminate the duplication of data entry or processing steps.

Integrated Database Application Programming Interface. *See* IDAPI.

integrated database. A database which has been consolidated to eliminate redundant data.

Integrated Digital Access. *See* IDA.

integrated digital network. IDN. A network using both digital transmission and digital switching.

integrated injection logic. A family of integrated circuits devised from diode transistor logic by combining some of the diode transistor logic components into single transistor units.

integrated modem. In data communications, a modem that is integral part of the device with which it operates.

integrated optical circuit. IOC. A monolithic optical circuit, composed of active and passive miniaturised components, employing planar waveguides for coupling to opto-electronic devices and providing signal processing functions such as modulation, multiplexing and switching.

integrated services digital network. ISDN. In communications, an integrated digital network in which the same digital switches and digital paths are used to establish different services. This concept represents a logical development in the provision of public communication services, taking into account the economy made possible by the advancement of digital technologies, the increasing demand for wide range of telecommunication services and the need to provide the customer with a single interface to which can be connected a wide variety of user communication devices such as alarm sensors, facsimile, telephone, teletext, videotex etc. The major advantages of integrated services digital network are:

(a) flexibility in the allocation of bandwidth to applications and specific routes;

(b) control over the allocation of network resources;

(c) reconfiguration of routes in a virtual private network and of the bandwidth allocations;

(d) cost control from the network management information;

(e) integrated network interfaces for a range of telecommunication types of a service;

(f) diversity in terms of alternate network routes; and

(g) opportunities of value-added services, voice prompts, database access, electronic mail etc.

integrated system. A system in which several elements are integrated and used for more than one function.

integrator. A device having an output variable whose value is:

(a) proportional to the integral of one variable with respect to another, or

(b) proportional to integral of an input variable with respect to elapsed time.

Intel 82C37A-5. A CHMOS version of Intel 8237A-5. It is pin-to-pin compatible with NMOS 8237A-5.

Intel 8086. The 16-bit microprocessor introduced in 1978; the least popular of the Intel chips because in the same year, IBM chose the Intel 8088 microprocessor for its personal computer. The 8088 offered 16-bit internal processing and 8-bit external processing, making it more compatible with peripherals available at that time.

Intel 8087. A high performance numeric data processor, which uses HMOS III technology and is packed in 40-pin package. It has been designed to work with 8086, 8088, 80186, and 80188 microprocessors. it has 68 numeric processing instructions whcih are added to 8086/8088 instructions set.

Intel 8088. The microprocessor used in original IBM Personal Computers, the 8088 offered one megabyte of random-access memory with 16-bit internal processing, and 8-bit external processing, making it more compatible with peripherals available at the time of its introduction in 1978. It operated at a slow 4.77 megahertz (MHz), although later versions had clock speeds approaching 10 MHz. The 8086 and 8088 microprocessors consist of two processing units: the execution unit (EU) which executes instructions, and the bus interface unit (BIU) which fetches instructions, read operands, and writes results.

Intel 8257/8257-5. The 4-channel DMA controller; 8257-5 is compatible with the 8085 processor. Each channel generates sequential memory address which permits the I/O device to transfer data to or from the memory. each channel contains two 16-bit registers, which are initialized before a channel is enabled.

Intel 8276. A small system CRT controller, meant to interface CRt raster scan displays with Intel 8085, 8086, 8088 microprocessors, and 8051 single-chip microcomputer.

Intel 80286. The microprocessor, which was introduced in 1984 and used for the IBM Personal Computer AT. The 80286 microprocessor is still being used, requiring 16-bit peripherals. It can address up to 16 megabytes of random-access memory although DOS can only use 640 kilobytes. 80286 chip is available in block speeds of 6, 8, 10, 12, 16, 20 megahertz, while 80386 is available in many clock speeds including 16, 20, 25, and 33 megahertz. When it was introduced, 80286 was a high-speed micropro-cessor, which pushed microprocessor-based systems to new performance levels.

Intel 80287. HMOS numeric processor extension for 80286 microprocessor with 80-bit internal architecture. It executes instructions in parallel with an 80286 processor.

Intel 80386 SX. The original Intel 80386 was designed to use a 32-bit data bus structure for internal and external communications. This made processing much faster. The SX version was introduced 20 June 1988 to take advantage of 32-bit internal processing, while restricting external communications to 16 bits- making it compatible with peripheral designed to operate on the 80286 microprocessor. The SX chip is available in clock speeds of 16/20 megahertz, while the 80386 comes in many clock speeds.

Intel 80386. The microprocessor, which was introduced in 1986 with a 32-bit data bus structure and the ability to directly address up to 4 gigabytes of random-access memory. A special mode enables 80386 to access more than one program at a time (such as a word processor plus a spreadsheet program) by separating blocks of 640 kilobytes of memory to be used by DOS as required. The 80386 microprocessor was first made available in the Compaq Deskpro 386. Intel designate the letters DX (80386DX) to this chip in order to distinguish it from the 80386SX chip.32-bit architecture provides the programming resources required to directly support large applications, those characterised by large integers, large data structures, large programs (or large numbers of programs), and so on. The 80386's eight 32-bit general registers can be used interchangeably both as instruction operands and addressing mode variables. Data types include 8, 16, and 32-bit integers and ordinals, packed and unpacked decimals, pointers, and strings of bits, bytes, words, and double-words.

Intel 80387 DX. A high performance 80-bit CHMOS IV numeric processor extension for 80386 processor. Its performance is 5-10 times more than that of 8087 and 80287. It directly extends 80386 DX CPU instruction set to include trigonometric, logarithmic, exponential, and arithmetic instructions for all types of data.

Intel 80387 X. A high performance 80-bit numeric processor extension for 80386 SX microprocessor. Its performance is 2-3 times more than that of 8087 and 80287, and is compatible with 80387 DX.

Intel 80486. A microprocessor with 32-bit data bus structure, having ability to directly address upto 64 gigabytes of random-access memory. A special mode enables the 80486 to run more than one program at a time (such as a word processor plus a spreadsheet program) by separating blocks of 640 kilobytes of memory to be used by DOS as required. It is also referred to as the i486.

Intel 82716. A low cost, highly integrated, video storage and display device. it displays graphics and texts, and can manage upto 16 display objects on screen, and can select upto 16 colours from a range of 4096. It contains on-chip DRAM controller and on-chip D/A converter, and can support upto 512 KB of display memory.

Intel 82786. CHMOS graphics coprocessor, which is compatible with all Intel microprocessors. It can support multiple graphics application, and has high speed character drawing capability, and can provide upto 256 simultaneous colours; contains 4 MB DRAM/VRAM controller for graphics memory.

Intel Hex. A format in data structures, for storing binary information. Some of the major features of this format include:

(a) ASCII code is used to encode all information;

(b) load addresses are included; and

(c) check sum bytes are included for error detection and recovery.

Intel. Maker of the 80×86 and Pentium lines of processors which are used in IBM PC and compatible computers.

Intelligent Character Recognition. *See* ICR.

intelligent device. Any device or peripheral, which can be programmed to give desired features.

intelligent disk server. IDS. A disk server, which can provide a mechanism for microcomputers in a network, to request and gain access to centralised peripherals and disk volumes. The system can manage efficient sharing of printers, tape drives, etc. and can provide security to by controlling individual user access to facilities.

intelligent display device. A display device directly supported by a computer that allows certain operation to be performed locally.

intelligent drive. An integrated storage element, such as those provided by Digital Equipment Corporation, which has some controller functionality built into the unit itself. These are called intelligent drives because they perform self-diagnosis, command queuing, seek optimisation, automatic on-board error detection and correction, and bad-block replacement, all without system or host adapter intervention. Most disk drives also include ancillary mechanism, such as power, temperature, and speed regulation.

intelligent hub. A hub that provides network management and intelligent path selection in addition to signal regeneration.

intelligent terminal. A device equipped with visual display unit, keyboard, processor memory, and local software, and is connected to a host computer. The terminal has sufficient processing ability to provide various functions, and can continue to operate in a limited mode without communication with the host computer.

IntelliMouse. A kind of mouse with a rotating wheel between two buttons, which allows to quickly scroll, pan, and zoom without using scroll bars or other on-screen controls. Office 97 applications supports this mouse.

Intelsat. International Telecommunications Satellite Organisation, an organisation founded in 1964 for developing global satellite communications system, At present, Intelsat has more than 120 members. Intelsat 1 satellite was launched in 1965. Intelsat VII is planned to replace the ageing Intelsat V-types which carry two-thirds of the world's telephone calls.

intensity modulation. IM. In an intensity modulation fibre-optics communications system, information is transmitted when a modulating electrical signal provides optical sources of variable intensity. Demodulation is achieved with a photo-detector whose electrical output is proportional to that of the optical input.

Interactive Maii Access Protocol. *See* IMAP.

interactive media. A software product that can react to and respond to input from the user.

interactive processing. The immediate processing of data at the time of entry; an application in which each entry elicits a response, as in an inquiry system or an airline reservation system. An interactive system may also be conversational, implying continuous dialogue between the user and the system.

interactive terminal facility. The capability of a computer system to allow a user at a local or remote terminal to elicit a response to any enquiry made of the system. It also allows for a continuous dialogue between the user and the system and provides for immediate diagnostic assistance to any errors made by the user. The device used for such purpose usually consists of a combination of a display and keyboard with at least one built-in microprocessor to provide facilities such as editing and prompts for the operator.

interblock gap. The space on a magnetic tape between the end of one block of data and the beginning of the next block.

interconnectivity devices. The devices that connect independent network; include routers, brouters, gateways, and CSUs/DSUs.

inter-digit pause. An interval of time experienced when telephone dialling, between the end of one set of pulses which represent a digit and the start of the next.

interface cancellation equipment. ICE. An electronic counter-counter measure system for very-high-frequency combat radio. The system can upgrade current equipment to meet electronic counter measures used against battlefield communications.

interface message processor. IMP. A computer that transmits data by means of addressed packets that occupy the channel just for the time taken to transmit the packet. It is used in an experimental data communication network funded by the Advanced Research Projects Agency.

interface. I/F. 1. A shared boundary between two related devices or components defined for specifying the operation between them. It might be a hardware component to link two devices, or it might be a portion of storage or registers accessed by two or more computer programs.
2. A common boundary between two systems or pieces of equipment where they are joined.
3. The link between computer program and the outside environment; common example is the RS232-C port or the AUI on LANs between the computer and transceiver. Knowledge systems have interfaces for development (the knowledge acquisition interface) and for users (the user interface). Some systems have interfaces that pass information to and from other programs, databases, display devices, or sensors.

interference. In signal transmission system, extraneous power from natural or man-made sources that interferes with reception of desired signals.

intergrated data management system. IDMS. In databases, a proprietary system, specified by CODASYL which provides facilities for structuring and using large databases.

Interior Gateway Protocol. *See* IGP.

nterior router. The router with an autonomous region, which may talk to each other to share the routing information. Such routers employ a class of routing protocols including RIP and OSPF.

interleaved memory. A process of dividing the dynamic random-access memory (DRAM) chip into two separate areas of storage so that the microprocessor can alternate between storage areas, thereby speeding up the rate of data access. While one area is being red, the other is being refreshed. This process became popular because DRAM requires its contents to be updated at least every one thousandth of a second. If this is not done, the capacitor used to represent memory-states would very quickly lose their electrical charge. However, introduction of static random-access memory (SRAM) eliminated the need for interleaved memory because SRAM chips can retain their contents until the power is switched off.

interleaving. A technique for obtaining multiprogramming in a relatively simple system without a supervisor program. Each of the programs that are to be run concurrently are broken down into segments that are then linked up into a single program. The function of each segment and order of linking is arranged so that maximum use is made of the processor time. A segment that initiates a transfer to a peripheral is linked to a segment of some other program for which processor activity is required. A multiplexer channel interface will interleave transfers from several slow peripherals.

interlocking. A mechanism by which one processor in a multiprocessing system can prevent another from accessing the same data. Processor operating independently in a multiprocessing environment must cooperate with one another when sharing resources such as primary memory. When multiple processors are executing a program, a mechanism must exist to control a sequence where processor 'A' waits to read data written by processor 'B'. A mechanism must also ensure that multiple processors do not attempt to write to the same location at the same time. Such sharing of data is made possible by interlocking. Interlock allows a processor to lock out the other processors while accessing the shared data.

intermediate distribution frame. IDF. A unit that provides for the interconnection, termination or cross-connection of cables and wires from units of telephone exchange equipment.

intermodulation noise. The noise resulting in a transmission path because of modulation, demodulation, and any non-linear characteristics of the electrical components or the transmission media.

intermodulation product. The frequencies in the output signal produced by intermodualtion. It is equal to the sums and differences of integral multiples of the frequency present in the input signal. The inter-modulation products are generally caused by nonlinear distortion.

intermodulation. The modulation of the frequency components of an electromagnetic wave, producing waves having frequencies equal to the sums and differences of integral multiples of the component frequencies of the original waves, such as by mixing or the use of non-linear circuits.

internal bias. The bias, either marking or spacing, that may occur within a start-stop teletypewriter receiving mechanism and which will have the same effect on the margin of operation as bias external to the receiver.

internal fragmentation. A form of fragmentation that arises when allocations are made only in multiples of a sub-unit. A request of the arbitrary size must be met by rounding up to the next highest multiple of the sub-unit, leaving small amount of memory that is allocated but not in use.

internal hard disk. A hard disk that is mounted and operated inside the chassis of computer or microprocessor.

internal label. A machine-readable label that is recorded on the same medium as the set of data, to which it refers.

internal modem. A communications device used to modulate data signals, it is mounted and operated inside the chassis of computer.

internal security controls. The hardware and softwares within an automated system that can restrict access to resources only to the authorized persons, programs, or devices.

International standard bibliographic description. ISBD. A convention employed in describing documents that is recognised internationally.

International standard book number. ISBN. A number used to aid the location of a particular book within a library or information retrieval system. Every book published is allocated its own unique number, consisting of ten digits.

International standard serial number. ISSN. A number used to aid communication between periodical publishers and libraries, to assist inter-library loan and maintenance of computer files. Every title published is given a unique number consisting of eight digits in two groups of four.

International standards organisation. ISO. A specialised agency of the United Nations, founded in 1947, and concerned with international standardisation across a variety of industries and their products.

Internet Activities Board. *See* IAB.

Internet address. An IP address assigned in blocks of numbers to user organisations accessing the Internet. Duplicate addresses can cause major problems on the network, but the NIC trusts organisations to use individual addresses responsibly. Each address is an eight- bit number (0 to 255). There are three classes: A, B and C, depending on how many computers on the site are likely to be connected.

Internet Control Message Protocol. *See* ICMP.

Internet Explorer. A proprietary Web browser from Microsoft Corporation.

Internet Group Multicast Protocol. *See* IGMP.

internet layer. The layer of TCP/IP stack, which provides logical addressing and routing.

Internet Packet Exchange. *See* IPX.

Internet Protocol Security. IPSec. A suite of cryptography based protection services and security protocols. It provides machine-level authentication as well as data encryption, for VPN connections that use the L2TP protocol. IPSec negotiates between the computer of the user and the remote tunnel server before L2TP connection is established.

Internet registry. The Internet registry assigns Internet addresses, registers unique domain names, keeps the main database, and performs other registry and organised tasks to allow smooth functioning of the Internet.

Internet Relay Chat. IRC. A world-wide part line protocol, which allows the user to converse with each other in real time. It is structured as a network of servers, each of which accepts connections from client programs, one per user.

Internet. 1. A world-wide collection of interconnected networks, so that they appear to be one continuous network, and can be addressed seamlessly at the network layer three of the OSI model. Typical Internets are built using routers, either to form a backbone network comprised of routers, or to link together LANs at the network layer. Internet carries messages, documents, programs, and data files that contain all kinds of information for bussiness, educational, and government institutions, and individual users. Internet functions as a single, co-operative virtual network. Internet provides universal connectivity and three levels of network services: connectionless packet delivery; full duplex stream delivery and application level services including electronic mail; and EDI. All computers on Internet use TCP/IP protocols to exchange command and data. The individual computers connect to local and regional networks, which are connected together through the Internet backbone. Every computer on Internet has a unique numeric IP address, and most also have an address that uses the Domain Nma e System. Most Internet programs use the client-server model; users run client programs that obtain data and services from a server.

internet. A collection of networks interconnected with routers. 'Small-i' internets are often used to refer to collection of LANs, metropolitan or campus networks, or other types of regional networks.

Internet-Draft. *See* I-D.

internetwork. Two or more independent networks that are connected and yet maintain independent identities. Internetworks are joined by the interconnectivity devices.

InterNIC. Internet Information Service.

interoperability. The ability to exchange information between two systems so that the information can be processed meaningfully.

interplanetary probe. An instrumented spacecraft that flies close to or lands upon a planet.

interpreter. A program that reads and executes source code one line at a time. Does not create an executable file that can run independently. Compare to compiler.

interpretive language. A programming language that is designed for or suited to interpretive implementation. In extreme cases, the language can only be implemented by means of an interpreter. BASIC is often interpreted on small computers.

inter-process communications. Communications between several programs based on one computer or across a number of machines. Alternatively, communication across a network between different processes of the same program between different computers running parts of a single program, or between two programs working together. The most common approaches to IPC in networking circles are probably Application Programming Interfaces such as APPC and NetBIOS.

interrupt handler. A code section, to which control is transferred when a processor is interrupted. It then decides what action should be executed. For example, a first level interrupt handler is the part of an operating system that provides the initial communication between a program or a device and the operating system. When an interruption occurs, the current state of the system is stored and the appropriate first level interrupt handler is executed; which leaves a message for the operating system and then returns, restoring the system to its original state and allowing the original task to continue as if no interruption has occurred. The operating system will periodically check for new messages and perform the appropriate actions.

interrupt mask. A means of selectively suppressing interrupts when they occur so that they can be acted upon at a later stage.

interrupt priority. An allocated order of importance to program interrupts; usually a system can only respond to one interrupt at a time but the rate of occurrence may be higher than the rate of servicing. The system control may arrange interrupt masks to suppress some types of interrupt if more important interrupt has just occurred.

interrupt request. Hardware lines over which devices can send interrupts. Typically, each device connected to computer uses a separate IRQ. Expansion cards such as Ethernet cards or token ring adapters also use IRQs. Setting the IRQ so that it does not conflict with other devices is an essential part of installing expansion cards and new devices.

interrupt vector. An address held in a special-purpose register or in memory that indicates the instruction to be executed on acceptance of the associated interrupt. It may be noted that the term 'interrupt vector' has also been used to describe an array of interrupt vectors that may be indexed.

interrupt. INT. 1. Normally initiated by an external signal, a discontinuity in the normal flow of system or routine, that can be resumed at a later time. 2. A specific control signal that diverts the attention of a microprocessor from the main program. It signifies that an asynchronous event has occurred. The current sequence of instructions is temporarily suspended and a sequence appropriate to the interruption has started in its place. On IBM and compatible computers, a signal that a device sends to the computer when the device is ready to accept or send information.

interrupted continuous wave. ICW. A type of controlled disturbance propagated through space (wave), used for radio telegraphy where the audio-frequency wave is keyed on and off.

intersatellite link. The transmission of messages between communications satellites.

intersegment linking. The links between the segments of a large program. If the segments are separately compiled, it is necessary to provide a mechanism for transferring control out of one segment and into another, usually by introducing a specific type of labeled statement which identifies the point at which a segment can be entered, and whose values can be made accessible to other segments when the program is link-edited.

interstage coupling. Coupling between two circuit stares, such as those of an amplifier. Common forms of interstage coupling are direct, capacitor, choke coil, transformer, neon bulb, and zener diode.

InterVU. An MPEG player that provides streaming MPEG audio/video downloads for Netscape Navigator. The user may play any MPEG file without requiring decoders. The InterVG plug-in is available for Macs and Windows NT/98 systems.

intranet. The inter-networked connection of local networks within a specific organisation.

invariant. A property which remains true across some transformation or mapping. In the context of program correctness proofs, an invariant is an assertion that is associated with some program element and remains 'true' despite execution of some part of that element. It may be noted that the invariant cannot accurately be described as 'true at all times', since individual operations may destroy and subsequently restore the invariant condition. However, the invariant is always true between such operations, and therefore provides a static characterisation by which the element can be analysed and understood.

inverse filtering. An image-restoration technique in which the distorted image is processed in a manner that reverses the transformations, which caused the original distortion.

inverted file. A file in which another of the data items in the records is used to sequence the records instead of the one originally used, e.g., a sequenced list of telephone numbers each of which is followed by the name of the subscriber to whom the number is assigned, rather than an alphabetical list of subscriber names each followed by the number assigned to them.

inverter. 1. A device for changing direct current to alternating current. 2. In computers, a device or circuit that inverts the polarity of a pulse. 3. A logic gate that inverts the signal it receives so that logic 1 (true) is converted to logic 0 (false) and vice versa. It therefore implements the logical NOT operation.

IO. Interpretive Operation.

IOA. Input/Output Adaptor.

IOBS. Input/Output Buffering System.

IOCS. Input/Output Controlling System.

IOMP. Input/Output MicroProcessor.

IONYL. Internal Organisation of the Network Layer, term for the Network Layer detailed architecture.

IOP. *See* input/output processor.

IOPS. Internet Official Protocol Standards.

IOQ. Input/Output Queue.

IOR. Input/Output register.

IOR. *See* input/output register.

IOREQ. Input/Output REQuest.

IOS. 1. Intermediate Open System.

2. Interactive Operating System.
3. Input/Output Selector.
4. Input/Output System.

IOT. Input/Output Transfer.

IP address. A logical address used to locate a computer on TCP/IP network; includes, a network ID number, identifying the network; a sub-net ID number, identifying a sub-net on the network; and host ID number, identifying the computer on the sub-net. It ensures that data can be delivered to the correct location.

IP address. The 32-bit address assigned to hosts that want to participate in a TCP/IP Internet. IP datagram; the basic unit of information passed across a TCP/IP Internet.

IP. Internet Protocol, the TCP/IP standard protocol that defines the IP datagram as the unit of information passed across an Internet and provides the basis for connectionless packet delivery service. IP includes the ICMP control and error message protocol as integral part. It provides the functional equivalent of ISO OSI Network Services. IP performs one set of tasks when transmitting data to a computer and a different set of tasks when receiving data from another computer. When sending data, IP on source computer must determine whether the destination computer is one the same network (local), or if it is on a different network. The three 32-bit fields within the IP software are integral to its operation. These are: IP address field: the unique 32-bit address assigned to a computer; sub-net mask field: 32-bit pattern of bits used to tell IP how to determine which part of the address is the network portion and which part is the host portion; default gateway field: the optional 32-bit address, which, if present, identifies the address of a router.

IPB. integrated Processor Board.

IPC. 1. InterProcess Communication, how the different programs, different computers, or several processes, which are instances of the same program on the same computer, talk to each other.
2. Information Processing Centre.
3. Industrial Process Control.
4. Independent Control Point.

IPE. In-band Parameter Exchange, the exchange of control data within a user channel.

IPL. *See* information processing language.

IPM SERVICE. InterPersonal Message service, provides a user with the features needed to communicate with other IPM service users.

IPM. 1. InterPersonal Message (MHS), application for personal messaging between individual users, based on the concept of a business memo.
2. Interruptions Per Minute.

IPM-UA. InterPersonal Messaging User Agent, the component of IPMs that represents the user in submission and delivery of messages.

IPRL. ISPICS Requirements List, a tabular form stating what protocol elements are mandatory or optical for each protocol in an International Standardised Profile.

IPS. 1. Inches Per Second; a measure of speed used to indicate the rate at which a magnetic tape passes a magnetic head.
2. Impulses Per Second.
3. Information Processing System, generic term used to describe any combination of hardware, software, and media in automation.

IPSB. InterProcessor Signal Bus.

IPSec. *See* Internet Protocol Security.

IPSIT. International Public Sector IT Group.

IPU. Instruction Processing Unit.

IPv6. A new standard for IP addressing

that features 128-bit IP addresses. The intent of IPv6 designers is for IPv6 to phase in gradually over the next several years.

IPX tunnelling. A method of supporting IPX/SPX on TCP/IP networks by interfacing IPX with TCP/IP transport layer.

IPX. Internet Packet Exchange, the native NetWare protocol used on many earlier Novell networks.

IR. 1. Index Register.
2. Interrupt Register.
3. Instruuction Register.

IRA. Information Resource Administration.

IRAM. Indexed Random Access Memory; a microchip that integrates a dynamic RAM and its control and refresh circuits on one substrate, creating a chip that has dynamic RAM density characteristics, but looks and operates like a static RAM chip. Before iRAM's introduction, users who built memory blocks smaller than 8 kilobytes typically used static RAMs.

IRC. 1. International Record Carrier, a public data carrier authorised to connect to carriers from different nations.
2. Internet Relay Chat.

IRD. Information Resource Dictionary.

IRIS printer. The printer used to produce high-resolution presentation graphics and coloured prints that resemble full-colour offset printed images. IRIS is a high-tone-high-tech form of inkjet printing in which individual sheets of paper are mounted on to a drum. The nozzles of the inkjet printing head pass from one of the spinning drum to the other spraying minute drops of coloured ink to form image with a resolution as high as 1800 dpi.

IRIX. A version of Unix for Silicon Graphics machines.

IRL. *See* information retrieval language.

IRN. Internal Routing Network.

IRQ. See Interrupt Request.

IRR. Interrupt Return Register.

IRS. *See* information retrieval system.

IRTF. Internet Research task Force, part of the Internet IAB responsible for research and development of the TCP/IP protocol suite.

IRV. 1. International Reference Version.
2. Interrupt Request Vector.

IS. 1. *See* information separator.
2. Inquiry Station.

ISA. Industry Standard Architecture, that specifies the architecture of the hardware; the 8/16-bit bus architecture originally developed by IBM and now standard in almost all personal computerss that use Intel's 8086 and 80×86 chips.

ISAL. Information System Access Line.

ISAM. *See* indexed sequential access method.

ISAR. *See* information storage and retrieval.

ISB. *See* independent side-band transmission.

ISBD. *See* International standard bibliographic description.

ISBN. *See* International standard book number.

ISDN modem. An interconnectivity device that connects a computer to an ISDN line.

ISDN. Integrated Services Digital Network, an approach to switched digital networking that can handle a range of digital voice, data and digital image transmission. It is intended to provide end-to-end, simultaneous handling of digitised voice and data traffic on the same digital links via integrated switches. There are different access channels, according to geographic location. These include Basic Rate Access, and Primary Rate Access (1.544 (US) and 2.048 Mbit/s (Europe). ISDN standards are defined in the ITU-TS's I-Series Recommendations.

Multilink dialling over ISDN combines multiple physical links in to a logical bundle. This aggregate link increases the bandwidth.

ISDN/AP. Integrated Systems Digital Network/Application Package, a hardware/software OSI-based package.

ISH. Intermediate System Hello, contains Network Entity Title and SNPA address for the sending IS, and the holding time for this information.

IS-IS. Intermediate System to Intermediate System protocol, the OSI protocol by which routing information is exchanged between ISs.

ISO 7. An Internationally agreed character code (ISO 646-1973), using seven bits for each character. The code includes certain positions designed for national use, to allow different countries to allow special characters for letters with diacritical marks, or currency symbols, etc. The US version of ISO-7 is ASCII, which is generally used in computing.

ISO 106-07. The ISP for FTAM.

ISO 646. ISO 7-bit coded character set for information interchange.

ISO 1155. Standard for the use of longitudinal parity for error detection.

ISO 2022. 7- and 8-bit coded character sets and code extension techniques.

ISO 2110. Specification for the functional interface standard, similar to RS-232-C or -D; specifies which signals will be carried on specific pins.

ISO 3166. Country codes alphabetic codes for representing country names.

ISO 3309 AD1. Data communications-HDLC Procedures;
Addendum 1: Start/stop transmission operation-Data link layer standard.

ISO 3309. Data communications-HDLC Procedures-Frame structure-Data link layer standard.

ISO 4217. Currency codes, codes for the representation of standards of currency.

ISO 4335. Data communications-HDLC Data link procedures Elements-Data link layer standard.

ISO 4902. Data communications-Standard for serial DTE/DCE communications using a 37-pin DB-37 connector, based on V.36.

ISO 4903. Data communications-Standard for serial DTE/DCE communications using a 15-pin DB-15 connector, based on RS-442.

ISO 6093. Specification for representation of numeric values in character strings for information interchange.

ISO 6160. (1987) PL/1 Programming language.

ISO 6429. The 7- and 8-bit coded character sets-additional control functions for character imaging devices.

ISO 6937. Code character set for text communications, defines several character set codes.

ISO 7478. Data communications-multilink procedures-data link layer standard.

ISO 7498 AD1. Addendum to reference model for connectionless operation.

ISO 7498 AD2. Addendum to reference model on multipeer data transmission.

ISO 7498-1. OSI basic reference model, seven-layer system; CCITT X.200.

ISO 7498-2. OSI reference model-security architecture.

ISO 7498-3. OSI reference model-naming and addressing.

ISO 7498-4. OSI reference model-management framework.

ISO 7776. X.25 Frame l-level protocol, a data link layer standard; approximately equal to ISO 8802/2 (808.2); talks up to ISO 8208, and down to X.21, EIA 530, EIA 449, etc.

ISO 7809 AD1. High-level data link control (HDLC) procedures.
Addendum 1: Consolidation of earlier draft addenda-data link layer standard.

ISO 7809 AD2. High-level data link control procedures.
Addendum 2: Optional functions description-data link layer standard.

ISO 7809 AD3. High-level data link control (HDLC) procedures-classes of procedures.
Addendum 3: Operation of start/stop transmission-data link layer standard.

ISO 7809. High-level data link control (HDLC) procedures-classes of procedures-data link layer standard.

ISO 7942. Graphical kernel system (GKS) functional description.

ISO 8072. Transport layer service definitions; CCITT X.214.

ISO 8073. Transport layer protocol specification; CCITT X.224.

ISO 8073/AD2. Operation of Class 4 over connectionless-mode network service.

ISO 8208 AD1. X.25 Packet-level protocol for data terminal equipment, Addendum 1: Alternative logical channel number allocation-network layer standard.

ISO 8208 AD2. X.25 Packet-level protocol for data terminal equipment, Addendum 2: Extensions for private and circuit switch use-network layer standard.

ISO 8208 AD3. X.25 Packet-level protocol for data terminal equipment, Addendum 3: Packet-level static conformance requirements-network layer standard.

ISO 8208. Connection-oriented network service protocol for X.25 packet-level protocol for data terminal equipment.

ISO 8211. Data descriptive file for information interchange, adopted in 1984 but never widely used; FIPS 123.

ISO 8326. Basic connection-oriented session service definition (Specification); CCITT X.215.

ISO 8327. Basic connection-oriented session protocol definition (Specification); CCITT X.225.

ISO 8348. Network service definition, CCITT X.213;
AD 1: connection-less-mode transmission,
AD 2: Network layer addressing, and
AD 3: Additional features of the network service.

ISO 8471. Data communications-high-level data link control (HDLC)-balanced classes of procedures-data link layers address resolution/negotiation in switched environments.

ISO 8473 AD2. Data communications-protocol for connectionless-mode network service,
Addendum 2: Formal description of ISO 8473-network layer standard.

ISO 8473 AD3. Data communications-protocol for connectionless-mode Network service,
Addendum 3: Provision of the underlying service assumed by ISO 8473, on point-to-point sub-networks network layer standard.

ISO 8473. Network layer protocol for providing connectionless-mode network service on X.25 packet net.

ISO 8509. OSI service conventions.

ISO 8571 AD1. FTAM-overlapped access.

ISO 8571 AD2. FTAM-filestore management.

ISO 8571. File transfer access and management.

ISO 8571-1. FTAM-Part 1: General description of file transfer access and management.

ISO 8571-2. FTAM-Part 2: Virtual filestore of file transfer access and management

ISO 8571-3. FTAM-Part 3: File service definition of file transfer access and management.

ISO 8583. Banking systems-Message interchange specification for messages originated by bankcards- Contents for financial transactions.

ISO 8613. Text and office systems-office document architecture and interchange format (ODA/ODIF), representation of document structure and content; there are 8 parts to the formal specification; CCITT T.410, ECMA-101.

ISO 8632. A standard for the transmission and storage of graphic images or files using GKS graphics encoding standard.

ISO 8648. Internal organisation of network layer.

ISO 8649 AD2. A-unit-data service.

ISO 8649. Service definition for association control service elements (ACSE); CCITT X.217.

ISO 8650 AD1. Authentication protocol.

ISO 8650. Protocol specification for association control service elements (ACSE); CCITT X.227.

ISO 8651. ISO 8651, rules for porting from GKS to specific languages, e.g., FORTRAN, PASCAL; companion standard to GKS.

ISO 8652. ADA programming language, ISO 8652:1983, ANSI/MIL-STD-1815A-1983.

ISO 8802/1. Local area networks-Part 1: Specification for layer management; equivalent to IEEE 802.1; handles communications between each layer and addresses security.

ISO 8802/2. Local area networks-Part 2: Common data link layer protocol-general principles; used by 802.3, 4, and 5, etc., it is a common interface for access to higher levels, called logical link control (LLC)-data link layer standard, equivalent to IEEE 802.2.

ISO 8802/2.2 AD1. Local area networks-Part 2: Logical link control (LLC1); Addendum 1: Techniques for flow control in multi-segment networks-data link layer standard.

ISO 8802/2.2 AD2. Local area networks-Part 2: Logical Link Control; Addendum 2: Type 3 operation, acknowledge connectionless-mode service-data link layer standard.

ISO 8802/3 AD1. Local area networks-Part 3: Carrier Sense Multiple Access and Collision Detect (CSMA/CD); Addendum 1: Medium attachment unit and baseband medium specifications for the networks using $10base_2$ connections-data link layer standard.

ISO 8802/3 AD2. Local area networks-Part 3:Carrier Sense Multiple Access and Collision Detect (CSMA/CD); Addendum 2: Specifications for Repeater Set and Repeater Unit for Use with $10base_3$ and $10base_5$ networks data link layer standard.

ISO 8802/3 AD3. Local area networks-part 3: Carrier sense multiple Access and collision detect (CSMA/CD); Addendum 3: Specifications for broadband MAU and medium for networks using 10broad36 connections data link layer standard.

ISO 8802/3 AD4. Local area network-Part 3: Carrier sense multiple access and collision detect (CSMA/CD); Addendum 4: Specifications for networks using StarLAN $10base_5$ connections-dataLink layer standard.

ISO 8802/3. Local area network-Part 3: Carrier sense multiple access and collision detect (CSMA/CD)-Data link layer standard; equivalent to IEEE 802.3.

ISO 8802/4. Local area networks-Part 4: Token passing bus access method LAN; equivalent to IEEE 802.4, ArcNet.

ISO 8802/5. Local area networks-Part 5: Token ring network access method and specifications for physical layer; LAN using passive hub connections (MAU), with shielded twisted pair and token passing access method; equivalent to IEEE 802.5, token ring.

ISO 8802/6. Local area networks-Part 6: Specification for metropolitan area network and specifications for physical layer using FDDI; equivalent to IEEE 802.6.

ISO 8802/7. Local area networks-Part 7: Broadband, slotted ring access method and physical layer specifications; equivalent to IEEE 802.7.

ISO 8802/8. Local area networks-Part 8: Fiber Optic Specifications. Equivalent to IEEE 802.8.

ISO 8802/9. Local area networks-Part 8: Integrated data and voice networks specifications; equivalent to IEEE 802.9.

ISO 8802/11. Local area networks-Part 11: Broadband, slotted ring access method and physical layer specifications; equivalent to IEEE 802.11.

ISO 8805. Graphical kernel system for three dimensions (GKS-3D).

ISO 8807. OSI-LOTOS-A Formal description technique based on the temporal ordering of observational behaviour.

ISO 8822 AD2. OSI-presentation layer-connection-oriented mode presentation service.

ISO 8822:1988. Connection-oriented presentation service definition.

ISO 8823 AD1. COPP specification-PICS performa.

ISO 8823 AD2. COPP specification-symmetric synchronisation.

ISO 8823. Connection-oriented presentation protocol specification (1988).

ISO 8824 AD1. ASN.1-specification addendum.

ISO 8824. Specification of ASN.1 language, CCITT X.208.

ISO 8825 AD1. ASN.1-Addendum to encoding rules.

ISO 8825. Specification of basic encoding rules for ASN.1.

ISO 8826. Specification of packed encoding rules for ASN.1.

ISO 8831. OSI job transfer and manipulation concepts and services.

ISO 8832. OSI specification of the basic class; class protocol for job transfer and manipulation.

ISO 8859. 8-bit character set; also known as Latin Alphabet-1.

ISO 8878 AD1. Data communications-Addendum 1: Protection and priority-network layer standard.

ISO 8878 AD2. Data communications-Addendum 2: The support of additional network service features-network layer standard.

ISO 8878. Use of X.25 packet net to provide OSI connection-oriented network service (CONP) including Annex A).

ISO 8879. Text and office systems-standard generalised markup language.

ISO 8880/1. Data communications-protocol specification for the provision and support of network services, Part 1: General principles-network layer standard.

ISO 8880/2. Data communications-protocol specification for provision and support of network services; Part 2: Connection-mode network service.

ISO 8880/3. Data communications-protocol specification for provision and support of network services, Part 3: Connectionless-mode network.

ISO 8881. Data communications-Use of X.25 packet-level protocol over a LAN-network layer standard.

ISO 8882/1. Data communications-X.25 DTE conformance testing, part 1: General principles-network layer standard.

ISO 8882/3. Data communications-X.25 DTE Conformance testing, Part 3: Packet layer-network layer standard.

ISO 8885 AD1. Local area networks-Procedures for high-level data link control-general-purpose XID Frame information field content and format; Addendum 1: Definition of a multi-link parameter negotiation data link layer sub-field and parameter negotiation data link layer sub-field: additional operational parameters.

ISO 8885 AD2. Local area networks-procedures for high-level data link control-general-purpose XID Frame information field content and format; Addendum 2: Operation of start/stop transmission.

ISO 8885. Local area networks-procedures for high-level link control-General-purpose XID Frame information field content and format-data link layer standard.

ISO 9040 AD2. Additional functional units.

ISO 9040. OSI virtual terminal basic class service.

ISO 9041. AD2. Additional functional units.

ISO 9041 AD3. The PICS Performa.

ISO 9041. OSI virtual terminal basic class protocol.

ISO 9066-1. The communication-reliable transfer part 1: Model and service definition; CCITT X.218.

ISO 9066-2. Text communication-reliable transfer, part 2: Protocol specification; CCITT X.228.

ISO 9068. Data communications-Provision of the connectionless-mode network service by using ISO 8208 (CONS)-network layer standard.

ISO 9069. Text and office systems; standard generalised markup language-SGM; document interchange format.

ISO 9070. Text and office systems-SGML-Registration procedures for public text owner.

ISO 9072-1. Text communication-Remote operation service specification; CCITT X.219.

ISO 9072-2. Text communication-Remote operation protocol specification; CCITT X.229.

ISO 9074. OSI-ESTELLE-A formal description technique derived from extended state transition model.

ISO 9075. Structured Query Language.

ISO 9314. Standard of FDDI, same as IEEE 802.6; metropolitan area network (MAN), using FDDI, in one of two configurations: single or double fibre link(s) (HDX or FDX); in full implementation also has a spare fibre.

ISO 9506. Manufacturing automation-specification for manufacturing message.

ISO 9542. Data communications-Intermediate system to end system protocol to be used with ISO 8208-network layer standard.

ISO 9545 AD1. OSI upper-layer architecture-application layer connectionless-mode operation.

ISO 9545. OSI upper-layer architecture-application layer structure standard.

ISO 9573. Text and office systems-SGML-techniques for using SGML.

ISO 9574. Data communications-Provision of connection-oriented mode network service where packet mode terminal equipment is connected to an ISDN-network layer standard.

ISO 9575. Data communications-the routing framework for OSI-network layer standard.

ISO 9577. Data communications-Protocol identification in the network layer-network layer standard.

ISO 9579. OSI remote database access.

ISO 9592. Programmer's Hierarchical Interactive Graphics System.

ISO 9594. The Directory. CCITT X.500.

ISO 9595 AD1. OSI management-common management information service definition;
Addendum 1: Cancel Get Function; CCITT X.710.

ISO 9595 AD2. The OSI management-common management information service definition;
Addendum 2: Add/remove function; CCITT X.710.

ISO 9595. OSI management-common management information service definition; CCITT X.710.

ISO 9596 AD1. OSI management-Common Management Information Protocol Specification, Addendum 1:Cancel Get Function. CCITT X.711.

ISO 9596 AD2. OSI management-common management information protocol specification; Addendum 2: Add/remove function.

ISO 9596. OSI management-common management information protocol specification; CCITT X.711.

ISO 9646. OSI conformance testing methodology and framework.

ISO 9735. Electronic data interchange (EDI) standards.

ISO 9804. OSI commitment, concurrency, and recovery service definition.

ISO 9805. OSI commitment, concurrency, and recovery protocol specification.

ISO 9834-1. OSI-Procedures for specific OSI registered authorities, Part 1: General procedures.

ISO 9834-2. OSI-Procedures for specific OSI registered authorities, Part 2: Registration of document types.

ISO 9834-3. OSI-Procedures for specific OSI registered authorities, Part 3: Joint registration authority procedures for object identifier values.

ISO 9834-4. OSI-Procedures for specific OSI registered authorities, Part 4: Procedures for abstract syntax.

ISO 9834-5. OSI-Procedures for specific OSI registered authorities, Part 5: Procedures for transfer syntax.

ISO 9834-6. OSI-Procedures for specific OSI registered authorities, Part 6: Procedures for application process and application entity titles.

ISO 9834-7. OSI-Procedures for specific OSI registered authorities, Part 7: Procedures for application contexts.

ISO 9834-8. OSI-Procedures for specific OSI registered authorities, Part 8: Procedures for system titles.

ISO 9834-9. OSI-Procedures for specific OSI registered authorities, Part 9: Procedures for VT profiles.

ISO 9834-10. OSI-Procedures for specific OSI registered authorities, Part 10: Procedures for VT control objects.

ISO 9945-2. Shell and utilities interface for POSIX.

ISO 9945-3. System administration for POSIX.

ISO 9955. Banking system-OSI applications in banking and guidelines for application protocol development for banking information interchange.

ISO 10021-1. Information processing systems-text communication message-oriented text interchange system. Part 1: Service and System Overview; CCITT X.400.

ISO 10021-2. Information processing systems-text communication message-oriented text interchange system. Part 2: Overall Architecture; CCITT X.402.

ISO 10021-3. Information processing systems-text communication message-oriented text interchange system. Part 3: Abstract service definition conventions; CCITT X.407.

ISO 10021-4. Information processing systems-text communication message-oriented text interchange system. Part 4: Message transfer system. Abstract Service Definition and Procedures; CCITT X.411.

ISO 10021-5. Information processing systems-text communication message-oriented text interchange system. Part 5: Message store: Abstract Service Definition; CCITT X.413.

ISO 10021-6. Information processing systems-text communication message-oriented text interchange system; Part 6: Protocol Specifications; CCITT X.419.

ISO 10021-7. Information processing

systems-text communication message-oriented text interchange system.
Part 7: Interpersonal messaging systems; CCITT X.420.

ISO 10022. Data communication-physical layer service definition- general.

ISO 10026-1. OSI distributed transaction processing, Part 1: Model.

ISO 10026-2. OSI distributed transaction processing, Part 2: Service.

ISO 10026-3. OSI distributed transaction processing, Part 3: Protocol.

ISO 10028. Data communications-Intermediate system functions for the network layer.

ISO 10029. Data communications-Operation of an X.25 interworking unit-Network layer standard.

ISO 10030. Data communications-Intermediate to end system routing exchange protocol for use with connectionless-mode network service.

ISO 10031. Text communication-Distributed office applications.

ISO 10031-2. Reference data transfer facility; allows efficient transfer of bulk data from a source to a sink (e.g., print server) at the request of a third party (i.e., users).

ISO 10033. Text and office systems-recording do documents whose format conforms to ISO 8616 (ODA) on flexible disk cartridge (floppies) which conform to ISO 9293.

ISO 10040. Systems management overview; CCITT X.701.

ISO 10160. Inter-library loan service-definition.

ISO 10161. Inter-library loan protocol specification.

ISO 10162. Application service for information systems-search, retrieve, and update, service definition.

ISO 10163. Application service for information systems-search, retrieve, and update, protocols.

ISO 10164-1. Systems management,
Part 1: Object management function; CCITT X.730.

ISO 10164-2. Systems management,
Part 2: State management function; CCITT X.731.

ISO 10164-3. Systems management,
Part 3: Attributes for representing relationships; CCITT X.732.

ISO 10164-4. Systems management,
Part 4: Alarm reporting function; CCITT X.733.

ISO 10164-5. Systems management,
Part 5: Event report function; CCITT X.734.

ISO 10164-6. Systems management,
Part 6: Log control function; CCITT X.735.

ISO 10164-7. Systems management,
Part 7: Security alarm reporting Function; CCITT X.736.

ISO 10164-8. Systems management,
Part 8: Security audit trail function; CCITT X.740.

ISO 10164-9. Systems management,
Part 9: Objects and attributes for access control function; CCITT X.74x.

ISO 10164-11. Systems management,
Part 11: Workload monitoring function; CCITT X.739.

ISO 10164-12. Systems management,
Part 12: Test management function. CCITT X.745.

ISO 10164-13. Systems management,
Part 13: Summarisation function; CCITT X.738.

ISO 10165-1. Management information services-Structure of management Information,
Part 1: Management information model.

ISO 10165-2. Management information services-Structure of management information,
Part 2: Definition of management information; CCITT X.721.

ISO 10165-4. Management information services-Structure of management information,

Part 4: Guidelines for the definition of information; CCITT X.722.

ISO 10165-5. Management information services-Structure of management Iniormation,

Part 5: Generic management information.

ISO 10165-6. Management information services-Requirements and guidelines for implementation conformance statement proformas associated with management information.

ISO 10166. Similar to DTAM (CCITT T.433), but provides for any type of file(s) transfer.

ISO 10175. Document printing application, transfer documents to a printer server along with user requirements.

ISO 10181-1 OSI. Security frameworks in open systems; Part 1: Overview.

ISO 10181-2. Authentication framework.

ISO TC97. ISO Technical Committee to issue International standardisation profiles.

ISO TR 9007. Technical report on concepts and terminology for conceptual scheme and the information base.

ISO TR 100000. Framework and taxonomy of International standardised profiles.

ISO. International Organisation for Standardization, an organisation responsible for creating International Standards in various disciplines, including computers and communications; founded in 1946. It is divided into technical committees, subcommittees, and working groups, as well as some joint technical committees.

isochronous transmission. IT. A transmission process in which there is always an integral number of unit intervals between any two significant instants. The mechanism is characterised by a constant pulse rate, a constant time interval or multiples thereof, between voltage or electromagnetic field intensity transitions, and a gating by a controlled clock.

isochronous burst transmission. IBT. The transmission that is performed by interrupting at controlled intervals, the data stream is being transmitted. The method of transmission enables communication between data terminal equipment and data networks that operate as dissimilar data signalling rates.

isochronous modulation. IM. Modulation or demodulation in which the time interval that separates any two significant instants is theoretically equal to the unit interval or to a multiple of the unit interval.

isochronous signal. A signal in which the time interval separating any two significant instants is theoretically equal to the unit interval or to a multiple of the unit interval. The variations in the time intervals are constrained within specified limits because there is no way of generating exactly equal unit intervals of time.

isochronous. A characteristic of a periodic signal in which the time interval that separates any two corresponding significant instants or transitions of signal level is equal to the unit interval or to the multiple of the unit interval.

ISODE. ISO Development Environment a non-proprietary implementation of some of the OSI protocols.

isolated. The state that exists at a point such that the state of the point cannot be changed or influenced by any stimulus from outside itself; that is, the point is not influenced by electrostatic, magnetic, magnetostatic, or electromagnetic field.

ISONET. International Organisation for Standardisation Network; the information network through which ISO co-ordinates the exchanges of information on international and national standards, technical regulations, and other standards-type documents, and which links the ISO and International Electrotechnical Commission's information centre in Geneva with similar centres in approximately 60 countries.

ISORM. ISO Reference Model, the seven-layer model of open systems.

isotropic source. A theoretical antenna, light source, or sound source, that radiates with equal power density in all directions, and which can only be approximated in actual practice. In true sense, the isotropic sources do not exist physically but they represent convenient reference sources for comparing and expressing the directional properties of actual sources such as radio antennas.

ISPATS. International Standardised Profile Abstract Test Suite.

ISPETS. International Standardised Profile Executable Test Suite.

ISPICS. ISP Protocol Implementation Conformance Statement.

ISPIXIT. ISP Protocol Implementation eXtra Information for Testing.

ISPX. ISN PBX, private branch-exchange to switch signals on ISDN-capable lines and terminal equipment.

ISS. 1. Information Sharing System.
2. Information Storage System.
3. Integrated Storage System.

ISSB. Information Systems Standards Board, one of eight standards boards within ANSI; oversees ASC X3, NISO (Z39) and AIIM.

ISSN. *See* International standard serial number.

ISUP. ISDN User Part, a part of Layer 7 of SS7; control signalling required by ISDN subscriber calls.

IT. 1. Information Technology, Technology, a generic term used broadly to cover any systematic means for organising, storing, and disseminating data.
2. *See* isochronous transmission.
3. Index Term.
4. Input Terminal.
5. Information Theory.

ITA. International Telegraph Alphabet, ISO.

ITA2. International Telegraph Alpha 2, character set used for telex.

ITAEGC. IT Advisory Experts Group on Certification, European group providing input on certification issues for Information Technology.

ITAEGS. IT Advisory Expert Group on Standardisation, European group that maintains functional standards work.

ITAEGT. It Advisory Experts Group on private Telecom networks, European group that maintains the directory of private telecom network standards.

ITC. Integrated Terminal Controller.

ITCA. International TeleConferencing Association, DC-based association that provides members with a directory of videoconferencing rooms around the world.

ITE. Information Technology Equipment, generic term to cover computer and communications equipment used for Information Technology.

item mark. A special character or item of information used as an indicator to designate the beginning or end of a set of one or more characters (field) that have related data or information; concerning a particular object, event, transaction or operation.

iteration. The repetition of a numerical or non-numerical process where the results from one or more stages are used to form the input to the next. Generally the recycling of the process continues until some present bound is achieved, or the process result is constantly repeated.

iterative impedance. In a pair of terminals of a four-terminal network, the impedance that will terminate the other pair of terminals in such a way that the impedance measured at the first pair is equal to the terminating impedance. The iterative impedance of a uniform line is the same as its characteristic impedance.

ITF. Interleaved Two of Five; a numeric bar code system adopted by American National Standards Institute in 1983; two of Five means that of a five-bar code, two bars (either black or white) must be larger than the rest. This bar code system was used for industrial applications such as labelling outer shipping containers; also popular in the automotive and paper industries.

ITI. 1. Interactive Terminal Interface, how a terminal interfaces with a host over a network.

2. The Industrial Technology Institute, an Ann Arbour-based research group involved in development and testing of OSI.

3. Industrial Training Institute.

i-time. Instruction time; when the central processor executes a computer program, the control unit receives an instruction, examines it, and then gives control to the arithmetic/logic unit. Instruction time is part of the machine cycle.

ITL. Intermediate Transfer Language.

ITM. Information Transfer Module.

ITP. Interactive Terminal Protocol.

ITR. Interrupt Control Unit.

ITRC. Information Technology Requirements Council, formerly the administrative wing of the North American MAP/TOP Users Forum.

ITSB. Imag Technology Standards Board, division of ANSI; oversees standards for photographic development, micrographics, and television studio practices.

ITSP. Information Technology and System Plan(ning), Treasury Board term; all Canadian government departments are required to have an OSI migration strategy as part of ITSP; obsolete term, now called IMP.

ITSTC. Information Technology Steering Committee, combination of CEN, CENELEC, and CEPT.

ITU. International Telecommunications Union, a body under United Nations, the parent organisation of CCITT.

IU. 1. Information Unit.

2. Input Unit.

3. interface Unit.

IUT. Implementation Under Test, in conformance testing, one or more adjacent protocols representing that part of a real system being tested.

IVDMS. Integrated Voice and Data Multiplexers, a way of connecting personal computers to a network supporting both voice and data.

IVDT. Integrated Voice/Data Terminal.

IVDTE. Integrated Voice/Data Terminal Equipment; the equipment capable of receiving voice and data information alternately or simultaneously; this term refers to the functionality of equipment necessary to receive or originate ISDN traffic.

IVID. Integrated Voice and Data, carry voice and data over the same circuit.

IVR. Interactive Voice Response, allows callers to manipulate computers from their telephone keypad.

IWB. Instruction Word Buffer.

IWF. InterWorking Function, a CCITT term for a component that supports operations between networks and/or computers.

IWU. InterWorking Unit, another name for an Intermediate System.

IX. 1. Inter-eXchange.

2. Inverted Index.

IXC. Inter-eXchange Control.

J

J.nnn. The CCITT J. Series Recommendations deal mostly with the quality of signalling over audible frequency media, including audible signals in association with television.

jabber control. A facility in data communications of a local area network, to interrupt automatically the transmission of an abnormally long-output data stream.

jabber. A malfunction on a network involving the continuous transmission of random data. A transmission by a data station beyond the time interval allowed by the protocol.

JAF. Job Accounting Facility.

jaggies. The rough or jagged edges which undesirably appear around images on the screen while using computer-generated graphics packages. Jaggies are especially noticeable when a diagonal line is drawn, showing a stepped (staircase) appearance. The automatic reduction or removal of the jagged edges is called 'anti-aliasing'.

JAI. Job Accounting Interface.

jam input. 1. A means of setting logic line to desired condition by simply applying desired high or low voltage. 2. The voltage so applied.

jam. A general term for a pile up of cards in a card reader.

jammer analyser. A device in which signal-processing methods are used to determine specific characteristics of received jamming signals.

jammer modulation. The specific modulation of the carrier wave that is transmitted by a jammer.

jammer. A transmitting system that is designed specifically for the jamming purposes.

jamming antenna. An antenna used for jamming purposes. The design of such an antenna includes the frequency, directivity, gain, polarization, power, and beam pattern requirements of the jamming signal.

jamming. A deliberate form of radiation interference aimed at radio, microwave or satellite transmissions. The use of high-energy transmitters forces the jammer to employ more powerful and hence more expensive transmission systems.

J-antenna. A radiating conductor with a length of about half a wavelength of the radiating frequency. It is fed at one end by a matched feeder a quarter of a wave in length.

janitor. *See* gods.

JAR. Jump Address Register.

JAT. Job Accounting Table.

Java. A 3rd generation platform-independent programming language, produced by Sun Microsystems. Java is built as a method to provide services over the WWW. It was designed to simplify object-oriented programming, promote portability, and limit spread of computer viruses. With Java, a Web site provides a Java application (called an applet) which is downloaded by the client and executed on the client machine. Java is specifically built so that an application can be run on any kind of system, so a separate Mac, Windows, Sun, etc. version is not needed. Java also has some security features built in, to make it more difficult for destructive applets to be written. Java is based on a subset of the C programming language.

Java applets. Java tools, which are influential in making more interactive material available to users of the Web. Applets allow the users to run applications from Web pages. These applications can be full-featured demos of products or simple animation applets.

JavaBeans. One of the recent technologies supported by Java; it allows developers to create reusable objects that can be used by most of the GUI development tools in the Java world. It also enables the creation of larger scale applications as well as allowing more RAD development.

JavaScript. The first client-side scripting language created in 1996. it is not related to Java programming language, although it does contain some similar syntax. Purpose of JavaScript is to provide a true programming language for use by Web page authors to add more interactive Web pages. It has full range of data structures, control structures, and conditional statements.

JScript. The Microsoft's implementation of JavaScript; contains the same syntax and structure JavaScript contains. Some of the JavaScript commands are not supported by JScript.

J-carrier system. In carrier-current telephony, a broad-band system which provides 12 telephone channels at frequencies up to 140 kHz.

JCB. Job Control Block.

JCL. *See* job control language.

JCN. Junction.

JCP. Job Control Program.

JCT. Job Control Table.

JD. Job Description.

JDL. *See* job description language.

JECL. Job Entry Control Language.

JEDI. Joint EDI task force under the United Nations, a committee set up to represent the United Nations in international EDI activities.

JES. Job Entry Subsystem.

JIB. Job Information Block.

JIP. Joint Input Processing.

JITEC. Joint Information Technology Experts Committee, ISO/IEC, a European committee set up by the ISO and IEC.

J-K flip-flop. A special form of flip-flop circuit that has two inputs, the J (set) and K (reset). At the application of a clock pulse, 1 on the J input and 0 on the K input will set the flip-flop at its 1 state. 1 on the K input and a 0 on the J input will reset to the 0 state. A 1 simultaneously on both the J and K inputs will cause it to change state regardless of the previous state. 0 on both the J and K inputs will prevent any change. Also known as a J-K bistable element.

JMUG. Japanese MAP/TOP User Group.

JNT. Joint Network Team, UK; predates JANET, but is involved in development of both WAN and LAN technologies used on JANET.

job control language. JCL. A computer language (designed by IBM) that interprets user instructions and processes them to instruct the central processor unit what to do with the user's program. A user-command is any instruction issued to the computer by user, such as 'find file' 'open file', 'sort file', print file', and close file'. Each line of instruction is called a 'job control statement', and these appear in a specific order so that the computer is able to process information in batches. If such information is issued on a regular basis, the commands may be stored in a job control file. Also called command language.

job description language. JDL. Similar to job control language, JDL is rather more general in that is covers all aspects of defining a task or job to a computer system.

job file control block. A set of memory locations containing information about a particular task or job; the information can be accessed by various programs, thus providing control of the operation of programs.

job file. A file containing in intermediate form one or more jobs awaiting execution. The jobs are generally presented as job-control language statements that may be pre-processed to eliminate the more blatant errors of syntax or other detectable errors being appended to the job file.

job mix. The set of jobs actually being executed within a multiprogramming system at any one instant.

job monitoring. The control of the jobs running within a system.

job priority. A value assigned to a job that determines the priority used in scheduling the job and allocating resources to it in a multiprogramming environment.

job step. A quantum of work associated with an application program.

job stream. The sequence of representations of jobs or parts of jobs to be performed, as submitted to an operating system.

job. A set of programs and the data to be manipulated by these programs. Also, he execution of the sét of programs. In the simplest form the job may consist of a loading a binary program and then executing the program on the data supplied.

joint communications. The common use of communication facilities by two or more services that belong to the same nation.

JOSS. Johnniac Open-Shop System. A time-sharing computer language modelled after formula translator (FORTRAN) or beginner's all-purpose symbolic instruction code (BASIC) that has been developed to make quick calculations.

journaling backup. A backup which records only the differences between a baseline version of a file and an updated version, unlike an incremental backup in which the volume's structure is scanned for all files created or modified since the date of the last backup (copying only those that have changed). This mode of backup) is most useful in applications which make relatively small numbers of random changes to large files.

JOVIAL. Jule's Own Version of IAL, a particular algorithmic language (ALGOL) used by the US Air Force in some of their systems. Its specific application has been in command and control systems. The language has also been used in scientific and commercial applications.

joystick. An input device, a movable handle that a person graphs and rotates to a limited extent in one or more degrees of freedom and whose variable position or applied force is measure, resulting in commands to a control system; used in video games.

JP. Job Processor.

JPEG. 1. A bitmap file format for compressed graphic images, which produces much smaller files than GIFs. The compression algorithm is a lossy one, however, which will not reproduce the original image exactly. Various settings are available, to allow more compression at the cost of a greater loss of image quality.

2. Joint Photographic Experts Group.

JPG. File name extension for a special compression format used to store photographs and pictures.

JPU. Job Processing Unit.

JPW. Job Processing Word.

JSL. Job Specification Language.

JTC. Joint Technical Committee (ISO and IEC).

JTC1. Joint Technical committee 1 on Information Technology, replaced ISO/TC97; joint IEC and ISO committee responsible for OSI, with ANSI as the secretariat.

JTM. Job Transfer and Manipulation, the OSI Application Layer specification that allows batch jobs to be distributed for processing on another system.

JTMP. Job Transfer and Manipulation Protocol.

jumbo payload. A datagram payload with a length exceeding the conventional limit of 65,535 bytes. IPv6 enables jumbo payload datagrams to pass through the network.

jump. A set of specific computer instruction that will cause the instruction at the memory location (address) specified in the jump, to be the next executed.

junction grammar. A model of language employed in analysing sentences, it allows a sentence to be reduced into its syntactic elements. It is used in computerised and other techniques for the automatic translation of text from one spoken language to another, machine-aided translation.

junction stage. A stage in the electrical layout of a system that represents a characteristic point that is identifiable and is accessible to a stage in the same or another system.

junction transistor. A transistor in which the emitter and collector consists of junctions between *p* and *n* semiconductor regions. It is the most common type of transistor, in which current flow depends on both the majority and minority carriers, with two junctions between *n*-type and *p*-type material, giving a sandwich form, either *n-p-n* or *p-n-p*.

junction. 1. The area of contact between two semiconductor materials having different electrical properties, or between semiconductor and a metal. Junctions play a fundamental role in semiconductor devices.

2. A circuit connecting two local telephone offices/exchanges, or local office and a tandem or trunk office/exchange.

3. Plane of transition between regions in a semiconductor.

4. Joint between waveguide sections.

5. Intersection of two pole routes.

JUNET. Japan Unix NETwork, a non-commercial research network.

justify. 1. To move the bit pattern stored in a register so that either the least or the most significant bit is at the appropriate end of the register. To shift the contents of a register so that the character at the specified end of the data is at a particular register position.

2. To shift the contents of a register to a specified position.

3. To set the lines of type to their full measure.

K

k. 1. kilo-. A decimal prefix used in association with a base unit in the SI system of units, indicating a multiplication factor of 10^3 of that unit.
2. In tape-relay system operations, the message pro-sign which is used to indicate an invitation to transmit. It is usually placed at the end of a transmission and indicates that a response is implied, necessary, requested, or expected.

K. *See* kilobyte.

K.nnn. The CCITT K. Series Recommendations deal with physical reliability standards for telephone network and related equipment, for example, resistance to over voltage and overcurrents, interference from RF broadcast stations, etc.

Ka band. The microwave frequencies in 12-30 GHz range.

KA9Q. TCP/IP and associated protocols for amateur packet radio systems. It is very popular with the home computer users.

Kalman filter. An algorithm which is used to process measurements to determine an optimum estimate of the past, present, or future state of a linear system by using a time sequence of measurements of the system behaviour, plus a statistical model that includes the system and measurement errors as well as initial condition information.

KB. 1. Keyboard.
2. Kilobyte.
3. Kilobit.

K-band. The band of frequencies occurring between 20-40 GHz, and comprise 10 numbered channels that are 2.0 GHz wide each. These frequencies overlap parts of the obsolete P- and K-bands, which comprised frequencies in the range from 10.9 GHz to 36 GHz between the old X- and Q-bands, and overlapping parts of the old X- and P-bands. The old K-band was divided into 12 sub-channels each designated by a distinctive letter.

kbps. Kilobit per second; in computing, it refers to 2^{10} (which equals (10^{24}), and is mainly used to express the speed of data transmission. When used as a plural, an 's' is not added. Also written as KBPS.

KBS. Kilobits Per Second.

KC. Kilocycle; a representation previously used to indicate one thousand cycles per second now deprecated in favour of kHz.

KCS. Kilo Characters per Second, that is, one thousand characters per second is a measurement of data transmission speed that enjoys general acceptance.

KCU. Keyboard Control Unit.

KDC. Key Distribution Centre, management and distribution of keys (passwords) used with encryption systems.

KDE. Keyboard Data Entry.

KDOS. Key Display Operating System.

KDS. Key Data Station.

KEP. Key Entry Processing.

kermit. A file transfer protocol capable of running on most of the operating environments; it is not same as file transfer protocol (FTP).

kernel. The lowest layer into which a large operating system is subdivided, each layer dealing with some aspect of the system hardware. The kernel is responsible for allocating hardware resources to the processes that make up the operating system and to the programs running under the operating system. It is the only part of an operating system that needs to be proved correct by rigorous program verification: the principal approach to providing the degree of security required in a computer system has been that of designing secure kernel.

kerning. A text editing feature in typography, the process of reducing space between certain character pairs which would normally seem badly spaced. Some page layout and word processing programs kern characters automatically. Characters typically requiring kerning are the capital pairs AW, WA, VA, etc. The word 'kern' comes from the French word *charne* meaning 'hinge'.

key issue tracking. A store of information held on computer files in the US, which provides continually-updated index of current important topics.

key matching. The technique of comparing the keys of two or more records to select some of them for a particular stage of processing and to reject the other ones.

key punch operator. A person who controls a device that perforates cards in specific positions. The device works under the guidance of a computer or a keyboard operator.

key status indicator. A symbol (such as flashing cursor) which appears on the screen to alert user which toggle keys are activated. Some modern keyboards also incorporate a light built into the key, highlighting the fact that a particular function is in use, for example, when the 'shift' or number lock' or scroll lock' keys are in use.

key to disk. A data entry system in which the data entered by a number of keyboard operators is accumulated on a magnetic disk.

key to tape. A data entry system in which the data entered by a number of keyboard operators is accumulated on a magnetic tape.

key variable. In aspreadsheet program like Lotus 1-2-3, a variable which may be referenced from anywhere within the spreadsheet, and which is stored in a single, separate cell. The key variable might be an interest rate and is particularly useful if the interest rate changes only the key variable needs to be updated, eliminating the need to scan through and change the figure at every affected point within the spreadsheet.

key word and context. KWAC. An index system that lists available computer programs or documents. It is similar to keyword in context indexing system, but each significant word is brought to the beginning is alphabetical order. The title has the keyword first, then the words that follow it, followed by the words that came before the keyword.

key word in context. KWIC. An index system that lists available computer programs or documents tabulated in alphabetical order of the most informative or significant word in the title of the information.

key word out of context. KWOC. An index that lists available computer programs or documents tabulated with the title used in full under as many significant or informative wordos from the title of the information as the compiler considers necessary.

key. 1. A switch with several contacts used on switchboards.
2. A manual switch to send signals.
3. A value used to identify a member of a set; usually the members of the set are records in which one of the fields holds the key.
4. One or more characters within or attached to a set of data that contains information about the set, including its identification.

keyboard buffer. A temporary storage area in memory that keeps track of keys that are typed, even if computer did not immediately respond to the keys when typed. It enables an operator to use the keyboard even when the processor is busy, a small area of primary storage is used to memorize the last set of keystrokes. When the processor is free again, the buffer transmits the keystrokes.

keyboard command. See shortcut key.

keyboard controller. A chip within the keyboard or the computer that receives the key stroke and generates the scan code.

keyboard control logic. In peripherals, the logic circuitry built into a keyboard for interpreting the individual keystrokes and converting them into electronic signals, needed to control computer to which the keyboard is connected.

keyboard input functions. In peripherals, the operating system subroutines that obtain the status of, or retrieve data from, a keyboard or keypad.

keyboard scan. In peripherals, the periodic sampling of the switches activated by the keys of a keyboard to determine whether a key has been depressed and, if so, its identity.

keyboard send/receive. KSR. A combination teletypewriter transmitter and receiver that has transmission capability manually from the keyboard only, but no means of automatic origination or retention in data.

keyboard type reperforator. KTR. A special kind of teletypewriter that receives, punches and types on paper tape. It can simultaneously punch and transmit.

keyboard. 1. Set of alphanumeric and functional keys.
2. The most common input device, which employs key depression as a means of entering letters, numbers, symbols, punctuation, commands, and generating the required code elements or signals.
3. An aray of keys that may be captioned buttons or marked areas on a plane each of which can cause a discrete signal action when pressed.

keyed sequential access method. KSAM. A group of computer library routines together with a structure that allows the storage of data under assigned names. This is turn allows the storage of data under assigned names. This in turn allows users to obtain records based on the ordering of key field contents.

keying. The process of converting data in to a machine-readable form.

keypad. A limited and compact form of keyboard with a small number (12-16) of captioned buttons or pressure-sensitive areas on a plane.

keypulse. To transmit information using a keyset as opposed to dialling.

key signal. A pseudo-random signal used in enciphering and deciphering procedures.

keyword parameter. A parameter of a subroutine, procedure, or macro that is identified by name rather than by its position in the parameter list.

keyword. A symbol in a programming language that has a special meaning for the compiler or interpreter. For example, keywords in BASIC include LET, IF, THEN, PRINT. The keywords guide the analysis of language, and in a simple language each keyword causes activation of a specific routine in the language processor.

keyword search. The use of a keyword or a logical combination of keywords to help a user to retrieve information by narrowing down the extent of search for the information required.

KF. Key Field.

K-factor. 1. In tropospheric ratio propagation, the ratio between the effective and the actual earth radius.

2. In ionospheric radio propagation, a correction factor applied in calculations involving a curved layer: it is a function of distance and the real height of reflection. Its use takes into account the effects of ducting.

KFAS. Keyed File Access System.

Khornerstone benchmark. A standard by which to test and compare a computer's overall performance such as the processor, memory access, and drive access speeds. Other benchmarks include the Whestone (speed of arithmetic operations), and the Dhrystone (microprocessor and memory performance).

KICU. Keyboard Interface Control Unit.

KIL. Keyed Input Language.

kill file. An automatically processed database; used to trim the information processing time, and to prevent to see/post the undesired mail.

killer, noise. A wave-shaping network added to a communications circuit to reduce interference caused by other nearby signals.

kilo instructions per second. KIPS. A method of rating the speed of a machine, standing for one thousand operations per second. Large-scale integration microprocessors can execute approximately 500 KIPS, whilst some of the larger computers can execute around 3000 KIPS.

kilobytes. One thousand bytes; in computer storage-capacity designation, this term is often used to designate 10^{24} bytes of storage capacity; used in discribing memory and hard drive storage.

kilohertz. kHz. A unit of frequency , equal to 1000 hertz.

KIPS. Knowledge Information Processing System; a computer system which uses inference capabilities in fifth-generation computer that are designed to work in conjuntion with very large knowledge bases at very high processing speeds.

KIPS. *See* kilo instructions per second.

KIS. Keyboard Input Simulation.

KISS. A colloquial expression for the jargon used in certain activities of computer programming, meaning 'Keep It Simple Sir'.

KIT. A colloquial expression used to describe a system that is assembled by the user. It does not necessarily imply an assembly of components or parts, as it is often applied to a marriage of stand-alone elements, or production equipment.

kkbps. Kilobytes per second. In computing, it refers to 2^{10} (which equals 10^{24}), and is mainly used to express the speed of data transmission. When used as a plural, an 's' is not added; for example, 1500 kbps.

KL. Key Length.

KLIC. A colloquial expression for Key Letter In Context; an index system that lists available computer programs or documents. It is similar to keyword in context (KWIC) indexing system but is based on letters rather than words. Permuted lists of terms are produced, sorted by each letter of every term, with the remainder of the term being entered.

kludge. The solution to a problem using conventional methods; the major problem of the kludges is that they may lead to unforeseen side effects or additional maintenance problems.

KMP. Key Management Protocol, the process for checking security key information in a secure data network.

Kn band. The microwave frequencies in the 10-12 GHz range.

knee. The bend in a response curve, usually indicating the onset of saturation cut-off, or levelling off.

knife edge effect. The transmission of signals in to the line-of-sight shadow region caused by the diffraction over an obstacle.

knowledge base. In programming, a database containing the codified knowledge of human expert(s). This contains all the information which help decide IF-THEN questions.

knowledge domain. The field of expertise for which an artificial intelligence system is designed. Due to the complexity of system programming for artificial intelligence, knowledge domains are usually very well focused on specific topics and operations.

knowledge information processing system. *See* KIPS.

Koan. A kind of MIDI music player formatted in Koan Music on all types of Windows systems. The music is generated locally in real-time by the computer's sound card.

KOPS. Kilo Operations Per Second.

KP. A term used in US to describe a signal that is sent forward down a telephone line to indicate that another signal identifying the party to be called or the onward route of the call is about to be transmitted.

KPIC. A colloquial expression for Key Phrase In Context, an index system that lists available computer programs or documents, similar to keyword in context (KWIC) and key letter in context (KLIC) indexing systems, but based on phrases rather than words or letters.

KPS. Knowledge Processing System.

Kramer system. A system of three-phase motor control providing constant horsepower and having a dc motor coupled to the shaft of a wound-rotor three-phase induction motor. The dc supply for the motor also supplies a rotary converter. The speed-control rheostat is connected in series with the field of the motor and the dc power supply.

KRL. Knowledge representation Language.

KSAM. *See* keyed sequential access method.

KSR. *See* keyboard send/receive.

KTR. *See* keyboard type reperforator.

KWAC. See key word and context.

KWIC. *See* key word in context.

KWOC. *See* key word out of context.

KYBD. Keyboard.

L

L.nnn. The CCITT L. Series Recommendations deal with physical reliability standards for telephone networks.

L band. Microwave frequencies occurring between 0.39-1.55 GHz and form the part of a larger continuous range of frequencies covering 0.225-100 GHz, which are usually subdivided into bands designated by letters.

L group. The 48 kHz bandwidth transmission path between two points (usually a standard 12-channel group), with standard terminal frequencies of 60-108 kHz.

L2 cache. Memory cache that is between CPU and main memory (level 1 cache is a memory cache that is onboard the CPU chip itself). L2 cache can provide faster CPU access to instructions and data in memory, thus increasing system performance. Also known as level-2 cache.

L2TP. *See* layer two Tunneling protocol.

LA. 1. Language.

2. Local Address.

3. Line Adaptor.

label. 1. A numeric or alphanumeric identifier associated with a line or statement in a program and used in other parts of the program to refer to the statement.

2. Information within a message used to identify specific information.

3. The descriptive text used in a spreadsheet cell to describe the data in a column or row.

4. A storage file on a magnetic tape containing the name and characteristics of either the entire tape or the data file immediately following.

5. A piece of information, which represents the security level of an object and that describes the sensitivity of the information in the object.

LAD. Logical Aptitude Device.

LADS. Local Area Data Set.

LAF. Long Address Form.

lag. 1. The time interval between the transmission of a signal and its detection at the receiving end.

2. Delay between correcting signal of a control system and its response.

3. Persistence of the electrical image in a television camera tube, which may be several frames in duration.

LAM. Loop Adder and Multiplier.

lambda calculus. A formalism for representing functions and ways of combining functions.

LAMP. Link Access Procedure for Modems.

LAN gateway. A functional unit that connects a local area network to another network using different protocols. It may be noted that the network may be another local area network, a public data network, or another network.

LAN group address. An address that identifies a group of data stations on a local area network.

LAN manager. LAN Network Operating System developed by Microsoft; it runs on top of OS/2 and Windows NT. LAN Manager is a high-performance, full-featured local area network operating system that provides advanced networking capabilities for DOS and OS/2 systems based workstations. LAN Manager package consists of a server component, which provides network services, administration, and management for workstations, and a redirector component, which enables DOS, Microsoft Windows, and OS/2 systems-based workstations to receive services from the server. It transforms OS/2 into multi-user network operating system, extending its power from the desktop to the workgroup. With OS/2 running on the server, LAN Manager can exploit protected mode multitasking and large memory support, both crucial for a high performance LAN operating system. LAN Manager is compatible with existing DOS-based LANs, such as Microsoft Networks and IBM PC-LAN Program.

LAN multicast. Sending of a frame that is intended to be accepted by a group of selected data stations on the same local area network.

LAN segment. A part of a LAN that is separated from the rest by one or more bridges.

LAN. 1. Local area network; a collection of computers and other devices (such as printers) connected to each other by wire (coaxial cable or fibre optics) or radio frequency devices, which usually cover a small geographical area. Devices linked by a LAN may be on the same floor or within a building or campus. It is user-owned and does not run over leased lines, though a LAN may have gateways to the PSTN or other, private, networks. Computers or workstations can communicate with one another. Some of the benefits of LAN are the ability for the users to share the same software, printers, mass storage, and other devices. This is done by connecting individual computers and peripherals to common central computer (file server). Where more than one computer system is available in an organisation, a terminal server is required. This allows users to connect to the computer of their choice. To ensure smooth communications within a network environment, industry standards (protocols) have been defined.

2. Lateral Access Network.

land. A flat area on the metal surface of a CD-ROM that reflects the laser light in to the sensor of an optical disk drive.

language construct. A synthetic structure or set of structures in a language for a particular class of operations, such as a loop construct.

language processor. A computer, microprocessor or other functional unit for processing programs written in specified programming language.

language. A set of characters, conventions, and rules used to convey information in programming and communications. A language may be formally considered to consist of pragmatics, semantics, and syntax.

language, plain. Intelligible text or language, not coded or encrypted.

LAP. 1. Link Access Procedure, the data link or OSI layer-2 protocol specified by the ITU-TS for the X.25 interface standard. The data link-level

protocol specified in the CCITT X.25 interface standard. The original LAP has been supplemented with LAPB (LAP-Balanced), and LAPD (a protocol designed for ISDN connections). 2. List Assembly Program.

lap. In printing, a small overlap where two colours touch each other to safe guard against a gap that might otherwise occur due to lack of register.

LAPADS. *See* lightweight acoustic processing and display system.

LAP B. Link Access Procedure Balanced, an HDLC substance used in X.25 as the Link Layer Protocol; it is full duplex, balanced, and connection oriented.

LAP D. Link Access Procedure-D; specified in CCITT I.441 or Q.921, services are given in I.440 or Q.920. A modification to HDLC for ISDN. It is a framed, bit-oriented protocol similar to Lap and Lap-B protocols specified for X.25 circuits.

Lap M. A variation of Lap-B used in the V.42 modem error control standard.

lap-top computer. A small, low-weight, battery-powered portable personal computer with a LCD screen, intended for use by travelling executives and marketing persons.

LAPX. Link Access Procedure half dupleX.

LARAM. *See* line-addressable random-access memory.

large interactive surface. LIS. The automated drafting table employed in plotting and/or digitising drawings in computer-aided design/computer-aided manufacture.

large optical cavity. LOC. A laser diode in which the material junctions are so arranged to provide a wide optical cavity for light waves to reflect back and forth, to provide the laser action. The cavity has a higher refractive index than the material surrounding it. The device provides an output beam and power greater than a light emitting diode.

large-scale integration. LSI. The design and production of integrated circuit or microcircuit chips. The solid state circuitry is produced on a single piece of material, normally silicon, LSI denotes circuits of complexity of up to 16 kilobits, and allows in the range of 10,000-100,000 transistors to be integrated on a single chip.

LARP. Local And remote Printing.

LARPS. Local And remote Printing Station.

LAS. Local Address Space.

laser beam recording. A technique employed in microfilm recorders where by the output characters from a computer are written directly to the microfilm by laser. Typically, the beam is divided into a number of separate rays which produce a dot matrix pattern.

laser diode. LD. A junction diode that consists of positive and negative charge carrier regions with a junction regions which, when injected with electrons, produces radiation at optical frequencies. In materials like gallium arsenide (GaAs) where emitted light is produced rather than heat, some reflected light trapped by polished ends is eventually emitted to produce laser action.

laser disc. In optical media, any disc recorded and read by a laser.

laser line follower. In peripherals, a graphic information input device in which a laser beam follows and traces continuous lines.

laser printer. A printer that uses a laser beam to produce fast, high quality output; a laser beam focused on an electrostatic drum creates an image to which toner adheres, which is then transferred to the paper. A colour laser printer works like a single-colour model, except that the process is repeated four times, and a different toner colour is used each time. The quality and speed of laser printer make them ideal for office environments.

LASER. *See* light amplification by stimulated emission of radiation.

LASERCOM. *See* light amplification by stimulated emission of radiation computer output microfilm.

LASP. Local Attached Support Processor.

last in first out. LIFO. 1. A method of queuing where the last item attached to queue is the first to be withdrawn. 2. A discipline of queuing in a computer where the newest entry in a file is the first to be removed.

last in last out. LILO. 1. A queuing method in which the last item attached to the queue is last to be withdrawn. 2. A discipline of queuing in a computer where the newest entry in a file is the last to be removed.

LAT. Local Area Transport protocol, a DecNET specific protocol for the exchange of small packets of data between typically Dec Vax host computers and terminal servers in a LAN.

LATA. Local Access and Transport Area, a term describing local versus long distance service areas.

latch. An electronic device that can store temporarily a single bit of data. It can be considered as a simple type of flip-flop. The storage is controlled by a clock signal, a given transition of which fixes the contents of the latch at the current value of its input. The contents will remain fixed until the next transition of the clock.

latency. The time taken for the start of a given sector of data on a storage disk or drum to reach the read/write head. It is measured form the instant when the head settles at the track within which the sector lies. The average latency is the time for half a revolution of the disk or drum.

LAU. Line Access Unit.

LAWN. Local Area Wireless Network, a local area network whose nodes or stations are connected by radio modems or other type of transmitter or transceiver.

layer two Tunneling protocol. L2TP. An industry-standard Internet tunneling protocol with almost the same functionality as point-to-point tunneling protocol (PPTP). Winddows 2000 implementation of L2TP is degigned to run natively over IP networks. A user can access a private network through the Internet or other public network by using a virtual private network (VPN) connection with layer two tunneling protocol.

layer. The description of divisions in specifications Such as OSI and SNA communications protocols. Functions are grouped together that comprise one step in the hierarchy necessary for successful data communications. In computer architecture, each part of the logical construction method, this provides an interface between, lower, more hardware-oriented entities, higher, more user-oriented entities, and higher, more user-oriented entities. For example, a physical layer might specify the hardware to be used, while a data link layer may exist immediately above this and pass data to the physical layer for transmission.

layered protocol. A set of rules governing communications between one or more devices. Network architectures are solving many incompatibility problems by isolating networking functions and establishing 'layers of protocols' to govern each set of operations. The layered approach to network architecture leads to the isolation of functions in a system and assignment of standard rules (protocols) to govern their operations. Layered protocols accomplish three objectives: they reduce the complexity of a network; they accommodate peer-to-peer interaction between nodes; and they allow changes in a layer without affecting other layers. The layered approach also permits the partitioning of the designed and development of many network components.

layer-to-layer transfer. In a roll of magnetic tape, unwanted transfer of data between adjacent turns on the reel. If severe, this transfer can cause drop-in or dropout in a computer. In audio applications, it can sometimes be heard as a delayed echo or a faint sound occurring just prior to the actual recorded sound.

LBN. Logic Bucket Number.

LBP. Laser Beam Printer.

LBR. Laser Beam Recorder.

LBT. Low Bit Test.

L-C network. The containing both inductance and capacitance. This form of tuned circuit has the product, L-C, of inductance and capacitance constant for a particular frequency.

LC. 1. Link Control.
2. Logical Channel, a logical rather than a direct connection between systems.
3. Line Control.
4. Line Connector.

LCA. 1. Line Control Adaptor.
2. Local Communications Adaptor.

LCB. 1. *See* line control block.
2. Logic Control Block.

LCC. *See* leadless chip carrier.

LCCC. *See* leadless ceramic chip carrier.

LCCD. *See* low complexity colour display.

LCD. Liquid Crystal Display; technology used for portable computer displays, as well as many electronics display applications, such as watches, etc. LCD displays for portables are usually active matrix, passive matrix, and dual scan displays.

LCDDS. *See* leased circuit digital data service.

LCF. 1. Log Control Function, used in Network Management to control what information about events or alarms gets logged.
2. Logical Channel Fill.

LCFS. Last Come First Served.

LCGN. Logical Channel Group Number, Field that identifies a logical channel.

LCI. Logical Channel Identifier, more frequently known as logical channel number.

LCL. 1. A colloquial expression for LoCaL; the mode of operation in some systems, in which information entered via the keyboard is displayed on a screen but not transmitted on a communication line.
2. Leakage Control Language.

LCM. Line Concentrating Module, telephony term.

LCN. Logical Channel Number used to identify a connection in X.25.

LCP. 1. Link Control Protocol, a protocol used by PPP to establish, manage, and terminate dial-up connections. PPP framing defines how data is encapsulated before transmission on the wide area network. PPP standard framing format ensures any vendor's remote access software that adheres to PPP standards. PPP and Windows 2000 use variants of High-level Data Link Control (HDLC) framing for serial or ISDN connections.
2. Language Conversion Program.

LCU. Line Control Unit.

LCW. Line Control Word.

LD. *See* laser diode.

LD4. In data communications, a high speed coaxial cable digital transmission system operating at 274 megabits per second.

LDD. Local Data Distribution.

LDDI. Local Distributed Data Interface, proposed ANS, Hyperchannel.

LDM. Limited-Distance Modem, a low-function DCE that provides relatively high bit transfer rates over short distances.

LDP. Language Data Processing.

LDR. Low Data Rate.

LDRI. Low Data Rate Input.

LDS. Large Disc Storage.

LDT. 1. Language Dependent Translator. 2. Long Distance Transmission.

LE. Local Exchange, term used in telephony to indicate a neighbourhood telephone office where calls are switched directly to the subscriber, i.e., exchange nearest the subscriber.

lead-in. The cable that connect the active part of an aerial to the transmitter or receiver.

leading zero. The zeros required by some programming methods in order to fill a numeric field, even when they do not seem necessary. For example, the number 76.88 may have to be written as 00076.88 in order to accommodate the program's limitations.

lead-in-track. A track on a compact disc, before the program tracks, containing the table of contents.

leadless ceramic chip carrier. LCCC. A particular mounting technique employing a high-density package for very-large-scale integration integrated circuits.

leadless chip carrier. LCC. A mounting technique employing a high-density package for very-large-scale integration integrated circuits.

leadless land grid array. LLGA. A particular mounting technique employing a high-density package for very-large-scale integration integrated circuits.

leadless. A raw semiconductor chip that is functionally complete except that it is non-capsulated and has no output leads affixed to the contact pads of the device. Leadless devices may be supplied by a manufacture when, for example, they are to be used to produce hybrid integrated circuits.

leaf. In data structures, the nodes at the end of a path in a tree structure.

leap second. A time step of one second used to adjust coordinated universal time to ensure approximate agreement with international universal time. An inserted second is called a positive leap second and an omitted second is called a negative leap second.

leased circuit digital data service. LCDDS. A service provided by British Telecom of high-speed, high-quality microwave data transmission links.

leased circuit. In data communications, a circuit hired by the subscribers for their exclusive use. It may be point-to-point or multi-drop connection.

leased line. Any communications line, designated to be at the exclusive disposal of an authorised subscriber.

leased network. A data network using circuits or channels leased from the network providers or major telecommunications carrier and dedicated to use solely by the lessee.

least recently used. A computer processing routine based on the length of time since the last access to a particular page or segment of main memory was made, in order to determine which part of the memory is to be overwritten.

least significant character. LSC. In a string where the position of a character determines its significance, the character at the end of least significance. Such a string is normally written with the least significant position on the right. For example, the least significant digit and the least significant bit contribute the smallest quantity to the value of a digital or binary number.

least significant digit. LSD. The significant digit that contributes the smallest quantity to the value of a number and in practice is the right-most digit.

least significant bit. LSB. The numerical, or binary digit in the binary scale of notation, that contributes the smallest quantity to the value of a number and in practice is the right-most digit.

LEC. Local Exchange Carrier, a carrier providing service within a local area.

LED display. A device used in some calculators digital watches, etc., to display numerical and alphabetical characters. It consists of an array of light-emitting diodes that emit light when a forward bias is applied; the colour of the light is usually red. LEDs are small, cheap, and have relatively low current and voltage requirements and long life. Their power requirements are, however, significantly higher than those of LCDs. In an LED display these diodes are arranged in such a way that by selectively illuminating individual ones in the array, simple characters are formed on the display. Seven diodes suffice to display the digits and some letters. *See also* light emitting diode.

LED. *See* Light-Emitting Diode. LED display.

left-to-right precedence. A simple form of precedence hierarchy, used in APL, in which operators are taken in the order in which they appear in the expression. Each operator takes everything to the right as right operand.

LEN. Low Entry Networking.

letters shift. A function initiated by a letters shift character and performed by a teletypewriter. It causes the machine to make a physical movement to lower case so that letters and lower case characters can be printed.

let-through current. The current conducted by a circuit breaker during a short-circuit.

level-2 cache. *See* L2 cache.

level alignment. Adjustment of transmission levels of single links and links in tandem to prevent overloading of transmission subsystems.

level measuring set. Instrumentation consisting of a receiving circuit calibrated in decibels (dB), which is used to measure the level of test-signals in telecommunication lines.

level 0. Transmission power at a reference point to which all other power measurements in the system are compared.

level 1. Pertaining to a videodisc player with freeze frame, picture stop, chapter stop, frame addressability and dual channel audio, but with limited memory and virtually with no processing power.

level 2. Pertaining to a videodisc player with level one facilities plus onboard, programmable memory and improved access times.

level 3. Pertaining to a level one or level two-videodisc player interfaced with an external computer.

level 4. Pertaining to a videodisc player with extensive memory, control and processing facilities.

level. A numerical value equal to one greater than the depth of the same node. The level of the root node is thus one; the level of any other node is one grater than that of its parent. In some texts, the term level is used as synonym for depth.

level-triggered flip-flop. A flip-flop that responds to voltage level rather than to the frequency of an input signal.

lexical analyser. The part of a compiler that breaks up the input into meaningful units, such as names, constants, reserved words, operators, etc. It also removes redundant characters such as spaces, and may deal with character-set mappings.

lexical scan. In programming, a stage in the compilation process in which source code statements are decomposed into essential components.

lexical uni. A language construct that, by convention, represents an elemental unit of meaning. Examples: a literal such as 'G25'; a keyword such as PRINT; a separator such as a semicolon.

LF. 1. Line Feed, ASCII character 10 decimal or ^J (control J); control character to move the print head one line forward.
2. Low Frequency, radio wave communications band, the exact range of which may vary from one country to another.
3. Linear File.
4. Logical File.
5. Line Feeder.

LFM. Local File Manager.

LFN. Logical File Name.

LFS. Local Format Storage.

LFSR. Linear Feedback Shift Register.

LGC. Line Group Controller.

LGN. Logical Group Number, an X.25 logical channel group.

LI. Length Indicator, where the size of an element within a PDU is carried.

LIFO. *See* last in first out.

lifter. In recording equipment, a device that removes the magnetic tape from contact with the head on fast wind and rewind.

ligature. In typography, the joining of two or more characters or symbols to form a new symbol used to form a mark, or for the purpose of decoration.

light amplification by stimulated emission of radiation computer output microfilm. LASERCOM. A device that combines LASER and dry film technologies, to enable the laser to mark or write directly onto microfilm. The system results in instant micrographic storage dispensing with any in-between steps.

light amplification by stimulated emission of radiation. LASER. An amplifier and generator of narrow coherent beam of electromagnetic energy in the optical or visible light region of the spectrum. Light from the laser is all the same frequency, has a high energy density and can travel great distances without any divergence from its tight beam. Lasers produce light in the visible, infra red, or less commonly in the ultra violet region of the electromagnetic spectrum. Some lasers are pulsed, and some are continuously operated. Laser beams can be modulated by very broadband input signals and are used in optical fibre communications links as pulsed sources of light.

light conduit. An assembly of fibres in a fibre optics cable which is used for the transmission of light sources rather than encoded optical signals.

light control. The control based on the use of light; or, the control of lighting levels.

light pen. A pen-like input device that is used with a cathode-ray tube display. It can be used to point to areas of the screen and thus indicate a selection from a displayed list, or it can be used to draw shapes. The light pen has a photosensor at the tip that responds to the peak illumination that occurs when the cathode ray tube scanning spot passes its point of focus. The display system correlates the timing of the pulse from the photosensor with the timing of the display scan to determine the position of the light pen.

light. An electromagnetic radiation with wavelengths between 400 nm (violet) and 740 nm (red) propagated at a velocity of ~300,000 km/s, and detected by the human eye as a visual signal. In the laser and optical communication fields, the term also includes the much broader portion of electromagnetic spectrum that can be handled by basic optical techniques used for visible spectrum. This is considered to extend from the near-ultraviolet region of approximately 300 nm through the visible region, and into mid-infrared region of 3.0-30 μm.

light-activated silicon controlled rectifier. LASCR. A silicon-controlled rectifier that functions both as a photosensor and a heavy-duty bistable electronic switch allowing heavy currents to be switched by means of a light beam.

light-emitting diode. LED. A *p-n* junction diode that emits light as a result of direct radiative recombination of excess electron-hole pairs. In direct-gap semiconductors, such as gallium arsenide, it is major part of recombination and a significant amount of light is emitted following injection of excess minority carriers. The amount of light produced in a forward-biased *p-n* junction diode formed from such material is proportional to the number of excess minority carriers. The light emitted by the diode is dependent on the optical quality of the crystal surfaces. These diodes with a light-producing characteristic provide light of different wavelengths (colours) by variations in their construction. The light-emitting diodes are widely used as indicators in panels and displays.

lightweight acoustic processing and display system. LAPADS. An antisubmarine system with a microprocessor unit that converts signals received from sonobuoys into digital form. It then carries out all the necessary filtering and analysis as well as processing the data for display.

LILO. *See* last in last out.

LIM EMS. Lotus-Intel-Microsoft Expanded Memory Specification; used to combat 640 kilobytes of random-access memory (RAM) limitations of DOS, the LIM EMS was introduced to enable computers fitted with expanded memory to work with up to 32 megabytes of RAM (LIM Version 4.0 introduced in 1987).

LIM-EMS. Lotus Intel Microsoft Expanded Memory Specification. *See* expanded memory.

limit check. A test on a number to see if it is within a stipulated range.

limited distance modem. A modem designated for operation over distances of about 50 km; used on privately owned line circuits. Also known as baseband modem; short-haul modem.

limited protection. A kind of short-term security, which warrants a degree of protection against simple analysis and easy exploitation; applied to data and acoustic communications.

limited syntax. A restricted range of sentence constructions; documents can be formed using this syntax to facilitate machine translation.

limiter circuit. A circuit of non-linear elements that restricts the electrical excursion of a variable in accordance with some specified criteria.

limiter. A device which automatically sets a boundary value(s) upon a signal. The term is usually applied to a device which, for inputs below a specified instantaneous value, gives an output proportional to the input, but for inputs above that value gives a constant peak output.

LINCMOS. LINear Complementary Metal-Oxide Semiconductor, a silicon-gate complementary metal-oxide semiconductor process technology. It combines the low power, low voltage and high input impedance of CMOS integrated circuits with offsets and voltage swings better than most bipolar devices, and is comparable to some devices.

line adapter. In data communications, a device used to convert signals so that transmission can take place. A modem acts as one form of line adapter between two computer devices, converting signals from digital to analog so that they may be transmitted via a telephone line for conversion at the receiving end.

line balance. The degree of electrical similarity of the two conductors of a transmission line.

line circuit. Equipment at a telephone exchange that acts to supervise the condition of a subscriber's line, when control signals are received.

line code. Code for the transmission medium and giving the equivalence between a set of digits generated in terminal or other processing equipment and the pulses chosen to represent the set of digits for line transmission.

line communications. Communications, such as through computers, telephones, between two nodes or points, by means of a physical path such as cable, fibre, or waveguide.

line conditioner. An electrical device (often part of a UPS) that ensures a constant level of electricity, by cleaning up any fluctuations in voltage.

line conditioning. A collection of techniques for keeping quality of transmissions within specified parameters.

line control block. LCB. An area of a memory containing control information for operations on a communication line. It can be divided into several groups of characters treated as a whole (field) most of which can be designated as generalised control blocks.

line control. The sequence of signals used to control a channel in data communications.

line editor. A text editor in programming where the user must select individual lines to modify text.

line feed. A specific control character used to advance one printing or display position to next position.

line filter. A filter in a transmission line, such as one that separates carrier frequencies from audio frequencies.

line finder. Any computer program that detects the lines in a grey-level array. It might look for the boundaries of regions of similar grey-level, or for a bar of similar grey-levels, etc.

line frequency. The number of horizontal scans per second.

line level. The signal level, usually in dB, at a particular point.

line loss. The total end-to-end loss in transmission line; expressed in dB.

line printer. A high-speed printer capable of printing an entire line of data simultaneously, 80-120 characters long, and then advancing to the next line. These printers normally use rotating drums or chains on which the necessary characters are located. They are normally associated with computers or medium to high-speed terminal services and are much faster than characters-at-a-time printers.

line protocol. A formally specified set of possible bit sequences that will guarantee that two ends of a communication link will be able to pass information between them in understandable manner. The standards which have been devised for implementation of such protocols include

BISYNC protocols, HDLC and ADCCP.

line spacing. The distance between lines of text in a document.

line speed. The rate, measured in bauds, at which signals may be transmitted over a given channel. It depends on the capabilities of the equipment and the extent of noise on the line.

line sweep. The horizontal movement of the scanning spot at line frequency in a television.

line switching. The most common form of concentration used to connect *n* transmitting devices to *m* receiving devices, where *n* is much greater than *m*. Buffering of data is done by the input devices if the transmission medium is busy.

line. 1. A string of characters accepted by the central computer as a single block of input entered prior to a carriage return command.

2. The path traced by a scanning spot in a television or facsimile.

3. A piece of conductor with supporting poles, used for transmission.

4. A device for transferring electrical energy from one point to another, such as a transmission line.

line-addressable random-access memory. LARAM. A block-access memory device consisting of a number of short charge-coupled device shift registers that has common input, output and regeneration circuits.

linear analog control. An analog system in which the functional relationships are of simple proportionality.

linear array. Another name for one-dimensional array, *i.e.*, for a vector.

linear channel. A transmission channel in which the information signal and the noise signal combine additively to form the output signal. In a *q*-ray linear channel, with a finite number, *q*, of amplitudes, the signals add modulo-*q*; in the binary case (q = 2), this has the same effect as an exclusive-OR operation between the signals.

linear circuit. A circuit in which the output varies continuously as a given function of the input.

linear codes. In coding theory, codes whose encoding and decoding operations may be expressed in terms of linear operations. The term is usually applied to certain error-correcting codes in which the encoding operation involves a generator matrix and the decoding operation involves a parity-check matrix.

linear information programming language. LIPL. A computer language that enables user to employ a notation with which he is already familiar.

linear integrated circuit. An integrated circuit designated for such operations as amplification, oscillation, non-digital regulation, analog instrumentation, and similar applications.

linear logic. A system of combinational and possibly sequential circuits in which the combinational components comprises exclusive-OR gates only. This is sometimes referred to as strongly linear logic in order to distinguish it from weakly linear logic in which inverters are permitted. In non-binary (*q*-valued) systems, the EXOR gates are generalised to modulo-q adders and substractors.

linear predictive coding. A technique used for the analysis of speech and its conversion into digital coded information.

linear programming. A technique employed in mathematics and operational research for determining or solving particular problems involving many variables, where it is required to find the best value or best set of values. The linear programming technique is not to be confused with computer programming, although problems using the technique can be programmed onto a computer. The mathematical technique used employs a series of linear equations to best allocate any limited resources.

linear time-base oscillator. A relaxation oscillator, which is used to generate a saw-tooth waveform for use as a time base.

linear. 1. Denoting any system, device, or apparatus which has its essential physical parts arranged in a line.
2. Describe any device that has an output directly proportional to the value of the input and varies continuously with it

linearity. 1. A constant ratio of incremental cause and effect.
2. The degree to which an input/output relationship is proportional.
3. The degree to which a motion intended to be in a straight line conforms to a straight line.

linearly polarised mode. In optoelectronics, a mode for which the field components in the direction of propagation are small compared to components perpendicular to that direction. Each LP mode consists of several phase degenerate modes. The LP description (which is an approximation for weakly guiding waveguides) becomes more accurate as the difference between the maximum and minimum values of the refractive index becomes a smaller fraction (typically less than 2%) of the mean index value across the profile. Also known as LP mode.

linearly-graded junction. A junction between two different polarity semiconductors in which the concentration of impurities varies linearly across the junction.

line-impedance stabilisation network. LISN. A network that simulates the normal impedance of a typical power source impedance. It is used for measuring the conducted emissions emanating from equipment to a power line.

lines per minute. LPM. 1. Usually used as a suffix forming an expression indicating the number of lines of text that can be dealt with by a printer or a teletypewriter.
2. Refers to the speed of operation of a line printer.

link access control. LAP. The data-link layer protocol which is a subset of HDLC and is used in X.25-base networks in setting up channels between DTE and DCE.

Link Access Protocol. *See* LAP.

Link Control Protocol. *See* LCP.

link editor. A utility program that combines several separately complied modules into one, resolving internal references between them. When a program is assembled or compiled, an intermediate form is produced into which it is necessary to incorporate library material containing the implementation of standard routines and procedures, and to add any other modules that may have been supplied by the user, possibly in other high-level languages.

link encryption. The application of on-line encrypto-operation to a link of communication system so that all information passing over the link is entirely encrypted.

link layer. The logical entity in the OSI model concerned with transmission of data between adjacent network nodes.

link loader. 1. A communication path that may be physical or either physical or logical.
2. A utility program that combines all the separately compiled modules of a program into a form suitable for execution.

link loss. The loss of signals in microwave transmission between the transmitting and receiving ground stations of communication satellite system.

link protocol. A set of rules for data communication over a data link specified in terms of a transmission code, a transmission mode, as well as control and recovery procedures.

link terminal. The ground station of an earth-to-satellite link.

link testing. Testing of a group of modules to ensure that the modules operate correctly in combination. It is generally performed after the individual modules have been tested in isolation and prior to the integration testing, which is performed for the whole system.

link. 1. The place in a hypermedia document that signals a connection to another hypermedia document. A link may be an image, text, or sound.
2. A communication channel or circuit that is used to connect other channels or circuits.
3. A path between two switches that form part of the central control system in automatic switching.
4. When a field of an item A in a data structure contains address of another item B, *i.e.*, of the first word in the memory, it contains a link to B.

linkage. 1. The meaningful combination of data or information from one information system with that from another system for the purpose of deriving additional information, such as combination of files from two or more sources.
2. Instructions, which connect one program to another, providing continuity of execution between programs.

linker. A program which can combine several machine language files into an executable program.

link-state algorithm. A routing algorithm such as OSPF which takes into account lowest delay when choosing a route: link speed and congestion as well as hop count.

lin-log receiver. A type of radar receiver which has a linear output for small input signals and a logarithmic output for the large input signals.

Linux. A UNIX-like operating system that has become quite popular in recent years. Like UNIX, Linux is a multi-user system with an easily extendable user interface.

LIPL. *See* linear information programming language.

liquid crystal display. LCD. A display that depends on an external light source for visibility and is based on materials that exhibit a regular crystal-like structure even in a liquid state. A normally transparent liquid is sandwiched between two glass plates that have a conductive material on their inner surfaces. When subject to an external electric field the liquid becomes opaque and reflective. As in other displays characters are normally built up from segments. As they require minimal power, LCDs are used in battery devices such as calculators, digital watches and portable digital instruments. A low-power-consumption panel that can provide a clear display even in bright sunlight is employed for this purpose. It is a development of a liquid crystal display screen that incorporates on a silicon wafer approximately 32 000 data and a very-light-sensitive large-scale integrated circuit.

LIS. *See* large interactive surface.

LISN. *See* line-impedance stabilisation network.

LISP. *See* list processing.

lister. A program, which lists code in a readable form.

list head. In many list representations, special header cells that are added to a list and possibly any sub-lists to management and traversal algorithms.

list processing. LISP. A computer language developed to manipulate symbolic strings of repetitive data and used primarily for research rather than for production programming. The basic data structure is a list whose elements are either atomic symbols or lists. An unusual feature of LISP is that programs are also expressed as lists, i.e., the programs and the data they manipulate have an identical language, having no assignment operator. LISP is used generally in the verification of mathematical proofs and for developing high-level languages in artificial intelligence research.

list sorting. A form of sorting that utilises a link field in each record. The links are manipulated so that each link points to the following record in the sorted file to form a straight linear list.

list. A finite ordered sequence of items. Unless stated otherwise, the items in a list can be arbitrary in nature.

listserv. An automated mailing list distribution system originally developed by BITNET/EARN network; it allows users to communicate with others on the list in an ongoing discussion. Listserver programs now also run on UNIX and other operating systems.

litera. A lexical unit that directly represents a value; for example, 15 represent the integer fifteen; APRIL represents string of character APRIL; 3.0005E2 represent the number 300.05.

LIU. Line Interface Unit.

LiveLink. A software program that allows a group of users to easily and automatically share and integrate many different types of data across different applications. An invisible link structure, in a layer beneath the data, 'connects' the local document to the remote data, enabling the user with access privileges immediate access to the most accurate, up-to-date data create by other applications that support LiverLink software.

LL parsing. One of the most powerful top-down parsing technique which proceeds without backtracking. An LL parser may be implemented as a push-down automation or by the method of recursive descent. In the former method, a stack is used to store that portion of leftmost derivation sequence that has not been matched against the input string. Initially the start symbol of the grammar is pushed onto an empty stack. Subsequently, if the top element of the stack is a terminal symbol, it is matched against the next symbol in the input string. If they are the same then the stack symbol is popped and the input marker advanced, otherwise there is an error in the input string.

LLA. Leased Line Adaptor.

LLC. 1. Logical Link Control, a data link protocol based or HDLC, developed for LANs by the IEEE 802 Committee and consequently common to all the LAN standards for Data Link OSI Layer Two transmission.

2. The sub-layer, which performs error-checking functions for frames delivered over the subnet and manages links between devices communicating on the subnet.

LLC1. Logical Link Control, connectionless.

LLC2. Logical Link Control, connection-oriented.

LLCs. Logical Link Control, Security, an IEEE 802.2 logical link control security feature.

LLG. Logical Line Group.

LLGA. *See* leadless land grid array.

LLI. Low Level Interface.

LLL. Low Level Language.

LLP. Lower-Layer Protocol; usually refers to OSI layers 1-3, and some times 4.

LLPDU. Logical Link Protocol Data Unit.

LM. 1. Layer Management, OSI Network Management specific to objects at given layer of the reference model.
2. Local Memory.

LME. Layer Management Entity, an entity that provides management functions, such as activation and error control, for objects within a given layer.

LMI. Layer Management Interface, how status information in frame relay is exchanged between user devices and the network.

LNB. Local Name Base.

LO. Location Code.

load and go. An obsolete method of operation in which program loading together with a possible compiling or assembling is followed immediately by the program's execution phase.

load and store. An obsolete method of operation in which program loading together with a possible compiling or assembling is concluded by the storage of the object code.

load characteristic. A characteristic curve for an electronic device showing the dynamic relationship between the instantaneous values of two variables when all the supply voltages are maintained constant.

load life. Time during which a device may dissipate power under specified operating conditions while remaining within its specified operational performance.

load point. The beginning of the recordable area on a magnetic tape.
It may be noted that some magnetic tape drives use a beginning of tape marker to indicate the position of the load point.

load sharing. A technique whereby computers on a network share work loads to attain a reasonably uniform distribution. It is generally achieved by the offloading of jobs from a heavily loaded computer to one that is lightly loaded.

load. 1. Any device/equipment that consumes power from a source of electrical signals.
2. The output power delivered by any electrical device, generator, transducer, electronic circuit, or device.
3. To put program, data, or software in to a register or storage.
4. The process of copying, from a disk to the computer's random-access memory, program instructions, or data sequences.
5. To transfer data into storage device or working registers.

loader. A utility program which sets up an executable program in main memory ready for execution. This is the final stage of compiling/assembly process.

loading, antenna. The addition of an inductance to enable an antenna to be tuned to a lower frequency than its natural frequency.

lobe. The cable between a token ring station and the trunk coupling unit to which it is connected. Lobe length comprises a patch cable from the TCU to the main wiring panel, the length of the main wiring to the user station's location, then a patch cable from a floor/desk socket to the station.

local and remote printing. LARP. he provision of a computer or word processor print-out or hard copy near the operator's terminal and if preferred at a more distant point.

local area connections. A type of connection that is automatically created and activated. Typically, the computers running Windows 2000 are connected toa local area network. When Windows 2000 is installed, the operating system detects network adapter and creates local area connection. It appears like all other connection types, in the network and dial-up connections folder. If the changes are made to the network, the user can modify the settings of an existing local area connection to reflect these changes.

local area data transport. LADT. A method of using local loop to provide both data and analog voice services for subscribers.

local area network. LAN. A computer network operating over a small area linking to computers, electronic mail and word processors and various the equipment. It can provide communication from site-to-site or provide access to other networks such as the public telephone network and a data transmission network.

local automatic message accounting. LAMA. A combination of automatic message accounting equipment and automatic number identification equipment housed in the same office. This American system can automatically process a telephone subscriber's dialled toll call for billing purposes without an operator's assistance.

local bridge. Bridge that links two local LANs: in the same room, for example.

local code. A digit, or a combination of digits, for obtaining an access to the exchange in an adjacent numbering area without using the national number.

local form control. A system for off-line data-entry operations by diskette storage of information and unchanging descriptions or specifications (fixed formats).

local security. A security method available for 386 and 486 servers running HPFS386. This method extends LAN Manager security measures to protect the files on a server by restricting access of the users working at the server. With local security, a user must be assigned permissions to access any file or directory in an HPFS386 partition, whether or not the resource is shared as part of a LAN Manager resource.

LOCAL. A colloquial expression for load on call. If a particular program is too big to be loaded into the core memory of central processor unit, sometimes it can be split into subprograms which can be held on disk or magnetic tape which can be loaded into memory on call.

local. A term applied to variables that are accessible only in restricted part of a program or area.

localtalk. The network hardware built into Macintosh computers. LocalTalk hardware handles the AppleTalk protocol. A 230Kbit/s-baseband network primarily for Mac computers and LaserWriter printers, it uses the CSMA/CA media access method. The current Phase II allows theoretically unlimited networks.

location operator. An operator in a programming language which yields the address of its operand.

lock up. An unwanted state from where the computer or microprocessor cannot escape.

locking. A term used for controlling the frequency of an oscillator by means of an applied signal of constant frequency from an external source.

locking-in. The process of synchronising the frequencies of two coupled oscillators, as in a frequency doubler, so that the two frequencies have a desired ratio, usually of two integral numbers.

lockout. 1. Programming technique used to prevent access to private or critical data by unauthorised terminals.

2. An arrangement of control circuits whereby only one receiver can feed the system at one time.

log. A record of a sequence of events or the jobs run through a computer.

logarithmic response. 1. Response in which the value of a dependent variable is at every point equal to the logarithm of the independent variable: y equals log x.

2. A kind of response in which a quantity (such as current) varies directly with the logarithm of another quantity (such as voltage).

LOGEL. LOgic GEnerated Language.

logger. A functional unit that records events and physical conditions, usually with respect to time.

logging. A record to keep track of events that take place with respect to system.

logic analyser. An electronic instrument which monitors the logic states of digital systems and stores the results for subsequent display.

logic board. Usually called a mother board, a logic board is one of the most important circuit boards in a computer, containing vital components including the central processing unit, microprocessor support chips, expansion slots, and some of the random-access memory.

logic bomb. A program used in a form of computer crime, which involves the use of an idle code which, when released, results in data destruction or other unauthorised functions. A logic bomb is a Trojan triggered by a set of conditions (such as the number of files on the disk, or a certain combination of letters being typed as determined by the programmer of the logic bomb).

logic card. A printed circuit board of standard size and carries a number of digital logic devices in a circuit arrangement capable of fulfilling a specific function.

logic circuit. Gating or switching electronic circuits which, in computer and control systems, perform such logical operations as AND, NAND, NOR, and OR. Logic circuits may employ diodes, transistors, charge-coupled devices, tunnel diodes, thyristors, ferroelectric elements, magnetic-core elements, or a combination of these. The term logic device is often used synonymously. A logic circuit is required to produce specified binary outputs as a result of specified binary inputs. This may be accomplished by using logic gates, producing what is called hardware circuitry. Alternatively the inputs may be associated with the address lines of a ROM and the outputs with the data lines of a ROM; this is called firmware circuitry. Hardware circuitry constructed from integrated-circuit packages on circuit boards requires two types of wiring. The first type carries two types of wiring. The first type carries the logical information between gates. The second type provides the power for the individual chips. The process of locating the power paths so that they do not interfere with the logic paths is called power routing. Logic circuitry may be mathematically analysed using Boolean (or switching) algebra. In this representation, the binary 1 is associated with the identity element and logic 0 is associated with the null element, *i.e.,* zero.

logic diagram. A diagram that displays graphically, the interconnection of logic symbols, the digital design of a logic circuit or system.

logic family. A range of electronic devices that is made by the same manufacturing technique and provides a number of logic functions. The range includes logic gates, flip-flops, and counters. Families in common use are ECL, TTL, and I^2L, which are all based on bipolar transistors, and the NMOS and CMOS families, which are based on MOSFETs.

Logic families vary in respect of switching speed, propagation delay, and power dissipation, although developments in the fabrication technology of the different families often improve these characteristics. A member of a logic family whose output changes state typically within a few nanoseconds (10^{-9} seconds) is considered a high-speed logic device. These devices are also characterised by short propagation delays, also in the order of a few nanoseconds.

logic function. An expression for an operation involving one or a combination of logic operators.

logic gate. A device, usually but not exclusively electronic, that implements an elementary logic function; examples include AND, OR, NAND, and NOR gates, and inverters. There are typically between two and eight inputs and one or two outputs. In order to represent the two logic states, true and false, in electronic logic gates, the input and output signals are held at either of two different voltage levels; a high voltage level usually represents true (logic 1) and a low level false (logic 0). Each type of logic gate has a logic symbol that conveys its logic function but does not indicate the electronic circuitry involved. The use of these symbols in circuit diagrams simplifies the understanding of a complex logic circuit and means that technological advances in electronics need not be taken into account. Logic gates based on fluid logic have been successfully used and optical logic gates, triggered by light, have recently been demonstrated.

logic instruction. An instruction that performs one of the class of logic operations on one or more specified operands. These operations may apply to a single variable, as in complementation, or more generally are defined on two variables.

logic level. In a combinational circuit, the maximum number of logic gates between any input and any output; the logic level represents a measure of delay time with the help of such circuits.

logic operation. An operation on logical values, producing a Boolean result. Operations may be unary or binary, and are denoted by symbols known as operations over one or two operands; they include AND, OR, NOT, NAND, NOR, exclusive-OR and equivalence. Logic operations involving more than two operands can always be expressed in terms of operations involving one or two operands.

logic probe. A probe using a light-emitting diode or light bulb to indicate whether a signal is 0,1 or undetermined.

logic state. The logical sense, true or false, of a given binary signal. A binary signal is a digital signal that has only two valid values. In physical terms, the logical sense of a binary signal is determined by the voltage level or current value of the signal.

logic symbols. A set of graphical symbols that express the function of individual logic gates in a logic diagram. The most common symbols are those for the simple Boolean functions and for flip-flops.

LOGIC. A programming language.

logic. 1. Science of reasoning, proof, thinking, or inference; in mathematical logic, investigation involves mathematical methods taken from algebra or theory of algorithms; two most common systems are pre-positional calculus and predicate calculus.
2. Process by which incoming digital information is transferred in to outgoing digital information or signals.

logical address. An address configured through the network software. In TCP/IP, a computer's logical address is called an IP address

logical data type. A data type comprising the values true and false.

logical error. A bug in which the code directs the computer to perform a task in a incorrect manner.

logical field. A database field that stores only one of two values, yes or no, true or false, on or off, and so on.

logical format. An operating system function in which tracks and sectors are mapped on the disk surface; mapping creates the boot record, FAT, root folder, directory, and the data area.

logical instruction. An instruction in a computer program, which is specifically logical and not purely arithmetic.

logical link control sublayer. A sublayer of OSI's data link layer; responsible for error checking and managing links between devices on the subnet.

Logical Link Control. *See* LLC.

logical one. The digit '1' used in binary notation, which is equivalent to true of a logical statement.

logical operator. An operator which can be used in a logical expression to indicate the action to be performed on the terms in the expression. Logical operators are AND, OR, and NOT.

logical record. A set of related data elements considered to be a record from a logical viewpoint.

logical shift. A shift operation which can take one of the two forms: left or right. The bits in a specified storage register are shifted a given number of places, in the appropriate direction, and the zeros are shifted in at the other end.

logical unit. The IBM SNA network function defined in layers four, five and six (Transmission Control, Data Flow Control and Presentation Services) of the SNA architecture. In the SNA network, corresponding LUs are able to exchange information. Originally, particular types of LU have specific functions: LU1 for printers, LU2 for displays and so on. As SNA has developed, new types of LU have been introduced that support a broader range of communications facilities. LUs are normally associated with particular physical units, or network devices. LUs provide the services required by Applications in the IBM SNA environment, sitting between the applications and the physical units. A dependent LU relies on the host for activation, physically and logically, while an independent LU can initiate a session without host involvement.

logical value. Either of the two values true or false, that indicate a truth value. Although a single bit is the most obvious computer storage structure that can be applied to the logical data, larger units of store, such as byte, are frequently used in practice since they can be addressed distinctly.

login. 1. The procedure used to establish the identity of the user and the levels of authorisation and access permitted to him.

2. Requests by the user for access to a computer usually time sharing system. Also known as logon.

logoff. In computing, the process by which a user terminates his session on computer. The term is also used as log off; log out; or sign off.

logon script. A batch program containing LAN Manager, NetWare and other operating system commands used to configure workstations. Logon scripts can be written for one or more users.

logon server. For a domain, a logon server is the primary domain controller and the backup domain controllers. For a user, the server that processes the user's logon request.

logon. *See* login.

long distance Xerox. A specific form of communication which combines facsimile and xerographic copying.

long waves. Low-frequency radio waves particularly those in the 30-300 kHz region (10^3-10^4 m).

long-haul optical transmission set. Capable of transmitting light wave signals for long distances via an optical cable, this type of optical link is used for telecommunications between distribution frames or switching centres.

longitudinal redundancy check. LRC. 1. An error-checking technique based on transmitted characters that follows pre-set rules. Information is accumulated at both sending and receiving stations during the transmission of a block. The accumulation is termed the block-check character and is transmitted as the last character in the block. A transmitted block-check character is compared with an accumulated block-check character to determine when a good transmission block has been made.

2. A procedure for checking errors in a computer program.

look aside cache. One of the basic decisions in designing a cache is how it fits onto bus between the microprocessor and main system DRAM (dynamic random-access memory). Caches can be designed with two basic read architectures: look through (serial) and look aside (parallel). In a look aside cache, the cache is designed to fit onto the memory bus in parallel with the microprocessor and main system memory. The cache does not interrupt memory request from the microprocessor to main system memory. Instead, all memory request from the microprocessor are sent simultaneously to the cache and main system memory.

look through cache. One of the basic decisions in designing a cache is how it fits onto bus between the microprocessor and main system DRAM (dynamic random-access memory). Caches can be designed with two basic read architectures; look through (serial) and look aside (parallel). In a look through cache, the cache is designed to fit in series between the microprocessor and main system memory. The microprocessor 'looks through' the cache to main system memory. All memory requests from the microprocessor are first sent to the cache then from the cache to main system memory.

look-ahead carry. A high-speed carry procedure in which a group of carry digits is formed in parallel from the respective input bits of the two groups that are to be added and if it exists, from the most significant carry digit that is previous to those groups.

loop switching system. LSS. A term used in the US to describe a system that accommodate more telephone subscribers than line pairs in the system. It is achieved by concentrating traffic from a remote terminal, onto a smaller number of lines, to a complementary terminal at the local exchange.

loop. 1. The repetition of a group of instructions in a computer routine.

2. Go and return conductors of an electric circuit; a closed circuit.

3. A single connection from a switching center or an individual message distribution point to the terminals of an end instrument.

4. In telephone systems, a pair of wires from a central office to the subscriber's telephone.

5. A closed path under measurement in a resistance test.

loopback. The routing of a channel back to its source, so that all data transmitted are immediately received again. The diagnostic test returns the transmitted signal back to the sending device after it has passed through a network or across a particular link. The returned signal can then be compared to the transmitted one. The discrepancy between the two helps to trace the fault. When trying to locate a faulty piece of equipment, loopbacks will be repeated, eliminating satisfactory machines until the problem is found.

LOS. Line Of Sight, in communications, a link in a straight line between two points, e.g., using microwave radio or infrared laser carrier.

LOSS. LOSs of Signal, used in performance management in Network Management.

lost time. The fraction of the scanning line period which is not available for transmission.

low-complexity colour display. LCCD. A form of high-quality colour television display providing well-defined alphanumeric and graphics, high-performance displays driven from a logic source, as well as high-quality legibility and sharper colour reproduction.

lower case. A character that can be printed on paper or displayed on a screen, which is not a capital letter and is not included in the upper case set of characters.

lowest useful high frequency. LUHF. Lowest specific frequency in the high-frequency band (*i.e.,* 3-30 MHz) that can be used for communication via the ionosphere at any particular time.

low-frequency compensation. 1. In video-amplifier design, the special measures such as the use of high coupling and bypass capacitance, to boost low-frequency gain. The compensation is designed to avoid distortion due to signal attenuation and phase shift caused by the reactance of coupling resistors.

2. Use of special circuits to increase the low-frequency response of an audio amplifier.

low-level language. A kind of programming language in which the control and data structures directly reflects the underlying machine architecture. Such languages are difficult to write, and their application is limited to specific hardware configurations.

low-level logic. LLL. In digital-computer practice, any logic system that operates at low voltage or current levels.

low-level modulation. LLM. A method of modulation whereby the modulation is produced at a stage in a system where the power level is low compared to the level of power that is output by the system.

low-level protocol. A protocol that is concerned with the mechanics of communications with a network.

low-level signal. LLS. 1. A signal with small amplitudes.

2. A signal with peak-to-peak voltage so low that it does not drive an

amplifier circuit out of the linear range of operation.

low-performance equipment. 1. Equipment with insufficiently exacting characteristics to permit their use in trunks or links.

2. Tactical ground and airborne equipment whose size, weight, and airborne equipment whose size, weight, and complexity must be kept to a minimum and where primary requirement is to operate in nets with similar minimum performance standards.

low-speed. Pertaining to the data communication systems that operate at less than 2400 bits per second.

low-VHF band. The part of the frequency band allocated in the U.S. by the FCC for VHF broadcast television, including television channels 2 through 6, or 54 through 108 MHz.

LPC. Linear Predictive Coding, a voice-to-digital sampling and encoding technique.

LPM. *See* lines per minute.

LPN. Local Packet Network, the nearby packet network, as opposed to the wider notion of packet networks linked together by X.75.

LPS. Laser Printing System.

LPT1. The name used by MS-DOS to refer to the first parallel port on a computer. The second parallel port, if there is one, is LPT2. The printer is usually connected to LPT1.

LR parsing. A bottom-up parsing technique; it is one of the most powerful left-to-right, no backtracking parsing method for context-free grammars.

LR. 1. Limit Register.

2. Logical Record.

LRA. Local record Address.

LRC. *See* Longitudinal Redundancy Check.

LRU. Least recently Used.

LS. Local Single-layer (abstract test method), one of the abstract test methods used in conformance testing.

LSA. Line Sharing Adaptor.

LSAP. Data Link Layer Service Access Point.

LSB. 1. Lower SideBand, a negative amplitude half (180 degrees) waveform used as a carrier; USB would be the upper or positive side-band.

2. Least Significant Bit (Byte), bit or byte representing the smallest amount, usually on the right when written.

LSDU. Data Link Service Data Unit.

LSE 1. Local System Environment, the hardware, operating system, and software tools making up the environment of a single system.

2. Local Single-layer Embedded [(abstract) test method], a variation on the LS abstract test method in conformance testing.

LSEL. Link Selector, a 1-byte value that combines with a 6-byte MAC address to make up an 802.3 sub-network point of attachment address, e.g., the LSEL 0XEE is used to select the ES-IS protocol.

LSI. *See* large-scale integration.

LSM. Linear Select Module.

LSR. 1. 1. Local Shared Resources.

2. Local Storage Register.

LSS. *See* loop switching system.

L-supergroup. A 60-channel (five group) FDM carrier system routed on a coaxial cable path.

L-system. A method of generating infinite sets of strings. L-systems are similar to grammars with the difference that, whereas for grammars each step of derivation rewrites a single occurrence of a non-terminal; in an L-system all non-terminals are rewritten simultaneously.

LT. 1. Lower Tester, used in conformance testing; refers to the tester that controls the PCO at the service connection of the layer below that which is being tested.

2. Line Termination, class of managed objects where a signal originates or terminates, or both.

3. Loop Termination, place at which the local loop ends, usually at an LTE, for example, data communications equipment, telephone, COC, etc.

4. Language Translation.

LTD. Line Transfer Device.

LTU. Line Termination Unit.

LU 6.2. An IBM SNA Logical Unit that provides general communications functions, including the communications functions necessary for peer-to-peer networking. Underlying LU 6.2 is a type of node: node type 2.1, which facilitates peer-to-peer networking. Two SNA units, which implement rode type 2.1, can set up a full peer-to-peer session without invoking SSCP capabilities in a host processor. This is defined as SNA low-entry networking.

LU. *See* logical unit.

LUB. Logical Unit Block.

luggable computer. Refers to a portable personal computer designed in the mid-1980s.

luminance. The measure of the brightness of a colour; corresponds to the total amount of light coming from a given surface area. Luminance, also called lightness or intensity, is used along with hue and saturation, in the HLS colour model.

lurking. In a mailing list or Usenet newsgroups, listening without responding publicly. It allows beginners to get feel for the response patterns of the participants of the groups, and lets them get up to speed on the history of the groups.

LVA. Local Virtual Address.

LWA. Last Word Address.

LX-band. A section of the L-band extending from 950 MHz to 1.15 GHz.

LY-band. A section of the L-band extending from 725 to 780 MHz.

LZ-band. A section of the L-band extending from 1.450 to 1.550 GHz.

M

μ. Micro; a decimal prefix commonly used in association with a base unit of the SI system of units, indicating a multiplication factor of one millionth, 10^{-6} of that unit.

M. Mega. 1. A decimal prefix commonly used in association with a base unit in SI system of units, indicating a multiplication factor of 10^{6} of that unit.
2. A prefix used in computing that denotes a multiple of 2^{30}. One megabyte equals 1,048,576 bytes.

m. milli; a decimal prefix commonly used in association with a base unit in SI system of units, indicating a multiplication factor of 10^{-3} of that unit

M.nnn. The CCITT M. Series Recommendations deal with standards for the control, monitoring, and maintenance of analog, digital, and mixed international telephone networks and equipment, for example, periodic testing of echo suppressers, maintenance of a coast earth station, etc.

M/S. More Segments flag in CLNP.

MA. 1. Memory Address.
2. Memory Assembler.

MAA. Major Sync Point Acknowledgement Session PDU.

MAB. Macro-Address Bus.

MAC. 1. Media Access Control, the layer-A sub-layer of the data link layer (Level Two) of the ISO OSI Model responsible for media control; it provides an interface with the network adapter. The network adapter driver, in fact, is sometimes known as MAC driver.
2. Memory Access Controller.
3. Message Authentication Code.

MACBASIC. Measurement And Control BASIC.

MacBinary. A file format for transferring Macintosh files between different computer platforms that allow the separate data and resource forks of the Macintosh to be stored together in a datafork. MacBinary is used to ensure that data and files created on the Macintosh (but stored and used by DOS based computers) maintain their original computer codes (including icons, graphics, creation date, and so on). MacBinary files are distinguished by the .bin file extension. Binhex is generally preferred over MacBinary.

MACF. Multiple Association Control Function, an Application Layer services for managing applications' associations with one another.

machine aided translation. MAT. A system of translation employing a computer-based multilingual lexicon. The system assists a human translator by providing the swift translation of particular words and/or terms, from one spoken human language to another.

machine check analysis and recording. MCAR. A diagnostic procedure initiated by an automatic interruption that occurs when the programmed checking of machine functions (machine check) circuits detects a machine error.

machine code. Set of coded instructions, which a machine can recognise, read, understands, interpret, and execute.

machine cycle. The combination of *i*-time and *e*-time (instruction time and execution time). After data and instructions are read by the input device and placed in primary storage, the control unit then:

(a) fetches the instructions from primary storage;

(b) decodes the instructions and makes the available data to the arithmetic/logic unit;

(c) instructs the arithmetic/logic unit to perform operation on the data;

(d) places the computation into primary storage.

The sequence of operations in a central processing unit that corresponds to one memory cycle, input/output (I/O) cycle or equivalent internal operation. It may be noted that an instruction may require one or more machine cycles for its execution and a machine cycle usually contains more than one clock cycle.

machine function. An operation which is performed by an equipment, or machine.

machine language. A computer-oriented language having instruction codes that are executed directly by a computer (machine); usually based on, or is a part of, internal circuitry design of a computer.

machine translation. Human language translation performed by computers or similar equipment.

machine-aided cognition. The application of computers that have artificial intelligence. The system exhibits characteristics commonly connected with human intelligence, including learning, logic, problem solving, reasoning and the ability to understand natural language.

machine-aided index. MAI. The use of a store of information held on a computer file to produce an index for documents. The documents are provided with titles that give an indication of their contents.

machine-orientated language. MOL. A method of notating information that is intelligible to a computer or specific machine. These languages often include information that directly controls machine operations.

machine-readable cataloguing. Developed by the British Library for the US Library of Congress, this system has been designed for the production of records which contain information of description of books, articles, journals, reports and documents that are capable of being read by a computer.

machine-readable data file. A file of information that is capable of being read by a computer.

Macintosh. Computer developed by Apple Computers, first released in 1984. The Macintosh was one of the first computers to use a graphical user interface. Today, Apple continues to produce many different models of Macintosh.

MacLink Plus. A file transfer utility used to transfer files from the Macintosh to the IBM Personal Computer or IBM-compatible. It also includes a translation facility.

MacOS. The operating system produced by Apple for their Macintosh computers.

macro call. A statement embedded in a source language, which is to be replaced by a defined statement sequence in the same source language. It may be noted that the macro call will also specify the actual parameters for any formal parameters in the macrodefinition.

macro. A sequence of commands and/or data input that has been stored for fast and easy playback.

MACRO. The short form of MACROcode or MACROprogram; a computer source-language statement, routine or program that is able to be understood by a computer compiler or processor with or without the assistance of another routine to decode instructions.

macrobend loss. In an optical waveguide, that portion of the total loss attributable to macrobending.

macrobend. In an optical waveguide, such as an optical fibre, a relatively large deviation of the optical axis from a straight line.

macroinstruction. A computer instruction that can be replaced by a specific sequence of instructions in the same language. It usually provides the parameters that are required for its own execution.

macroprocessor. A processor that allows a programmer to define and use macroinstructions; usually the macroprocessor is a portion of an assembler.

MACSYM. Measurement And Control SYsteMs.

MacWeb. The EINet's full-featured World Wide Web browser, that can be obtained from: ftp.einet.net.

Maczila. A music player that supports many audio formats from QuickTime, MIDI background sound, WAV, AU, and AIFF audio, MPEG and the AVI video on Macintosh.

MAD. Multiple Access Drive.

MADA. Multiple Access Discrete Address.

MADAM. Multi-Purpose Automatic Data Analysis Machine.

magic eye. A small cathode ray tube used as an indicator of received signal strength, used to tune in radio receivers accurately. In addition, a light-sensitive or infrared sensitive device used in a burglar alarm or other devices, to trigger action when a beam is interrupted.

magic-tee. A four-branch waveguide assembly which, when its branches are correctly terminated, will effect the transfer of energy from one branch to two other branches.

magnetic bubble memory. MBM. A memory device employing a very thin layer of magnet garnet set out in its natural state as ribbon-shaped strips or magnetic domains. When an external magnetic field is applied to the material the domains contract into cylinder, which when viewed from the top under a microscope look and behave like bubbles. When influenced by the external fields the bubbles can be manipulated to represent information binary digits. The bubbles are tiny circular areas (stable magnetic domains) in which the medium is magnetised in the reverse direction to the rest of the medium. Bubble memory thus differs from magnetic tape and disk stores. in which the medium moves and the data bits are stationary with respect to it. It belongs to the class of magnetic domain memory but is the only form in current use.

magnetic bubble. A solid state memory device, which depends on the magnetic polarization of domains, usually in garnet-type material. The magnetic bubble is caused to move through the material by an external field, and the direction of polarization of individual domains, read off as each passes a sensing device, represents two logical states of 0 or 1.

magnetic card. A card with a magnetizable surface layer on which data can be stored by a magnetising field and read by a sensing device.

magnetic centring. Centring the beam in television picture tube by means of an electromagnetic focusing coil, a permanent magnetic core memory.

magnetic disk. A flat, circular surface that spins around its centre, and has a magnetizable coating on which data may be recorded as magnetised spots; disk rotates permitting data to be recorded in a set of concentric tracks.

magnetic head. An electromagnet that is capable of reading, writing, or erasing data in the form of magnetised areas on a magnetizable surface, such as on magnetic tape, disk, drum, or card.

magnetic ink character reader. MICR. A device capable of converting into a machine code characters which are printed in magnetic ink and are readable by humans; used by banks to enable cheques to be handled automatically.

magnetic storage. Storage in which the magnetic properties of materials are used to store data, usually in the form of magnetised areas or spots on a surface coated with a magnetizable material, such as magnetic tapes, drums, disks, cards, and thin films; or as magnetised cores and slugs.

magnetic tape. A plastic substrate on which a magnetic medium is formed by depositing an oxide such as ferric oxide (Fe_2O_3). Recent tapes use particles of metal. The tape may be wound onto reels either in a closed cassette container with 4 mm tape or an open reel-to-reel with 12 or 25 mm tape. Generally cassettes are used for low to medium quality or domestic audio or microcomputer recording while reel-to-reels are used with high-quality audio or large mainframe computers. Also known as magtape.

magnetic thin-film storage. The storage in which data are stored by magnetic recording on film of molecular thickness, of the order of 1 micron; used for combinational circuits as well as for storage elements.

magnetic-film memory. A magnetic memory in which memory cells consists of a thin film (thick film in some instances) of a magnetic material deposited on a substrate. Information is written into and read out of the cell through coils. Also known as thin-film memory.

magnetic-tape drive. A mechanism capable of controlling the movement of magnetic tape for reading, writing, and erasing data while the tape is moved past a magnetic head.

magnetic-tape leader. The portion of the magnetic tape that precedes the beginning of tape and is used to thread the tape on a tape handler, or on a reel.

magnetic-tape parity. As a safeguard against losing information between magnetic tape and a memory device, a technique in which an extra bit is generated and added to characters under certain conditions to make the output uniform temporarily. Lack of uniformity in output then serves as an error indicator. The original quantity is recovered by dropping the extra bit following a parity check.

magnetic-tape trailer. The portion of the magnetic tape that follows the end of tape mark and is used to retain the tape on the reel or on the tape handler.

magnetic-tape unit. MTU. A piece of equipment that records electrical signals on a magnetic tape, using the tape as a storage medium. The tape, which is flexible, is wound on reels and passes over a read/write head. High tape speeds can be used, as there is no physical contact between the tape and the read/write head.

magneto-optical disk. A storage medium having the capacity of an optical disk, but can be rewritten with the ease of a magnetic disk; data is written to disk when a laser melts the plastic coating encasing the magnetically sensitive metallic crystals, allowing a magnet to change the orientation of the crystals.

magtape. *See* magnetic tape.

MAI. Multiple Access Interface.

mail merge. The process of combining a text document, such as a letter, with the contents of a database, such as an address list. It allows user to send a personalised letter to several people without having to type the letter more than once. The addressing details are left out of the main letter. Instead, main letter contains codes in place of specific addressee details. These codes are used to automatically combine (merge) these details from a database file, which only contains addressee details. The addressee file is usually called secondary file.

mailbox facility. A store-and-forward communication system service feature in which a message from a originator is held in storage until the destination user requests access to read the message. Also known as electronic mail.

mail server. An Internet term for the server on which messages received from the post office server are stored until the recipients access their mail box and retrieve messages.

main distribution frame. MDF. A distribution frame that has connections on either side. The lines external to the telephone exchange are connected on one side and the internal cables of exchange equipment are connected on the other. MDF is used for associating any outside line with any other outside line or with any cable terminal. It functions as a test point between line and central office.

main file. *See* master file.

main lobe. In an antenna radiation pattern, lobe containing the direction of maximum radiation intensity. For a light source energising an optical fibre, bundle, or cable, the main lobe directed into the fibres. The horizontal directivity pattern is specified as the angle encompassed between the points where the radiation has fallen to 3 dB below the maximum value.

main station. A user end instrument, such as a telephone set or terminal, with a distinct call-number designation, connected to a local loop, which is used for originating calls, and on which incoming calls from the local exchange are received.

main storage. The storage, which is considered to integral part of the computer, communication, or data processing system.

mainframe. A large and fast central computer which offers superior data processing capabilities. They are usually installed in very large organisations. The term 'mainframe' was originally used to refer to the metal framework (cabinet) which housed the computer's circuits, but today it refers to the computer itself.

maintainability. The ease with which maintenance of a functional unit can be performed in accordance with prescribed requirements.

maintenance. Any activity intended to retain a functional unit in, or to restore it to, a state in which it can perform its required function. It may be noted that maintenance includes keeping a functional unit in a specified state by performing activities such as tests, measurements, replacements, adjustments, and repairs.

MAL. 1. Macro Assembly Language. 2. Memory Access Logic.

MAM. Memory Access Multiplexer.

MAMMAX. MAchine-Made and Machine-Aided indeX, a form of machine-aided index (MAI) in which documents in machine readable form are scanned by a computer, and entries are written into the index in a form that complies with instructions in a particular extraction program.

MAN. Metropolitan Area Network; a complete communications network set up by a local company to service the customers in regional locations, providing them with microwave and satellite relay stations, fibre optics, and cellular radio services within a 50 kilometre range (operating at speed from 1-200 megabit/s. MAN is larger than local area network (LAN), but smaller than a wide area network (WAN). IEEE has defined its 802.6 standard for MANs based on Distributed Queue Dual Bus technology.

management information base. MIB. A hierarchical address space, the set of variables or database that a gateway running CMOT, SNMP, or CMIP network management protocols maintains. It is a virtual database used to define the functional and operational aspects of network devices. It defines variables needed by the SNMP protocol to monitor and control components in a network. Managers fetch or store into these variables. MIB-II refers to extended SNMP management database that contains variables not shared by CMOT and SNMP. CMIP and SNMP MIB formats differ in structure and complexity.

management information system. MIS. 1. A type of data processing system designed to provide management and other specified supervisory personnel with information of desired nature. 2. A process of communication where data is processed and recorded and any problems are flagged in order that higher-level decisions can be made, and also so that management can review overall progress of project.

Manchester encoding. A data-encoding scheme in which data and clock pulses can be combined into a single self-synchronising bit stream and in which each encoded bit contains a midpoint transition, first half being the complement of the bit value and second half being the true bit value.

man-machine interface. MMI. A device, which helps a computer (system software) communicate with the user in plain language. These include voice synthesising devices as used in talking calculators.

manual exchange. Telephone exchange in which the connections between the incoming and outgoing lines are manually controlled by an operator.

manual hold. When a call is made via the operator in an automatic telephone system, manual hold is established when the telephone caller's line is held in the busy state until the operator releases it.

manual. A unit of documentation; one is on the shelf; while someone has the other copy. It is help in using the equipment/software.

MAP. 1. Manufacturing Automation Protocol, an industry profile for use in factory environments; mostly OSI-based in origin.
2. Major sync Point Session PDU; a confirmation must be received for this PDU before more data can be sent.
3. Macro Assembly Program.
4. Memory Allocation Processor.
5. Multifunction Adaptive Processor.

MAPDU. Management Application Protocol Data Unit, a PDU containing management information.

MAPI. Messaging Application Programming Interface, Microsoft's standard for the applications interface to e-mail.

mapped buffer. A display buffer in which each storage location has a corresponding display position on the display surface of a display device. Thus, a character stored at a location in the buffer will be displayed in a corresponding position on the screen.

MAR. *See* memory address register.

MARC. MAchine-Readable Cataloguing, maintained by the Network Development and MARC Standards Office of the US Library of Congress.

margin. 1. The allowable error rate.
2. The maximum degree of signal distortion which can be tolerated without affecting the restitution.

marginal test. A technique in which certain operating conditions, such as temperature, humidity, pressure, voltage or frequency supplied, are varied about their nominal values in order to detect and locate components with incipient faults.

MARISAT. MARItime SATellite service, which make use of geo-stationary satellites over the Pacific and Atlantic oceans. This service enables communications to be established between ships in either ocean.

mark scanning. The automatic optical sensing of marks recorded on a data medium.

mark sensing. The detection, by an optical device, of marks on a piece of paper, commonly used to collate questionnaires or school examinations where a student, using a pencil, marks certain boxes on the examination answer sheet.

mark. 1. A symbol which indicates the beginning or the end of a field, word, data item, or data set.
2. One of the two significant conditions of modulation.

M-array signalling. The transmission of digital data in a way that permits the pulses to take on with equal probability any of *m* rather than 2-amplitude levels. This multilevel system implies three or more transmitted conditions.

MAS. 1. MacroASsembler.
2. Modular Application System.

MASER. Microwave Amplification by Stimulated Emission of Radiation; a term used to describe a general class of microwave amplifiers, which are based on molecular interaction electromagnetic radiation. It is non-electronic in its working principle, providing low-value noise emissions, especially if operated at very low temperatures.

masking. A logical operation carried out on a byte, word, or field of data in order to modify or identify a part of it. A bit pattern-the same length as the item to be masked-is generated and stored in a register as a mask. By use of the appropriate operation, *e.g.*, subtract, logical AND, logical OR, the mask can be used to suppress bits in the data, or set them to zero, etc. The process is used for purposes such as identifying the presence of high-priority bits in a status byte or resetting interrupts.

MASS. *See* multiple access sequential selection.

master antenna television. MATV. Television network similar to a community antenna television, a master antenna television is designed to provide television pictures but is on a much smaller scale than a community system. A typical example would be a antenna serving a block of flats.

master control program. MCP. A program that control all phases of job. It directs all equipment functions and the flow of all data; provides for automatic error detection and correction; also directs the operator with printed instructions and adjusts system operation to changes in system environment.

master file. A relatively permanent file of essential data used as primary or main file in support of a given job or set of jobs. Also known as main file.

master instruction tape. A tape, most often a magnetic tape, onto which all the programs for a system of various computer runs are recorded. It is considered to be a fundamental part of an operating system.

master pages. The special pages created in desktop publishing software that contains elements common to all the pages in the document, such as page numbers, headers and footers, margins, and layout guides.

master station. A device that controls/polls the nodes in multi-point circuits or, in point-to-point circuits, the unit that controls the slave station. In LAN terms, the device on a token passing ring that enables recovery from error conditions, such as lost, busy or duplicate tokens, usually by generating a new token. Servers are sometimes called master stations.

MAT. 1. Machine Aided Translation.
2. Memory Address Test.

MATD. Maximum Acceptable Transit Delay, the lowest throughout acceptable, when proposing a network connection.

math coprocessor. *See* Floating Point Unit.

mathematics markup language. An XML application for marking up mathematics. It is an extremely interesting application in that it uses parallel markup structures to address both the presentation and semantic structures of mathematics.

matrix switching. A form of data switching at the heart of ATM, enabling the appropriate of bandwidth to be available end-to-end for the duration of the session without contention.

mature. Adjective used to describe anything that nobody uses anymore.

MAU. 1. Multi-station Access Unit, a token ring passive hub.
2. Medium Attachment Unit, a transceiver (transmitter/receiver) comprising hardware circuitry that provides the correct electrical or optical connection between the computer and IEEE 802.3 LAN media. Since MAUs typically support only one type of network medium, a choice of MAUs is available to support different media. It detects carrier and collision activity, passing the information to Computer. It can be standalone unit or incorporated in a circuit board inside the computer. Also known as media access unit; transceiver.
3. Memory Access Unit.

Maving. A popular TinyMUDder who sometimes accidentlly left a colon on the front of a whisper, thus directing private mesages to the whole room.

maxicomputer. An old-fashioned name used to refer to supercomputers.

maximal code sequence. A binary digit code sequence that is the longest which can be generated by a given spread-spectrum code-sequence generator before the sequence is repeated.

maximum access time. Maximum allowable waiting-time between initiation of an access attempt and access success.

maximum justification rate. In pulse code modulation multiplexing, the maximum rate at which justifying digits can be inserted or deleted.

maximum keying frequency. The frequency (in hertz) that is numerically equal to the spot speed divided by twice the scanning spot *x*-dimension. The term is generally used in context of facsimile- transmission systems.

maximum modulating frequency. The highest picture frequency which is required for a given facsimile-transmission system. The maximum modulating frequency and the maximum keying frequency may or may not be equal.

maximum rating. 1. The highest value of a quality (*e.g.,* current, voltage, or power) which may safely be used with a given device.

2. The highest value of a quantity afforded by a given device, *e.g.,* maximum capacitance.

maximum stuffing time. The maximum rate at which bits can be inserted into or deleted from a data stream.

maximum usable frequency. MUF. The upper limit of the frequencies that can be used at a specified time for ratio transmission between two points and involving propagation by reflection from the regular ionised layers of the ionosphere. A higher frequency would penetrate the ionosphere and be lost in space. The maximum useable frequency is usually the optimum frequency to use for long-distance communications.

Mb. *See* megabyte.

M-band. The band of frequencies in the range from 60-100 GHz, comprising 10 numbered channels that are each 4 GHz wide. The old M-band comprised frequencies in the range from 10 GHz to 15 GHz, overlapping the parts of the old X-band and the old P-band.

MBC. Memory Bus Controller.

MBI. Memory Bank Interface.

M-BIT. More data bit, used in X.25 to indicate whether more data PDUs are coming.

MBM. *See* magnetic bubble memory.

MBOS. Multi-user Business Operating System.

Mbps. Megabits per second (one million bits per second); speed at which data is transferred. As modems and serial transmissions become faster, Mbps is used to discuss their speed.

MC. 1. Magnetic Card.

2. Main Channel.

3. Master Control.

4. Memory Control.

MCAI. MicroComputer Assisted Instruction.

MCAR. *See* machine check analysis and recording.

MCB. MicroComputer Board.

MCC. Multiple Chip Carrier.

MCCU. Multiple Channel Control Unit.

MCL. Microprogram Control Logic.

MCM. Memory Controlled Module.

MCP. 1. Master Control Program.

2. Message Control Program.

MCR. 1. Magnetic Card Reader.

2. Memory Control Register.

MCRR. Machine Check Recording and Recovery.

MCS. Master Control System.

MCU. 1. Memory Control Unit.

2. Master Control Unit.

3. Microprocessor Control Unit.

MCVF. Multi-Channel Voice Frequency.

MD. 1. Management Domain, the one or more network entities managed by the same organisation.

2. Mediation Device, in a managed network, the device that performs mediation functions.
3. Message Data.

MDA. Multi-Dimensional Array.

MDAS. Modular Data Acquisition System.

MDCU. Magnetic Disc Control Unit.

MDD. Magnetic Disc Drive.

MDES. Multiple Data Entry System.

MDF. Main Distribution Frame, a connecting apparatus for communications circuits.

MDL. Macro-Description Language.

MDLC. Multiple Data Link Controller.

MDM. Multiplexer/DeMultiplexer.

MDMS. Multiple Database Management System.

MDR. 1. Message Detail Recording.
2. Memory Data Register.
3. Magnetic Disc Recorder.
4. Modular Disc Storage.

MDS. 1. Modular Data System.
2. Modular Disc Storage.
3. Multiprocessor Distributed System.

MDSE. Message Delivery Service Element, in X.400, the means by which delivery is effected.

MDT. Mean Down Time.

MDU. Maintenance Diagnostic Unit.

Mean Time Between Failures. *See* MTBF.

mechatronics. The study devoted to the design, development, fabrication, functioning, and use of systems or devices in which mechanical electronic components are integrated, usually the electronics for control, sensing, and decision making, and the mechanism for the motion and force development, such as mouse, light pen, and other pointing devices.

media access control driver. The LAN device driver that works directly with the network adapter cards, acting as an intermediary between the transport driver and the hardware.

media access control sublayer. A sublayer of OSI's data link layer, which is responsible for the interface with the network adapter.

Media Access Control. *See* MAC.

media access unit. A device that both transmits and receives data, providing the electrical and physical interface to the network cable. Also known as 'transceiver.

media. Items used to hold data, including floppy disks, hard disks, tapes, CD-R0Ms, etc.

medium attachment unit. *See* MAU.

medium frequency. The frequencies between 300-3000 kHz, forming part of a larger continuous range of frequencies. Medium frequencies are considered by International agreement to be radio frequencies in band number 6 and have wavelengths of between 100-1000 m.

medium. The physical method or equipment used for transmission, from a tangible fibre optic or copper cable to a satellite link.

medium-interface connector. In LAN/MAN system, the connector at the interface point between the bus interface unit, and the terminal, that is, at the medium-interface point.

medium-scale integration. MSI. The design and production of integrated circuits or microcircuits The solid state circuitry is produced on a single piece of material normally silicon. Medium-scale integration denotes circuits of medium complexity, *i.e.,* fewer component in a given area than large scale integration.

medium-wave. Pertaining to wavelength corresponding to medium frequencies *i.e.,* those in the 100-1000 metres range.

megabyte. Mb. The number of bytes given by 2 raised to the 20th power. One megabyte is 1,048,576 bytes, or

1.048576 million bytes; usually abbreviated Mb or MB as in 100 MB; employed as a measure of the storage capacity of a device. The memory of most artificial intelligence systems reaches the megabyte level.

megaFLOPS. MFLOPS. Million Floating Points Operations Per Second, a measure of computing power; specifically, the speed at which certain mathematical functions are performed.

megahertz. MHz. The speed at which a computer runs; does not take the speed at which a processor runs to be absolute. For instance a machine with a PowerPC processor running at 90 MHz may perform some tasks more quickly than an Pentium machine running at 120 MHz, and the Pentium may be faster at others.

member server. The server in a domain that keeps and uses a copy of the domain's user accounts database but does rot validate logon requests.

membrane keyboard. A pressure-sensitive two-dimensional keyboard covered with a dust-proofed and dirt-proofed plastic sheet. Although these keyboards are not designed for fast typing, they are useful in environments susceptible to dust and dirt, such as on a factory floor or in restaurants, where users may not have clean hands. Membrane keyboards are also used in hand-held input devices and in telephones because of their space saving feature.

memo field. A database field that stores text information of variable length.

memory address register. MAR. A special memory storage area, used to hold identification of the location of a selected word either to be read from or to be written into the main memory.

memory date register. MDR. A special memory storage area that holds the last data word read from a written into the location addressed by the contents of the memory address register.

memory management program. A utility program that uses a portion of a hard disk for the extension of the random-access memory (RAM) so that the size of RAM appears larger. Sometimes, sections of expanded memory and extended memory are used by this utility.

memory map. A listing of addresses, or symbolic representations of addresses, which define the boundaries of the memory address space occupied by a program or a series of programs.

memory protection. A capability of some operating systems to control a program's access to memory, so that one program cannot corrupt the memory allocated to another program. Memory protection will often allow a single program to crash without affecting other programs, or the system as a whole.

memory segment. A block of memory that is identified by a base address and has been allocated for a specific purpose. In common usage different portions of memory may be designated as, for example, data segment, and stack segment.

memory, internal. Memory unit which is under the direct control of a processor and which forms part of the centralised complex.

memory, random access. Memory system, for which the address of the particular section holding the information in question, or into which new information is to be stored, must be specified for each action.

memory. 1. A collection of chips on the motherboard or on a circuit board attached to the motherboard where all computer processing and program instructions are stored while in use. RAM, ROM, conventional memory, expanded memory, and extended memory are all different types of memory. RAM and hard disk space should not be confused. RAM is temporary storage while the hard disk offers semi-permanent storage.

2. In robotics, a unit into which a piece of data is entered, in which it is held, and form which it retrieves later. The robot memory is part of the controller, storing commands that have been programmed in and through the controller and telling the robot what to do and when to do it.

menu bar. A one-line, horizontal menu at the top of the screen; usually found in GUIs.

menu item. One of the command choices on a display menu which can be selected by an operator of a computer or data processing system.

menu. A screen image displaying display elements, display groups, or display images, usually displayed on the display surface of the display device, one of which can be chosen, by means of picking, to indicate one or more subsequent actions.

merge. To combine the items of two or more sets of data that are in the same given order into one set in that order, usually ordered according to some predefined sequencing criterion.

merged transistor logic. MTL. A form of logic that employs two multi-collector transistors. It evolved from diode transistor logic, a family of bipolar integrated circuits which are very compact and provide high speed operation along with a functional packing density. MTLs use less power, are more stable and cheaper, and are two orders of magnitude faster than transistor logic. Also known as integrated injection logic.

merge-sort. A sort in which the items in a set are divided into subsets, the items in each subset are then sorted, and finally the resulting sorted subsets are merged.

MESFET. MEtal Semiconductor Field-Effect Transistor, a junction field-effect transistor that has a barrier formed by a junction between metal and semiconductor (a Schottky barrier) as a gate electrode rather than a semiconductor junction.

message address. Address component of a message; usually consisting of one or more identifiers for originator, action addresses, information addresses, and exempted addresses.

message buffering. The placement of messages in a spooler for transmission at an optimum rate and at an appropriate time.

message control routine. 1. A specially designed routine or program used to control the sending or receiving of communications or messages to or from a remote terminal.

2. A supervisory routine in a program consisting of a series of subroutines. It controls the linking of the other subroutines and controls the overlaying of the various segments of memory as required.

message feedback. A method of checking the accuracy of transmission of data in which the received data are returned to the sending end for comparison with the original data.

message handling systems. MHS. X.400 refers to a series of CCITT Recommendations defining Message Handling Systems. The ISO term MOTIS, Message-Oriented Text Interchange Systems, is usually used synonymously and refers to a series of ISO standards 10021. X.400 is often used interchangeably with electronic mail or e-mail as well, but it encompasses a much wider range of messaging applications.

X.400 provides a general Message Transfer Service and content-specific user agents. The user agents aid a user, which can either be a human user or an application process, in originating and receiving messages. MTS is considered general because it can be used to carry messages from many different applications. User agents are designed for specific application and generate messages for that application (e.g., interpersonal Messaging, or Inter-Library Loan messages). Each application user agent creates messages with format and header fields specific to the type of message to be transferred.

The application type is identified as a content type of the MTS. the only content type defined in the first (1984) release of X.400, and hence the most common content type, is interpersonal messaging. The MTS, based on information in the envelope, transfer the message to a Message Transfer Agent (MTA) that can deliver it to the appropriate UA for the addressed recipient. Reliable Transfer Service is used to connect adjacent MTAs.

The initial release of X.400 was in 1984, in the CCITT Red Book series of recommendations. It was one of the first OSI Application Layer standards to be finalised and become widely accepted. Because of the timing, it did not follow the strict OSI Reference Model, not using a full presentation Layer and writing its own interface directly to Session. This was because the specifications for these layers were being developed at the same time. Essentially, X.400 took the Application Layer and divided it into sub-layers:

User Agent Layer (UAL) and
Message Transfer Layer (MTL).

The idea was that the user had a generic message transfer service in Application Layer that could carry all kinds of different messages. For many reasons, including time constraints and the necessity of starting with a limited scope, only one message content type was released with 1984 X.400 Recommendations. This was the interpersonal messaging service (IPMS). Again, this content type was simplified in order to reach agreements within the time allotted, and only business-style user names were standardised.

1984-88 CCITT study period saw additional development of the X.400 series of Recommendations. Enhancements were made, but more importantly, the X.400 model was redesigned using an object oriented approach. The idea of sub-layers within the Application Layer disappeared. The Application Entities that made up those layers still exist, but instead they are described in terms of objects and refined objects. In addition, X.400 was brought into alignment with progress that had been made in the development of the Presentation Layer and ACSE in the Application Layer.

message mode. A method of operating in a communication network in which message switching is used rather than packet switching.

message. The data package passed from the application layer to the transport layer. The term is also used to describe a message from one entity to another on the network.

Messaging Application Programming Interface. *See* MAPI.

meta-data. Data about data records, *e.g.*, the contents of an IRD.

meta-language. A programming language, usually non-procedural, that is used to describe computer programs. It is also used to describe the sequence in which application programs are executed to perform a computer system transaction.

METAPLAN. Methods of Extracting Text Automatically Programming LANguage; a computer programming language used for the retrieval of required portions of text.

metering pulse. A pulse sent periodically over a telephone line to determine the duration of the call.

metric wave. An electromagnetic wave with a wavelength between 1 metre and 10 metres, that is, a wave that has a frequency of 30-300 MHz and therefore lies in the very-high-frequency (VHF) range.

Metropolitan Area Network. *See* MAN.

MF. 1. Mediation Function block, provides translation of information being transferred between NEs and OSs in a managed network.
2. Medium Frequency, below HF and above LF.

MFLOP. *See* million floating point.

MFLOPS. *See* megaFLOPS.

MFM. *See* modified frequency modulation.

mget. UNIX program used in line mode to do multiple gets.

MH. 1. Manual Hold.
2. Message Handling.

MHP. Message Handling Processor.

MHS. Message Handling System, the engine underlying an electronic messaging system; also a proprietary e-mail integration scheme developed by Action Technologies.

MHS. *See* Message Handling Systems.

MHz. *See* megahertz

MIA. 1. MInor sync Acknowledgement session PDU, optionally used to acknowledge receipt of a Minor Sync Point PDU.
2. Multiplex Interface Adaptor.

MIB. *See* management information base.

MIC. 1. Medium Interface Cable.
2. Microwave Integrated Circuits.
3. Multichip Integrated Circuits.

MICR. *See* magnetic ink character reader; magnetic ink character recognition.

micro manager. The person employed to manage the purchase, maintenance, and modification of personal computers for an organisation, including the training of staff in the use of application programs.

micro. A colloquial expression often used as an abbreviation for a microcomputer or a microprocessor.

MICRO. *See* multiple indexing and console retrieval operation.

micro-bending. In an optical waveguide, sharp curvatures involving local axial displacements of a few micrometers and spatial wavelengths of a few millimetres. Such bends may result from waveguide coating, cabling, packaging or installation.

micro-channel architecture. MCA. A 32-bit PC bus standard developed by IBM for the high-end models of their PS/2 line of personal computers; it allows expansion boards to be configured by the software instead of manually; MCA is no longer used.

micro-channel. A proprietary bus developed by IBM for its PS/2 computer family's internal expansion cards. It offers improved performance over ISA-based machines like IBM PC/AT.

micro-chip. A small, silicon object containing microscopic circuitry.

micro-circuit. An integrated circuit, generally one performing a very complex function. An example is a microprocessor comprised of arithmetic logic unit, control circuits, registers, program counter, and memory, all within a single integrated circuit.

micro-code. A representation of the

microprogram, for example, the representation in coded form of a microprogram in a storage medium.

micro-computer. A computer having a microprocessor, storage, and input-output facility, all of which may be integrated on a single chip.

micro-fiche management system. MMS. A system employed for the storage and retrieval of information held in microfiche; similar to computer output microfilm.

micro-fiche. A method of storing printed information on small film-cards. The pages are reduced and arranged in order from left to right and top to bottom. The card is interested into a projecting machine to allow retrieval of the information. The photographic method is similar to that employed in microfilm.

micro-film. A method of storing printed to photographic information. The pages are reduced and arranged sequentially on a strip of film, usually 35 mm size. The film is inserted into a projecting device for retrieval of the information.

micro-form. Any data medium that contains micro-images, such as microfiche, microfilm, and microimage chips.

micro-image chip. A microform consisting of a small piece of material on which is recorded an image, which requires the use of a high-powered optical system to render the image legible to the human eye.

micro-processing unit. The main hardware constituent of a microcomputer; normally assembled on a printed circuit board, the micro-processing unit is not housed in an enclosure and does not have a power supply. It consists of a microprocessor, a main memory, input/output interface devices and a clock circuit. There are also a buffer, drive circuits and various passive circuit elements.

micro-processor development system. Essentially a system for producing software for micro-processors. A computer-controlled system which employs various devices or peripherals to aid the application development of micro-processors.

micro-processor. An arithmetic, logic, or control unit which is constructed on a semiconductor chip, or chip set, and implements the central processor of a computer. It contains all the essential elements of a central processor unit, this integrated circuit includes the control logic, instruction decoding and arithmetic processing circuitry. But in order to be useful the micro-processor chip or combination of chips is married with memory and input/output circuit chips to produce a microcomputer. Micro-processors are characterised by speed, word length (internal and external), architecture, and instruction set, which may be either fixed or micro-programmed. It is the combination of these characteristics and not just the cycle time that determines the performance of a microprocessor.

micro-program control unit. The system used in bipolar micro-processors, this functional unit maintains and generates micro-program addresses. It is also used to control carry-and-shift operation, and in conjunction with an interrupt control unit sets up the interrupt structure.

Microsoft Access. *See* MS-Access.

Microsoft Challenge Handeshake Authentication Protocol. MS-CHAP. A protocol created to authenticate remote windows workstations, providing the functionality to which LAN-based users are accustomed while integrating the encryption and hashing algorithms used on Windows networks. It uss a challenge-response mechanism with one-way encryption on the response. Its response packect is in a format specifically designed for NT and Windows 2000, and Windows 95 and later, networking products. In addition, MS-CHAP does not require the use of plaintext or reversibly encrypted passwords.

Microsoft Office. A Windows based software, which brings together full-featured programs and seamlessly integrates them to allow them to do a lot more. It gives an easy access to powerful, user-friendly tools that allow focusing on getting on to the jobs. Also known as MS Office. Its latest version is Office 2000, which is soon to be followed by Office XP.

Microsoft Windows. *See* Windows 3.11; Windows 95; Windows 2000; Windows NT; Windows NT 4.0.

Microsoft. A software company founded and run by Bill Gates. Microsoft produces MS-DOS and Windows. Microsoft also produces a number of applications including Word for Windows and Macintosh, Excel for Windows and the Macintosh, and Flight Simulator. The latest version of Windows has completely redesigned and redefined the desktop with added working support.

micro-software. The software designed and packaged, usually on diskettes, for installation and use on a personal computer.

microsyn. A device that translates rotational positions into an electrical signal; similar to a selsyn; used for for rotator-direction reading.

micro-wave integrated circuits. MIC. A diverse range of fabrication techniques which range from micro-strip circuits through various thin-film technologies employing glass and alumina substrates, up to monolithic microwave integrated circuits employing bulk silicon bipolar, silicon-on-sapphire and gallium arsenide processes. At present the majority of microwave integrated circuits manufactures produce hybrid devices utilising a mixture of thin-film and stripline techniques, achieving such circuit functions as oscillators, mixers and amplifiers in combinations to suit many applications and for frequencies up to 60 GHz or more.

micro-wave. An electromagnetic wave having wavelength 0.003m-3m, and frequencies from about 0.1-100 GHz, thus covering wavelengths from very high frequency (VHF) to extremely high frequency (EHF).

MICS. 1. Management Information Conformance Statement, states what is supported in relationship to objects supported; this includes information about attributes and attribute groups, notifications, and actions.
2. Management Information and Control System.

MID. 1. File name extension for data confirming to the protocol for interaction between digitized musical instruments and a computer.
2. Message Input Description.

MIDA. Message Interchange for Distributed Application, OSI.

midband. MB. The region whose limits are immediately above and below a mid-frequency, the limits usually being specified for a particular case.

MIDDLE. MIcroprogram Design and Description Language.

MIDI. Musical Instrument Digital Interface, a standard protocol for communication between electronic musical instruments and computers. MIDI has become a standard tool for musicians, enabling them to compose complex music on a piano-style keyboard, and then capture that information using a computer, which can be used to automatically write the score. The data is stored on standard floppy disk, and every aspect of the music can be edited, including orchestral arrangement, tempo, pitch, and key.

MIDMS. Machine-Independent Data Management System.

MidPlug. A kind of MIDI music player that plays MIDI background music on PowerMacs and Windows 95.

MIL. 1. Management Information Library. 2. Micro-Implementation Language.

million floating point. MFLOP. A measure of computing power that refers to the number of operations per second made when the position of the decimal point of stored numbers changes during computing.

Milnet. Military Network, originally part of Arpanet, Milnet was partitioned in 1984 to make it possible for military installations to have a reliable network service while the Arpanet continued to be used for research. Under normal circumstances, Milnet is part of the Internet.

MIM. Management Information Model, part of the OSI management standards, ISO 19165-1.

MIME. Multipurpose Internet Mail Extension. A standard for transferring binary information (such as sound and graphics files, or word processing files with embedded formatting codes) over e-mail.

MIMO. Man In/Machine Out.

MIND. Modular Interactive Network Designer.

mini supercomputer. A supercomputer capable of operating at no more than 100 million floating point operations per second.

minimum distance code. A binary code in which the signal distance does not fall below a specified value and which can be interpreted even under noise conditions.

minimum standard antenna. A directional antenna having specified minimum characteristics as regards directive gain and service sector at its operating frequency or frequencies.

MIO. Multiple Input/Output.

MIOP. Master Input/Output Processor.

MIP. 1. Manual Input Processing. 2. Matrix Inversion Program. 3. Mixed Integer Programming.

MIPE. Modular Information Processing Equipment.

MIPS. Millions of Instructions per Second; execution speed of a computer; for example, 1 MIPS is 1,000,000 instructions per second. The personal computers often perform at 100 MIPS. MIPS rates are not uniform. Some are averages while some are peak performances. In addition, it takes more instructions on some machines to perform the same function (RISC vs. CISC, mainframe vs. micro). As a consequence of this, MIPS are sometimes known as MisInformation to Promote Sales. MIPS rate is just one factor in overall performance. Bus and channel speed and bandwidth, memory speed, memory management techniques and system software also affect the complete performance of the computer.

MIR. 1. Memory Information register. 2. Memory Input Register.

MIRA. Microprocessor Implementation of Reliable Architecture; a system which offers very high 'system availability' consisting of two Micro VAX systems which are linked together by means of an Ethernet, a watchdog timer, and switching modules.

mirroring. 1. A fault-tolerance feature that sets up primary and secondary partitions on a physical drive. The drive that duplicates data on the

primary memory is called the secondary partition.
2. The process of keeping a constant backup of the server data on another server. Every change to the data made to the primary drive is immediately communicated to the backup mirror server so that if primary server fails for any reason, the mirror can take over immediately.

MIRTOS. MInimum Real Time Operating System.

MIS. 1. Management Information Services, information services used to monitor, control, and coordinate resources like network and its entities.
2. Management Information System.

MISR. Multiple Input Signal Register.

MIT. Management Information Tree, the logical structure of information in a management information base.

M-IT-02. Memorandum of the CEC on Information Technology Policy, program under which much of the work on European functional standards has been developed.

M-IT-03. Memorandum of the CEC on Certification of Information Technology Products.

MIU. Model Interface Unit.

MIW. Micro-Instruction Word.

mixed base system. A numeration system in which a number is represented as the sum of a series of terms each of which consists of a mantissa and a base, the base of a given term being constant for a given application but the based being such that there are not necessarily integral ratios between the bases of all the terms.

MKH. Multiple Key Hashing.

ML. Machine Language.

MLD. Machine Language Debugger.

MLI. Machine Language Instruction.

MLIP. Message Level Interface Port.

MLP. MultiLink Procedure, an extension to LAPB that allows multiple single links to be managed as a logical whole.

MLPP. MultiLevel Precedence and Preemption service.

MLS. MultiLevel Security, provision of security by multiple means which may be combined or used individually.

MLU. Memory Logic Unit.

MMAR. Main Memory Address register.

MMD. MultiMedia Documnet, for example, an X.400 message carrying different types of body parts, like IA5 and fax or voice.

MMFS. Manufacturing Message Format Standard, part of MAP.

MMI. 1. Man-Machine Interface, obsolete term for user interface.
2. Main Memory Interface.

MMJ. Modified Modular Jack, a connector similar to the standard modular jacks for RJ-45 and RJ-11, which has an attachment clip offset to one side instead of in the centre.

MML. Man-Machine Language, obsolete term for command language.

MMS. 1. Manufacturing Messaging Specification.
2. Manufacturing Message Service.
3. Manufacturing Message Standard.
4. *See* microfiche management system.

MMU. 1. Main Memory Unit.
2. Memory Management Unit.

MNF. Multi-system Networking Facility.

MNP 2-4. MNP protocols included in V.42 specification; originally, Microcom Network Protocol.

MNP. Microcom Networking Protocol, a series of protocols designed by Microcom to support the error control and data compression for asynchronous modem transmission.

MO. Managed Object, that can be controlled or provide reports in Network Management.

MOAC. Message Origin Authentication Check, a security service available in X.400.

mobile communication equipment. The communication equipment, which is installed in one or vehicles and can be operated, that is, it can transmit and receive messages and signals, even when the vehicle is in motion.

MOBL. Marco Orientated Business Language, a specific computer programming language that permits users to employ a notation with which they are already familiar.

MOCS. Managed Object Conformance Statement, a statement about what managed objects an implementation supports; similar to PICS for objects instead of protocol.

MOD. Message Output Description.

Modelling Tool. A software product for business analysis; also used for generating complete applications based on business analysis. It tends to be complex, and generally requires business and data modelling expertise in order to be used effectively.

modem approval group. An organisation established in January 1993 to raise awareness of the law against connecting unapproved devices to the PSTN, this group demands a level playing field in the modem market with better law enforcement or more open standards.

modem eliminator. A device that can replace a modem in some instances when the distance to be covered is short. It takes the power it needs to operate from the transmission line.

modem patch. A patch that electrically connects two points, two paths, or two conductors by means of two modems which are connected back-to-back.

modem. MOdulate-DEModulate, a communications device named from an amalgam of the words modulator and demodulator. A modem modulates an outgoing binary bit stream or to an analog carrier, and demodulates an incoming binary bit stream from an analog carrier. The term can also be applied to units carrying out other functions like multiplexing.

Generally, a modem provides network access through a telephone line. However, the more recent modems are installed on the cable lines, which provide network access through a cable line. Modems are used primarily for converting digital signals into quasi-analog signals for transmission and for reconverting the quasi-analog signals into digital signals; although many additional functions may be added to provide for customer service and control features.

2. In frequency division carrier systems, devices that change the frequency of a signal; voice band on one side, and the carrier frequency with either erect or inverted sidebands on the other side.

MODI. Modular Optical Digital Interface.

modified frequency modulation. MFM. Two standard data-recording techniques used to combine clock and data information for storage on a floppy disk. The single-density technique is referred to as frequency modulation encoding. In frequency modulation encoding, a double frequency encoding technique is used that inserts a data bit between two adjacent clocks bits. (The presence of data bits represents a binary 'one' while the absence of a data bit represents binary zero.) The adjacent clock bits are referred to as a bit cell, and except for unique field identifiers, all clock bits written on the disk are binary 'ones'.

In frequency modulation encoding, each data bit is written at the centre of the bit cell and the clock bits are written at the leading edge of the bit cell. The encoding used for double-density recording is termed MFM encoding (for modified FM). In MFM encoding, the data bits are again written at the centre of the bit cell. However, a clock bit is written at the leading edge of the bit cell only if no data bit was written in the previous bit cell and no data bit would be written in the present bit cell.

modifier keys. The part of a keyboard used in conjunction with other keys to execute a command, such as Shift, Ctrl, and Alt.

modular programming. A technique for developing computer programs or operating systems as a collection of components.

modular. Pertaining to the composition of a system by means of assembled and interconnected modules, each of which can be individually replaced.

modulated beam. 1. An electron beam which is intensity modulated by desired signal.
2. A light beam whose intensity is modulated for communications or control purposes.

modulated carrier. The carrier wave whose amplitude frequency, or phase is modulated at a (usually) lower-frequency rate to convey intelligence.

modulated continuous wave. A particular carrier wave, that is modulated by a steady audio frequency tone.

modulation, delta. A code, representing the difference between the amplitude of a sample and the amplitude of the previous sample. It operates well in the presence of noise but requires a wide frequency band.

modulation, double. Modulation carried out in two stages. First the sub-carrier is modulated by the information-carrying modulating signal, then the modulated sub-carrier is used to modulate a higher frequency carrier.

modulation, high-level. Modulation carried out at a power level comparable with final output power of the unit.

modulation, low-level. Modulation carried out at a low power level point in the system so that final stages of amplification operate on the modulated signal.

modulation, phase. A type of modulation in which the angle relative to the unmodulated carrier is varied in accordance with the instantaneous value of the amplitude of the modulating signal.

modulation, velocity. Modulation of an electron stream by varying the field acting on the stream so as to accelerate or decelerate it, causing the bunching of electrons.

modulation. The process of varying one signal, called the carrier, according to the pattern provided by another signal. The carrier is usually an analog signal selected to match the characteristics of a particular transmission system. Modulation signals and techniques may be combined to produce composite signals carrying many independent channels of information.

MOLDS. Management OnLine Data Systems.

monitor. A hardware device used to display the visual output of a computer using a cathode ray tube or LED dispaly.

monochrome. A monitor that displays only one colour. Some monochrome monitors can also display various shades of grey and are called grey-scale monitors.

monolithic driver. A network device driver that acts as network adapter card driver and transport protocol driver combined.

monospaced font. *See* fixed-width font

MOP. Multiple Online Processing.

MOR. Memory Output Register.

MOS. 1. Master Operating System. 2. Multiprogramming Operating System. 3. Management Operating System.

MOSAIC. Macro-Operation Symbolic Assembler And Information Compiler; a freeware Web browser, developed by the NCSA (National Centre for Supercomputing Applications). It supports World Wide Web, Gopher, and FTP directly, and other protocols either by emulation or through public gateway. It can be down-loaded from: ftp.ncsa.uiuc.edu.

most significant bit. The numeral or binary digit in the binary scale of notation that contributes the largest quantity to the value of a number and in practice is the left-most digit.

most significant character. The character in the left-most position in a number or word.

most significant digit. The significant digit that contributes the largest quantity to the value of a number and in practice is the left-most digit.

mother board. A printed circuit that in general will carry all the major functional elements of a computer system, *e.g.*, the central processing unit, memory, keyboard, etc., and may thus act as a stand-alone unit. The board's functions may be enhanced by the addition of modular elements, known as daughter such as memory extension or disk control and that communicate to the mother board via sockets onto a standard bus.

Motorola. Manufacturer of computer chips, makes the 680×0 chip family, and is part of the industry group that developed the PowerPC chips.

mouse. A mouse is a pointing device with a ball on the bottom, and is used to control the position of the pointer on the screen without using the keyboard. It is moved by hand to indicate precise position on a digital data tablet. The device has a transparent panel engraved with a fine cross and has several switches arranged under the fingertips. The data tablet and associated processor can correlate the function indicated by the switches with the precise position of the cross intersection.

The near-hemispherical shape and trailing cable suggest the similarity to an animal mouse. When the mouse is moved across a surface, the ball turns, turning receptors inside the mouse. These receptors send signals to the computer, which cause a pointer or cursor on screen to move in a manner, which corresponds to the direction and speed the mouse was moved.

There are also optical mouse, that track the motion of the mouse by reflecting light off of a special mouse pad. In a graphical user interface environment like Macintosh or MS-Windows, a graphics object (icon) is displayed on the screen to represent a series of instructions or programs. The user selects the icon by moving the cursor to point to the icon with a mouse, automatically activating a set of commands without the user having to enter complex instructions. The mouse can also be used to open menus, select text for editing, move objects on the screen, and draw images or diagrams. A mechanical mouse uses a rubber-coated ball on the under-side. The movement of this ball sends electrical signals to the system unit which cause the cursor, or pointer, to move in a corresponding fashion.

There are normally two buttons on the top of the mouse. The application program determines how the buttons function. In contrast, an optical mouse (opto-mechanical) uses diodes to emit light on to a metal pad. performing the same task, but usually with greater accuracy. With a mouse, the cursor can be moved very quickly to any point on the screen. This is very useful in drafting, engineering, and publishing applications where geometric figures and text must be placed in the correct position. Newer operating system environments also encourage the use of a mouse to make screen selections from graphics menus. The term 'mice' is generally used when referring to more than one mouse. A hand held locator operated by moving it on a surface. It may be noted that a mouse generally contains a control ball or pair of wheels.

moving domain. MOD. A memory device that is non-volatile like a core memory but much smaller, and is reasonably fast in operation. Unlike bubble memory, it requires no magnetic bias to form and hold domains and can be batch-fabricated using conventional microcircuit techniques.

MP. 1. MicroProcessor.
2. MicroProgram.
3. Multiprocessor.
4. Managing Process, part of an OSI application that handles OSI Management.
5. Machine Processable, highly structured, easy to use as input to a computer translation system, for example, TTCN-MP.

MPC. MicroProgram Control

MPCC. Multi-Protocol Communications Controller.

MPCM. MicroProgram Control Memory.

MPDT. Multipeer Data Transmission.

MPDU. Message Protocol Data Unit, data unit carrying X.400-related information.

MPE. Memory Parity Error.

MPEG. Moving Pictures Experts Group, a standard for compressed audio and video data. This is "lossy" compression scheme, which means the data loses some quality in compression. The standard specifies a bandwidth of 150 Kbytes per second, which is the data rate of audio CD's.

MPEG-2 format. A multimedia data compression standard used to compress broadcast-quality video.

MPG. File name extension for compressed video data.

MPL. MicroProgramming Language.

MPMC. MicroProgram Memory Control.

MPR. Message Processing Region.

MPS. MicroProcessor System.

MPT. Memory Processing Time.

MPTM. MultiParty Test Method, a method for conformance testing when more than two peer entities are required, as, in application relay testing.

MPU. Memory Protection Unit.

MPX. Multiplexer.

MR. 1. Mask register.
2. Message Retrieval, part of the P7 protocol for retrieving messages from a message Store.

MRAD. Mass random Access Disc.

MRC. Machine Readable Code.

MRDOS. Mapped Real time Disc Operating System.

MRI. Memory reference Register.

MRSE. Message Retrieval Service Element the means by which UV can retrieve messages from the MS.

MS. 1. Main Storage.
2. Message Storage, X.400 facility that allows storage separate from that provided by proprietary means with either UV or MTA. Formally defined as the automatic storage for later retrieval of information objects conveyed by means of message transfer.
3. Acronym for MicroSoft.

MS-Access. Microsoft Access, a relational database management system (RDBMS) under Windows; used for manipulate large amount of data, which is stored in multiple tables; MS-Access allows to set up relationship between tables to facilitate data retrieval. It is an object-oriented program, in which each object has properties that define how it appears and what work it performs. This program has a number of components.

MSAP. MAP Sublayer Service Access Point.

MSAT. Mobile service SATellite, refers to mobile services satellites, as distinct from mobile earth stations.

MSAU. Multi-Station Access Unit, a wiring concentrator on a Token Ring network that allows devices, typically eight to 12 Token Ring stations, to be connected to the ring. Relays in the MAU ensure the integrity of the network when devices are attached or removed. Managed Multi-Port/Multi-Station Access Unit has built-in network management support.

MSB. Most Significant Bit (Byte), the bit or byte representing the highest value in the string, usually that on the left when written.

MSC. Mass Storage Controller.

MS-CHAP. *See* Microsoft Challenge Handeshake Authentication Protocol.

MS-CHAP v2. New version of Microsoft Challenge Authentication Protocol, which provides mutual authentication, stronger initial data encryption keys, and different encryption keys for sending/receiving. To minimise the risk of password compromise during MS-CHAP exchanges, MS-CHAP v2 drops support for MS-CHAP password change and does not transmit the encoded password.

MSDB. Main Storage DataBase.

MS-DOS. Microsoft Disk Operating System, the most common operating system for IBM and compatible PCs; produced by Microsoft; sometimes referred to simply as DOS.

MSF. 1. Mass Storage facility.
2. Measurement Summarisation Function, service of Network Management.

MSI. *See* medium-scale integration.

MSL. Machine Specification Language.

MS-Net. Microsoft DOS-based networking system software product (Microsoft Network).

MSO. Multiple System Operator.

MSP. Message Security Protocol, developed by the US National Security Agency as part of Secure Data Network System to provide end-to-end security at layer-7 of an X.400 system.

MSS. Mobile Satellite Service, refers to using mobile earth stations and geostationary satellites to establish a communications service at any location for voice, data, video, etc.

MSSE. Message Submission Service Element, how a message is passed from an originating UA or MS to the initial MTA in X.400.

MSSSE. Message Submission and Storage Service Element, applications service element by which a UA effects the submission (origination) and storage of messages and probes in the MS.

MSU. Mass Storage Unit.

MT. 1. Machine Translation.
2. Message Transfer, the service of moving messages from one MTA to another, which is provided by MTS.

MTA. Message Transfer Agent, a functional component within the MTS that conveys information objects to users and distribution lists; uses P3 to interface with remote UAs and MSs, and P1 to communicate with other MTAs within the MTS.

MTAE. Message Transfer Agent Entity, an implementation of MTA process.

MTBF. Mean Time Between Failures, a term describing the reliability of equipment established by testing kit to its limits and promoting the MTBF as a selling point. As most users know, however, laboratory and operational environments have little in common.

MTBO. *See* mean time between outages.

MTCN. Minimum Throughout Class Negotiation facility, used to negotiate quality of service on the network.

MTL. Message Transfer Layer, MHS. In 1984 X.400, that portion of the Application Layer which contains MTAs and provides the message transfer service for X.400.

MTL. *See* merged transistor logic.

MTNL. Mahanagar Telephone Nigam Limited; a unit of Government of India, that provides telephone and Internet Services in major Indian cities.

MTP. Message Transfer Part, the lower three layers of the SS7 protocol stack; provides reliable datagram service.

MTS. Message Transfer System, one or more MTAs which provide store and forward message transfer between UAs, MSs, and AUs.

MTSE. Message Transfer Service Element, the means by which message PDUs are moved from one MTA to another MTA.

MTSL. Message Transfer Sub-Layer, an obsolete term, referring to the message transfer portion of the Application Layer running X.400.

MTTR. Mean Time To Repair, term used in specifications for equipment indicating the estimated average time between repairs.

MTTS. Multi-Task Terminal System.

MTU. Maximum Transmission Unit, largest unit of data that an be sent on a given physical medium.

MUD. Multiple User Dimension, generic term for a whole range of interactive environments. It is also known as MOOs, MUSHes, MUCKs, TinyMUDs, AberMUDs, etc; the name varies depending on the software underlying the shared environment. In a MUD, the user type commands to manipulate objects, make a general announcement, or whisper. In India, most of MUDding is restricted because of bandwidth problems, as a result of this, most MUDders use hidden/illegal resources to perform their activities.

MUD Archive. A webpage with a lot of information related to MUDs and MUDding;
http:/www.ccs.neu.edu/home/lpb/muddex.html.

MUDCaller. A MS-DOS based MUD program; it requires an Ethernet card and does not work with a modem. Its features include scripting, multiple connections, triggers, macros, scrollback, logging, and command-line history. This program may be found at:
ftp://ftp.tcp.com/pub/mud/Clients.

MUDSock. A MUD program that runs on MSWindows using Winsock; works mainly with TinyMUCK. The program can be seen at the site:
http://www.cyberspy.com.

MUDWin. A MUD program that runs on MSWindows using Winsock; some of its features include command history, macros, and logging. The program can be seen at the site:
ftp://ftp.microserve.com/pub/msdos/winsock.

MULDEM. MULtiplexor-DEMultiplexor; analogous to a modulator/demodulator (MODEM), a device or equipment that contains both a digital multiplexor and a digital demultiplexor.

multi-cast bit. A bit found in the Ethernet addressing scheme that indicates that the message is to be sent to all stations.

multi-cast message. A message that is intended for set of stations on network.

multi-channel bundle cable. In optical

fibre-systems, two or more single-bundle cables all combined in a single outside jacket.

multi-channel cable. In optical-fibre systems, two or more cables combined in a single jacket, harness, strength-member, cover, or any other unitising element.

multi-chip microcircuit. A microcircuit containing two or more monolithic integrated circuit chips bonded to a common substrate.

multi-drop. Referring to a circuit in communications line which is a type of multi-point link where the telephone company 'drops' several sets of local-loops into various customer sites at secondary stations. This is in contrast to a standard multi-point link where there is only one set of local-loop connections at each end of the telephone network.

MultiFinder. A utility used in Apple Macintosh computers as the operating system's shell for file and memory management, and user interaction.

multi-frequency signalling system. A system that transfers information using alternating currents with frequencies in telephone speech band, to set up, control and release calls. The information is represented by compound signals, made up of a number of voice-frequency currents chosen from set of available currents.

multi-layer board. A special type of printed circuit board, with two or more layers of circuit tracks, which is able to increase logic speed and packing density, whilst cutting electrical crosstalk.

multi-layer device. An electronic device that is fabricated by a technique that involves the deposition of a number of layers of conductive track onto an insulating substrate, the individual layers being separated by a layer of insulating material. Interconnections are made to the various conductive layers by means of holes in the insulating material. The technique is used to produce compact multilayer circuit boards for hybrid integrated circuits and to fabricate multilayer CMOS integrated circuits.

multi-loading operating system. An operating system which permits the user to open more than one application program at a time.

multimedia authoring. A process that combines text, graphics, animation, video, and sound data developed with various softwares to create a composite product.

multimedia authoring software. An application that allows the user to incorporate animation, images, text, sound, and vedio, to produce a multimedia product.

multimedia. the computer applications involving text, graphics, audio and video, or computers that are (or claim to be) designed to provide high quality graphics and audio. Multimedia is largely associated with CD-ROM, because the large amounts of data involved are provided best by CD-ROM. Applications to exploit multimedia to the full are emerging in the wake of advanced switching techniques and develop merits in desktop and server processing architectures. It may be essential to a physically separated group that communicates as if it was physically networked.

multi-mode distortion. In an optical waveguide, that distortion resulting from the superposition of modes having differential modal delays. The term multi-mode dispersion is often used as a synonym but is erroneous since the mechanism is not dispersive in nature.

multi-mode facility. A facility which is capable of handling more than transmission mode, such as telephone, facsimile, radio, etc.

multi-mode optical waveguide. An optical waveguide which will allow more than one bound mode to propagate. It may be either a graded index or step index waveguide.

multi-mode. Term used to describe an optical waveguide that permits the propagation of more than one mode.

multi-path fading. Fading of a received radio communications signal because incoming signals are received via more than one path. Since path lengths differ the different incoming signals do not always assist each other; they sometimes cancel each other out.

multiple access sequential selection. MASS. A particular method of storing and retrieving information that is used by a computer.

multiple homing. 1. The connection of a terminal facility so that it can be served by any one of several switching centres. This service may use a single directory number.
2. The connection of a terminal facility to more than one switching centre by separate access lines. Separate directory numbers are applicable to each accessed switching centre.

multiple indexing and console retrieval operation. MICRO. Interacting directly with the central processor unit of a computer, a MICRO is designed to retrieve, rank and qualify document entries in an index.

multiple on-line programming. A facility providing interactive programs development to a number of user terminals simultaneously.

multiple routing. A method of message routing in which more than one destination address is specified in the header.

multiple unit steerable aerial. A directive antenna that can be altered or steered to its direction of maximum sensitivity by adjusting the phase relationship between the units from which it is assembled.

multiple unit steerable array. A line of identical rhombic antennas, intended for communications reception, which have their outputs combined to provide steerable properties to the array.

multiple-access computer. A computer system that can receive or despatch input or output information from more than one location or terminal. Also known as multi-access computer.

multiple-frequency-shift keying. A form of communication where a separate frequency is used to transmit a digital data input code. Ten discrete frequencies are used for the ten numerals of the decimal system of notation.

multiplex link. A link that enables data terminal equipment to have several access channels to a network over a single circuit.

multiplexer. A device capable of sending several signals over a single line; it is separated by a similar device at the other end of the link. This can be done in a variety of ways: time division multiplexing, frequency division multiplexing and statistical multiplexing. Multiplexers are also becoming increasingly efficient in terms of data compression, error correction, transmission speed and multi-drop capabilities.

multiplexing. Creation of datalinks, circuits, or channels employing a set of equipment and applying various means of increasing the capacity of the physical equipment to carry messages. Several individual information-carrying channels are combined for transmission over one bearer (line, fibre or radio), using frequency division or time division techniques.

multiplier. 1. A device having two or more inputs and that produces an output of magnitude equal to the product of magnitudes of input signals. 2. A device or circuit that produces an output equal to a specified multiple of the input signals.

multiply. MPY. An operation performed in computing by two binary digits whereby the result is 1 (true), if and only if both digits are 1 (true). If either or both digits are 0 (false), the result is 0 (false).

multi-point connection. Single channel or circuit interconnecting devices in different locations. This usually means using polling techniques with each terminal a unique address. Also known as multi-drop line.

multi-point. A link that connects more than two points. Interchangeable with multi-drop.

multi-port repeater. An Ethernet wiring centre that allows multiple devices to be attached at one point on an Ethernet. A managed multi-port repeater has network management capabilities.

multi-processing. 1. The simultaneous execution of two or more computer programs by a computer, or multiprocessor.
2. One of the modes of operation in which parallel processing is performed simultaneously by two or more processors of a multi-processor.

multiprocessor. A computer system that uses more than one CPU running in parallel for faster performance.

multi-programming system. The computers capable of providing a technique for handling the concurrent execution of a number of routines of programs. The system accomplishes this by overlapping or interleaving their execution, so that one program is executed during the input/output waiting time of another program.

multi-star topology. In local area network, a star topology is one in which each device is connected to a central device (computer) through which all data must pass. In a multi-star arrangement, several host computers are linked together, each having its own star topology network.

multi-sync monitor. A colour display monitor designed to adjust to several frequencies so that it can receive input from various adapters.

MultiSync. In a monitor, the ability to run at different scan rates, allowing the monitor to display different resolutions.

multi-tasking. The concurrent execution of two or more tasks, or the concurrent use of a single program that can carry out many functions. There are different types of multitasking. Co-operative multi-tasking requires a program to be written to allow other programs to access the system. In pre-emptive multitasking, the system can suspend any program to allow other programs access. Preemptive multitasking provides better performance, as programs can switch with fewer overheads. Macintosh and Windows 3.1 use co-operative multitasking. Windows 95 and Unix use pre-emptive multitasking.

multi-threading. The ability to have more than one task occurring in an application. For example, you could have calculate a large spreadsheet values while continuing to use that spreadsheet or print a complicated document while continuing to work on that document. OS/2 has multithreading capabilities. Applications must be written according to certain specifications in order to multithread.

mush area. A region where signals from two or more synchronised transmitters are comparable in strength, producing fading and distortion of received signals.

MUSHes. Theme-based MUD programs.

MULTI-L. A website for the discussion of multilingual education: listserv@barilvm.bitnet.

muting circuit. 1. An interference preventing device that automatically shuts off a radio receiver during the operation of a transmitter, and vice-versa.

2. An electronic element that cuts off all audio when no signal is present or when the receiver is being tuned between carriers.

muting. 1. Disabling a receiver or amplifier under no-signal or weak signal conditions.

2. Softening or muffling a sound.

MUTT. Multi-User Trivial Terminal, a MUD program that runs on MS Windows using WinSock; its features include scripting, multiple connections, triggers, macros, and logging. This program may be found at: ftp://ftp.graphcomp.com/pub/msw/mutt.

mutual exclusion. A principle requiring that, at given time, only one asynchronous procedure may access the same shared variable, or execute members of a group of critical sections.

MUX. Multiplexer, device connecting more than one channel or circuit over the same line, a way of sharing resources; sometimes MPX.

MV. Mean Value.

MVDS. Modular Video Data System.

MVS. Multiple Virtual Storage

MXE. Mobile Electronic Exchange.

MXU. Mobile Exhibition Unit.

Mycalex. An insulating material consisting of mica bonded with glass; its dielectric constant is ~6-8, and the resistivity is 10^{13} ohm-cm.

Mylar. A tough, plastic insulating material commonly used as a base for magnetic coatings for making magnetic tapes; its dielectric constant is ~2.8-3.7, and dielectric strength is 7000V/mil.

N

***n,k* code.** A coding arrangement where in a block of *n* bits, *n-k* of the bits are used for parity checking..

N. Symbol for negative of sign flag; usually the most significant bit, this denotes the sign of a word in two's complement notation.

n. Nano, a decimal prefix commonly used in association with a unit of SI system of units, indicating a multiplication factor of 10^{-9} of that unit.

N.nnn. The CCITT N. Series Recommendations deal with standards for International Sound Program Transmission.

NA. 1. Not Applicable.
2. Numerical Analysis.

NAC. Network Access Controller.

***n*-address instruction.** A computer program instruction, which has *n* address parts, where *n* is whole number.

***n*-adic Boolean operation.** A Boolean operation in which there are exactly *n* operands, where *n* is whole number.

NAD. Node ADministration.

NAF. Network Access facility.

NAG. *See* numerical algorithms group.

NAK. Negative AcKnowledgement, a response to a PDU indicating that a problem was encountered such as receipt of corrupted packet of information; used in the transport layer.

NAL. Network Access Layer; the layer of TCP/IP stack that provides an interface with the physical network.

NAM. *See* network access machine.

name key. In computers, a key that, when depressed while the system is in an applicable mode, will cause the system to display names that have been assigned to groups of data.

name resolution. The mapping of the domain names to its corresponding IP address.

name service. A service, which associates human friendly alphanumeric names with network, addresses.

name space. A commonly distributed set of names in which all names are unique.

named pipe. A connection used to transfer data between separate processes, usually on separate computers. Named pipes are the foundation of inter-process communications and underpin Microsoft's LAN manager numbers.

named range. In data processing and computers, specified group of storage locations which has been given a name, so that the data in these locations can be called in a function, moved elsewhere, or printed as a single unit by using assigned name.

NAN. 1. Network Application Node. 2. National Area Network, a generic term describing a wide area network specifically restricted to within a political boundary, and used by one or more enterprises.

nano-code. A level of programming deeper than the micro-code; each individual level of the micro-code is executed by a separate nano-code program.

nano-computer. The future fourth-generation computer whose main processing chip may contain at least 100,000,000 electronic components.

NAP. Network Access Protocol.

narrow band frequency modulation. NBFM. A frequency modulation form in which the frequency change is kept at such a level that the signal occupies the same bandwidth as an amplitude modulated signal carrying the same information.

narrow band modem. A modem whose output signal has a frequency spectrum which is limited to that, which can be wholly contained within, and transmitted through a voice channel with a nominal 4-kHz bandwidth.

narrow band private. Referring to communications lines, that are leased for low-speed devices. Narrow band private lines provide a private line service for transmission from one teletype device to another, transmitting upto 300 bits per seconds.

narrow band. 1. In data transmission, describing circuits able to carry digital transmission systems up to 2400 bits per second.

2. A frequency band in which the difference between upper and lower limits is only a few Hz or kHz, with respect to bandwidths usually encountered in the service specified.

3. Any standard bandwidth whose limits have been reduced from a prior standard. In amateur radio FM practice, for example, narrow band means 5 kHz at vhf and uhf, whereas wide band implies a 15 kHz bandwidth.

narrow casting. CATV term distinguishing cable from broadcasting, it describes the function of distributing a range of TV channels or programs designed for minority interests rather than mass appeal.

narrow-beam antenna. An antenna having high directive gain, that is, its radiative energy is confined to small solid angle and thus has a narrow main lobe.

***n*-ary code.** A code in which each code element may be any of *n* distinct kinds or values, where *n* is an integer.

***n*-ary digital signal.** A digital signal in which a signal element may assume *n* discrete states, where *n* may be any integer.

NAS. Network Application Support; a comprehensive set of software that enables application integration across a distribution, multi-vendor environment. It consists of well defined programming interfaces, toolkits, and products that help developers build applications that are well-integrated and easily portable across different systems.

NASORD. A colloquial expression for Not in Sequential ORDer. A reference made in computer programming to a file not in sequential order.

natural language software. An artificial intelligence application designed to enable users with little or no programming skills to write English-like computer commands which will be easily recognised and converted by the computer as legitimate enquiries.

natural language. A language in which the rules reflect current usage without being specifically prescribed. The language employed by the users in normal communication as compared with the restricted language used for communication with computers, indexing documents etc.

navigation. The process of moving through a software program.

NBFM. *See* narrow-band frequency modulation.

***n*-bit byte.** A byte which is composed of *n* binary digits, where *n* is a positive integer, generally not greater than 16.

NBNS. NetBIOS Name Server, a server that provides a NetBIOS name to IP address mapping.

NBS. National Bureau of Standards, U.S., obsolete, now known as NIST.

NC. 1. Network Control.

2. Network Connection, an association established at Network Layer for transfer of data between two or more network users, transport entities.

NCB. Network Control Block.

NCC. Network Control Centre, location of systems providing manager services in a managed network.

NCFTP. A line-mode program for anonymous FTP that doens not require the user to be able to spell anonymous. It automatically enters the e-mail address as the password.

NCH. Network Connection Handler.

***n*-channel MOSFET.** A metal-oxide silicon field-effect transistor in which all conduction is through *n*-type silicon.

NCL. Network Control Language.

NCM. 1. Network Control Module.

2. Network Connection Management.

NCMS. Network Control and Management Systems.

NCN. Network Control Node.

NCOP. Network Code of Practice, a voluntary code of practice for the design of networks covering transmission quality, safety and technical standards.

NCP. 1. Network Control Program, used as a generic term.

2. *See* Network Control Protocol.

NCSL. National Computer System Laboratory, formerly ICST, a part of NIST.

ND. Network Digit, the fourth digit in an X.121 address.

NDBS. Network Database Management System.

NDIS. Network Driver Interface Specification, a *de facto* standard interface specification developed by Microsoft to separate communications protocols from PC networking hardware. The driver can also run multiple stacks concurrently.

NDL. Network Database language, a language used for network databases.

NDN. NonDelivery Notification, in X.400, a service message saying that a message could not be delivered to the requested recipient UA.

NDR. *See* non-destructive read.

NDRO. *See* non-destructive read out.

NE. Network Element, an object in a managed OSI network.

near-end crosstalk. Crosstalk which is propagated in a disturbed channel in the direction opposite to the direction of propagation of the electric current in the disturbing channel. Terminals of disturbed channel, at which the crosstalk is present, and the energised terminal of disturbing channel, are generally quite near each other.

near-field region. The region of the field of an antenna between the close-in reactive field region and the far-field region wherein the angular field distribution is dependent upon distance from antenna.

near-letter quality. Dot matrix printers produce characters by forming dots closely together. In general, closer are dots, better is the reproduction. Earlier dot matrix printers had to run slowly for good letter quality, but now high-speed printers are being produced. These are termed as near letter quality machines.

necessary bandwidth. In electromagnetic wave transmission, the bandwidth which is just sufficient to ensure that the transmission of information is at the speed and of the quality required.

NEF. Network Element Function block, the function block that communicates monitor and control information between an NE and the network.

negative acknowledge. NAK. 1. The opposite to acknowledge. In the method of error control that relies on repeating any message with errors, the return signal that reports the error in negative acknowledges.

2. A signal sent from receiver to transmitter indicating that message with detectable errors has been received.

negative disclosure. A type of personal disclosure by which it is possible to deduce that an individual does not have a particular attribute.

negative entry. The entry of a number along with an associated negative indicator.

negative feedback. A signal that is returned to an earlier stage of an amplifier opposing the input signal at that point. Negative feedback. reduces gain in the return or feedback loop, improves linearity and provides more level frequency response. The feedback circuits is built from passive components which are independent of active devices in the feedback loop. It is also known as 'degenerative feedback.

negative logic. 1. Logic system in which the normal meanings of the binary signal levels are interchanged, *e.g.* high voltage equals logic 0, low voltage equals logic 1.

2. A logic system in which all the Boolean variables and Boolean functions behave as though they were complements.

neighbour contification. In a token-ring network, the process by which each data station identifies the next active station so that all stations that are affected by a hard failure can be informed that a failure has occurred.

***N*-entity.** In the OSI-RM model, an active element in the *n*-th layer which interacts directly with elements of the layer immediately above and below it. It is defined by a unique set of rules and information formats, it performs a defined set of functions.

neper. Np. A dimensionless unit used in telecommunications to express gain, loss, and other relative ratios. It is the natural logarithm of the square root of the power ratio; similar to bel, except that the natural logarithm, *ln* is used.

nest. To embed a subroutine in a larger routine or to embed a loop instruction inside another loop instruction.

nested phrase-indexing system. An automated system of indexing subjects listing all the words in the title of a document. It is arranged so that every word appears in turn.

nested transaction. A sequence of operations within a transaction that can be aborted without aborting the entire transaction; useful for the application programmer because it allows the program to have two ways of performing a transaction.

nested. A statement contained within a branch of another statement.

nesting. A feature of language design in which constructs can be embedded within the instances of themselves, *e.g.*, nested loops.

net call sign. In a radio net, a call sign, which uniquely identifies each station in the net.

net use. A net command used to establish or drop a mapped drive letter connection to a specific share point.

net view. A net command, which allows viewing the share point names on a server. It does not require a user ID or password.

net. An organisation of stations capable of conducting communication operations in accordance with a protocol and usually on the same channel.

NetBEUI. NetBios Extended User Interface, a network device driver or transport protocol that is the transport driver supplied with LAN Manager, It can bind with as many as eight media access control drivers.

NetBios Extended User Interface. *See* NetBEUI.

NetBIOS name. A 16-character name that allows the user-assigned name for a computer to be up to 15 character in length; the 16th character is used by the underlying application and in general is not directly configurable by the user.

NetBIOS. Network Basic Input/output Operating System, a collection of network services and an interface to those services used on some networks. It refers to session layer that resides in the application layer of the TCP/IP model application-programming interface developed by IBM. It has its own method of addressing for computers on a network. It uses NetBIOS names instead of IP addresses to identify and locate other computers. UNIX computers and other operating systems can be integrated in to a NetBIOS environment, but it requires extra efforts.

It was developed by IBM to provide vendor-neutral program interface for LAN based proprietary protocols. To resolve NetBIOS computer names to IP addresses, network needs entire name resolution system, which is different from DNS. This NetBIOS based name resolution is provided in a layer logically located between the transport layer and NetBIOS interface, called NetBIOS over TCP/IP or NBT.

NETBLT. Network Block Transfer, a transport level, flow controlled, bulk data transfer protocol used with TCP/IP internets. NETBLT controls the rate at which data is sent to allow a steady, high-speed flow,

net-control station. A station which maintains control of an operational network with two or more facilities.

Netlogon service. LAN Manager Service that implements logon security. This service verifies the usernarne and password supplied by each user logging on to the local area network. *See also* LAN Manager.

net-loss variation. The maximum change in net loss, which occurs in a specified portion of a communication system during a specified period.

NETNORTH. A research computer network in Canada, run as a consortium.

Netscape. The short name of Netscape Navigator, the commercial web browser developed in 1995, for Macintosh, Windows, and X-windowing system. Netscape is currently free to educational institutions. It can be obtained from the main Netscape archive at:

ftp.netscape.com.

To install Netscape in Windows 95 or Windows NT, 32-bit Navigator should be used.

netscapisms. Extensions made to HTML that extend beyond the HTML standard. These extensions give the Web browser, Netscape, a competitive advantage

NetStat. A utility displaying statistics related to IP, TCP, UDP, and ICMP protocols. It displays numerical counts for items such as datagrams sent, datagrams received, and a variety of errors that could have occurred.

NetView. IBM's network management system; a text message-based system that monitors, manages and controls SNA networks. It is an implementation of IBM's Open Network Management Architecture. The term NetView is normally associated with the focal point of the architecture.

NetView/PC. An implementation of IBM's NetView running on an OS/2 PC-based platform that allows non-IBM networks and equipment to be managed via an SNA network management station. NetView/PC is a service point in IBM's Open Network Management Architecture.

NetWare. LAN Network Operating System and related products developed by Novell. There are three main product lines:

NetWare 2.X designed to run on a Intel 80286 platform and above;

NetWare 3.X (latest version NetWare 3.11), designed to run on an Intel 80386 platform; and

NetWare 4.0. NetWare is currently installed on more than 70% of LANs worldwide.

Network Access Layer. *See* NAL.

network access machine. NAM. A computer programmed to generate the specific procedures necessary to gain access to a network that connects a number of computers, and to enable the user to interact with the network.

network adapter card driver. A network device driver, which controls the physical functions of a network adapter card.

network adapter card. A printed circuit board, installed in a computer, enabling the computer to join the LAN.

network address. A group of characters that uniquely identify the location of a node on a network.

network architecture. The communication equipment, protocols and transmission links that constitute a network, and the methods by which they are arranged; also include specification for access method, data frame, and network cabling.

Network Block Transfer. *See* NETBLT.

network cluster. A final circuit group along with all the high usage circuit groups which have at least one terminus in common with it, and for which the final circuit group is in the last-choice route.

Network Code of Practice. *See* NCOP.

network computing. A term analogous to client/server computing.

network configuration. A schematic presentation of elements of a network. In particular, it is the arrangement of the nodes and branches of a network.

network connectivity. The topological description of a network which specifies the interconnection of the nodes of the network in terms of circuit parameters, such as location, termination, and quantity.

network control centre. NCC. A location in computer network that controls and in part monitors operations.

network control channel. A channel between nodes which carries information concerning status of network.

network control program. NCP. The specific computer program which allows process-to-process communication over a computer network.

Network Control Protocol. NCP. One of various protocols designed to interface PPP with specific protocol suites. Network control protocol establish and configure different network protocol settings for TCP/IP,

IPX, NetBEUI, and AppleTalk. Some of the network control protocols used with a PPP connections are:
Internet Protocol Control Protocol (IPC),
Internet Packet Exchange Control Protocol (IPXCP),
IPX WAN Protocol,
NetBEUI Control Protocol (NBTP), and
AppleTalk Control Protocol (ATCP.

network controller. A physical device usually controlled by a programmed computer, which directs the operation of data links of a communication network.

network database. An organisation of data relationships such that any record, except the root, may have more than one parent record, and there may be several access to a given record.

network delay. The transit time for a packet, in a packet-switch network; it is defined as the interval between the time that the last bit of the packet leaves the source node and the time at which the first bit enters the destination node.

network device driver. A program that enables the operating system software to communicate the network adapter cards. Also a software module running on a host or workstation that is responsible for the communications between the computer and the network or a device attached to the network.

network device. A computer, peripheral or other related communications equipment attached to a network.

Network Driver Interface Specification. *See* NDIS.

network element. A piece of network equipment that can be managed through an element manager as part of a network management system.

Network File Systems. *See* NFS.

network ID. A portion of the IP address, which refers to a given physical network. All computers on a network should contain an IP address with the same network ID.

network integration. Close co-operation between telephone and and Internet providers, not just interconnection, but technical as well as economic integration.

network interface card/controller. Circuitry connecting a node to a network, usually in the form of a card in a PC expansion slot. In conjunction with the nos and PC operating system it helps transmit and receive messages on the network.

network interface. Point of interconnection between one network and another network or portion thereof, *i.e.*, interconnection between a network communications facilities and terminal equipment, protective apparatus or wiring at subscriber's premises.

network layer level. The layer in the OSI stack responsible for the necessary routing and relaying through one or more networks in multiple link or wide area environments.

network layer. The third layer of the OSI (Open Systems Interconnection) model. The network layer maps out packet routing between networks or from node to node within a network, defining all possible routes that a message packet could travel to reach its destination. In so doing, this layer must account for all the transmission technologies and network types it might encounter en route. It must also segment and reassemble data units to expedite delivery and some limited error checking.

network management console. A workstation running network management software that is used to centrally monitor, maintain, and configure a large distributed network.

network management integration. The highest level of network management system that brings together information from a number of Element Management Systems.

network management protocol. Protocol used to transfer network management NetView, and HP OpenView.

network management. The systematic procedures necessary to plan, organise, and control an evolving communication network with optimum costs and performance. Under the OSI model network management takes account of five key areas: configuration management, fault management, performance management, accounting management, and security management. A major challenge and often a headache to users because there are no complete answers today, only a patchwork of systems covering different parts of the subject. Vendors either concentrate on the physical (hardware) elements or logical (control and management of inter-process communications) sides. ITU-TS is slowly considering standards for public networks.

network manager. A person who is responsible for ensuring that the network remains operational; special network monitoring software utilises network management protocols to monitor and notify the network manager automatically when unusual events occur.

network measurement centre. A location on an advanced research projects agency network packet-switched computer network used to measure performance, normally by means of relatively long-term test.

network monitor. A utility included with Windows NT server; it is representative of a class of utilities known as sniffer. They capture datagrams from the network into a buffer or file. Network monitor may be used to check the physical address of the datagram's source and destination, and to find out how many bytes of data the Ethernet frame is carrying.

network operating system. A generic term employed to describe distributed software for the control of the operation of a computer network.

network protocol. A set of standards used for network communications.

network redundancy. The property of networks that have more links than are necessary to connect the nodes, thus enabling network to continue to function if certain links fail.

network slowdown. A mode of reduced operations in communication network when congestion occurs; for example, when the buffer availability drops below a threshold or traffic capacity is insufficient to handle the demands.

network sniffer. A diagnostic application, capable of capturing and displaying the contents of the datagrams. *See also* net work Monitor.

network software. A computer program that controls the hardware functions of a network.

network terminating unit. The part of telecommunications network equipment that connects directly to data terminal equipment. It operates between local transmission lines and a telephone subscriber's interface.

network time protocol. NTP. A protocol defined in STD 12, RFC 1119, that assures accurate local time keeping with reference to radio and atomic clocks located on the Internet. This protocol is capable of synchronising distributed clocks within milliseconds over long duration.

network timing. The timing signals transferred from data circuit terminating equipment to data terminal equipment to control the transmission of digits across the transmitted and received data circuits.

network topology. The physical and logical relationship between nodes in a network, *i.e.*, geometrical arrangement of nodes and links in a communication network, such as a ring, bus, star, tree, or hybrid.

network user address. NUA. A set of packet assembler-disassembler parameters that identifies the computer with which a local area network (LAN) wide area network (WAN) user wishes to communicate.

network user identity. NUI. A set of packet assembler/disassembler parameters that provide a local area network (LAN) or wide area network (WAN) user with a recognisable identity.

network version. A version of application software written especially for concurrent access, enabling several users to access and modify information in one session. Software written for single-user applications may not be licensed for use on a local area network, and may not run efficiently.

network. 1. A system of consisting of terminals, nodes and interconnected facilities, including lines or trunks, satellites, microwave, medium, and longwave radio, etc.

2. A group of computers connected by cables or other means and using software, enabling them to exchange information and share equipment (such as printers and disk drives).

3. A series of interconnected points.

network-access line. A line which connects the communication facility of an organisation to a communication network.

neuro-computer. Referring to computer which is much more powerful than a supercomputer and in which the term 'neuro' implies that the computer behaves and calculates at the speed of nerve tissues of the human brain.

neutral transmission. A form of signalling employing two distinct states, one of which is the absence of signal.

new line character. A functional character that controls or demands action of a printer or display, by causing the printing or display position to be moved to the next printing or display line. It combines the functions of a carriage return and a line feed.

news database. In an online information retrieval, a full-text database comprising daily and weekly newspaper editions.

NeXT. Defunct computer designed by Steve Jobs, one of the originators of the Macintosh. The company that made NeXT computers. The NeXT was a workstation running NeXTStep, a version of UNIX. NeXTStep uses a GUI, and runs Display PostScript. NeXTStep is still available for machines running on the 486, SPARC, and HP Alpha processors.

NEXT. Near-End CROSSTalk, an unwanted energy transfer from a disturbing circuit to a disturbed circuit, where the energy travels in a directions different from that of the signal in the disturbing circuit.

NF. Not Finished Session PDU, essentially a refusal to terminate a Session connection.

NFAM. Network File Access Method.

NFAP. Network File Access Protocol.

NFS. Network File Systems, a networking protocol suite developed by Sun Microsystems; used widely in the Unix world. It uses RPC calls between the offering systems of two computers to transparently allow the user of an NES client computer to access files located on a remote NFS server computer. This system has been designed to be independent of the operating systems, the transport protocols, and physical network architecture, and allows the VFS client to inter-operate with any NFS server. Before remote files and directories can be used on the NFS file system, they must undergo a process known as mounting. After that the remote files and directories appear and operate as if they were located on the local file system.

NFT. Network File Transfer.

NGP. Network Graphics Protocol.

NI. Network Interface, generic, how a device interacts with a network.

nibble. In data structures, a term used to describe a 4-binary digit word in contrast to a byte, which is generally considered to be an 8-binary digit word.

NIC. 1. Network Information Centre, directory information services for DDN and the Internet.
2. Network Interface Control.

nickel-cadmium cell. A secondary cell having potassium hydroxide as electrolyte, positive plate of nickel-oxide/nickel-hydrate mixture, and a negative plate or cadmium. It can provide a high rate of discharge along with a steadily maintained voltage, properties brought about by the use of cadmium. It gives the cell a lower charging voltage than a nickel-iron cell and reduces internal resistance.

nickel-iron cell. A secondary cell capable of delivering heavy currents using potassium hydroxide as its electrolyte. The cell has a positive plate made from a nickel-oxide/nickel-hydrate mixture and the negative plate is of iron oxide. The cell is lighter, more durable and can operate at lower temperatures (-30°C) than a lead-acid cell, but is more expensive.

night effect. The phenomenon by which, at frequencies below 0.5 MHz, direction-finding signals received between sunset and the following sunrise seem to come from a transmitter that moves slowly back and forth in a line perpendicular to the line between transmitter and receiver. It happens due to variations in the state of polarization of electromagnetic waves which are reflected by the ionosphere.

NIM. Network Interface Machine, same as a PAD.

NISO. National Information Standards Organisation, US, a standards promotion organisation, one part of which is Z39.

NJE. Network Job Entry.

NJI. Network Job Interface.

***N*-key rollover.** A keyboard action which produces coded signals in the correct sequence when *N* keys are depressed virtually simultaneously.

NL. Network Layer, layer-3 of the OSI Reference Model; it provides end-to-end connections for the transport entities.

NLM. Netware Loadable Module, an installation module used as part of NetWare setup.

nm. Abbreviation for nanometre (nm); one thousandth of a millionth of a metre, that is 10^{-9} m. It is a convenient unit for designating the wavelength of light; also equal to 10 angstroms and is synonymous with millimicron.

NM. ISO Network Management is a series of standards. ISO 9595 and 9696 define a common management information protocol (CMIP) and service (CMIS), which is a very basic means of using remote operation service elements (ROSE) operations to carry information about management activities. With CMIP one can basically do gets, sets, creates, and deletes on managed objects and their attributes and can send event reports. On any given association, one network entity is serving as a manager and the other as a managed object or its agent. In general, the entity doing the managing involves activities and the agent responds; the agent, on the other hand, initiates most reports. CMIP and CMIS are then used in turn to actually provide management functionality in a variety of functional areas. ISO has partitioned Network Management into five specific management functional areas (SMFAs) for convenience in developing specific requirements: configuration management (CM), fault management, performance management, security management (SM), and accounting management. These make use of system management functions which provide a generic platform of common Network Management capabilities available to any management application. ISO 10164 is a multi-part standard defining system management functions. There are seven stable SMF international standards, including Object Management, State Management, Attributes for Representing Relationship, Alarm Reporting, Event Report Management, Log Control, and Security Alarm Reporting. These system management functions provide most of the functionally required for the current work on CM and FM. Additional requirements identified by other SMFAs may develop into additional system management functions. Work is currently being done on security audit trail, accounting metering, workload monitoring, confidence and diagnostic testing.

NM. Network Management, OSI management standards.

NMF. New Master File.

NMFORUM. OSI Network Management Forum.

NMOS RAM. N-channel Metal-Oxide Semiconductor Random-Access Memory; a kind of RAM that uses NMOS technology of high speed and low power; competes with bipolar units for many high-speed cache applications. It is housed in a standard 16-pin package and requiring a single 5V supply, a typical NMOS RAM has an access time of less than 100 nanoseconds, a maximum power dissipation of less than 600mW and fully static operation.

NMOS. N-channel Metal-Oxide Semiconductor; metal-oxide semiconductor device made on a *p*-type substrate whose active carriers, electrons, migrate between *n*-type source and drain contacts. NMOS are the newer variety of large scale integration chips. They are transistor-transistor logic compatible and use one power supply and have gats about half the size of *p*-channel metal-oxide semiconductor device gates.

NMP. Network Management Protocol, protocol for carrying information about monitoring and control of objects on a network.

NMSIG. Network Management Special Interest Group, the technical group within the OIW working on agreements for OSI Network Management.

NN. Negative Notification, a type of EDI notification that says that an EDI message was not received.

NNTP. Network News Transfer Protocol, common way of transferring news feeds over TCP/IP networks.

NNX. A general way of referring to three digits representing the central office code in a telephone number.

NOC. Network Operations Centre, responsible for providing monitoring and control, user assistance, etc., for a network; generic term, also specifically used to refer to the Internet NOC.

NOCP. Network Operator Control Program.

nodal operation. Refers to remote location and control of line groups.

node. A point of interconnection to a network having significance of data routing; also, an entity on two or more access paths. A point of contact, each TCP/IP address becomes an end point for communication. Most computers have one node, but others such as servers and routers may have more than one IP addresses, and therefore many nodes. Node is often used instead of workstation.

noise bar. A momentary distortion of the picture in video recording, during playback of a helical scan device. It generally occurs during still framing.

noise equivalent power. NEP. A measurement of the minimum detectable signal that can be found amongst noise in detection and multiplication processes. It can be defined as the amount of light falling on a photodetector, required to produce an output signal equal to the noise output. It is usually expressed in nanowatts. In opto-electronics, it is the radiant power, at a given modulation frequency and for a given bandwidth, that produces a signal-to-noise ratio of 1 at the output of a given detector. In this sense, it is the minimum detectable power at the given frequency and for the given bandwidth.

noise factor. The amount of noise added by the signal-handling equipment to the noise existing as its input, usually expressed in dB, thus being equal to the signal-to-noise ratio at input divided by the signal-to-noise ratio at output. It is a measure of the deterioration of the signal-to-noise power density ratio that occurs during the process of amplification.

noise immunity. A measure of the magnitude of external disturbances, which a digital circuit can tolerate without producing errors.

noise jammer. A jammer that emits a signal in which the power is randomly distributed over a wide range of frequencies.

noise level. 1. The amplitude of ambient electrical noise generated outside an electronic system of interest.

2. Amplitude of electrical noise generated in an electronic system.

3. Intensity of ambient acoustic noise.

noise margin. The maximum noise voltage that can be added or subtracted from the logic signal before a threshold voltage for a logic state is passed.

noise strobe. Scanning of the frequency spectrum for the noise levels.

noise suppression. A receiver circuit arrangement which automatically reduces the noise output of a device, such as an amplifier, antenna, transmission line, or channel, during periods when a carrier is not being received or transmitted.

noise window. A trough in the noise frequency spectrum characteristic of a device, such as an amplifier, channel, receiver, or transmitter, from external sources or internal sources. It is usually represented as a band of low amplitude noise in a wider band of higher amplitude noise.

noise, ambient. Acoustic noise, that is a part of the environment in which a system transducer is located.

noise, background. System noise in the absence of a signal.

noise, broadband. Noise with a spectral intensity, significant over a band where the upper frequency is many times higher than the lower.

noise, carrrier. Noise resulting from variations in carrier level.

noise, cosmic. The random noise picked up at microwave frequencies, particularly between 20-100 MHz, when the antenne are directed towards the Milky Way.

noise, granular. A quantising noise resulting from the transition from a signal continuously varying in amplitude into the one, which has discrete sampling steps.

noise, intermodulation. Sum-and-difference frequencies produced by every non-linear device through which a multichannel carrier signal passes.

noise, intrinsic. Noise normally present in a device or circuit which is not caused by modulation and is not affected by input signal. Idle noise or background noise.

noise, modulation. Noise in a modulation system which is associated with the signal and varies in strength with the strength of the signal.

noise. 1. Any signal that occurs in an electronic or communication system and is considered extraneous to the desired signal being propagated. Noise can be introduced, for example, by external disturbances and may be deleterious in a given system since it can produce spurious signals, such as errors.

2. A (usually interfering) random-frequency current or voltage signal extending over a considerable frequency spectrum and having no useful purpose, unless it is intentionally generated for test purposes.

3. Dissonant, interfering, disagreeable sound, unlike harmonious sound.

4. Extra bits or bytes that must be removed from digital data before it can be useful.

noise figure. A measure of the noise in dB, generated at the input of an amplifier as compared with the noise generated by an impedance-method resistor at a specified temperature.

noiseless coding. The use of a code to improve the efficiency of a communication system in which noise is almost negligible.

noise-power density. The noise power in a bandwidth of 1 Hz, that is, the noise power per hertz. The noise power density of the internal noise that is contributed by a receiving system to an incoming signal is expressed as the product of Boltzmann's constant *k*, and the equivalence noise temperature, T_n.

noisy mode. A method of operation, which is sometimes, used when normalising a floating-point number. If the mantissa is shifted *m* bits to the left during normalisation, then in noisy mode the digits generated to fill the *m* rightmost bits in the normalised mantissa are not necessarily zeros.

nominal bandwidth. 1. For a filter, the difference, fc_1 - fc_2, where fc_1 is nominal lower cut-off frequency and fc_2, nominal upper cut-off frequency.

2. For an allocated communication channel, total bandwidth including upper and lower guard frequencies.

3. The intended and named bandwidth of given wavelength or channel, regardless of the bandwidth of a given wavelength or channel, regardless of the bandwidth of the signal on that frequency at any given time.

nominal bit stuffing rate. Rate at which stuffing bits are inserted (or deleted) when both the input and output bit rates are at their nominal values.

nominal black. In display systems, a characteristic or value, such as signal level or frequency, this corresponds to the darkest black that can be transmitted by a transmitter.

nominal justification rate. In pulse code modulation multiplexing, the rate at which justifying digits are inserted (or deleted) when both the tributary and the multiplex digit rates are at their nominal values.

nominal white. In display systems, a characteristic or value, such as signal level or frequency, this corresponds to the brightest white that can be transmitted by a transmitter.

nominal-Q. The rated (nameplate) value of Q of a capacitor, inductor, transformer winding, or tank circuit.

non-add function. On a printing calculator, and function that allows the printing of characters without affecting the calculations.

non-blocking. Pertaining to a communication system in which 100% of all access attempts are completed.

non-centralised operation. A control displine for multi-point data communication links in which transmission may be between tributary stations or between the control station and a tributary station.

non-conjunction. The dyadic Boolean operation whose result has the Boolean value 0, if and only if each operand has the Boolean value 1.

non-destructive cursor. A cursor, which does not erase the symbols or characters at its current display position nor at any of the display positions through which it passes.

non-destructive read out. NDRO. The sensing of information contained in the internal storage of a computer and the transmission of that information to an external storage unit which inherently does not destroy or erase the record of data that has been read. Reading is usually achieved on tapes, drums, disks and other similar devices, as hard copy on paper or as a display on a cathode-ray tube.

non-destructive read. NDR. A process of reading information in a memory location without erasing or altering that information in any way.

non-equivalence operation. The dyadic Boolean operation whose result has the Boolean value 1 if and only if the operands have different Boolean values.

non-escaping key. A key, which permits a character to be typed or printed without a subsequent change in the print position.

non-interactive. Pertaining to an application or mode of operation of a system in which there is no interaction between the system and an operator, except perhaps to initiate the application or operation.

non-linear device. A device in which the change in the input signal does not necessarily produce a proportional change in the output signal.

non-linear distortion. Distortion caused by non-linear response of an amplifier or component. Non-linearity causes different parts of the signal to be amplified or transmitted by different amounts; therefore, the amplitude variations in the output signal differ from those in the input signal.

non-loaded line. A communication line, which does not have loading coils connected to it.

non-maskable interrupt. A signal sent from an input/output device or chip to a microprocessor unit to request a service (an interrupt) at the highest priority that is not affected by an interrupt mask. It is typically used in case of a power failure.

non-memory reference instruction. An instruction which can be carried out without having to obtain an operand form, or return a result to, memory.

non-operational load. The power which is required for the administration, support, housing of the communication system. Also known as unity load.

non-pollable terminal. A hardware device that cannot buffer or store messages cannot recognise an identification code in a poll or select message. Such a device is also known as a 'dump terminal' Terminal of this type are usually restricted to point-to-point operation.

non-printing character. A control or function character transmitted as part of a message but not reproduced in the printed copy.

non-procedural language. A computer language in which the user specifies the nature of the desired end result rather than the processes required to attain it.

non-return-to-zero (change) modulation. The modulation of a signal parameter which is used in a bit stream in which one of the binary digits is represented by a transition to a specified signal condition from a given condition, such as magnetisation, electric field intensity, magnetic field intensity, or electric current or voltage amplitude; and the other binary digit is represented by a transition from the specified condition back to the given condition. The conditions may be a finite value of a signal parameter and a zero value, two finite values, two polarities, or opposite directions.

non-return-to-zero (mark). A method of writing information on a magnetic surface in which a change in the condition of magnetisation represents 1 and no change represents 0.

non-return-to-zero binary code. A code in which there are two and only two states of a signal parameter, which is used to represent data, a state that is termed as 0 and a state that is termed 1, and no other state is possible, such as a neutral or rest condition. Also known as NRZ binary code.

non-return-to-zero inverted. A method of writing information on a magnetic surface in which the state of magnetisation representing either 0 or 1 changes only when a 1 is transmitted.

non-return-to-zero. NRZ. 1. A signal presented in the digital form having pulses which are full-symbol-length so that there is no alteration of signal level when a symbol is repeated, *i.e.*, there is not return to zero level. 2. A method of writing information on a magnetic surface where the current passing through the write head winding does not return to zero after the write head winding does not return to zero after the write pulse. The reference condition is represented by the change in state of magnetisation between the 1 and 0 condition.

non-standard sector. A floppy disk which has been formatted in a non-standard manner for the purpose of software protection, and hence cannot be copied using operating system utilities.

non-terminal node. Any node which is not a terminal node and hence has one or more branching.

non-transparent mode. A mode of operating a data transmission system in which control characters are treated and interpreted as such, rather than simply as data or text bits in a bit stream.

non-volatile memory. NVM. A permanent memory storage medium, which is able to retain information in the absence of power and allows data to be available when power is restored. Memory chips (such as read-only memory) which retain their information even after the electrical power has been switched off. This contrasts with volatile chips (such as random-access memory) which lose their information when the power is switched off.

non-volatile random-access memory. A particular combination of random-access memory and read only memory which produces a device with RAM attributes that is unaffected by the loss of power, in that is does lost is contents. It is therefore termed non-volatile.

non-volatile storage. A storage device whose contents are not lost when power is cut off.

no-op. *See* no-operation.

no-operation. An instruction that is used to force a delay of one instruction cycle without altering in any way the status flags or the contents of a memory location. It causes no action to take place in the computer except for consumption of time and instruction storage space. There are several uses for this instruction including time adjustment of a program, filling out program space in a system where instruction boundaries do not always coincide with word boundaries, and replacement of unwanted instructions without having to recompute all other program addresses. Also known as no-op.

Norton SI. Norton System Information, designed by Peter Porton to benchmark a computer's throughput. This is included in the Norton Utilities program to rate the speed of internal processing and the speed of a hard disk drive. The original IBM XT computer is used as a base reference point, with rating referring to the comparative speed. A Norton SI rating of 40 means the tested computer performs 40 times faster than the IBM XT, which has a rating of 1.0.

NOS. Network Operating System, the software that connects all the devices on a network so that resources can be shared efficiently and files can be transferred. It handles administration of all network functions, Network operating systems are usually in two parts; server and client/requester. The requester puts the workstation on the server machine and makes disks, software, ports and other facilities available to a node on request. Each device's services requested by a PC are accessed via the requester software.

NOTA. Novell Open Technology Association, a group of companies that have adopted a suggested software platform suggested by Novell that will lead to the development of a new range of CTI applications.

notch filter. A filter capable of passing all frequencies except for a single extremely narrow band. The frequency-response curve is constant over all frequencies, except at a narrow band, where the response curve dips to zero and recovers, giving the appearance of a deep trough or valley.

notch. In a frequency spectrum, consisting mainly of white noise though not necessarily of uniform amplitude, a narrow band of the spectrum in which amplitudes of the waves are low or zero, that is, they may not be present.

notched noise. The noise which is distributed over a wide range of frequency spectrum and in which one or more narrow bands of frequencies have been removed.

notebook computer. Lightweight full-function personal computer, so named because of its size *i.e.*, smaller than a portable. Measurements are usually about 8.5×11 inches.

notepad. A part of the software, which reserves a portion of main memory as an aide memory for the user in MS-windows environment.

NP. 1. Network Provider, normally refers to a PTT, but could be any organisation providing a network service. 2. New Project, in ISO, a proposal for a new program of work.

NPA. Numbering Plant Area, the telephone numbering system used in the United States and Canada.

NPD. Network Protective Device.

NPDU. Network Protocol Data Unit.

NPL. National Physical Laboratory, U.K. government body involved in the development of conformance test tools for OSI.

NPP. Network Protocol Processor.

NPU. Network Processing Unit.

NRS. 1. Name Registration Service, domain naming scheme used on JANET and defined in the Grey Book. 2. Network Registration Service, an on-line database for registration of interoperability testing by OSINET members.

NRZ. *See* non-return-to-zero.

NRZI. Non Return to zero Inverted.

NS Lookup. A utility that enables to query DNS servers and view information such as their resource records, and is useful when troubleshooting DNS problems.

NS. Network Service, the service provided to transfer data between network users at the service boundary between the Network and Transport Layers.

NSAP. Network Service Access Point, the NSAP address is unique in the global domain of OSI network addressing.

NSDU. Network Service Data Unit.

NSEL. Network SELector, usually the last octet of an NSAP address, which identifies the network type, e.g., CLNP.

NSF. National Science Foundation, an organisation that now controls NSFNET, the transitional successor to ARPANET.

NSP. 1. Network Service Part of SS 7. 2. NATO Standardised Profile, functional profile for military communications agreed to by the NATO countries.

NSSDU. Normal Data Session Service Data Unit, data unit that carries data between two Session service users.

NT. Network Termination, and point in standards under ISDN; in the same way a telephone or PAD terminates its respective circuit, there are standards for ISDN termination.

NT1. ISDN NT Type 1 interface between customer and provider; terminates the public network on customer premises.

NT2. ISDN NT Type 2, subscriber-owned device like a PBX which terminates the customer network and provides switching within a customer site.

NTM. Network Traffic Management, a function of OSI Network Management.

NTN. Network Terminal Number, part of X.121, the protocol for X.25 addresses.

NTP. 1. Network Terminal Protocol. 2. Network Time Protocol.

NUA. Network User Address.

null modem cable. An RS232 cable that has pins 2 and 3 reversed so that the two connected computers are under the impression they are linked using modems. A device connects two DTE devices directly by emulating the Physical connections of a DCE unit.

null string. In data structures, a string having no characters.

null suppression. The bypassing of the null characters to be stored or transmitted to save transmission time or storage space.

null. 1. A computer instruction to do nothing, except proceed to the next sequential operation. Null characters can be inserted into, or removed from, a sequence of characters without the meaning of sequence being affected although the control of equipment or the format may be altered.
2. The absence of information, as opposed to a zero or blank, which indicate presence of no information.
3. The deflection from a centre or end position.

number, binary. A number expressed to the base 2.

number crunching. Processing activities involving a high proportion of mathematical operations on the data. Such applications make heavy use of the central processing unit and involve lesser input/output operations.

number unobtainable. A tone used in telephone communications indicating to a caller, by use of an audible signal, that a call cannot be completed. There are four possible reasons; the line required is either faulty or out of commission; a non-existent or invalid number has been dialled; equipment has been wrongfully operated or has malfunctioned; access to the required number is banned. The tone is also relayed if a caller does not send an effective signal during a certain period.

numbering plan area. Part of a national of integrated telephone numbering plan, it is an area that consists of further numbered subdivisions that are identified by a particular number-plant trunk code.

numeric field. A database field that stores numeric.

numerical algorithms group. NAG. A body which has provided a collection of library routines for a number of numerical functions for use on a variety of computers.

numerical analysis. The study of methods relating to the development of quantitative solutions to mathematical problems, including the study of errors and efficiency of the methods in terms of the total computational effort.

numerical code. A code whose target alphabet contains only digits and/or strings of digits, *e.g.,* binary code.

NVT. Network Virtual terminal.

Nyquist criterion. The statement that when a continuous-time band-limited channel is to be sampled, the sampling process may or may not cause information to be lost according to whether the sampling rate is less than, greater than, or equal to twice the bandwidth.

Nyquist interval. The maximum time interval between adjacent, equally spaced samples of a signal that will permit the waveform to be completely determined and hence reproduced when the samples are detected. It is equal to the reciprocal of twice the bandwidth of the sampled signal.

NZT. Non-Zero-Transfer.

O

O. Operand.

O.nnn. The CCITT O. Series Recommendations deal with equipment for measurement distortion and related effects on telephone circuits.

O/R. Originator/Recipient, users in X.400.

OA. 1. Office Automation.

2. Operand Address.

OAAC. Objects and Attributes for the Access Control, used in the Network Management.

OAF. Original Address Field.

OAM&P. Operations, Administration, Maintenance, & Provisioning, what T1M1 calls Network Management.

OAS. Office Automation System.

OB. 1. *See* occupied bandwidth.

2. Octal to Binary.

3. Output Buffer.

4. Output Bus.

OBCR. Optical Bar Code Reader.

object code. The code produced, usually from a source code, by hardware or software, such as the output code from an assembler or compiler, which can be executed as a machine code or which can be processed to produce executable machine codes. In general, it refers to the program which computer actually executes after translating it from a higher-level programming language (source code).

object embedding. The process of integrating a copy of the data from one application into another, such as from a worksheet to a word processor.

object language. 1. A language which is specified by a meta-language.

2. A language into which statements are translated.

object linking. The process of integrating a opy of data from one application into another so that the data retains a link to the original document; change in the original document also appears in the linked data.

object linking and embedding. OLE. A proprietary software system from Microsoft; it allows applications to transfer and share information. When a change is made to a shared object in the original application, any document that contains that object is updated automatically to reflect the changes.

object module. 1. All or part of an object program sufficiently complete for linking. It may be noted that assemblers and compilers usually produce object modules.

2. A program unit that is the output of an assembler or a compiler and, that is suitable for input to a linkage editor.

object program. An assembled, compiled, or translated computer program that is ready for execution and loading onto a computer. It may be noted that an object program may or may not require linking.

objective C. A programming language based on the "C" programming language, featuring a greater emphasis on hierarchical design of programs.

object-oriented database. A database structure in which data items, their characteristics, attributes, and procedures are grouped into units called objects.

object-oriented graphics. Graphic designs that are handled by the computer as mathematically-described shapes, rather than as collections of pixels; often referred to as drawing as opposed to painting.

object-oriented programming. A programming technique that makes use of reusable, modular components, includes encapsulation and inheritance and ability to create an object before its exact character is known.

object-oriented technology. The art and science of manipulating data, like programming, in the form of objects, streamlining ways of identifying and addressing business problems and creating applications. Its applications are built up from objects containing both information and the intelligence needed to process that data in a single unit; particularly useful in workgroups where it lets a document contain its own security and routing information. Standards are being discussed by several bodies including the Object Management Group with its Object Management Architecture.

OC. 1. Optical Carrier, the carrier frequency used to transmit signals through an optical waveguide.
2. Operating Characteristics.

OC-1. Optical Carrier level 1, the lowest optical transmission rate in the incipient Sonet standard at 51.48Mbit/s.

OC-3. Optical Carrier level 3, the second fastest optical rate in incipient Sonet standard at 155.52Mbit/s.

OCC terminal. The location from which another common carrier provides service to the users.

OCCAM. A concurrent programming language; named after European philosopher.

occupied bandwidth. OB. The frequency bandwidth which is bounded by limits such that below its lower limit and above its upper limit the mean power radiated are 0.5% of the total mean power that is radiated. Thus, it is band of frequencies which is occupied by an emission constituting 99% of the total radiated power.

occurrence time. The date/time of an event when it is referred to a particular time scale in communication systems.

OCG. Optimal Code Generation.

OCL. Operator Control Language.

OCP. Output Control Program.

OCR WAND. *See* optical character reader WAND.

OCR. 1. Optical Character Recognition, the software converting scanned images of documents into text files, which can be word-processed.
2. *See* optical character reader.

OCS. Office Communications System.

octal base. A 8-pin base.

octal notation. The representation of numbers in the positional number system with radix 8. The octal digits are denoted by 0-7. Any octal number may be simply converted into its binary equivalent, and any binary number into its shorter octal equivalent. Number in the system express values with each digit position representing successive powers of eight.

For instance, decimal 85 would be written as 125, representing 1 times 64, 2 times 16, and 5′1. If used as a shorthand method of writing binary digit strings, the bit string 001,010,101 can be written as octal 85, whereas in straight binary it is 1010101.

octal-to-decimal conversion. Conversion of numbers in the octal number system to numbers in the more familiar decimal number system; done by expressing octal number serially in powers of eight. Thus, octal 12
$= (1'8^1) + (2'8^0)$
$= 8 + 2$
= decimal 10.

octect alignment. Alignment of bits in to sequences of 8 binary digits.

octet timing signal. OTS. A signal which identifies each octet in a contiguous sequence of serially transmitted octets. It generally identifies the first bit in each octet.

octet. A group or byte that consists of 8-binary digits and is usually operated upon as a single entity. An octet is a string of eight ones and/or zeros, such as 01111100. In networking, this term is sometimes used instead of byte, because some systems have bytes that are not 8-bits long.

octode. A device having eight electrodes, such as an octode tube, in which the principal electrodes are anode, cathode, and primary control electrode in addition to five auxiliary electrodes.

ODA. 1. Office Document Architecture, defined in ISO 8613 and related standards. ODA provides architecture for representing electronic documents with one or more content types. There is a related interchange format (ODIF) for exchanging electronic documents for processing and/or presentation. It covers aspects such as layout, physical rendition, structure, and content of complex documents. ODIF defines the rules for constructing a linear message stream to represent the elements and content of the electronic document. ODA does not specify the actual means for transferring the document from one system to another. It may be carried by one of the communication applications like MHS or FTAM. 2. Operational Design and Analysis.

ODB. 1. *See* output to display buffer. 2. Output Data Buffer.

ODBC. Open Database Connectivity, non-proprietary programming SQL interface specified by Microsoft for database connectivity. It offers access to a variety of PC, minicomputer and mainframe systems, plus Apple networks.

ODC. Output Data Control.

odd parity. Parity in which number of 1s, or marks, in a group of binary digits, or in a group of mark and space signalling elements, such as those which comprise a character or word, is always maintained as an odd number, including the parity bit itself.

ODDD. Optical Digital Data Disc.

odd-order harmonic. Any odd multiple of the fundamental frequency of a signal. For example, if the fundamental frequency is 1 MHz, then the odd-order harmonics occur at frequencies of 3 MHz, 7 MHz, and so on. The push-pull circuit accentuates the odd harmonics, and is used as frequency tripler. The push-push circuit tends to cancel out the odd harmonics in the output. A half-wave antenna operates at all odd-harmonic frequencies, assuming it is a full-size antenna. The impedance at the centre of such antenna is purely resistive at all odd-harmonic frequencies. At the odd harmonics, the dipole antenna presents a slightly higher feed-point resistance than at the fundamental frequency, but the difference is not large enough to cause an appreciable mismatch when the antenna is operated at the odd harmonics.

ODE. Online Data Entry.

ODF. Original Data File.

ODG. Offline Data Generator.

ODIF. Open Document Interchange Formation ODA/ODIF. The ODIF portion defines the format for documents during transfer between systems.

ODLI. Open Data Link Interface, a Novell technique similar in concept to Microsoft's NDIS, it enables PC adapter cards to support ODLI and so run multiple protocols to access various implementations of NetWare.

ODP. 1. Optical data Processing.
2. Open Distributed Processing; ISO SC21/WG7 is currently working on a ODP reference model, and will try to coordinate it with CCITT's Distributed Application Framework.

ODR. Output Definition Register.

ODS. Open Data Services, Microsoft software supporting access from Microsoft's SQL Server to wide range of data sources and formats, including information from major mainframe databases.

ODT. Online Debugging Technique.

ODU. Output Display Unit.

OEAP. Operational Error Analysis Program.

OEM. Original Equipment Manufacturer, the maker of equipment marketed by another vendor, usually under the name of the reseller. The OEM may make only certain components or complete devices, which can then be configured with software and/or hardware by the reseller.

OF LIN PS. Open Frame LINear Power Supply; low cost, very simple construction power supply unit that employs linear techniques. Normally mounted on a single open chassis without a cover, this type of unit has a power rating of up to 150 watts.

OF SMPS. *See* open-frame switch mode power supply.

off-centre feed. A method of applying power to an antenna at a current or voltage loop not at the centre or end of the radiating element. Off-centre feed is also called window feed. For the off-centre feed to be possible, an antenna must be at least 1 wavelength long. 1-wavelength antenna has current loops at distances of 1/4 of the wavelength from either end.

off-hook signal. A signal in switching systems which indicates the seizure of a line, a request for a service, or a busy condition. The signal is usually transmitted when user actuates a switch on an end instrument.

off-line equipment. 1. Equipment which provides data to, or accepts data from, intermediate storage and not directly to or from a transmission line.
2. The equipment which is not under direct or continual control of computer or data processing system.
3. An equipment, which is not connected to a transmission line. Thus, signals cannot pass to or from the equipment and the line without the intervention of the operator.
4. Disconnected from a system, not in operation, and may be without power supply.

off-line operation. The method of operation in which the messages/data is handled separately from their transmission, with the encrypted messages passed on for decryption.

off-line recovery. The process of recovering data by using an off-line processor or central processing unit.

off-line storage. The memory not directly accessible or under the control of a central processor.

off-net extension. The ability of an exchange or switching centre to extend an incoming call into another network. Generally, off-net calling from outside the net calling persons may not be within the mission requirements of the local net.

off-state. Condition of an on-off circuit or device, such as a flip-flop, that is off.

Office 97. A Windows based software, which brings together full-featured programs and seamlessly integrates them to allow them to do a lot more. It gives an easy access to powerful, user-friendly tools that allow focusing on getting on to the jobs. Office 97 works with corporate networks and the Internet. It includes new features like Active Web technology, Office Web FindFast, and Outlook. A major component of Office 97 is its Windows 95 compliant interface. The standard edition of Office 97 has tools namely Excel, PowerPoint, Outlook, and Word.

Office Assistant. A feature of Office 97 that unifies online help interface; it is visible by default after installing Office 97. User may click the Assistant to ask questions, and the Assistant finds relevant topics in the help.

office information system. OIS. A general term that can be applied to any of the integration of several applications of computers and networks employed in a variety of office functions. The processes concerned can include information retrieval, telecommunications or word processing, financial accounting, management information system, etc.

Office Systems Node. *See* OSN.

OFTS. Optical Fibre Transmission System.

OH. Octal to Hexadecimal.

OIB. Operation Instruction Block.

OID. Object IDentifier, in ASN.1, an order list of component values that provides the path from the root to a specific registered information object. The path usually includes the registration authority along the way.

OIDI. Optically Isolated Digital Input.

OIS. *See* office information system.

OIW. OSI Implementers Workshop, sponsored by NIST. Regional workshop in North American for establishing OSI Implementers Agreements which can be harmonised with those of the other regional workshops and fed into ISO to become ISPs.

OL. 1. On Line.
2. Open Loop.

OLB. On Line Batch.

OLE. Object Linking and Embedding, a Microsoft specification for implementing object-oriented software developments. An improved form of DDE, it adopts a layered approach and allows a file or program to be embedded as an object in another file. OLE2 (the most recent version) and ODBC drivers altered without affecting core software applications from different vendors to be accessed seamlessly. More and more organisations are adopting this set-up.

OLM. On Line Monitor.

OLOE. On Line Order Entry.

OLP. On Line Programming.

OLRT. On-Line Real-Time operation, a method of operation whereby results from a computer are obtained during the progress of an event. Input data are passed directly from a measuring device to the computer.

OLS. On Line Search.

OLT. On Line Test.

OLTS. On-Line Test System, the running of a whole system against test data with a verified solution, or the complete simulation of an actual running system to test out the adequacy of the system. The system runs at speeds compatible with a computer and is connected directly to the main processing unit.

OM. 1. Operations Manual.
2. Output Module.

OMAC. On Line Manufacturing Control.

OMAP. 1. Operations, Management, and Administration Part.
2. Object Module Assembly Program.

OMD. Object Macro definition.

Omega. A global radio navigation system which provides position information by measuring phase difference between signals radiated by a network of eight transmitting stations deployed all over the world.

OMG. Object Management Group, a vendor and user consortium of over 100 members.

omni-directional antenna. An antenna that intercepts or radiates equally well in any azimuth, or compass, direction. It may be a transmitting or receiving antenna that is capable of transmitting or receiving electromagnetic signals in many or all directions with nearly equal power in each direction. An isotropic antenna is a true omni-directional antenna, but it exists only in theory. An isotropic antenna radiates with equal field strength in all directions.

omni-directional signalling system. OSS. A signalling system in which signals are transmitted in nearly equal intensity or power density in all directions, or at least in a given plane such as the horizontal plane.

omni-directional. 1. A device that responds equally well to acoustic or electromagnetic energy from any direction in three dimensions.
2. A device that radiates acoustic or electromagnetic energy equally well in any direction in three dimensions.

OMPR. Optical Mark Page Reader.

ONA. Open Network Architecture, the extension of the concept of an open system to the network architecture itself.

one state. The high, on or true logic state of a bistable device such as a flip-flop.

one-address instruction. A computer program instruction in which the address part contains only one address, such as the address of an operand.

O-network. A network consisting of four impedance connected to form a closed loop or square. It has an input applied across one element and the output (O,2) taken across the opposite element.

one-way communication. The communication information can be transferred in only one pre-assigned direction.

one-way operation. In a communication system, pertaining to a transmission operation between two points such that transmission takes place only from one point to the other and not back, regardless of the transmission equipment capability to perform.

ONI. Operator Number Identification.

on-line help. A utility available to the user when difficulty is encountered with a computer network or an application program. Most software applications offer on-screen help-messages to guide the user through the different tasks. A special help command will display an index of all the help functions available, and the user is expected to nominate in which area help is required.

on-line real-time branch information. *See* ORBIT.

on-line real-time operation. *See* OLRT.

on-line storage. Storage which is connected and immediately accessible to a system, such as a static magnetic storage unit in a computer.

on-line test system. *See* OLTS.

on-line. 1. Connected to, served by, or

available through a networked computer system.

2. In automation theory, describing an automaton that, having read the first k symbols of the input string, has already produced the first k symbols of the output string. The concept of being on-line is analogous to the initial subwords-preserving property of GSM-mappings.

3. Pertaining to the direct connection, operation, and control of devices and components for immediate use on demand by a system, usually without human intervention.

4. Pertaining to operations, equipment, or devices that are under the direct control of, or in direct communication with a processor.

5. A method of transmission in which the signals from communication equipment are passed directly to a channel or circuit to operate one or more compatible pieces of equipment at one or more distant locations.

ONMA. Open Network Management Architecture, IBM's network management architecture comprised of Entry Points, Service Points and Focal Points - implemented as NetView.

ONP. Open Network Provision, defines the access conditions and quality of service for valued-added service providers across Europe. The EC plan for common interfaces and tariffs in the EEC.

ON-TAP. An expression for ON-line Training And Practice, a specific set of information held on computer files containing data from a number of other stores of information held on computer file. It is designed to help train personnel in the uses of direct searching of computer files.

OOD. Object-Oriented Design, a method for modelling a concept as objects.

OOP. Object-Oriented Programming.

OOS. Out Of service.

OPDU. Operation Protocol Data Unit.

open architecture. A type of IBM PC and compatible architecture that allows third party manufacturers to produce additional interior add-ons (usually circuit boards), and to allow users to easily install these add-ons.

Open Data Link Interface. *See* ODLI.

Open Database Connectivity. *See* ODBC.

Open Network Management Architecture. *See* ONMA.

Open Shortest Path First. *See* OSPF.

open software description. OSD. An XML application for describing software components, their versions, structure, and relationships to other components. When combined with channel definition format (CDF), it allows software applications to be automatically installed and upgraded over the Internet.

open system interconnection. OSI. A term used to describe the technique employed for the construction and connection of a computer network, in which the types of interconnected computer systems employed are different. It refers to a suite of protocols and proposed specifications of such a system have been drafted by the International Standard Organisation.

Open Systems Interconnection model. *See* OSI model.

open waveguide. A waveguide in which electromagnetic waves are guided by a refractive index gradient so that the waves are confined to the guide by refraction within, or reflection from, the outer surface of the guide.

open. To display the contents of a file in an application or to start an application.

OpenDoc. A standard for applications and documents created by a consortium of Apple, IBM, and Novell. It is intended to provide more cross platform and cross application integration, by splitting components of documents (text, sound, graphics, etc.) and providing separate access to each component through modular software.

operand. Any of the various qualities arising out of, or resulting from the execution of a computer instruction, a constant, a parameter, the address of any of the quantities, or the next instruction to be executed.

operating environment. An intuitive graphical user interface that overlays the operating system but does not replace it, such as Microsoft Windows.

operating point. The point on family of characteristic curves of an active electronic device, such as a transistor, that represents the magnitudes of voltage and current when designated operating conditions and applied to the device. The choice of operating point determines the class of operation of the amplifier. Certain transducers and semiconductor devices require direct-current bias for proper operation. When the signal is applied or received, the instantaneous current fluctuates above and below the no-signal current. The no-signal is called the operating current or operating point. The correct choice of operating point ensures that the device will function according to its ratings.

operating ratio. For a given period, the ratio t_1/t_2 as a percentage, where t_1 is the time during which an equipment is operating correctly, and t_2 is the duration of the period.

operating signal. A group of characters, which are employed in communication operations to convey orders, instructions, requests, reports, or other information.

operating system. OS. That part of computer software necessary to simplify administrative procedures for input/output, data-conversion and other routines. The operating system provides interfaces for the user, software, hardware, and for file management. The functionality of the operating system can be extended with the addition of utilities.

A section of the software allows the computer to communicate with the user (computer operator). The operating system is usually loaded (booted) each time the computer is switched on. This is generally an automatic loading procedure controlled by the read-only memory chip. During the booting process, several diagnostic tests are performed to check on the order of internal and external devices such as printers or disk drives. The operating system manages all of the other programs that are running. It also provides system-level services to those programs, including file management, memory management, and printing. It also allows programs to share information. In Windows 3.1, 3.11, NT, and 95, sharing is accomplished through the Clipboard and OLE.

Operating systems coordinate flow of data to and from central processing unit, and from input and output devices such as a mouse or a printer. They also assign and recall memory addresses, and in multi-user systems, they prevent users from obstructing each other, or overwriting data on a file as it is being read by another user.

The operating system uses interrupt requests to maintain organised communication with CPU and other hardware components. Each of the hardware devices is controlled by another piece of software called the driver, which allows the operating system to activate and use the device. The operating system also provides the software necessary to link computers to form a network. Operating systems have gradually included more features such as file defragmentation, data compression, backup, data recovery, protection against viruses, and screen saving.

There are a number of different operating systems, which have different design philosophies, provide different facilities, and have different facilities. Among popular operating systems are MacOS, MS-DOS, the various versions of Windows, such as Windows 3.1, 3.11, NT, 95, and Windows 2000. UNIX was the first multiuser, multiprocessing operating system, but is gradually losing the market share. The manufacturers of PC operating systems such as Microsoft, IBM, and Apple, come up with new and more capable versions of their operating systems almost every year.

operation code trap. A specific value that replaces the normal operation part of a machine instruction at a particular location to cause an interrupt when that machine instruction is executed.

operation code. 1. The portion of the instruction word that specifies the operation to be performed by the instruction.
2. The set of such portions available for a particular computer, and defining the repertoire of operations it can perform.

operation part. The part of the computer program instruction word which contains the operator or which specifies the operation that is to be performed with or on operands whose addresses are also given in the address parts of the instruction word.

operation register. A memory storage location used to hold the operation code of computer instructions.

operation table. A table consisting of permissible combinations of operators and all possible values of operands and indicating the result for each of the combinations listed.

operation time. The time duration to interpret and execute a specified operation; such as time required to select a storage location and store a number or time required to add numbers, including the access time for operating the operands and storing the results.

operation. A function from some domain S^m into S itself, where S is some set specific to the function. Such a function is usually referred to as an m-ary or m-adic operation over S; m being some positive integer. The most common operations are binary (or dyadic) operations that map S X S into S and the unary (or monadic) operations that map S into S.

operational research. OR. Scientific methods applied to the solving of problems that concern the allocation of resources. They make use of mathematical models and analytical methods to provide logical basis for solving operational problems as well as for making sound predictions and decisions that have been designed for and are used by management.

operations per minute. The number of defined actions executed in one minute.

operation support systems. Software programs which help in operating the systems and the networks.

operator number identification. Equipment at a local dial central office that permits an operator to break-in for sufficient time to identify and acquire the calling telephone number. This is done so that the number may then be dialled into centralised automatic message accounting equipment.

operator. A person who interacts with the system to ensure successful operation of the system.

optical character reader WAND. A hand-held optical character reader, such as a bar code scanner, which can read documents encoded in a special bar code, at speeds of hundreds of characters per second.

optical character reader. OCR. A device used to produce coded signals, in digital form, from printed characters, numbers of symbols on paper, that are suitable for a given computer. It usually requires source material in a specially designed typeface for maximum efficiency.

optical character recognition. OCR. The use of optical means by which a machine scans, recognises, and encodes information printed or typed in alphanumeric characters.

optical chopper. A device for periodically interrupting a light beam. For example, a rotating disk with radial slots through which a collimated beam must pass, or an electronically controllable coupler that utilises piezoelectric effect to move a mirror or change the refractive index and thus interrupt a light wave.

optical communication. Application of light beams for sending and receiving messages. The modern optical communication systems use modulated-light sources and receivers sensitive to rapidly varying light intensity. Lasers and light-emitting diodes is the favoured method of generating modulated light because they have rapid response time and emit light within narrow range of wavelengths.

optical conductor. The materials, which offer low optical attenuation to transmission of, light waves. The optical conductors may be single fibres, bundles, single-channel single-bundle cables, multi-channel single-fibre cables, single-channel single-fibre cables, multi-channel bundle cables, and multi-channel cables.

optical coupling. A method of transferring signal from one circuit to another, by converting it to modulated light and then back to its original form. The signal is first applied to a light-emitting diode or other light-producing device. Resulting modulated-light signal propagates across a small gap, where it is intercepted by a photocell, phototransistor, or other light-sensitive device and converted back to electrical pulses. Optical coupling is used when it is necessary to prevent impedance interaction between two successive stages in a multistage circuit. It also facilitates coupling between circuits at substantially different potentials.

optical data bus. An optical-fibre bus, which interconnects stations, nodes, or terminals in such a manner so that any station, node, or terminal can communicate with any other.

optical data processing. The performance of the data processing operations that simulate actual systems that represented by the mathematical functions and the relationships governing the the behaviour of light passing through the optical elements, such as by making use of interference or diffraction patterns.

optical disk. A circular, flat disk coated with a photosensitive material on which binary digits in the form of light and dark spots may be stored by modulation of light from source such as laser.

optical fibre bundle. The collection of a number of optical fibres in a single protective sheath or jacket. The number of fibres varies from a few to several thousands, depending on the requirement and the characteristics of the fibres.

optical fibre junction. An interface formed by joining the ends of two optical fibres in a coaxial butt joint for direct fibre-to-fibre transmission.

optical fibre merit figure. A figure which indicates ability of an optical fibre to handle high-frequency signals over given distances with specified distortion limits or error rates.

optical fibre transfer function. A constant for a particular optical fibre. When a light wave enters an optical fibre the fibre brings about a transformation upon it. If the input composition and the transfer function are known, then the output can be determined.

optical fibre. A single discrete optical transmission element or waveguide that is generally cylindrical in shape, usually consisting of fibre core and a fibre cladding that can guide a light wave. It consists either of a cylinder of transparent dielectric material of a given refractive index whose walls are in contact with a second dielectric material of a lower refractive index; or of a cylinder whose core has a refractive index that gets progressively lower away from the centre. The fibre utilises internal reflection to transmit light along the axial length. The light enters one end of the fibre and emerges from the opposite end with losses depending upon the length, absorption, scattering, and other factors. Optical fibre is used as the physical layer of several LAN standards. 10Base-FP Ethernet physical layer standard uses optical fibre operating with an 850 nm source. The 100Base-FX Fast Ethernet physical layer standard uses two fibres. It is also the preferred medium for Gigabit Ethernet.

optical filter. A device, which transmits a range of wavelengths, while blocking adjacent wavelengths.

optical isolator. An optical transmission system, such as a fibre-optic link, inserted into or between wire communication systems for the purpose of preventing electrical contact between systems or parts of systems.

optical junction. Any interface in an optical system.

optical lever. The means of amplifying small angular movements by reflecting a beam of light.

optical link. Any optical transmission channel designed to interconnect two end terminals, or to be connected in series, as part of a circuit, with other channels.

optical mixing. 1. The production of electrical current proportional to the frequency difference between two monochromatic light waves incident upon the same photo-conductor.
2. The production of dichromatic or polychromatic radiation from monochromatic radiation by using a mixing box, mixing rod, or any other means.

optical multi-mode dispersion. A dispersion of the constituent frequencies of pulses in an optical waveguide caused by mode mixing when two or more transmission modes are supported by the same fibre. It is greatly reduced in graded-index fibres and slightly reduced by employing monochromatic light source such as laser.

optical neurocomputer. Computer which combines both optical and electronic systems (or devices), using light and electricity to transmit signals.

optical pattern recognition. OPR. A technique in which an optical scanning device is used to convert scanned information into digital signals; normally used for computer recognition of pattern by comparison to a known reference, for classification, identification or sorting.

optical reader. A device capable of reading or sensing hand-written, typed, or printed characters by being able to distinguish between light and dark areas on a data medium.

optical repeater. An optical/optical, optical/electrical, or electrical/optical signal amplification and processing device.

optical rotor. A connector which permits optical signals propagating in an optical fibre to pass across an axial interface between two fibres that are axially rotating at different speeds, such as between a fibre rotating about its central longitudinal axis and a stationary fibre.

optical scanner. 1. A scanner that uses light for examining patterns.
2. A device that scans optically and usually generates an analog or digital signal.

optical shaft encoder. In digital radios, frequency adjustment is in discrete steps. In high-frequency gear, the usual increment is 10 Hz. At 6 m and above, 10 or 100 Hz increments are used for code, radio-teletype, and single sideband; 5 kHz increments are common for frequency modulation. For tuning, an alternative to mechanical switches is optical shaft encoder. It has a light-emitting diode, a photoconductor, and a chopping wheel.

optical space-division multiplexing. OSDM. Bundles of independent fibres that provide optical paths for independent channels. In practice this is a single cable with overall sheathing and strengthening made from a collection of fibres.

optical switch. A switching circuit that enables signals in optical fibres and integrated optical circuits to be selectively switched from one circuit or path to another or to perform logic operations with these signals by employing electro-optic effects, magneto-optic effects, or other effects or methods that operate on transition modes, such as transverse electric versus transverse magnetic nodes, type and direction of polarization, or other characteristics of electromagnetic waves.

optical video disk. A dish having on its surface a spiral or concentric circles of recorded digital data at a high packing density. The information is recorded in spots using a laser beam. Using a suitable machine the disk can be used to provide television programming playback.

optical waveguide. Any structure capable of guiding optical power along a path parallel to its axis and that can contain the energy within or adjacent to its surface. In optical communications, the term generally refers to a fibre designed to transmit optical signals.

optical-mark reader. A device that recognises graphite marks, which are normally produced by a pencil on card or paper, and converts the information into digital signals for input to a computer.

optical-mark recognition. A technique in which a device scans and recognises graphite marks on a document and converts the information into digital signals for input to a computer.

optical-pulse stretching. The increase in optical-pulse length in terms of duration or width, caused by transmission through a length of optical fibre, or through a series of fibres connected in tandem.

optimisation. A process or operation by which a set of parameters is adjusted for the most efficient, the maximum, or the minimum result. Optimisation is partly determined by calculation, but often it is a trial-and-error procedure.

optimum working frequency. OWF. In high frequency transmissions, a frequency that is lower than the maximum useable frequency by an amount sufficient to allow for expected variations in the propagation conditions that may occur during the working period of operation. The optimum working frequency depends on the distance between the transmitting and receiving stations, the time of day, the season, and the level of sunspot activity. In general, the optimum working frequency is increased, as the station separation becomes greater. It is usually greater during the day than at night; it is higher in summer than in winter; and is the highest during periods of peak sunspot activity.

opto-electronic coupler. An assembly consisting of LED and a phototransistor. An input signal causes the diode to glow, and the light activates the transistor, which in turn delivers an output signal of higher amplitude than that of the input signal.

opto-electronic device. A device responsive to electromagnetic radiation (light) in the visible, infrared or ultraviolet spectral regions, emits or modifies non-coherent or coherent electromagnetic radiation in these same regions, or utilises such radiation for its internal operation.

opto-electronic directional coupler. A directional coupler in which coupling function is electronically controllable, usually with photodetector which permits an electronic circuit to be driven by the coupler by tapping some of the passing optical power.

opto-electronics. The technology concerned with generation, processing, and detection of optical signals that represent electrical quantities. Its areas for application of this technology include communications, where electrical signals may be transmitted along fibre-optic cables and where two unconnected electrical circuits may exchange signals by means of an optical link yet remain electrically isolated; these latter devices are called opto-isolators. The technology is also being used to implement logical gating functions employing lasers and liquid crystals the advantages being high speeds of operation.

opto-phone. A photoelectric device for converting light into sounds of proportionate pitch to enable blind persons to see by ear.

OPUR. Object Program Utility Routines.

OR. *See* operational research.

ORAP. O/R Address Prefix, a sequence of the most significant O/R address attributes which identifies one or more MTs users.

ORBIT. An expression for On-line Real-time Branch Information. A computer language developed by International Business Machines (IBM) to search information stored on computer files.

order code. Another name for operation code.

order. 1. A means of indicating the way a function varies in magnitude as its argument tends to some limits, usually zero or infinity.

2. Another name for operation code.

ordering relation. A relation that is reflexive, anti-symmetric, and transitive. The relation 'less than or eual to' on integers is an ordering relation.

orderwire. The channel or path used for signals to control, or direct the control of, system operations in a communication system.

ORG. ORGanization name, one of the attributes used in X.400 naming.

.org. One of the various domain types for organizations that do not fit the commercial or educational institutions.

Original Equipment Manufacturer. *See* OEM.

OROM. Optical Read Only Memory.

orthogonal multiplex. One of the methods of time division multiplexing in which pulses with orthogonal properties are used in order to avoid intersymbol interference.

ortho-mode transducer. A device which is a part of an antenna feed and combines or separates orthogonally polarised signals.

OS. Operations System, a managing object in an OSI managed network. *See* operating system.

OS/2 Warp. The later version of OS/2, which has received attention as a possible replacement (and improvement) for both DOS and Windows since it can run DOS, Windows, and OS/2 applications.

OS/2. Operating System/2, a single-user, multi-tasking and multi-threading operating system with point-and-click interface; devised by Microsoft and IBM for computers based on Intel's 80286 and 80386 microprocessors. It supports multi-tasking and programs needing more than 640 kbytes of memory, as well as program to program communications. Its designers claim that it is better than Windows 95 at running older DOS-based programs and that it performs more efficient multitasking. OS/2.2 is the current version. OS/2 EE (Extended Edition) IBM's extended version of the original OS/2 with enhanced communications facilities.

OS/9. An operating system which performs the basis for interactive compact disc operating system.

oscillation. Any repeating, periodic effect, such as the swinging pendulum, the back and forth motion of a spring, or the continual back and forth movement of electrons in an electrical conductor. Circuits can be made to oscillate deliberately at a precise frequency.

OSCL. Operating System Control Language.

OSD. *See* open software description.

OSF. Open Software Foundation, a consortium of hardware manufacturers aimed at setting common standards for open systems, including operating systems and networks. The OSF has defined the Distributed Computing Environment.

OSI basic reference model. Open Systems Interconnection Reference Model, an architectural model describing how communications can be achieved between different vendors' systems. This provides common basis for the coordination of standards development by dividing the large problem of data communications into smaller, more manageable sub-problems, isolating them from each other in order to prevent changes and advances in one area from impacting on unrelated areas. It is a logical structure for network operations standardised within ISO and containing seven primary layers. It enables any OSI compliant computer or device to communicate with other OS1-compliant equipment. The seven Layers, starting with the lowest are the Physical, Data Link, Network, Transport, Session, Presentation and Applications. The OSI physical layer is responsible for turning the data frame into a stream of bits suitable for transmission medium.

OSI model. *See* OSI basic reference model.

OSI. *See* open system interconnection.

OSIE. Open Systems Interconnection Environment.

OSIL. Operating System Implementation Language.

OSIONE. An association of six regional networks which demonstrates worldwide interoperability of OSI products.

OSIRM. OSI Reference Model.

OSITOP. A European TOP user group promoting standards in IT.

OSL. Operating System Language.

OSM. Operating System Monitor.

OSN. Office Systems Node, an IBM concept describing a set of functions and services provided to connected nodes in an IBM office system. OSN has central role in Document Interchange Office systems with more limited IBM function sets are termed Source or Recipient Nodes. A typical A user at workstation, using commands defined in DIA, can request an OSN to supply document library, document distribution, fibre transfer and applications processing services. DIA enables an SNA network to build an office systems network with multiple remote locations sharing an OSN.

OSN. Output Sequence Number.

OSPF. Open Shortest Path First, a protocol for optimising routing on TCP/IP networks. It is gradually replacing RIP on many networks.

OSS. 1. Operations Support System, a system used to support administrative management of network resources.

2. *See* omni-directional signalling system.

3. Operating System Support.

OT. Output Terminal.

OTD. *See* optical time domain.

OTF. Optical Transfer Function.

OTL. OSI Testing Liaison, provides interpretation of accreditation requirements for Information Technology laboratories in communication testing services in Europe.

OTS. *See* octet timing signal.

OTSS. Open Transport and Session Support.

OU. 1. Organisational Unit, one of the attributes used in X.400 naming to provide hierarchical information within an organisation.

2. Operation Unit.

outage. 1. A state that occurs when a system denies service to at least one user for a period. This clearly interrupts the user's work and leads to a loss of personnel time, business, money, customer goodwill, or other valuable resources; period of time is not precisely defined and varies based upon application requirements.

2. A communication service condition during which a user is completely deprived of service due to any fault or any other reason within the communication system. Also known as outage stage.

outboard components. 1. Discrete components (capacitors, coils, resistors, or transformers) which are connected externally to an integrated circuit.

2. Discrete components which are connected externally to any existing electronic device.

outdoor antenna. An antenna which is placed outside a building. In general, outdoor antennas are preferable to indoor antennas because there are fewer obstructions for the transmission or reception of signals in most outdoor locations as compared with most indoor antennas.

outgoing access. The capability of a user in one network to communicate with a user in another network via networks to which they are connected.

outline font. A font (set of characters of a typeface) whose characters are generated by a mathematical formula.

The outline of each character is then filled in by the printer depending on the printer's maximum resolution. Unlike bitmapped fonts, the size of an outline font is easily changed without distortion through a mathematical formula stored either in the printer or in the memory of the personal computer. Adobe Systems Incorporated is a leading supplier of outline fonts.

outline utility. In word processing, a mode which hides all text, and displays on-screen only the headings and sub-headings available in a document.

outlining. A spreadsheet tool that collapses spreadsheet data, so that only the cells with pertinent data, such as tools, are visible; used to analyse trends and view spreadsheet structure.

OUTLOOK. A new Workflow Manager in Office 97; it takes the place of Schedule, offering calendar, contact, and task management features. Outlook can be used to send and receive all the e-mail, and acts as mail server. It can be used to keep a track of all the tasks. it helps to share work on the network using Microsoft's Exchange Server, public folders, and Outlook's built-in-view of the computer's file system and the network.

out-of-band signalling. An extra signal transmitted alongside the information signal to monitor and control the transmission. It uses separate channel of LAN and allows network management devices to access LAN devices even when the LAN itself is not functioning, so providing an additional layer of resilience.

output area. The region of the main memory that is allocated for the storage of data prior to transfer to an output device.

output device. 1. A load device, such as a resistor, loudspeaker, lamp, relay, motor, or the like, that utilises the output energy delivered by a generator, amplifier, or network.
2. A device, such as an output transformer, that serves to transfer energy or information from a circuit or device.
3. A device, which presents the results of computer operation in a comprehensible form, such as readouts, typewriters, tape recorders, card punchers, tape punchers, and so on.

output enable. An output control signal that provides a completely separate means of controlling the output buffer of a memory device, so eliminating the need for bus connections.

output process. The process that consists of the production of data from any component part of computer.

output subsystem. The part of a process interface system that transfers data from the process computer system to a technical process.

output to display buffer. ODB. Peripheral to a computer, this data storage area holds information whilst it is being transmitted from an output to a display device.

output. 1. The result of data processing activity when it is presented external to the system, or the process of presenting the data externally. The output from a computer can be in a form for use by people, *e.g.* printed or displayed, or it may be ready for input to another system or process, when it may be encoded magnetically on a tape or disk or punched into a card or paper tape.
2. Signals produced by a device that are used to drive peripheral devices.
3. Information transferred from the internal storage of a computer to secondary or external storage.
4. A channel for expressing a state on a device or logic element.

output-limited process. A process whose speed of execution is limited by the rate at which output data can be accepted.

outsourcing. The use of outside expertise to accomplish a task.

overflow check. A limit check to determine whether a representation of data exceeds a stipulated length.

overflow indicator. 1. In a digital calculator, a display that indicates that a numerical value is too large or too small to be shown with the available number of decimal places.
2. The display that indicates the presence of too many bits or characters for the available storage capacity.

overflow. An over-capacity, for instance the generation in an arithmetic operation of a quantity beyond the capacity of the memory store or location to receive it. Fields that are longer than field locations will overflow, for example, a 10-digit product will overflow an 8-digit accumulator.

overhead bit. Any bit which is not an information bit and that is contained in a message. The bit may be a part of user overhead or it may be a part of system overhead.

overlap. 1. A kind of parallelism in which events that are not mutually dependent take place concurrently in order to increase the performance of the computer.
2. The ability of two or more windows to be overlaid without any loss of data along the sides where the windows overlap.

overlay program. A computer program that has two or more control segments, which can be, stored in the same storage locations at different times during execution of program.

overlay. 1. A segment of the program which is not permanently stored in internal storage.
2. The process of repeatedly using the same areas of internal storage during different stages of the execution of a computer program.

over-loading. The result of an attempt to draw too much current from a source of power, or to apply excessive voltage to a load.

over-modulation. Modulation in excess of a prescribed level, especially amplitude modulation greater than 100%; results in distortion of the output signal.

over-run. Loss of data which occurs when a receiver is unable to accept the data at the arriving signalling rate.

over-voltage protection unit. A circuit or device that comes into operation when the supply voltage in a particular circuit rises above a predetermined value. Such units are used to protect computers and delicate equipment from short-duration transients (spikes) in supply voltages.

over-voltage protection. The action of defending a circuit from voltages larger than the predetermined requirements.

overwrite. To store or record data in a storage location or data medium in such a manner that the data originally stored or recorded in that location, are lost; *i.e.*, to write data to a secondary storage device (or random-access memory) so that the new data replaces the old.

O-wave. One (the ordinary) of the pair of components into which ionospheric radio wave is divided by earth's magnetic field.

OWF. 1. One-Way Function, an easy-to-compute mathematical function whose inverse cannot be computed.
2. Optimum Working facility.
3. *See* optimum working frequency.

OWL. Online Without Limits.

P

p. *See* pico.

P.nnn. The CCITT P. Series Recommendations, dealing with the noise and audibility characteristics related to the telephone sets and telephone components.

P1. X.400 Message Transfer protocol between MTA and MTA.

P1000.3. Synonymous with IEEE 10003,3, Test Method and verification for Portable Operating Systems.

P1003.1. Synonymous with IEEE 1003.1.

P1201.x IEEE standard for X-Windows; defines the interface between client and server.

P2. Content type for X.400 Interpersonal Messaging protocol between UA and UA.

P3. X.400 Submission and Delivery protocol between MTA and UA. MHS, UA(1), MTA, MS, X.411 (1984), X.419 (1988).

P6. See Pentium Pro.

P7. 1. The code name for a central processing unit chip from Intel.
2. X.400 Message Store protocol between MS and UA.

PA. 1. Program Access.
2. Program Address.

PAA. Peer Access Approval, the process by which peer communicating entities in a Secure Data Network System authenticate each other's identity when establishing an association.

PABX. Private Automatic Branch eXchange; privately owned automatic branch telephone exchange that provides access to and from the public telephone network without operator intervention. It handles calls automatically i.e., unattended; generally, a manual, user-owned exchange. Also known as PBX.

PAC. Personal Analog Computer.

PACC. *See* product administration and contract control.

PACCEPT. Presentation ACCEPT PDU, PDU providing a positive response to a request to establish a Presentation Association.

pack. To convert data to compact form in storage medium by taking advantage of known characteristics of the data and of the storage medium, in such a way that the original form of the data can be recovered. Example: To make use of bit or byte locations that would otherwise remain unused.

packed decimal notation. A binary-coded decimal notation in which two consecutive decimal digits, each having 4-bits, are represented by one byte.

packet alteration line. PAL. A system for 625-line colour television transmission. Signals are much less susceptible to transmission problems than in other systems, as the technique that is used inverts the phase of one of the two chrominance signal components every alternate line.

packet assembler/disassembler. PAD. A device that converts computer data into packets for transmission, and also changes received packets back into computer data. It is analogous to a radioteletype terminal unit.

packet assembly. The conversion of a message signal into smaller packets of data, usually 8000-bits each so that they can be transmitted independently and efficiently over a network.

packet assembly/disassembly. The circuitary arrangement provided in a packet-switching exchange, a packet assembly/disassembly facilitates communication between two terminals of a different nature. It has two basic functions, firstly to assemble received data into packets for onward transmission and secondly to disassemble these packets and transmit to various other terminals.

packet buffer. Memory space reserved for storing a packet awaiting transmission or for storing a received packet.

packet disassembly. The re-grouping of packets of data in their correct order after they have been successfully received, so as to make up the original full-length message.

packet radio. A transmission method that makes use of radio broadcast signals carying packets of data. There is no assurance that only a single transmitter is active at a time, so it is necessary to have a convention for the action to be taken when packets collide. Logically packet radio is essentially equivalent to bus architeture networks that are used in some local network architectures. Packet radio provides rapid, error-free transmission and reception of messages. Complex and massive antenna systems, high-powered amplifiers or sophisticated radios are not required. A modest setup can serve as a packet station, which has computer, a transceiver, and a terminal node controller. In order to make a packet network function, all the computers must use protocols that adhere to a standard model; most widely accpted standard is the open systems interconnection reference model (OSI-RM).

packet switching. A method of switching data in a network. Individual packets of a set size and format are accepted by the network and delivered to their destination. The sequence of packets is maintained, and destination established, by the exchange of control information (also contained in the packets) between the sending terminal and the network before the transmission starts. The network is open to all users, all the time, with packets from the various nodes being interleaved throughout the network. The packets can be sent in any order, as the control information sent at the beginning of the transmission ensures they are interpreted in the correct order at the receiving end. Because each packet carries its own control instructions, it can use any route to reach its destination. The link lasts only as long as the transmission. An ITU-TS standard for packet switched networks information.

packet. A collection of bits, including the address, data and control, that are switched and transmitted together. The terms frame and packet are often used synonymously. Any message that exceeds the maximum size is partitioned and carried as several packets.

packet-radio bulletin-board system. A set of stored messages, accessible by means of a personal computer. Many personal computer users use modems to connect their computers to telephone lines, via which the bulletin-board system is accessed.

packet-switching exchange. A group of network nodes (intersections of number of networks), at one location. Splitting of information into packets for transmission is often done at the packet-switching exchange.

packet-switching system. A data transmission system that provides for the transfer of discrete groups or packets of information along a channel, which is occupied only for the duration of the transmission of the packet. The packet itself contains address information and the channel is available for transfer of other packets, providing communications through the network to other users without the need for a two-way transmission path.

packing density. The number of discrete packaged circuits within a given surface area or volume.

packing fraction. A ratio of the active core total cross-sectional area of a bundle of optical fibres or cable cores, to the total cross-sectional area of the bundle. The packing fraction can be expressed as $PF = N(A/D)^2$ where N is the number of cores, A is the diameter of each core and D is the diameter of the whole bundle or assembly.

pad. 1. A passive attenuator network, which displays no reactance, reduces the power level of a signal and may match impedance. Since its components are purely resistive, its does not introduce different attenuation at different frequencies. Pads are often used between radio transmitters and external linear amplifiers to regulate the amplifier drive. Pads are also used in some receiver front ends to reduce or prevent overloading in the presence of extremely strong signals.

2. In computer practice, to make a record a fixed size by adding blanks or dummy characters to it.

3. To lower the frequency of an LC circuit by adding capacitance to an already capacitively tuned network.

PAD. Packet Assembler/Disassembler, a device used in packet switched network to convert data to appropriate format so that a non X.25 (non-packet switching) device can send information over X.25 (packet switched) network. It is responsible for call setup and addressing routines.

padding. 1. The process of precisely adjusting a circuit by means of small, series or parallel components.

2. A process in which blanks or other meaningless data characters are added toa file to make the file a certain standard size.

PAE. Peer Access Enforcement, the process by which incoming and outgoing PDUs are checked for conformance with the security policies in place for a given association between communicating entities in a Secure Data Network Service.

PAF. Peripheral Address Field.

page description language. A programming language (such as PostScript) that uses special commands to describe how an image will be printed on a page. Output to any printer which contains an interpreter for the same page description language can drive that printer, regardless of its make or model. This means all processing is transferred from the computer to the printer which has its own central processing unit and random access memory for converting the mathematical representation of images.

page footing. A record of information of data situated and printed at bottom or foot of page(s) of a document.

page heading. PH. A record of information or data that is situated and printed at the top or head of a page or pages in a document.

page view terminal. A visual display unit that allows the user to display pages of text, one page at a time.

page. In a virtual storage system). A fixed-length block that has a virtual address and that is transferred as a unit between real storage and auxiliary storage.

page-mode RAM. Page-mode random-access memory; a spatial static RAM chip that carries information without having to rely on the central processing unit to refresh it several thousand times per second (as is the case with dynamic RAM). Page-mode RAM is used with very fast processors (such as the Intel 80486) to ensure that the processor does not have to ensure that the processor does not have to wait for information when it is needed, thereby reducing or eliminating the wait state. 'Fast page-mode RAM' refers to the column address strobe (CAS) cycle time of dynamic memory incorporated in a personal computer. With shorter CAS pre-charge time, the access time to the system memory is reduced if the second or subsequent address is close to the initial memory access. As a result, total cycle time for reading and writing back is reduced, leading to faster memory performance.

pager. A small electronic radio signal receiver which can be activated to alert the carrier that message awaits. More sophisticated pagers are used as alternatives to cellular radios (portable phones) because messages (data) can be sent in digitised format and viewed on liquid crystal display screens. Pagers are sometimes called 'beepers' because of the sound they emit when activated.

paging technique. A real storage allocation technique by which real storage is divided into page frames.

paging. A one-way alert or alphanumeric message service. Messages are normally left via a bureau with a human or automatic operator.

PAGODA. Profile Alignment Group for Office Document Architecture, a group to harmonise ODA profiles.

pair-select ternary. PST. A pseudo-ternary code where pairs of binary digits are coded together, making a third value, in such a way that the resultant signal has no long strings of zeros. A ternary code has three possible values, e.g., + 1 V, 0 and -1 V.

PAL D. Acronym for Phase Alteration Line Delay; a method of decoding signals used in the Phase Alternation Line (PAL) colour television system, that reduces colour errors.

PAL S. Acronym for Phase Alternation Line Simple; a process of decoding signals used in the Phase Alternation Line (PAL) colour television system, that requires the observer by sight to optically integrate any switched, line-by-line colour errors.

PAL. 1. Programmed Array Logic. 2. *See* packet alteration line.

PAM. Pulse Amplitude Modulation, a form of communications where the amplitude of a pulse (either peak voltage or audio volume) indicates whether it is a binary 1 or 0; a simple example would be RS-=232.

PAN. 1. Peripheral Area Network, a generic term for a network which specifically connects remote sites to a central network.

2. Polled Access Network.

3. Permanent Account Number.

PANDA. Prestel Advanced Network Design Architecture; a particular design of construction for interconnecting Prestel devices.

panel call indicator. PCI. Relays or switches at a terminating office that registers detection of a direct current pulsing system. In this system, information digits are each transmitted as a series of our four marginal, polarised pulses.

panel electronic circuit. A printed wiring panel that has components mounted upon it.

panning. Progressively translating the display image to give visual impression of lateral movement of the image. It may be noted that Panning may be restricted to a viewport.

panoramic receiver. A device that allows continuous visual monitoring of a specified band of frequencies. Most receivers can be adapted for panoramic reception by connecting a specialised form of spectrum analyser into the first intermediate-frequency chain.

pantone. System of colour matching designed to ensure that colour output would be the colour intended whether on-screen or in output from a printer.

PAP. 1. Phase Advance Pulse.

2. *See* Password authentication protocol.

paper advance. Usually a key or button provided on a printer that moves the paper or printout forward independently of the action of the printing head or impressing device.

paper-tape reader. A popular low cost input device that senses and translates the holes or information provided in a paper tape into machine code. The use of a paper-tape punch and a paper-tape reader combination has now been generally superseded by magnetic tape cassette units.

paper-tape-punch. An output device that punches or encodes machine-readable output data in the form of holes into paper tape. It has been a very popular device for producing physical data storage.

Paradox Application Language. A high-level programming language that also serves as an extension of Paradox's script-recording capability. Paradox Application Language (PAL) is designed as productivity tool to enable advanced Paradox users to customise Paradox to their style of working. It is also part of a complete application development environment including a built-in script editor and interactive debugger. Numerous built-in functions are available, as are third-party (non-Borland) application development tools. PAL support procedure concepts, including selective definition of local and global variables, and dynamic scooping of variables.

parallel access. Access to a storage device in which a number of bits are transferred simultaneously rather than sequentially; e.g., access to semiconductor memory almost invariably yields a number of bytes in parallel; by contrast access to the contents of a disk is usually serial in nature.

parallel conversion. A method of transferring to a new computer system or software program, whereby organisation chooses to use the old and new system side by side (in parallel). Once new system proves to be stable and satisfactory, the old system is either phased out, or immediately abandoned. Although this procedure is much more expensive than other methods, it is the safest.

parallel data transmission. Transmission method where data is transmitted one byte at a time, each of the bits making up byte being transmitted simultaneously over a separate path. The information can be transmitted along a single line or along two or more lines. The first method is known as serial data transfer, and the latter is called parallel data transfer. Parallel data transfer has the advantage of being more rapid than the serial transfer. However, more lines are required, in proportion to the factor by which the speed is increased.

parallel elements of processing ensemble. PEPE. An early method of executing a number of processes in a computer, in parallel.

parallel feed. The presentation of parallel ac and dc voltages to a device or presentation of dc operating voltage in parallel with the ac output voltage of the device (as in a parallel-fed amplifier or oscillator).

parallel in parallel out. PIPO. A term used to describe a shift register that can be loaded in parallel and also read in parallel, in addition to which (by implication) data can enter and leave the device serially.

parallel in serial out. PISO. A class of digital devices that can accept parallel *n*-bit data words and convert them into serial sequential *n*-bit data streams. These devices often consist of an *n*-bit shift register that is parallel loaded with the data word. This data is then clocked out of the register in serial form.

parallel input/output. PIO. An interface that permits a computer to input and output data bits simultaneously to and from external parallel devices, such as a visual display unit or a keyboard. It is a circuit in a computer system or a separate unit that is bus compatible with various microcomputers and peripheral devices. Most are programmable to operate in static, clocked or discrete modes.

parallel interface. A channel through which 8 or more data bits can flowsimultaneously, as for the computer bus, commonly used for connecting printers to the computers. Probably the best known parallel interface of all is the one developed by Centronics, a printer manufacturer, that has 36-pins and can handle a byte of data at a time. The transmission of the data is controlled by a computer generated strobe pulse. Also known as parallel port.

parallel leads. When two or more wire leads are used together in a circuit, with their ends joined, the leads are said to be parallel.

parallel port. A connection on an IBM or compatible computer usually named LPT1, where you plug in a cable for parallel printer. Some computers have more than one parallel port and are labelled LPT2, LPT3, etc. See also parallel interface.

parallel printer. A printer with a parallel interface, which you connect to a parallel port.

parallel processing system. PPS. A system including a CPU, random-access memories, read-only memories, clock-circuits, with circuits that can be used to build equipment requirements into digital data processing equipment. Such systems can be found in calculators, general-purpose data processors, and process controllers.

parallel. 1. Pertaining to the concurrent or simultaneous operation of two or more devices or to the concurrent performance of two or more activities in a single device.

2. Pertaining to concurrent or simultaneous occurrence of two or more

related activities in multiple devices or channels.

3. Pertaining to the simultaneity of two or more processes.

4. Pertaining to the simultaneous processing of the individual parts of a whole such as the bits of a character and the characters of a word, using separate facilities for the various parts.

parameter. 1. Information passed to a subroutine, procedure, or function. The definition of the procedure is written using formal parameters to denote data items that will be provided when the subroutine is called, and the call of the procedure includes corresponding actual parameters.

2. A quantity in a function or mathematical model whose value is selected or estimated according to the circumstances. Parameters should be distinguished from constants, that are fixed for all uses of the function or model, and variables, which are actual recorded measurements involved in the function or model.

Parc Universal Packet. *See* PUP.

PARD. *See* periodic and random deviation.

parity bit. An extra bit added to a group of bits, usually to a seven-bit byte. The parity bit can be of 0 or 1 value so that every byte will then add up to an odd or even number, depending on whether odd or even parity is chosen. Sometimes, the addition of parity bits is used as a means of checking the accuracy of a received digital signal. When the transmitting device frames a character, it counts the numbers of 0s and 1s in the frame and attaches the appropriate parity bit. The recipient counts all the 0s and 1s and compares the total to the odd or even message contained in the parity bit. If there's a discrepancy, the recipient asks the data to be resent.

parity. An error-checking procedure in which the number of 1s must always be the same- either even or odd- for each group of bits transmitted without error. The parity setting is often important in communications. If the users are having difficulty with a modem, parity may be checked; it can be odd, even, or none.

park. To move the read/write heads of a hard disk to a stationary position in a designated landing zone to guard against possible damage during the movement or transportation of a personal computer.

partition. Before a hard disk can be used for the first time, it must be partitioned and then formatted. Partitioning is a software function that involves dividing the storage space into usable sections, with each section assigned a letter as though it was a separate drive. This process conceivably allows each partition to be assigned to a different operating system. However, even if the entire disk is to belong to same operating system, partitioning must still be performed. DOS command 'FDISK' command also specifies the partition from which the operating system is to boot (this is called active partition), and specifies the drive letter assignments. Normally the command automatically assigns letters may be assigned if there are multiple hard disks. After a hard disk is partitioned, each partition must be formatted by the operating system to which it is dedicated. Under DOS, the 'format' command lays out the DOS structure on the disk and establishes how and where files can be stored. Note that the DOS 'format' command works differently on a floppy-disk drive as opposed to a hard disk drive. On a floppy disk drive, the command performs both low-level formatting involves creation of sectors complete with their address markings (initialising). High-level formatting lays out the operating system structure on the disk and establishes how and where files are stored.

A new hard disk normally comes with low-level formatting already done. Consequently, the format command on a hard disk only performs high level formatting. Utility programs (such as MultiDisk) are available to manage the partitioned disks.

partitioned data set. PDS. A computer file that is divided into sub-files which are able to be referenced as a group or individually.

PASCAL. A computer language designed originally to enable the teaching of programming as a systematic discipline and to allow those being taught to do systems programming. It is based on an algorithmic language (ALGOL).

passband. 1. The number of hertz, expressing the difference between the limiting frequencies at which the desired fraction (usually half power) of the maximum output is obtained. In a superheterodyne receiver that has a narrow bandpass filter, the passband can be as small as a few hundred hertz for continuous signals, or as wide as 5-10 kHz for amplitude-modulated signals.

In a receiver designed for the reception of frequency-modulated signals, the passband can be as wide as 100 kHz or more.

In a television receiver, the passband is ~6 MHz wide. If the passband is too wide for a given emission mode, excessive interference is received, reducing the sensitivity of the receiver. If the passband is too narrow, the full signal cannot be received, and again, the sensitivity is degraded.

2. A range of frequencies with a lower limit and an upper limit, such that all frequencies between these limits (but not necessarily excluding other frequencies) are passed, with little attenuation, by a filter or a channel.

3. The band of radio frequencies accepted by a radio receiver for amplitude modulation signals and measured at the detector input. It is limited by the two frequencies for which the attenuation exceeds that of the most favoured frequency by some agreed value. In general, this value is 6 dB. In high quality radiotelephony receivers, the value is 2 dB.

password authentication protocol. PAP. A protocol that uses plain text (encrypted) passwords and in the least sophisticated authentication protocol. It is used if the connection and the server cannot negotiate a more secure form of validation.

password. A secret word or phrase spoken to a guard to gain admission. In Internet Terminology. The secret number or word is assigned by the system administrator or key distribution program. Passwords are commonly used these days to protect computer resources. The user may need to enter password when he turns on the computer, to use a printer, or to gain access to a network resource.

It is recommended that while selecting a password, name of the user or any part of it should be used. Also, do not use words that are found in a dictionary or that are common around the office environment. Secure passwords should contain a combination of upper and lower case letters and may contain symbols or numbers.

paste. An application command that copies data from clipboard and places it in the document at the cursor.

PAT. Public access terminal; a computer terminal accessible to anyone. These may be positioned in a public library or in the foyer of a building. IN years to come, public access terminals will be as common as public telephones.

patch cord. A length of conductor or cable, usually equipped with plugs on both ends, and used for the purpose of making temporary connections between circuits.

PATCH. A colloquial expression;
(a) normally employed to describe a non-standard or unusual correction to a computer program that corrects a bug or unexpected function,
(b) employed to describe an extract connection or link that was not intended at the design stage but enables a circuit or a printed circuit board to function.

path control layer. Each of the layers of IBM's Systems Network Architecture (SNA) has its own set of rules for communicating with its peer layer in the other node. The layers communicate with each other by adding header information to user data. The path control layer (third layer) is responsible for the routing of messages and defines the class of services offered.

path. Specifies the location of a file; for example in MS-DOS, the path of the file KMC.DOC, which is located in document directory in the institution directory on C drive, is:
C:\INSTITUTION\DOCUMENT\KMC.DOC.
Paths are applicable to every operating system that uses directories.

PATRICIA. Practical Algorithm To Receive Information Coded In Alphanumeric; a set of simple procedures or rules for receiving alphabetical and numerical information.

PATSY. Programmer's Automatic Test System; a procedure that assists people who prepare programs for a computer, in debugging routines.

pattern articulation unit. PAU. A microprocessor capable of converting graphics images into a stream of data or information. It can also reverse the process, *i.e.*, reconstruct graphics images from converted information.

pattern recognition. The process of detecting the presence of a specified pattern in a signal, or assigning a probability to its possible presence. For example visual pattern recognition involves the identification of two-dimensional patterns in a grey-level array. The specification of one of more patterns is done either analytically, or, by the provision of templates, which are model patterns for comparison. Pattern recognition employs the techniques of digital signal processing picture processing, and artificial intelligence.

PAU. *See* pattern articulation unit.

PAX. *See* private automatic exchange.

payload. the actual data that is transmitted across a network.

P band. A band of microwave frequencies that range 0.225-0.390 gigahertz and form part of a larger continuous range of frequencies covering 0.225-100 gigahertz which are usually subdivided into bands designated by letters. The bands are commonly used subdivisions but are not internationally agreed. P band frequencies have wavelengths of between 133.3 and 76.9 cm.

PB. *See* peripheral buffer.

PBX. Private Branch eXchange, a privately owned phone system, usually connected by one or more loops to the public telephone network.

PC card. A standard for hardware expansion, mainly for notebook computers. It is supported by Macintosh and IBM compatible notebooks, and features ease of use. Also known as PCMCIA.

PC. 1. *See* personal computer.
2. Peripheral Controller.
3. Program Controller.

PCB PS. *See* printed circuit board power supply.

PCB. 1. *See* printed circuit board.
2. Page Control Block.
3. Program Control Block.

PCC. Primary category Code.

PC-DOS. Personal Computer Disk Operating System; a version of MS-DOS licensed by IBM for use on its personal computers.

PCE. Peripheral Controller Enclosure.

PCEI. Presentation Connection End point Identifier, identifies a terminator at presentation service access point.

PCEP. Presentation Connection End Point, identifies the terminator at one end of a presentation connection.

PCI. 1. Peripheral Component Interconnect, a new standard computer bus, common to newer Macintosh and Pentium machines. This bus features faster bus throughput, as well as hardware compatibility across computer platforms, so a card could be used on both a PCI Mac and a PCI Pentium machine, though different software drivers would be needed.
2. Program Check Interruption.
3. *See* panel call indicator.

PCLA. Process Control LAnguage.

PCM. 1. Plug-compatible manufacturer; a peripheral equipment manufacturer (PEM) that makes compatible plug-in devices, that can be used interchangeably between different computers.
2. Pulse Code Modulation, a modulation technique in which an analog signal is sampled and the magnitude of each sample is quantified and converted to a coded digital signal. It usually samples at 8,000 times per second; each sampling representing 8bits. This produces a transmission rate of 641Kbit/s, with the traffic on the line in interleaved data format. At the receiving end, the interleaved signals are separated and converted back to analog.

PCMCIA. *See* PC card.

PCN. Personal Communications Networks, micro-cellular communications concept, developed in the UK, which allows pocket-sized or smaller telephone to have a permanent number.

PCO. Point of Control and Observation, term used in conformance testing of OSI products to describe the location of the upper and lower testers in relation to the IUT.

PCONNECT. Presentation CONNECT PDU, PDU requesting the establishment of an association between application entities.

PCOS. Acronym for Process Control Operating System.

PCP. Primary Control Program.

PCR. Page Control Register.

PCRAM. Page Composition Random Access Memory.

PCS. Personal Computing System.

PCSN. Private Circuit-Switching Network, a circuit-switched network, not owned by the government.

PCT. Peripheral Control terminal.

PCTR. Protocol Conformance Test Report, used in conformance testing, a report of what test cases were executed and their verdicts.

PCW. Program Control Word.

PCX. File name extension for a bitmap image, a kind of graphics file.

PD. Physical Delivery, when a message is printed and delivered as paper mail.

PDA. 1. Physical Device Address.
2. *See* problem determination aid.

PDAD. Proposed Draft ADdenum, an ISO term.

PDAU. Physical Delivery Access Unit, under X.500, an access unit that prints messages and introduces from into a hard-copy messaging service, e.g., the country's postal service for delivery.

PDB. Program definition Block.

PDC. Parallel Data Controller.

PDD. *See* post dialling delay.

PDES INC. Product Data Exchange Standard using STEP, an industry consortium.

PDES. Product Data Exchange Standard.

PDF. 1. Portable Document Format, a text format designed by Adobe, to be read by the Adobe Acrobat Reader. PDF is designed to be portable across computer platforms.
2. Process Defined Function.

PDISP. Proposed Draft ISP, often written as pDISP.

PDL. *See* print definition language.

PDM. Pulse Duration Modulation, a form of communications where the duration of a pulse indicates whether it is binary 1 or 0; a simple example is Morse code.

PDN. 1. Public Data Network, a network established by a PTT, PTO or TA to provide data transmission services for public use, carrying traffic for paying customers.
2. Packet Data Network or Packet-switched Data Network.

PDP. *See* programmed data processor.

PDS. 1. Physical Delivery Service, a service supporting delivery of paper mail, such as national postal service.
2. *See* partitioned data set.

PDTR. Proposed Draft Technical Report; ISO technical reports are for guidance rather than standards.

PDU. 1. Protocol Data Unit, a data unit that carries protocol control information and optionally user data between peer OSI entities in a given layer.
2. *See* pilot display unit.

PE. Parity Error.

peak current. The maximum instantaneous value reached by the current in an alternating or pulsating waveform. In a symmetrical alternating-current sine wave, the peak current is the same in either direction, and is reached once per cycle in either direction. In non-symmetrical waveforms, the peak current can be greater in one direction than in the other. The peak current in a sinusoidal waveform is 1.414 times the root-mean-square current, assuming there is no direct-current component associated with the signal.

peak. An instantaneous or local maximum or minimum in a waveform or other changing parameter. The value of parameter falls off on either side of a maximum peak, and rises on either side of a minimum peak. A waveform peak usually has infinitesimal, or nearly zero, duration. In some cases a peak can be sustained for a certain length of time. A peak may be negative or positive in terms of polarity or direction of current flow.

peak-to-peak value. The difference between the maximum positive instantaneous value and the maximum negative instantaneous value in a fluctuating or alternating waveform.

peak-to-valley value. The comparison or difference between the greatest instantaneous value (peak value) and the least instantaneous value (valley value) of a time-dependent quantity.

PEDI. Protocol for Electronic Data Interchange, content with for carrying EDI over the X.400 MTS.

peek. A term used in computer programming; it instructs a processor to read information from a particular memory store.

peer-to-peer network. A network environment in which all nodes on the network have equal access to atleast some of the resources on all other nodes.

PEL. Production Error Log.

pel. *See* Pixel.

PEM. *See* privacy enhanced mail.

pen recorder. A device for graphically plotting the magnitude of a parameter as a function of time. The device is a form of analog meter.

Pentium Pro. A central processing unit chip utilising 132-bit microprocessor; produced by Intel; it has some substantial architectural changes from the Pentium, including a built in L2 cache. It can achieve faster clock speeds, the earliest model was packaged with a 133 MHz clock. It is capable of processing 3 program instructions in a single clock cycle and utilises dynamic execution. Pentium Pro was called P6 during its development.

Pentium. A central processing unit chip introduced by Intel, used in IBM compatible machines. The Pentium is the equivalent of 586 (of 80×86 chip family). Pentium runs application programs approximately five times faster than a 486 at the same clock speed. A part of Pentium's speed comes from a superscalar architecture, which allows chip to process more than one instruction in a single clock cycle.

PEP. Platform Environment Profile, a POSIX term for a profile that provides a general base platform to be used by more specific application profiles.

PER. 1. Packed Encoding Rules, an extension to the basic encoding rules for ASN.1 that makes better uses of the communications link.

2. Program Execution Request.

peripheral buffer. PB. An input/output buffer situated within the memory store of a peripheral device. It permits data-word transfers to and from the computer memory without the need of main program attention.

peripheral interchange program. PIP. A series of computer programs that transfer information from one device to another.

peripheral interface adaptor. PIA. A device that will permit parallel orientated peripherals to be connected to various microprocessors usually without any additional circuits. It consists of a set of electronic circuits fitted to a processor or a peripheral to achieve compatibility between the interfaces. The interface offered by the vendor of a peripheral may not be appropriate for direct connection to a given system for several reasons: the system manufacturers may have designed a unique interface to prevent the connection of unauthorised peripherals, or the interface fitted may have been optimized for low cost and short cable length, *e.g.* parallel input/output, and thus be incompatible with a peripheral interface optimised for long lines or network connection.

peripheral interface device. PID. Interface printed circuits, compatible with a set of standard peripherals, that can all be plugged into a chassis assembly. It may sometimes be a separate unit.

peripheral processor. PP. A device used in association with one or more pieces of computer peripheral equipment, this processor helps the peripheral to function semi-autonomously, not under the control of the central processor unit.

peripheral. A hardware item that can be attached to a computer to increase its functions, such as a printer or monitor. The devices normally perform input/output operations, such as disk drives or paper tape readers.

permanent virtual circuit. *See* PVC.

permanent virtual terminal. *See* PVT.

personal computer. PC. Strictly speaking, the IBM PC, which is any IBM-manufactured personal computer made prior to PS/2 Series. Usually personal computer refers to any personal computer compatible with IBM machines. It is also used to refer to any small, low-cost computer (relative to standard and mini systems) available as ready-built units or in the form of kit. Its applications include professional business, small business, hobbyists and home, the individual software being orientated towards single user applications. The two major categories are those that:
(a) have their own cathode-ray tube display and cassette or floppy disk facilities for program storage and exchange; and
(b) rely on domestic television as an output display and an audio cassette for program storage and exchange. Both are able to accommodate peripheral devices such as standard or purpose designed printers.

personal computing system. A relatively low cost portable computer that has software designed for single-user applications, personally controllable and easily used. There are several classifications of systems, which include home, hobbyist, professional and small business.

personal digital assistant. A small portable computer designed to be held in one hand; used to perform specific tasks. Also known as palmtop.

personal electronic transaction computer. PET. A popular personal home computer, based on the 6502 8-binary digit microprocessor manufactured by Commodore Business Machines.

personal information retrieval system. PIRS. A software package used together with a mini or microcomputer to order and index information for storage on a magnetic medium.

personal productivity applications. The application software installed on business computers, which are designed to help individual employees do their work more efficiently . The database management systems may be considered personal productivity applications, though in business, large database management systems are often vertical applications.

PERT. *See* program evaluation and review technique.

PES. Program Execution System.

PET. Personal Electronic Transactor; a Commodore personal computer manufactured by Commodore Business Machines; PET offered 8 kilobytes of random-access memory and 14 kilobytes of read-only memory.

PETS. Parameterised Executable Test Suite, using the test suite parameter values from PICS and PXIIT to parameterise an executable test suite for testing a specific IUT in conformance testing.

PEU. Port Expander Unit.

PF. Programmable Function.

PFA. Program and File Analysis.

PFK. Programmed Function Key.

PFM. *See* pulse frequency modulation.

PFP. Program File Processor.

PFR. *See* power fail recovery.

PGA. *See* pin grid array.

PGI. Parameter Group Identifier, an identifier for a parameter field that contains a set of parameters.

PGP. Pretty Good Privacy, a freeware system for providing security for file transfers (e-mail, etc.) through file encryption.

PGS. *See* program generation system.

PH. Packet Header, protocol control information for a Network Layer Protocol data unit.

phase modulation. PM. A method of modifying a sine wave signal to make it carry information in which the phase of the carrier current is varied with the frequency of the modulating voltage. Phase modulation is accomplished by an instantaneous carrier-frequency change, which is proportional to the amplitude and frequency of the modulating voltage. For digital transmission, 2, 4, or 8 different phases can be employed. In angle modulation, the phase angle of a sinusoidal carrier is caused to vary from a reference carrier phase angle by an amount proportional to the instantaneous amplitude of the modulating signal.

phase opposition. When two signals are exactly 180 degrees different in phase, they are said to be in phase opposition. It results in net amplitude that is the absolute value of the difference in amplitudes of two signals having identical frequency. The phase of the resultant signal is the same as the phase of the stronger of the two constituent signals. If the two signals have the same amplitude, they combine in phase opposition to produce no signal. This effect is called phase cancellation.

phase shift. A change in the phase of a signal; it can occur over a small fraction of one cycle, or it can occur over a span of many cycles. Phase shift is generally measured in degrees. One degree of phase shift corresponds to 1/360 (0.00278) cycle. Phase shift can be used to convey information via radio-frequency carrier waves. In such a system, the instantaneous phase of a carrier wave is made to follow the waveform of some input signal, such as a human voice.

phase. 1. Any distinguishable state in a periodic phenomenon. 2. Time displacement between two currents or two voltages, or between a current and a voltage measured in electrical degrees, where an electrical degree is 1/360 part of a complete cycle. 3. The number of separate voltage waves in a commercial alternating current, designated as single phase, three-phase etc.

phased array. An antenna having two or more driven elements. The elements are fed with a certain relative phase, and they are spaced at a certain distance, resulting in a directivity pattern that exhibits gain in some directions and little or no radiation in other directions.

phase-shift keying. A process whereby the phase of a modulated carrier wave is changed between a specified set of predetermined values. In phase-shift keying, the carrier is transmitted at constant amplitude. During the space, or key-up, condition, the wave is at one phase; during the mark, or keydown, condition, the phase is altered by a predetermined amount. The phase-shift keying can be used in place of frequency-shift keying in certain applications. The primary advantage of phase-shift keying is that it can be accomplished in an amplifier stage, whereas the frequency-shift keying cannot.

PHIGS. Programmer's Hierarchical Inter-active Graphics System; a sophisticated, three-dimensional graphics and modelling support system that allows an application to use a graphics coprocessor without being tied to a single kind of hardware. It also controls the definition, modification, and display of hierarchical graphics data. PHIGS includes extensions to the ISO standard to provide capabilities for hidden-surface removal, shading, and depth cueing.

PHY. A prefix referring to the Physical Layer.

physical address. A permanent address incorporated into the network adapter during its manufacture.

physical control layer. Each of the layers of IBM's Systems Network Architecture (SNA) has its own set of rules for communicating with its peer layer in the other node. The layers communicate with each other by adding header information to the user data. The physical control layer (first layer) defines the physical, electrical, mechanical, and functional procedures used to connect the equipment. This is where RS-232-C (or the equivalent CCITT interface) is located. Also known as physical layer.

physical layer. *See* physical control layer.

physical optics. The branch of optics in which light propagation is treated as a wave phenomenon rather than a ray phenomenon, as in geometric optics.

physical signalling sub-layer. In a local area network, that portion of the physical layer that interfaces with the medium access control sub-layer and performs bit symbol encoding and transmission, bit symbol reception and decoding, and optional isolation functions.

PI. 1. Parameter Identifier, an identifier used to indicate the type of information contained in an associated parameter field; used in protocols like Session and Transport.
2. Programmed Instruction.
3. *See* programmed interrupt.

PIA. *See* peripheral interface adaptor.

PIB. Programmable Input Buffer.

PIC. 1. File name extension for a Lotus vector image, a kind of graphics file.
2. Personal Identification Code.
3. *See* priority interrupt control.

pick device. An input device used to specify a particular display element or segment. Example: a light-pen.

PICKS. Public Key Crypto System, encryption system that uses a public and private password (key).

pico. *p.* A decimal prefix commonly used in association with a base unit in SI system of units indicating a multiplication factor of 10^{-12} of that unit.

PICTEL. PICture TELephone; the name suggested and used by US General Telephone and Electronics Company to describe its experimental video telephone that permits the user to see as well as talk with another party.

picture element. The smallest detail in a picture area, comprising a television facsimile (FAX) or other transmitted picture, that can be resolved by the scanning system without loss of amplitude; also known as 'pixel'.

picture signal. A general term referring to any of a variety of different methods of conveying visual images by modulating electromagnetic waves. Also known as video signal.

PICU. Parallel Instruction Control Unit.

PID. 1. Protocol IDentifier.
2. *See* peripheral interface device.

PIE. Parallel Interface Element.

PIF. Program Information File, a file that provides information about how Windows should run a non-Windows application. For example, you use a PIF to direct Windows to run an MS-DOS application in a full screen rather than in a window, or to specify a start-up directory.

PIFT. Protocol Inter-bank File Transfer, a swift proprietary file transfer system.

PIL. *See* precision-in-line.

pilot display unit. PDU. A display unit mounted in a cockpit on which information is projected in the pilot's line of sight and superimposed over his view of the real world.

PIM. 1. Processor Interface Module.
2. *See* pulse interval modulation.

pin grid array. PGA. A mounting technique employing a high-density package for very-large-scale integration integrated circuits.

PIN. Personal Identification Number used with some applications such as ATM machines, as a kind of password.

Pine. A terminal-based email reader program, that runs on UNIX box; it allows to read, write, and exchange email messages with others. It accepts simple one-character commands in conjunction with Ctrl key. Pine accepts and responds to either uppercase or lowercase characters. With the help of Pine, the user can compose and read e-mail messages, maintain address books, create and manage folders, add attachments to email messages, perform spell-check, and reply and forward messages to others.

ping. A utility for determining if the local host is capable of exchanging datagrams with another host. Using such information, one can infer that certain TCP/IP configuration parameters are properly configured and operating in the correct manner. This utility is of great use in checking a computer's capability to communicate. It only requires that the bottom two layers of TCP/IP stack are operational. Ping, by default on Windows NT, sends four ICMP echo requests with 32-bytes data. It also displays the time in ms, from the time echo was sent until the echo reply is received. A successful ping returns 4 replies, while ping that return 3, 2, or 1 replies indicate some problem. A ping with zero reply is definitely a failure.

PING. Packet INternet Groper, a test to check whether a node on the network is responding.

PIO. *See* parallel input/output.

PIOC. *See* programmable input/output chip.

PIOU. Parallel Input/Output Unit.

PIP. *See* peripheral interchange program.

pipeline processor. A processor in which instruction execution takes place in a series of units, arranged so that several units can be simultaneously processing the appropriate parts of several instructions.

PIPO. *See* parallel in parallel out.

PIQ. Parallel Instruction Queue.

PIRS. *See* personal information retrieval system.

PISO. *See* parallel in serial out.

PIT. *See* programmable interval timer.

PITR. Product Interoperation Test Report, a report stating what interoperability tests were passed between two OSI implementations.

PIU. *See* programmable interface unit.

Pixel. The smallest graphic unit that can be displayed on the screen, usually a single-coloured dot. More and smaller rectangles are necessary to achieve higher resolution. Therefore, a sharper picture requires more computer memory to store the pixels. Also known as pel or picture element.

PIXY. Three-dimensional SPRYTe.

PKE. Public Key Encryption.

PL. 1. Presentation Layer, layer 6 of the OSI Reference Model, concerned with the presentation of information being transferred between open system application entities.
2. Private Line, used in telephones.

PL/1. Programming Language One; an interactive computer programming language developed by International Business Machines in the mid-1960s, this is a high-level computer language employed in a varied range of scientific and commercial applications. A version now exists for microcomputers. PL/1 was developed to overcome the inadequate file handling capabilities of FORTRAN, and the inadequate scientific calculation capabilities of COBOL. PL/C is the name given to the version created at Cornell.

PL/M. *See* programming language for microprocessor.

PL/SQL. Oracle's procedural extensions to the SQL language; contains if-then and other control constructs that SQL does not, and allows the definition and use of local variables. PL/SQL may be sent to database server in single anonymous block, and some tools contain their own local PL/SQL engines, allowing the execution of PL/SQL on the client machine.

PLA. *See* programmable logic array.

PLATO. *See* programmed logic for automatic teaching operations.

PLCP. Physical Layer Convergence Protocol, maps a signal onto a DS-1 or DS-3 signal.

plesiochronous. The relationship between two signals whose corresponding significant instants occur at nominally the same rate, any variation in rate being constrained within specified limits. Two signals having the same nomi~al digit rate, but not stemming from the same nominal digit rate, but not stemming from the same clock or homochronous clocks, are usually plesiochronous.

PLF. Page Length Field.

PLI. Private Line Interface.

PLJ. Permanent Loop Junctor.

PLL. Phase-Locked Loop, a type of electronic circuit used to emit a stable constant frequency without using a crystal or analog.

PLM. *See* pulse length modulation.

PLP. 1. Packet Layer Protocol, part of layer 3 or X.25. 2. Presentation Level Protocol.

PLR. Program Lock-in Register.

PLS. PhysicaL SIgnaling, IEEE 802.

PLSAP. Physical Layer Service Access Point.

Plug and Play. PnP. A hardware standard for auto configuration, which requires operating system support. Currently, Windows 95 as well as Windows 98 supports Plug and Play. Also slang for autoconfig.

plug compatible manufacturer. A manufacturer of peripheral equipment that produces item fully compatible with a particular computer, the computer being made by another manufacturer. The devices simply plug into the computer.

plug compatible peripherals. Peripherals to a computer, which can include main memory, that simply plug in. The plug-compatible peripherals are made by a different manufacturer that that of the computer.

plug-in component. Any component that can be removed for easy replacement. Some transistors are of the plug-in type. Many integrated circuits are installed in sockets, and thus they may be called plug-in components.

PM. *See* phase modulation.

PMA. Physical Medium Attachment, a Physical Layer connector used in an IEEE 802.3 local area network.

PMBX. *See* private manual branch exchange.

PMD. 1. Program Module Dictionary. 2. *See* post-mortem dump.

PMD. Physical Media Dependent layer, a Physical Layer component used in the ANSI FDDI standard.

PML. Physical Memory Level.

PMT. Packet-Mode Terminal; use with ISDN is specified in I.462.

PMX. Private Message eXchange.

PN. 1. Positive Notification, a type of EDI notification that says an EDI message was received.

2. Personal Name, one of the attributes used in X.400 naming, made up of surname, and optionally given name, and generational qualifier.

PNA. Private Network Adapter.

PNC. Personal Number Calling.

PNCC. Partial Network Control Centre.

PNIC. Private Network Identification Code, X.121.

PnP. *See* Plug and Play.

PNT. *See* project network techniques.

POA. *See* point of action.

POAC. Probe Origin Authentication Check, security service available in X.4000 (1988).

POF. Point Of Failure.

point of action. POA. Describes displays and readouts sited where processes such as manufacturing actually take place. They are characterised by housings, which can stand environmental hazards such as impact and the ingress of dust and water. They have bright wide-angle characters that are often laid out in a single line, so the messages are received by operators without the need to look closely at visual display units

point size. The height of a printed character specified in points. Also known as font size.

Point to Point Tunnelling Protocol. *See* PPTP.

point. In typography, a universal unit of measure in which 72 points equals one inch.

pointer. *See* cursor.

pointing device. An input device used to move pointer on the screen, choose commands, press buttons, select text, create drawings, and so on; for example, mouse in a pointing device.

point-to-point connection. A connection consisting of two communicating devices sharing a transmission line. A point-to-point connection is simpler than a LAN-based configuration because it does not have to provide a means for multiple computers to share the transmission medium.

point-to-point protocol. *See* PPP.

point-to-point tunneling protocol. PPTP. A protocol that enables the secure transfer of data from a remote computer to a private server by creating a virtual private network (VPN) across TCP/IP-based data networks. It supports on-demand, multiprotocol, virtual private networking over public networks, such as Internet. It is developed as extension of the point-to-point protocol (PPP), PPTP adds a new level of enhanced security and multiprotocol communications over the Internet. PPTP tunnels or encapsulates, IP, IPX, or NetBEUI protocols inside of PPP datagrams. The tunnel server performs all security checks and validations, and enables data encryption, which makes it safer to send information over non-secure networks. In PPTP, the details of the LAN address space are hidden from the Internet because the LAN header is enclosed in a PPP packet, which is then enclosed in an IP datagram.

point-to-point. The transmission of data between two points. It can also relate to the single physical line, switched or non-switched, that connects a remote terminal to a computer.

POKE. A command used in Beginner's All-purpose Symbolic Instruction Code (BASIC). This self-modifying feature will cause a computer or microcomputer to change a section of its own program in a manner the programmer commands. It is used to modify the contents of an absolute memory location from a high-level language, usually by means of a procedure of this name whose two arguments are the address in question and the value to be deposited there.

POL. *See* problem orientated language.

polling. Controlling terminals on a multi-point line by which a computer acting as master calls or polls each of the terminals in turn to find out if they have any data to send. This method is used in star topology networks but is generally being superseded by the preferred interrupt method. Network manager can control the sequence and frequency of polling to allow some users longer transmission time. On a multi-point connection or a point-to-point connection, the process whereby data stations are invited one at a time to transmit.

POP. 1. A colloquial expression for the retrieval of information from a push down stack, in order to place it in a particular memory location or register (as opposed to entering information which is pushed).
2. Point Of Presence, where a long distance carrier connects to a local exchange carrier in telephony.
3. *See* post office protocol.

Pop-up Program. *See* TSR.

port (I/O port). 1. A connection point with associated control circuitry that allows I/O devices to be connected to the internal bus of a microprocessor. Plug and its associated circuitry in a computer's hardware, used for sending data from computer to its peripherals or to other computers. Serial, parallel, and SCSI ports are commonly used ports. Generally the port can be switched to input or output and is often associated with a peripheral interface adapter. The PIA has connections compatible with the I/O port on one side and one or more interfaces to suit various peripherals on the other.
2. An internal address, which provides an interface between an application and TCP/IP's, transport layer.

portability. The ease with which an application can be moved from one hardware/software system environment to another. It refers to the ability to compile and run unaltered source programs on any platform and execution environment with identical behaviour. True portability is extremely difficult to achieve, and when one speaks or portability, it would be a more accurate measure if one could estimate the degree of compatibility, and the degree of change required when one program is ported (moved) from one environment (computer system) to another.

portable computer. A hand-held micro or personal computer; typically these devices can accommodate add-on printers or cassette units. In addition to being small and light, portable computers are designed to withstand physical abuse such as vibration, temperature, and humidity extremes.

POS. 1. Point Of Sale, used in banking applications; potentially related to OSI because of EDI.
2. Primary Operating System.

POSH. Permuted On Subject Headings; an index that lists all the subject headings of a document's title so that each heading appears, in turn, as the leading word followed by the remaining words.

position-independent code. The code which can execute properly wherever it is loaded in memory without modification or relinking; generally utilises addressing modes that form an effective memory address relative to central processor's program counter.

positive logic. A logic system in which all the Boolean variables and Boolean functions behave. Normally, the logic 1 is the more positive of the voltage levels in a binary circuit, and the logic 0 is the more negative.

positive modulation. In amplitude-modulated TV transmission, the increase in transmitted power when the brightness of the scene increases.

post office protocol. POP. A protocol to allow single user machines to download e-mail from a server.

post office server. The server on which the messages received from a sender's communications software are stored before being routed to the recipient's mail server.

post sending delay. A time interval that occurs between the finish of dialling on a telephone and the reception of a return signal, which could be a ringing tone or a busy tone.

POST. Power-On Self-Test; test of internal circuitry, memory, and installed hardware that a computer does to itself when turned on.

post-amble. A sequence of bits recorded at the end of each block on a magnetic medium, for synchronisation when reading backward.

post-mortem dump. PMD. The transfer of the contents of the computer memory instantaneously to a peripheral unit, performed at the end of a machine run. It is used to provide information for locating, diagnosing, and correcting errors.

post-mortem. 1. An analysis undertaken of an event or operation after the completion of that event or operation.

2. In a computer system, a check routine that provides information concerning the contents of all or a particular section of storage after a problem has ceased to exist. It assists in locating a program error or machine malfunction.

post-script. A language designed for describing text and graphics, usually built into high-end output devices such as laser printers and typesetters. Display postscript is the use of postscript for the computer's own display (on a monitor).

potting. Sealing of electronic components under a plastic cover to protect from moisture.

power fail recovery. PFR. A system containing automatic switching and charging circuits, designed to protect computer systems by detecting a drop in input voltage, which signals an imminent power failure. This provides several tens of ms during which all the memory locations can be maintained by a battery backed-up memory, or preserved in non-volatile memory and then automatically restarted when the power is restored. Also known as power fail restart.

power fail restart. *See* power fail recovery.

power supply unit. PSU. 1. A device, such as a generator or a transformer-rectifier filter arrangement, that produces the power needed to operate an electronic equipment. All electronic devices and circuits require some form of external power source. The voltages required are the range 1.5V-25kV or higher, and the currents can range from a few microamperes to several tens of amperes. Power supply units can be produced to cover all these requirements. Most electronic circuits run off the 240V, 50Hz supply via a power supply unit, the simplest form of which consists of a transformer that produces alternating current, which is in turn rectified by a rectifier circuits to give off direct current. The high ripple content of the rectifier's output is removed by a smoothing circuit to provide a stable supply. Also some form of stabilisation is provided as the direct current output has to remain substantially constant free from the effects of changes in load current, mains input and temperature.

2. A reserve of available power, *e.g.*, the power line, an installation of batteries, etc.

PowerPC Platform. PPCP. A standard hardware architecture developed by a consortium including Apple, IBM, and several other companies. PPCP machines use the PowerPC central processing unit (CPU) and a PCI bus. A number of operating systems, such as Copland, AIX, Windows NT, etc. should be able to run on PPCP machines. Also known as Common Hardware Reference Platform (CHRP).

PowerPC. A family of central processing unit (CPU) chips, produced by an industry group including Motorola, IBM, and Apple; used in IBM, Macintosh and other computers.

PowerPoint. One of the tools available in Microsoft Office 97; it can be used to complete an entire conference in a short time, and brings presentations to life with multimedia and sound, eliminating the boring slide-after-slide presentations. PowerPoint 97 has been enhanced and improved to make the daunting job of preparing presentations easier. It has very powerful formatting tools and multimedia capability, and has a liberty of colourful backgrounds, several groups of templates, and access to Office ClipGallery. Its Presentation Manager allows making presentations over network or review presentations with a remote group simultaneously.

PP. 1. Parallel Processor.

2. *See* peripheral processor.

PPCI. Presentation Protocol Control Information.

PPCP. *See* PowerPC Platform.

PPDU. Presentation Protocol Data Unit.

PPI. 1. Programmable Peripheral Interphase.

2. *See* plan position indicator.

PPL. Polymorphic Programming Language.

PPM. 1. Presentation Protocol Machine.

2. *See* pulse position modulation.

PPN. Private Packet Network, the packet network carrying data only for the operating organisation.

PPP. Point to Point Protocol, addition to the Internet protocol suite to help connect devices where dissimilar transport protocols exist; an implementation of TCP/IP protocol to be used over serial lines (modems); for example for the transfer of routing the range of actions a user can perform on the network. It more effective than the SLIP.

PPS. 1. Packets Per Second, a measurement of throughput.

2.*See* parallel processing system.

PPSU. *See* programmable power supply unit.

PPTM. Protocol Profile Testing Methodology, conformance testing to a profile.

PPTP. *See* Point to Point Tunnelling Protocol.

PPU. Peripheral Processing Unit.

PPX. Packet Protocol Extension.

PRA. Primary Rate Access, an ISDN access method that uses maximum data rates of 2.048 Mbit/s in Europe, or 1.544 Mbit/s in the US and Japan.

PRA. Primary Rate Access, in ISDN, a T1 link, several 64-kbaud channels (about 1.5 Mbaud) on one line.

PRADMD. PRivAte Directory Management Domain.

PRAM. Parameter RAM; a special part of RAM on the Macintosh computer, where some system parameters are stored. This RAM is battery backed, to save the information even when the machine is turned off. P-RAM can become corrupted, causing erratic system behaviour. A process called zapping the P-RAM can be used to clear the RAM area.

preamble. 1. A series of bits marking the beginning of a data frame transmission.

2. A series of bits recorded at the beginning of each block on a magnetic medium, for the purpose of synchronisation.

pre-coordinate index system. A system of indexing documents in which terms are combined as the index is being compiled to provide the entries.

predictive dialling. Automated dialling feature in which the systems predicts from pre-set algorithms when an agent/operator will become free and makes the call in advance.

pre-emphasis. In frequency modulation, introduction of a rising response characteristic. (Response rises as modulation frequency increases). Also called accentuation, pre-distortion, or pre-equalisation.

pre-emptive multitasking. A multitasking environment in which the OS prioritizes system and application processes and performs them in the most efficient order.

PREFUSE. Presentation REFUSE PDU, PDU indicating a negative response to a request to establish a presentation connection.

PReP. PowerPC Reference Platform, a system standard developed by IBM, to ensure compatibility between PowerPC computer systems. PReP has largely been superseded by PPCP (which integrates the PReP standard).

presentation layer. The sixth layer of the OSI (Open Systems Interconnection) model. The presentation layer ensures that the receiving station understands what was sent by the transmitting station. The communicating parties negotiate how the data will be sent (for instance, ASCII-coded characters instead of binary) and which end will do the translation, if necessary. This layer also allows the application to interpret the information to be transferred (such as code conversion, file format, and character sets).

presentation services layer. Each of the layers of IBM's Systems Network Architecture (SNA) has its own set of rules for communicating with its peer layer in the other mode. The layers communicate with each other by adding header information to user data. The presentation services layer (sixth layer) formats data for different presentation media and co-ordinates the sharing of resources.

preserved context index system. A system of indexing information in which various groups or strings of items are arranged with respect to their linguistic function. This permit a computer to use the information strings so that the user can find a term which is of primary interest.

press. An action performed using the mouse. It is performed by clicking the mouse button but not releasing it. The mouse button is held in pressed position for duration of an operation. Pressing is used in selecting items from menus, dragging items, and using scroll bars.

preview dialling. Automated dialling feature in which the system determines the next call to be made but allows the agent/operator as a supervisor to check and activate the call.

PRI. Primary Rate Interface, ISDN's carrier or large user-interface comprising 30BD channels in Europe, supporting around 1,920Mbit/s.

PRI. Primary Rate Interface.

PRID. PRotocol IDentifier, an identifier used to select the protocol to be used between peer entities on a specific connection of the layer below.

primary channel. A transmission channel having the highest signalling rate capability of all the channels sharing a common interface.

primary control program. A particular sequence of instructions that prescribe the series of steps to be taken by a computer system, the system having been designed to perform one task or job at a time.

primary domain controller. A LAN Manager term for the server at whom the master copy of a domain's user accounts database is maintained. The primary domain controller also validates logon requests.

primary frequency standard. An equipment for generating precise frequencies. The heart of device is usually a highly stable 50 or 100 kHz crystal oscillator, which can be referred to a time standard and periodically corrected. A string of multivibrators, together with harmonic amplifiers and buffers, subdivide basic frequency to provide a variety of precise lower frequencies. These low frequencies, in company with the harmonics of 100 kHz oscillator, provide highly accurate frequency-spectrum checkpoints.

primary name server. While implementing DNS on the network, one needs to choose at least one server to be responsible for maintaining its domain. This is referred to as its primary name server, and it gets all the information about the zones it is responsible for from local files. Any changes made to the domain are made on this server.

Primary Rate Access. *See* PRA.

Primary Rate Interface. *See* PRI.

print contrast signal. A value of a measured difference between the contrast of a character that ha been printed and the contrast of a character that has been printed and the contrast of the paper on which that character appears.

print definition language. PDL. A language used by a computer to define printer characteristics including lines, columns, page and overflow print conditions.

print queue. A list of files that have been sent to a printer; the list indicates the file currently printing and those waiting to be printed.

print server. 1. A computer and/or software to provide users or network with access to a central printer. The printer server acts as a buffer, holding the information to be printed out in memory until the printer is free. It is possible to program the printer server to print jobs in the order they arrive or to give priority to particular users who, in effect, jump the queue. The advantages of a printer server include maximum exploitation of expensive resources like laser printers and not having to retry if the printer is initially busy.

2. A device and/or program that manages shared printers.

printed circuit board power supply. PCB PS. A power supply unit mounted on a single printed circuit board or card.

printed circuit board. PCB. A circuit or part of a circuit formed on an insulating board or card, in which all the interconnecting wires have been replaced by conductive strips the conducting interconnecting paths that have been printed or etched. Printed circuit boards may be single-sided, double-sided or multilayer for high-density applications. Printed circuit boards are fabricated by first drawing an etching pattern. The pattern is then photographed and reproduced on clear plastic. The plastic is placed over a copper-coated glass epoxy or phenolic board, and the assembly undergoes a photochemical process. This can be done on one side of the board only. If the circuit is too complicated to be drawn on a single plane surface without crossing foil runs, the etching is done on both side of the board.

printer driver. A program that controls printing and sets options such as print quality and paper size for a particular printer. For example, in LAN Manager, each printer queue has a single printer driver associated with it.

printer fonts. Fonts that are stored in printer's memory or soft fonts that are sent to your printer before a document is printed. Because the font works only with the printer, either the operating system (or environment) must approximate the font on-screen or separate screen versions must be installed.

print preview. A feature that allows the user to dispaly the document in reduced view so that the full document page or facing pages can be seen on the screen at a time; used to view page formatting prior to printing.

printroller. A device, which prints out, usually on a tape, the record of all faults detected by the routiner.

priority interrupt control. PIC. A special chip in a microcomputer that manages several, normally eight, external attention signals sent from a input/output device or chip to the microprocessor unit to obtain service.

privacy enhanced mail. PEM. The e-mail that provides confidentiality, authentication, and message integrity employing various encryption methods.

privacy protection. The implementation of appropriate administrative, technical, and physical safeguards to ensure the security and confidentiality of data records, and to protect both security and confidentiality against any threat or hazard that could result in substantial embarrassment, harm, inconvenience, or unfairness to any individual about whom such information is maintained.

private automatic exchange. PAX. A dialled telephone exchange that provides a private service within an organisation, but does not allow calls to be transmitted to or from the public telephone network.

private branch exchange. PBX. A private telephone exchange located on subscriber's premises that has access to public telephone network. The term can be applied to automatic or manual exchanges, although in India an automatic exchange is referred to as PABX and manual exchange is referred to as PMBX.

private exchange. A telephone exchange that serves a particular organisation and has no means of connection with the public telephone network.

private line. A dedicated voice or data circuit usually leased from a Common Carrier. Also known as dedicated line.

Private Line. A trademark of Motorola; the term is commonly used to describe a radio telephone tone-squelch system.

private manual branch exchange. PMBX. A private telephone exchange located in subscriber's premises, operated manually and providing access to the public telephone network.

private wire. A specific channel along with the necessary equipment that is intended for the exclusive use of a particular subscriber. Application of such a line can include a telephone link, a facsimile or telecommunications link.

privilege level. For user-level security, one of three settings -user, admin or guest is assigned for each user account. The privilege level defines interfaces, known as Recommendation X.25. Hence packet switched networks are often referred to as X.25. In some cases, X.25 is being superseded by frame relay and eventually by ATM.

probe. A device intended for picking off a signal from a specific point for test purposes. The probe normally does not disturb the operation of the circuit. Probes are employed to measure direct-current voltages; and with ohmmeters to determine the resistance between two points in a circuit.

problem determination aid. PDA. A device or routine that assists the procedure which is to be adhered to in order to determine cause of an error.

problem orientated language. POL. A computer language designed for the solutions of a given class of problems. Although elaborate it should be easily understood and usually allows the solution to a problem to be expressed in the same terms as the problem.

process control interface. A device manufactured in the form of a circuit on a board, it can provide computer with an interface to a number of electromechanical devices such as relays, switches, motors, contractors, thermostats and various other devices.

processor status word. PSW. A register held in a central processor unit containing the status of the most recent instruction execution result. It can record error and exception conditions that are able to be dealt with by the operating system.

processor-controller. With reference to computer systems, a processor-controller can be used for direct control, data analysis, and supervisory control or editing.

producer. An asynchronous procedure that provides data to be used by other asynchronous procedures.

product administration and contract control. PACC. A method of control employed by a data management system in business environment.

product detector. Single-sideband continuous-wave and frequency-shift-keyed signals require a special form of detector for reception. Such a detector must supply an unmodulated local signal, and must provide for some means of mixing this signal with the incoming signal. This type of detector is called product detector.

production run tape. PRT. A tape, containing a verified and checked schedule for a production run, and able to run on a variety of computers.

profile. A set of parameters defining the way in which a device performs; in LAN world, a profile is often used by one or more workstations to determine the connection they will have with other devices. Profiles work like batch files, executing a number of commands to save a user time and effort.

program address counter. A sequential counter that is able to keep track of the location of the next instruction to be executed from a program memory.

program check interruption. PCI. The interruption caused by unusual conditions experienced in a computer program, this interruption is usually due to an incorrect operand.

program control flow. The order in which the program statements are executed. Programs rarely execute a single sequence of commands from beginning to end; instead, program control flows through loops and branching structures.

program counter. A processor register that is automatically advanced, usually by 2, every time the processor retrieves an instruction. This information is then used in connection with operating modes.

program evaluation & review technique. PERT. Software that provides a method of analysis and reporting for overall project administrators. Areas that impose the greatest time restriction for completion of a project as well as those with excess time for completion can be highlighted.

program file. On an IBM or compatible computer, an executable file that starts an application or program. A program file has .EXE, .PIF, .COM, or .BAT filename extension.

program generation system. PGS. Allowing the user to select a particular area of memory and output it in a particular format, this system will then load programs into memory. It can load self-produced programs and others produced elsewhere.

program information file. *See* PIF.

program reference table. A particular kind of memory-storage area, which is used for storing the operands, array references, file references and the references to segments of a computer program. It allows programs to be independent of the memory location actually occupied by part of the program and data.

program status word. A sector of main memory storage that is used as a computer system status indicator in relationship to a specific program.

program storage unit. A chip that principally provides for the storage of programmed instructions and various non-volatile data constants of a program. It can be interfaced directly with a central processor unit without the need of buffer circuits.

program test system. Capable of automatically verifying and checking programs, this specific system is able to assist in the organisation of a production run by providing diagnostic information.

program. 1. A set of data bits, comprising a unit of information and/or instructions to perform a specific task. In computers, a program tells the device what to do. One of the program called assembler is used to derive the mechanical language of the computer from the assembly language. Another program, called the compiler, converts higher-order language to mechanical language. Most of the programs are application programs, which are designed to help users perform specific tasks.
2. A radio or television broadcast, intended for reception by the public and conveying a message.

programmable array logic. PAL. Programmable equipment used to provide the discrete logic required to link large scale integration circuit packages and to tie a total system together.

programmable input/output chip. PIOC. An input/output chip, in most cases an 8-binary digit interface chip that multiplexes a connection to a data bus, which is capable of transferring data to and from the central processor unit and peripheral devices, into two or more ports.

programmable interface unit. PIU. A programmable large scale integration device used to eliminate the hardwire logic often needed for communication interfaces, between processors and various other system components.

programmable interval timer. PIT. A chip that has a separate timing clock and a number of special memory storage locations. These are used independently of the microprocessor unit to count time for real-time application. They can store the time-elapsed or generated signals, at the completion of a period.

programmable logic array. PLA. An orderly arrangement of logical AND functions and logical OR functions, which are constructed using metal-oxide semiconductor or bipolar circuits. They are used as alternatives to random-access memories, which use standard logic networks programmed to perform a specific function.

programmable multiplex. PMUX. A device, which gives flexibility of routing of outputs; once programmed for a particular pattern, it cannot be changed.

programmable peripheral interface adaptor. PPIA. A peripheral interface adaptor that can provide control over connection of parallel orientated peripherals to various microprocessors.

programmable power supply unit. PPSU. A particular type of laboratory power supply unit that has an internal memory which can be programmed with the value of voltages, each with an associated current-limit and dwell time. A typical unit has an IEEE-488 interface and a memory that once loaded can be stepped through, run continuously, or run in a single slot mode. Such features make programmable power supply unit devices ideal for use with automatic test equipment.

programmable read-only memory. PROM. Memory which can be programmed after manufacture by external equipment; the fusible link connecting a memory cell can be disconnected to produce a logic 0 instead of 1. It refers to any memory device that is not recorded during manufacture, but requires some form of physical operation to be programmed. Special processes can allow some programmable read-only memories to be erased and reprogrammed. They are used to form read-mostly memories (RMM) of which the most common type is floating-gate programmable read-only memory, which employs the metal-oxide semiconductor as its basic memory cell.

programmable uni-junction transistor. PUT. A form of uni-junction transistor with variable triggering voltage. The triggering voltage is set by means of an external voltage divider.

programmed data processor. PDP. A group of computers, from large mainframes to minicomputers.

programmed interrupt. PI. A software technique often used as a fast method of transferring control to an error routine, a programmed interrupt is caused deliberately by a computer program (as opposed to one caused by an external event).

programmed logic for automatic teaching operations. A computer language and also a system of computer-aided instruction.

programmed logic. In general, programmable devices that are more complicated (logical) than read-only memories, including programmed logic arrays, programmed gate arrays, programmed-array logic, and uncommitted logic arrays.

programming language for microprocessor. PL/M. A high-level programming language that permits users to employ a notation with which they are already familiar; developed by Integrated Electronics, for use on its microcomputer systems, from a dialect of programming language one (PL/1).

programming languages. The means of of sending instructions to a computer. To be sure that the computer understands these instructions, programmers use defined languages to communicate with the computer. Hundreds of the programming languages have been developed. These languages fall in to any of the following categories:

Machine languages

Assembly languages
Higher-level languages.

The only language that a computer understands is its machine language.

project network techniques. PNT. A group of techniques that considers the logical inter-relationship of all project activities. It is used for the description, analysis, planning and control of projects. The group includes techniques concerned with time, resources, costs and other uncertain factors.

PROLOG. PROgramming in LOGic; a high-level non-procedural programming language developed in the early 1970s, for use in artificial intelligence research and applications such as expert systems. LISP, a similar language developed in the 1960s, rivals Prolog, but the decision by Japanese fifth-generation computer designers to work with Prolog has given Prolog a temporary lead in the industry.

PROM. *See* programmable read-only memory.

prompt. A short message sent from a process to a user, indicating that the process expects the user to present fresh data. The prompt frequently has some mnemonic content indicating the type of data expected.

proportional font. The font in which different characters have varying widths; e.g., Helvetica, Times Roman, Times New Roman.

prospero. A distributed file system, which provides user with the ability to create multiple views of a single collection of files distributed across the Internet.

protected mode. An IBM or compatible computer's operating mode that is capable of addressing extended memory directly; keeps applications in memory from addressing the same memory location.

protocol converter. A communications control unit, which can convert information from one coding system to one recognised by the computer or communications device. For example, a protocol converter, if necessary, can convert code from ASCII to EBCDIC format so that it can be processed.

protocol independent routing. A proprietary routing method designed for IBM networks developed by General DataCom, improving on Source Routing. Router checks all LAN packets for their source address contained in each frame. Adopting the proprietary DSPF (Discover Shortest Path First) router-to-router protocol, a PIR router finds the best path between pairs of LANs, rather than simply between pairs of routers as OSPF (Open Shortest Path First). Because a router can have several LANs connected to it, OSPF does not necessarily produce the best result, whereas PIR load-balances across each available LAN link for improved throughput and performance. From a Token Ring LAN, PIR looks like a Source Routing bridge; in an Ethernet environment, PIR appears as a transparent bridge.

protocol stack. A layered set of protocols that work together to provide a set of network functions. Computers must have the same protocol stacks in order to communicate with each other. Most Internet networks use TCP/IP stack.

protocol system. A system of standards and procedures, which enables computers to communicate over network.

protocol tunnelling. *See* encapsulation.

protocol. A formal description of message formats and set of rules governing the information flow within a communications infrastructure, often known as data link control. Protocols control format, timing, error essential correction and running order. They are essential for a device to be able to interpret incoming information. Suites of protocols are often used in networks, with each protocol responsible for one part of a communications function.

proxy agent. A network management agent that sits in front of a device attached to a network that needs to be managed, but has no intrinsic network management capabilities. The proxy agent provides network management "by proxy" for that device.

PRT. *See* production run tape.

PRU. Physical Record Unit.

PS. 1. Parallel to Serial.
2. Programming System.

ps. Symbol for pico-second; one millionth of a second, *i.e.*, 10^{-12} second.

PSAM. Partitioned Sequence Access Method.

PSAP. Presentation Service Access Point, normally a numeric address that identifies the Presentation Layer.

PSD. Protection Switching Duration, used in performance management in Network Management.

PSDN. Packet-Switched Data Network; carries packet messaging.

PSDU. Presentation Service Data Unit.

PSE. Packet Switching Exchange.

pseudo-code. An informal, English-like language used instead of flowcharting when designing a computer program; used when programmers are working out of the logic of a program. This is sometimes known as fake code.

pseudo-random number sequence. A sequence of numbers that has been determined by some defined arithmetic process but is effectively a random number sequence for the purpose for which it is required.

PSIC. Process Signal Interface Controller.

PSLI. Packet Switch Level Interface.

PSN. 1. Private Switching Network, not necessarily packet-switching.
2. Packet-Switched Network, the data network that employs packet-switching technology.
3. Packet-Switching Node, a node in MILNET.

PSN. Packet Switching Node, the name of an ArpNET packet switch; PSNs were formerly called IMPS.

PSPDN. Packet-Switching Public Data Network.

PSTN. Public Switched Telephone Network.

PSU. 1. Packet Switching Unit.
2. *See* power supply unit.

PSW. 1. Program Status Word.
2. *See* processor status word.

PT. 1. Please Token Session PDU.
2. Pass Through, a prefix used in system management to indicate that the service is mapped directly onto the services of CMIS.

PTB. Physical transaction Block.

PTC. Public Telephone Companies.

PTI. Program Transfer Interface.

PTL. Process and Test Language.

PTM. *See* pulse time modulation.

PTP. Point-To-Point, connection logically made from source to destination, as opposed to store and forward.

PTS. Profile Test Specification, a conformance test suite geared toward a profile rather than the base standard.

PTT. Postal, Telephone, and Telegraph administration, refers to the government agency responsible for these services in a country.

PTTXAU. Public TeleTeX Access Unit, an access unit enabling a telemetric terminal user to send messages to an IPM service user within X.400 system.

PTXAU. Public TeleX Access Unit, provides an interface for telex users not registered in an IPM service to send messages to and receive them from IMP users.

PU. 1. Peripheral Unit.
2. Processing Unit.

Public Data Network. *See* PDN.

public domain software. Software available for use free of charges because it is not protected under copyright. It differs from shareware, which makes available protected software on a trial basis, on the condition that if the program is adopted, user will forward payment to the author.

public switched network. A switching system made available by a common carrier for circuit switching many subscribers.

PUC. Program Under Control.

PUL. Program Update Library.

Pulse Code Modulation. *See* PCM.

pulse position modulation. Modulation in which information is conveyed by varying the time of occurrence of pulses in relation to a reference without varying their length.

pulse width. The temporal duration or spatial length of a pulse, measured in time or distance units.

punch-down block. A term describing the connector arrangements for distributing and connecting UTP/STP wiring inside a building. Typically, found in telephone wiring closets.

punched-card system. A system for encoding information onto cards in the form of holes. The pattern of positions punched

PUP. Parc Universal Packet; in Internet system developed by Xerox Corporation, PUP is the fundamental unit of transfer, just as the IP datagram in a TCP/IP Internet.

pure code. In programming, a code that is never modified in execution.

pure notation. A notation that is exclusively alphabetical or exclusively numeric.

pure tone. In acoustics, a single-frequency sound without overtones.

purging. The removal of obsolete data by erasure, by overwriting of storage or by resetting registers.

PUSH. An instruction that is used to deposit a word on the top of a stack or push-down list (as opposed to POP).

push-down list. A list that is constructed and maintained so that the next data element to be retrieved is the most recently stored. It may be noted that This method is characterised as 'last in, first out' (LIFO).

push-down storage. A storage device in which data are ordered in such a way that the next data element to be retrieved is the most recently stored. It may be noted that it is characterised as 'last in, first out' (LIFO).

push-up storage. A storage device in which data are ordered in such a way that next data element to be retrieved is the one stored first. It may be noted that this method is characterised as 'first in, first out' (FIFO).

PUT. *See* programmable uni-junction transistor.

PV. 1. Path Verification.
2. Parameter Value, value associated with a parameter field in the given instance.

PVC. Permanent Virtual Circuit, a fixed virtual circuit between the two users, the public data network equivalent of a leased line; a virtual circuit which is not disconnected when not in use. No call set-up or clearing procedures is needed.

PVI. Programmable Video Interface.

PVR. Process Variable record.

PVT. Permanent Virtual Terminal, a VT, which is created permanently and not, simply deleted when the application no longer requires.

PW. Pulse Width.

PX. Private eXchange.

PZT. PieZoelectric Transducer.

Q

Q. 1. A comparison made between two or more units of quantitative data to discover if they are equal or unequal.
2. A register used as an accumulator extension, which is necessary for efficient multiple-divide computer programming.
3. Symbol for queue, arranged in sequence, a collection of items that has two ends which are the head and the tail. New items are added to the tail. Items can be removed from either the head or the tail.
4. An address, or source location in internal storage in some forms of computer equipment from which data can be transferred.

Q.nnn. The CCITT Q. Series Recommendations; deal with signaling within public telephone systems.

Q adjustment. Separate null adjustment for Q value of a component being tested in an impedance bridge having separate resistive and reactive balance.

QA. *See* quality assurance.

QADS. Quality Assurance Data System.

QAM. *See* quadrature amplitude modulation.

Q-axis. Chrominance axis that corresponds to the coarse chrominance primary in the National Television System Committee of colour television transmission system. Also known as narrow-band axis.

Q-band. Q-band microwave frequencies occur between 36-46 GHz and form part of a larger continuous range of frequencies covering 0.225-100 GHz which are usually subdivided into bands designated by letters. Q-band frequencies have wavelengths between 0.834-0.652 cm.

Q-bit. In X.25 networks, bit 8 in an octet of packet header; used to indicate if a packet contains control information. Also known as qualifier bit.

Q-factor. A measure of the ratio of energy stored in a system, circuit, component or device in comparison to the energy dissipated. The energy dissipation could be due to resistance, electromagnetic radiation or other factors.

QC. *See* quality control.

QCB. *See* queue control block.

QED. *See* quick text editor.

QIC. Quarter-Inch Cartridge Drive Standards; an international trade association incorporated in November 1987 to encourage and promote the widespread use of quarter-inch data cartridge tape drives and media, as used for computer data backup, secondary storage, and software distribution. The primary purpose of QIC is to provide a forum for technical discussions that lead to the generation of industry standards, providing compatibility among various manufacturers' tape cartridges, drives, and systems.

A quarter-inch cartridge system consists of a drive unit and one or more removable, portable tape cartridges which contain integral tape motion and guidance mechanisms, and are loaded with up to 305 metres of quarter-inch magnetic-coated tape. Single-capstan drive units, which contain magnetic read/write heads, electronics for read/write, motion control, and system interface functions, are available in 2.5-inch, 5.35-inch or 8-inch form factors for installation within computer system hardware or as stand-alone, plug-compatible units. Data are recorded on up to 32 tracks along the tape, usually in a serial fashion. Data storage capacities, which earlier ranged from 10 megabytes to 150 megabytes, increased to 1 gigabyte in 1990. The industry has now extended quarter-inch cartridge tape technology to achieve capacities in excess of 2.7 gigabytes. Quarter-inch Cartridge Drive Standards are supported by system manufacturers such as Apple, AT&T, Compaq, Data General, Hewlett-Packard, IBM, ICL, NCR, NEC, and Olivetti.

QL. Query Language.

QLLC. Qualified Logical Link Control, the routines to provide Synchronous Data Link Control.

Q-matching section. A linear, *r-f* impedance-matching transformer consisting of two parallel lengths of metal tubing used to match a feeder line to an antenna. The length and spacing of the tubes are such that the surge impedance of the matching section is the geometric mean of the feeder-line surge impedance and the radiation resistance of the radiator.

Q-modulation. Amplitude modulation obtained by varying effective Q of an *r-f* tank in step with a modulating component.

QOS. Quality of Service, refers to certain characteristics, such as throughput, error rate, etc., of a given connection within a protocol.

Q-phase. A colour-TV carrier signal which is 147 degrees out of phase with the colour sub-carrier.

QPSK. Quadrature Phase Shift Keying, a type of carrier modulation where the fourth part of each carrier cycle is phase shifted to indicate a binary 1 or 0 similar to QAM.

QRP. One of the ham radio signals meaning 'reduce power', used in code communications. The main advantage of QRP is that it allows the use of battery power.

QRT. Queue Run Time.

QSAM. *See* queued sequential access method.

Q signal. 1. In colour television, the quardature component of chrominance signal, equal to + 0.48 (R-Y) and to + 0.41 (B-Y), where *B* is blue camera signal, *R* red camera signal, and *Y* luminance signal.

2. The signal that represents the chrominance information along the green-magenta axis in colour television transmission system.

3. A set of abbreviated signals used in radiotelegraphy. Each Q signal consists of letter Q, followed by two more letters. Although Q signals were originally designed for radiotelegraph use, many radioteletype and radiotelephone operators also use them.

QSL. Queue Search Limit.

QSPX. Queued Synchronous Packet eXchange, a protocol used in conjunction with the 802.6 MAN standard, developed by QPSX Communications of Western Australia.

Q-switch. A device that prevents pulsed laser emission being achieved until a certain required energy level is reached in the lasing material. It provides shorter and more intense pulses at the high repetition rate than could be reached by pulsing the lasing material. In a pulsed laser, a Q-switch increases peak power by shortening pulse duration.

Q-switching. A laser-switching action obtainable with Kerr cells or rotating reflecting prisms, which consists of holding the Q of the laser cavity to a low value during an ion-population build-up and then abruptly switching the Q to a higher value.

QTAM. *See* queued telecommunications access method.

quad-in-line-package. QUIP. Having two rows of pins along each longitudinal edge of its package, rather than one row as in a dual-line package, this 64-lead integrated circuit package was developed jointly by Integrated Electronics (INTEL) and 3M.

quadrature amplitude modulation. QAM. A high-speed modulator/demodulator modulation technique used in digital transmission where two sinusoidal carrier waves having a phase difference of 90° between them are amplitude modulated by independent signals and resulting components are summed to produce output signals; used in colour television transmission.

quadriphonic. Pertaining to four-channel sound system; two sets of two interrelated channels are used to obtain a panoramic sound reproduction effect.

quadruple diversity. The simultaneous combining of, or selection from, four independently fading signals and their detection, using space, frequency, angle, time or polarization characteristics or combinations thereof.

qualification. A mechanism for referencing a component of a language object by means of a reference to the object and an identifier declared for the component. Examples: Used for referencing record components (B OF A in COBOL), members of a library, language objects in a module.

qualifier bit. *See* Q bit.

quality assurance. QA. Methods employed in a systematic manner to provide the necessary confidence that an item itself has been tested or is constructed of components, which have been tested, and will perform satisfactorily.

quality control. QC. Workmanship, processes and materials that have been monitored by an organised and formal process to produce consistent and uniform products. The process can involve the keeping of evaluation records, batch logs, and error summary reports.

quantization noise. The effective continuous noise power, the addition of which to a continuous signal has the same effect as amplitude quantization to which the signal is subjected. The effect of time quantization may also be described by the addition of noise, but in a more complex way.

quantization. The process of constructing a discrete representation of a quantity that is usually regarded as continuous. A process by which the continuous range of values of a signal is divided into non-overlapping, but not necessarily equal, subranges, and a discrete value of the output uniquely assigned to each sub-range. Whenever the signal value falls within a given sub-range, the output has the corresponding discrete value. For example, the measurement of the amplitude of a signal at discrete intervals of time, when the signal at discrete intervals of time, when the signal occurs over continuous time, is called time quantization, or sampling; the measurement of the brightness of picture elements (pixels) in space-continuous picture is called space quantization, or pixelization. The term quantization without the predication of time or space usually refers to the quantization of amplitude; the same applies to digitisation, which is nearly synonymous with quantization.

Quark XPress. A professional page layout program originally developed for Apple Macintosh environment (competing with Aldus PageMaker) that provides word processing functions with advanced typographic features plus colour separations, graphics, scaling, and cropping.

quartet signalling. Part of 100BaseVG-AnyLAN proposed standard involving transmission over all four-wire pairs simultaneously in voice-grade UTP cable, expanding its capacity to 100Mbit/s.

Quattro Pro. The three-dimensional spreadsheet program designed by Borland International for use on personal computers using DOS.

quenching action. Typical operation of a super-regenerative circuit in which regeneration is increased to nearly the point of oscillation and then reduced; this action is repeated at a supersonic frequency and results in very high sensitivity.

query key. In computers and communications, a key that will when pressed, cause data in certain previously specified storage locations to be displayed on a screen.

query language. A language, which is used to interrogate a system, such as a language that enables a user to interact directly with database-management system and to retrieve or modify stored data.

query language. QL. A very-high-level programming language introduced to assist programmers to access data from a computer. It is considered the highest level language because it uses simple English commands, which resemble a conversation. Database management systems (DBMS) each have their own query language to enable users to quickly search through a set of information in order to access particular data, which may be grouped in a variety of ways. For example, in a financial system, one query might ask for a particular customer's investment status, while another query might list all customers, who meet a certain set of criteria (such as those who purchased more than a certain number of shares of a particular stock on a specific day).

queue control block. QCB. A memory storage location that holds information in a condensed form, which is used to regulate the sequence in which entries in a list waiting for service are processed.

queue. 1. A list of string of items in which items that are to be processed are taken only from ends, or from the top or bottom.

2. A collection of items that are arranged in sequence.

3. A list of files that have been sent to a device such as a printer. The list indicates the file currently being acted on by the device (printed) and those waiting to be acted up on (printed).

queued access method. QAM. A term applied to any data access method that is able to synchronise the data transfer between the user program and input/output devices and reduce input/output delays.

queued sequential access method. QSAM. A type of the basic sequential access method, which uses blocks formed from queus of input data which uses blocks formed from queues of input data which are waiting for processing, or output data blocks which have been processed and are waiting for transfer to output devices or other auxiliary storage.

queued telecommunications access method. QTAM. A method of transferring data between main computer storage and remote terminals. It uses an application program with specific macro instruction that requests the transfer of data, which is performed by a message control program that also synchronises the transfer, which in turn eliminates delays for input/output operations. The technique is employed for data collection, message switching and other teleprocessing uses. It provides the capabilities of basic telecommunications access method as well as the ability of queued messages on direct-access storage devices.

quick text editor. QED. A high-speed system that provides the user with a flexible source text generation system. Source statements are entered which can be output, statements added, or groups of statements altered.

quick-connect. Terminal block into which insulated wires can be pushed. The insulation is cut as the wires are pushed in, and a reliable low-resistance contact is established.

QUICKTRAN. Short form of QUICK forTRAN, a development of the formula translation (FORTRAN) programming language designed primarily for running from remote terminal.

quintet. A byte that is composed of five binary digits, such as 10011.

QUIP. *See* quad-in-line-package.

QUIPU. An X.500 product running on ISODE.

quit command. In data processing and communications, a command to the system to leave the current mode or status and return to another, usually higher, command level or mode.

quite automatic gain control. QAGC. A delayed automatic gain control combined with a signal suppresser in such a way that the output of a receiver is suppressed for inputs too weak to operate the automatic gain control.

QWERTY. A standard English-language computer terminal keyboard or typewriter keyboard on which the keys are arranged such that the top row below the numerals begins with the letters Q-W-E-R-T-Y, reading left to right. Such keyboards are mainly used in the UK, US and many other English-speaking countries.

QWERTZ. A German-language computer or typewriter keyboard with the keys arranged in such a manner, so that the top row below the numerals begins with the letters Q-W-E-R-T-Z, reading left to right. It normally contains some additional letters of the German language, as well as instructional keys with notations in German.

R

R.nn. The CCITT R. Series Recommendations deal with methods of telegraphy, transmission standards, and quality testing, for example, VFT, AMVFT, FMVFT, TDM.

R/W. Read/Write. The function of the small electromagnetic heads, which read, record (write) or erases the polarised areas on a magnetic surface usually tape.

RA. 1. Record Address.
2. Relocation Address.

RA0. Rate Adapter type 0, for connecting asynchronous bit streams to ISDN B channels.

RA1. Rate Adapter type 1, for connecting low-speed synchronous bit streams to ISDN B channels.

RA2. Rate Adapter type 2, for connecting medium-speed synchronous bit streams to ISDN B channels.

RAA. Random Access Array.

RAAR. RAM Address Register.

RACE. *See* random-access computer equipment.

raceway. A linear enclosure or channel used to hold and protect wires, cables, buses, and power and communication lines.

RACF. Resource Access Control facility.

rack-and-panel construction. A method of building electronic equipment on a chassis attached horizontally or vertically to a vertical panel. After completion of a unit, the panel is fastened in place on a rack. Several such panels fill the rack.

radio beam. A radiation pattern from a directional antenna such that the energy of the transmitted electromagnetic wave is confined to a small angle in at least one dimension.

radio communication. The use of electromagnetic waves in free space for communication purposes, *i.e.*, use of radio waves that are not guided between transmitting and receiving antennas by physical paths, such as wires, waveguides, or optical fibres.

radio control. The control of a mechanism by electromagnetic waves, such as the control of the movement of an aircraft, vehicle or missile, from a radio station on the ground or in another mobile unit.

radio fadeout. The situation in which incoming radio signals fade away because a sudden and unusual ionisation change in the ionosphere has increased the absorption of radio waves which would normally have been reflected by the ionosphere.

radio frequency. RF. 1. The frequencies of the electromagnetic spectrum normally associated with radio wave propagation. Sometimes defined as

transmission at any frequency at which coherent electromagnetic energy radiation is possible, usually above 150 kHz.
2. A frequency of electromagnetic radiation or alternating circuit within the range of 3 kHz to 300 GHz. By international agreement radio frequencies occupy bands numbered between 5-11 (inclusive) and have wavelengths 100-1 mm. Each band extends from 0.3×10^n Hz to 3×10^n Hz where n is the specific band number.

radio horizon range. The distance at which a direct radio wave can reach a receiving antenna of given height from a transmitting antenna of given height.

radio link. The accessible link between two points by a radio, for the purpose of communication.

radio navigation system. A computerised avionics system for small military and commercial aircraft designed to work with conventional cockpit interments. It enables a pilot to fly along any course without manual calculations or reference to maps and is able to provide dead reckoning navigation when temporarily outside the range of a radio beacon.

radio net. An organisation of radio stations broadcasting common programme over different frequencies at different locations, not necessarily simultaneously.

radio pager. A pocketsize radio receiver capable of alerting its possessor that there is a phone call, either from a displayed phone number or to a predesignated number.

radio range. A radio aid to air navigation that creates an infinite number of paths in space throughout a given sector or azimuth angle by various methods of transmission and reception of electromagnetic waves.

radio recognition. The radio determination of the character, individuality, or nature of a received radio signal and concluding the information concerning the transmitting station and its operators based on signal analysis.

radio telecontrol. Control of devices, equipment, components, mechanisms, and systems by radio waves sent to the items over greater distances than are involved in radio control.

radio telephone. A combined and complete radio receiver and transmitter required at one station for two-way communication.

radio teletypewriter. A teletypewriter that operates via radio circuits employing frequency-shift keying and also audio frequency-shift keying.

radio transmission control. The control and limitation that is imposed upon radio operation.

radio window. Radio frequencies, which are not reflected by the ionosphere and so cannot be used for long-range terrestrial radio communications links. The window ranges from approximately 10 MHz to 40 Ghz.

radio. A method of communicating over a distance by modulating electromagnetic waves by means of an intelligence-bearing signal and radiating these modulated waves by means of a transmitter and an antenna.

radio-frequency interference. RFI. 1. The distortion or impairment of a desired transmission or signal brought about by radio frequency disturbances such as atmospheric noise.
2. Undesired radio-frequency signals that compete with desired ones in amplifiers, receivers and instruments.

RADIR. *See* random-access document indexing and retrieval.

radix complement. A complement obtained by subtracting each digit of the given number from the number that is one less than the radix of that digit place, then adding one to the least significant digit of the result and executing any carries required; for example, 830 is the ten complement, *i.e.*, the radix complement of 170 in decimal numeration system using three digits.

radix complement. In fixed radix numeration system, a complement that can be derived from a given number by subtracting it from a specified power of the radix. Example: 830 is the radix complement of 170 in the decimal numeration system using three digits, the power of the radix being 1000. It may be noted that The radix complement may be obtained by first deriving the diminished radix complement, then adding one to the least significant digit of the result and executing any carries required.

radix numeration system. A position representation system in which the ratio of the weight of any one digit place to the weight of the next lower digit place is a positive integer. The permissible values of the character in any digit range from zero to one less than the radix of that digit place.

radix. In radix numeration system, the positive integer by which the weight of any digit place is multiplied to obtain the weight of digit place with next higher weight. Example: In the decimal numeration system the radix of each digit place is 10. It may be noted that the term 'base' is deprecated in this sense because of its mathematical use.

radome. A cover protecting an antenna, light source, or any radiation receiver from the environmental damage; designed to avoid signal distortion.

radux. A continuous-wave, low-frequency radio-navigation system; the position is determined by comparing the phase of two signals sent from different locations.

RAG. Registration and Advisory Group, term used by ISO.

ragged left. In typography and word processing, the positioning of text on a page so that all the text is aligned to the right margin, leaving a ragged left margin. Compare indent, justification, flush left and ragged right.

ragged right. In typography and word processing, the positioning of text on a page so that all the text is aligned to the left margin, leaving a ragged right margin. Compare indent, justification, flush left and ragged left.

RAI. Random Access and inquiry.

RALU. *See* register and arithmetic logic unit.

RAM cache. An area on random-access memory chip reserved for use when the central processing unit (CPU) is using the disk drives. RAM cache is used to improve the performance of a computer by temporarily acting as the hard disk because RAM can transfer data and program instructions to the CPU hundreds of times faster than a disk drive. RAM cache chip continues to carry data that is most frequently required by the CPU so that waiting time is minimised. This technique is also used when writing to a disk drive because RAM cache can accept data much faster than a disk drive.

RAM disk. A portion of RAM that is used as if it were a disk drive; RAM drives are much faster than hard disks because computer can read information faster from memory than from a hard disk. However, information on a RAM drive is lost when the computer is turn off or rebooted. Also known as virtual drive.

RAM. Random Access Memory; a direct-access memory device that is used where it is required to change the binary digit location during the routine operation of the memory. It is a mass storage device designed so that the location of stored data is independent of content and any location may be directly accessed without having to work through from the beginning. Large-capacity memories are formed as two-dimensional arrays of these cells. An individual cell is identified uniquely by row and column addresses, which are derived by decoding a user-supplied address word. The fast access to any storage location is provided by means of vertical and horizontal co-ordinates and information is written in or out using the same procedure. The term "Random Access" refers to the ability of a processor to immediately access any part of the memory.

Many people confuse RAM and hard disk. RAM is temporary storage while hard disk is semi-permanent storage. One way to understand the difference between the two is to relate RAM to short term memory and the hard disk to long term memory. Just as many memories are stored in your brain, lots of information is stored in a computer's hard drive. However, you can only actively think about and use a small portion of what you remember at any given time. This is similar to RAM. When a computer is using an application, it is loaded into RAM. Also known as random-access/read-write memory.

RAMIS. *See* random-access management information system.

RAM-resident. A program remaining in memory after it has returned control of the computer back to the operating system. RAM-resident programs either wait or operate in the background while applications are active. Also known as TSRs (Terminate and Stay Resident) in IBM and compatible computers.

random access memory. *See* RAM.

random access. 1. A type of memory access for which the access time to any item of information is independent of the address of that item and of the address of any previous item referred to.

2. In COBOL, an access mode in which specific logical records are obtained from a place in mass storage file in a non-sequential manner.

random bit-stream signalling. A communication method which makes use of bit-intermittent transmission of signals on a unit interval basis without regard to the presence or absence of a code or alphabet.

random file. Data records stored in a file without regard to the sequences of the key or control field.

random noise. Noise that consists of impulses that occur at random time; it consists of a large number of transient disturbances with a statistically random time distribution.

random number. A number selected from a known set of numbers in such a way that the probability of occurrence of each number in the set is predetermined.

random process. A process in which the output cannot be fully determined from knowledge of system variables.

random signal. A sequence of pulses such that each pulse does not have a fixed time relationship with any other pulse, and their individual occurrence time is unpredictable.

random-access computer equipment. RACE. Computer equipment in which information can be introduced and stored, where any location can be read from, or written into, in a random access method. It is used where the information to be obtained is unrelated to the location of previous information.

random-access discrete address. RADA. A particular location in a random access memory (RAM).

random-access disk. *See* rapid-access disk.

random-access document indexing and retrieval. RADIR. A system for creating an index of documents, in which access to data to be obtained is unrelated to the location of previously accessed information.

random-access management information system. RAMIS. A system providing information in response to user's requests in which the computer files store management data in a random-access memory (RAM).

random-access/read-write memory. *See* random-access memory.

rank. 1. A measure of relative position in an array, group, series or classification.

2. To arrange in ascending or descending order according to some predefined criterion.

rapid-access disk. A memory storage device often a magnetic disk that provides rapid access to a memory location, and retrieval of data, a procedure that is often synonymous with random access or direct access. It is contrasted with sequential access in that it does not depend upon the access of preceding data. Also known as random-access disk.

RAR. Return Address Register.

RARP. Reverse Address Resolution Protocol, the TCP/IP protocol a diskless machine uses at start-up to find its IP address. It performs the reverse function as ARP, and is used when the IP address is known but the physical address is not known. It is also used in conjunction with the BOOTP protocol and is used to boot diskless workstations.

RAS. 1. Rapid Access Storage.

2. *See* row address strobe.

RASTAC. Random Access STorage And Control.

raster font. *See* screen font

raster-mode graphic display. A technique for displaying computer generated images. For a black/white picture, the image is conceptually divided up in a matrix of dots. A frame store holds 0s, or 1s, in the memory locations corresponding to the locations of the dots. Display controller scans the frame store a line at a time, and switches the electron beam of a cathode ray tube on and off, during the scan. The presentation of graphical or pictorial images in the desired shape is built up by means of a succession of parallel movements of the pen of a plotter or the spot on a visual display unit, in a similar manner to television picture, *i.e.* without each line being traced as a continuous movement of pen or spot.

rate. A measure of the average number of bits of information in each character of a message.

rated output power. The power that s available at a specified output terminal of a device under specified conditions of operation.

RATFOR. RATional FORtran. A structured development of formula translator (FORTRAN) which is translated or compiled into standard FORTRAN) by a processor.

RAW. Read After Write.

RB. A command statement used in computers meaning Return to Bias. A mode of recording where the state of medium used for recording alters from a bias state to another state, and then returns to record a binary 1.

RBA. Relative Byte Address.

RBE. Remote Batch Entry.

RBS. Remote Batch System.

R channel. One of the eight compact disc sub-codes channels (P-W).

RC-6. Coaxial cable used primarily for CATV (cable television) for extended distance segments, 75W, per U.S. MIL-C-17-F.

RCB. Remote Control Block.

RCC. 1. Remote Communications Concentrator.

2. *See* remote centre compliance.

RCI. Remote Control Interface.

Rcp. A remote file transfer utility, which provides remote access to UNIX systems. It is not as versatile as FTP, but is still sometimes used for file transfer in the UNIX systems.

RCP. Recognition and Control Processor.

RCV. A command statement used in computers meaning receive; the process of obtaining a transmitted signal, as contrasted with sending or transmission.

RD. 1. Read Data.

2. Receive Data.

RDA. Remote Database Access is defined in ISO 9579; provides a standard means of accessing a database server from an intelligent workstation in a client/server model.

R-DAT. One of the proposed formats for digital audio tape recording. In this format, a helical scan similar to video tape recorders, is implemented to provide the required 20 megha bits per second data transfer rate.

RDB. Relational DataBase.

RDE. Remote Data Entry.

RDF. 1. Record Definition Field.

2. *See* repeater distribution frame.

RDL-SQL. Relational Database Language-Structured Query Language.

RDMBS. Relational database management system; a program in which several items of information may be joined together to form a new data file, even though each resides on a different database. For example, in a library-book tracking program, report can be generated to list all scientific books, and another to list all science members. The two databases can be joined to report on members who have overdue books.

RDN. Relative Distinguished Name, a name that uniquely identifies a directory entry as distinct from all other entries with the same immediate superior entry.

RDOS. An expression for Real-time Disk Operating System. A disk operating system that operates in real time.

RDP. Reliable Data Protocol, a connection-oriented transport protocol on the Internet.

RDT. 1. Resource Definition Table.

2. Referenced Data Transfer.

RDY. The control signal meaning ready, used in some systems, for slow memory to indicate if data is valid.

RE. 1. Routing Element, in X.400, composed of member MTAs or MDs, which share a consistent strategy for routing messages.

2. Reference Equivalent, OSI.

read access. In computer security, the permission to read information.

read around ratio. The number of times a specified spot, digit, or location in electrostatic storage may be consulted before a spillover of electrons, causes loss of data stored in surrounding spots. The surrounding data must be restored before the deterioration results in any loss of data.

read error. In peripherals, an error in reading of data from storage medium.

read head. A magnetic head used to read data or signals from a magnetic recording medium.

read only. Data access that allows the data to be examined or read, but does not permit any modifications to be made.

READ. An expression for Real-time Electronic Access and Display; acquisition of information from a storage device or a peripheral unit, which is produced on a visual display unit. The whole operation taking place in real time.

reader only. The function of a paper-tape reader, which is a device that senses and translates the holes or information on a paper tape into computer machine code, but is unable to punch holes or put information on blanch tape.

reader punch. The function of a paper tape reader punch. It can punch holes in blank paper tapes and is capable of sensing and translating holes on a tape into computer machine code.

read-in. To sense information contained in some source and to transfer this information by means of an input device to internal storage.

read-modify-write. A refresh cycle used in the operation of a random-access memory.

read-mostly memory. RMM. A memory device used where lone-term storage of information of required. Thus, stored information is altered very infrequently, so allowing for a device that has the write time much greater than the access time.

read-only file. A file that can be read only but no changes can be made to it.

read-only memory. ROM. A non-volatile semiconductor memory device, used for the storage of data that will never require modification: the memory contents are permanently built into the device during its manufacture according to a specially created pattern or mask. It stores permanent set of information written into it, whose contents under normal conditions are not intended to be alterable by the instructions. In general, there are three groups of ROMs:

masked programmed,
fusible link, and
alterable.

The mask programmed ROM is programmed by a mask pattern, as a part of its final manufacturing process. The fusible link is permanently programmed by electrical pulse or mechanical means. The alterable device undergoes changes, which are induced electrically.

read-out. To transfer data from internal storage to an external storage device, or to display processed data by means of a printer, etc.

read-protection. The prevention of reading of data, such as file or record; it is invoked to prevent unauthorised access.

read-write memory. RWM. A type of memory that, in normal operation, allows the user to access (read from) or alter (write to) individual storage locations within the device. The choice of read or write operation is normally determined by a read/write signal applied to the device. RAM devices are typical read-write memories. Where the application for a small computer system is needed, it would have a read-only memory program memory. Where it is necessary to change the system application by an operator read/write memory is employed. The read/write memory has provided advancement in small computer system complexity for hardware and programs.

read-write protection. The preventing of reading data from and writing data on a data medium. It is invoked to prevent unauthorised reading of files and records, as well as unauthorised changing of contents of the files.

real audio. *See* RealAudio

real storage. Main storage in a virtual storage system. It may be noted that physically, real storage and main storage are identical. Conceptually, however, real storage represents only parts of the range of addresses available to user of a virtual storage system. Traditionally, the total range of addresses available to the user was provided by the main storage.

real time. A computer system response which occurs at the same rate as that of data input. Remote control or automatic guidance systems by necessity operate in real time. Term real time is also used to describe systems operating in conversational mode and processes that can be influenced by human intervention while they are in progress.

RealAudio. A plug-in for playing live, on-demand, real-time audio over 28.8 Kbps or faster connection to the Internet. This software system is used for playing sound files in real time over the Internet; produced by progressive networks. RealAudio players and creation software are available for Windows systems. RealAudio is supported on Netscape Navigator, Cello WWW browser, Microsoft Internet Explorer, and NetCruiser. It can be down-loaded at: http:/www.realaudio.com.

REALCOM. REAL-time COMmunications, a communication system in which response occurs at the same rate as that of the data input.

real-time clock. A device that produces readable digits or periodic signals that allow computer to recognise elapsed time between events, and indicate the performance of time initiated or time related processing.

real-time data processing. Data processing in which the processed data originate from a process in real time and the results of the data processing are used to influence or control the process or related processes while they occur.

real-time executive. A system of computer software that provides an overall guidance for scheduling, handling and program capabilities.

real-time operating system. RTOS. Software that is required to manage the hardware resources of a computer system, which is capable of real time task management. The management can include scheduling, real-time event counters and event scheduling.

real-time. Referring to transactions being made by the computer fast enough that records are activated or updated immediately- as external events occur. Real-time systems must be able to provide quick and precisely predictable response times, and communicate with the external sensor and actuators required by the application. Real-time applications provide the intelligence for scientific, medical, automated factories, and many other devices that perform data acquisition and analysis. In contrast, batch processing is a technique in which transactions are collected into groups so that they can be processed or updated as a single job.

reasonableness check. A check to determine whether a value conforms to specified criteria.

receive only. Printer unit in data processing, or a radio receiver in telecommunications that can only receive messages and is unable to generate them.

receive. To accept an entity, such as message, signal, or electromagnetic wave, that has been transmitted from another point.

received noise power. 1. The absolute power of the noise which is measured or calculated at the receiving end.

2. The value of the noise power from all sources measured at the line terminals of a listening user's set.

receive-only page printer. The teleprinter used at communications stations that are unable to generate messages, this type of teleprinter unit has a printer only.

receiver incremental tuning. A control that permits the frequency received in a transmitter/receiver to be carried on one side or the other of the transmitted frequency.

receiver threshold. The minimum input carrier-to-noise ratio at a receiver demodulator for acceptable signal-to-noise ratio in the baseband output.

receiver. A unit or circuit in a communications system that converts incoming electrical signals into audible signals. Normally on communications equipment a green panel indicator shows that an receiver circuit is in operation.

reception. Listening to, accepting, copying, collecting, recording, or viewing received signals.

recognition memory. REM. A simplified associative memory designed to interface with ordinary computers.

RECOL. REtrieval COmmand Language, a computer language employed to interrogate the store of data held on the computer files within an information retrieval system.

reconfiguration. The process of physically altering the location or functionality of network or system elements. Automatic configuration describes the way sophisticated networks can readjust themselves in case of a link or device failing, enabling the network to continue operation.

record separator. A particular control character that is used to indicate logical division between separate areas of records.

recording line rate. The scanning line rate during the recording of an image.

recording trunk. A trunk between telephone exchanges, such as between two telephones switching centres or private branch exchanges used only for communication between operators.

recovery management support. RMS. When operations fail due to some hardware error, this facility gathers information concerning hardware reliability and allows the operations to be attempted again.

recovery process. The action that are taken to restore a system's operational capability after a failure or penetration.

recovery routine. A routine that is entered when incorrect results are obtained. It isolates the cause, assesses the significance, indicates courses of action, attempts to make corrections, and causes resumption of the operation.

recursive filtering. The image-filtering technique in which the function that operates upon distorted image, to produce less distorted image, is based upon a statistical estimation and smoothing technique involving recursive functions that make use of linear combination of previous estimates.

recursive function. A function whose values are natural numbers that are derived from natural numbers by substitution formulas in which the function is an operand.

recursive. Pertaining to a process in which each step makes use of the results of earlier steps.

recursively defined sequence. A sequence of terms in which each term after the first is determined by an operation in which operands include some or all of the preceding terms. It may be noted that in a recursively-defined sequence, there may exist a finite number of non-defined terms, possibly greater than one.

red circuit. The circuit, which can carry classified or sensitive communications in clear language form.

redirect. A packet switching function that routes a call to an alternative network address, if the link to the original address is not working. It is carried out by end-point switches.

redirector. A LAN device driver that translates operating system requests into network events and transmits them to the right protocol stack. It enables the user to access network resources as if they were part of the local environment. For example, a remote disk drive may appear as a local disk drive on the client computer. Redirector is sometimes referred as requester or shell.

reduced carrier. A carrier wave that is transmitted at a power level that is usually between 6-32 dB, preferably between 16-26 dB, below the peak envelope power level. It is usually transmitted in order to achieve automatic frequency control or automatic gain control at the receiver.

redundancy. The characters and bits that can be removed from a transmission without affecting the message; in data processing and data communications, it means providing backup for components: should one of them fail, the system continues to run without operation. Total redundancy is usually impractical, but financial institutions and other organisations with mission-critical applications attempt to install a high level of redundancy on the basis that downtime loses money, lives, depending on the business.

redundant code. A code in which more signal elements are used than are necessary to represent the intrinsic information content of a given amount of text.

reed switch. A frequency-sensitive switch in which the movable contact is mounted on the tip of a thin, metal strip (reed), which is actuated by an ac coil. Reed vibrates most vigorously and closes the contacts when the ac excitation is at the natural frequency of the reed.

re-entrant program. A program that may be entered repeatedly and may be entered before prior executions of same computer program have been completed, subject to requirement that neither its external program parameters nor any instructions are modified during its execution.

re-entry point. In the execution of a computer program, the point, place, address, or label of instruction at which the computer program is continued after a temporary departure from the program.

reference antenna. A theoretical antenna, that has a radiation pattern that can be used as a basis of comparison for other antenna radiation patterns.

reference circuit. A hypothetical circuit of specified length and configuration with a defined transmission characteristic, used primarily as a reference for the performance of other circuits and as a guide for planning and engineering of circuits and networks.

reference edge. The edge of a data carrier or data medium that is used to establish specifications or measurements for the layout of data on the carrier or medium.

reflected code. A cyclic code such as if the code words are listed in a column, there is a line that can be considered as a mirror, above and below which the code words appear to be in reflected pairs if the most significant digits are ignored.

refresh rate. The number of times per second that each pixel on the screen is scanned; measured in hertz.
refresh. 1. To replenish the charge on the storage capacitors used in dynamic memory cells and other similar devices; some devices are provided with internal circuitry that automatically refreshes dynamic cells whenever these cells are read. The word refresh is also used as a noun. 2. To repeat at regular intervals the display of digital information on a cathode ray tube or television monitor in order that the display can appear continuous.
REFS. Remote Entry Flexible Security.
regeneration. 1. Process of restoring data to the latest undeteriorated state. 2. The gain that results from coupling the output of an amplifier to its input. 3. A method of boosting a digital signal. Remote bridge LAN-to-LAN bridge that links geographically distant LANs across a wide area link.
regenerative repeater. A device used to amplify, retime and retransmit received signal impulses at their original strength or level.
regenerative track. Part of a track on magnetic drum or magnetic disk used in conjunction with a read head and a write head that are connected to function as a circulating storage.
register and arithmetic logic unit. RALU. An assembly of logic elements including accumulators, stack and arithmetic logic units which together provide both storage and processing functions. All the elements of the unit are married by a set of buses. Also known as register-equipped arithmetic logic unit.
register length. The storage capacity of a register.
register transfer module. RTM. A functional register unit designed for the construction of register logic systems.
register. A part of computer's processor that holds information for a while. Number of registers in a given system is *N*-3 where *N* is the number needed to efficiently implement a function. It is a short-term memory-storage device that has specified storage capacity, such as a bit, a byte, or a numeral, and has a specific purpose. A number of registers store data for the CPU.
register-equipped arithmetic logic unit. *See* register and arithmetic logic unit.
registration marks. The marks inserted in a document by DTP software and used to align colour separations and multiple page layouts for printing.
REJ. Radio Frequency, frequencies used as carriers to transmit information electromagnetically through the air, as differentiated from audio frequencies, those, which can be heard.
relational database. A database in which the relationships among files, records, or other data items are specified explicitly. Like the network database, the relational database can define multiple and complex relations among different data. However, whereas the network database model predefines those relationships in a way that is efficient for the computer to process but difficult for the user to change, the relational database model predefines the relationships in a very flexible way, using tables. A table also called a 'relation') is a collection of rows and columns. At each row-column intersection, a user can store a single data item (such as a specific employee's surname). Each table typically contains many individual data records (for example, one record for each customer).
relational operator. An operator that operates on two or more operands,

yielding a true or false value, and is usually placed between the operands.

relative address. An address that is expressed as a difference in relation to a base address.

relative cell reference. A spreadsheet cell reference that changes with respect to its relative position on the spreadsheet when copied to a new location.

relay satellite. A satellite that has a radio-relay station on board, *i.e.*, a satellite station that accept messages and retransmits or rebroadcasts them.

relay. 1. A device, usually electromagnetic, by which current flowing in one circuit causes contacts to operate which control the flow of currents in other circuits.

2. To retransmit a message through an intermediate point: a repeater or regenerator.

relocate. To move a computer program, routine, subroutine, database, or parts thereof, and to adjust necessary references so that they can be used after being moved.

relocation dictionary. A section of a program that contains the information necessary to alter the label identifying the location of where it is stored, after it has been placed in new location, *i.e.*, relocated.

remapping. In spread-spectrum systems, a process of correlation in which a spread-spectrum signal is converted into a coherent narrowband signal and undesired signals are converted into wider bandwidths.

remodulation. A transponder that is usually in satellite or line-of-sight radio relay links, and in which the incoming signal is first down converted to an intermediate frequency, amplified, and demodulated to obtain the baseband. The baseband is then used to modulate a radio frequency carrier that is up converted for transmission.

remote access utilities. A collection of utilities designed to support remote access. Such utilities grew around UNIX but have been extended to other operating systems. The purpose of such utilities is to give a remote user some of the powers a local user might have.

remote access. The use of a terminal that is capable or providing access to a computer from a point that is physically distant to the computer.

remote axis admittance. RAA. A unit that performs fine motions of parts mating, that can be mounted on the end of a robot arm, and that will perform the final phases of assembly when parts are in close proximity and in contact. The RRA can be adapted to a number of different types of tasks, including simple insertion. The RAA can be used together with different types of robot arms to perform parts fetching and assembly.

remote batch entry. The transfer of a group of records to be processed as a single item, over a distance by means of communications link.

remote centre compliance. RCC. A compliant unit for interfacing a robot or other mechanical workhead to its tool or working medium by permitting a gripped part to rotate about its tip or to translate without rotating when pushed laterally at its tip. The RCC provides general lateral and rotational float and greatly eases robot or other mechanical assembly in the presence of errors in parts, jigs, pallets, and robots. It is particularly useful in performing very close clearance or interference inserting.

remote copy. A UNIX-based utility, which allows to copy files between computers using syntax that is similar to log in prior to initiating the file copy process.

remote electrical alphanumeric display. A visual display, normally on a visual display unit, of numerical and alphabetical details, that is provided at a location physically distant from the computer.

remote job entry. The action of a remote device that provides input or job information to a main computer system.

remote method invocation. RMI. A JAVA specific version of CORBA framework; an object on one system can call a method in an object somewhere else on the network. It sends over parameters, and get a result back automatically. RMI directly supports client/server systems in JAVA. It differs form opening a socket to the server in that RMI is a higher level interface built on top of sockets. RMI is similar to remote procedure calls (RPC) with an object-oriented style. It is very simple to setup and use.

Remote Procedure Call. *See* RPC.

Remote Program Load. *See* RPL.

remote sensing. The technique whereby sensors located remotely from a computer are used to produce inputs for digital system. These inputs are then transmitted either by wire or radio techniques to the computer.

remote terminal. A terminal that is physically distant from the process or computer system it is accessing. The link can be made via cable or a broadcast transmission.

REMSTAR. Remote Electronic Microfilm in Storage Transmission And Retrieval, a computer output microfilm station that is physically distant from the main system. It is able to provide necessary distribution and storage functions.

repeater distribution frame. The frame provides interconnection for various items of apparatus or equipment, which include signalling units, amplifiers and transformers; it is usually housed in a telecommunication repeater station.

repeater. A device used in networks to extend cabling distances by amplifying or regenerating signals; used to join lengths of network cables, or to split the network cable into multiple segments. The repeaters are useful when employed for different types of cable in the network. For example, one could connect an Ethernet network with 10Base-T cable to one on a thick cable. In fibre networks, it is an opto-electrical module that receives an optical signal and converts it into an electrical form.

repetitive strain injury. RSI. An injury to the nerves and muscles of neck, hand, wrist, arm, and fingertips, which it is believed to be caused by excessive keyboarding operations.

report program generator. RPG. 1. A processing program that provides a convenient method for producing a variety of reports. The generator can vary from a listing of a magnetic tape reel to a very formal, calculated and edited table of data provided from a number of inputs.

2. A computer programming language that helps the user by providing facilities for assimilating data, producing printed reports and creating, updating and maintaining files.

requester. *See* redirector.

request-to-send signal. A signal which is generated by a receiver in order to condition a remote transmitter to commence transmission.

RER. Residual Error Rate.

RES. A command statement used in computers meaning:

1. To return a device or circuit to its initial state.

2. To return a counter or timer to zero.
3. To return a register, trigger or error correction signal to zero or to a specific initial condition.
4. To place a zero in a binary cell.

reserved word. A word of source language whose meaning is fixed by the particular rules of that language, and which cannot be altered for the convenience of any computer program expressed in source language. Computer programs expressed in the source language may also be prohibited from using such words in other contexts in the computer program; for example, SINE may be a reserved word to call a subroutine for computing the sine function; in COBOL, the COBOL words are reserved.

residual current circuit-breaker. RCCB. A term used in switching terminology that is superseding earth leakage contact-breaker and conforms to current regulations. Residual current circuit-breakers can provide user's with protection against serious electrocution either from appliance or cable by tripping out well before a serious shock can be received, typically in 30 ms and at 30 mA.

residual frequency modulation. The modulation of fundamental frequency of a klystron by noise voltages, a.c. heater voltage, and the like.

residue check. A validation check in which an operand is divided by a number to generate a remainder that is then used for checking.

resistor-transistor logic. RTL. An early logic family usually produced in integrated-circuit form, whose principal component parts consist of integrated resistors and bipolar transistors; which was sometimes used to provide NOR and NAND gates before integrated circuits became readily available. There is a family of resistor-transistor logic integrated logic circuits in which the input is through a resistor into the base of an inverting transistor. Input to a pair of transistors is via resistors.

resolution. A term referring to the number of dots (or pixels) that make up an image on a screen or printer. The higher the resolution, the finer and smoother images can appear when displayed at a given size.

resource allocation. The assignment of the facilities of a computer system for the accomplishment of jobs. Example: The assignment of main storage, input/output units, files.

resource record. The entries contained in a zone file; different resource records are used to identify different types of computer services.

resource. Any of the component parts of computer system and the facilities that it offers. All computer systems must include one or more processors, which actually manipulate the stored information, some form of memory in which to store both instructions for the processors and data awaiting manipulation, and input/output devices capable of reading information from the outside world and writing results to the outside world.

return loss. The ratio, at the junction of a transmission line and a terminating impedance, of the amplitude of the reflected wave to the amplitude of the incident wave; expressed in decibels, nepers, or as a percentage. It is a measure of the dissimilarity between the two impedance.

return-to-zero. RZ. A signal presented in a digital form having pulses, which are not full symbol length, *i.e.,* they are shorter than the spacing between the symbols. Intervals occur between successive binary 1 symbols, *i.e.,* the signal returns-to-zero.

reusable program. Any computer program that may be loaded into main storage once and then executed repeatedly, if the program parameters, such as addresses and instructions that were modified, are returned to their original states after each use.

reusable resource. A resource, such as a central processing unit or tape transport, that is not rendered useless by being used. A magnetic tape or disk can be used often indefinitely and are to be regarded as reusable resources.

Reverse Address Resolution Protocol. *See* RARP.

reverse channel. Referring to the transmission of a circuit-assurance-signal, over two-wire dial-up line in a direction opposite to that of the data low. The feature gives the secondary receiving station notification of any error conditions as they arise. Generally, use of this technique is limited to remote stations that do not have the ability of communicate error status by line protocol.

REW. A command statement meaning rewind; to return a magnetic tape, film or paper tape to its beginning, or some other initial data point.

Rexec. A remote command-execution utility, which instructs the remote computer to execute a command.

RF. *See* radio frequency.

RFA. Remote File Access.

RFC. Request For Comment; an official technical document, which provides relevant information on TCP/IP or the Internet.

RFC 822. The Internet Standard format for e-mail message headers.

RFI. Request For Information.

RFMS. Remote File Management System.

RFP. Request For Proposal, document issued to request bids for products or services.

RFS. Random Filing System.

RFT. Revisable Format Text, text that carries codes for formatting that allow one to edit the text and easily retain the format style, for example, use of tab and centre codes rather than spaces.

RG-59. Coaxial cable used primarily for cable television, 75Ω, per US MIL-C-17-F.

RG-62. Coaxial cable generally used for ARC-NET, 93Ω, per US MIL-C-17-F.

RG-8. Thick-wire coaxial cable (coax); specification calls for heavy, brightly coloured coax, with a contrasting marker ring every 1.5 m, 50Ω, per US MIL-C-17-F.

RGB. Red, Green, Blue. A standard way of specifying colours on a computer monitor. Stands for the three (additive) primary colours; *i.e.*, the primary colours when light is added together to produce the colour. Red, yellow, and blue are the primary colours when ink is blended and put onto (white) paper. CYMB (Cyan, yellow, magenta, black) is the colour model used for printing (this does correspond to the standard blue, yellow, red usage). An alternative model is saturation, hue, and luminance.

RHOB. Relevant Hierarchical Operational Binding, either an HOB or an NHOB, depending on the context.

RIB. Routing Information Base.

RIMS. Remote Information Management System.

ring in and ring out. Token Ring connectors on the MSAU connecting the unit to trunk cabling. The Wrap feature is implemented at these interfaces.

ring modulator. A modulator with two pairs of diode elements so arranged that current flows in one direction, or its reverse, under the control of the modulating current. Ring modulators are much used in FDM multiplexing equipment.

ring network. A network constructed as a loop of unidirectional links between stations. It generally uses a bit-serial medium such as twisted pairs or coaxial cable.

ring topology. A layout scheme in which the network takes the form of a closed loop with the devices attached into ring. Every workstation is linked to two others, one on each side. All data is passed from node to node in one direction only, each computer acting as a repeater for the next one in the loop. Response time is determined by the number of stations on the ring; the more there are, the slower it works. With this methodology, each node examines data that is sent through the ring. If the data is not addressed to the node examining it, that node passes it along to the next node in the ring. If one computer fails, the loop is broken, though most rings have self-healing capacity to reconfigure and continue operation. IBM's Token passing ring ensures that the failed station is removed and its neighbours are then directly connected. It has substantial advantage over bus topology, as there is no danger of collisions because the data always flows in one direction. One drawback, however, is that if a connection is broken, the entire network goes down.

RIP. Routing Information Protocol, a common distance-vector interior routing protocol. This is common TCP/IP routing protocol, which is gradually being replaced by newer protocols such as OSPF. RIP is derived from an earlier protocol of the same name developed at Xerox.

RIPE. Reseaux IP European, a European TCP/IP network operated by EUNET.

RIR. Relative Index Register.

RISC. Reduced Instruction Set Computer. A type of central processing unit architecture in which the central processing unit has a small set of computer instructions that it can perform. Different instructions are combined to provide the functionality of other central processing units with more instructions. The greater speed that the instructions can be carried out at is thought to more than make up for the fact that fewer instructions are supported. There is a growing consensus that RISC processors have more potential for speed than CISC processors do.

RISC. Reduced instruction set computing. Most personal computers have a central processing unit based on complex instruction set computing, capable of recognising over 100 instructions for immediate computation.

rise time. In the approximation of a step function, the time required a signal to change from a specified low value to a specified high value. It may be noted that usually these values are 10% and 90% of the step height.

riser. A cable that runs vertically, usually inside a building, to carry signals to the various parts of the building.

RJ. 1. ReJect Transport PDU, PDU that may be used to request retransmission or as part of resynchronisation.
2. Registered Jack.

RJ-11. Modular jack or plug used in telephony and networks; normally has four positions tined or wired, but accommodates six.

RJ-12. RJ-11 with six positions filled.

RJ-45. Modular plug with eight positions; larger jack will fit RJ-11 and 12 plugs; normally wired with outside-to-inside pair groupings.

RJ-71. Telco 50-pin, ANSI-type, D-type connector (like Centronix but longer).

RJE. Remote Job Entry.

RJO. remote Job Output.

RLCM. Remote Line Concentrating Module, telephony term.

Rlogin. A remote login utility, used to connect with a UNIX host that, is running the server daemon. It serves the same purpose as Telnet, but Rlogin is less versatile, as it does not provide some of the configuration negotiation features available with Telnet. Although Rlogin offers essentially the same service as Telnet, it is superior because the software passes information about the user's environment to the remote machine.

RLRE. ReLease-REsponse application protocol data unit, the PDU used to accept the release of an ACSE association.

RLRQ. ReLease-ReQuest application protocol data unit, PDU used to initiate release of an ACSE association.

RM. 1. Reference Model, used often in OSI documents and specifications in referring to the seven-layer OSI model.

2. Register Memory.

3. Resource Manager.

RMA. random Multiple Access.

RMDM. Reference Model of Data Management, extension to the OSI Reference Model used in papers by the OSI database working group.

RMI. *See* remote method invocation.

RMM. *See* read-mostly memory.

RMON. Remote Monitoring, SNMP specification for multi-vendor statistics-gathering by a standards-based management station from de facto standard (RMON)-compliant devices.

RMS. 1. Record Management System.

2. *See* recovery management support.

RN. 1. Record Number.

2. Receipt Notification, in MHS, a user agent Service PDU returned to say the message was received.

RNAC. Remote Network Access Controller.

RNR. Receiver Not Ready, PDU in HDLC and X.25.

ROAC. Report Origin Authentication Check, security service available in X.400.

roaming. The ability of a mobile communications device to move freely from one part the whole of a network operator's system or another.

robot. A machine equipped with sensing instruments for detecting input signals or environmental conditions, but with reacting or guidance mechanisms that can perform sensing, calculations, and so on, and with stored programs for resultant actions; for example, a machine running itself.

robustness. The extent to which hardware or software continues to perform correctly despite some violation of its specifications, such as incorrect data input, operator commands, or environmental conditions.

ROIV. Remove Operations InVoke, PDU that requests a remote operation.

roll back. A programmed return to a prior point in the sequence of instructions, usually to check point or a restart point.

roll in. To transfer back to main or internal storage, data computer programs that previously have been rolled out.

roll out. To transfer data or computer programs from main to the auxiliary storage or from internal to external storage.

ROM. *See* read-only memory.

root compiler. In computer programming, a compiler whose object language is a machine-independent, intermediate-level language.

root folder. Top-level folder of a disk.

root segment. The part of an overlay program that remains in storage during the entire execution of the overlay program.

root. The top-level directory of a disk; in UNIX, it is also name for the super user account.

ROPM. Remote Operations Protocol Machine.

RORE. Remote Operations Return Error, PDU that returns an error in dictation to a remote operation.

RORJ. Remote Operations ReJect, PDU that indicates that an ROIV was not acceptable.

RORS. Remove Operations ReSponse, PDU that responds to a remote operation request.

ROS. 1. Read Only Storage.
2. Remote Operations Service.

ROSE. Remove Operations Service Element, a generic ASE that works like a remote procedure call.

rotation position sensor. A feature of some disk drives that allows the central processor to be made aware that a required sector is about to come under the read head of the drive.

rotational position sensing. A technique for continuously monitoring a disk position to indicate the position currently available for reading and writing. It may be noted that this technique uses continuous comparison of the read/write head position with appropriate synchronisation signals.

round-trip propagation time. Twice the time required for a bit to travel between the two most distant data stations in a bus network. It may be noted that In a network using carrier sense, each frame must be long enough so that a collision or jam signal may be detected by the transmitting station while this frame is being transmitted. Its minimum length is therefore determined by the round-trip propagation time.

route matrix. The record of interconnections between pairs of nodes in the network. The status of these interconnections is used to produce direct route, alternate route, and available route from point to point.

route. 1. Path used to move information from one place to another.
2. In a packet switching network, it is the list of nodes that a particular packet or class of packets is to follow or has followed.

router. Hardware and software that routes data between similar or dissimilar networks on the protocol level. Routers can support more than one protocol. It can read logical addressing information and direct data across the network. It divides the local subnet from the larger network. It operates at OSI Network Layer (Level Three) that supports a particular Network Layer protocol and related stack, such as TCP/IP, DecNet, XNS, SNA, OSI IP, IPX. These days routers tend to support multiple protocols by a variety of methods, such as Protocol Independent Routing. A router can be used to link LANs together locally or remotely as part of a WAN. A network built using routers is often termed an inter-network. Routers can actively direct messages between separate networks (for example, an Ethernet network and a token ring network). They make decisions about which path through the network traffic will follow. Each network connected by the router has a unique identity with its own Internet address. The router receives data from one of its attached networks and passes it up the protocol stack to the Internet layer. The router checks destination address in IP header. If the destination is on the network from whence the data came, router discards the data that has already presumably reached its destination because it was transmitted on the network of the destination computer. If the data is destined for a different network, the router consults a routing table to determine where to forward the data. After the router determines which of its adapters will receive the data, it passes the data down through the appropriate Network Access Layer software for transmission through the adapter.

routine. A sequence of computer instructions that is designed to accomplish a specific purpose or task or that is used frequently.

Routing Information Protocol. *See* RIP.

routing protocol. One of the several protocols used by routers to assemble route information.

routing table. A matrix associated with a network-control protocol that gives the preferred ongoing line preference at each node in the network. It is used to select the most appropriate route to forward information along.

routing. The procedure used to determine the route taken by a packet in a packet switching computer network. Routing may be fixed or dynamic. It may be centralised or distributed.

row address strobe. RAS. A signal used in dynamic random-access memories (DRAM) this is employed to reduce the number of pins necessary, by multiplexing the address.

row binary. Pertaining to binary representation of data on cards on which the significance of punch positions are assigned along card rows.

row. A string of items such as characters, whose orientation in space is such that the line of items is parallel to the inter-pupillary line of the perversion viewing the string.

RP. Remote Processor.

RPC. Remote Procedure Call, a means of communication between two tasks running on separate computers linked by a LAN. One computer can request a service, typically computation, from the other, by executing a high-level request known as a language procedure call. RPCs are underlying architectural element of distributed processing and client/server computing.

RPG. *See* report program generator.

RPL. Remote Program Load, starting a computer and loading the operating system into memory when the operating system software is provided by a server on the network.

RS PPDU. ReSynchronize Presentation PDU.

RS. Record Separator.

RS-232. An interface standard, which defines the physical and electrical interface used to connect data communications equipment and data terminal equipment. This is the most commonly used interface, especially between modems and computers. RS232 is suitable for both synchronous and asynchronous communications and specifies a 25-pin connector, traditionally the DB-25. 20 of the pins carry out routine system operation while the rest are reserved for modem testing or unallocated. For this reason, it is never safe to assume that two RS232 devices will work together. Newer, more compact RS232 interfaces have nine pins only and an adapter card is needed. It is functionally similar to the ITU-TS's V.24 and V.28 standards.

RS-232C. A standard for the interconnection of computer terminals, input/output devices, data terminal equipment, cathode-ray tubes, displays, modulator/demodulators, teletypewriters, peripheral devices, and data communication equipment. RS-232C is an electrical standard and the suffix C denotes the latest revision.

RS-422. A high-speed serial interface used to connect data communications equipment (such as the Apple Macintosh). RS-422 governs the asynchronous transmission of computer data at speed of up to 920000 bits per second.

RS-423. A communications interface with greater sensitivity for a distance of up to 300 m, longer than an RS-232. By design, RS-423 interface is compatible with most RS-232 hookups. RS-423 is the standard interface for DEC type serial communications.

RS-449. A new standard designed to replace RS-232.

RSA PPDU. ReSynchronize Acknowledge Presentation PDU.

RSC. Remove Switching centre, term for a switch located somewhere other than at a central office.

RSDP. Remote Site Data Processing.

RSE. Remote Single-layer Embedded, a variation on the RS abstract test method used in conformance testing.

Rsh. A remote command-execution utility, which allows to execute a single command on remote computer without logging in to the remote computer.

RSTS. Resource Sharing Time Sharing.

RSU. Register Storage Unit.

RTAB. Reliable Transfer ABort Application protocol data unit, PDU that refers to either provider or user abnormal termination of activity in the Reliable Transfer service.

RTBM. Real Time Bit Mapping.

RTF. Rich Text Format, a word processing file standard; attempts to maintain some aspects of document formatting during transfers and conversions.

RTL. Real Time Language.

RTN. Remote Terminal Network.

RTOAC. Reliable Transfer Open ACcept Application protocol data unit.

RTORJ. Reliable Transfer ReJect Application protocol data unit.

RTORQ. Reliable Transfer Open ReQuest Application protocol data unit.

RTS. Request To Send, a pin or connection defined in the RS-232 specification; when asserted by the DTE, it indicates that the DTE wishes to transmit data.

RTTR. Reliable Transfer Token Response Application protocol data unit.

RTU. Remote Terminal Unit.

RUF. Resource Utilisation factor.

run time. RU. Time, at which a program is executed, in contrast to the time at which it may have been submitted, loaded, compiled, or assembled. Also known as execution time.

run. Transmission of a complete message or the continuous transmission of a group of messages or packets.

run-length encoding. A data-compression technique for reducing the amount of information in a digitised binary image. It removes redundancy that arises from the fact that such images contain large regions of adjacent pixels that are either all white or all black. The brightness information is replaced by a sequence of small integers that tell how many consecutive black and white pixels are encountered while traversing each scan line.

run-to-run totals. The utilisation of output control totals resulting from one process as input control totals over subsequent processing.

Ruptime. A utility that displays system information on uptime and the number of connected users.

Rwho. A utility that displays information on currently connected users.

RZ. Return to Zero, signal where the waveform returns to a quiescent or zero amplitude between bits or at the beginning and end of each bit frame.

S

S.nnn. The CCITT S. Series Recommendations; deal with standards related to telegraphy, for example, International Telegraph Alphabet, answer back units, teleprinter control.

S/D. Signal to Distortion Ratio.

S/M. Sort/Message.

S100 bus. A bus originally designed for the ALTAIR system and now standardised as the IEEE-696 bus. In S-100 bus each logic card has a 100-contact edge connector on the bottom (50 contacts on each side). It is derived from the backplane used in the original Altair 8080-based microcomputer, but has been expanded to accommodate 16-bit processors multiple processors, a 24-bit address space, and direct memory access.

SA. Source Address; network address of host initiating network connection.

SAA. Systems Application Architecture, IBM's common application development environment, enabling software to be developed to run on broad range of IBM hardware, under a range of operating systems: MVS/ESA, VM/ESA, OS/400 and OS/2.

SAB. Stack Access Block.

SABM. Set Asynchronous Balanced Mode, HDLC PDU used in establishing a connection.

SABME. Set Asynchronous Balanced Mode Extended.

sabotage. The pre-mediated destruction of personnel, property or physical plant in an effort to disrupt or terminate manufacturing or other operations by the government or a private enterprise.

SAC. 1. Single Association Concentrator, used in FDII.
2. Simplified Access Control, a pared-down version of the access control provided in X.500 1992 extensions.
3. Storage Access Channel.

SACF. Single Association Control Function, an application layer service for managing an application association.

SAD. System Analysis and Design.

SADT. Structured Analysis and Design Technique.

SAF. Sub-network Access Facility, sublayer of layer 3 of the OSI reference model.

SAK. Selective AcKnowledgement, not commonly used, but the complement of Selective Reject.

SAL. 1. Structured Assembly Language.
2. Symbolic Assembly Language.

salami shaving. A form of computer crime which involves the unauthorised withdrawal of money from a group of bank accounts so that it can be deposited into the criminal's account.

SAM. 1. File name extension for a particular type of word processor file. 2. Sequential Access Method. 3. *See* serial-access memory.

SAMBA. A basic browser available from www.Org; it does not support many advanced features of the internet. To install SAMBA on computer system, MacTCP must be installed first.

SAMICS. Solar Array Manufacturing Industry Costing Standards; a technique that employs a computer program, providing a common ground for the comparison of the economic aspects of several alternate approaches to the production of silicon cells. It can provide some of the best documented and validated costing of the process sequences involved in fabricating solar modules.

sampling. The process of obtaining a group of representative measurements in relation to some function in order to develop information on that system.

SAO. Single Association Object.

SAP. 1. Structural Analysis Program. 2. Symbolic Address Program. 3. Service Access Point, the point at which service is provided the adjacent layer.

SAPI. Service Access Point Identifier, indicates the type of layer 3 protocol being used in LAPD.

SAR. 1. Segment Address Register. 2. Source Address register.

SARF. Security Alarm Reporting Function, term used in Network Management.

SARM. Set Asynchronous Response Mode, an HDLC link initialisation frame.

SAS. SEF/AIS Severely errored framing Alarm indication Signal second, used in performance management in Network Management.

SASE. Specific Application Service Elements, capabilities required for a specific application, such as file transfer, database access, etc.

SASFE. SAS Far End, used in performance management in Network Management.

SASO. Saudi Arabian Standards Organisation, national member of ISO.

SAT. System Access Technique.

SATF. Security Audit Trail Function, used in Network Management.

SATS. Selected Abstract Test Suite, only those tests from an ATS that will be run based on information in the PICS.

saturation testing. A technique in data communications, for checking the performance of communications network by means of a large bulk of messages. It is undertaken to check system faults that only arise in certain circumstances.

saturation. The purity of a colour's hue, moving from grey to the pure colour. A high saturation corresponds to a strong colour. Hue and luminance also affect the appearance of a colour, in the HLS colour model.

SAU. Smallest Addressable Unit.

save. In computing, to store a computer program or data on an auxiliary device, such as disk or tape.

SBA. Shared Batch Area.

S-band. Microwave frequencies that occur between 1.55 and 5.20 GHz and form part of a larger continuous range of frequencies covering 0.225-100 GHz which are usually subdivided into bands designated by letters. S-band microwave frequencies have wavelengths of between 19.3-5.77cm.

SBC. Sytem Bus Controller.

SBE. System Buffer Element.

SBI. Single Byte Interleaved.

S-box. Substitution box; in data security, a component of an encryption algorithm that performs a substitution cipher on the input signal.

SBR. Storage Buffer Register.

SBT. Six-Bit Transcode.

S-channel. One of the eight compact disc sub-code channels (P-W). At present, it is only allocated to disc graphics.

SC. SubCommittee, technical group under ISO, as in TC97/SC21/WG3.

SC15. ISO Subcomittee for Labelling and File Structure.

SC18. ISO Subcommittee for Text and Office Systems, has six active and three inactive WGs studying ODA-related standards.

SC2. SubCommittee on Character Sets and Information Coding, ISO, has eight WGs and one Registration and Advisory Group (RAG).

SC21. ISO Subcommittee on Open Systems Support Services, JTC1/SC21.

SCA. 1. Short Code Address.
2. System Control Area.

SCAI. Switch to Computer Application Interface, a working group within ANSI T1S1.1 to develop standards for intelligent co-operation between computers and network switches.

scalar processor. A supercomputer, which processes collections (scalars) of data simultaneously at speeds of 100 MFLOP. The common computer is known as a vector processor because it can handle only single-dimensional items of data at any one time.

scaleable typeface. A set of letters, numbers, punctuation marks, and symbols (a font) that are a given design but can be scaled to any size.

scan code. The code generated by the keyboard controller that tells the keyboard buffer which key has been pressed.

scan. 1. In data structures, a procedure to investigate every node in the structure.
2. In television, the horizontal sweep of an electron beam across a television screen.

scanner. 1. A device that examines an object, image, or three-dimensional space in a regular manner and produces analog or digital signals corresponding to a physical state at each part of the search area.
2. A device used to intercept radio communications usually in the citizen band, cellular radio, police, fire, and ambulance transmission areas.
3. A peripheral input device used to assist in the entry of data into a computer system. In desktop publishing, a scanner may be used to digitise artwork or photographs so that they can be merged with text. 4. A device that examines a special pattern, one part after another, and generates analog or digital signals corresponding to the pattern.

scanning density. The number of lines per inch in facsimile image communications. In general, higher is the scanning density, better is the quality of image. The typical scanning density for a FAX signal is in the range of about 80-200 lines per inch.

scanning line. In television, a single horizontal line traced across the face of a television screen by an electron beam.

scavenging. In computers, searching through residue for the purpose of unauthorised data acquisition.

SCB. Segment Control Bit.

SCC. Satellite Communications Controller.

SCCC. Single Channel Communications Controller.

SCCP. Signalling Connection Control Part, part of the third layer in ISDN that adds addressing and connection-oriented services.

SCCS. Source Code Control System.

SCCU. Single Channel Control Unit.

SCDAM. *See* static column dynamic access memory.

schema. In database, map of the overall logical structure of a database.

SCI. System Control Interface.

SCL. Sequential Control Logic.

SCN. Shortest Connected Network.

SCOBOL. Structured COBOL.

scope. A range of addresses controlled by a DHCP server. These IP addresses are intended for lease to DHCP client computers. It is that portion of a program, within which the declaration applies. It may be noted that:

(a) The scope of an identifier is used as a synonym for the scope of its declaration.

(b) A language object may not be referable throughout its scope since it may be hidden by the declaration of the same identifier in an inner block.

SCP. 1. Service Control Point.

2. Secure Conversion process, an extension to X.400 conversion to ensure that it meets military security requirements, defined by MMHS.

3. Secondary Cross-connection Point.

scrambler. In communications, an encoding device applied to communication links for security purposes, or to avoid harmful repetitive patterns of the digital data. Such repetitive patterns may arise in phase-modulated systems and produce a zero phase shift over a comparatively long period, with a resultant loss in synchronisation between the transmitter and receiver decoders.

scratch file. In programming, a file used as a memory workspace.

scratch pad memory. A small, high-speed memory used as a temporary storage for working data.

scratch. To free an area of storage so that it may be used for another application.

screen buffer. A buffer used to store the data that is displayed on the screen of a visual display unit. The display unit accesses this buffer in each display scan.

screen dropping resistor. The resistor connected in series with the dc plate supply and the screen grid of an electron tube. Screen current passing through this resistor creates a voltage drop which corrects the value of applied dc screen voltage.

screen font. Also called a raster font. The font that is displayed on your screen, which may approximate a printer font so that document looks approximately the same on the screen as they do when printed.

screen modulation. A method of modulation in which a modulation voltage is superimposed upon the dc screen voltage of an amplifier or oscillator.

screen saver. A moving picture or pattern that appears on your screen when you have not moved the mouse or pressed a key on the computer for a specified period. Screen savers prevent screen damage that is caused when the same areas of light and dark are displayed for long periods of time. Be careful when using a screen saver on a computer with an LCD screen (most laptops and notebooks). A pixel on an LCD screen is on when its dark; therefore, blacking the screen as some screen savers do would cause more damage.

scroll arrow. An arrow on either end of a scroll bar that is used to scroll through the contents of a window or list box.

scroll bar. A bar that appears at the bottom and/or right (or left) edge of a window whose contents is not entirely visible. Each scroll bar contains a scroll box and two scroll arrows. Also known as scroller.

scroll box. In a scroll bar, the small box, that shows the position of information currently in the window or list box relative to the contents of the entire window.

scroll mode. Pertaining to a terminal with no intelligence; when a key is pressed a character is sent over a line, and when it is received, it is displayed.

scroll. 1. To move through text or graphics (up, down, left, or right) in order to see parts of the file or list that cannot fit on the screen.
2. In computer graphics, the continuous vertical or horizontal movement of display elements within a window in a manner such that new data appear at one edge of the window as old data disappear at the opposite edge. The window may include the entire display surface.
3. A graphic display technique whereby the generation of a new line of alphanumeric text at the bottom of a display screen automatically regenerates all other lines of text one line higher than before and deletes the top line.

scroller. *See* scroll bar.

SCS. System Conformance Statement, in conformance testing, a short summary of the SCTR.

SCSI. Small computer system interface; an interface standard for connecting peripheral devices (such as hard disks and printers) to a computer. For modern high-speed personal computers to work efficiently with mass storage devices there must be an effective means of transferring data between the device and the computer; pronounced as "scuzzy." Instead of plugging cards in to the computer's bus via expansion slot, SCSI extends the bus outside the computer by way of a cable. It is just like an extension cord for the data bus. To provide a computer with a SCSI port, a SCSI adapter board is inserted in the expansion slot. Many devices use the SCSI interface. Fast, high-end hard disk drives, scanners, tape drives, and optical storage devices such as CD-ROM drives, often have SCSI interfaces.

SCTR. System Conformance Test Report, in conformance testing, a summary of PCTRs stating how the entire system conforms.

SD. 1. Send Data.
2. Search Date.
3. Starting Delimiter, a control field used in IEEE 80-2.3 local area network protocols.

SDA. 1. Security Domain Authority, the authority administering a security policy for a set of elements.
2. *See* source data acquisition.

SDAP. Standard Document Application Profile, profile of an exchange format for SGML.

S-DAT. In recording, one of the proposed formats for digital audio tape-recording; in this format a 3.81 mm tape is used but, unlike conventional compact cassette formats, 22 tracks are recorded across the width of the tape. The tracks are recorded longitudinally and read by a multi-track stationary read/write system.

SDB. Segment Descriptor Block.

SDE. 1. Submission and Delivery Entity, in X.400, a remote UA using P3 to submit and deliver messages to MTS.
2. Source Data Entry.
3. System Development Engine.

SDF. 1. Standard Data Format.
2. *See* super-group distribution frame.

SDFS. Standard Disc Filing System.

SDH. Synchronous Digital Hierarchy, ITU-TS synchronous transmission standards aligned with Sonet above 155Mbit/s. aimed at network operators; designed with ATM in mind, SDH has many advantages over the presently available transmission technologies including flexibility in managing transmission, reconfiguration, control and switching at data rates to 622Mbit/s and beyond. SDH-based networks are being implemented by operators in various parts of Europe and developed by major players such as Alcatel and Northern Telecom.

SDIF. SGML Document Interchange Format, ISO 9069.

SDL. Software Design Language.

SDL/GR. SDL/Graphical Representation.

SDL/PR. SDL/Phrase Representation.

SDLC. Synchronous Data Link Control, an IBM protocol for use in SNA (System Network Architecture) environments. It controls an individual link while catering for other network needs and can operate over full or half-duplex lines. SDLC is bit oriented protocol, using a variety of patterns to flag the beginning and end of a frame or packet. Different bit patterns are used to convey address, control and header fields, which accompany the transmission and guide the frame to its destination. 2. Systems Development Life Cycle, systems analysis methodology.

SDMA. Shared Direct Memory Access.

SDN. *See* synchronous data network.

SDP. Source Data Processing.

SDSI. Shared Data Set Integrity.

SDU. 1. Service Data Unit; the data, that is passed from one layer to the layer below, to be carried intact to the peer entity.

2. Source Data Utility.

SE. Session Entity, OSI entity providing Session Layer services.

sealed data module. A sealed data module is a unit wherein the access arm and the magnetic data disk are enclosed in one unit (a fixed disk). This is referred to as Winchester technology.

search cycle. The sequence of events of a search that is repeated for each data element.

search engine. Any program that is used for searching the information on the Internet

search program. In databases, a program which can search a data file or database to find a key word or key phrase supplied by an operator or another program.

search. The examination of one or more data elements of a set to find those elements that have a given property.

SECDED. *See* single-error-correction double-error detection.

second read rate. SRR. A second read rate scanner is a bar code scanner which translates code on the second read rate should the 'first read rate' be unsuccessful.

second window. Characteristic of an optical fibre having a relatively high transmittance surrounded by regions of low transmittance surrounded by regions of low transmittance in the wavelength range 1,200-1,350 nm.

second. s. The SI unit of time; it is defined as duration of 9,192,631,770 periods of the radiation of the ceasium-133 atom. Formerly it was defined as 1/86,400th of the average solar day.

secondary channel. A data channel derived from the same physical path as the main data channel, but completely independent from it. It carries auxiliary information at a low data rate, dealing with device control, diagnostics, etc. It has lower signalling rate capability than the primary channel in a system in which two channels share a common interface.

secondary failure. The failure of the components due to the malfunctioning of some other component.

secondary frequency standard. A device for generating signals of accurate frequency, but which does not possess the high stability and extreme accuracy of primary frequency standard. The secondary standard is periodically referred to primary standard and appropriately corrected. The secondary standard usually consists of 50, 100, 1000, or 5000 kHz crystal oscillator (with or without temperature control and supply-voltage regulation). Some units subdivide the oscillator frequency and deliver lower-frequency signals. Harmonics from the oscillator provide numerous high-frequency checkpoints.

secondary index. An index in data structures, that holds the key or locations of all records which have a particular value for a specified field.

secondary storage. Units such as disks, which hold permanent or semi-permanent data, sometimes referred to as auxiliary storage. In contrast, primary storage is used only temporarily by the control unit (located inside the central processing unit).

secondary time standard. A time standard, which requires calibration.

sector allocation. Pertaining to allocation of free magnetic disk sectors to a file that is to be written to disk.

sector interleave factor. The ratio of the number of sectors traversed by a read/write head to the number of sectors written. For example, if the interleave factor is 5:1, then the disk would write to the first available sector then skip four sectors and write on the fifth, then skip another four, and so on. Although an interleave factor of 1:1 is optimal, manufacturers may set a higher ratio in order to slow down the data flow to ensure the computer can keep up with the fast rate of data transfer.

sector interleaving. The initial formatting of a floppy disk determines where sectors are located within a track. It is not necessary to allocate sectors sequentially around the track. It is often advantageous to place the sectors on the track in non-sequential order. Sequential sector ordering optimises sector access times during multi-sector transfers (such as when a program is loading) by permitting the number of sectors specified (up to an entire track) to be transferred within a single revolution of the disk.

sector. Smallest unit of absolutely addressable information on a read-only memory or interactive compact disc. It is the portion of a rotational magnetic storage device, which can be accessed by the magnetic heads in the course of a particular rotation. Magnetic disks are divided into circular tracks and each track is then subdivided into sectors holding a block of data. Most of the personal computers use sectors, which can store 128 or 256, or 512 or 1024 bytes of information. The sector size is specified when the track is initially formatted by the controller. Each sector within a track is composed of the following four fields: (a) Sector ID field. This field, consisting of seven bytes, is written only when the track is formatted. The ID field provides the sector identification that is used by the controller when a sector must be read or written. The first byte of the field is the ID address mark, a unique coding that specifies the beginning of the ID field. The second, third, and fourth bytes are the cylinder, head, and sectors addresses, respectively, and the fifth byte is the sector length code. The last two bytes are the 16-bit cyclic redundancy check (CRC) character for the ID field. During formatting, the controller supplies the address mark. The cylinder, head, sector addresses, and the sector length code are supplied to the controller by the processor software. The CRC character is derived by the controller from the data in the first five bytes. (b) Post ID field gap. This is written initially when the track is formatted. During subsequent write operations, the drive's write circuits are enabled within the gap and the trailing bytes of the gap are rewritten each time the sector is updated (written).

security filter. A set of software routines and techniques in computer security, employed in automatic data-processing systems to prevent automatic forwarding of specified data over unprotected links or to unauthorised persons.

security host. An authentication device that verifies whether a connection is authorised to connect to a remote server. This verification supplements security already supplied by Network and Dial-up connections by Windows 2000 server. There are two kinds of security hosts; those which perform authentication checks during a modem call, and those which are called during the authentication process of the connection.

security label. A sensitivity indicator permanently associated with protected data, processes and/or other resources and may be used in enforcing security policy.

security modem. A modem installed in a user's terminal with integrated security functions. Such modems incorporate outbound call-screening security to control host access from the user end. User enters a password for a given host computer, the security modem checks password against host computer telephone numbers, if it matches, the modem dials up the computer and initiates logon procedures.

security techniques. General term for the procedures such as redundancy in design, replication, encryption of messages, use of passwords and personal identification numbers, and scrambling of voice signals.

SEEA. Software Error Effects Analysis.

seed. In applications, a number supplied to a random-number generator to commence the sequence.

seek time. 1. Time required to reposition the heads of a magnetic disk unit in order to read or write data on a different track.

2. The time required to find a record of data, generally used in reference to disk files.

SEF. Standard External File.

segment. 1. A section of message that can be held in a buffer.

2. A self-contained portion of a computer program that can be executed without the entire program necessarily resident in the internal store at any particular moment.

3. Data package passed from TCP at the transport layer to the Internet layer.

4. A bus LAN term, referring to the electrically continuous piece of the bus. Segments can be joined together using repeaters or bridges.

seize. To gain control of a communication channel in order to transmit a message or program.

select. To mark an item so that a subsequent action can be carried out on that item. You can usually select an item by clicking it with a mouse or pressing a key. After selecting an item, you choose the action that you want to affect the item.

selection structure. The structures built around a condition statement; if the condition statement is true, certain lines of a code are executed. If the condition statement is false, those lines of the code are not executed. The two most common selection structures are If and If-Else.

selective calling. An automatic method of sending messages to specific points, without causing interference to other stations.

selective combiner. A circuit or device for selecting one of two or more diversity signals in such a way that only the signal having the most desirable characteristics is used.

selective dump. A dump of one or more selected areas of storage.

selective fading. Fading at different rates of signals of different frequencies within the same modulation envelope. When a signal is propagated via ionosphere, fading is commonly experienced at the receiving station. This fading usually does not occur at the same time at all frequencies. For example, for a given communication circuit, fading will not be observed at 5 MHz and 7 MHz at the same time.

selector channel. A channel designed to operate with only one input/output device at any one particular instant.

selector. A device that responds to the presence of a control pulse in a pulse train, and consequently directs the pulse train to the appropriate one of the two lines.

self-relocating program. A program, which can be loaded in any location of the main storage. At initialisation the program adjusts its address values so that it can be executed at that location.

self-synchronising. A property of cipher, which provides for an automatic recovery after an error has occurred.

self-test. The series of testing operations performed by the memory controller when a computer is powered up to ensure that the memory modules are operating properly. Self-test reads and writes every dynamic random-access memory (DRAM) location several times. Any detected hard failure are logged in the control status register (CSR) and reported to the operating system. The operating system isolates the areas in which any hard failures have occurred by marking them as bad blocks. Bad blocks are then mapped out by the memory controller, allowing the system to operate normally, ignoring the faulty memory cells.

selsyn. An indicating device used to show the direction in which an object is pointing. It consists of a synchronous motor system, with the transmitting unit at the movable device and the receiving unit where the operator can easily detect it.

SEN. Software Error Notification.

sensitive software. Any data-processing software, which can bypass, penetrate, or damage data-processing security controls.

sensitivity. 1. A general term that applies to many different electronic devices. In general, sensitivity is an expression of the change in input necessary to cause certain change in the output of a device.

2. In a radio receiver, the minimum input signal required to produce a specified output signal having a specified signal-to-noise ratio.

3. In opto-electricity, an imprecise synonym for response.

4. In an amplifier, sensitivity is expressed in terms of the input-signal voltage that is needed to produce a certain signal-to-noise ratio, in decibels, at the output.

5. In a microphone or other transducer, sensitivity is expressed as the

acoustic pressure, light intensity, or other flux required to produce certain amount of signal at the output.
6. The current required to produce a full-scale deflection.

sentinel. A marker indicating the beginning or end of a section of information accessed by a program.

septet. A group of seven binary digits treated as an entity.

SEQUEL. Structured English QUEry Language.

sequence codes. In sequence-starting with one-without concern for the classification or order of the subjects being coded. It is useful for any short list of names, products, or accounts where the only object is the application of simple code numbers, and where the arrangement of data is not important.

sequence number. A unique number associated with a byte transmitted through TCP.

sequence structure. The structure defining the default control flow in a program.

sequence. A list of items arranged according to a specified set of rules.

sequence-control register. A specific storage location or register that holds the location of a specified item in a memory, containing the next instruction to be executed.

sequential access memory. A form of memory in which data channels can be recalled only in a certain predetermined order. Any form of memory can have sequential access. The most common forms of sequential access memory are the first-in/first-out memory and the pushdown stack.

sequential access. An access mode in which records are obtained from, or placed into, a file in such a way that each successive access to the file refers to following record in the file.

sequential computer. A computer in which events occur one after the other with little or no provision for simultaneous or overlapping events.

sequential file. If files in secondary storage and arranged in a particular order (sequence), they can be accessed by going directly to the required file without having to read every file preceding (as the case with magnetic tape reels). Sequential files each contain a unique identifier.

sequential logic. A logic circuit in which the output depends upon the previous states of the inputs. A sequential logic circuit has one or more inputs, and one output. The present state of the output depends on the present state of the inputs, and also on the immediately previous state of the output.

SER. *See* serial.

serial interface. An interface between a computer and a serial device, such as a printer or modem, by which the computer sends single bits of information to the device, one after the other.

serial interface. Hardware for sending and receiving data one bit at a time.

Serial Line Internet Protocol. *See* SLIP.

serial mouse. A mouse designed to be connected directly to the computer's serial port for transmitting data asynchronously (one bit at a time).

serial operation. The sequential or consecutive execution of two or more operations in a single device.

serial port adapter. A connection on a computer (or peripheral device) that can send and receive data one bit at a time. On early personal computers, the serial port adapter was offered as an optional plug-in board. On modern personal computers, these circuits come as standard, often combined on a board with other functions. When personal computer transmits data, the adapter converts the data from a parallel format into bit-serial format required for transmission over a single telephone line. When receiving data, the adapter circuits are also responsible for controlling the modem and performing some data formatting and error checking functions.

serial port. A port that transmits data a bit at a time used for modems, mice, certain printers and communication devices.

serial processing. Traditional serial processing methods use one central processing unit to carry out several instructions one after the other. Limitation of serial processors is that circuit-switching speeds ultimately reach their limits. Their components on the microprocessor are positioned closer and closer together to reduce the distance that electrical signals must travel. However, the generated heat becomes more difficult to dissipate. Parallel computers, on the other hand, distribute processing task to a series of processors (nodes or computers) to simultaneously share the processing of a large task.

serial transmission. A method of information transfer in which each bit of a character is sent in sequence.

serial. SER. 1. Pertaining to the sequential performance of two or more activities in single device. In English, the modifiers serial and parallel usually refer to devices, as opposed to sequential and consecutive, which refer to processes.

2. Sequential or consecutive occurrence of two or more related activities in a single device or channel.

3. Pertaining to the sequential processing of the individual parts of a whole such as the bits of a character or the characters of a word, using the same facilities for successive parts.

serial-access memory. SAM. A memory-storage device in which the information is entered in sequence. This results in sequential processing of the data.

series circuit. A circuit in which the components are connected end to end so that the same current flows through each of them.

series compensation. In a wide-band amplifier, such as a video amplifier, frequency compensation provided by an inductor and capacitor connected in series between stages.

series feedback. A feedback system in which the feedback signal is presented to the output point in series with the input signal.

series modulation. Amplitude modulation obtained with a triode inserted in series with the dc supply of the modulated *r-f* amplifier. An *a-f* modulating voltage applied to the grid of the series tube varies the tube's internal plate resistance (and, accordingly, the plate current of the *r-f* amplifier) at the audio frequency.

Server Message Block. *See* SMB.

server. A unit at the node of a computer network, which provides a specific service for network users. Servers include file servers, disk servers, print servers, etc. It may be considered as a node that permits other nodes on the LAN to access its resources.

The server may be dedicated, in which case this is its sole function, or non-dedicated, where the node can be used in other ways, such as a workstation. The server handles the work of locating and extracting the information. The term is also used to refer to the computer running a server program, particularly, if it is used only for thatpurpose.

serving area. The geographic area handled by the service provider.

service point. IBM network management term for a system that allows non-SNA equipment and network components to be incorporated into an SNA management structure.

service software. In programming, software designed specifically for service and repair work.

services. A general term for resources made available by a server to other nodes on the network. In Microsoft LAN Manager terminology, this concept is broadened to include all main components of the LAN Manager software.

servo system. A complete electromechanical system, incorporating one or more servomechanisms, including all of associated circuits and hardware; can be used for variety of purposes, such as temperature regulation, frequency control, voltage regulation, or transmitter tuning.

SES. Severely Errored Second, used in performance management in Network Management.

SESFE. Severely Errored Second Far End, used in performance management in Network Management.

SESP. Severely Errored Second-Path, used in performance management in Network Management.

session layer. The fifth layer of the OSI (Open System Interconnection) reference model. The session layer is responsible for establishing, managing, and terminating conversations between stations, and for mapping logical names on to physical addresses. Logging on and off a network is an example of a session layer operation. Dialogue may process in either full duplex or half-duplex mode.

session. 1. A logical connection between two nodes on a network for exchanging data; alternatively, any live link between any two data devices, such as minicomputer and a dumb terminal. A session is also used to describe connection time. Session Layer Level Five of the OSI data communications model, drawn up by the ISO, ensures the management of dialogue between applications by providing protocols for assembling physical messages into logical messages to all dialogue between end systems.

2. A connection between two stations/centres that allows them to communicate.

set. An operation on a bit, in binary arithmetic, to adjust its value to 1.

SETS. Selected Executable Test Suite, in conformance testing, those tests selected to be run based on the PICS.

settle time. The time taken by the read/write heads to stabilise (settle) once they are correctly positioned over a particular track of a magnetic/optical disk. This is one of the many factors, which governor the access speed.

settling time. Following the initiation of a specified input signal to a system, the time required for the output signal to enter and remain within a specified narrow range centred on its steady-state value. It may be noted that the input may be a step, impulse, ramp, parabola, or sinusoid.

sextet. A group of six binary digits treated as an entity.

SF. 1. Short Format.

2. Store and Forward.

3. SubFile.

SFA. Segment Frequency Algorithm.

SFC. Sectored File Controller.

SFD. Simple Formattable Document, CCITT Recommendation X.420.

SFI. Single Frequency Interface.

SFQL. Structured Full-text Query Language, ANSI standard developed by X3H2.

SFS. Symbolic File Support.

SFU. Special Function Unit.

SG I. Study Group One, produces F. Series of CCITT Recommendations about operations are quality service for telemetric services.

SG VII. Study Group Seven covers public data networks and produces the X. Series of CCITT Recommendations, e.g., X.400, X.25, Transport and session Layers.

SG VIII. Study Group Eight develops terminal equipment T. Series of CCITT Recommendations for telemetric services; involved with the upper four layers of the OSI Reference Model.

SG XI. Study Group Eleven works on CCITT Recommendations for switching and signalling for telephony; covers ISDN services and protocols.

SG XVII. Study Group Seventeen develops the V. Series of modem and interface CCITT Recommendations; works with data transmission over telephone networks.

SG XVIII. Study Group Eighteen works with digital network and ISDN CCITT Recommendations.

SG. 1. System Gain.
2. Study Group, Special Group, technical body under CCITT.

SGISP. OSI Special Group on International Standardised Profiles.

SGML. Standard Generalised Markup Language, a language format meant for designing other markup languages; it is based upon the use of a special file called a document type description (DTD) document. DTD describes the structure of a document, much like the a data description document describes the the structure of a database.

SGML-B. A binary version of SGML; a proposed annex to ISO 8879.

SGMP. Simple Gateway Monitoring Protocol, a predecessor of SNMP.

shadow memory. Shadow memory is sometimes used with 32-bit microprocessors, which use only a 16-bit bus architecture for their read-only memory (ROM) routines. Shadow memory is area of the random-access memory (RAM) which is set aside to temporarily store some ROM routines, thereby doubling such processing speeds because the RAM chip operates with the full 32-bit bus architecture.

shadow ROM. The Shadow Read-Only Memory is installed in some computers to increase overall system speed by copying the system BIOS (basic input/output system) and Video Graphics Array BIOS directly into system random-access memory) at the time the system is booted. RAM typically runs two to three times faster than the ROM that holds the BIOS. Therefore, the system's response to all BIOS calls is much quicker.

shadow server. *See* back-up server.

shadow. Shadowing BIOS in RAM; when an IBM or compatible computer boots, the BIOS code which is located in relatively slow read-only memory (ROM) is copied into write-protected memory locations in much faster RAM. This allows BIOS functions to execute more quickly.

shannon. A unit of logarithmic measure of information equal to the decision content of a set of two mutually exclusive events expressed as a logarithm to base 2; for example, the decision content of a character set of 8-characters is equal to 3 shannons.

shape factor. The attenuation-versus-frequency response of a bandpass filter, especially in a communication receiver. The shape factor determines the extent to which the response is rectangular. It is generally expressed as the ratio of the bandwidth of a filter at the -60 dB points to the bandwidth at the -6 dB points.

share point. A named location on a computer with SMB server service. A share point is a location to which client computers can connect.

shared disk. A magnetic disk, used for information storage by two or more computers at the same time.

shared file. A file that may be accessed by two systems. It can provide a means of communication between two computer systems.

shared logic. A computer system in which units operate under a central control sharing the processing power of the central unit.

shareware. Software, which is protected under copyright and made available to users on a trial basis, on the condition that if the program is adopted, user will make payment. Payment may or may not buy additional functionality or support. Shareware is often distributed via mail order, or copied from public bulletin boards. In some cases, it can also be downloaded form the Internet. This differs from public domain software, which is available free, for use because it is not protected under copyright.

shell account. A kind of Internet access used by remote terminal connections; operates from a host computer running UNIX or similar operating system.

shell. 1. A program providing interface between user and operating system. 2. *See* redirector.

shielded cable. An inner conductor cable surrounded by an outer grounded metallic braid to protect signals from interference.

shielded twisted pair. A twisted pair of cables surrounded by a wire gauze shield, commonly used by IBM.

shift codes. A method of increasing the number of characters that can be associated with given number of bits.

shift key. A control on a keyboard to enable an alternate character set to be used.

shift register. A register designed for shifting of data to the left or right.

shift. To move bit pattern of a word, either to the left or right.

Shiva password authentication protocol. SPAP. A protocol with which clients can dial into computers running the Windows 2000 server, and who can dial into Shiva servers.

shortcut key. A key or combination of keys that are pressed to carry out a command or action. In Windows and on the Macintosh, if a command has a shortcut key, the key combination is listed to the right of the command name on the menu. On the NeXT, a key is listed to right of the command name on the menu. You press the Command key along with that key. In MS-DOS and many DOS applications, one letter of a command is bolder, a different colour, or underlined. To select that command, you may press that letter. Other operating systems may have other methods.

shoulder tap. A technique enabling one processor to communicate with another.

S-interface. An integrated services digital network terminal interface for TE1 equipment.

SI. 1. Serial Input.
2. Step Index.
3. Session PDU Identifier, field at the beginning of a Session PDU that identifies the type of PDU.

SIA. Stable Implementation Agreements, the OIW Implementers Agreements go stable at the end of each year.

SIB. Serial Interface Board.

SICS. Service Implementation Conformance Statement, in Network Management, a statement similar to PICS that states to which services in implementation claim conformance.

side lobe. One of the lobes between main and back lobes of an antenna pattern.

sideband frequency. The frequency of the modulation-generated signal accompanying a carrier on either side. On a given carrier, one sideband frequency is that of the carrier less that of the modulating signal another is the sum of the carrier and the modulation frequency.

sideband transmission. That method of transmission in which frequencies produced by amplitude modulation occurs above and below the carrier frequency. Frequencies above the carrier are called upper sideband and those below are called lower sideband.

sideband. In communications, frequency bands on both sides of the carrier frequency within which fall the frequencies of the wave produced by the process of amplitude modulation.

sidetone path. Special bypass circuit in a four-wire telephone instrument, which feeds into the local receiver circuit part of the signal produced by the local microphone.

SIG. Special Interest Group, within OIW and AOW, the technical group developing IAs for a given protocol area.

sigma memory. A storage device in calculators used to accumulate the results of a series of calculations.

sign bit. The bit designated to indicate the numerical sign of the binary number with which it is associated.

sign position. A position normally located at one end of a numeral, that contains an indicator denoting the algebraic sign of the number represented by the numeral.

signal generator. A device for producing waveforms of various shapes, frequencies, and amplitudes; generally used for test equipment.

signal processing. The processing of signals by means of hardwired of programmable devices, the signals being regarded as continuous or discrete and being regarded as continuous or discrete and being approximated by analog or digital devices accordingly. Filtering and picture processing are examples of signal processing.

signature. The message at the bottom of an e-mail message or a Usernet article that identifies the sender.

SILS. Standard for Interperable LAN Security.

SIM. 1. Set Initialisation Mode, an HDLC control frame.

2. Synchronous Interface Module.

SIMD. Single-instruction, multiple-data processing; in the parallel processing, more than 65000 processors may be engaged to simultaneously share a processing task. The specialised softwares manages this process by allocating equal portions of the raw data to the processors. Once this is done, it issues one single instruction to all processors simultaneously. An even more common method used with parallel processing is multiple-instruction, multiple-data processing, a method of issuing several instructions attached to groups of data.

SIMM. Single In-line Memory Module. This technology involves surface-mounting individual random-access memory chips onto tiny circuit boards called carrier modules, creating component module that can be plugged into sockets on a personal computer's system board. The key advantage of this approach is that the modules are simple to install. A memory board must be designed specifically to use SIMMs. Many computers use SIMMs, though some now use DIMMs.

Simple Network Management Protocol. *See* SNMP.

Simplex. A communications system or link which can only carry a signal in one direction.

simulation. In computing, a technique by which a system is represented as a mathematical model. The model is then programmed on a computer so that the behaviour of the original system may be studied.

simultaneous computer. A computer that contains a separate unit to perform each portion of the entire computation concurrently, the units being interconnected in a way determined by the computation. At different times in a run, a given interconnection carries signals representing different values of the same variable; for example, a differential analyser.

simultaneous processing. In computing, the performance of two or more computing tasks at the same instant.

simultaneous transmission. In data communications, a technique in which the transmission of messages in one direction is accompanied with transmission of control characters or data in the other.

SINAD. SIgnal to Noise And Distortion; an expression frequently used to define the sensitivity of a frequency-modulation receiver at very-high and ultra-high frequencies; usually, SINAD sensitivity of a receiver is given as the signal strength in μV at the antenna terminals that results in signal-to-noise-and-distortion ratio of 12 dB at the speaker terminals.

single-address instruction. A machine language instruction which contains only one operator and one address.

single-error-correction double-error detection. SECDED. An error correction and detection code that can detect and correct one-bit errors and detect but not correct two-bit errors. Simple parity checks can only detect but not correct one-bit errors whereas two-bit errors cannot even be detected.

single-frequency signalling. In communications, the use of tones to give information for control and supervisory purposes on a channel.

sink tree. Set of all paths to a destination in a communication network, when fixed routing tables are used.

sink. A memory or recording device in which information can be stored.

SIO. 1. Serial Input/Output.
2. Start Input/Output.
3. Step Input/Output.
4. Security Information Object, used with Security Exchange ASE.

SIR. 1. Speaker Independent voice Recognition, technologies for the automated conversion of speech to accurate and meaningful textual information, typically ASCII. It typically accepts input from callers to voice processors where callers are using rotary dial instead of DTMF telephones. SIR products have deliberately limited vocabularies, but are increasing due to the vast installed base of non-DTMF telephones.
2. Segment Identification register.
3. Selective Information Retrieval.

SIS. 1. Structured Information Store of conceptual communications area of virtual terminal.
2. Signalling Interworking Subsystem.

SIU. System Interface Unit.

SKB. SKew Buffer.

SKINNEYNET. Thin Ethernet standard used over TCP/IP.

SL. Session Layer, layer 5 of the OSI Reference Model.

slave. A remote system or terminal whose functions are controlled by a central master system.

slice network. A self-contained modular unit, which is capable of being located in as many places as necessary, and in the event of being cut off from rest of the system, will continue to operate independently.

sliding window protocol. When used in reference to error correction protocols, a protocol which allows several blocks of data to be transmitted before acknowledgement is required from the receiver. If very few errors are detected on a communications path, the size of the window may increase so that data throughput is increased. If a significant number of errors occur, the size of the data window may decrease to ensure data integrity and maintain throughput.

SLIP. Serial Line Internet Protocol, an early TCP/IP-based modem protocol, which can be used over RS-232 to support IP; made obsolete by Point-to-Point Protocol. The purpose of SLIP is to transmit IP datagram across a modem line. SLIP provides no physical addressing or error-control and depends on upper-layer protocols for error-controlled functions. It simply sends the data then sends a signal marking the end of the data, and allows direct access to the Internet over a modem. The user may configure a computer running Windows 2000 as a SLIP server, and must use TCP/IP protocol and a serial COM port to connect to a SLIP server.

slope detector. An AM receiving circuit de-tuned to one side of resonance (*i.e.*, to a point along the skirt of the selectivity curve) to detect the FM signal. FM swing occurs along the slope of the resonance curve. Slope detection is useful in narrow-band FM when conventional FM circuitry is not available.

slotted ring network. A ring network with unidirectional data transmission in which data is transferred in the predefined slots in the transmission stream.

slotted ring. A LAN architecture that continually carries a constant number of fixed length packets or slots round the ring. The nodes then use, by replacement, empty slots as they pass through, to transmit data. All the nodes have the ability to recognise empty slots or addressed to them. This network architecture is also known as a Cambridge Ring.

slotted-ring network. A ring network that allows unidirectional data transmission between data stations by transferring data in predefined slots in the transmission stream over one transmission medium such that the data return to the originating station. It may be noted that in a slotted-ring network, a slot is a kind of frame.

SLU. Special Line Unit.

SM. Single Mode.

SMAE. System Management Application Entity, an application entity for communication of systems management information.

SMAL. 1. Store Multiple Access Control. 2. Structural MacroAssembly Language.

SMAP. System Management Application Process.

smart card. A plastic card similar in appearance to the normal credit card, but has an integrated circuit embedded in the plastic. The circuit has two broad functions: intelligence and memory. The card is activated when it is inserted into terminal. It receives signals from the terminal, performs functions according to those signals, and a program stored in the card's internal memory, sends out response signals and updates its internal memory. The memory of the card may be partitioned for secret data, protected data and a working space. The smart cards are used as high-security keys, allowing access to telephone networks, corporate data banks, and restricted locations. The most advanced smart cards (sometimes called IC cards) have a small liquid-crystal display, which in the future will be able to digitise versions of their owner's signatures, retina prints, or fingerprints.

386 smart cache. A cache chip produced by Intel Corporation to integrate entire cache subsystem onto single chip: control logic, 16-kilobytes data SRAM (static random-access memory), a four double-word writ buffer, and a four double-word line buffer. The 80486 central processing unit's on-chip cache architecture is utilised by the 386 Smart Cache, allowing it to achieve equal or greater performance than previous 64- and 128-kilobytes caches.

smart machine. Any device, which uses a microprocessor to evaluate the input and make decisions about which path to take. For example, a smart car headlight can be designed to automatically monitor the level of external light. When it becomes sufficiently dark outside, the microprocessor switches on the driving lights, and continues to monitor the environment in order to switch the light off when the sun rises.

smart wiring hub. A network concentrator, enabling multiple media to be supported and managed from a central location. When supporting structured wiring systems, smart hubs provide port management.

SMASE. System Management Application Service Entity, the application entity that makes use of CMISE to provide specific management functions.

SMB. Server Message Block, a Microsoft originated distributed system protocol, which enables access to another computer's files and peripherals over the network as if they were local; enables computers to share directories with other computers via the network. NetBIOS is based on SMB, and Windows NT uses SMB.

SMD. Storage Modular Device.

SMDL. Standard Music Description Language, a specific application of SGML.

SMDR. Station Message Detail Recording detailed records of calls made from a telephone station, including time of call and duration.

SMDS. Switched Multi-megabit Data Services, a public packet-switched high-speed data service that extends LAN-like performance to MANs and WANs with no distance limit. Although reflecting DQDB MAN standards, SMDS can also run over ATM. It offers variable data packet size, Virtual Private Network and Closed User Group features, transmission rates up to 34Mbit/s today and 150Mbit/s in the future.

SMF. System Management Function, a set of logically related user requirements in the systems management.

SMI. 1. Structure of Management Information, set of standards in the OSI management.

2. Structure of Management Information, in SNMP, defines the relation between network objects, written in ASN 1.

SMIB. System Management Information Base, definition of objects used in system management.

SML. Symbolic Machine Language.

SMM. Shared Mutiport Memory.

SMO. System Management Overview.

SMP. 1. Session Protocol Machine.

2. System Modification Program.

SMP. Standby Monitor Present MAC frame.

SMPDU. 1. System Management Protocol Data Unit.

2. Service Message Protocol Data

Unit, a delivery or non-delivery report about a message in X.400.

SMS. 1. Service Management System.
2. Storage Management System.

SMT. Station ManagemenT, the station management entity in an IEEE/ANSI/ISO local area network.

SMTP. Simple Mail Transfer Protocol, an early messaging standard used over TCP/IP; the protocol used to transfer e-mail between computers on the Internet. It is a server to server protocol, so other protocols (like POP) are needed to transfer the E-mail to a client machine.

SN. 1. Sub-Network, a set of one or more physical open systems which can provide network connections and relaying services for end systems; can refer to either a public or a private network.
2. Source Name.
3. Subject Name.

SNA. Systems Network Architecture, a networking standard by IBM.

SNAP. 1. Standard Network Access Protocol.
2. Sub-Network Access Protocol.

SNARE. Sub-Network Address Resolution Entity.

SNDCF. Sub-Network Dependent Convergent Facility, Sub-layer of layer 3 of the OSI Reference Model.

SNDCP. Sub-Network Dependent Convergence Protocol, a translation function for CLNS over X.25.

sneakerNet. Hand-carrying documents or diskettes between computer systems; slang.

SNICF. Sub-Network Independent Convergence Facility, a sub-layer of layer 3 of the OSI Reference Model.

SNICP. Sub-Network Independent Convergence Protocol, a sub-layer of layer 3 of the OSI Reference Model.

SNMP. Simple Network Management Protocol, one of the protocols within the TCP/IP suite utilising UDP port 161 for communication. Most network analyser software can interface to SNMP, and an SNMP monitor is a very useful tool in a network of more than moderate complexity. SNMP provides three ways to access management information:

1. Request/response interaction in which a manager sends a request to an agent and the agent responds to the request. The agent must always reply using a Response-PDU.

2. Request/response interaction in which manager sends a request to another manager and the latter responds to the request. The request is usually to notify a manager of management information associated with the same manager, using InformRequest-PDU.

3. Unconfirmed interaction in which an agent sends an unsolicited Trap-PDU to a manager. This request is usually to notify a manager of an exceptional situation that has resulted in changes to the management information associated with the network device.

SNOBOL. A string-oriented symbolic language designed for advanced string manipulation; used in artificial intelligence, compiler construction applications.

snow. A type of TV picture interference caused by a weak video signal; it is characterised by a screen whose image is superimposed by countless tiny out-of-focus light spots whose random pulsing resembles falling snow.

SNRM. Set Normal Response Mode, an HDLC link initialisation frame.

SO. 1. Send Only.
2. Serial Output.

soak. A method of detecting program errors and problems by running the program under normal operating conditions, and closely supervised by the programmer.

SOAP. Symbolic Optimum Assembly Programming.

SOB. Start Of Block.

SOF. Start Of Frame.

soft copy. The information displayed on screen or in audio format.

soft data. The data, such as routing data, that is semi-permanent in the system, and which is under the control of the administrative program.

soft error. An error that occurs sporadically and that may not appear on successive attempts to read data. It can be corrected by re-reading the sector or by moving the read/write head back and forth.

soft font. Any of the various font, usually provided by a font vendor, that must be installed on the computer and sent to the printer before it can be printed. Also known as downloadable font.

soft lifting. The illegal copying of the licensed software for personal use.

soft sectoring. The identification of sector boundaries on a magnetic disk by using recorded data.

software engine. Borland's software product, which allows applications to access common data; it is designed to be incorporated into a variety of different applications. For example, the Paradox Engine is built into Paradox, Quattro Pro, and Sidekick for Presentation Manager. It allows Borland products and programs written in C, C^{++}, and object Pascal to access data kept in Paradox tables.

software package. A complete and documented set of programs supplied to several users for a generic application or function. It may be noted that some software packages may be alterable for a specific application. The software packages are generally mainstream applications that fall in any of the following categories:

Operating systems
Software development systems
Word processors
Internet browsers
Spreadsheets
Database managers
Communications applications
Graphics applications
CAD software
Educational software
Multimedia software
Entertainment software
Utilities.

software vending machine. A novel method of purchasing software, in which the purchaser inserts bank notes or a credit card into the payment slot of the machine, chooses the required software by menu selection and keyboard action, inserts a floppy disk, or cassette into the machine and the program is then written to the tape or disk.

software. The programs, procedures, rules, routines, and possibly documents associated with the operation of the data-processing system. Programs, operating systems, device drivers, and macros are all software.

SOGT. Senior Officials Group for Telecommunications, made up of European government representatives; they monitor standards in the public telecom sector.

SOH. Start Of Header, ASCII character decimal 1 or ^A (control A); not a printed character but a "control" character.

Solaris. The Sun workstation operating environment, including SunOS and the Open Windows windowing environment.

solid colour. A colour that appears on a display when all pixels are the same colour. On a monochrome display, there are only two solid colours, black and white. Contrast to nonsolid colour or dithered colour.

solid state disk. SSD. A secondary storage device that uses semiconductor memory as its storage medium (rather than a magnetic disk) providing performance 10-30 times better than that of a magnetic disk. Solid state disks provide a significant perfor-mance boost in environments where shared files cause a throughput bottleneck. solid state disks are also useful in reducing bottlenecks in situations where input/output system is constantly required to provide access to small amounts of data, such as application and system software control files.

SOM. Start Of Message.

SONET. Synchronous Optical NETwork, a family of Physical Layer interfaces for optical fibre.

SOP. Standard Operating Procedure.

sorting order. The order in which records are sorted, either ascending or descending.

sorting. The procedure for arranging records in a particular order according to the contents of one or more fields.

SOS. Sophisticated Operating System.

SOT. Start Of Text.

sound card. An expansion card that records and plays back sound by translating the analog signal from a microphone in to a digitised form that the computer can store and process and then translating the modified data back in to analog signals.

SOUP. SOftware Utility Package.

source code analyser. A real time saver for the programmers, that examine a program and generates a report on many aspects of that program.

source code. The set of instructions written in high-level language, which is yet to be translated (assembled) into machine language (object code). In order to run the program, source code must be translated into machine code by either an interpreter or a compiler.

source data acquisition. SDA. Information being entered directly into a computer at the location where the data originates. An example of this is a point-of-sale system.

source data automation. The coded recording of information on tags, paper tape, or punch cards, which can be used repeatedly without rewriting being necessary in order to produce other records of data.

source file. The file that stores instructions for the computer to execute.

source follower. An amplifier circuit in which the output is taken from the source circuit of a field-effect transistor. The output impedance of the source follower is low, and the voltage gain is always less than 1.

source language. A language in which the user's program is written. In machine translation, the language from which translation is to be made.

source program. A computer program written in a source language.

source suppression. In communications, the design of circuitry and layout so that no compromising signals are emitted.

source user. The user providing the information to be transferred to the destination user during a particular information transfer.

source. A point of message entry into the system.

SP. Security Protocol, part of Secure Data Network Systems.

SPAP. *See* Shiva password authentication protocol.

SPARC station. A Sun workstation model using the SPARC CPU

SPARC. The RISC CPU used in newer Sun workstations.

SPB. Stored Program Buffer.

SPDU. Session Protocol Data Unit.

special characters. 1. The printable symbols often used with numeric characters. They include the dollar sign ($) comma (,), and percentage sign (%).
2. A graphic character that is not a letter, digit, or blank character, and usually not an ideogram. Some of the commonly used space characters include a currency symbol, a percent sign, and a mathematical symbol.

SPECmark. Systems Performance Evaluation Cooperative MARK; suite of 10 benchmarks that test integer (SPECint) and floating point (SPECfp) performance of a computer. A VAX-11\780 is a one-SPECmark machine.

spectral envelope. The envelope function of a frequency spectrum representing energy distribution as a function of frequency.

speed dialing. Dialing at a rate faster than 10 impulses per second.

speed matching. The ability of several switched data services to interconnect terminals with different operating speeds.

SPF. 1. Shortest Path First, one of the rules used in packet-switched networks when selecting a route for a packet to its destination.
2. Standard Program Facility.

SPL. Simulation Programming Language.

SPLC. Standard Point Location Code.

split screen. A facility that juxtaposes two or more displays on the screen of a visual display unit.

SPN. Signal Processor Networking.

spoofing. The deliberate inducement of a user or a resource to take an incorrect action.

spool. Simultaneous Peripheral Operation OnLine; to transfer data intended for a peripheral device (usually a printer) into temporary storage. From there the data can be transferred to the peripheral at a later time, without affecting or delaying the system as it performs other operations. When several programs are running in the same, operating system and files need to be printed, or when different users are attached to the same printer, files are spooled to ensure they are printed quickly and correctly. To spool the files, they are sent to the printer-buffer (memory) and queued until they can be printed. One advantage of spooling is that the relatively slow printer does not hold up the computer because files can be sent down to the buffer very quickly. Processing then occurs between the buffers and the printer, thereby freeing the computer to proceed with its normal tasks.

spooling. The use of auxiliary storage as a buffer storage to reduce processing delays when transferring data between peripheral equipment and the processor of a computer.

spot modulation. In a cathode-ray tube, modulation of the brightness of the spot (and, accordingly, of the image) produced on the screen by the electron beam.

SPR. Storage Protection Register.

SPRYTE. Two-dimensional graphical representation which can be moved over another graphic image, either stationary or another SPRYTE.

SPS. Symbolic Program System.

SQA. Software Quality Assurance.

SQE. Signal Quality, IEEE 802.3 transceiver heartbeat sent to terminal via AUI; must be disabled when transceiver is used with repeater.

SQL. Structured Query Language, standardised language used in various DBMS packages

SQL2. Addendum to SQL with various enhancements.

SQL3. Addendum to SQL2, designed at the feature level.

S register. Any of the register of a modem which allow the user to tailor the modem to particular applications. The information is retained by the modem in its own non-volatile memory. For example, S Register 0 contains a decimal value (from 0-255) equivalent to the number of rings the modem will wait before answering an incoming call. Thus, if S Register 0 contains a value of 5, the modem will go online immediately after the fifth ring of an incoming call. If this register contains a zero value, the automatic answering operation will be disabled. Allowable values however, depend on the local environment.

SREJ. Selective REJect, selectively sending a negative acknowledgement of one protocol data unit.

SRM. System Resource Manager.

SRR. Second read rate; refers to a bar code scanner which translates code on the 'second read rate' should the 'first read rate' be unsuccessful.

SRT. Source Routing Transparent, a routing algorithm that is transparent to the end user, implemented in a bridge or router.

SR-UAPDU. Service Report User Agent Protocol Data Unit, a receipt or non-receipt notification in X.400.

SS. 1. Signalling System, generic, a physical and/or logical system to transmit information, such as Morse or radio.

2. Session Service, provides dialogue management for presentation entities; define by layer 5 of the OSI Reference Model.

SS7. Signalling System No. 7.

SSA. Segment Search Argument; defines database segment to be accessed by a program.

SSAP. Session Service Access Point, address for a session entity, normally expressed as an integer.

SSB. Single SideBand, in radio frequency communications, the technique of using only half of a carrier frequency's waveform as a carrier.

SSBM. Single SideBand Modulation.

SSBSC. Single SideBand Suppressed Carrier.

SSD. *See* solid state disk.

SSDU. Session Service Data Unit.

SSEL. Session SELector, used by the Session to identify a Presentation Layer entity. An SSEL and a TSAP address make up a SSAP address.

SSI. Small-Scale Integration, *i.e.* integration of generally less than 100 transistors on a single chip.

SSP. Service Switching Point.

ST-506 disk interface. The original interface between a hard disk and its controller, named after the model number of an early drive from Seagate Technology. For modern high-speed personal computers (PCs) to work efficiently with mass storage devices there must be an effective means of transferring data between the device and the PC. The format and speed of this data transfer is determined by the type of device interface built-into the electronics on the drive and its controller board.

stack. 1. A data structure, in which items are added at the end of a sequential and can only be retrieved from the same end; refers to the computer memory that is used for the purpose of short-term data storage. In a stack, items are removed in a last in, first out (LIFO) manner. In contrast, a queue removes items in a first in, first out (FIFO) manner. Random access is not possible. A magnetic-core memory is often called a stack.

2. A memory space used to entertain the programmers and management by overflowing or being subjected to mismatched PUSH/POPs.

standalone terminal. A terminal that can be directly connected via a modem and is not, therefore, a member of a cluster.

standard binary-coded-decimal interchange code. A computer code in most second-generation computers which is an expansion of the binary-coded-decimal system. The significant difference in the standard BCD code is the use of zone bits. The zone also bits of an alphanumeric character perform a code function similar to the zone positions of a punched card. They are used in combination with digits to represent the letters of the alphabet or special characters.

standard document. The primary document which is used in automatic letter writing and is merged with variable information to produce final letter.

Standard Generalised Markup Language. *See* SGML.

standard mode. In Windows, an operating mode that provides access to extended memory and also enables you to switch between non-Windows applications, but it does not provide virtual memory or enable non-Windows applications to run in the background or in a window. Hint. You can tell what mode your copy of Windows is running in by choosing About Program Manager... from the Help menu in the Program Manager.

standby. A condition in which a complete resumption of stable operation is possible within a short time.

star bit. A bit used in asynchronous transmission preceding a serial character and signalling the start of that character.

star signal. In star-stop transmission, a signal at the beginning of a character that prepares the receiving device for the reception of the code elements. It may be noted that a start signal is limited to one signal element generally having the duration of a unit interval.

star topology. A network topology in data communications, in which each node is connected only to one central controller. Such network is commonly employed when a number of terminals are connected to single host computer and the majority of the traffic is concerned with host-terminal rather than terminal-terminal communication.

StarLAN 10. A higher-performance version of StarLAN, transmitting at 10 megabits per second, developed by AT&T.

StarLAN. A star topology local area network using baseband CSMA/CD, running on twisted pair cable (1 megabit per second) where the maximum cable distance between a device and the central controller is 500 m.

start-up disk. Also called a system disk. A disk that contains files necessary to start up a computer. A Macintosh start-up disk must contain a System file and the finder file. An MS-DOS start-up disk must have the invisible system files (IO.SYS and MSDOS.SYS) and COMMAND.COM file. The user should have an extra system disk around in case the system files on the hard drive that starts the computer are damaged. Without a system disk, the user can not access and fix the hard disk.

static column dynamic access memory. SCDAM. A dynamic random-access memory organised as 64K X1 using one transistor cell arrays and housed in 16-pin package. The memory on the same row address can be accessed only by selecting column address without the aid of a clock, as on static random-access memory. In this mode cycle, time can be equal to an access time while DRAM usually requires a cycle time of twice the access time. Therefore, the access time becomes competitive to current high-speed static column dynamic access memory.

static dump. In computing, a dump performed at a particular point in time relative to a machine run.

static input. In a digital-logic circuit, a static input produces an output state that depends on whether the input is logic low (0) or logic high (1). It is triggered by the actual signal level, rather than by a change of signal level.

static routing. A routing method in which the routing information is input manually by network administrator.

static test mode. That set-up mode of an analog computer during which special initial conditions are set in order to check the patching, and consequently, the proper operation of all computer devices except integrators.

statistical database. A database containing aggregate information concerning large subsets of entities. Such data can be misused to reveal information concerning individuals unless some form of inference control is employed.

status. One or more data bits showing which one of a class of operations is being performed, has been completed or is recognised by the central processing unit.

STB. 1. Segment Tag Bits.
2. Start of Text Block.

STC. Switching and Testing Centre.

STD. 1. Synchronous Time Division, a basic form of multiplexing.
2. Subscriber Trunk Dialling.

STDM. Statistical Time Division Multiplexing, basic form of multi-plexing.

STE. Signalling Terminal Equipment, X.75.

steady-state condition. 1. In a communication circuit, a condition in which some specified characteristic of condition-such as value, rate, periodicity or amplitude-exhibits only negligible change over an arbitrarily long period of time.
2. In an electrical circuit, a condition occurring after all initial transient or fluctuating conditions have damped out, in which currents, voltages or fields remain essentially constant or oscillate uniformly without changes in characteristics such as amplitude, frequency, or wave shape.
3. Equilibrium mode distribution.

steganography. The concealment of the existence of the messages in the management of data security. This can be done by filling in inter-message gaps with padding characters.

STF. Short Title File.

STM. 1. Synchronous Transfer Mode, traditional multiplexing based on fixed frame size and fixed channels.
2. Short Term Memory.

STO. Segment Table Origin.

STOL. System Test and Operation Language.

stop bit. A bit used in asynchronous transmission for indicating the end of the character.

stop-and-wait protocol. A flow control algorithm in data communications in which the sending host awaits acknowledgement, from the receiving host, that the error-free frames have been received before transmitting further frames.

storage capacity. The amount of data that a particular store can accommodate, generally mentioned in bytes.

storage devices. The devices that can receive data and retain it for subsequent retrieval. Such devices cover a wide range of capacities and speeds of access. The semiconductor devices used as the main memory for the processor may take only a few nanoseconds to retrieve data but the cost of storing each bit is very high by comparison with the devices used as backing store, which may take milliseconds or even many seconds to retrieve data. Two main categories used to store data are magnetic and optical storage. Although devices that store data typically employ one or the other, some combine both the technologies. The primary types of magnetic storage are:

Diskettes
Hard disks
Removable hard disks
Magnetic tapes.

Primary types of optical storage are:

CD-ROM
WORM
Magneto-optical disks.

store-and-forward. The communications in which messages are held, or stored, for transmission at a later stage. The most common store-and-forward scheme is packet radio.

STP. Signal Transfer Point.

strap. 1. A connection link between two tags, terminals or items of equipment. 2. In printing, a subheading used above the main headline in a document or article.

stream cipher. A method of encryption in data security, with the capability of providing perfect secrecy. The plain text is encoded into numbers, usually binary, and a key stream of random numbers is combined with the plain text to form the cipher text. The receiving end is supplied with an identical key stream of random numbers, and the mathematical inverse combination of cipher text and key stream reveals the plain text.

StreamWorks. A music player that is high-end counterpart to RealAudio system. StreamWorks plug-in supports high speed digital Internet connections not supported by RealAudio, including 44.1kHz CD-quality stereo sound transmitted over 128 Kbps ISDN line.

stripping. An action taken by an originating data station to remove its frames from the network after a successful revolution on the ring.

stroke character generator. A character generator that generates character images composed of line segments.

structured flowchart. A flowcharting technique, which uses control structures to minimise the complexity of the programs, thereby reducing error rates. It is related to structured programming, a method of breaking a program into logic sections, using universal programming standards.

structured language. A technique, which uses control structures in a language to minimise the complexity of the programs, thereby reducing error rates. It is related to structured programming, a method of breaking a program into logic sections, using universal programming standards. These sections, sometimes managed by different programmers, make it easier to write, check, and maintain a complex program.

structured programming. A technique for organising and coding programs that reduces complexity, improves clarity, and makes them easier to debug and modify. Typically, a structured program is hierarchy of modules that have a single entry point and a single exit point; control is passed downward through the structure without unconditional branches to higher levels of structure; synonymous with GOTO-less programming.

Programs may be written with any of the following control structures:
Sequence structure
Selection Structure
Repetition structure.

STS. Shared Tenant Service, a term describing the backbone of the "smart building" concept.

style sheet. A collection of styles, or design elements, created for a specific document. Once the style are set up, one can apply them simply selecting the style from a menu. It is a big time saver if universal changes to the document are to be made.

style. A named collection of character and paragraph formats that determine the appearance of a text block. Styles allows the user to apply the same sets of formatting choices over and over with a single keystroke.

SU. Service User, entity above a given layer in the OSI Reference Model making use of the service provided at the lower layer.

SUABORT. Session User ABORT, PDU to indicate that the user of Session Layer wants to abnormally terminate an activity.

sub notebook. A portable computer, that is usually weighing less than 2 kg. Sub-notebooks often have fewer ports than a notebook, and no internal floppy drive.

sub-code channel. One of the eight compact disc sub-channels (P-W) that exist in parallel to the main channel. They are used for control and display information.

sub-directory. A directory within another directory.

sub-frame. A sequence of non-contiguous sets of digits assembled within a pulse code modulation multiplexing frame, each set being repeated at *n* times the frame repetition rate where *n* is an integer > 1.

sub-menu. A secondary menu that appears while dragging and holding over an item in a menu. It gives you choices of options that apply to the item you are selecting in the menu. Also known as hierarchical menu; submenu.

sub-net mask. *See* address mask.

sub-net. A network segment, which has a portion of the total number of addresses assigned to the network ID; created using routers or gateways on networks with high traffic. Gives better administrative control and improves performance. Subnetting is very beneficial because it reduces congestion, supports different technologies, handles technology-imposed limits, increases security, and reduces disruption from broadcasts.

sub-program. A part of larger program that can be compiled independently.

sub-routine. A sequence of instructions to perform an action that is frequently required in a program, or set of programs.

subsequent address message. A message used in common-channel signalling following an initial address. It contains one or more additional digits of address information along with or instead of an end-of-pulsing signal.

subsidiary feedback. Feedback other than the main feedback in a system. Thus, feedback within a single amplifier stage that has overall feedback, is subsidiary.

substitution cipher. A cipher in which each character or fixed group of characters is substituted by another character or group of characters.

summation check. A comparison of checksums, computed on the same data on different occasions, or on different representations of the data, to verify data integrity.

summer. A functional unit whose output analog variable is equal to the sum, or a weighted sum, of the input analog variables.

Sun. Sun Microsystems. Makers of high-end UNIX workstations.

SunOS. A version of UNIX produced for the Sun workstations.

super drive. A floppy disk drive in Macintosh computers that enables it to read 400K, 800K, and 1.44MB disks; also allows (with proper software) to read MS-DOS disks.

super large-scale integration. Pertaining to a fabrication technology capable of producing well in excess of 100,000 transistors per chip.

superband. The frequency band in the range 216-600 MHz, used for fixed and mobile radios and additional television channels on a cable system.

supergroup distribution frame. SDF. The frame used in a frequency-division multiplexing system, it provides for the interconnection of equipment and apparatus which transmit signals having frequencies in the 60-channel basic supergroup range.

supergroup. A collection of five channel groups occupying adjacent bands in the spectrum for the purpose of simultaneous modulation and demodulation. A subgroup comprises 60 voice channels.

SuperVGA. Super Video Graphics Array; specifications for video output that expanded the VGA specifications on IBM and compatible computers to more than 640×480 resolution, and more than 256 colours. There is not a single SuperVGA standard, so not all SuperVGA devices have compatible features.

superzapping. 1. The process of making a direct change to object or machine code.

2. Pertaining to operations that misuse the computer universal access program in order to bypass normal security arrangements and then make illegal modifications to programs or data. It involves the use of a computer network's 'superzap program' - master control program used by senior computer maintenance professionals in disaster recovery, or when a computer system cannot be started in the normal way after it crashes. Criminals with access to the superzap codes are able to perform any unauthorised transaction very quickly, being in a position to escape before they can be caught.

surge suppresser. An electrical device that electronic equipment can be plugged into. A surge suppresser includes a circuit breaker that will protect equipment from damage from a surge in electricity (from, e.g., a lightning strike).

SUT. System Under Test, the real open system containing an implementation to be test for conformance.

SVC. Switched Voice Circuit, Switched Virtual Circuit.

SWAN. Satellite Wide Area Network.

swap file. An area of your hard disk that is set aside for virtual memory. Swap files can be either temporary or permanent.

swap in. To load essential parts of a program in to the memory as required for use.

swap out. To unload, or remove non-essential parts of a program from memory to make space available for necessary functions.

swapping. Interchanges in the contents of an area of main storage with the contents of an area of auxiliary storage.

symbolic inference. The process by which lines of reasoning are formed; for example, syllogisms and other common ways of reasoning systematically from premises. In the real world, knowledge and data-premises-are often inexact. Thus, some inference procedures can use degrees of uncertainty in their inference making. In an expert system, the inference subsystem in an expert system is one of three subsystems necessary to achieve expert performance; the other two subsystems are the knowledge base management subsystem and the human interface subsystem.

symmetric binary channel. A channel that is designed to convey messages consisting of binary characters and that has the property that conditional probabilities of changing any one character to other character are equal.

symmetrical binary code. A pulse code derived from a binary code in which the sign of quantized value, positive or negative, is represented by one digit, and in which remaining digits constitute a binary number representing the magnitude. In a particular symmetrical binary code, the order of the digits and the use made of the symbols 0 and 1 in the various digit position must be specified.

SYN. A control flag signifying that sequence number synchronisation is taking place. The SYN flag is used at the beginning of TCP connection as part of the 3-way handshake.

sync pulse. 1. A pulse used to control the frequency or repetition rate of an oscillator or other generator.

2. A pulse transmitted as part of the composite video signal to control scanning.

synchronisation. A relationship between processes such that one process cannot proceed beyond a particular point until another process has reached a particular point. For example, when one process is writing data in a buffer to be read by another process, the two processes must be synchronised so that the reading process does not attempt to read the buffer beyond the point at which the writing process has written data in the buffer. Synchronisation can be achieved by using a semaphore.

synchronise. To cause two systems to operate at the same speed.

synchronising level. A processor timing level during which repetitive programs are run as initiated by a real time clock, which interrupts the processor at a regular rate.

synchronous computer. A computer in which each event is constrained to wait upon the arrival of timing signal.

synchronous counter. A counter consisting of an interconnected series of flip-flops in which all the flip-flop outputs change state at the same instant, normally on application of a pulse at the counter input.

synchronous data link control. SDLC. A bit-oriented uniform discipline employing synchronous data techniques to transfer data between stations in a multi-point, point-to-point or loop configuration.

synchronous data network. SDN. A data network which uses a method of synchronisation between data circuit-terminating equipment and the data switching exchange, as well as between data switching exchanges. The data signalling rates are controlled by timing equipment within the network.

synchronous data. Any data, usually digital, that is transmitted according to a precise time function. In some synchronous-data communication circuits the receiver is kept in step with the transmitter by means of pulses sent at the beginning and/or end of each character, or at regular intervals. In communications, some codes use such pulses to indicate the start and finish of each character. The television transmitters send out synchronising pulses to keep the receiver scanning properly.

synchronous detector. A circuit that operates in a manner similar to a product detector; a local oscillator signal is mixed with the incoming signal to recover the sidebands. It uses a phase-locking system, which keeps the local-oscillator output in exact synchronisation with the carrier wave of the incoming signal. This ensures that the output of the detector will be identical with the original modulating wave.

synchronous digital hierarchy. *See* SDH.

synchronous modem. A modem with an internal clock, which produces a continuous stream of data at a fixed transmission rate. Synchronisation is required at the bit, byte, and message level.

synchronous multiplex. A form of time division multiplex in which two or more signals are transmitted over a single circuit at the same time. The signals are split into discrete intervals having equal duration, and interwoven at a higher speed.

synchronous operation. Method of data transmission in which both terminals are kept in step by time pulses.

synchronous transmission. A transmission method in which each bit is transmitted according to a given time sequence. It can provide a higher bit rate than asynchronous transmission.

syntax error. A programming error, other than logical error, in a computer program caused by, for example, spelling, or grammatical mistakes.

syntax. The relationships among characters or groups of characters, independent of their meanings or manner of their interpretation and use.

synthesis. A cognitive process that involves rearranging elements, parts, items, into a new and integrated whole.

SYS. File name extension for a system file, one that specifies device drivers, operating parameters, etc. for a computer or program.

SYSIN. SYStem INput.

SYSOUT. SYStem OUTput.

System 7. The current generation of the Macintosh operating system. There are several versions of System 7, such as 7.0, 7.1, 7.5, 7.5.2, and 7.5.3.

system clock. The computer's internal clock, used to time processing operations; the time intervals are based on the constant, unchanging vibrations of molecules in a quartz crystal; measured in megahertz.

system design. A process of defining the hardware and software architecture, components, modules, interfaces, and data for a system to satisfy specified requirements.

system disk. *See* Startup Disk

system file. On an MS-DOS system, a file that contains information required for running the MS-DOS operating system. A system file is hidden, that is, it is not shown in the directory listing (unless the :/a option is used).

system generation. The selection optional part of an operating system and of creating a particular operating system tailored to the requirements of a data processing installation.

system lifecycle. The course of developmental changes through which a system passes from its conception to the termination of its use.

system software. The set of programs necessary to run the computer. System software provides the interface to the computer and controls basic operations like saving and printing. Such programs (usually prepared and supplied by the manufacturer of a computer) provide the link between user programs and the computer hardware, *e.g.*, the programs that control the operation of the computer itself and compilers for the high-level programming languages that can be used with it.

system support. The continued provision of services and material necessary for the use and improvement of an implemented system.

system. 1. An essential file (program) which makes up part of the MacOS. The system file controls the basic operation of the computer at a low-level, such as printing, saving, etc. 2. Generic term for an operating system. 3. A collection of personnel, machines, methods, and softwares, organised to accompalish the given set of specific functions.

SYSTEM.INI file. A Windows initialisation file that contains settings that can be used to customise Windows for the system's hardware. It can be edited manually, but this should only be attempted if the user knows what he is doing, and even then, he should be sure to have a backup copy.

systems analysis. Analysis of an activity to determine precisely what must be accomplished and how to perform it.

systems analyst. A professional whose task it is to determine (analyse) why a particular set of procedures is required, and how best to design a computer program which will improve the method of operation (system). The systems analysts are responsible for thinking of possible solutions when an information system needs to be updated, modified, or completely revamped. After users or managers identify a need, systems analysts discuss the business, scientific, or engineeringproblem, and spend a significant amount of time and labour at the beginning of the projects defining the goals and issues of a new information system.

Systems Application Architecture. *See* SAA.

systems approach. A term used to denote the systematic application of instructional technology to an educational or training programmes, starting by identifying input and output and then determining how best to convert the former into the latter by employing an appropriate instructional system.

systems development life cycle. SDLC. An organised way to build an information system; it is composed of various phases:

Phase 1	Needs analysis
Phase 2	System design
Phase 3	Development
Phase 4	Implementation
Phase 5	Maintenance

systolic array. VLSI architecture utilising regular array of identical processing elements with common control and timing so that each element performs the same function simultaneously but on different data items.

SYSTRAN. A widely used machine translation system providing translation between pairs of languages such as English, French, Russian, and Spanish.

SZ-band. A section of the S-band extending from 3900 to 4200 MHz.

T

T. *See* tera.

T 1. The basic 24-channel 1.544 Mb/s pulse code modulation system; represents a higher level of the ISDN standard service.

T.nnn. CCITT T. Series Recommendations; define terminal equipment and control procedures for the telematic equipments.

T1E1. Technical subcommittee on network interfaces under the Exchange Carriers Standards Association; they feed into ANSI.

T1P1. Technical subcommittee on personal communications under the Exchange Carriers Standards Association; they feed into ANSI.

T1Q1. Technical subcommittee on performance under the Exchange Carriers Standards Association; they feed into ANSI.

T1S1. Technical subcommittee on services, architectures, and signalling under Exchange Carriers Standards Association; they feed into ANSI.

T1X1. Technical subcommittee on digital hierarchy and synchronisation under Exchange Carriers Standards Association; they feed into ANSI.

T1Y1. Technical subcommittee on specialised subjects under the Exchange Carriers Standards Association; they feed into ANSI.

T2. High-speed data link service for 6.312 Mb messaging.

T^{2}L. *See* transistor-transistor logic.

T3. 45-Mb fibre- or RF-delivered digital signal service; DS-3 is the standard packet format; actually 44.736 Mb/s.

TA. 1. Terminal Adapter, used both is ISDN generic.
2. Transferred Account, OSI.

TAA. Typical Address Access.

table. A collection of data, each item being uniquely identified either by some label, or by its relative position.

tablet. A sensitised drawing area used in conjunction with a mouse or light pen to input/manipulate data on the screen. A graphics tablet is a popular input device that consists of a flat drawing surface, and a pointing device similar to a pen that translates motion into digital data. The majority of graphics tablets are dedicated to the computer-aided design and the computer graphic applications.

tab stop. A preset position in a document to which the cursor moves when the Tab key is pressed.

TAC. Telenet Access Controller.

TACS. Total Access Communication System.

tactical digital information link. A class of data links having rigidly controlled protocol.

tactical load. Part of the operational load consisting of command control systems and related functions.

tactile keyboard. A keyboard that is laid on a flat surface and activated by touch rather than by physical movement of keys.

tag. 1. The identifying digits or characters forming part of a record.

2. An encoded price tag, *i.e.*, a perforated one, the retailer can detach for presentation to a data processing system, for inventory management.

3. One or more characters attached to a group of data, that provides information about that group.

TAG. 1. Time Automated Grid.

2. Technical Advisory Group, used with ISO.

tail. 1. A specified data item that indicates the end of a list.

2. A series of codes to denote the end of the message.

TAL. Terminal Application Language.

Talk. Internet tool used for private, individual-to-individual communications that may be authoritative.

TAM. Terminal Access Method.

tandem centre. 1. An installation in a communication system in which switching equipment connects trunks to trunks, but does not connect customer loops.

2. An exchange used primarily as a switching point for traffic between other exchanges.

tap. 1. A branch or intermediate circuit.

2. To monitor conversations on a line.

TAP. Terminal Access Processor.

tape deck. An audio tape recorder that requires ancillary equipment (usually amplifier and loudspeaker system) to produce an audio signal.

tape drive. 1. Mechanism in an audio/video tape recorder, which moves the tape past the heads, usually a capstan of some sort.

2. A mass-storage magnetic device used to store large amounts of data on a tape cartridge for the purpose of archiving important files. The magnetic tape is available in many sizes, and resembles the tape found in videocassettes. To protect against a media failure in the hard drive, this procedure would typically be performed on a daily basis, with the tape being continually reused. Unlike other mass-storage devices, a tape drive is not intended for use with an executing application program because random data cannot be accessed quickly.

tape row. A group of binary characters recorded or sensed in parallel on a line perpendicular to the reference edge of a magnetic tape.

tapped coil. An inductor to which one or more intermediate connections (taps) are made at appropriate turns to provide intermediate values of inductance.

.tar. Extension for the UNIX files that are compressed by UNIX tape archive format and need to be processed with UNIX tar utility for using.

TAR. Terminal Address Register.

TARR. Test Action Request Receiver, in Network Management, the ability of a managed object to perform test management requests.

TASC. TAbular Sequence Control.

task list. In Windows, a window that shows a list of all of the applications currently running. It enables you to switch between them. On Macintosh System 7, the Application menu (the icon at the far right of the menu bar) performs a similar function.

TAT. Trans-Atlantic Telecom, e.g., TAT-8.

TAU. Telematic Access Unit, an access unit providing connection between telematic service and X.400.

TBC. Token Bus Controller, a part of the Arcnet specification.

TBM. Tone Burst Modulator.

TC PPDU. Capability Data Presentation PDU.

TC. 1. Tag Code.
2. Terminal Control.
3. Test Conductor, in test function of Network Management a manager that issue test operation requests.
4. Transport Connection.
5. Technical Committee, used in ISO and ETSI, equivalent of Study Group in CCITT.

TCB. Task Control Block.

TCC PPDU. Capability Data Acknowledge Presentation PDU.

TCCCC. Technical Committee for Computer Communications, body under the Computer Society of IEEE that developed 802 standards for LANs.

TCM. Time Compression Multiplexing, a form of multiplexing.

TCN. 1. Throughput Class Negotiation facility.
2. TeleCommunications Networks.

TCP. 1. Test Coordination Procedure, used in conformance testing to coordinate activity on upper and lower testers while executing a test suite.
2. Transmission Control Protocol; a connection-oriented transport protocol in the TCP/IP suite.
3. Task Control Program.

TCP/IP implementation. The software component, which performs the functions that, enables a computer to participate in a TCP/IP network.

TCP/IP standard. A system of rules defining communication on TCP/IP networks. The purpose of TCP/IP standards is to ensure the compatibility of all the TCP/IP implementations regardless of version.

TCP/IP. Transmission Control Protocol/Internet Protocol. A network protocol system used on. Internet; a collection of protocols which support network communications. TCP/IP and its related protocol form a complete system defining how data should be processed, transmitted, and received on a TCP/IP network.

TCU. 1. Trunk Coupling Unit, used in IEEE 802.4.
2. Terminal Control Unit.

TD PPDU. Presentation DATA PDU.

TD. Typed Data Session PDU.

TDB. Terminology DataBase.

TDE. Total Data Entry.

TDG. Test Data Generator.

TDI. Transit Delay Indication utility.

TDM. Time Division Multiplexing.

TDMA. Time division multiple access; an integrated services digital network (ISDN) service used primarily for international public-switched telephones of very large volume.

TDS. Transit Delay Selection utility.

TDSAI. Transit Delay Selection And Indication facility, used as a guideline in allocating resources for a virtual call in DTE.

TE PPDU. Expedited Data Presentation PDU.

TE. Terminal Equipment, the equipment at the end of an ISDN local loop.

TEBOL. Terminal Business Oriented Language.

TEI. Terminal End-point Identifier, identifies a specific end point within a service access point.

TEL. Task Execution Language.

telecommunication. Any process that enables a correspondent to relay written or printed matter, fixed or moving pictures, words, music, or visible or audible signals or signals controlling the functioning of mechanisms, etc. by means of an electromagnetic system.

teleconferencing. A computer-based system enabling geographically-separated users to participate in an activity, such as the management of a complex project, despite being separated in space and/or time. Users will typically be provided with access to a computer terminal, which will allow them to communicate with other members of their team, often but not necessarily simultaneously. Data communication lines are used to transmit the conference information between participants. The system is controlled by a manager whose functions is to organise the participants and allow them access to the conference and to transmit their inputs to other members. Such a conference may use audio links only, or may use both audio links and slow-scan television links.

telelecture. An arrangement, which enables a speaker to communicate with several classes in different locations simultaneously, using public telephone links.

TELEMAIL. Electronic mail service of US.

telemetry. The transmission of quantitative information from one point to another by electromagnetic means. It is used in space flights, both manned as well as unmanned, to keep track of all aspects of the equipment and the physical condition of astronauts.

TELEPACK. Telecommunication Service of US.

telephone seminar. A seminar in which participants are connected via public telephone system.

telepresence. A form of virtual reality where a person is separated from the world that they are in, then remapped into a computer program that enables them to believe that they are elsewhere.

teleprocessing system. A method of centralising a computer system through the use (sharing) of communication lines such as common telephone lines. It became popular in the 1960s.

teleprompter. A device that was originally developed to feed cues and other information to television presenters, newsreaders, etc. It reveals text in front of a speaker at the same rate at which he/she is speaking. Also known as autocue.

telerecording. The process of recording television pictures on motion picture film. It is carried out by filming the image produced on extra-high-definition cathode ray tube using a special motion picture camera.

teletext. A system for one-way broadcast transmission of information, primarily in text form but with primitive graphics capability, using spare television channel capacity and adapted domestic TV receivers. On a channel offering teletext, a number of pages of information are transmitted in a continuous cycle, concurrently with the normal TV signal and leaving it unaffected while the receiver is used for normal viewing. Having selected teletext mode on the control pad, it is then possible to select any page number; when the selected page next arrives in the transmission cycle, it is stored in local memory in the set and displayed indefinitely (until the user selects another page or exits from teletext mode. A special decoding unit in domestic receivers permits selection and display on the screen. All the information is transmitted on a cyclic repetition basis by the broadcasting station without need of a telephone line.

television conference. A conference between geographically-separated individuals or groups that is made possible by setting up two-way television links between the locations involved. For practical reasons, such conferences are usually restricted to a limited number of venues.

television. The transfer of moving visual images from one place to another; used not only for broadcasting, but also for two-way communications. The television systems can be categorised as either fast-scan or slow-scan. In order to get the realistic impression of the motion, it is necessary to transmit at least 20 still pictures per second, and the detail must be accurate. A fast-scan television system provides 30 images, or frames per second. There are 525 or 625 lines in each frame, running horizontally across the picture, which is usually 1.33 times as wide as it is high. Each lines contains shades of brightness in a black-and-white system, and shades of brightness and colour in the colour system. The image is sent as amplitude-modulated signal, and the sound is sent as a frequency-modulated signal.

telex. A world-wide communication system that employs the teleprinters linked by a dedicated hardwire telegraph network.

TELNET. A remote terminal utility comprising a set of components that provides terminal-like access to a remote computer. Telnet is also a protocol, a system of rules defining the interactions between Telnet servers and clients. The Telnet protocol is defined in a series of RFCs. Because it is based on a well-defined open protocol, it has been implemented on a wide range of hardware and software systems. Its basic purpose is to provide a means by which keyboard commands typed by a remote user can cross the network and become input for a different computer. On graphics-based platforms such as Microsoft Windows, a Telnet application may have its own icon and run in window, but the underlying commands and processes are same as with text-based system.

template. A preformatted document used to quickly create a standard document, such as a memo or report.

temporal locality. Locality in time; the tendency of data and subroutines that have been used recently to be used again in the near future. Data retrieved from primary memory is written to cache memory, where it is then read by the processor. Any data modified by the processor is also written to the cache.

tens complement. The number that result when nine is subtracted from each digit of a decimal number and one is added to the digit in the rightmost position of the result, *e.g.*, the tens complement of 365 is 635, = (999 - 365 + 1 = 635).

TEP. Terminal Error Program.

TER. Third version of a standard.

tera-. T. SI prefix for one trillion (10^{12})..

terminal emulator. TEP. A program which enables a personal computer to surrender its processing powers to allow it to act like a dumb terminal so that it can communicate with a mainframe or minicomputer.

terminal server. A device that connects many terminals to LAN through one network connection; terminal server can also connect many network users to its asynchronous ports for dial-out capabilities and printer access.

terminal. Input/Output device connected to a processor or computer in order to communicate with it and control processing.

terminal-node controller. TNC. A device that act as the interface between a communications terminal and a radio transceiver. It contains memory circuits and allows messages to be held for later transmission. It can also store an incoming message and send it out later.

terminate. To connct a line to a terminal or to equipment.

Terminate-and-Stay-Resident Program. *See* TSR.

ternary signal. A signal that can assume one of the three conditions of power level, phase position, pulse length, frequency value, or other parameter at any given instant.

tertiary storage. Storage which is generally used for archival purposes, that is as a backup for secondary storage. Tertiary storage products include a variety of open-reel and cartridge magnetic tape drives as well as optical products such as CD-ROM and WORM devices. Generally, tertiary products provide access to vast amounts of data in a small space, but at slower access speeds than magnetic disks.

TES. Text Editing System.

test loop translator. A unit that is fed with a sample of a transmitted signal that it translates to another frequency The new frequency is then fed to a receiver that is being tested, which also receives the originally transmitted frequency in a test loop configuration, thus enabling analysis of the performance of the transmitter and receiver.

test signal. 1. A signal employed in making a test.

2. In radiotelegraphy, a special signifying that the transmitting station is testing equipment.

text editor. An application used to create, view, and modify text files. For example, Notepad in Windows, Edit in MS-DOS, simple text on the Macintosh, or VI on Unix. Text editors do not support the formatting functions of word processors.

text file. *See* ASCII Text File.

text mode. In MS-DOS, the mode that enables applications to display text but not graphic images

text. The part of a message which contains the information to be conveyed.

TFA. Transparent File Access, defines a specification for file system semantics which are required for file sharing within a distributed environment.

TFM. Tape File Management.

TFTP. Trivial File Transfer Protocol, one of the Internet standards used with TCP/IP; a client server utility and protocol used to transfer files between two computers. It employs UDP, as a transport and, unlike FTP, does not require a user log on. It can only read and write files, and can not list the contents of directories, create or remove directories, or allow a user to log on as FTP protocol allows. This protocol is primarily used in conjunction with RARP and BOOTP protocols to boot diskless work-stations.

tfVMS. A software for connecting to MUDs; VMS version of TinyFuge.

.tga. Extension for true vision targa files from the Amiga family of computers; used as input to create other utilities, such as programs to generate fractals.

thick Ethernet. Ethernet cabling which uses half-inch diameter coaxial cable to connect computers. The connector, DB-9, resembles a serial port.

thimble map. A computer program that directs a computer printer to substitute other characters for those that the printer is set to print.

thin Ethernet. Ethernet cabling which uses thin coaxial cable to connect computers; uses a T-shaped connector.

thin-film memory. A memory device whose individual elements are formed by evaporating a thin film of a magnetic material onto a glass substrate. The status of each element may be interrogated or changed by the application of a direct-current magnetic field parallel to the surface of the device. Large-capacity memories having many thousands of elements can be formed in a single operation using this process.

thin-film optical modulator. A device of multi-layered films of material of different optical characteristics capable of modulating transmitted light by using electro-optic, electro-acoustic, or magneto-optic effects to obtain signal modulation.

thin-film optical multiplexer. A multiplexer consisting of layered optical materials that make use of electro-optic, electro-acoustic, or magneto-optic effects to accomplish the multiplexing. Thin-film optical multiplexers may be component parts of integrated optical circuits.

thin-film semiconductor. A thin film of semiconductor material, such as single-crystal silicon, electro-deposited on a substrate.

thin-film transistor. A transistor fabricated by thin-film techniques.

third-generation computer. The computer generation, started after 1964, in which integrated circuits replaced the wired transistors.

third-generation languages. The computer languages having the capability to support structured programming, which means, they provide explicit structures for branches and loops. Third-generation languages include:

BASIC
COBOL
FORTRAN
PASCAL
C
C++.

THP. Terminal Handling Processor.

thrashing. A computer data processing system operating condition in which little useful work is accomplished because of the excessive time spent in transferring data and programs among storage units and areas, such as extensive paging.

threading. The act of pulling a cable in, around, over, under, through various obstacles in order to use a single piece of cable from one distant point to another without splicing.

three-address instruction. A computer program instruction whose address part contains three addresses, such as the addresses of two operands and the address for the results.

throughput. The number of bits, bytes, blocks, calls, characters, messages, words, or other units of data that pass through all or part of a computer or communication system when the system is working at optimum capacity.

TI. Terminal Interface.

TIA. Telematic Interworking Application, a set of applications provided to telematic users.

TIAS. Telematic Interworking Abstract Service, the description of the service provided by a telematic network.

tie trunk. A telephone line that directly connects either two private branch exchanges or two private exchanges.

TIFF. Tagged Image File Format, a very large, high quality image format to exchange image data files between systems.

tikker. An early radiotelegraph detector consisting of a stationary wire or blade in light contact with a motor-driven metal disk rotating at high speed. The received rf signal passes through the tikker and head-phones, connected in series, and the make-and-break action of the chattering contact chops the signal and makes it audible in the headphones.

tile. In Windows, a method of arranging open windows so that no windows overlap but all windows are visible. Each window takes up a portion of the screen.

time base corrector. An electronic device for synchronising the frame speed of a video signal with that of the system into which it is being fed.

time block. An arbitrary grouping of several consecutive hours of a day, usually for a particular season, during which it is assumed that propagation data are statistically homogeneous, and therefore somewhat predictable during a period of several hours.

time code resolution. The time interval between two successive time code states. It is determined by the most rapidly changing symbol position within the time code.

time code. A time format used for transmission and identification of timing signals.

time out. A network parameter related to an enforced event that is designed to occur at the conclusion of a predetermined elapsed period of time.

time sharing. *See* time slicing.

time slicing. A method in which two or more processes are assigned interleaving time on the same processor. Sometimes called time sharing.

time slot. 1. The time interval that can be recognised and uniquely defined. 2. An interval in time domain capable of providing a channel.

time standard. A stable device that emits signals at exactly equal intervals such that their count can be used as a precision clock.

time zone. An adopted relation of local time to Greenwich time (GMT) for a particular geographical area.

time-derived channel. A channel obtained by time-division multiplexing another channel, a line or circuit.

time-division duplexing. TDD. Duplexing that is accomplished by the simultaneous transmission and reception of two signals each representing different information over a common path by using different time intervals for each signal.

time-division multiplex access. TDMA. The use of time interleaving to provide multiple and apparently simultaneous transmission, in a single transponder with minimum interference.

time-division multiplexing. TDM. A time-sharing technique in which several terminals use same channel by transmitting data at regular, staggered intervals, *i.e.,* one is active while the others idle, but the effect is apparent simultaneous operation.

timing recovery. The derivation of a timing signal from a received signal.

timing signal. A signal used to synchronise interconnected equipment. Also the output of a standard clock.

TINT. A program for connecting to TinyMUD-style MUDs. Some of its features include simple macros, gags, and screen mode.

TinTin. A program for connecting to MUDs; runs on BSD. Some of its features include macros, triggers, logging, and X-Windows interface.

TinTin++. A program for connecting to MUDs; runs on BSD or SysV. Some of its features include macros, triggers, logging, and X-Windows interface; additional features include faster triggers, and a split screen mode.

TinySex. Act of performing MUD actions to imitate having sex with another person, usually consensually, sometimes with one hand on the kyboard.

TinyTalk. A software to connect to MUDs. Some of its features include line editing, command line history, auto-login, and simple macros.

TIO. Terminal Input/Output.

TIP. Technical Information Program.

TIQ. Task Input Queue.

title bar. Area at the top of a window which indicates name of that window.

In most GUIs, the title bar is dragged to move the window. Title bars, in most GUIs, have an area to click on to close the window as well as an area that will resize it if clicked.

TIU. Terminal Interface Unit.

TL. 1. Transport Layer, layer 4 of the OSI Reference Model.
2. Transaction Language.

TLA. Three-Letter Acronym.

TLC. 1. Task Level Controller.
2. Type, Length, Value, the format used in ASN.1.

TLFF. Technical Level Feeders Forum, a group that feeds technical information to the ISO SGFS.

TLI. 1. Transport Layer Interface.
2. Transport Library Interface, Unix.

TLM. TeLeMatic, the functional object that corresponds to a terminal defined in the CCITT T. series.

TLX. TeLeX.

TLXAU. TeLeX Access Unit, an access unit providing connection between the Telex network and an X.400 MTA.

TM mode. A mode of electromagnetic propagation in a waveguide in which the wave is transverse magnetic wave.

TM. 1. Terminal Management.
2. Test Management, used in conformance testing, how the lower tester co-ordinates what happens with the upper tester.
3. Test Mode.

TMF. Test Management Function, used in Network Management.

TMP. Terminal Management Program.

TMPDU. Test Management Protocol Data Unit, carrier TMP.

TN3270. A variant of the Telnet program that allows to attach to IBM mainframes and use the mainframe as if using a 3270 or similar terminal.

TNC. Terminal Node Controller, a modem used for converting/encoding data into radio signals over packet radio networks.

T-network. Network with two series branches and one shunt branch. The shunt joins the network at the point between the two series units.

TO. Test Object, a managed object that is created only for a test invocation in test function of Network Management.

token bus network. A local area network using a bus topology, which uses the token-passing access method. The IEEE 802.4 token bus access method is deterministic. This means that each station is assigned a logical position and therefore each station is allowed the right to use the channel in predetermined order.

token ring network. A local area network (LAN) using a ring topology, which uses the token-passing access method. IEEE 802.5 token ring access method is deterministic, meaning that each station is assigned a logical position and therefore each station is allowed the right to use the channel in a predetermined order. On a token ring network, token-passing operates by allowing each node the chance to transmit on a 'round robin' basis. It can use twisted pair, coaxial cable, or fibre optic cable. Token ring can operate at data rates of 1-16 Mb/s.

token ring. A hardware system for networking; developed by IBM; constructed as a ring of daisy chained nodes. Each node passes a control message (token) around the ring. Whichever node has the token can send a message.

TOL. Test Oriented Language.

tone control. A facility for modifying an audio signal by boosting or suppressing certain frequencies; for example, the bass (tone) control and treble (tone) control are incorporated in most audio amplifiers and tape recorders.

tone diversity. A method of voice-frequency telegraph transmission (VFTG) in which two channels of a 16-channel VFTG carry the same information.

tone signalling. The use of voice frequency tones to carry signalling information on an in-band basis.

tone. An audio signal of identifiable frequency or periodicity.

TOOL. Test Oriented Operator Language.

TOP. Technical Office Protocol(s), facilitates graphics and image messaging as well as data (EDI); an industry functional profile originally championed by Boeing.

topology. The physical layout of network cabling.

TOS. Technical and Office Systems.

TOSL. Terminal Oriented Service Language.

touch-tone device. Portable unit, which can be carried in a briefcase and used to send data from remote locations to a central computer via normal phone.

TP monitor. Transaction processing monitor; a software product that provides, in a single bundled package, all the elements of an environment in which transaction processing application programs can be designed and run efficiently. Its essential purpose is to optimise the use of system resources for the specialised way transaction processing applications tend to use a computer. Hence, it is usually a layered software package, used in conjunction with a particular base operating system, an may provide a standard interface between the application program and such facilities as the terminal and the database.

TP. 1. Transaction Processing; defined in ISO 10026, parts 1-3. A transaction is defined as a set of operations characterised by the ACID properties, atomicity, consistency, isolation, and durability. TP allows any number of systems to co-operatively process a transaction. Transaction commitment and recovery features are built in, to help ensure consistency and integrity of data.

2. Transport Protocol, protocol for layer 4 of the OSI Reference Model.

3. Terminal Processor.

4. Text Processing.

TP0. Transport Class 0, basic transport, provides only connection establishment, data transfer with segmentation, and protocol error reporting.

TP1. Transport Class 1, adds basic error recovery to Transprot.

TP2. Transport Class 2, adds multiplexing with or without flow control, but no error detection or recovery.

TP3. Transport Class 3, adds multiplexing and error recovery for network errors.

TP4. Transport Class 4, adds error detection and recovery at the Transport Layer to the services provided with TP3.

TPDU. Transport Protocol Data Unit.

TPE. Twisted Pair Ethernet.

TPL. Terminal Processing Language.

TPT. Third-Party Transfer Application Entity, OSI.

TPU. Task Processing Unit.

TR. 1. Technical Report, used by ECMA and ISO.

2. Test Responder, in conformance testing, a program to be ported to run ton the SUT to be the upper tester.

TRAC. Technical Recommendations Applications Committee.

trace program. A diagnostic program that can monitor the execution of some or all of the instructions of a computer program and record the effects of each step; provides information on the dynamic behaviour of that system in the form of a trace.

TraceRoute. A command used to trace the route (path) taken by datagrams as they move from one computer through multiple gateways to their destination. It works by leveraging an ICMP message in which a router sends a time exceeded message to the source IP when a TTL datagram at the router reaches 0. It sends the first datagram with a TTL of 1.

track. The portion of a magnetic storage medium that is accessible to read/write heads. In magnetic disks, the tracks are concentric and circular.

track-and-hold unit. In analog systems, a device whose output analog variable is either the input variable or a sample of the input variable sampled by the action of an external signal. When tracking, the device follows the input analog variable. When holding, the device holds the value of the input analog variable at the instant of switching.

trackball. A pointing device that works like an upside-down mouse; to move cursor around the screen, the ball is rolled with the thumb. Since the whole device is not moved, a trackball requires less space than a mouse.

tracking mode. A mode of operating a system in which it is operating within specified limits relative to a reference. In tracking supplies, the usual manner of operation in which the output of each of the separate supplies automatically follows that of the one being adjusted.

tracking symbol. A symbol that is visible in the display space on the display surface, which can be moved and used to indicate the position of a pointer. The pointer may be stylus, joystick, control ball, or mouse.

tracking. A text editing feature in typography, used for adjusting letter spacing, rather than making adjustments between individual characters. It is a general setting for an entire block. Tighter tracking squeezes all the letters closer together, fitting more type in to a given space. Loose tracking expands the space between the letters, making the page look less dense.

trackpad. A stationary pointing device that works like a mouseused in laptops.

traffic capacity. The maximum traffic per unit time that a specified communication system, subsystem, or device can carry under specified conditions.

traffic control. A term sometimes used in reference to the control of input and output; covers both the hardware and software necessary to achieve the orderly and correct movement of data in a multiprogramming system.

traffic load. The total traffic carried by a trunk or trunk group during a specified time interval.

traffic overflow. A condition in communication systems in which the traffic offered to the system or component exceeds its capacity. The excess traffic may be blocked or it may be provided with an alternate route.

traffic. The system control and user information that is moved in the form of data or signals over a communication path.

Trailer Boss. IBM's internal code name used to describe the project and the product that was introduced to replace the 3990 disk controller.

trailer label. A sentinel which occurs at the end of data organised in sequential form.

transaction routing. The routing of messages individually according to processed keys, destination names, or other data placed in the message heading by the originator, source user, or originating office.

transaction. A single coherent action on a file or database; different transactions can be carried out sequentially without interfering with one another.

transceiver. Acronym for transmitter and receiver; device that can both transmit and receive signals on a communication medium. It consists of a combination of transmitting and receiving equipment in one housing. It employs common circuit components for both transmitting and receiving and employs simplex operation. The word is usually used in describing radio equipment but is sometimes also used in data networks to describe a device for transmitting and receiving data signals, usually baseband signals. Many communication devices, including modems, are transceivers.

transcoder. An electronic system for transforming a television signal from one colour standard to another.

Transfer Access and Management. *See* FTAM.

transfer. In communications, to move a data unit in its entirety from one location to another.

trans-horizon propagation. Propagation over paths extending beyond the normal radio horizon. It may include a variety of mechanisms such as diffraction, forward scatter, specular and diffuse reflection, and ducting.

trans-information content. The difference between the information content that can be conveyed by the occurrence of an event and the conditional information content that can be conveyed by the occurrence of the same event but given the occurrence of another event.

transistor-transistor logic. TTL. The widely used family of logic circuits that is produced in integrated-circuit form and whose principal switching components are bipolar **transistors**, and in which the multiple-diode cluster of the diode-transistor logic circuit has been replaced by a multiple-emitter transistor. Also written as T^2L.

transit time. The time taken for a signal to propagate from one earth station to another via a satellite link; approximately 1/3 of a second for geostationary earth satellites.

transition fibre. An optical element of such geometrical shape at input and output ends that it enables coupling between an element in an integrated optical circuit and an optical fibre.

translation table. A table of information stored within a processor or a peripheral that is used to convert encoded information into another form of code with the same meaning.

translation. 1. Conversion of a program in one computer programming language to another program that will produce the same results when executed but is in another language. 2. The process of changing frequency without altering the baseband data or the type of modulation.

translator. A network/system so connected that input signals expressed in a certain code cause output signals to appear which represent the same information in a different code.

transliteration. 1. To change the characters in one alphabet or code system to the characters in a different system. 2. The function that maps the characters in one alphabet or code system to those in another.

transmission channel. All the transmission facilities between the input of an initiating node in a communication network and the output of a terminating node of the network.

transmission control layer. Each of the layers of IBM's System Network

Architecture (SNA) has its own set of rules for communicating with its peer layer in the other node. The layers communicate with each other by adding header information to user data. The transmission control layer (fourth layer) is responsible for session set-up and disconnection, and the overall end-to-end connectivity. It paces data exchanges to match the processing capacity at the end point of a session. This layer will also code data for security if needed.

transmission efficiency. The number of good or correct bytes, bits, characters, words, or other data units received at a point divided by the total number of the same units that were transmitted to the point.

transmission flexibility. Multiplexing, demultiplexing, encoding, decoding, semi-permanent inter-connection, or any combination of these.

transmission level. The signal power at a given point in a transmission system relative to the signal power at an arbitrary selected or specified point, such as at the beginning of a transmission line, or relative to an arbitrary selected power level such as 1 W or 1 mW.

transmission loss. The decrease in the power of a signal during transmission from one point to another; usually expressed in decibels.

transmission mode. 1. In a transceiver, the condition in which transmitter is enabled and the receiver is disabled. 2. In a waveguide, propagation via transverse waves.

transmission rate. The speed at which information may be transferred from a device or via a circuit. The unit used is usually related to the amount of information transferred per cycle, *e.g.* characters per second or bits per second.

transmission routing. Assigning a path between two terminal transmission nodes; it may be provided over two or more transmission sections connected end-to-end.

transmission time. The time required for a message to pass a point in the transmission medium. It is a function of the length of the message and the signalling speed.

transmission-control character. A character used to control or facilitate the transmission of data over communication networks.

transmit flow control. A control of the rate at which data may be transmitted from one point so that it is equal to the rate at which it can be received or buffered at another terminal.

transmitter start code. A code that is sent by switching centre and is used for polling all stations. If a polled station has no message to transmit, it responds with an answer-back code.

transmitter. A device capable of generating, modulating, and sending a signal for communication, control, or other purpose.

transparency. The property of communication systems that allows transmission of signals without changing their electrical characteristics or coding beyond the specified limits of system design.

transparent interface. An interface which allows interconnected equipment on both side of the interface to operate without modification of the input, output, circuitry, or operational procedures, after installation of the interface.

transparent mode. A mode of operating a data transmission system in which all the data or text bits are transmitted as bit stream without distinction, including control and other special purpose characters.

transponder. A radio or radar transmitter-receiver that is capable of transmitting signals automatically when the proper signals are received. It depends on some frequency memory or timing procedure to affect on-frequency retransmissions.

transport layer. The layer of TCP/IP stack which provides error checking and acknowledgement and serves as an interface for network applications.

transposition. 1. In data transmission, a transmission defect in which, during one character period, one or more signal elements are changed from one significant condition to the other, and an equal number of elements are changed in the reverse manner.

2. An interchange of positions of several conductors of a circuit between successive lengths. This interchange is used to reduce inductive interference on communication circuits.

transverse jitter. In facsimile transmission systems, an effect due to the irregularity of the scanning pitch that results in concurrent overlap and underlay in the reproduced image.

transverse parity check. A parity check performed on a group of binary digits recorded on parallel tracks of a data medium, such as a magnetic disk, tape, drum, or card.

trap. A fault detection mechanism designed to isolate various abnormal operating conditions.

trapdoor. A term used to identify computer crime, which involves the use of trapdoors (accidentally or intentionally left behind by programmers) to gain unauthorised access to certain parts of programs which may contain valuable confidential or proprietary information. Breach in computer, data processing and communication security, that is created intentionally in a system for the purpose of collecting, delaying, or destroying data that is done so far for unauthorised purposes. When developing complicated computer programs, trapdoors are sections of code used by programmers as diagnostic tools, which enables them to gain access to certain parts of a program. Before programs are sold, trapdoors should be removed for security purposes.

trap interrupt. An interruption when there is a hardware or software error.

treble. A term used to denote the highest frequencies of the audio spectrum.

tree file. A file that is divided into subsections that are further subdivided, and so on, for the entire file.

tree grammar. A generalisation of the notion of grammar, applying to trees rather than strings. A regular tree grammar is the corresponding generalisation of the notion of regular grammar.

tree search. Any method of searching a body of data structured as a tree; a search in which it is possible to decide, at each step, which part of the tree may be rejected without a further search.

tree. A finite set of one or more nodes such that firstly there is a single designated node called the root and secondly the remaining nodes are partitioned into *n* greater than or equal to 0 disjoint sets, where each of these sets is itself a tree.

tree-and-branch system. A cable television distribution system in which users are connected to the distribution system by a branching system of coaxial cables.

triad. A group of three binary digits that can be operated or treated as a single entity by electronic circuits.

triangular random noise. Random noise that has a frequency distribution in which the noise power per unit bandwidth is proportional to the square of the frequency.

triaxial connector. A male or female connector-jack or plug-having three concentric contacting surfaces. By contrast, the coaxial jack and coaxial plug have only two such surface.

Trivial File Transfer Protocol. *See* TFTP.

Trojan horse. In computer and communication security, a computer program that is apparently or actually useful and at the same time contains a trap door.

tropospheric scatter. 1. The propagation of radio waves by scattering because of irregularities or discontinuities in the physical properties of the troposphere.

2. A method of trans-horizon communications utilising frequencies from approximately 350-8400 MHz.

troubleshoot. To locate and eliminate bugs in hardware or software, that is, to remove errors in computer programs, or correct faults in a computer, line, or circuit.

true power gain. An expression of the extent to which the amplifier can increase the realisable power of a signal; usually expressed in decibels.

true type fonts. Fonts that are scaleable and sometimes generated as bitmaps or soft fonts, depending on the capabilities of the printer. TrueType fonts can be sized to any height, and they print out exactly as they appear on the screen.

truncation. A term used in data transmission, meaning the deliberate removal of intelligence signal components without the loss of message intelligibility.

trunk circuit. In telephone switchboard operations, a circuit that directly connects two exchanges.

trunk code. A digit or digit combination (not including the trunk prefix) which characterises a particular numbering area within a country. The trunk code must be dialled before the called subscriber's number is dialled when the calling and called subscribers are in different numbering areas.

trunk feeder. A transmission line used to interconnect two electric power stations or two electric power distribution networks.

trunk. 1. A single or multi-channel communications medium between terminal facilities where channels can be tested, re-routed, dropped out, or switched to another route.

2. A circuit between two ranks of switching equipment in the same office, or between different switching centres or different central offices.

trusted access. A security system in which a system administrator designates remote hosts and users who are trusted to access the local system.

truth table. 1. A tabular description of a logic operation such as AND, OR, NAND, listing all possible combinations of truth values, of the operands together with the truth value of the outcome for each of the possible combinations.

2. A tabular description of a combinational circuit such as AND gate, OR gate, NAND gate, listing all possible states of the input variables together with a statement of the output variables for each of those possible states.

TS. 1. Time Sharing.

2. Transport Service, service provided by layer 4 of the OSI Reference Model.

TSAP. Transport Service Access Point.

TSDU. Transport Service Data Unit.

TSE. Terminal Source Editor.

TSEL. Transport Selector, used to identify Session Layer entity. A TSEL and an NSAP address make up a TSAP address.

TSM. Terminal Support Module.

TSN. Task Sequence Number.

TSR. Terminate-and-Stay-Resident program; the MS-DOS program that is loaded into memory and is available even as another application is active; usually activated by an event such as keystroke or interrupt. Also known as memory resident or pop-up program.

TSS&TP. Test Suite Structure and Test Purposes, the first couple of steps in developing an abstract test suite for conformance testing.

TSSDU. Typed Data Session Service Data Unit.

T-tap. A passive line interface for extracting data from circuit or optical signals form a fibre line.

TTCN. Tree and Tabular Combined Notation, supposedly information notation for describing abstract test cases.

TTCN.GR. TTCN Graphical Representation, the form of TTCN that contains tables and lines for ease of readability by humans.

TTCN.MP. TTCN Machine Processable format, the form of TTCN that is meant to be easily manipulated by computer rather than easily read by a human.

TTD PPDU. Presentation Typed Data PDU.

TTD. Target Transit Delay.

TTD. Temporary Text Delay.

TTX. TeleTeX.

TTXAU. TeleTeX Access Unit, an access unit for providing connection between a teletex network and an X.400 MTA.

TTY. TeleTYpe, or telegraphy.

TU. Timing Unit.

tuning. Adjusting a circuit for resonance or best response.

tunnel erase. The use in floppy-disk drives of an auxiliary erase head that follows the write head and is designed to erase the edges of the written pattern of magnetisation, thus defining it more accurately and reducing cross-talk between adjacent tracks. Also known as trim erase.

tunnelling. The encapsulation of protocol A within protocol B, such that B treats A, as if it were its own; used to receive data between administrative domains that use a protocol not supported by Internet, and to make pseudo-connections between connectionless protocol systems like Internet.

TUP. Telephone User Part, part of level 4 of ISDN; responds to a user with a telephony device.

turn-around time. 1. The time between submission of a job, task, or program, and the return of completed results. 2. Time required to reverse direction of transmission, usually including propagation time, line effects, modem timing, and machine reaction time.

TUsh. A program for connecting to MUDs; runs on BSD or SysV. Some of its features include auto-login, macros, triggers, logging, line editing, and command history.

TWA. Two-Way Alternate, use of session when either side can send data, but only one at a time when the sender has the token.

twin cable. A cable composed of two insulated conductors that are laid parallel to each other and that are either attached to each other by insulation or are bound together with a common covering.

twisted pair wire. The wires commonly used for network wiring. Twisted pair consists of two pairs of wires, one for transmitting and one for receiving data. The wires in each pair are twisted together to reduce induction between them. 10Base-T Ethernet cable is twisted pair.

two-frequency half-duplex. Pertaining to a communication circuit with two-way simultaneous traffic capacity in which different frequencies are used for two directions of transmission.

two-level grammars. A generalisation of context-free grammars that enables non-context-free aspects of a language to be specified.

two-level memory. A memory system with two memories of different capacities and speeds.

two-level optical signal. A modulated lightwave carrier that is either one of two different intensities or power density levels at a given instant.

two-out-of-five code. A binary-coded decimal notation in which each decimal digit is represented by a binary numeral consisting of five bits out of which two are of one kind, conventionally ones, and three are of the other kind, conventionally zeros. It may be noted that the usual weights are 6-3-2-1-0 except for the representation of zero, which is then 00110.

two-phase. Pertaining to circuits or devices in which two components (two voltages, two currents, or a current and a voltage) are 90 degrees out of phase with each other.

two's complement. The complement of a binary number obtained by adding 1 to the least significant digit of its one's complement and propagating the carries only as far as they go.

two-way communication. A telecommunication system in which signals may be transmitted between two points in both directions.

two-way merge. An algorithm that merges two files into one single sorted file.

TWS. Two-Way Simultaneous, use of session when both sides can send data at the same time.

TWX. TeletypeWriter eXchange.

TXT. File name extension for a text file that can be displayed or printed without requiring processing by any utility. These files should be retrieved in text/ASCII mode.

U

U.nnn. The CCITT U. Series Recommendations deal with international Telex services, such as, automatic switching, signal quality, maritime satellite interface, store and forward, etc.

UA. 1. In data communications, user agent in the CCITT X.400 message handling standard; the functional object or component in MHS, which enables a single user to engage in, message handling.
2. Unnumbered Acknowledgement.

UAE. Unrecoverable Application Error; occurred often in Windows 3.0 and below. UAEs would bring the entire machine down causing loss of data. Windows 3.1 greatly improved the handling of UAEs. While UAEs still occur (much less that previously), they crash only that application and not Windows or the entire machine.

UAL. User Agent Layer, 1984 portion of the Application Layer in which UAs reside.

UAP. User Area Profile.

UAR. Unit Address Register.

UART. Universal Asynchronous Receiver/Transmitter; a logic circuit, usually an integrated circuit, that will convert an asynchronous serial data stream into a byte-parallel form and vice versa. The normal application is in the interfaces for data transmission lines and peripherals.

UAS. UnAvailable Second, used in performance management in Network Management.

UASFE. Unavailable Second Far End, used in performance management in Network Management.

UASL. User Agent SubLayer.

UBC. Universal Book Code.

UCB. Unit Control Block.

UCF. Utility Control Facility.

U-channel. One of the eight compact disc sub-code channels (P-W); generally allocated to compact disc graphics.

UCM. Unit Control Module.

UCW. Unit Control Word.

UD. Unit Data, information conveyed as a single entity, *e.g.*, a Protocol Data Unit, an integer.

UDK. User Defined Key.

UDL. Uniform Data Language.

UDP. User Datagram Protocol, a connectionless protocol. It is faster than TCP, but is not as reliable; it offloads more of the error-checking responsibilities to the application.

UDR. Universal Document Reader.

UE. User Element, layer 7, part of an application process that uses application service elements to accomplish communication purpose of that process.

UF. Utility File.

UFD. User File Directory.

UFP. Utility Facility Program.

UHF. Ultra High Frequency, radio communications above the VHF carrier band range, generally used for mobile communications.

UI. 1. User Interface, prompts and commands with which a human interacts with a computer program.
2. Unit Interval.
3. Unnumbered Interrupt.
4. Unix International, an industry consortium dedicated to developing and promoting open software solution based on Unix platforms.

UIG. User Instruction Group.

UIR. User Instruction Register.

UJCL. Universal Job Control Language.

ULA. Upper-Layer Architecture.

ULCT. Upper-Layer Conformance Testing, a group under ISO SC21 developing abstract test suites for FTAM and is supporting upper layers.

ULP. Upper-Layer Protocol.

ultrafiche. In micrographics, microfiche images reduced by more than 90x.

ultra-high frequency. UHF. Frequency range of 300-3000 MHz. In televisions, frequency range 470-884 MHz.

ultra-large-scale integration. In microelectronics, a fabrication technology that produces well in excess of 100,000 transistors per chip.

ultra-low frequencies. Frequencies lower than those in the audio frequency spectrum, *e.g.*, between 0.001 and 1 Hz. Also known as subsonic frequencies.

ultrasonic cleaning. A method of cleaning delicate or intricately structured items, such as dentures, contact lenses, or jewellery, in which the soiled items are immersed in a fluid which is agitated by ultrasonic transducers; the foreign particles are shaken away.

ultrasonic filter. 1. A bandpass filter whose operation is based upon the natural (ultrasonic) vibration frequency of small disks or rods of mangetostrictive metal.
2. Generally, a filter operating at ultrasonic frequencies.

ultrasonics. 1. The branch of electronics concerned with the application of ultrasonic-frequency energy in industry, medicine, research, and the home.
2. The use of ultrasonic energy for medical diagnosis and treatment.
3. The branch of physics dealing with ultrasonic phenomena.

ULTRIX. The BSD-based version of UNIX that runs on DEC VAXs and MicroVAXs.

U-matic. The commercial name of the most widely used U-format videocassette recording system.

umbrella antenna. A wire antenna that is used mostly at low and very low frequencies. It consists of several wire conductors and a metal mast. The mast and the wires all radiate and serve to support each other. The conductors extend from the top of the mast to the points at ground level. The wires and the mast are inductively loaded so that they are 1/4 electrical wavelength at the operating frequency.

UMPDU. User Message Protocol Data Unit, in MHS, the PDU carried in the content field of the P1 envelope.

unaffected level. The absolute level (at a point of zero relative level on the line between the compressor and the expander of a signal at 8000 Hz which remains unchanged whether the circuit is operated with the compressor or not.

unbalanced transmission. A data communication technique employing one wire for each signal and a common return path for all signals.

unbound mode. In fibre optics, any mode which is not a bound mode; a leaky or radiation mode of the waveguide.

unbounding. The separation of system software charges from hardware charges in the marketing of computer systems.

unconditional jump. An instruction to jump to another specified instruction.

underflow. In an arithmetic operation, a result whose absolute value is too small to be represented within the range of the numeration system in use. The condition which arises when the result of an arithmetic operation is smaller than the allowable range of numbers that can be represented, or the result so obtained.

underware. A term sometimes applied to those aspects of instructional technology which underlie the use of hardware and software, but which cannot be placed in either category, that is, the principles and methodologies of the field.

uniform encoding. 1. The generation of character signals representing uniformly quantized samples.
2. An analog-to-digital conversion process in which all of the quantization sub-range values is equal.

UniForum. A Unix trades association, formerly called/user/group.

UNIMARC. UNIversal MARC, developed in 1985/86 to improve the standardisation of information exchange between libraries.

unipolar signal. A signal, whose signalling elements are constrained to lie either between zero volts and some arbitrary positive voltage or less commonly between zero volts and some negative voltage; used in data-communication systems.

UNIVAC. UNIVersal Automatic Computer; a first-generation computer (using vacuum tubes) which processed both numerical and a alphabetical calculations with ease.

universal access number. The single number which, when dialled from anywhere, will reach a customer with several installations in different parts of the country. Calls from subscribers on exchanges in predetermined areas will be routed to installations chosen (within certain restrictions) for the area in question by the customer having the facility.

universal administration. Address administration in which all LAN individual addresses are unique within the same or other local area networks.

universal coupler. 1. An arrangement of one or more inductors and variable capacitors for matching a transmitter to virtually any antenna. One such device is the Collins coupler.
2. A device for matching numerous generators output impedance to numerous load impedance.

universal product code. UPC. Variable-width-bar code appearing on price tags or product labels, and yielding such information as cost, size, and colour, when read by optical character recognition equipment. Also known as universal vendor marking (UVM).

UNIX. An operating system developed by AT&T; it features multi-user support, pre-emptive multitasking, and strong networking capabilities; written in platform-independent programming language C, and is easily portable to different hardware systems. UNIX is older than all the other PC operating systems, and in many ways it served as a model for them. Although it is an extremely robust and capable operating system, command-line UNIX is quite complicated, because it requires many commands to do even simple operations. UNIX configuration takes place within configuration files. Many versions of UNIX, and UNIX-like clones, have been produced through the years, including System V, BSD, NetBSD, Linux, AIX, A/UX, MINIX, SunOS, etc. UNIX windowing system called X-Windows has brought a GUI to UNIX computers, but it has remained an operating system for engineers and technical users. It has gradually lost ground to operating systems such as DOS, Windows, which are easier to learn and use.

UNJEDI. United Nations joint EDI committee, reporting to UN/ISO to develop EDIFACT and data dictionary for international use.

unlock. An indivisible operation by which a process indicates that has completed its access to a particular resource.

unnumbered command. A command that does not contain sequence numbers in the control field.

unnumbered response. A response that does not contain sequence numbers in the control field.

unpack. To convert from a packed format to a form in which individual items are directly accessible.

unpacked decimal notation. A binary coded decimal notation which each decimal digit is represented by one byte.

unscheduled down-time. A computer system is said to be 'available' if it delivers correct service to its users when service is required. Despite strong efforts, not all systems can be available 100% of the time because unexpected faults may occur and lead to their failure, or partial failure.

UNTDI. United Nations/Trade Data Interchange, one of the Electronic Data Interchange formats.

up. A term applied to a computer or other system, which is operational at the time in question.

UPC. Universal Product Code.

updating. Any process that changes the state of a system in an irreversible manner; or to make changes that has been modified to comply current information or some other change in circumstances.

upgrade. To improve service by offering better facilities.

UPL. User Programming Language.

upline. The direction from a remote node toward a central or controlling node in a hierarchical network.

uplink. A term used to refer to the band on which an active communication satellite receives its signals from earth-based stations. Uplink frequency is much different from the downlink frequency, on which the satellite transmits signals back to the earth.

upper memory area. On IBM and other compatible computers, the 384K area of address space adjacent to the 640K of conventional memory (these two total 1 Megabyte). This area is usually reserved for running your system's hardware, such as your monitor, and is not considered part of total memory because applications cannot store information in this area. In 386 enhanced mode, Windows can access unused portions of this area. Some memory managers also allow applications access to unused portions of this area.

upper memory blocks. On IBM and other compatible computers, areas of the upper memory area that contain general-purpose memory and that can be used to hold device drivers or other memory-resident programs in order to leave more conventional memory available for applications.

upper sideband suppressed carrier. USSC. A single-sideband transmission technique in which the upper sideband is transmitted the lower sideband is suppressed, and the carrier is suppressed.

upper sideband. USB. The group of frequencies immediately above the carrier frequency. The upper sideband frequencies result from additive mixing between the carrier signal and the modulating signal.

UPS. Uninterruptible Power Supply, backup power unit that provides continuous power when the normal power supply is interrupted. UPS systems can be stand-by, only supplying power when the regular supply is interrupted, or full-time, relying on regular power and/or batteries to supply it while it supplies power to the protected device. UPS is not necessary on most computer systems, but can be important on systems that need to be up 24 hours a day, such as servers.

upstream. In a broadcasting network, a signal from a transmitting station to a headend.

uptime. The time or percentage of time during which a computer system is actually operating in correct manner. It is the uninterrpted period of time that a etwork or computer resources are accessible and available to a user.

UPU. Universal Postal Union.

upward modulation. Modulation in which the output current of the modulated circuit increases during modulation. Upward modulation is not the only means by which a carrier wave can be amplitude-modulated; information can also be impressed on a carrier by decreasing the amplitude.

UQT. User Queue Table.

URC. Unit Record Control.

URL. Uniform Resource Locator; used with the WWW to identify the type and location of a multimedia resource on the internet. For example, the URL <FTP.< STRONG>//mirrors.aol.com/pub/info-mac/help/faq-of-faqs.txt> identifies a file named faq-of-faqs.txt, available via ftp, located on the site mirrors.aol.com, in the directory /pub/info-mac/help/.

usability test. A test to determine whether an implemented system fulfils its functional purpose as determined by its users.

USB. Upper SideBand, a positive amplitude or upper half (180 degrees) waveform used as a carrier.

useful bandwidth. The bandwidth available for information-carrying signals, bearing in mind the fact that guard bands are needed between channels and groups.

USENET. A UNIX based international network, handling mail and news, based on the UNIX program for file transfer; provides a large number of newsgroups, that discuss a variety of topics, including technical computer, scientific, recreational, and social areas. Usenet can be accessed with a number of programs on different computer platforms.

user area. The portion of main memory of a computer that is available for use by the user's programs; a significant portion of the main memory may be utilised for the operating system and the facilities that it requires.

User Datagram Protocol. *See* UDP.

user friendly. A term applied to a machine or system, which is specifically designed to be as simple to operate or use as possible.

user ID. An account name or login name.

user information. Information transferred across the functional interface between a sources user and a telecommunication system for ultimate delivery to a destination user. In data telecommunication systems, user information includes user overhead information.

user information bit. A bit transferred from a source user for ultimate delivery to the destination user.

user information block. A block that contains at least one user information bit.

user interface. UI. The aspect of a computer or program that is visible to the user, giving and accepting information from him or her. User interfaces are,. broadly, CLIs and GUIs.

user manual. A document that describes how to use a functional unit, and may include description of the rights and responsibilities of the user, owner, and the supplier of the unit.

user number. In computer security, a code or password by means of which an authorised user can gain access to a computer or to stored information.

user part. Functional part of a common channel signalling system, which transfers signalling messages via message transfer part.

user. A person, organisation, or other group, that employ the services of a network or communication link, for the transfer of informations.

USG. User Support Group.

USI. User System Interface.

USSC. *See* upper sideband, suppressed carrier.

UT. Upper Tester, in conformance testing, that which controls the upper service boundary of the IUT.

UTC. Coordinated Universal Time; also Greenwich Mean Time (GMT).

utility programs. The collection of programs that forms part of every computer system and provides a variety of generally useful functions, including copying and deleting, text preparation, and program cross-referencing etc.

utility routine. A routine (a computer program) that provides general, frequently needed services for computer users and services personnel. Examples: An input routine; a diagnostic program; a trace program; a sort program.

utility. A program intended to make the use of a computer or of an application program easier.

UTOL. Universal Translator Oriented Language.

UTP. Unshielded Twisted Pair, a type of cable that can support either data or voice; it can be used in wiring a building for LANs.

UUCP. UNIX-to-UNIX Copy Protocol. Networking software used to transmit data over phone lines. UUCP is not used much now.

UUencode/UUdecode. A system for encoding binary files as ASCII files for easy transfer between computer systems; widely used on Unix systems.

UUNET. A subscription service providing connections, mail, and news feeds to the Internet and various international networks, mainly for Unix hosts.

UWA. User Working Area.

V

V.21. The CCITT standard covering 300 bits per second communications over the public telephone network or 2-wire leased-line circuits. Since the public telephone lines are designed to carry analog voice information, the serial digital data from the adapter must be converted into analog audio tones. This is the function of the modem. When receiving data, the modem performs just the opposite function: it converts data from analog to digital. Many modems used with personal computers are classified as 'medium speed', meaning they can send and receive data at either 1200 or 2400 Bps. For 2400 Bps operation, all manufacturers follow a standard signalling scheme. This means that different modems can function together. At 1200 Bps, however, there are several different signalling standards, causing potential compatibility problems.

V.22bis. CCITT standard covering 2400/75 bits per second communications over the public telephone network.

V.24. A standard electrical interface by the CCITT for interconnecting data terminal equipment to a modem. The interface includes definition of control signals as well as clocking and data signalling standards.

V.32. A modem communications standard, which supports 9600 bps.

V.32bis. A modem communications standard, which supports 14.4K bps.

V.34. A modem communications standard, which supports 28.8K bps.

V.42. A modem communications standard, which supports error detection and data compression.

V.DOT terms. A series of modem communications standards.

V.nnn. The CCITT V. Series Recommendations define data communications over telephone lines. Several definitions deal with types of modems, which have become increasingly more popular since their introduction as standards.

VA. Virtual Address.

VAA. Voice Access Arrangement.

VAC. *See* value-added carrier.

vaccine. A computer program written to search for unusual disk activity, and report to the user on any presence of a disk infection such as a virus. The known virus can be detected quickly, but authors of computer viruses are constantly designing new viruses with which to cause malicious and widespread computer damage.

validation. A process used to determine if data are inaccurate, incomplete, or unreasonable. It may be noted that data validation may include format checks, completeness checks, check key tests, reasonableness checks, and limit checks.

validity check. Any check that some entity respects the constraints applying to that entity.

value-added carrier. VAC. Common carrier which employs the basic services leased from other carriers and adds special features to these, (usually computer-oriented) before renting these out to users.

VAM. Virtual Access Method.

VAMPIRE TAP. Cable-piercing transceiver connection.

VAN. Value Added Network, often used in reference to X.25 packet-switched networks.

VANS. Value Added Network Services.

variable. A string of characters used to denote some value stored within the computer and may be changed during execution. A variable may be internal to the program, in which case it is held in the memory, or external if the program must perform an input operation in order to read its value.

variable-length code. A code in which a fixed number of source symbols are encoded into a variable number of output symbols. This variable number may be made to depend on some property of the source symbols input to the encoder, often their relative frequency of occurrence.

VAS. Value Added Service, enhanced unregulated services offered to network subscribers by value-added carriers.

VAT. Virtual Address Translator.

VAX Notes. An electronic conferencing software that allows to create and access online conferences/meetings.

VAX Rdb/VMS. A full-function relational database management system designed for VMS and Micro VMS operating systems. It is intended for general purpose, multi-user, centralised, or distributed applications offering high data capacity (up to 50 gigabytes) and through put for general purpose, multi-user, centralised, or distributed applications.

VB. Voice Band.

VBP. Virtual Block Processor.

VBScript. A scripting language based up on Microsoft's Visual Basic programming language; allows programmers to use a language with which they are familiar. It is supported in Microsoft's Internet Explorer browser. VBScript does not contain all the same commands that Visual Basic contains. Also, because of the unique environment for VBScript scripts, there are a few new built-in functions that are not a part of Visual Basic.

VCBA. Variable Control Block Area.

VCI. Virtual Cannel Identifier, similar to the LCN of X.25, identifies a channel in asynchronous transfer mode.

VCS. Validation Control System.

VD. Virtual Data.

VDAM. Virtual Data Access Method.

VDU. Video Display Unit, generic term to indicate a monitor or screen; this term is somewhat outdated but appears in a wide body of information technology literature.
2. *See* visual display unit.

VEA. Virtual Effective Address.

Veitch diagram. A means of representing Boolean functions in which the number of variables determines the number of squares in the diagram: the number of squares needed is the number of possible states, that is two, raised to a power determined by the number of variables.

vertical antenna. Any antenna in which the radiating element is perpendicular to average terrain. The simplest form of vertical antenna is a quarter-wave radiator mounted at ground level.

vertical applications. The programs that perform every phase of a critical business function, such as accounting, order entry, or payroll. These programs are sometimes called mission-critical applications because the success of the business depends on the business functions these applications tools handle. A typical vertical application might be the bank's accounting system that records all the transactions that have occurred during a specified period and makes necessary adjustments to the account balances. In most cases vertical applications are database-management systems.

vertical block line. A development of the magnetic bubble which greatly increases storage capacity, giving the potential of storing 1.6 Gbit of data on single chip one centimetre square. The chip, its driver and ancillary circuits will occupy a single printed circuit board about 10 cm × 10 cm.

vertical dipole. A half-wave dipole antenna, fed at the centre, and oriented vertically.

vertical mode index. VMI. In laser printer technology, the amount of space that a cursor moves in vertical direction in increments of 1/48th of an inch, with the minimum vertical modex index being 0 and the maximum being 125.

vertical sweep frequency. The frequency at which vertical sweep takes place. In a TV receiver, it is 60 Hz. Also called vertical sweep rate.

vertical sync pulse. In a video signal, the pulse that synchronises the vertical component of scanning in a TV receiver with that of the camera, and which triggers vertical retrace and blanking.

vertical-hold control. In a TV receiver, the control for adjusting the frequency of the vertical oscillator, so the picture can be locked to prevent vertical roll.

very large scale integration. VLSI. The use of chips each providing a very large number (typically several thousand) of active elements or logic gates. $VLSI^2$ is VLSI with more than 1,000,000 logic gates, sometimes called very large scale integration indeed.

very low frequency. VLF. A radio frequency in the band 3 kHz to 300 kBz.

very-high frequency. VHF. A radio frequency in the band 30 MHz to 300 MHz; below the UHF carrier band range and above HF; generally used for mobile communications. Also television channels 2 through 13.

VESA. Video Equipment Standards Association.

VEX. Video Extensions to X-Windows.

VF. Voice Frequency, frequencies typically between 30 and 8000 cycles per second.

VFS. Virtual File Store, in FTAM, the concept of file storage, distinct from the way it is represented on a specific computer's file system.

VFT. Voice Frequency Telegraph, covered in CCITT Recommendations R.30-R.35.

VGA. Video Graphics Array; specifications for video output on IBM and compatible computers, which features 640×480 resolution and 256 colours (8 bit graphics).

VHF. *See* very-high frequency.

VHLL. Very High Level Language.

VHOL. Very High Order Language.

video display board. An electronic circuit board that resides in the computer as part of its hardware to generate the images (text and/or graphics) on the monitor. Using a special section of the computer's memory, the video display board also controls the resolution and colours on the monitor.

video graphics array. A graphics display standard introduced in 1987 by IBM for their PS/2 line of personal computers. Video Graphics Array (VGA) offers improved graphics and text resolution and an expanded number of available colours for both text and graphics while maintaining software compatibility with most CGA and EGA applications. It has maximum screen resolution of 640×480, or 720×400 pixels where each character is formed in a 9×16 pixel matrix. A maximum of 256 colours can be displayed at once, from a selection of 256000 colours.

video teleconferencing. Real time and usually two-way transmission of video images between two or more locations. Transmitted images may be of full TV standard or freeze-frame, where the picture is repainted every few seconds. The bandwidth requirements may be as low as 56 kbit/s for freeze-frame transmission.

video terminal. A visual display unit that displays information on a cathode-ray tube and generally has an associated keyboard.

videotext. A system that enables a keyboard to be used in conjunction with an ordinary television receiver and a telephone, forming a terminal that provides interactive dial-up access to one or more remote services providing information. The videotext system allows TV viewers to dial up special material, such as stock market quotations, weather data, sports scores, and the like.

ViewMovie. A shareware plug-in, that lets Macs view Quick Time movies, whether linked with anchors or embedded as active images directly on the page, as it is downloaded.

vines. Virtual Networking System; a network operating system from Banyan System Incorporated. It is based on UNIX, and allows file and printing services, among others, for DOS, OS/2, and Apple workstations.

VIO. Voice Input/Output.

Virtual 86. The capability of Intel 80386 chips to establish an 8086 environment. Two generations of the Intel 86 family processors have proceeded the Intel 80386 microprocessor. These are the 80286 and the 8086. The 80386 is compatible at the binary level with both of them. This compatibility preserves software investments, allows rapid market entry, and can provide access to the vast library of software written for computers based on the 86 family. The 80386 can run 8086 programs; it can also run 80286 and 80386 programs concurrently. But the 80386's most innovative compatibility feature is Virtual 86 capability, which establishes a protected 8086 environment within the 80386 multitasking framework.

virtual drive. *See* RAM disk.

virtual memory support. Virtual memory enables the maximum size of a program, or a mix of programs, to be governed by available disk space rather than size of physical memory (random-access memory), which is about 7-8 times more expensive. The resulting flexibility benefits manufacturers, programmers (who can leave storage management to the operating system, rather than writing overlays), and end-users, who can run larger applications without being concerned about running out of memory.

virtual memory system. VMS. Digital Equipment Corporation's generation-purpose operating environment for development and execution of a wide range of applications that run across the entire line of the VAX family of processors.

virtual memory. VM. A system in which a process workspace is held partly in high-speed memory and partly on some slower, and cheaper, backing-store device. In Windows, the amount of virtual memory available equals the amount of free RAM plus the amount of disk space allocated to the swap file. In Macintosh System 7, virtual memory is controlled in the Memory Control Panel. The default setting is twice the amount of RAM in the machine. However, the amount of RAM plus the amount of virtual memory together is the amount of disk space you must allocate. For example, if you have 4 MB of RAM and set virtual memory at 8 MB, 12 MB of disk space is allocated.

virtual private network. *See* VPN.

virtual reality. VR. An emerging technology that attempts to fully immerse the user in an interactive computer generated environment. Virtual memory is rather ill-defined, but focuses on a more complex interaction with the computer, featuring at least 3D interactive video. In computing, the term 'virtual reality' refers to a computer program, coupled with other tools and devices, that enable a person to perform tasks 'virtually' with all the function and effectiveness of a real.

virtual storage. The storage space that may be regarded as addressable main storage by the user of a computer system in which virtual addresses are mapped into real addresses. It may be noted that the size of virtual storage is limited by the addressing scheme of the computer system and by the amount of auxiliary storage available, and not by the actual number of main storage locations.

virus. A parasitic program buried within another legitimate program or stored in a special area of a disk called boot sector. Executing the legitimate program or accessing the disk activates the virus without user's knowledge. The viruses may:

copy themselves to other programs;
display information on screen;
destroy data files;
erase entire hard disk; and
lie dormat for a specified time or until a given condition is fulfilled.

A system may be infected by the viruses, by:

receiving a disk from another user. In this case, the virus could be in boot sector of the disk or an executable file on the disk; or

downloading an executable file form another user, an online service, or Internet. The best protection for viruses is to treat all disks as potential carriers of viruses. Some of the commonly available anti-virus programs include:

McAfee
Norton Antivirus
Virex
disinfectant
Symantec Antivirus for Macintosh.

Visicalc. The first electronic spreadsheet, that spelled success and paved the way for further research. Also known as visible calculator.

visual display unit. VDU. An output device that can display information; the information can be both alphanumeric and graphical, and can be erased or changed under the control of a processor that may be remote or part of the unit. Most devices have a selection of display attributes that can be used to emphasise or differentiate items of information, such as blink or flash, brilliance, reverse video, or colour.

VL. Virtual Link, in data communications, a connection between two addresses on a network which are not physically connected.

VLSI. *See* very large scale integration.

VM. 1. Virtual Machine, OSI.
2. Virtual Memory, when a computer allows one to use more memory than it really has by paging some out to disk when not actually active.

v-mail. Voice mail; a voice messaging system with telephone answering machine is the most basic form of voice mail. More sophisticated systems are commonplace at an office. Through the PABX, each staff member is able to send a spoken message to any or all other staff members. Messages are stored digitally in security-coded memory chips or a disk storage device, which can only be accessed by the addressee from any touch-tone telephone.

voice mailbox. The code number determining the store in which incoming voice messages have been stored for later retrieval.

VMD. Virtual Manufacturing Device, used in manufacturing message systems.

VMS. Voice Messaging System.

vocoder. A device for reducing speech to frequencies low enough for efficient transmission through a limited-bandwidth channel. The term is an acronym for voice coder. Vocoder does not encode the human voice directly, as in pulse code modulation, but rather attempts to measure certain parameters of the voice and transmit these via a slow digital bit stream. The receiving end then uses these measurements to synthesise key features of the original voice using an electronic circuit to imitate the human vocal cord and throat. Also known as voice-operated coder.

voder. A speech synthesiser intended for the transmission of recognisable voice signals over a channel having a narrow bandwidth. The voder is similar to vocoder, except that the voder produces entirely synthesised signals.

vogad. A type of automatic gain control for audio amplifiers and modulators. In a radio transmitter, it maintains 100% modulation of the carrier, even when the speaker's voice level varies widely. The name is an acronym for voice-operated gain adjusting device.

voice frequencies. The frequency range of speech, roughly in the range 62-8000 Hz. Within these limits, the range of human speech varies considerably with individual talkers, the average peak energy in the male speaking voice being at about 130 Hz, and in the female speaking voice at 300 Hz.

voice-operated coder. *See* vocoder.

volatile memory. A type of memory whose contents are destroyed on the removal of power to the memory. When volatile memories are used for crucial applications, they can be backed up with temporary battery-power supplies.

volatile. A term applied to information held in memory store, which depends on power being continuously available; referring to memory chips such as random-access memory which lose their information when the electrical power is switched off. This contrasts with non-volatile chips such as read-only memory chips, which retain their information even after the power has been switched off.

VPN. Virtual Private Network, a private connection over a public network, *i.e.*, a connection that achieves virtual privacy even though it shares the transmission medium with a greater network.

VRML. Virtual Reality Modelling Language; originally, is called Virtual Reality Markup Language; an evolving language specification to provide virtual reality resources on internet. Currently, VRML provides support for interactive 3D graphics data.

VROOM. Virtual Runtime Object-Oriented Memory Manager. This object-oriented technology was developed by Borland International, Incorporated. It allows Borland's software to make the most efficient use of personal computer memory. By swapping small code objects in and out of memory on an 'as-needed' basis, software incorporating VROOMM technology makes the trade-off between program code and application data residing in memory.

VSAT. Very Small Aperture Terminal, used with rented satellite telephone channels, typically 19.2 kbps.

VT. Virtual Terminal, defined in ISO 9040 (services) and 9041 (protocol). Virtual Terminal provides a way for computers to log on to a remote host and be treated like a terminal on that host. There are several different types of profile that can be supported. For example, TELNET profile provides a simple line-at-a-time or character-at-a-time dialogue. The Forms profile supports forms-based applications, with the terminal system providing local entry and validation of data. Transparent profile allows for the use of embedded control characters to control the terminal. The X3 profile provides supported for CCITT X.3 PAD compatible operation.

VTAM. Virtual Telecommunications Access Method; a set of IBM mainframe programs that control communications between application programs and terminals by providing SNA services such as managing communication sessions and API (Application Program Interface - a programming language interface that allows a user-written application program to access the functions of a hardware or software system).

VTP. Virtual Terminal Protocol.

VTS. Virtual Terminal Service.

VWS. Variable Word Size.

W

WAD. Word and Author InDEX.

WADS. Wide Area Data Service.

wafer. A thin slice of semiconducting material, used as the substrate for manufacturing chips.

WAIS. Wide Area Information Server. An information retrieval system used on the internet, which features text search facilities to identify the documents that the user wants to find.

wait state. A processing cycle programmed in the computers which does nothing, but occupy time for the purpose of waiting for other components such as the dynamic random-access memory (DRAM) chip to refresh its contents and catch up to the central processing unit. Although wait states force a very fast processor (cycling at over 25 megahertz) to waste time, they are necessary to ensure that errors do not occur as a result of one component processing too fast for others to catch up. Static random-access memory (SRAM) chips and page-mode RAM chips are becoming popular because they store information without the need for the central processing unit to refresh them several thousand times per second, thereby reducing or eliminating the wait state.

WAK. Write Access Key.

walking code. A binary code that gives the appearance of walking bit-by-bit through a register, one bit for each number change.

walkthrough. A critical examination of a design or product undertaken to ensure that it is of adequate quality and meets the desired specifications.

WAN. *See* Wide Area Network.

wand. A stick-shaped, hand-held device, usually long and narrow, which can be used to read optically-coded labels such as bar code labels.

wander. Long-term random variations in the values, conditions, or characteristics of a signal, such as significant instants of a digital signal from their ideal position in time.

WAP. Work Assignment Procedure.

warm boot. *See* warm start.

warm start. If computer processing is interrupted in a minor way, a 'warm start' (function reset) is sufficient to result from where an operator left off. A 'cold start' (total system reset) would be required if all the power was switched off, or if a system crashed during processing and required rebooting. Also known as warm boot.

WAV. File name extension for files storing data in the form of sound.

waveguide. A transmission line consisting of a hollow metallic conductor-generally rectangular, elliptical or circular-within which electromagnetic waves may be propagated. It is often used at ultra-high and microwave frequencies. It consists of a hollow metal pipe, usually having a rectangular or circular cross section. The electromagnetic field travels down the pipe, if the wavelength is short enough. It provides excellent shielding and low loss, and may be used as filters and attenuators.

WC. Word Count.

WCL. Word Control Logic.

WCM. Writable Control Memory.

WCR. Word Count Register.

WD. 1. Working Document, ISO term for a standard. This is an earlier stage than a Committee Draft.
2. WorD.
3. Write Data.
4. Write Direct.

WE. Write Enable.

web browser. A program that accesses the WWW, allowing the user to use the multimedia resources of the Internet. A web browser will require Internet access (either Ethernet hardware or PPP/SLIP), and sufficient graphics hardware.

web crawler. A program that travels around the Internet and gathers the required information.

web page. The pages of information placed on the network for the perusal by other people, companies, and organisation. A page may include graphics, sounds, text, and movies.

Web. The most commonly used shortened name for World Wide Web.

Weitek 3167 coprocessor. Many personal computers provide a separate socket on the memory cache controller board for the high-powered Weitek 3167 coprocessor. An accelerator typically used in mini computers; Weitek coprocessor is a very powerful tool for speeding up performance when running one of the many floating point-intensive applications that have been designed to take advantage of this capability. The ideal applications for the Weitek options are CAD/CAE, scientific/engineering, and solids modelling.

wetware. A term used in the artificial intelligence and similar fields to denote the biological equivalent of hardware, such as human brain.

WFL. Work Flow Language.

WFMTUG. World Federation of MAP/TOP users group.

WG. Working Group, in ISO/IEC, a division of subcommittee.

WG3. Common acronyms for the database working group under SC21 of ISO/JTC1.

white noise. Random noise (acoustic or electric) equally distributed over a given frequency band, such as the noise resulting from random motion of free electrons in conductors and semiconductors. Noise occurring in a channel and regarded as continuous in time and continuous in amplitude, the noise being uniform in energy over equal intervals of frequency.

white signal. In facsimile transmission, the signal resulting from the scanning of a minimum-density area of the subject copy.

white transmission. A form of amplitude-modulated facsimile signal in which the greatest copy density or dark shade, corresponds to the minimum amplitude of the signal.

WHOIS. An Internet program that allows users to find names of companies or individuals that match criteria that is submitted to a WHOIS server.

wide area network. WAN. The network linking computers, terminals, and other equipment over a large geographic area. A linking together of metropolitan area networks, which enables data terminals in one city to access data resources in another city or country. Inter-city links are usually digital circuits (*e.g.,* at 56 kbit/s, 64 kbit/s, 1.5 Mbit/s, 2 Mbit/s) leased from common carriers or telecommunications administrations.

wideband communication system. A communication system which is capable of handling, making use of, or requires a wide range of frequencies and usually provides numerous channels of communication that use frequency division multiplexing.

wideband modem. A modem that has a modulated output signal frequency spectrum that is wider than that which can be wholly contained within, and faithfully transmitted through a voice channel with a nominal 4-kHz bandwidth.

wideband. Passing or processing a wide range of frequencies; the meaning varies with the context. In an audio system, wideband can mean a band of up to 20 kHz wide, but in television system, the band can be many megahertz wide.

Widget. A term used in GUI environment to refer to any thing on the screen that can be manipulated by the user, such as buttons, checkboxes, scroll bars, etc.

wildcard character. A character which represents one or several unknown characters. Wildcard characters are especially used in databases when search are being made.

wildcard. A character that can be used to represent any other character or series of characters in a statement. For instance, the wildcard "*" allows "DAN*Y" to refer to both "DANNY" and "DANDY." It is useful in searches when the user does not know the exact text he is looking for, and in specifying and action to be performed on a group of files.

WIMP. Windows, Icons, Mouse, and Pull-down menus; an acronym used generically to refer to any system designed to offer easy-to-use interface between the user and the operating system through the use of on-screen graphics (icons) which represent certain files or commands, which are accessible to user through a point device such as a mouse.

Winamp. A music player for Windows. Some of the features of the version 2.6 include, massively improved CD audio support complete with menu option to play CD. New splash screen (smaller) and about box effect; removed unused links stuff in about box; improved Jump (to file) dialog (hit J key); and bookmarking system. It has the facility to fix to mp3 plug-in. Now won't stop after failed shoutcast stream. It can updates to URLs used in player for web site integration, and new SuperPiMP installation system.

WIN.INI file. A Windows initialisation file that contains settings you can use to customise your Windows environment. It can be edited manually, but this should only be attempted if you know what you are doing. Even then, you should be sure to have a backup copy.

window. In computers, a specified area, showing a section of a program or document that is selected for working, such as enlargement, thus effectively defining a window through which that particular portion of the display can be viewed in more detail.

windowing. The ability to have several individual 'screens' on one display; a facility available with microcomputers whereby multiple inlays can be incorporated in existing screen displays, the user then being able to work on any chosen section of the display. In linked windowing systems, altering one section automatically brings about corresponding changes in other parts of the system. Microsoft's Windows, Digital Research's Gem Desktop, Quarterdeck's DESQview, and IBM's Topview, are all windowing environments which offer alternative operating environments. These systems move away from using test-based commands. Instead, they interface with their operating systems through a menu-oriented 'desktop' for selecting and running computer applications.

Windows 3.11. The Microsoft Windows Operating Environment before Windows 95.

Windows 95. The Microsoft Windows Operating Environment. Windows 95 features full 32-bit design, pre-emptive multi-tasking, and multi-threading. Windows 95 is successor to Windows 3.1 and Windows for Work-groups, but it does not replace Windows NT. As a result of the 16-bit code, Windows 95 can run almost any DOS or Windows program.

Windows 95 has a graphical interface. Windows 95 also allows users to type the file names of up to 256 characters and to have spaces in those names. In addition, it offers a plug-and-play standard for connecting new hardware. With Windows 3.0 and 3.1, users often faced complexities when installing disk drives, sound cards, modems, printers, CD-ROM drives, and other hardware.

Another feature of Windows 95 is its compatibility with networking software such as Novell NetWare, and Microsoft Windows NT Server.

Windows 2000. The most manageable, reliable, and secure version of Windows; the improved hardware and increased software compatibility make using Windows 2000 easy. Windows 2000 has Universal Serial Bus (USB); when the user attach hardware to a USB port, Windows 2000 automatically detects the new device and installs the necessary drivers without restarting the computer. It includes hundreds of new printer, modem, and other hardware drivers, making hardware installtion and setup easy and efficient. Add/Remove wizard automatically detects and configures new devices. Add Printer wizard helps in changing printer settings from within applications. Windows 2000 also includes improved printing support such as Internet printing, image colour management, and new font technologies. Because the Internet is integrated in to Window 2000, one can browse through computer as effortlessly as one browse through the Web. Also it supports OpenGL specifications, 3-D graphics standard used for computer aided design and scientific applications. The cameras and scanners are easy to is\nstall in Windows 2000. User can configure the scanners and cameras features to automatically launch the program of his choice he scans the image. This version of Windows also adds support for Universal Disk Format, a new file system designed for interchanging information between DVD and CD-ROM media.

Before you install Windows 2000, make sure the following minimum hardware requirements are met:

133 MHz Pentium or higher processor.
64 MB RAM.
2 GB hard disk with 650 MB of free space.

VGA or higher resolution monitor.
Keyboard.

Windows NT 4.0. The newer version of Windows NT, by which clients take full advantage of all incoming connection features except dynamic allocation of multilinked lines, extensible authentication protocol (EAP), IPSec client to the server data security, and L2TP for tunneling across intervening networks.

Windows NT. An operating system developed by Microsoft, designed to provide networking services, and to be atleast somewhat processor independent. It is 32-bit operating system, and was originally designed to be successor to DDOS, but by the time, it was ready for release, it had become too large to run on most of the PCs. NT shares a common interface with Windows 3.1, but does not require MS-DOS. Windows NT runs on Intel processors (386 and above), MIPS, and the DEC Alpha. Support for the PowerPC is planned. Windows NT version 3.1 clients do not support the point-to-point protocol (PPP) introduced in Windows NT 3.5.

Windows. Operating Environment written by Microsoft; a graphical user interface that runs on top of MS-DOS.

WINS configuration property sheet. The property sheet that allows enabling or disabling WINS resolution. To enable WINS resolution, the user enters IP addresses for one or two WINS servers in the primary WINS server and optionally secondary WINS server fields.

WINS. Windows Internet Naming Service, a registered Microsoft implementation of NetBIOS name server, and can be installed on Windows NT servers. It maintains a database of registered NetBIOS names for a variety of objects including users, computers, services running on those computers, and workgroups. Instead of the entries in this database coming from manually edited text files, as in DNS, client computers register their names and IP addresses with WINS server dynamically when they start up, thus making it less time consuming to maintain than a DNS server.

Winsock. A Windows programming interface, that provides access to TCP and UDP ports.

WKS. File name extension for the spreadsheet files.

WMF. 1. File name extension for a bitmapped image, a graphic file.
2. Workload Monitoring Function, used in Network Management.

WO. Write Only.

WOM. Write Only Memory.

WOOD. Write Once Optical Disk; a type of digital optical disk on which a user can record data, but, once recorded, it cannot be erased or re-recorded. It comes in various sizes from 2-14 inch, and has data storage capacities in the megabyte-gigabyte range.

Word for Word. A file conversion utility used to read files created by one word processing program and convert them so that they can be read by another word processing program.

word processing. WP. Use of computers and microprocessors for writing and editing letters and manuscripts.

word processor. WP. Application which provides you with the tools necessary to create and edit and format text. Word processors commonly include an area to enter text, the ability to control the format of text (bold, italics, size), indenting, margins, the ability to check spelling, etc. Many word processors also handle graphics to a varying degree.

word wrap. One of the great time-saving features of word processing, that moves text from end of a line to the beginning of a new line as you type. With word wrap, you do not need to press ENTER at the end of each line in a paragraph.

WORD. One of the tools in Microsoft Office 97; it is the centrepiece of Microsoft Office suite, partly because it is the oldest of the applications, and partly because almost anyone who uses a computer must have a word processor. It is a collection of objects designed to present a central theme, and is one of the tools for unifying the various elements of a document. Word 97 has several features such as Natural Language Checker and Automatic Grammar Checking. Word 97 allows to enter text, cut it, copy it, and print it. It also allows sending e-mails, or merging it with data from another Office 97 applications. Word 97 also incorporates a collection of templates designed to make it easy to give a document a particular look. It also allows creating macros to automate repetitive actions or handle complex editing.

word. In computing, data storage, etc., an ordered set of bits representing a unit of data and occupying one storage location within the system. It is usually treated by the computer as a single unit, and transferred as such. Microcomputers commonly use 8-bit and 16-bit words; minicomputers commonly use 16-bit words; the super computers commonly use 64-bit words. As technology develops, these figures keep on changing.

Wordstar. A registered word processing program for microcomputers with CP/M operating system.

work file. A file used to provide temporary storage space for data that is required only for the complete execution of one job.

work group applications. The programs designed to make combinations of individuals more effective as they work together toward common goals. Many of such aplications require special equipment and significant computing power. The workgroup computing is often document-oriented. With a workgroup application, many people on a product team can focus on the same information. By working together efficiently, team members can shorten the process of specifying the parts of their products.

work space. The area of a window that displays the information contained in the application or document you are working with.

work station. A terminal whereby an individual can have access to facilities of a computer, word processor, data base, video system, etc., or to a combination of systems. As personal computers have continued to become more powerful, the distinction between personal computers and lower end work stations has blurred.

working memory. That part of the memory in central processing unit of a computer that is actually available to the user at any given time. It is always less than the total memory capacity of the central processing unit, exact amount available depending on how much of the memory is taken up by the operating programs that are being used at that time.

world coordinate. A device-independent Cartesian coordinate used by the application program for specifying graphical input and output.

World Wide Web. WWW. An amalgam of Internet sites offering text, graphics, sound, and animation resources through the http protocol. More generally, all ftp, gopher, and WAIS sites are also included.

worm drive. A mechanism for transferring motion from a tuning-knob shaft through a right angle to the shaft of an adjustable component, such as a potentiometer or variable capacitor. The knob turns a worm, which mates with a gear wheel.

worm. A web-based computer program that replicates itself and is self-propagating; worms, as opposed to viruses, are meant to spawn in network environments.

wow. Periodic variations in the operating speed of recording or a playback system in frequency ranges 1-10 Hz.

WP. 1. Word Processing.
2. Word Processor.
3. Write Protocol.

WPD. File name extension for a word processor file.

WPG. File name extension for a Word Perfect vector image, a kind of graphics file.

WPM. Words Per Minute.

WPS. Word Processing System.

wrap around. Making that part of an image, which lies outside an edge of the display space, be displayed at the opposite edge of that space.

write once optical disk. *See* WOOD.

write. To make a permanent or transient recording of data in a storage device or on a data medium. It may be noted that the phrases 'to read to' and 'to read from' are often distinguished from the phrases 'to write to' and to write from' only by the viewpoint of the description. For example, transfer of a block of data from internal storage to external storage may be called 'writing to the external storage' or 'reading from the internal storage', or both.

write instruction. A program instruction that causes an item of data to be recorded in some form of storage.

write-through caching. Primary memory must be kept up-to-date (coherent) with any new data written to the cache. Two basic strategies are used for coordinating writes to the cache with primary memory: write-through caching and write-back caching. Most processors use a write through cache, meaning the processor writes the modified word unit to both the cache and primary memory to ensure that both memories always have updated copies of the word unit.

write time. The elapsed time during which a given amount of data is being recorded in the storage device; does not include the latency or check read time.

WSF. WorkStation Function, term used in Network Management.

W-type fibre. A doubly-cladded optical fibre with two layers of concentric cladding, and in which the core has the largest refractive index while the inner cladding has the lowest refractive index.

WWW. *See* World Wide Web.

WYSIWYG. What you see is what you get; in a graphical user interface, the method of displaying (on screen) an image of what the output will look like, very closely resembling the size, appearance, and position of the finished output.

X Window. A graphic-based user interface often associated with UNIX and Linux. It has brought a GUI to UNIX computers, but has remained an operating system for technical users.

X

X Windowing System. A GUI developed to work with different operating systems, and to support networking. That is, one machine may be running an application, and the user interface to the application can be running on another machine.

X.3. ASC X3, ANSI Accredited Standards Committee for the Information Processing Systems.

X.12. ANSI X12, one of the common EDI formats and one that can be carried over X.400 with X.435.

X.25. The CCITT standard defining accessing protocol for public packet-switching networks. X.25 is a dynamic standard with many variations in different countries. X.25 recommendation specifies a three-level structure for the transmission of data between data terminal equipment and data circuit equipment. It consists of three levels of protocol: the physical layer, the link layer, and the network layer. These layers parallel the bottom three layers of the Open Systems Interconnection (OSI) reference model. Significance for X.25 is that the highest level of protocol it defines, level three (packet level), provides all OSI network (level three) functions and some transport (level four) functions.

Remote access clients running Windows 2000 Professional or Windows Server can use either an X.25 card or dial into X.25 PAD to create connections. To accept incoming connections on a computer using X.25 running Windows 2000 Professional or Windows 2000 server, one must use X.25 card.

X.25 level 1. One of the three levels of the CCITT standard that defines the accessing protocol for public packet-switching networks. The physical level specifies the physical and electrical characteristics of the data terminal equipment (DTE) and data circuit equipment. The CCIIT X.25 recommendation specifies that a duplex synchronous link should be used to provide a physical transmission path between the DTE and the network. CCITT also specifies the use of X.21 and X.21 'bis' as the standard interface to digital and analog networks.

X.25 level 2. One of the three levels of the CCITT standard that defines the accessing protocol for public packet-switching networks. The link level provides the packet layer with a reliable error-free facility to move packets across the physical link.

X.25 level 3. One of three levels of the CCITT standard that defines the accessing protocol for public packet-switching networks. The packet level defines procedures for constructing and controlling a data packet. The packet level describes the formats of packets passed between data terminal equipment (DTE) and data circuit equipment. These formats are used to set up and clear virtual calls.

X.75/X.121. The CCITT X.75 'recommendation' defines the procedures for the interconnection of separate packet-switched networks. Networks that are interconnected by X.75 subscribe that are interconnected by X.75 subscribe to yet another CCITT standard called 'X.121'. This describe the international numbering plan for public data networks.

X.nnn. The CCITT X. Series of Recommendations for data communications networks, services, and protocols.

X/OPEN. Unix Open Applications Group, initially an association of European EDP vendors committed to creation of open systems environment.

X.121. An international standard for numbering networks and stations that will be interconnected using the X-25 and related protocols.

X.400. A standard for electronic mail developed by CCITT.

X.3S3. Data Communications subcommittee of ANSI X3.

X3S3.1. Data Communications Planning technical committee under ANSI X3S3.

X3S3.2. Data Communications Vocabulary technical committee under ANSI X3S3.

X3S3.3. Network Layer technical committee under ANSI X3S3.

X3S3.7. Public Data Network Access technical committee under ANSI X3S3.

X3SX.5. Communications Systems Performance technical committee under ANSI X3S3.

X3T5. ASC Specification for Open Systems Interconnect (OSI).

X3V1. Technical committee under ASC X3 for Text Processing; Office and Publishing Systems.

X.75. The CCITT standard interface protocol for packet switching networks that defines the message structure required for gateway nodes of public packet networks to intercommunicate.

X-band. The frequencies in the range 5.2-10.9 GHz, between the old S- and K-bands and overlapping parts of the old C-, G-, J-, H- and M-bands.

XCU. Cross-point Control Unit.

XDUP. Extended Disc Utilities Program.

Xfer. Transfer.

XID. Exchange Identification, an LLC PDU.

XIT. Extra Input Terminal.

XL. Execution Language.

XLS. File name extension for a spreadsheet file.

XM. Expended Memory.

XML. Extensible Markup Language, a language developed to fill the gap between the power and complexity of SGML at one end, and the inadequacy and simplicity of HTML at the other end. It provides a means to define applications and the markup language so that the information can be encoded in the Web document far more precisely than can be done in HTML. Combining XML with the processing power that languages like Java and ActiveX can provide, and the user has the means to produce intelligent documents, the documents that can be understood by the user applications so that the information can be processed in ways that would be absolutely impossible with HTML. XML is not intended to a replacement for HTML; it is meant to be a supplement and alternative to HTML.

The two languages can very well co-exist, each being used for what is most suited. XML provides much more powerful links than either SGML or HTML, and allows any element type to act as a linking element. This is achieved by specifying the reserved attribute XML-LINK for each element that is to act as a linking element. XML is being used for a number of applications such as:

Channel Definition Format (CDF)
Open Software Description (OSD)
Chemical Markup Language (CML)
Hand-held Device Markup Language (HDML).

XML document. A document consisting of a mixture of text and markup (tags). An XML document need not necessary look different from an HTML document, and can be converted in to HTML document. AN XML document has an entity called document entity, which serves as the starting point for the XML processor. The logical and physical structures in an XML document must be synchronous. The tags and elements each must begin and end in the same entity, but they may refer to other entities internally. A well-formed XML document must fulfill the following:

It must start with a required markup declaration that says that a DTD is not required.

It must contain one or more elements.

It must have all the elements nested inside each other, and all tags must be balanced.

It must have all attribute values enclosed in quotation marks.

It must have empty element start tags closed with special /> string, or they must be made nonempty by adding a specific closing tag.

It must not have any markup character in character data.

All the element attributes must be of character data type, because there is no way to define them as being otherwise without a DTD.

XMODEM protocol. A public-domain data transfer technique which permits protocol matching between systems, detects errors introduced during transmission and causes retransmission until the transmitted data are correctly received, error-free transmission is assured, and conventional file transfer protocol and handshaking is eliminated.

XNA. Xerox Network Architecture, proprietary-networking system developed by Xerox.

XPG. X/Open Portability Guide, a series of books providing standards for application portability.

XPSDU. Expedited Presentation Service Data Unit.

XR. IndeX Register.

XT. Second generation of IBM computers, distinguished by a hard disk and an eight-bit bus. 'XT' can also be applied to any IBM-compatible computer based on the Intel 8088 CPU.

XTC. External Transmit Block.

XUI. X User Interface Toolkit; X Window standard services that support the development of user interfaces for any hardware that supports the X Window System.

Extensible Markup Language. *See* XML.

Y

Y/N. Yes/No.

YACC. A widely used compiler provided as part of the UNIX operating system environment.

Yagi. A directional antenna used for television reception; consists of a dipole with parasitic directors in the front, and reflectors at the rear side.

YEC. Youngest Empty Cell.

YModem. An extension of the original XModem transfer protocol. YModem was developed by Chuck Forsburg in the early 1980s. YModem added features such as transfer of file names, multi-file transfers, increased reliability of error checking, and increased data throughput.

YMU. Y-NET Management Unit, a central unit in Belgium to coordinate and manage the Y-NET project.

Y-NET. An ESPRIT project for establishing an OSI infrastructure across Europe for X.400, FTAM, and X.5000 services.

yon plane. In three-dimensional computer graphics display, the imaginary plane behind the screen which defines the rearmost limit of the display.

Z

.Z. UNIX files that are compressed and require the UNIX uncompress utility before they can be used.

Z.nnn. The CCITT Z. Series Recommendations for specific several languages and meta-languages.

zap. To erase data from a computer storage.

Z-axis intercept. In communication, the intersection of a satellite's Z-axis and the earth's surface. It defines an antenna's pointing direction.

ZBID. Zero Bit Insertion/Deletion.

z-clipping. Defining the front and rear limits of a 3-dimensional display to set planes parallel to the view plane.

ZCR. Zero Crossing Rate.

Zeeman effect. The splitting of electromagnetic radiation in to its component frequencies.

zero address. A term referring to an instruction format with no operand addresses.

zero address instruction. A machine instruction that has no address part.

zero crossing. A term referring to a point or line in a filtered image between two pixel groups, one of which is all positive, and the other all negative, and can be used to determine edges in the original image when the filtering procedure is adequate.

zero fill. To character-fill with the representation of the character that denotes zero.

zero function. The function whose value is zero for every element in its domain. This function is basic to the theory of recursive and primitive recursive functions.

zero output. The signal condition given by a magnetic cell representing zero when a read pulse is applied.

zero rew. The third row of punching positions in a punched card.

zero state. The state of a binary memory cell when 0 is stored therein.

zero suppression. The deletion of non-significant zeros in a numeral signal which has been transmitted. While numerical data is being processed, it may be expanded to uniform number of digits by the addition of non-significant zeos to the left of the most significant digit. For print out or display, these non-significant zeros are suppressed.

zero transmission level. An arbitrarily chosen reference point in a circuit to which all relative transmission levels are referred.

zero wait state. *See* ZWS.

zero word. A word consisting entirely of zero digits. It lies at the origin of Hamming space.

zeroize. To restore a storage unit, or the contents of a storage unit, such as a register, to a condition in which all zeros are stored. Also, degaussing, erasing, or over-writing electronically stored data.

ZIF. Zero Insertion Force.

zig-zag book. A scrambled text in which pages are divided in to cut sections, which can be turned forwards or backwards in an independent manner.

zimdex. A cueing technique used in audio instruction; involves numbers or pulses being recorded on one track of an audio-tape in order to mark or index the contents of the other track.

ZIP code. A decimal-digit numeral (in India, 6-digit) that is assigned to each post office in a country. It is used to expedite the transfer and forwarding of mail. It is equivalent to the address designator and address-indicating group that are used on messages for electrical transmission.

zip. The file extension given to a particular kind of compressed file. To use a file with this extension, it is necessary to unzip it with a decompression program.

Z Modem. A file transfer protocol developed by Chuck Forsburg in the mid-1980s. It was designed to rectify some of the limitations associated with YModem as well as to provide support for high speed, packet and network communications environments.

ZOH. Zero Order Hold.

zone bit. Bits in a word used to alter the significance of the non-zone bits.

zone digit. A digit punched in a zone.

zone file. The configuration files used by servers. These textural files are used to configure DNS servers. One zone file is created for each domain name. Single DNS server can support multiple domains and therefore multiple zone files simultaneously. In a domain with small number of computers, the zone file probably contains all the entries for the domain. this often the case, and is easy to confuse a zone and a domain for the same thing. However, the computers in a domain could be separated in to two zones with each zone residing on a different DNS server.

zone. Any defined region or area in time or space, or any other domain such as frequency, temperature, velocity, pressure, or any other measurable or defined quantity.

zoom. A visual effect in computer graphics, which in volves continuously scaling of the elements of display image to more clearly percive and manipulate details not readily perceived in the previous view.

Z-parameters. Device or network parameters expressed as impedance.

ZRM. Zone Reserved for Memory.

ZWS. Zero wait state; referring to a central processing unit which is capable of processing information at its optimal speed without having to wait for other components (such as dynamic random-access memory) to catch up.

ZX80. A small microcomputer aimed at initial use by novice computer users.